D0850034

Supplement to
A Lithuanian Bibliography

Supplement to
A Lithuanian Bibliography

A further check-list of books and articles
held by the major libraries
of Canada and the United States

The University of Alberta Press
gratefully acknowledges the
support of the Multiculturalism
Program, Government of Canada.

Adam and Filomena Kantautas

The University of Alberta Press   1979

First published by
The University of Alberta Press
Edmonton, Alberta, Canada.   1979

Copyright © 1979 The University of Alberta Press

This book has been published with the help of a grant
from the Lithuanian Canadian Foundation.

ISBN   0-88864-068-4

Canadian Cataloguing in Publication Data

Kantautas, Adam.
    Supplement to A Lithuanian bibliography

    Supplement to: Kantautis, Adam. A Lithuanian
bibliography.
    Includes index.
    ISBN 0-88864-068-4

    1. Lithuania—Bibliography—Union lists.
2. Catalogs, Union—Canada. 3. Catalogs,
Union—United States. I. Kantautas, Filomena.
II. Kantautis, Adam. A Lithuanian bibliography.
III. Title.
Z2537.K332   016.947'5   C79-091229-5

Printing in Canada by
Hignell Printing Limited
Winnipeg, Manitoba.

TABLE OF CONTENTS

INTRODUCTION

The Supplement volume to the Lithuanian Bibliography includes and covers the materials related to Lithuania that were acquired and catalogued by the libraries of Canada and the United States since 1 January, 1972 and up to 31 December, 1977.

The cut-off date is not necessarily the same as the imprint date, as the libraries are steadily acquiring and processing new and old books with a great variety of imprint dates.

The methods, policies, and rules in compiling the Supplement were the same as those described in the Introduction to the main volume, but there are a few deviations from the previous work that should be mentioned here.

The Analytical Table of Contents serves almost as the subject index, with the exception that it is not alphabetically arranged. Two new subject headings are added:

    (a) VII.9.g   Soviet Lithuanian foreign relations, and

    (b) XIII.5.c.8 Lithuanian authors writing in foreign languages

Forty-five works have been listed under more than one subject area in this Supplement, since they are concerned with more than one subject. Under both subject areas, the entry is recorded in full and the sequential entry number assigned.

Twelve titles erroneously assigned in the main volume were added to the Supplement in order to change the subject area.

One hundred and thirty-two entries with imprints 1971 and 1972 were selected from the main volume and re-entered in the Supplement for reasons of clarification, correction, or providing a more complete record of libraries that are holding these materials.

We are indebted to many people for their assistance, advice, and co-operation and to many librarians, who were kind enough to answer

our letters, who sent us photocopies of catalogue cards on Lithuanian topics, or who granted access to their libraries and helped us
in collecting the material we needed.

Special thanks are extended to Dr. Vincas Maciūnas, University
of Pennsylvania Library, Philadelphia, for his valuable advice and
help in collecting the materials for the Supplement; to Mr. Jonas
Sakas of Chicago, Illinois, for his contribution; and to Doreen Youngs
(Mrs. C. W. Youngs) for the typing of the manuscript.

The appearance of this Supplement has been made possible with
the help of a grant from the Lithuanian Canadian Foundation, Toronto,
Ontario.

ANALYTICAL TABLE OF CONTENTS

VI. THE PEOPLE

VII. THE STATE

VIII. SOCIETY, SOCIAL STRUCTURE AND CONDITIONS

IX. ECONOMY

X. HISTORY

ABBREVIATIONS

Abdr. Abdruck, reprint, offprint
akad. akademiia, akademia, academy
akd. akademik, akademika member of
the Academy of Sciences
& and, et, und.
Assoc. Association
ats. atsakingasis, responsible
ats. atsakingasis redaktorius,
red. editor-in-chief
atsak. atsakingasis redaktorius,
red. editor-in-chief
Aufl. Auflage, edition, issue,
printing
Ausg. Ausgabe, edition, printing
avg. avgust, August
avtoriz. avtorizovannyĭ perevod
per

b. bei, near
b-vė,-s bendrovė bendrovės, company, company's
bal. balandis, April
Bd. Band, volume
bearb. bearbeitet, revised, rewrit-
ten, edited
birž. birželis, June
Br. Breisgau (Germany)

CPXIX Lietuvos TSR Mokslų akademija,
Vilna. Geologijos ir geo-
grafijos institutas. Colec-
ted papers for the XIX International Geographical Congress
CPXXI Lietuvos TSR Mokslų akademija,
Vilna. Geologijos ir geo-
grafijos institutas. Collected papers for the XXI session of the International Geological Congress
Calif. California
cap. caput, chapter
Co. Company
col. coloured
comp. compiler
Conn. Connecticut

d. diena, day
Dr. daktaras, daktaro, Doctor's
degree
diagrs diagrams
dop. dopolnenie, supplement
dop. dopolnennoe izdanie, enlarged
izd. edition
dr. drugie, others
Druk. Drukarnia, Printing house

ed., edition, edition, editor
ed.
ekon., ekonom. ekonomicheskoe, economic

Eng. England
et al. et alii, and others
etc. et cetera, and so forth

F-no fortepiano, piano
fasc. fascicle, fascicule, part.
number
facsim. facsimile
Feb. Februar, February
fold. folded

g. god, year
g. gorod, city, town
gg. gody, years
gaz. gazeta, gazety, newspaper
geg. gegužis, May
geogr. geograficheskii, geografi-
cheskoi, geographical
Ger. Germany
gł. główny, main chief, principal, central
Gos. gosudarstvennyi, gosudarstvennoe, state, national
Gos. izd vo polit. i nauch. lit-ry
Gosudarstvennoe izdatel'stvo
politicheskoi i nauchnoi
literatury, Publishing
house of the political and
scientific literature
Gos. sots.-ekon, izd-vo Gosudarstvennoe sotsialialistiches-
ko-eko-nomicheskoe izdatel'
stvo, Publishing house of
the socio-economic literature
Gos. ucheb.-pedagog. izd-vo
Gosudarstvennoe uchebno-peda-
gogicheskoe izdatel'stvo,
Publishing house of educational literature
GPO Government Printing Office
Govt. Print. Off. Government
Printing Office
gr. gruodis, December

Hft. Heft, part, number, issue
hrsg. herausgegeben, edited, published, edited

i dr. i drugie, and others
i.e. id est, that is
incl. includes, included
il. illiustratsiia, -tsiĭ,
illiustration, -s
ill., illius. illiustratsiia,
illiustrirovannyĭ, illus-
tration, illustrations,
illustrated
illus. illustration, -s, illustrated

im. imienia (Polish), imeni (Russian), name, of the name
Imp., Imperat. Imperator, imperatorskii, imperatorskaia, imperatorskoe, imperial, Emperor
imp., imprimé, imprimerie, imprimeur, printed, printing,
impr. printing firm, printer
in-t institut, institute
in-tov institutov, of the institutes
Inaug. Inaugural-Dissertation, in-
-Diss. augural dissertation
ispr. ispravlennyĭ, corrected, revised
izd. izdanie, edition
izd-vo izdatel'stvo, printing firm, publishing house, publisher

Ja., Jan. Januar, January
Jg., Jahrg. Jahrgang, year, annual publication

khud. khudozhnik, artist
khudozh. khudozhestvennaia, khudozhestvennoĭ, khudozhestvennyĭ, artistic khudozhestvennoe proizvedenie, work of art
khudozh. lit-ra, khudozh. lit-ry, khudozhestvennaia literatura, khudozhestvennoĭ literatury, belle-lettres, of belleslettres
kn. knyga, kniga, knyha, book, volume
ks. ksiądz, księdza, priest, priest's
Kun. Kunigas, priest, reverend

lapkr. lapkritis. November
litov. litovskii, litovskaia litovskaia, litovskoi, Lithuanian
LitNIGRI Litovskii nauchno-issledovatel'skiĭ geologo-razvedochnyĭ institut
LitSSR Litovskoĭ SSR Lithuanian SSR
lit-ra lit-ry liteᵣatura, literatury. literature, of literature
LKMAM Lietuvių katalikų mokslo akademija, Rome. Metraštis
LKMASD Lietuvių katalikų mokslo akademija. Suvažiavimo darbai
LTSR Lietuvos Tarybų Socialistinė Respublika

m. metai, year, years, annual publication
Me. Maine
mėn. mėnuo, month

Nakł. Nakład, edition, impression

nauch. nauchnyi, nauchnoi, scientific
n.d. no date of publication
n.F. N.F., NF. neue Folge, new series
no. numero, number, -s
nos. numbers
Nov. November
n.p. no publisher, no place
Nr. Nummer, number
nr. nummer, numeris, number
n.s., ns new series
ns. nouvelle serie
N.Y. New York
N.T. New Testament

Ont. Ontario
otd-nie otdelenie, Division, Branch Section
O.T. Old Testament
otv. red. otvetstvennyi redaktor, editor-in-chief

PLB Pasaulio lietuvių bendruomenė, World Lithuanian community
PWN Panstwowe Wydawnictwo Naukowe
p. page, -s
part. col. partly coloured
Pa. Pennsylvania
pedagog. pedagogicheskiĭ educational
prim. pirmininkas, chairman
port., ports, portrait, -s
posleslov. posleslovie

Pr. Preussen, Prussia
predislovie predislovie, preface
pt. part
pts parts

r. rok, year
R.C. Roman Catholic
red. redagowany, redakcja, redaktsiĩa, redakᵗsiei, edited, editorial office
red. redaktorius, redaktor, editor
rpm. revolution per minute
rugp. rugpiūtis, August
rugs. rugsėjis, September

s. seria, series
S.-Peterburg Sanktpeterburg
s.d. san datum, no date
s.l. san loco, no place
s.n. san nomine, no name
Šv. šventas, holy
sas. sasiuvinys, fascicle, part, issue, number
saus. sausis, January
ser. serija, series
ser. series

Skł. Skład, Publisher, Publishing
      house
sog. sogennant, sogennante, so-
      called
sokr. sokrashchenie, sokrashchen-
      nyĭ, abbreviated
sots.-ekon. sotsial'no-ekonomi-
      cheskoĭ, -kogo, social eco-
      nomic
sov. sovetskaia, -oĭ, Soviet
spec. specialusis redaktorius,
  red. special editor
St.   Saint
Sv.-Dukh Sviatogo Dukha, Holy
      Spirit, Holy Ghost

T., t. tom, tomas, tome, volume
tip. tipografiia, tipografia,
      printing firm
Tow. Towarzystwo, Association
t.p. title page
t.p. tak potem, and so forth
tr.   translated, translator
TSKP Tarybu Sąjungos Komunistu
      Partija, jos Communist
      Party of the Soviet Union
tract. tractatus, treatise, essay
t-va, t-vo tovarichestva, tovari-
      chestvo, Association,
      Society

übers. übersetzt, translated
Übers. Übersetzer, translator
univ. universitetskaia, universi-
      tet, University, Universi-
      ty's
un-t universitet, university
unver.,unverand. unverandert,
      unchanged, unaltered
uppl. upplage, edition

v.,vol. volume, -s
verm. vermehrte, enlarged
VGLL Valstybine grožines litera-
      turos leidykla
voen. voennyĭ, voennoe, voennoĭ,
      military
vstup. vstupitel'nyi, introductory
vstup. stat'ia vstupitel'naia
      stat'ia, introduction,
      introductory article
Vyp., vyp. vypusk, issue, number,
      part, fascicle, edition

Vyr. redaktorius Vyriausias
      redaktorius, editor-in-
      chief
Vses. Vsesoiuznyĭ, -ia All-
      union, USSR

wyd. wydał, wydanie, edited,
      edition
wydawn. wydawnictwo, publishing
      house

X.   Książę, Księtwo, Duke,
      Duchy
XX   Księży, Księże, priests'
      priests

yr   year

zesz. zeszyt, fascicle, part
ZMNP Zhurnal ministerstva na-
      rodnago prosveshcheniia
      (Russia, Ministerstvo
      narodnogo prosveshcheni-
      ia. Zhurnal)

LIST OF SYMBOLS FOR CANADIAN

AND AMERICAN LIBRARIES

CANADIAN LIBRARIES

ALBERTA

CaAEU   University of Alberta, Edmonton

BRITISH COLUMBIA

CaBVa   Vancouver Public Library
CaBVaS   Simon Fraser University, Vancouver
CaBVaU   University of British Columbia, Vancouver
CaBVi   Victoria Public Library
CaBViP   Provincial Library, Victoria

MANITOBA

CaMW   Winnipeg Public Library
CaMWU   University of Manitoba, Winnipeg

NEW BRUNSWICK

CaNBFU   University of New Brunswick, Fredericton

NOVA SCOTIA

CaNSHD   Dalhousie University, Halifax

ONTARIO

CaOHM   McMaster University, Hamilton
CaOKF   Canadian Army Staff College, Kingston
CaOKQ   Queen's University, Kingston
CaOLU   University of Western Ontario, London
CaOOC   Ottawa Public Library
CaOOG   Geological Survey of Canada, Ottawa
CaOOGB   Water Sector Library, Department of Energy, Mines and Resources, Ottawa
CaOON   National Science Library, National Research Council, Ottawa (Formerly National Research Council)
CaOONL   National Library of Canada, Ottawa
CaOONM   National Museum of Canada, Ottawa

CaOOP   Library of Parliament, Ottawa
CaOOSC   Supreme Court of Canada, Ottawa
CaOOU   University of Ottawa
CaOPAL   Lakehead College, Port Arthur
CaOTP   Toronto Public Library, Metropolitan Bibliographic Centre
CaOTR   Ryerson Institute, Toronto
CaOTRM   Royal Ontario Museum, Toronto
CaOTU   University of Toronto
CaOTY   York University, Toronto
CaOWA   University of Windsor
CaOWtU   University of Waterloo
CaWtU   Obsolete. See CaOWtU

QUEBEC

CaQMAI   Arctic Institute of North America, Montreal
CaQMBN   Bibliothèque nationale du Quebec, Montreal. (Formerly Bibliothèque Saint-Sulpice)
CaQMG   Sir George Williams College, Montreal
CaQML   Loyala College, Montreal
CaQMM   McGill University, Montreal
CaQMSS   Obsolete. See CaQMBN
CaQMU   Université de Montreal

SASKATCHEWAN

CaSRL   Legislative Library of Saskatchewan, Regina
CaSSU   University of Saskatchewan, Saskatoon

UNITED STATES LIBRARIES

ALABAMA

A   Obsolete. See A-Ar.
A-Ar   Alabama Department of Archives and History, Montgomery
AAP   Auburn University, Auburn
ABS   Birmingham-Southern College, Birmingham
AMAU   Air University, Maxwell Air Force Base, Montgomery
AU   University of Alabama, University

ARKANSAS

ArU   University of Arkansas,
          Fayetteville

ARIZONA

AzTeS   Arizona State University,
          Tempe
AzU   University of Arizona,
          Tucson

CALIFORNIA

C   California State Library,
          Sacramento
CBGTU   Graduate Theological Union,
          Berkeley
CBPac   Pacific School of Religion,
          Berkeley
CCC   Honnold Library, Claremont
CDU,cdu Disregard-not library symbols
CFS   Fresno State College, Fresno
CL   Los Angeles Public Library
CLI   Immaculate Heart College,
          Los Angeles
CLL   Los Angeles County Law
          Library, Los Angeles
CLS   California State College at
          Los Angeles
CLSU   University of Southern
          California, Los Angeles
CLSU-H ---Hancock Library of Bio-
          logy and Oceanography
CLU   University of California,
          Los Angeles
CLgA   Alma College, Los Gatos
CLobS   California State College at
          Long Beach. (Formerly Long
          Beach State College, Long
          Beach)
CMC   Obsolete. See COMC
CNoS   San Fernando Valley State
          College, Northridge
CPT   California Institute of
          Technology, Pasadena
CSf   San Francisco Public Library
CSfA   California Academy of Scien-
          ces, San Francisco
CSmH   Henry E. Huntington Library,
          San Marino
CSt   Stanford University, Palo
          Alto
CSt-H   ---Hoover Institution on War,
          Revolution and Peace
CStbS   University of California,
          Santa Barbara
CStcIU University of Santa Clara
CU   University of California,
          Berkeley
CU-A   University of California,
          Davis
CU-AL   ---Law Library
CU-CS   University of California,
          Berkeley. Center for
          Chinese Studies

CU-I   University of California,
          Irvine
CU-L   University of Caligornia, Law
          Library, Berkeley
CU-Riv University of California,
          Riverside
CU-S   University of California,
          San Diego
CU-SC   University of California,
          Santa Cruz. (Includes Lick
          Observatory)

COLORADO

CoCC   Colorado College, Colorado
          Springs
CoDI   Iliff School of Theology,
          Denver
CoDGS   U.S. Geological Survey, Fe-
          deral Center, Denver
CoDMS   Colorado Military School,
          Denver
CoDMSC Metropolitan State College of
          Denver
CoDU   University of Denver
CoDuF   Fort Lewis College, Durango
CoFS   Colorado State University,
          Fort Collins
CoG   Colorado School of Mines,
          Golden
CoGrS   Colorado State College,
          Greeley
CoU   University of Colorado,
          Boulder

CONNECTICUT

Ct   Connecticut State Library,
          Hartford
CtHC   Hartford Seminary Foundation,
          Hartford
CtHi   Connecticut Historical Socie-
          ty, Hartford
CtHT   Trinity College, Hartford
CtHW   ULS symbol for CtHT-W
CtNIC   Connecticut College, New
          London
CtPAM   ALKA Museum, Putman, Conn.
CtTMF   Marian Fathers, Thompson, Conn.
CtW   Wesleyan University, Middle-
          town
CtY   Yale University, New Haven
CtY-D   ---Divinity School
CtY-KS ---Kline Science Library
CtY-L   ---Law Library

DISTRICT OF COLUMBIA
WASHINGTON, D.C.

DA   Obsolete. See DNAL
DAU   American University
DCE   Obsolete. See DSI
DCU   Catholic University of
          America
DCaE   Canadian Embassy

DDO   Dumbarton Oaks Research Library of Harvard University
DFo   Folger Shakespeare Library
DGS   Obsolete. See DI-GS
DGU   Georgetown University
DGW   George Washington University
DGW-C   ---Carnegie endowment for International Peace Collection
DI   U.S. Department of the Interior Library
DI-GS   ---Geological Survey Library
DLC   U.S. Library of Congress
DLC-L   ---Law Library
DLC-P4 ---Priority 4 Collection
DLL   Lithuanian Legation, Washington, D.C.
DN   U.S. Department of the Navy
DNAL   U.S. National Agricultural Library
DNIH   U.S. National Institutes of Health, Bethesda, Md.
DNLM   U.S. National Library of Medicine
DNW   U.S. National War College, Fort McNair
DS   U.S. Department of State Library (Division of Library and Reference Services)
DSG   Obsolete. See DNLM
DSG   ULS symbol for DNLM
DSI   Smithsonian Institution
DSI-E   Bureau of American Ethnology Library. Obsolete. See DSI
DSI-M   Obsolete. See DSI
DWB   Obsolete. See DAS

DELAWARE

DeU   University of Delaware, Newark

FLORIDA

F   Florida State Library, Tallahasse
FDS   Stetson University, Deland. (Formerly John B. Stetson University)
FM   Miami Public Library
FMU   University of Miami, Coral Gables
FTS   ULS symbol of FTaSU
FTaSU   Florida State University, Tallahassee
FU   University of Florida, Gainesville

GEORGIA

GA   Atlanta Public Library
GAT   Georgia Institute of Technology, Atlanta
GDS   Agnes Scott College, Decatur
GEU   Emory University, Atlanta
GEU-T   ---Candler School of Theology

GOU   ULS symbol for GAOC
GOgU   Obsolete. See GAOC
GU   University of Georgia, Athens
GU-L   ---Law Library

HAWAII

H   Library of Hawaii, Honolulu
HU   University of Hawaii, Honolulu

ILLINOIS

I   Illinois State Library, Springfield
IC   Chicago Public Library
ICBM   Balzekas Museum of Lithuanian Culture, Chicago
ICCC   St. Casimir Convent, 2601 West Marquette Road, Chicago
ICD   DePaul University, Chicago
ICF   Chicago Natural History
ICIU   University of Illinois at Chicago Circle, Chicago
ICJ   John Crerar Library, Chicago
ICJS   College of Jewish Studies, Chicago
ICLJF   Lithuanian Jesuit Fathers, Chicago
ICMcC   McCormick Theological Seminary, Chicago
ICN   Newberry Library, Chicago
ICRL   Center for Research Libraries, Chicago. (Formerly Midwest Inter-Library Center
ICU   University of Chicago
ICWA   World Lithuanian Archives, Chicago
ICarbS Southern Illinois University, Carbondale
IEG   Garnett Theological Seminary, Evanston
IEN   Northwestern University, Evanston
IEN-L   ---Law Library, Chicago
IEdS   Southern Illinois University, Edwardsville Campus
INS   Illinois State University Normal
IRA   Augustana College, Rock Island
IU   University of Illinois, Urbana

IOWA

IaAS   Iowa State University of Science and Technology, Ames
IaDL   Luther College, Decorah
IaGG   Grinnell College, Grinnell
IaU   University of Iowa, Iowa City
IaU-L   ---College of Law

IDAHO

IdB	Boise Public Library
IdPI	Idaho State University, Pocatello
IdU	University of Idaho, Moscow

INDIANA

In	Indiana State Library, Indianapolis
InCW	Wabash College, Crawfords-ville
InIA	Indiana Academy of Science, Indianapolis
InLP	Purdue University, Lafay-ette
InNd	University of Notre Dame, Notre Dame
InRenS	St. Joseph's College, Rensselaer
InS	South Bend Public Library
InU	Indiana University, Bloom-ington

KANSAS

KAS	Saint Benedict's College, Atchison
KEmT	Kansas State Teachers College, Emporia
KMK	Kansas State University, Manhattan
KStMC	Obsolete. See MoSU-D
KT	Topeka Public Library
KU	University of Kansas, Lawrence
KU-M	---School of Medicine, Kansas City

KENTUCKY

KyLo	Louisville Free Public Library
KyLoU	University of Louisville
KyLx	Lexington Public Library
KyLxCB	Lexington Theological Seminary, Lexington. (Formerly College of the Bible)
KyU	University of Kentucky, Lexington
KyWAT	Asbury Theological Seminary, Wilmore

LOUISIANA

LN	New Orleans Public Library
LNHT	Tulane University, New Orleans
LNL	Loyola University, New Orleans
LU	Louisiana State University, Baton Rouge
LU-L	---Law Library
LU-NO	Louisiana State University in New Orleans

MASSACHUSETTS

MA	Amherst College, Amherst
MB	Boston Public Library
MBA	American Academy of the Arts and Sciences, Boston
MBAt	Boston Atheneum
MBC	American Congregational Association, Boston
MBCo	Countway Library of Medicine (Harvard-Boston Medical Libraries), Boston
MBMu	Museum of Fine Arts, Boston
MBN	Boston Museum of Science
MBU	Boston University
MBU-T	---School of Theology Library
MBdAF	U.S. Air Force Cambridge Research Center, Bedford
MBtS	Saint John's Seminary, Brighton
MCM	Massachusetts Institute of Technology, Cambridge
MH	Harvard University, Cambridge
MH-A	---Arnold Arboretum
MH-AH	---Andover-Harvard Theological Library
MH-BH	---Blue Hill Observatory
MH-F	Farlow Reference Library
MH-G	---Gray Herbarium
MH-L	---Law School
MH-P	---Peabody Museum
MH-Z	---Museum of Comparative Zoology
MHi	Massachusetts Historical Society, Boston
MNF	Forbes Library, Northampton
MNS	Smith College, Northampton
MNtcA	Andover Newton Theological School, Newton Center
MShM	Mount Holyoke College, South Hadley
MSM	ULS symbol for MShM
MSohG	Gordon-Cornell Theological Society Library, South Hamilton, Mass.
MU	University of Massachusetts, Amherst
MWA	American Antiquarian Society, Worcester
MWC	Clark University, Worcester
MWM	Worcester Art Museum
MWalB	Brandeis University, Waltham
MWelC	Wellesley College, Wellesley
MWhB	Marine Biological Laboratory, Woods Hole
MWiCA	Sterling and Francine Clark Art Institute, Williamstown, Mass.
MWiW	Williams College, Williamstown

MARYLAND

MdAN	U.S. Naval Academy, Annapolis
MdBE	Enoch Pratt Free Library, Baltimore

MdBJ	Johns Hopkins University, Baltimore		MONTANA
MdBP	Peabody Institute, Baltimore	MtBC	Montana State University at Bozeman
MdU	University of Maryland, College Park	MtU	University of Montana at Missoula

MAINE

NEW YORK

MeB	Bowdoin College, Brunswick	N	New York State Library, Albany
MeP	Portland Public Library	NAW	ULS symbol for NAurW
MeU	University of Maine, Orono	NAurW	Wells College, Aurora
		NB	Brooklyn Public Library
		NBB	Brooklyn Museum

MICHIGAN

MiD	Detroit Public Library	NBC	Brooklyn College, Brooklyn
MiDW	Wayne State University, Detroit	NBG	Brooklyn Botanic Garden
		NBM	Medical Research Library
MiEM	Michigan State University, East Lansing	NBSU-M	Obsolete. See NBM
		NBu	Buffalo and Erie County Public Library, Buffalo
MiMtpT	Central Michigan University, Mount Pleasant	NBuB	Buffalo Society of Natural Sciences, Buffalo Museum of Science
MiU	University of Michigan, Ann Arbor		
MiU-C	---William L. Clements Library	NBuC	State University of New York College at Buffalo
MiU-L	---Law Library	NBuG	Grosvenor Reference Division, Buffalo and Erie County Public Library, Buffalo

MINNESOTA

		NBuU	State University of New York At Buffalo
MnHi	Minnesota Historical Society, Saint Paul	NCH	Hamilton College, Clinton
		NFQC	Queens College, Flushing
MnM	Minneapolis Public Library	NGrmUN	Obsolete. See NNUN
MnSJ	James Jerome Hill Reference Library, Saint Paul	NIC	Cornell University, Ithaca
		NIC-A	---Obsolete. See NIC
MnSSC	College of Saint Catherine, Saint Paul	NN	New York Public Library
		NNA	American Geographical Society, New York
MnU	University of Minnesota, Minneapolis	NNAL	American Academy of Arts and Letters, New York
MnU-L	---Law Library	NNB	Association of the Bar of the City of New York

MISSOURI

		NNBG	New York Botanical Garden, Bronx Park
MoK	Kansas City Public Library	NNC	Columbia University, New York
MoKL	Linda Hall Library, Kansas City	NNC-L	---Law Library
		NNC-M	---Medical Library
MoSA	Obsolete. See MoSU	NNC-T	---Teachers College
MoSB	Missouri Botanical Garden, Saint Louis	NNCFR	Council on Foreign Relations, New York
MoSCS	Concordia Seminary, Saint Louis	NNCU-G	Graduate Center Library, City University of New York
MoSU	Saint Louis University, Saint Louis	NNCoC	ULS symbol for NNCoCi
		NNCoCi	City College of the City University of New York
MoSW	Washington University, Saint Louis	NNCoo	Cooper Union for the Advancement of Science and Art, New York
MoU	University of Missouri, Columbia		
		NNE	Engineering Societies Library, New York

MISSISSIPPI

		NNF	Fordham University, New York
		NNG	General Theological Seminary of the Protestant Episcopal Church, New York
MsSM	Mississippi State University, State College		
MsU	University of Mississippi, University	NNJ	Jewish Theological Seminary of America, New York

NNM   American Museum of Natural History, New York
NNQ   Obsolete. See NJQ
NNStJ   Saint John's University, Jamaica
NNU   New York University Libraries, New York
NNU-C   ---School of Commerce
NNU-H   ---University Heights Library
NNU-W   Washington Square Library
NNUN   United Nations, New York
NNUN-W   ---Woodrow Wilson Memorial Library
NNUT   Union Theological Seminary, New York
NPV   Vassar College, Poughkeepsie
NR   Rochester Public Library
NRRI   Rochester Institute of Technology
NRU   University of Rochester
NSU   ULS symbol for NSyU
NSbSU   State University of New York at Stony Brook
NSyU   Syracuse University, Syracuse
NWM   U.S. Military Academy, West Point
NYBT   Boyce Thompson Institute for Plant Research, Yonkers

NEBRASKA

NbU   University of Nebraska, Lincoln

NORTH CAROLINA

Nc   North Carolina State Library, Raleigh
NcC   Public Library of Charlotte & Mecklenburg County, Charlotte
NcD   Duke University, Durham
NcD-L   ---School of Law
NcGU   University of North Carolina at Greensboro
NcGW   Obsolete. See NcGU
NcRS   North Carolina State University at Raleigh
NcU   University of North Carolina, Chapel Hill
NcWsW   Wake Forest College, Winston-Salem

NEW HAMPSHIRE

Nh   New Hampshire State Library, Concord
NhD   Dartmouth College, Hanover
NhU   University of New Hampshire, Durham

NEW JERSEY

NjMD   Drew University, Madison
NjNbS   Gardner A. Sage Library, New Brunswick Theological Seminary, New Brunswick
NjNbT   Obsolete. See NjNbS
NjP   Princeton University, Princeton
NjPT   Princeton Theological Seminary, Princeton
NjR   Rutgers-The State University, New Brunswick

NEW MEXICO

NmLcU   New Mexico State University, Las Cruces
NmU   University of New Mexico, Albuquerque

NEVADA

NvU   University of Nevada, Reno

OHIO

OAU   Ohio University, Athens
OAkU   University of Akron
OC   Public Library of Cincinnati and Hamilton County, Cincinnati
OCH   Hebrew Union College, Jewish Institute of Religion, Cincinnati
OCU   University of Cincinnati
OCl   Cleveland Public Library
OClCS   Obsolete. See OClW
OClJC   John Carroll University, Cleveland
OClMA   Cleveland Museum of Art
OClND   Notre Dame College, Cleveland
OClU   Cleveland State University, Cleveland. (Formerly Fenn College)
OClUR   Ursuline College for Women, Cleveland
OClW   Case Western Reserve University, Cleveland
ODW   Ohio Wesleyan University, Delaware
ODa   Dayton and Montgomery County Public Library, Dayton
OEac   East Cleveland Public Library
OKentU   Kent State University, Kent
OO   Oberlin College, Oberlin
OOxM   Miami University, Oxford
OU   Ohio State University, Columbus
OWorP   Pontifical College Josephinum, Worthington
OYesA   Antioch College, Yellow Springs

OKLAHOMA

OkS	Oklahoma State University, Stillwater
OkTU	University of Tulsa
OkU	University of Oklahoma, Norman

OREGON

Or	Oregon State Library, Salem
OrAshS	Southern Oregon College, Ashland
OrCA	Obsolete. See OrCS
OrCS	Oregon State University, Corvallis
OrLgE	Eastern Oregon College, La Grande
OrMonO	Oregon College of Education, Monmouth
OrP	Library Association of Portland
OrPR	Reed College, Portland
OrPS	Portland State College, Portland
OrSaW	Williamette University, Salem
OrStbM	Mount Angel College, Saint Benedict
OrU	University of Oregon, Eugene

PENNSYLVANIA

P	Pennsylvania State Library, Harrisburg
PBL	Lehigh University, Bethlehem
PBa	Academy of the New Church, Bryn Athyn
PBm	Bryn Mawr College, Bryn Mawr
PCC	Crozier Theological Seminary, Chester
PCM	PMC Colleges, Chester
PCM	Pennsylvania Military College, Chester
PCaD	Obsolete. See PCarlD
PCamA	Alliance College, Cambridge Springs
PCarlD	Dickinson College, Carlisle
PEL	Lafayette College, Easton
PHC	Haverford College, Haverford
PIm	Immaculata College, Immaculata
PLatS	Saint Vincent College and Archabbey, Latrobe
PP	Free Library of Philadelphia
PPA	Athenaeum of Philadelphia
PPAN	Academy of Natural Sciences, Philadelphia
PPAP	Obsolete. See PPAmP
PPAmP	American Philosophical Society, Philadelphia
PPC	College of Physicians of Philadelphia
PPB	Philadelphia Bar Association
PPD	Drexel Institute of Technology, Philadelphia

PPDrop	Dropsie College for Hebrew and Cognate Learning, Philadelphia
PPF	Franklin Institute, Philadelphia
PPG	German Society of Pennsylvania, Philadelphia
PPGeo	Geographical Society of Philadelphia
PPGi	Girard College, Philadelphia
PPL	Library Company of Philadelphia
PPLT	Lutheran Theological Seminary, Krauth Memorial Library, Philadelphia
PPLas	LaSalle College, Philadelphia
PPM	Mercantile Library, Philadelphia (No longer in existence)
PPT	Temple University, Philadelphia
PPULC	Union Library Catalogue of Pennsylvania, Philadelphia
PPWe	Westminster Theological Seminary, Philadelphia
PPi	Carnegie Library of Pittsburgh
PPiD	Duquesne University, Pittsburgh
PPiPT	Pittsburgh Theological Seminary
PPiU	University of Pittsburgh
PSC	Swarthmore College, Swarthmore
PSc	Scranton Public Library
PSt	Pennsylvania State University, University Park
PU	University of Pennyslvania, Philadelphia
PU-L	---Biddle Law Library
PU-MU	---University Museum
PU-W	---Wharton School of Finance and Commerce
PV	Villanova University, Villanova
PWcS	West Chester State College, West Chester

RHODE ISLAND

RP	Providence Public Library
RPB	Brown University, Providence
RPJCB	John Carter Brown Library, Providence

SOUTH CAROLINA

ScCleU	Clemson University, Clemson
ScU	University of South Carolina, Columbia

TENNESSEE

TMG	Goodwyn Institute, Memphis
TNG	George Peabody College for Teachers, Nashville. See also TNJ-P
TNJ-P	Joint University Libraries, Nashville, Peabody College
TNV	Obsolete. See TNJ
TNV-M	Obsolete. See TNJ-M
TOU	Oak Ridge Associated Universities, Oak Ridge
TU	University of Tennessee, Knoxville

TEXAS

TxBeal	Lamar State College of Technology, Beaumont
TxCM	Texas A & M University, College Station
TxDaM	Southern Methodist University, Dallas
TxDW	Texas Woman's University, Denton
TxDaM-P	Southern Methodist University, Dallas. Perkins School of Theology
TxFTC	Texas Christian University, Fort Worth
TxHR	Rice University, Houston
TxHU	University of Houston
TxLT	Texas Technological College, Lubbock
TxU	University of Texas, Austin
TxSaT	Trinity University, San Antonio

UTAH

ULA	Utah State University, Logan
UPB	Brigham Young University, Provo
UU	University of Utah, Salt Lake City

VIRGINIA

VHS	ULS symbol for ViHdsC
VU	Obsolete. See ViU
ViBlbV	Virginia Polytechnic Istitute, Blacksburg
ViHarEM	Eastern Mennonite College, Harrisonburg
ViLxW	Washington & Lee University, Lexington
ViRUT	Union Theological Seminary, Richmond
ViU	University of Virginia, Charlottesville

VERMONT

VtMM	ULS symbol for VtMiM
VtMiM	Middlebury College, Middlebury
VtU	University of Vermont and State Agricultural College, Burlington

WISCONSIN

WAL	Lawrence University, Appleton
WE	Eau Claire Public Library
WLacU	Wisconsin State University, LaCrosse
WM	Milwaukee Public Library
WU	University of Wisconsin, Madison

WASHINGTON

Wa	Washington State Library
WaE	Everett Public Library
WaS	Seattle Public Library
WaSp	Spokane Public Library
WaSpG	Gonzaga University, Spokane
WaT	Tacoma Public Library
WaTC	University of Puget Sound, Tacoma
WaU	University of Washington, Seattle
WaU-L	---Law Library
WaWW	Whitman College, Walla Walla

WEST VIRGINIA

WvU	West Virginia University, Morgantown

WYOMING

Wy	Wyoming State Library, Cheyenne
WyU	University of Wyoming, Laramie

LIBRARIES IN OTHER COUNTRIES

Au.GU	Universitäts-Bibliothek, Graz, Austria
Au.InU	Universitäts-Bibliothek, Innsbruck, Austria
Au.WLH	Landwitschaftliche Hochschule, Wien, Austria
BM	Britisch Museum Library, London, W.C.L., England

BN	Bibliothèque National, Paris France	Ger.HmbU	Universitäts-Bibliothek, Hamburg, Germany
Fr.StU	Université de Strasbourg, France	Ger.MnsU	Universitäts-Bibliothek, Münster, Germany
Ger.BlU	Universitäts-Bibliothek, Berlin, Germany	Ger.TU	Universitäts-Bibliothek, Tübingen, Germany
Ger.BU	Universitäts-Bibliothek, Bonn, Germany	It.RG	Pontificia Universitas Gregoriana, Rome, Italy
Ger.DaTH	Technische Hochschule, Darmstadt, Germany	Lith.VU	University of Vilnius Library, Vilnius, Lithuania
Ger.FBrU	Universitäts-Bibliothek, Freiburg im Br., Germany	Swz.FU	Universitäts-Bibliothek, Fribourg, Switzerland
Ger.HlbU	Universitäts-Bibliothek, Heidelberg, Germany		

I. BIBLIOGRAPHIC AIDS

I. 1. GENERAL BIBLIOGRAPHIES

1. BIRŽIŠKA, Vaclovas. Lietuvių bibliografija. Kaunas, Švietimo ministerijos leidinys, 1924-1929 [Xerox copy, 1976] 3 v. Contents:-- T.1. XVI-XVIII amž.--T.2. 1800-1864 m.--T.3. 1865-1904 m. Z2537.B55 1924a PU

2. CHERNEVSKII, Petr Osipovich. Ukazatel' materialov dlia izuchenii severo-zapadnogo kraia (Kovenskaia, Vilenskaia i Grodnenskaia gub.) v arkheologichesko-etnograficheskom otnoshenii. In Pamiatnaia knizhka Kovenskoi gubernii. Kovno, 1882. DK511.K55P32 DLC; PU

3. GOLDAS, M. Tarybų Lietuva; literatūros rodyklė, 1965-1970. Vilnius, 1972. 200 p. At head of title Lietuvos TSR Valastybinė respublikinė biblioteka. M. Goldas ir E. Lagauskienė. [Soviet Lithuania; bibliography, 1965-1970] Z2537.G58 DLC; MH; WU

4. KANTAUTAS, Adam. A Lithuanian bibliography; a check-list of books and articles held by the major libraries of Canada and the United States. [By] Adam and Filomena Kantautas. Edmonton, Alta, University of Alberta Press, 1975. xxxix, 725 p. Z2537. K33 DLC; CaAEU; OKentU; PU

5. REKLAITIS, Povilas Viktoras. Litauische Bibliographie, 1970-1972 in Auswahl. In Zeitschrift für Ostforschung (Marburg-Lahn, Ger.), 1974, p. 364-381. See serials consulted.

6. --- Litauische Bibliographie, 1973-1974 in Auswahl. In Zeitschrift für Ostforschung (Marburg-Lahn, Ger.) Jahrg. 26, 1977, p. 173-192. See serials consulted.

7. RISTER, Herbert. Schrifttum über Litauen, 1943-1953. In Zeitschrift für Ostforschung (Marburg-Lahn, Ger.) v.4, no.2, 1955, p.305-320. See serials consulted.

I.2. SUBJECT BIBLIOGRAPHIES

8. THE AMERICAN BIBLIOGRAPHY OF SLAVIC AND EAST EUROPEAN STUDIES FOR 1958. Joseph Shaw, ed. Bloomington, Ind., Indiana University Press, 1957-112 p. (Slavic and East European series, no. 18) Z2483.A65 DLC; CaBVaU; CaAEU; KEmT; NSyU; TxU; UU

ARMON, Witold. Wybrana bibliografia etnograficzna Litwy za lata 1949-1965. In Etnografia Polska. Warszawa, 1968. v.12, p. 475-490. GN585.P6E8 DLC; see also serials consulted.

10. BIENHOLD, Marianne. Quellen und Literatur. In Her Entstehung des litauischen Staates in den Jahren 1918-1919 im Spiegel deutscher Akten. Bochum, 1976. p.367-408. A bibliography on the question of German politics toward the Lithuanian State. DK511.L26B58 1976 CaAEU; DLC; PU

11. BIRŽIŠKA, Vaclovas. The American-Lithuanian publications, 1875-1910. [Boulder, Colo., 1959] p.396-408. Reproduced by xerography from Journal of Central European Affairs, 1959, v. 18, no.4, in 1972. PG8740.B5 PU

12. BUFIENĖ, Teklė. Lietuvos TSR rašytojai, literatūrinių premijų premijų laureatai; rekomenduojamosios literatūros rodyklė. [The writers of the Lithuanian SSR who received literary awards; recomended bibliography] Vilnius, 1969. 187 p. ports. Z2537.B93 DLC; MH; NNC

13. DILYS, Povilas, comp. Mokslo personalo spaudinių bibliografija 1922-1924-1971) In Čepėnas, P. ed. Lietuvos Universitetas. Chicago,Ill. 1972. p.785-816. [A bibliography of publications by the academic staff of the University of Vilnius, 1922-1971] LA853.L48C4 PU; CaAEU; InNd; NjP

14. DUBINSKI, S. A. Bibliografiia po arkheologii Belarusi i sumezhnykh krain. Mensk, 1933. Mu913.476.D853 PU

15. GEOLOGICHESKAIA IZUCHENNOST' SSSR. t.6: Kaliningradskaia oblast' RSFSR. Period 1946-1960. Vyp. 1. Pechatnye raboty. Vil'nius, 1966. 137 p. QE276.G415 DLC; CaAEU; MiU; OClW

16. INGLOT, Mieczysław. Polskie czasopisma literackie ziem litewsko-ruskich w latach 1832-1851. Warszawa, Państwowe Wydawn. Naukowe, 1966.

375 p. ill., facsims., ports. Pracownia historii czasopiśmiennictwa Polskiego XIX i XX wieku PAN. Materialy i studia do historii prasy i czasopiśmiennictwa polskiego, zeszyt 5. PN5355.P6I52 CaAEU; CLU; CU; ICU;

17. KAMIŃSKI, A. Materiały do bibliografii archeologicznej Jaćwierzy od I do XIII w. In Materiały starożytne (Warszawa), tom 1, 1956, p. 193-273. DK409.M3 DLC; see also serials consulted.

18. KANET, Roger E. Soviet and East European Foreign policy; a bibliography of English and Russian language publications, 1967-1971. Santa Barbara, Calif., Clio Press, 1974. 208 p. Z2510.K3 DLC

19. KOLUPAILA, Steponas. Lietuvos upių monografijos. [The monographs of Lithuanian rivers. In Židinys (Kaunas), no.7, v.14, 1931, p.20-29 and v.16, no.8-9, 1932, p.131-145. See serials consulted.

20. KUCHARZEWSKI, Jan. Czasopiśmiennictwo polskie wieku XIX w Królestwie, na Litwie i Rusi oraz na emigracyi; zarys bibliograficzno-historyczny... Warszawa, Gebethner i Wolff, 1911. 121 p. Reprinted from Przegląd Narodowy. *QO p.v.12,no.2 --NN

21. LEVICKAITĖ, Danutė. Lietuvių rašytojai vaikams (proza). Vilnius, Lietuvos TSR Valstybinė respublikinė biblioteka, Vaikų literatūros skyrius, 1972. 112 p. [Lithuanian authors of childrens literature] Z2537.L4 PU

22. LEWICKI, Józef. Bibliography of prints having reference to the Commission of national education in Poland, first instruction department in Europe from 1773-1794. Bibliografia druków odnoszących się do Komisyi edukacyi narodowej... [Lwów, B. Połonieckiego, 1908] 3 p. .,[3]-172, [4] p. Z5815.P7L5 DLC; NN

23. LIETUVOS TSR MOKSLŲ AKADEMIJA, VILNA. LIETUVIŲ KALBOS IR LITERATŪROS INSTITUTAS. Lietuvių literatūros mokslas ir kritika, 1971-1973; bibliografinė rodyklė. [Lithuanian literature and criticism, 1971-1973; a bibliography. Sudarė Eugenijus Stančikas. Redagavo Jonas Vosylius] Vilnius, Vaga, 1976. 428 p. Sequel to: Tarybinis lietuvių literatūros mokslas ir kritika apie literatūrinį palikimą and Tarybinė lietuvių literatūra ir kritika. Z2537.L517 PU

24. LIETUVOS TSR MOKSLŲ AKADEMIJA, VILNA. LIETUVIU KALBOS IR LITERATŪROS INSTITUTAS. Tarybinis lietuvių literatūros mokslas ir kritika apie literatūrinį palikimą, 1959-1970; bibliografinė rodyklė. [Soviet Lithuanian literature and criticism, 1959-1970; a bibliography. Sudarė Eugenijus Stančikas. Redagavo Jonas Vosylius] Vilnius, Vaga, 1975. 430 p. Z2537.L516 PU

25. LITOVSKAĨA SSR; period 1966-1970. [Otv. redaktor A. A. Grigĩalis sostavitel' I.IŪ. Skuodienė] Vil'-nius, Periodika, 1975- . v. Geologicheskaĩa izuchennost' SSSR; t. 43) At head of title, v.1- : Ministerstvo geologii pri Sovete Ministrov Litovskoĩ SSR. Litovskiĩ nauchno-issledovatel'skiĩ geologorazvedochnyĩ institut. Partial contents.--Vyp.1. Pechatnye raboty. QE276.G415 t.43, 1966-1970, vyp.1 DLC

26. MASIOKAS, M. Specialus pramoninių katalogų fondas, 1973. Vilnius, LIMTI, 1973. 35 p. At head of title; Lietuvos mokslinės techninės informacijos ir techninės ekonominės analizės mokslo tyrimo institutas. Z7914.M3M37 DLC

27. PLEKAVIČIENĖ, Birutė. Kultūros-švietimo darbuotojui; rekomenduojamos metodinės literatūros rodyklė. Vilnius, Lietuvos TSR Valstybinė respublikinė biblioteka,1973. 85 p. [A bibliography for the educator and social worker] At head of title: Lietuvos TSR Valstybinė respublikinė biblioteka. Z2537.P55 PU; DLC; WU

28. POŠKUTĖ, B. Techninės literatūros bibliografiniai šaltiniai; trumpas bibliografinis vadovas. [Bibliographic sources of the technical literature...] At head of title Lietuvos TSR Valstibinė respublikinė biblioteka. B. Poškutė. Vilnius, 1967. 122 p. Z7911.A1P67 DLC

29. RAČKAUSKAS, Jonas A. Bibliografija. [A bibliography of the Primary education in Lithuania] In Lietuvių Tautos Praeitis (Chicago, Ill.), v.3, kn.1, 1971, p. 125-132. See serials consulted.

30. ŠIUPŠINSKIENĖ, KLARA. Pjesės; bibliografinė rodyklė (1945-1970) Vilnius, Lietuvos TSR Valstybinė respublikinė biblioteka, 1972. 179 p. [Drama; a bibliography, 1945-1970] Z2537.S57 PU

31. SPITRYS, Chuanas. Rusų rašytojai lietuvių kalba, 1940-1970;

bibliografija. [Russian literature
in Lithuanian, 1940-1970] Vilnius,
Lietuvos TSR Valstybinė respublikinė
biblioteka, 1974. 313 p.
Z2054.T7S65 PU

32. Cancelled.

33. VAŠTOKAS, Joan M. M.K. Čiurlionis: a preliminary bibliography.
In Lituanus (Chicago, Ill.), v.21,
no.2, 1975, p. 51-54. See serials
consulted.

34. VILNA. VALSTYBINE MOKSLINĖS
MEDICINOS BIBLIOTEKA. Lietuviškoji
medicininė bibliografija. [A Lithuanian medical bibliography. Ats.
red. M. Maslauskienė] Vilnius,
1959- . v. At head of title:
Lietuvos TSR Sveikatos apsaugos ministerija. V. Šimkūnas, M. Maslaus-
kienė] Lithuanian and Russian.
Z6661.L75V5 DLC(2-); DNLM(1-); MH(1-)
PU(1-); CaOTU(3-)

35. VILNA. ŽEMĖS ŪKIO EKONOMIKOS
MOKSLINIO TYRIMO INSTITUTAS. Lietuvos žemės ūkio ekonomikos mokslinio
tyrimo instituto leidinių bibliografija, 1959-1971. Bibliografiia iz-
daniĭ Litovskogo nauchno-issledovatel'skogo instituta ėkonomiki sel's-
kogo khoziaĭstva. Lietuvos žemės
ūkio ekonomikos mokslinio tyrimo institutas. Sudarė R. Bitinaitė, A. Bra-
šiškienė, J.Kerbelytė] Vilnius, Periodika, 1973. 155 p.
Z5075.L55V56 1973 DLC

36. WERMKE, Ernst. Bibliographie
der Geschichte von Ost- und Westpreussen für die Jahre 1967-1970,
nebst Nachträgen aus früheren Jahren.
Bearb. im Auftrag der Historischen
Kommission für ost- und westpreussische Landesforschung. Marburg-Lahn,
Johann Gottfried Herder-Institut,
1972. xii, 364 p. DR10.W5 nr.93 PU

37. --- --- für die Jahre 1939-
1970. Bearb. im Auftrag der Historischen Kommission für ost- und west-
preussische Landesforschung. Bonn,
Verlag Wissenschaftliches Archiv,
1974. xv, 1153 p. Originally issued
in 5 parts, 1953-1970.
Z2527.P78W47 PU; DLC; NRU

38. WIEDEMANN, Oskar. Sprachver-
gleichende Werke. In His Handbuch
der litauischen Sprache. Strassburg,
1897. p. 4-6. 491.92W63 NbU; MiU;
OClW; OCU; OU; InU; GU; NN; NRU

39. ŽEBRYTĖ, Jonė. Pažinkime gim-
tąjį kraštą; literatūros rodyklė.
[Let's know the native land; a bib-
liography] Vilnius, Lietuvos TSR Kultūros ministerija, 1974. 277 p.

At head of title: Lietuvos TSR Valstybinė respublikinė biblioteka.
Z2557.Z4 DLC

I.3 BIBLIOGRAPHIES OF INDIVIDUAL
AUTHORS

40. ANDRIULIS, V., comp. Augustinas Janulaitis, 1878-1950; biobibliografija. [A. Janulaitis, 1878-1950;
a biobibliography. Sudarė V. Andriulis. Spec. red. J. Basiulis] Vilnius,
[s.n.], 1972. 67 p., port.
Z8449.45.A53 DLC; PU

41. BAGDANAVIČIUS, Vytautas Jonas.
Raštų bibliografija, 1945-1972 m.
[Bibliography of V.J.Bagdanavičius
writings, 1945-1972] Chicago, Ill.,
1973. 126 leaves. Z8062.6.B3 PU;
CaAEU

42. BUŠMIENĖ, Stasė. Eduardas Volteris; biobibliografija. [E. Volter;
a biobibliography] Vilnius, Lietuvos TSR Valstybinė respublikinė biblioteka, 1973. Z8945.2.B8 PU

43. KURLIANDSKIENĖ, Birutė. Juo-
zas Žiugžda; literatūros rodyklė.
[Juozas Žiugžda; a bibliography] Vil-
nius, Lietuvos TSR Mokslų akademijos
Centrinė biblioteka, 1974.
Z8998.35.K8 PU

44. KUZMICKAS, Vincas and ŠEŠEL-
GIS, Aleksandras. Jurgis Zauerveinas
medžiaga bibliografijai. [Jurgis
Zauerveinas; a bibliography] Vilnius,
Lietuvos TSR Mokslų akademija, Lietuvių kalbos ir literatūros institutas,
1975. 204 p. Z8784.55.K8 PU

45. MACIŪNAS, Vincas. Antano Strazdo bibliografija. [A bibliography
of A. Atrazdas] Chicago, Ill., 1970.
13 leaves. Xerox copy of clippings
from Draugas, 1970, no.2 and 8.
Z8850.05.M3 PU

46. PLACE, Georges G. Milosz
[bibliographie] Paris, Editions de
la chronique des lettres françaises,
1970. 52 p. In Talvart, Hector.
Bibliographie des auteurs modernes
de langue française... Paris, 1963.
Tome 15, p. [153]-188.
PQ226.Z T15 T.15 CaAEU; MWH; NNC

47. SAMULIONIS, Algis Romualdas.
Balio Sruogos raštų bibliografija.
[A bibliography of the works of Balys Sruoga] Vilnius, Mintis, 1970.
231 p. At head of title: Lietuvos
TSR Mokslų akademija. Lietuvių kalbos ir literatūros institutas. Summary in Russian. Z8832.78.S35 DLC;
CtY; CU; MH; NjP; PPiU

48. SKARDŽIUS, Pranas. J. Jablonskis. J. Jablonskio bibliografija. [A bibliography of J. Jablonskis by A. Merkelis] In Archivum philologicum Kaunas), kn.2, 1931, p. 5-37. See serials consulted.

49. VAITIEKŪNIENĖ, Aldona, comp. Knygų, straipsnių ir kitų darbų apie Vaižganto kūryba bibliografija. [A bibliography of books, articles, etc about Vaižgantas (J. Tumas)] In Her Vaižganto apysaka "Dėdės ir dėdienės" Vilnius, 1964. p. 259-273. PG8721.V3215V3 DLC; PU; PPULC; OU

50. VALENTĖLIENĖ, Petronėlė. Juozas Matulis; literatūros rodyklė. [Juozas Matulis; a bibliography of his works] Vilnius, Lietuvos TSR Mokslų akademijos Centrinė biblioteka, 1973. 143 p., port. Lithuanian and Russian. Z8554.713.V34 PU; DLC

51. VILNONYTĖ, Valerija and LUKOŠIŪNAS, Algimantas. Petras Cvirka; bibliografija, 1924-1970. [P. Cvirka; a bibliography] Vilnius, Vaga, 1974. 630 p. PG8721.C8Z9 PU; DLC; WU

I.4. LIBRARY CATALOGUES AND GUIDES TO COLLECTIONS

52. BALYS, Jonas. Lithuanian materials available in the Library of Congress. [By] John P. Balys. In Lituanus (Chicago, Ill.), no.4, v.20, 1974, p. 32-41. See serials consulted.

53. BOSTON. PUBLIC LIBRARY. Dictionary catalog of the music collection. Boston, Mass., G.K. Hall, 1972. 20 v. Lithuania is in v.10, p. 231-232. ML136.B7B74 1972 CaAEU; DLC; CU; GU; IU; IaU; MB; MU; MiU; NcD; UU

54. CADZOW, John F. The Lithuanian periodical holdings in the Kent State Library. In Journal of Baltic Studies (Brooklyn, N.Y.), no.3, v.5, 1974, p. 264-275. DK511.B25B78 DLC; see also serials consulted.

55. --- The Lithuanian collection in the Kent State University Library. In Lituanus (Chicago, Ill.), no.1, v.21, 1975, p. 40-44. See serials consulted.

56. GIDŽIŪNAS, Viktoras. Lietuvos istorijos šaltiniai Vatikano archyve. Sources of Lithuanian history in the Vatican Archives. In Lituanistikos Instituto suvažiavimo

darbai. Chicago, Ill., 1971. p.227-235. Summary in English. DK511.L2I57 DLC; CaAEU; InNd; MiU; NIC; NRU; PU

57. HARVARD UNIVERSITY. LIBRARY. Finnish and Baltic history and literatures. Cambridge, Mass., Distributed by the Harvard University Press,1972. 250 p. (Its Widener Library shelflist, 40) Z881.H32 v.40 CaAEU; AAP; CaBVaU; CaQMM; CLSU; CoU; CtY; CU;CLU CSt-H; DLC; FU; FMU; IaU; ICU; InU;IU IaAS; IEN; GU; KU; LU; MB; MH-AH; MH-Ed; MiEM; MiU; MnU; MoU; MoSW; NN;NNU NBuU; NRU; NjP; NbU; NIC; NjR; NcD; NcU; OKentU; OU; OCl; OClW; OCU; OU; OOxM; OrPS; PU; PSt; UU; ViU; ViBlbV; WU; Wau

58. KANTAUTAS, Adam. Lithuanian materials in United States and Canadian Libraries and Archives. In Lituanus (Chicago, Ill.), no.4, v.20, 1974, p. 20-31. See SERIALS CONSULTED.

59. KARVELIO, J., IR J. RINKEVIČIAUS KNYGYNAS, Kaunas. Knygų katalogas nr.1. Kaunas, 1932. 32 p. [Book catalogue no.1] Z2537.K3 1932 PU

60. LASSNER, Franz G. Baltic archival materials at the Hoover Institution on War, Revolution and Peace. In Lituanus (Chicago, Ill.), no.4, v.20, 1974, p. 42-47. See serials consulted.

61. KUKK, Hilja. The monograph and serial holdings at the Hoover Institution pertaining to Baltic area studies. In Lituanus (Chicago, Ill.), no.4, v.22, 1976, p.60-64. See serials consulted.

62. LITHUANIAN LITERATURE HOLDINGS in the Memorial Library of the University of Wisconsin at Madison. In Lituanus (Chicago, Ill.), no.4, v.23, 1977, p. 65-82. SEE serials consulted.

63. MASINĖS BIBLIOTEKOS KATALOGAS. [Public library catalogue. Katalogo sudarytojai M. Goldas et al.] Vilnius, Lietuvos TSR Valst. respublikinė biblioteka, 1974. 811 p. At head of title: Lietuvos TSR Kultūros ministerija. Lietuvos TSR Valstybinė respublikinė biblioteka. Z2537.M37 DLC;PU

64. METROPOLITAN TORONTO, Ont. LIBRARY BOARD. LANGUAGES AND LITERATURE CENTRE. Books in Lithuanian; additions. Toronto, Ont. querterly (irregular) Ceased with July-Oct. 1969 issue. Z883 CaOTP

65. MILOVIDOV, Aleksandr Ivanovich. Opisanie slaviâno-russkikh
staro-pechatnykh knig Vil'enskoĭ pu-
lichnoĭ biblioteki 1491-1800 gg.
Vil'na, Tip. A. G. Syrkina, 1908.
160 p. Z939.V5 DLC; NN

66. NEW YORK (City). PUBLIC LIB-
RARY. SLAVONIC DIVISION. THE RE-
SEARCH LIBRARIES. Dictionary catalog of the Slavonic Collection. Second ed., rev. and enlg. Boston,
Mass., G.K. Hall, 1974. v.22, p.51-
114. Z881.N53S6 1974 CaAEU; IEN

67. PIASECKAITĖS-ŠLAPELIENĖS M.
Knygynas, Vilna. M. Piaseckaitės-
Šlapelienės knygyno katalogas. Vil-
nius, 1910. [Xerox copy, 1975] 80 p.
Z2537.P5 1975 PU

68. RIVADENEIRA, Pedro de. Bibliotheca scriptorum Societatis Jesu,
post excusum anno MDCVIII catalogum
[Ed. by] Philippo Alegambe. Antver-
piae, apud Ioannem Meursium, 1643.
[24], 585 p. Some biographical and
bibliographical information on the
Lithuanian writers of those days.
Z7840.J5R4 DLC; DGU; CLgA; CtY; InU;
MH; N; NcU; PU; RPJCB

69. SENN, Alfred Erich. The Senn
Lithuanian Collection at the University of Wisconsin. In Journal of
Baltic Studies (Brooklyn, N.Y.),no.4,
v.7, 1976, p. 352-366. See serials
consulted.

70. ŠEŠPLAUKIS, Alfonsas. Litua-
nika Europos bibliotekose. [Litua-
nica in European Research libraries]
In Institute of Lithuanian Studies.
Lituanistikos Instituto 1971 metų
suvažiavimo darbai. Chicago, Ill.,
1971, p. 236-246. Summary in English.
DK511.L2I57 DLC; CaAEU; InNd; MiU;
NIC; NRU; PU

71. SPAUDOS FONDO KNYGŲ KATALOGAS,
1928-1930. [Book catalogue of Spaudos Fondas] Kaunas, Spaudos Fondas,
1930. 96 p. Z2537.S63 PU

72. TORONTO. UNIVERSITY. LIBRARY.
Baltic material in the University of
Toronto Library; a bibliography com-
piled by Elvi Aer, Betty McKinstry,
Vida Mockus [and] Emilija Ziplans.
[Toronto] Printed for the Association
of Baltic Studies and the University
of Toronto Library by the University
of Toronto Press [1972] 125 p.
Z2531.T67 PU; CaAEU; CaBVaU; CaOTU;
CaOTY; CSt; CU-SB; CLSU; CLU;CSt-H;
DLC; DGU; GU; FU; IU; InNd; InU; ICU
IaU; NBuU; NSyU; N; NcD; NRU; NIC;
MB; MnU; MdU; MiU; MiEM; MoU; MoSW;
MU; OKentU; OCU; OkS; OkU; OClW;
OrU; PU; PPT; PPiU; RPB; TNJ; ViU

I.5. BIBLIOGRAPHIES OF SERIALS

73. KUBICKA, Weronika. Czasopiś-
ma bibliologiczne litewskie. In Roczniki biblioteczne (Wrocław), rok 15
zesz.1-2, 1971, p. 275-289.
Z671.R66 DLC; CLU; CU; ICU; InU; IU;
MH; NcD; NIC; NjP; NN; PU;
Z671.R66 DLC

I.6. INDEXES TO PERIODICAL ARTICLES

74. BALYS, Jonas. The American
Lithuanian Press. [By] J.P. Balys.
In Lituanus (Chicago, Ill.), no.1,
v.22, 1976, p. 42-53. See serials
consulted.

I.7. BIBLIOGRAPHIES OF MANUSCRIPTS

75. MACIŪNAS, Vincas. Dr. Jurgio
Šaulio archyvas. The Dr. Šaulys archive. In Institute of Lithuanian
Studies. Lituanistikos instituto
1973 metų suvažiavimo darbai. Chicago, Ill., 1975. p. 39-64. Summary
in English. DK511.L2I63 1975 CaAEU;
PU

I.10. LITHUANIAN BIBLIOGRAPHY, ITS
HISTORY AND CRITICISM

76. LIROVAS, Viktoras. P. Litva
v pechati SSSR i zarubezhnykh stran
sotsializma; voprosy razvitiiâ bibliografii lituaniki. Moskva, 1964.
19 p. Microfilm Slavic 6198 Z DLC

77. ŽUKAS, Vladas. Lietuvių bibliografijos istorija iki 1940 m.;
metodiniai nurodymai. [History of Lithuanian bibliography until 1940]
Vilnius, Vilniaus Vinco Kapsuko universitetas, 1976. 238 p. ill. At
head of title: Lietuvos TSR Aukštojo ir specialiojo vidurinio mokslo
ministerija. Z2537.Z84 DLC; PU

II. GENERAL REFERENCE AIDS

II.1. ENCYCLOPEDIAS

78. LIETUVIŠKOJI TARYBINĖ ENCIKLO-
PEDIJA. [Soviet Lithuanian encyclopedia. Vyriausias redaktorius J.Zin-
kus] Vilnius, Mokslas, 1976- . v.
AE35.55.L53 DLC; CaAEU; PU

79. MAŽOJI LIETUVIŠKOJI TARYBINĖ enciklopedija. [Concise Soviet Lithuanian encyclopedia] J. Matulis, vyriausiasis redaktorius. Vilnius, Mintis, 1966-1971. At head of title Lietuvos TSR Mokslų akademija. 3 v.
----- Abėcėlinė vardų rodyklė. [Alfabetical index] Rodyklę sudarė J. Bernotienė (grupės vadovė) et al. Vilnius, Mintis, 1975. 222 p. DK511.L2M33 DLC; CaAEU; CaOTU; CtPAM CLU; CU; CtY; GU; InU; ICBM; ICU; IU; MiU; MU; NN; NNC; NjP; OU; PU

II.2. DIRECTORIES, HANDBOOKS AND MANUALS

80. BIRŽIŠKA, Vaclovas. Lietuviškieji slapyvardžiai ir slapyraidės. [Lithuanian pseudonims] Kaunas, 1943. [Photomechanical reproduction 1976] "Bibliografijos žinių" priedas. Z1073.8.B5 1943a PU

81. FRANCISCANS. CUSTODY OF ST. CASIMIR. Catalogus independentis Commissariatus Lithaniae S. Casimiri Ordinis Fratrum Minorum sedem habens in Statibus Foederatis Americae Septentrionalis. Kennebunk Port, Me., 1954. [16] p. BX3650.S23A4 DLC

82. JOPSON, N. B. The survey of Lithuanian studies. In Slavonic and East European review (London, Eng.), v.3, 1924-1925, p. 642-656. See serials consulted.

83. LITHUANIA. SVEIKATOS DEPARTA-MENTAS. Lietuvos medicinos, farmacijos ir veterinarijos personalo ir įstaigų sąrašas. [Directory of Lithuania's medical, pharmaceutical and veterinarian professions] Kaunas, Varpo b-vės spaustuvė, 1922-1923. R713.67.L5A5 1922 DLC

84. PASAULIO LIETUVIŲ KATALIKŲ žinynas. World Lithuanian Roman Catholic Directory. [Editor Casimir Pugevičius. Brooklyn, N.Y., Lithuanian Roman Catholic Priests' League of America] 1975. 102 p. DK511.L223P36 PU; DLC

85. SABONIENĖ, A. and DAUBARAS,F. Santrumpų ir mokslo simbolikos rodyklė studijuojantiems vokiečių kalbą. [Abbreviations and symbols in the German language] Vilnius, Lietuvos TSR Mokslų akademija, [Užsienio kalbų katedra], 1973. 141 p. PF3693.S3 PU

II.3. DICTIONARIES, GLOSSARIES, ETC.

II.3.a. BILINGUAL, POLYGLOT, ETC.

86. ANGLŲ-LIETUVIŲ KALBŲ ŽODYNAS; apie 60,000 žodžių. English-Lithuanian dictionary. Sudarė A. Laučka, B. Piesarskas, E. Stasiulevičiūtė. Vilnius, Mintis, 1975. 1094 p. PG8679.A58 PU

87. B.S., pseud. ANGLIŠKAI-LIETU-VIŠKAS žodinėlis. [English-Lithuanian dictionary] Bologna, 1946. 176 p. 491.923.B1 CtTMF

88. BARAVYKAS, Vaclovas. Trumpas mokyklinis anglų-lietuvių ir lietuvių-anglų kalbų žodynas. [A concise English-Lithuanian and Lithuanian-English dictionary for the school] Sudarė V. Baravykas ir B. Piesarskas. [2. leidimas]. Kaunas, Šviesa, 1971. 331 p. PG8679.B3 1971 DLC; CtY;InU; ICIU; MB

89. --- --- 3. leidimas. Kaunas, Šviesa, 1973. 331 p. PG8679.B3 1973 DLC

90. ČERNIUS, Rimas. Namų ir artimiausios aplinkos žodynėlis. [Lietuviškai angliškas ir angliškai-lietuviškas. Lithuanian-English and English-Lithuanian dictionary of simple words, mostly in daily use] Chicago, Ill., JAV Lietuvių bendruomenės Švietimo taryba, 1977. 75 p. PG8679.C4 PU

91. IEŠMANTIENĖ, Marija and IEŠ-MANTA, Albinas. Lenkų lietuvių žodynas. Słownik polsko-litewski. Słowa litewskie akcentowane. 4300 wyrazów z dodaniem podstawowych zasad gramatyki jęz. litewskiego. [By] M. ir A. [pseud.] Vilnius [1940] 448 p. PG8682.P6M2 PU

92. NESSELMANN, Georg Heinrich Ferdinand. Wörterbuch der Littauischen Sprache. Walluf bei Wiesbaden, Ger., M. Sändig [1973] xi, 555 p. Reprint of the 1851 edition. PG8681.G5N45 1973 PU; CSt

93. PETRAITIS, Alfonso D. and JODE-LIS, Lucia. Mokyklinis lietuvių-portugalų kalbų žodynas. Pequeno dicionario escolar lituano-portugues. Sao Paulo, Brazilijos Lietuvių bendruomenė, 1974. 184 p. PG8681.P67P48 PU

94. PRANCŪZŲ-LIETUVIŲ KALBŲ ŽODY-NAS. [French-Lithuanian dictionary] Apie 50,000 žodžių. Sudarė A. [Elena] Juškienė, M[arija] Katilienė, K[uni-gunda] Kaziūnienė. Vilnius, Mokslas,

1976. 955 p. PG8681.F7P7 PU

95. SEREISKIS, Benjaminas. Lietuviškai-rusiškas žodynas. [Lithuanian-Russian dictionary. Nandeln, Lichtenstein, Kraus, 1969] 1096 p. Reprint of the 1933 ed. published by A. Lapinas ir G. Volfas, Kaunas. PG8682.R8S3 CaAEU; ICU; NN; WaU

96. ŠIRVYDAS, Konstantinas. Dictionarium trium linguarum in usum studiosae iuventutis. Auctore Constantino Szyrwid. Vilnae, 1677. 396 p. PG8681.P6S55 1677a PU(Positive photocopy)

97. --- --- 5. editio recognita et aucta. Vilnae, Typis Academicis Societatis Jesu, 1713 [Xerox copy, 1975] 464 p. PG8681.P6S55 1713a PU

98. ŠLAPOBERSKIS, Dovydas. Vokiečių-lietuvių kalbų žodynas. [German-Lithuanian dictionary] Apie 60,000 žodžių. 2. leidimas. Vilnius, Mintis, 1972. 1039 p. PG8681.G5S55 1972 PU; DLC

II.3.b. SPECIAL AND SUBJECT DICTIONARIES

99. AGAPOV, Sergeĭ Vasil'evich. Geografijos žodynas. [Geographic dictionary. Skiriamas vidurinės mokyklos mokiniams. Vertė V. Kvietkauskas. Vertimą redagavo V. Gudelis. By] S.V. Agapov, S.N. Sokolov, D.I. Tikhomirov. Kaunas, Šviesa, 1972. 268 p. G103.A4175 PU

100. BURAČAS, Antanas. English-Lithuanian dictionary of economic terms for students. Vilnius, Vilnius State University, 1975. 131 p. At head of title: The Ministry of High and Special secondary education of the Lithuanian SSR. Vilnius State University, Institute of economics of the Lithuanian Academy of Sciences. HB61.B853 PU; DLC

101. ELISONAS, Jurgis. Zoologijos sistematikos terminų žodynėlis. [Dictionary of terms in zoology] Kaunas, 1920. (Švietimo Ministerija. Knygų leidimo komisijos leidinys nr.14) Bw91 # 30p CtY

102. JUREVIČIUS, A. Aiškinamasis tekstilės terminų žodynas. [A dictionary of terms in textile] Vilnius, Respublikinis mokslinės-techninės informacijos ir propagandos institutas, 1962- . v. TS1309.J8 DLC

103. KISINAS, Izidorius. Bibliotekinė ir bibliografinė terminologija. [Library and bibliographic terminology] 1.sąsiuvinis. Vilnius, Lietuvos TSR Knygų rūmai, 1956. 47 p. No more published. Z1006.K55 PU

104. KRUTULYS, Antanas. Muzikos terminų žodynas. [Dictionary of musical terms] 2.pataisytas ir papildytas leidimas. [Redagavo Jonas Kazlauskas] Vilnius, Vaga, 1975. 257p. ML108.K75 1975 PU

105. MIKALAJŪNAS, Mykolas. Rusų-lietuvių kalbų meteorologijos terminų žodynas. Apie 10,000 žodžių. [A Russian-Lithuanian meteorological dictionary. About 10,000 words] Vilnius, Mintis, 1975. 219 p. QC854.M5 PU

106. PETRAUSKAS, Mikas. Mažasis muzikos žodynėlis. [Concise dictionary of music] So. Boston, Mass., Lietuvių muzikos konservatorija,1916. 32 p. The words are principally Italian, with definitions in Lithuanian and English. 4049.413 MB

107. POVILAITIS, V. Anglų-lietuvių kalbų bendramokslinės leksikos minimalus žodynas. [English-Lithuanian dictionary of science. By] V. Povilaitis, I. Pulokienė, A. Svecevičienė. PG8679.P6 PU

108. PRIČINAUSKAS, J. Pramonės prekių ydos. Mokymo priemonė studentams neakivaizdininkams. [The defects of the industrial goods...] Vilnius, 1967. 115 p. At head of title: LTSR Aukštojo ir specialiojo vidurinio mokslo ministerija. Vilniaus Valstybinis V. Kapsuko vardo universitetas. Prekių mokslo katedra. TS9.P75 DLC

109. ROZENTAL', Mark Moiseevich. Filosofijos žodynas. [By] M. Rozentalis. [Dictionary of philosophy. Iš trečiojo leidimo vertė K. Gavenis, M. Joffé, J. Montrimas, J. Petronis, V. Andrijauskas. Lietuviškąjį leidimą redagavo R. Plečkaitis] Vilnius, Mintis, 1975. 486 p. B48.R9R719 PU

110. ŠALKAUSKIS, Stasys. Bendroji filosofijos terminija; LKD Terminologijos sekcijos apsvarstyta, papildyta ir priimta. [General terminology of philosophy...] Kaunas, V. D. Universiteto Teologijos ir filosofijos fakultetas, 193-. PG8685.S3 PU

111. SKARDŽIUS, Pranas. Lietuviš-kitarptautinių žodžių atitikmenys. [Lithuanian equivalents of interna-

tional words] Chicago, Ill., [Pedagoginis Lituanistikos Institutas] 1973. 100 p. PG8664.A3S5 PU; DLC; InNd

112. TREČIOKAITĖ, A. Informatikos terminų žodynas. [A dictionary of computing science] Vilnius, Mintis, 1969. 96 p. PG8674.T7 PU

113. ŽEMAITIS, Zigmas. Geometrijos ir trigonometrijos terminų rinkinėlis. [Dictionary of terms in geometry and trigonometry] Kaunas, 1920. [Xerox copy, 1977] 99 p. PG8685.Z4 1920a PU

II.3.c. DICTIONARIES WITH DEFINITIONS IN SAME LANGUAGE

114. KLIMAS, Antanas and BARZDUKAS, Stasys, eds. Lietuvių kalbos žodynas; mokyklai ir namams. Lithuanian dictionary. Illus. Zita Sodeikienė. Chicago, Ill., JAV Lietuvių bendruomenės Švietimo taryba, 1974. xx, 200 p. ill. PG8675.K5 DLC; PU

115. LIETUVOS TSR MOKSLŲ AKADEMIJA, VILNA. LIETUVIŲ KALBOS IR LITERATŪROS INSTITUTAS. Dabartinės lietuvių kalbos žodynas. Apie 60000 žodžių. [Dictionary of the Lithuanian language: about 60,000 words] 2. papildytas leidimas. Red. kolegija: J. Kruopas (atsak. redaktorius) [ir kiti] Vilnius, Mintis, 1972. xxiv, 974 p. PG8675.L5 1972 DLC; CaAEU; CaBVaU; CSt; CU; IU; InU;MB; MiDW; MH; MiU; N; NIC; NNC; NjP; OrU; PU; PPiU; PSt; WU; WaU; CtY; ICU

116. VITKAUSKAS, Vytautas. Šiaurės rytų dūnininkų šnektų žodynas. [Dictionary of the dūnininkų dialect.] Vilnius, Mokslas, 1976. 559 p. PG8693.S3V51 PU; DLC

II.4. STATISTICS

117. LITAUEN. In Ostland. Reichskommissar. Ostland in Zahlen. Riga, 1942, p. 114-152. HA1448.B308 1942 DLC; CSt-H; PU

II.5. GAZETTEERS, GEOGRAPHIC DICTIONARIES

118. GEDGAUDAS, Česlovas. 1559 M. G. Valavičiaus vardynas modernaus

Baltų kalbotyros mokslo šviesoje. [The place names in the work of M.G. Valavičius from 1559...] In Varpas (Brooklyn, N.Y.), no.13, 1975, p.124-137. See serials consulted.

119. TARVYDAS, Stasys. Lietuvos vietovardžiai. Litauische Ortsnamen. In Basalykas, A., ed. Lietuvos TSR fizinė geografija. Vilnius, 1958. v.1, p. 31-41. GB276.L5B3 DLC; CU; NN; NNC; WaU

120. UNITED STATES. GEOGRAPHIC NAMES DIVISION. U.S.S.R.; official standard names approved by the United States Board on Geographic Names. 2d ed. Washington, D.C.,1970-7 v. (U.S. Board of Geographic Names. Gazetteer, no. 42) Includes geographic names of Lithuania and other Baltic countries. DK14.U562 DLC; CaAEU; DI-GS; DS; NBuU; NbU; NBuC

II.6.BIOGRAPHIES

II.6.a. GENERAL BIOGRAPHIES

121. DAGYTĖ, Emilija and STRAUKAITĖ, Danutė. Tarybų Lietuvos rašytojai; biografinis žodynas. [Soviet Lithuanian authors; biography. Žodyno autorė Emilija Dagytė ir Danutė Straukaitė] Vilnius, Vaga, 1975. 190 p., [4] leaves of plates, ports. PG8709.D3 DLC; PU

122. DAMBRAUSKAS, Aleksandras. Užgesę žiburiai; biografijų ir nekrologų rinkinys [By] Aleksandras Dambrauskas-Jakštas. [Extinguished lights; a collection of biographies and obituaries] Roma, Lietuvių katalikų mokslo akademijos leidinys, 1975. 502 p. ports. (Negęstantieji žiburiai: 1 t.) Reprint of the 1930 ed. published by Zavišos ir Steponavičiaus spaustuvės Kaune, which was issued as no.1 of Lietuvių katalikų mokslo akademijos leidinys. DK511.L28D27 1975 DLC

123. DERNAŁOWICZ, Maria. Portret familii. Warszawa, Państw. Inst.Wydawniczy, 1974. 346 p.,[56] leaves of plates. ill. DK413.8.D47 DLC

124. DEUTSCHBALTISCHES BIOGRAPHIsches Lexikon, 1710-1960. Im Auftrage der Baltischen Historischen Kommission begonnen von Olaf Welding und unter Mitarbeit von Erik Amburger und Wilhelm Lenz. Köln, Böhlau Verlag, 1970. xiii, 930 p. DK511.B3D396 DLC; CaBVaU; CaOTP; CU; ClSU; CLU; CtY; CSt; CSt-H GU; InU;

IU; KyU; MB; MH; MH-AH; MnU; MeU;
MiDW; MoU; MdBJ; MU; NN; NNC; NIC;
NjP; NcU; NcD; OKentU; PSt; TxU; ViU
WU

125. GRICKEVIČIUS, Valentinas.
Dešimt kelių iš Vilniaus. [Ten
roads radiating from Vilnius] Vil-
nius, Mintis, 1972. 222 p. ill.
DK511.L25G74 DLC; IU; MH; NjP;OKentU
Wu

126. JUCEVIČIUS, Liudvikas Adomas.
Mokyti žemaičiai. [Educated Žemaičiai (Samogitians)] Vilnius, Vaga,
1975. 266 p. (Lituanistinė biblioteka, 14) DK511.L28A15 DLC

127. MACIJAUSKAS, Jonas and VA-
SERDAMAS, E., comp. Ąžuolai nelink-
sta; biografinė apybraiža. [Oaks
don't bend; biographical sketch.]
Vilnius, Vaga, 1967. 255 p. MH

128. MEYSZTOWICZ, Walerian.
Poszło z dymem; gawędy o czasach i
ludziach. Londyn (London), Polska
Fundacja Kulturalna, 1973-1974. 2 v.
illus., facsims. Vol.2 has title:
To co trwałe. DK4130.M49 DLC; CLU;
InU; MH; MiU NN; NNC; NBuU; WU;WaU

129. SABALIAUSKAS, Algirdas. No-
ted scholars of the Lithuanian language; biographical sketches. Translated by William R. Schmalstieg and
Ruth Armentrout. Published jointly
by Akademinės Skautijos leidykla and
Dept. of Slavic Languages, Pennsylvania State University. Chicago,Ill.
Philadelphia, Pa., 1973. 168 p.
Translation of Žodžiai atgyja, Vilnius, 1967. OU; ICU; PSt; ICIU

130. SAVICKAS, Augustinas. Bespokoĭnoe puteshestvie. Avtorizovannyĭ perevod s litovskogo D. Kyĭv.
Moskva, Sov. khudozhnik, 1977. 324
p. illus. ND699.S34A42 DLC

131. STADELNINKAS, Algimantas Antanas. Mokslininkų šeima. [The Lithuanian scientists] Vilnius, Mintis, 1967. 49 p. Q141.S75 DLC

132. TARYBŲ LIETUVOS RAŠYTOJAI.
[Authors of Soviet Lithuania; auto-
biographies. Autobiografijos. Red.
komisija: Juozas Baltušis (pirmininkas), Jonas Lankutis, Alfonsas
Maldonis. Sudarė A. Mickienė ir A.
Paraščiakas] Vilnius, Vaga, 1977.
2 v. PG8701.T32 1977 PU

133. TUMAS, Juozas. Lietuvių literatūros draudžiamojo laiko paskaitos: Antanas Vienažindys, Antanas
Kriščiukaitis, Martynas Jankus, Ksaveras Sakalauskas. [Lectures on Lithuanian literature: A. Vienažindys,

A. Kriščiukaitis... By] Vaižgantas,
[pseud.] Kaunas, Valstybės spaustuvė, 1925 [Xerox copy, 1977] 175 p.
PG8709.T8 1925a PU

134. YLA, Stasys. Vardai ir veidai mūsų kultūros istorijoje, nuo
Mažvydo ligi Skvirecko. [Chicago,
Ill.] Lietuviškos Knygos Klubas,
[1973] 345 p. illus. [Names and
faces in our cultural history]
DK511.L28A18 PU; DLC; InU; MB

135. ŽIRGULYS, Aleksandras. Literatūros keliuose; memuarinės-biografinės apybraižos. [In the literary
field-biographical sketches] Vilnius
Vaga, 1976. 227 p. DK511.L28A185 PU

II.6.b. INDIVIDUAL BIOGRAPHIES

136. ABRAMAVIČIUS, Girša and KAŽU-
KAUSKAS, Vytautas. Laiko vartus at-
kėlus; Pijus Glovackas 1918-1926.
[...Biography of Pijus Glovackas]
Vilnius, Vaga, 1970. 169 p. illus.
Bibliography: p. 158-166.
DK511.L28G63 DLC; NNC

137. ABRAMAVIČIUS, Vladas. Tadas
Vrublevskis. [Biography of T. Vrub-
levskis] Vilnius, Valstybinė politinės ir mokslinės literatūros leidykla, 1960. 36 p. illus., facsims.,
port. At head of title: Lietuvos TSR
Politinių ir mokslinių žinių skleidi-
mo draugija. CT1232.W73A63 DLC

138. --- Valeriĭ Vrublevskiĭ
[1836-1908] Moskva, Mysl', 1968.
159 p. illus. At head of title: V.
E. Abramavichiĭus, V.A. D'iakov. Bib-
liography: p. 151-[158] DK436.5.W7
A64 DLC; CLU; CaOTU; CaBVaU; CSt-H;
CtY; ICU; InU; IEN; IU; KU; MH;MdBJ;
NNC; NjP; NSyU; NcD; OrU; OU; PPiU;
WU; WaU

139. ALEKNA, Antanas. Žemaičių
vyskupas Motiejus Valančius. [Motie-
jus Valančius, Bishop of Žemaitija
(Samogitia)] 2. leidimas. Su Vinco
Trumpos įvadu ir dokumentų priedais.
Čikaga, Lituanistikos Institutas,
1975. xxx, 300 p. illus.
PG8721.V327Z6 1975 PU CaAEU

140. AMBRAZAS, Algirdas. Íuozas
Gruodis; ocherk zhizni i tvorchestva.
Leningrad, Muzyka, 1964. 63 p. ill.
MH; WU

141. AMŽIAIS SU GIMTINE. [Always
with his homeland. Sudarytojas Vytautas Kazakevičius] Vilnius, Vaga,
1970. 205 p. illus. Rojaus Mizaros atminimui. E184.L7A73 DLC; MH;
NN; NjP; PU; OKentU

142. ANTANAS BUDRIŪNAS; straipsniai: amžininkų atsiminimai. [A.Bud-
riūnas, his life and works. Sudarė
ir parengė S. Yla] Vilnius, Vaga,
1974. 271 p., [9] leaves of plates.
M1423.B83A8 DLC; PU

143. ARKIVYSKUPAS MECISLOVAS REI-
NYS. [Archbishop M. Reinys. Chicago, Ill.] Lietuvių krikščionių demokratų sąjunga [1977] 245 p.
BX4705.R43A7 PU

144. AUDĖNAS, Juozas. Darbo žmonių Lietuva; Albino Rimkos siekimus
prisimenant. [Lithuania, the country of peasants and workers...] In
Varpas (Brooklyn, N.Y.0, no.12, 1973,
p. 15-38. See serials consulted.

145. BAGDANAVIČIUS, Vytautas Jonas.
Krupavičiaus kunigystė. [Krupavičius
as a priest] In Tėvynės Sargas
(New York, N.Y.), no.1, 1972, p. 10-
31. See serials consulted.

146. BAGDONAS, Juozas. Juozas
Bagdonas. [Parašė ir suredagavo Paulius Jurkus. New York, N.Y., Lietuvių Bendruomenės Vaižganto Kultūros
klubas New Yorke, 1972. 80 p.
N6999.B33J87 DLC; OKentU; PU

147. BAL'CHIŪNENE, Galina Iosifovna. M.K. Chiūrlenis; k 100-letiiu
so dnia rozhdeniia. Moskva, Znanie,
1975. 20 p., [8] leaves of plates.
illus. (Novoe v zhisni, nauke, tekhnike. Seriia iskustvo; 5(1975)
NX6.N6 1975, no.5 DLC

148. BALKŪNAS, Jonas. Dr. Antanas Trimakas, 1902-1964. In Tėvynės
Sargas (New York, N.Y.), no.1, 1969,
p. 185-198. See serials consulted.

149. BALTINIS, Andrius. Vyskupo
Vincento Borisevičiaus gyvenimas ir
darbai. [Bishop V. Borisevičius,
his life and works] Roma, Lietuvių
katalikų mokslo akademija, 1975.
ix, 178 p., [6] leaves of plates.
illus. (Negęstantieji žiburiai,t.6)
At head of title: Lietuvių katalikų
mokslo akademija. Summary in English.
BX4705.B655B34 DLC; PU

150. BALTRUŠAITIS, Jurgis. Autobiographical notes. Tr. by B. Vaškelis. In Lituanus (Chicago, Ill.),
no.1, v.20, 1974, p. 9-13. See serials consulted.

151. CANCELLED..

152. BIELIAUSKAS, Feliksas. Karolis Petrikas. Vilnius, Mintis, 1973.
93 p. illus.
MH

153. BINKIS, Kazys. Motiejus Valančius, 1875-1935. Šešių dešimčių
metų mirties sukaktuvėms paminėti.
[Bishop Motiejus Valančius, 1875-
1935; sixtieth anniversary of his
death] Kaunas, Autoriaus leidinys,
1935. 63 p. PG8721.V327Z65 1935a
PU (Xerox copy)

154. BIRŽIŠKA, Mykolas. Duonelai-
čio gyvenimas ir raštai su kalbos pa-
aiškinimais. [Donelaitis, his life
and works] Kaunas, Švyturio b-vė,
1921. 2 v. WU

155. BIRŽIŠKA, Vaclovas. Vyskupo Motiejaus Valančiaus biografijos
bruožai. [Brief biography of Bishop
Motiejus Valančius] In Aidai (Kennebunk Port, Me), no.8(42), 1951,
p. 346-356; no.9(43), 1951, p. 408-
419; and no.10(44), 1951, p. 455-
463. Mr. Liūdas Kairys (Chicago)
no.328; see also serials consulted.

156. BRAZAITIS, Juozas. Dinamiš-
kasai asmuo mūsų visuomenėje. [The
dynamic man (Pakštas) in our socie-
ty] In Aidai (Kennebunk Port, Me.),
no.8(64), 1953, p. 337-341.
Mr. Liūdas Kairys, Chicago, no.330;
see also serials consulted.

157. --- Jurgis Savickis. In Aidai (Kennebunk Port, Me.), no.2,
1953, p. 70-73. Mr. Liūdas Kairys,
Chicago, no. 330; see also serials
consulted.

158. BUDRECKAS, Ladas. Juozo Nau-
jalio muzikinė veikla Lietuvoje.
[Juozas Naujalis and his life as a
musician in Lithuania] In Aidai
(Brookly, N.Y.), no.8, p. 356-365.
See serials consulted.

159. BUDRYS, Stasys. Piatras
Rimsha. [P. Rimša his life and
works] Moskva, Sovetskii Khudozhnik, 1961. 61 p. port., illus.
MH

160. BUŠACKIS, Brunonas. Radvila Juodasis, patriotas ir protestan-
tas; biografija. [Radvila Juodasis
as a patriot and protestant] Chicago, Ill., Devenių kultūrinio fondo
leidinys, 1977. 263 p.
DK511.L28R25 PU

161. BUŠMIENĖ, Stasė. Eduardas
Volteris; biobibliografija. [Eduar-
das Volteris; a biobibliography]
Vilnius, Lietuvos TSR Valstybinė res-
publikinė biblioteka, 1973.
Z8945.2.B8 PU

162. BŪTĖNAS, Julius. Maironis.
Vilnius, Valstybinė politinės ir
mokslinės literatūros leidykla,1957.

37 p. At head of title: Lietuvos
TSR Politinių ir mokslinių žinių
skelbimo draugija. PG8721.M3Z6
OKentU; MH

163. CAP, Biruta. A survey of
studies on O.V. Milosz. In Lituanus
(Chicago, Ill.), no.2, v.22, 1976,
p. 67-75. See serials consulted.

164. ČIURLIONIS, Mikalojus Konstantinas. Laiškai Sofijai. [Sudarė
ir parengė V. Landsbergis] Vilnius,
Vaga, 1973. 170 p. illus. Contains correspondence as well as ex-
cerpts from the memoirs of various
individuals pertaining to the author.
ND699.C6C58 DLC

165. ČIURLIONIUI 100. [Čiurlio-
nis, the 100th anniversary of his
birth. Sudarė Jonas Bruveris] Vilnius, Vaga, 1977. ND699.C6C49 PU

166. ČIURLIONYTĖ, Jadvyga. Atsiminimai apie M.K. Čiurlionį. [Remi-
niscences about M.K. Čiurlionis]
2-as papildytas leidimas. Vilnius,
Vaga, 1973. 351 p. with illus. and
music. ML410.C6C6 1973 DLC

167. --- Vospominaniia o M.K.
Chiurlenise. [Adviga Chiurlenite;
per. s litov. A. Berman. Vil'nius,
Vaga, 1975. 367 p. illus.
ML410.C6C68 DLC

168. ČIŽIŪNAS, Vaclovas. Antano
Smetonos gimimo šimtmečiui. The 100th
anniversary of the birth of Antanas
Smetona. In Varpas (Brooklyn, N.Y.)
no.13, 1975, p. 58-70. See serials
consulted.

169. GAUDRIMAS, Juozas. Balys
Dvarionas. Moskva, Sovetskiĭ Kom-
pozitor, 1960. 29 p. ports.
ML410.D98G4 DLC; CtY; FMU; IU; NIC

170. GERULLIS, Georg. Kazimieras
Būga. In Indogermanisches Jahrbuch
(Strassbourg), v.10, 1926.
Z7049.A7I8 DLC; see also serials
consulted.

170a. --- Zu Johannes Bretke. In
Studi Baltici (Roma), v.5, 1935-1936,
p. 48-61. See serials consulted.

171. GIMBUTAS, Jurgis. Steponas
Kolupaila. [By] Jurgis Gimbutas ir
Juozas Danys. Čikaga, Akademinės
Skautijos leidykla, 1974. 464 p.
illus. Bibliography: p. 399-445.
Summary in English. DK511.L28G49
1974 CaAEU; InNd

172. GIRA, Liudas. Kun. Tumo-Vai-
žganto gyvenimas ir darbai. [Rev.
Tumas-Vaižgantas, his life and works]

Kaunas, Pažangos b-vės leidinys,1930.
[Xerox copy, 1977] 64 p.
PG8721.T77Z7 1930a PU

173. GIRNIUS, Juozas. Pranas Dovydaitis. Chicago, Ateitis, 1975.
776 p., [8] leaves of plates. illus.
Bibliography: p. 717-761.
QH31.D65G57 DLC; PU

174. GIRNIUS, Saulius A. Bishop
Motiejus Valančius: a man for all
seasons. In Lituanus (Chicago, Ill.)
no.2, v.22, 1976, p. 5-28. See serials consulted.

175. GODOY, Armand. Milosz, le
poète de l'amour. Paris, A. Silvaire, 1960. 282 p. illus.
PG2625.I558Z7G5 CaAEU; ICU; InU;MH;
NIC; NNC; OrU

176. GORSKI, Tadeusz. Paskutinis
Vilniaus Vyskupas Jurgis Matulaitis-
Matulevičius (1918-1925) In Lietuvių
Tautos Praeitis (Chicago, Ill.),Bk.1,
v.4, p. 97-104. See serials consul-
ted.

177. GRINIUS, Jonas. Pranas Die-
lininkaitis. In LKMASD, v.4, p.224-
227. See serials consulted.

178. GUDELIS, Martynas. Povilas
Mileris; biografijos bruožai. Chicago, Ill., Chicagos lietuvių literatūros draugijos leidinys, 1973. 232
p. illus. DK511.L28M544 DLC

179. GULBINAS, Konstantinas P.
Das pädagogische Lebenswerk der litau-
ischen Dichterin Marija Pečkauskaitė.
Paderborne, Ger., Ferdinand Schöningh
1971. 174 p. Thesis--University of
Münster, Ger. Ger.MnsU

180. JAKŠTAS, Juozas. Leonas Karsavinas, istorikas-filosofas ir Europos kultūros istorijos autorius. Leonas Karsavinas; historian-philosopher
and the author of the Cultural History of Europe. In Lietuvių Tautos Praeitis (Chicago, Ill.), Bk.1, v.4,
1977, p. 53-71. See serials consulted.

181. --- Vyskupas Motiejus Valančius savo laikuose ir dabar. Bishop
Motiejus Valančius in his time and
today. In Lietuvių Tautos Praeitis
(Chicago, Ill.), Bk.4, v.3, 1976, p.
9-26. See serials consulted.

182. JANULAITIS, Augustinas. Ki-
prijonas Juozas Zabitis-Nezabitaus-
kas, Žemaičių rašytojas ir politikos
veikėjas, 1778-1837. [K.J. Zabitis-
Nezabitauskas as an author and poli-
titian] Padidintas ir pataisytas at-
mušimas iš "Tautos ir Žodžio" V ir

VI tomų. Kaunas, A. Janulaitis,1931.
[Xerox copy, 1977] iv, 136 p.
PG8721.N45Z75 1931a PU

183. JASAITIS, Domas. Aleksandras Stulginskis. In Tėvynės Sargas
(New York, N.Y.), no.1, 1970, p. 156-
177. See serials consulted.

184. JASINSKAS, Jurgis. Julius
Janonis, poetas ir revoliucionierius;
monografija. [J.Janonis a poet and
revolutionist] Chicago, Ill., J.Ja-
šinskas, 1975. PG8721.J3Z75 PU

185. JATULIS, Paulius. Kardinolo
Jurgio Radvilo veikla lietuvių tar-
pe. [The role of cardinal Jurgis
Radvila among Lithuanians] Roma,
Lietuvių Katalikų Mokslo Akademija,
1972. 32 p. Atspaudas iš L.K.M.
Akademijos Suvažiavimo darbų VII t.
BX4705.R2865J35 PU

186. JUODAKIS, Virgilijus. Balys
Buračas. [Balys Buračas; a biogra-
phy] Vilnius, Vaga, 1971. 45 p.,
illus., 73 leaves of illus. Summaries in Russian, English, and German. TR140.B87J86 DLC; IU; KU; MH;
ICIU; NN; NjP; OKentU

187. JUODPUSIS, Vaclovas. Juozas
Pakalnis. Vilnius, Vaga, 1972. 75
p. illus., music, 8 leaves of illus.
ML410.P143J8 DLC

188. JUOZAPAVIČIUS, Pranas. Adomas Mickevičius Kaune. [A. Mickiewicz in Kaunas] Vilnius, Mintis,
1970. 62 p. with illus.
PG7158.M5Z7J95 1970 CaAEU; NN; NjP

189. JUREVIČIUS, Juozas. Juozas
Tūbelis-valstybininkas, visuomeninkas, 1882-1939. [J. Tūbelis as a s
statesman...] In Naujoji Viltis
(Chicago, Ill.), no.1, 1970, p.94-
97. See serials consulted.

190. JURGINIS, Juozas. Pasmerkimas pasakojimas apie Kazimierą Liš-
činskį. [Condemnation; story about
K. Liščinskis] Vilnius, Vaga, 1976.
148 p. BL2790.L9J81 PU

191. JURGIS PABRĖŽA, 1771-1849.
[Vyr. red. K. Jankevičius] Vilnius,
Mintis, 1972. 121 p. illus. At
head of title: Lietuvos TSR Mokslų
akademija. Botanikos institutas ir
Lietuvos botanikų draugija. Summaries in Russian, German, English,
and French. Bibliography: p. 95-
[114] QH31.P12J87 DLC; CU; MH;PU

192. KAUNECKIS, Jonas. Prelatas
Olšauskis; dokumentinė apybraiža.
[Msgr. Olšauskis...] 2. leidimas.
Vilnius, Valstybinė grožinės litera-

tūros leidykla, 1962. 280,[4] p.
BX4705.O486K3 1962 DLC

193. KAUPAS, Antanas. Mykolas
Akelaitis; šviesoj laiškų pas Kraševs-
skį. [M. Akelaitis in the light of
letters to Kraszewski. By] Selimas
[pseud.] In Tėvynė (Plymouth, Pa.),
nos.7-9, 1898, p. 247-249, 281-283,
311-313. NN; CtTMF; ICWA

194. KIRKOR, Stanisław. Kirkoro-
wie litewscy; materiały do monogra-
fii rodziny kresowej. [Londyn,1969]
2 v. in 1. MH; CtY

195. KRAUJELIS, Petras. D-ro Jono Basanavičiaus laidotuvės. [Fune-
ral of Dr. J. Basanavičius] By P.
Vieštautas, [pseud.] Vilnius, "Ruch"
spaustuvė, 1927. [Xerox copy, 1974]
20 p. DK511.L28B35 1974 PU

196. KUZMINSKIS, Vytautas. Pranas Mažylis. [Autoriai]: V. Kuzminskis, K. Vaitkevičius [ir] J.Žu-
kauskas. Vilnius, Mintis, 1970.
166 p. ill. DNLM

197. LAPELIS, Petras. Prelatas
Kazimieras Šaulys, vienas iš didžių-
jų Nepriklausomos Lietuvos kūrėjų,
Vasario 16-sios dienos akto signata-
ras; keletas būdingesnių bruožų iš
jo gyvenimo bei nuopelnų Tautai ir
Bažnyčiai. [Msgr. K. Šaulys, his
life and works. By] Vaidevutis-La-
pelis, [pseud.] South Boston, Mass.,
Spauda Darbininkas, 1949. 67 p.
DK511.L28S3 PU

198. LAURYNAITIS, Vincas. Dioni-
zas Poška. Vilnius, Valstybinė politinės ir mokslinės literatūros leidykla, 1959. 37 p. PG8721.P66Z75 PU

199. LIŪDŽIUVIENĖ, Petronėlė. Atsiminimai apie Juozą Liūdžių. [Re-
miniscences about J. Liūdžius] Chicago, Ill., 1961.
891.92.L793.yL PU

200. LIULEVIČIUS, Vincentas, ed.
Jurgis Krasnickas. 50 metų mirties
sukakčiai atminti. [Jurgis Krasnic-
kas; 50th anniversary of his death]
Chicago, Ill., Studentų Ateitininkų
Sąjunga [1972] 192 p.
DK511.L28K7 PU; DLC

201. MACEINA, Antanas. Tasai ne-
pažįstamasis Ivinskis. [Zenonas
Ivinskis] In Aidai (Brooklyn, N.Y.)
no.4, 1972, p. 126-143. See serials
consulted.

202. MACIŪNAS, Vincas. Dvidešimt
septyni Žemaitės laiškai. [Twenty
seven letters of Žemaitė] In Lituanistikos Darbai (Chicago, Ill.), v.3,

1973, p. 73-132. See serials consulted.

203. --- Mano tėvas; vieno gydytojo gyvenimo ir jo laikų istorija. [My father; a story of a physician and his time. Philadelphia, Pa., Author, 1975. Xerox copy of an article from Draugas (Chicago, Ill.), March,22, 28; April 5, 12, 19, 26; May 3, 1975. DK511.L28M15 1975 PU CaAEU

204. MALDEIKIS, Petras. Mykolas Krupavičius. [Chicago, Ill.], Lietuvių Krikščionių Demokratų Sąjunga, 1975. 493 p. ill. Bibliography: p. 480-488. DK511.L28K76 PU; DLC

205. MATIJOŠAITIS, J. Knygnešių tėvas kun. Martynas Sederevičius. Kaunas, 1932. 45 p. DK511.L28S52 PU

206. MATULAITYTĖ, A. Konstantinas Galkauskas. Vilnius, Vaga, 1975. 117 p. ML410.G155M3 PU

207. MATULEVIČIUS, Jurgis, Abp. In the service of the Church: The servant of God George Matulaitis-Matulewicz; biographical sketch and Spiritual diary [by] Vincenzo Cusumano. Chicago, Ill., [Lithuanian Catholic Press, 1974] 145 p. illus. The original edition of In the service of the Church was published in Italian in 1963 by Ancora, Milan, Italy, under the title: Innamorato della Chiesa. InNd

208. MERKYS, Vytautas. Simonas Daukantas. Vilnius, Vaga, 1972. 333 p. DK511.L28D37 PU; DLC;OKentU

209. MIKŠYTĖ, Regina. Antanas Baranauskas. Kaunas, Šviesa, 1972. 55 p. PG8721.B325 PU

210. MILUKAS, Antanas. Daktaras Petras Šatulaitis. A. Miluko paskaita. Philadelphia, Pa., Žvaigždė, 1926. 891.92.M426.yM PU

211. --- Kun. dr. Gustaitis. Philadelphia, Pa., Žvaigždė, 1915. 891.92.G976.yM PU

212. --- Kun. Martynas Sideravyčius ir jo padėjėjai. Philadelphia, Pa., Spauda Žvaigždė, 1925. 891.92.Si12.yM PU

213. --- Kun. Silvestras Gimžauskas. A. Miluko paskaita. Philadelphia, Pa., Spauda Žvaigždė, 1925. 891.92.G427.yM PU

214. MŪSŲ VYTIS; skautiškos minties žurnalas, nr.4, 1963. Numeris

skirtas Prof. M. Biržiškai atminti. 891.92.B535.yM PU

215. MYKOLAITIS, Vincas. Vinco Mykolaičio-Putino laiškai Australijon; sesei Magdalenai Slavėnienei ir jos šeimai, 1957-1967, redagavo Jurgis Janavičius. Canberra, Australijos Lietuvių bendruomenės Canberros apylinkė, 1971. 72 p. Letters of Vincas Mykolaitis-Putinas to his sister in Australia... PG8721.M9Z53 1971 DLC

216. NARBUTIENĖ, Ona. Juozas Indra. Vilnius, Lietuvos TSR Teatro draugija, 1975. 117 p. ML420.I57N3 PU

217. ---, comp. Juozas Naujalis; straipsniai, laiškai, dokumentai, amžininkų atsiminimai, etc. Sustatė Ona Narbutienė. Vilnius, Vaga, 1968. 333 p. illus., port., music. Bibliography: p. 318-[324] ML410.N287N4 DLC; CtY; ICLJF; OKentU

218. NARUSZEWICZ, Adam Stanisław, Bp. Hystoria Jana Karola Chodkiewicza...1560-1621; wojewody wileńskiego, hetmana wielkiego W.X.Litewskiego. Warszawa, T. Mostowski, 1805. 2 v. (Wybór pisarzów polskich. Historya) 917.52.C459.yZ PU

219. --- Wyd. nowe Jana Nep. Bobrowicza z popiersiem Chodkiewicza. W. Lipsku, Breitkopf & Haertel, 1837. 2 v. port. (Życia sławnych polaków, t.1-2). DK430.2.C5N37 1837 CtY

220. --- Żywot J.K. Chodkiewicza; wojewody wileńskiego, hetmana wielkiego W.X.Litewskiego. Wydanie Kazimierza Józefa Turowskiego. Przemyśl, M. Dzikowski, 1857-1858. 2 v. (Biblioteka Polska) *QY--NN; MH

221. --- --- W.Ks.Lit. Kraków, Wydawn. Biblioteki Polskiej, 1858. 2 v. in 1. DK430.2.C5N3 DLC; InU; IU; OU

222. NERAMIOS ŠVIESOS PASAULIAI; knyga apie dramaturgą Juozą Grušą. Parengė Algis Samulionis. [Juozas Grušas, the dramatist] PG8721.G7Z8 PU

223. NEZABITAUSKIS, Adolfas. Basanavičius. [Kaunas] Spaudos Fondas [1938] [Xerox copy, 1977] 541 p. J. Basanavičius, his life and works. DK511.L28B36 PU

224. PAKSTIENĖ, Janina. Jaunystė; autobiografinių atsiminimų antroji dalis. [Adolescence; autobiography. By] Janina Narūnė, [pseud.] Brooklyn, N.Y., Pranciškonų spaustuvė,

1978. 232 p. PG8749.P33J3 PU

225. --- Trys ir viena; jaunystės atsiminimai. [Three and one; reminicences. By] Janina Narūnė [pseud.] [Chicago, Ill.], Chicagos lietuvių literatūros draugijos leidinys, 1972. PG8709.P35 PU

226. --- Vaikystė; autobiografiniai atsiminimai. [Childhood; autobiography. By] Janina Narūnė [pseud] [Brooklyn, N.Y., Spaudė Pranciškonų spaustuvė, 1975] 164 p. PG8749.P33A3 PU

227. PEČKAUSKAITĖ, Marija. Marijos Pečkauskaitės laiškai Janinai Kairiukštytėi-Tumėnienėi. [Letters of M. Pečkauskaitė to J. Tumėnienė] Spaudai paruošė Juozas Eretas. [Kaunas, 1937] 152 p. Atspaudas iš Atheneum, t.8, Kaunas, 1937. PG3721.P4Z5 OKentU

228. PETRIKA, Antanas. Bronius Vargšas-Laucevičius. apysakininkas, dramaturgas, visuomeninkas. [Bronius Vargšas-Laucevičius, the novelist, dramatist, etc.] Chicago, Ill. Išleido Vilnis, 1943. 32 p. port. *Q p.v. 1926--NN

229. PETRULIS, Algirdas. Algirdas Petrulis; reprodukcijos. Vilnius, Vaga, 1972. 15 p. 16 col. plates. Lithuanian, Russian, and English. Text by Pranas Gudynas. DK699.P45G8 PU

230. PIROČKINAS, Arnoldas. Prie bendrinės kalbos ištakų; J. Jablonskio gyvenimas ir darbai 1860-1904 m. [J. Jablonskis his life and works] Vilnius, Mokslas, 1977. PG8517.J3P52 PU

231. PREIKŠAS, Kazys. Kazys Preikšas. [Sudarė M. Kaniauskas ir J.Lebedys] Vilnius, Mintis, 1964. 350 p. illus., ports. DK511.L27P67 DLC; MH; OKentU

232. PRZECŁAWSKI, Józef. Kaleĭdoskop vospominaniĭ TSiprinusa. Moskva, Tip. Gratševa, 1874- . v. DK511.L28P7 DLC

233. PUZINAS, Jonas. Dr. Jonas Basanavičius-founder of Aušra. In Lituanus (Chicago, ILL.), no.3, v. 23, 1977, p. 5-13. See serials consulted.

234. RABIKAUSKAS, Paulius. Konstantino Širvydo biografinės datos. [Biographical data of Konstantinas Širvydas] In Aidai (Kennebunk Port, Me.), no.4(149), 1962, p. 147-154. Mr. L. Kairys, Chicago, Ill.no.339.

235. RAČKAUSKAS, Vladas Karolis. Kunigas maištininkas; biografinė apybraiža. [Revolutionary priest; a biography] Vilnius, Vaga, 1967. 238 p. illus., ports. CT1218.DR3 DLC; PU; OKentU

236. RAGAŽINSKAS, Povilas. Ignas Domeika kaip lietuvis ir mokslininkas. [Ignas Domeika as a scientist and patriot] In Tautos Praeitis (Chicago, Ill.), kn.3-4, v.2, 1967, p. 123-153. QE22.D73R3 PU(Offprint) see also serials consulted.

237. RAGUOTIS, Bronius. Antanas Bimba; gyvenimo, veiklos, kūrybos bruožai. [Antanas Bimba, his life and works] Vilnius, Mintis, 1974. "A. Bimbos knygos ir leidiniai": p. 126-[127] E184.L7B547 DLC

238. RUTENBERG, Gregor. Simanas Daukantas, lietuvių pranašas. Su Mykolo Biržiškos prakalba. [S. Daukantas, the Lithuanian prophet. By] G. Rutenbergas. Kaunas, 1922. [Xerox copy, 1977] 64 p. DK511.L28D375 1922a PU

239. SENN, Alfred Erich. Vincas Krėvė's journey to America. In Journal of Baltic Studies (Brooklyn, N.Y.) no.3, v.7, 1976, p. 255-263. See serials consulted.

240. SKOLEVIČIENĖ, Jovita and JASIULIS, Leonas. Napoleonas Petrulis. Vilnius, Vaga, 1975. Summary in English and Russian. NB699.P45S5 PU; DLC

241. SLAVĖNIENĖ, Magdalena. Putinas mano atsiminimuose. [Putinas(V. Mykolaitis). My recollections. By] M.M. Mykolaitytė-Slavėnienė. [London] Nida [1977] 447 p. PG8721.M9Z8 PU

242. SMIRNOV, Anatoliĭ Filippovich, writer of history. Kastus' Kalinovskiĭ. Moskva, Izd-vo sotsial'noekon. lit-ry, 1959. 93 p. illus., ports. DK507.6.K3S6 DLC; CSt-H; CtY IU; MH; NN; NNC;

243. ŠMULKŠTYS, Liudas. Mykolas Šleževičius, 1882-1939. In Sėja (Chicago, Ill.), no.1-2, 1972, p. 20-26. See serials consulted.

244. SOMMER, Erich Franz. Apie vieno rusų metafiziko gyvenimą ir mirtį-Leono Karsavino pavėluotas nekrologas 1952.VII.12. The life and death of one Russian methaphysic-the belated necrology of Leonas Karsavinas who died July 12, 1952. In Lietuvių Tautos Praeitis (Chicago, Ill.), Bk.1 v.4, 1977, p. 72-80. See serials consulted.

245. SRUOGIENĖ, Vanda (Daugirdaitė). Balys Sruoga musų atsiminimuose. [Balys Sruoga in our memories] Spaudai paruošė Vanda Sruogienė. Chicago, Ill., Sruoga, 1974. 552 p. illus., facsims, ports.
PG8721.S68Z89 DLC; InNd; WU

246. --- Viktorijos Goesaitės-Gravrokienės gyvenimas ir darbai. [Viktorija Goesaitė-Gravrogkienė, her life and works] In Sėja (Chicago, Ill.), no.3, 1974, p. 25-45. See serials consulted.

247. ŠVARPLAITIS, Jonas. Lietuvių rezistencijos didvyris, aviaci jos kapitonas Albertas Švarplaitis. [The hero of the Lithuanian resistance, air force captain Albertas Švarplaitis] In Karys (Brooklyn, N.Y.), no.1, 1973, p. 1-6. See serials consulted.

249. TAMULYTĖ, Loreta. Vytautas Klova. Vilnius, Vaga, 1973. 63, [4] p., 5 leaves of plates. illus. ML410.K54T3 PU; DLC

248. TADAS IVANAUSKAS; gyvenimas ir veikla. [Tadas Ivanauskas, his life and works. Sudarė: Rimantas Budrys, Janina Prūsaitė] Vilnius, Mokslas, 1976. 337 p.
QL31.I85T3 PU

250. TARVID, Richard T. Captain Alexander Bielaski; a profile. In Lietuvių Tautos Praeitis (Chicago, Ill.), Bk.1, v.4, 1977, p. 138-143. See serials consulted.

251. TĖVAS JONAS BRUŽIKAS, S.J. [Father J. Bružikas, S.J. Spaudai paruošė T. Br. Krištanavičius] Čikaga [Išleido Tėvai Jėzuitai] 1974. 180 p. BX4705.B893T48 PU; DLC.

252. TRUMPA, Vincas. Motiejus Valančius istorijoje ir istorikas. Motiejus Valančius in history and as a historian. In Institute of Lithuanian studies. Lituanistikos instituto 1975 metų suvažiavimo darbai. Chicago, Ill., 1976. p. 9-15. Summary in English. DK511.L2I64 1975 CaAEU; PU.

253. TUMAS, Juozas. Antanas Baranauskas, 1835-1902. [By] Vaižgantas, [pseud.] Kaunas, Vaivos b-vė, 1924. [Xerox copy, 1975] 117 p. (His Lietuvių literatūros paskaitos. Draudžiamasis laikas) PG8721.B325T83 1975 PU; CtTMF(original); WU(original)

254. --- Jaunosios Antano Smetonos dienos. 25(1906-1931) metams jo rašto darbo paminėti. [By] Vaižgantas,

[pseud.] Kaunas, Žemės ūkio akademijos lietuvių studentų tautininkų Jaunosios Lietuvos leidinys, 1931. [Xerox copy, 1974] 31 p. [A. Smetona as a young man; a 25th anniversary of his creative writing]
DK511.L28S64 PU(Xerox)

255. --- L.Ivinskis. Kovotojai. [Lectures on Lithuanian literature ...L. Ivinskis. By] Vaižgantas, [pseud.] Kaunas, 1924. [Herox copy, 1975] 67 p. (His Lietuvių literatūros paskaitos. Draudžiamasis laikas) PG8721.I85T8 1975 PU(Xerox); WU(orininal)

256. UMBRASAS, Kazys. Žemaitė; biografija ir kūrybos ištakos. [Žemaitė (Julija Žymantienė); a biography. Parengė: V. Galinis, V.Kubilius, R. Mikšytė] Vilnius, Vaga, 1975. 317 p. PG8721.Z9Z9 PU; DLC

257. VAITKŪNAS, Gytis. Mikalojus Konstantinas Čiurlionis. [Übersetzung aus dem litauischen Manuskript Edmund Danner. Aufnahmen Klaus G. Beyer. Dresden, Ger., Verlag der Kunst [1975] 278 p.
ND699.C6V42 PU; DLC.

258. VALANČIUS, Grigas. Žemaičių didysis; istoriografiniai pasakojimai. Vysk. Motiejaus Valančiaus mirties šimtmečiui paminėti. [The great Samogitian;....Bp. Motiejus Valančius. Los Angeles, Calif.,] Autorius ir LŠST J. Daumanto kuopa,1977- v.1- . PG8721.V327Z9 PU

259. VALONIS, K. Pralotas Olšauskas. [Msgr. Olšauskas] Chicago, Ill. Vilnis [1929] 64 p. illus.
LB1.OLS ICLJF

260. VIENAS IŠ REZISTENTŲ KARTOS: Dr. Pranas Padalis, 1911-1971. [Dr. P. Padalis one of the Lithuanian resistance members. Spaudai paruošė J. Brazaitis. Brooklyn, N.Y., Pranciškonų spaustuvė, 1974] 78 p.
DK511.L28P27 PU

261. VYTAUTAS PUTNA. [V. Putna; a biography] Vilnius, Valstybinė politinės ir mokslinės literatūros leidykla, 1962. 150 p. illus., port. CtPAM

262. YUKNIS, Anthony D. Thaddeus Kosciuszko; the champion of freedom. [s.l.] J.K. Tautmyla, 1966. 16 p. port. DK434.8.K8Y95 1966 CaAEU; OKentU.

263. ŽEMAITĖ (Julija Žymantienė); archyvinė medžiaga, atsiminimai, straipsniai. [Žemaitė; her life, archival material, essays and remi-

niscences of her contemporaries.
Edited by] K. Doveika. Vilnius,
Vaga, 1972. 550 p.   WU

264. ŽVIRBLIS, Kazimieras. Tėvas
Bonaventūra Pauliukas, O.P., Lietuvos dominikonų Angelo Sargo provin-
cijos atnaujintojas ir pirmasis jos
provinciolas; biografija. [Father
Bonaventūra Pauliukas, O.P.,... ; a
biography] Washington, D.C., Tėvų
Dominikonų leidinys, 1973. 128 p.
BX4705.P38Z9 PU

III. GENERAL WORKS

III.1. BALTIC COUNTRIES IN GENERAL

265. BOETTCHER, Erik. Völkerschik-
sale im baltischen Raum. In Baltische Hefte (Grossbiewende, Ger.), Jg.
2, no.4, Juli 1956, p. 24-30. See
serials consulted.

266. ERETAS, Juozas. Les Baltes
oubliés. Traduit par Pierre Maurice.
Montréal, Que., Éditions Notre-Dame
de la Porte de l'Aurore, 1975. 30 p.
port., map. At head of title: Joseph
Ehret "Sous le parrainage de Irena
et Dr. Leonas Krauceliūnai" Translation of Die vergessenen Balten.
DK511.B3E67F8 1975 CaAEU

267. --- The forgotten Balts. Tran-
slated from German by Algis Mickūnas.
Chicago, Ill., Lithuanian American
Council, Inc., 1974. 26 p. map.
"On the occasion of the European Se-
curity and Cooperation Conference."
Bibliography: p. 24-26. At head of
title: J. Ehret. DK511.B3E6 InNd

268. --- Die vergessenen Balten.
Basel, "Civitas", 1969. 11 p.
DK511.B3E45 PU; OKentU.

269. --- Von Adam der Europäer.
Basel, 1978. 46 p. At head of title: Joseph Ehret. DK511.B3E47 PU

270. FORSTEN, Georgiĭ Vasil'evich.
Baltiĭskiĭ vopros v XVI i XVII sto-
lietiĭakh, 1544-1648. S.-Peterburg,
Tip. V.S. Baklasheva, 1894.
947.52.F776.2 PU

271. HELLMANN, Manfred. Die bal-
tischen Völker; Preussen, Letten und
Litauer. In Die Deutschen und ihre
östlichen Nachbarn. Ein Handbuch.
Frankfurt a.M., 1967. DR36.D4 DLC;
CU-SC; MU; NjP; OU; ViU.

272. HERMANN, Joachim. Ostsee-
ein völkerverbindendes Meer im früh-

en Mittelalter. In Altertum (Akademie der Wissenschaften, Berlin. Sektion für Altertumswissenschaft.) Bd.
21, Hft.3, p. 133-142. See serials
consulted.

273. ILERMAN, B. Swedish Viking
colonies on the Baltic. In Eurasia
Septentrionalis Antiqua; v.9, 1934,
(Bulletin et mémoires consacrés à
l'archéologie et l'ethnographie de
l'Europe orientale et de l'Asie du
Nord, Helsingfors) See serials consulted.

274. INFLUENCE OF EAST EUROPE AND
the Soviet West on on the USSR. E-
dited by Roman Szporluk.
New York, N.Y., Praeger, 1975, c1976.
x, 258 p. (Praeger special studies
in international politics and government) DK276.I48 DLC; CaAEU.

275. KALNIŅŠ, Bruno. Die sowjetische Nationalitätenpolitik im Baltikum. In Acta Baltica (Königstein,
Ger.), v.15, 1975, p. 133-139. See
serials consulted.

276. KARVELIS, Petras. Die Frei-
heit der baltischen Völker eine Ge-
wissensfrage für die freie Welt. In
Acta Baltica (Königstein, Ger.), v.11
1971, p. 9-19. See serials consulted.

277. KASLAS, Bronius J. Power
politics on the Baltic. In Poska,
Jüri G., ed. Pro Baltica. Stock-
holm, 1965. p.155-160. DK511.B25P6
DLC; CaAEU; CLU; CU; CtY; ICU; InU;
MiU-L; NN; PU.

278. KIPARSKY, Valentin. Die Ku-
renfrage. Helsinki, 1939. 474 p.
fold.maps. (Suomalainen tiedeakatemian toimituksia, ser. B, v. 42)
Q60.H35 v.42 DLC; CSt; CaOON; CtY;
DSI; MH; MdBJ; NN; NjP; OCl; WU.

279. KONOPCZYŃSKI, Władysław.
Kwestia bałtycka do XX w. Gdańsk,
Instytut Bałtycki, 1947. xi, 216 p.
fold.maps. (Prace Naukowe informacyj-
ne. Seria: sprawy Morskie) Biblio-
graphy: p. 200-206. DL47.K65 DLC;
CtY; CSt; CoU; IU; ICU; MH; MU; NN;
NNC; NIC; WU.

280. KORSTS, Voldemars. The Bal-
tic States; a case study of modern-
day colonialism in Europe. Toronto,
Ont., Latvian National Federation of
Canada and Latvian Relief Society of
Canada, 1967. 1 v. (unpaged)
DK511.B3K84 CaAEU

281. LANDSMANIS, Arturs. De miss-
tolkade legionärerna. Ett baltisk
debattinlägg. Stockholm, Lettiska

Nationella Fonden; [Solna, Seelig], 1970. 83 p. "Denna skrift kommenterar problem som tagits upp i romanen-Legionärerna-eller berörts i pressen och i debatten." DL658.8.L35 DLC; IU; MnU; NNC; WU; WaU.

282. LIETUVIS, pseud. S Germaniei ili s Rossiei Blizhaisiia sudby Pol'shi, Ukrainy, Finlandii, Litvy, Bielorusii, Estonii, Latvii, Kavkaza, Kryma. Petrograd, [Sotrudnichastvo, etc] 1918. 87 p. Slavic unclassified DLC

283. MAČIUIKA, Benediktas Vytenis. The role of the Baltic Republics in the economy of the USSR. In Journal of Baltic Studies (Brookly, N.Y.), no.1, v.3, 1972, p. 18-25. See serials consulted.

284. MATULIS, Anatole C. Balten in Leben und Werk von Alexander Solschenizyn. In Acta Baltica (Königstein, Ger.), v.14, 1974, p. 197-207. See serials consulted.

285. MAŽEIKA, Povilas A. Russian objectives in the Baltic countries. In Conference on Baltic Studies, 3d, University ofToronto, 1972. Problems of mininations... San Jose, Calif., 1973. p. 123-128. HC243.C65 1972 DLC; CaBVaU; CSt; CtY CU; GAT; ICIU; IU; InU; ICarbS; InNd MB; MH; MiU; NNC; NN; NBuC; NBuU;NjP NmU; OkU; RPB; UU; WU; WaU.

286. MEISSNER, Boris. Die baltische Frage in der Weltpolitik. In Acta Baltica (Königstein, Ger.),v.16 1976, p. 111-123. See serials consulted.

287. NAMSONS, Andrivs. Die bürgerliche Bewegung in Sowjetrussland und in den baltischen Ländern. In Acta Baltica (Königstein, Ger.), v.14, 1974, p. 138-183. See serials consulted.

288. NERMAN, Birger. Balticums rält. Stockholm, 1944. 947.N3581 PU

289. --- Den svenska expansinen over Ostersjön. In Nordisk Kultur (Clara Lachmanns fond) (Stockholm), v. 1, 1936. See serials consulted.

290. PASHUTO, Vladimir Terent'evich. Geroicheskaia bor'ba russkogo naroda za nezavisimost' XIII v. Moskva, Gos. izd-vo polit. lit-ry, 1956. 278 p. illus., mps. Information on Baltic area p. 92-118. DK90.P3 DLC; CaAEU; CaBVaU; CaOTU; IaU; IU; MiU; MnU; NN; WaU.

291. PASSARGE, Ludwig. Aus Balti-Landen; Studien und Bilder. Glogau, Ger., C. Flemming, 1878. 551 p. DD491.Q343P34 PU; DLC-P4(4DK306)

292. RATHFELDERS, Hermanis. Die ehemaligen Grenzen der Balten. In Acta Baltica (Königstein, Ger.), v.16, 1976, p. 255-279. See serials consulted.

293. RENNER, Hans von. Die wirtschaftliche und politische Entwicklung in Baltikum seit 1939. In Jahrbuch des baltischen Deutschtums, 1970. Lüneburg, Ger., 1969. p. 80-107. DK511.B25J3 DLC; CaBVaU; ICU; See also serials consulted.

294. RIMSCHA, Hans von. Die Politik Paul Schiemanns während der Begründung der baltischen Staaten im Herbst 1918. In Zeitschrift für Ostforschung (Marburg-Lahn, Ger.), 1956, Bd.5, p. 68-82. DR.1.Z4 DLC; AMAU; CaQMM; CtY; CU; InU; MH; MiDW; NN; NIC; NjP; PU.

295. ROHRBACH, Paul, ed. Baltenbuch; die baltischen Provinzen und ihre deutsche Kultur. Dachau, Ger., W. Blumtritt, 1916. 61 p. illus. DK511.B28R74 CaAEU; CtY; CoU; DLC; GU; IU; ICJ; MH; MWiCA; NcD; TxU.

296. TAAGEPERA, Rein. Dissimilarities between Northwestern Soviet Republics; Karelia, Estonia, Latvia, Lithuania, Belorussia. In Conference on Baltic Studies, 3d, University of Toronto, 1972. Problems of mininations... San Jose, Calif., 1973. p. 69-88. HC243.C65 1972 DLC; CaBVaU; CSt; CtY; CU; GAT; ICIU; IU; InU; ICarbS; InNd; MB; MH; MiU; NN; NNC; NBuC; NBuU; NjP; NmU; OkU; RPB; UU; WU; WaU.

297. TORNIUS, Valerian Hugo. Die baltischen Provinzen. Leipzig, Ger., B.G. Teubner, 1915. 104 p. illus., maps. (Aus Natur und Geisteswelt,42) DK511.B28T6 CaAEU

298. --- --- 3. Aufl. Leipzig, Ger., B.G. Teubner, 1918. vi, 111 p. illus., maps. (Aus Natur und Geisteswelt; Sammlung wissenschaftlich-gemeinverständlicher Darstellungen, Bdchen 542) DK511.B28T6 1918 DLC

299. VARDYS, Stanley V. The Baltic nations in search of their own political systems. In East European Quarterly (Boulder, Colo.), Jan. 1974, p. 399-406. See Serials consulted.

300. VILIAMAS, Vladas. Das baltische Grenzraum und die Ostgrenze der

baltischen Staaten. Thesis-Universi-
ty of Berlin, 1936. Ger.BlU

301. VUORJOKI, Asko. The Baltic
question in today's world. In Baltic Review (New York, N.Y.), no.38,
1971, p. 2-7. See serials consulted.

302. WARNER, Oliver. The sea and
the sword; the Baltic, 1630-1945.
New York, N.Y., Morrow, 1965. xiv,
305 p. illus., maps, ports.
DL53.W3 1965 DLC; AU; CaAEU; CaOTP;
CLU; CU; CtY; DS; DSI; FTaSU; FU;GU;
GAT; IaAS; IU; InU; IaU; IEN; IdU;
KU; LU; MB; MH; MnU; MiU; MU; MoSW;
MoU; N; NIC; NNC; NcU; NBuU; NjR;
NRU; OCU; OCl; OkU; OO; OrPS; PPULC
PU; RP; ScU; TNJ; TU; TxFTC; ViU;
ViBlbV; WaU.

III. LITHUANIA IN GENERAL

III.2.a. GENERAL STUDIES

303. AKSTINAS, Bronius. Glimpses
of Lithuania. Vilnius, Gintaras,
1972. 237 p. illus.
DK511.L2A59 DLC; CtY; DSI; InU; IU;
MH; MnU; MoU; NcD; NjP; PPiU.

304. KRAŠTOTYRA; [straipsnių rinkinys. Kraštotyra (Know your country); a collection of articles) Vyr.
redaktorius E. Dirvelė] Vienkartinis
leidinys. Vilnius, 1963. 169 p.
illus. At head of title: LTSR Kraštotyros draugija. DK.L2K712 DLC;
CaAEU.

305. --- ; straipsnių rinkinys
skiriamas TSRS įkūrimo 50-mečiui.
[Kraštotyra (Know your country);
a collection of articles dedicated
to the founding of TSRS: 50th anniversary. Vyr redaktorius Bronius
Vaitkevičius] Vilnius, 1971. 417
p. illus. At head of title: Lietuvos TSR Paminklų apsaugos ir
Kraštotyros draugija.
DK511.L2K714 DLC; MH; WU.

306. --- [Kraštotyra (know your
country)]Vyr. redaktorius Bronius
Vaitkevičius]. Vilnius, LTSR Paminklų apsaugos ir kraštotyros draugija
1975. 378 p. illus.
DK511.L27K64 DLC.

307. RABIKAUSKAS, Paulius. Lithu-
ania. In New Catholic Encyclopedia.
New York, N.Y., 1967. v.8, p. 841-
845. BX841.N53 v.8 CaAEU; AAP;
CtY-D; CBPaC; CMenSP; CSaT;CoU; DAU;
DSI; DPU; FTaSU; GAT; GU;IaU; IdU;

ICU; IEG; IEN; KU; LU; MB; MoU; MiU;
MnU; MsSM; MtU; MeU; N; NNC; NSyU;
NjPT; NbU; NcD; NNMM; OCH; OKentU;
OCl; OO; OrU; OrPS; ODW; OOxM;OrStbM
PPULC; ScU TU; KyU; KyLxCB; KEmT;
Wa.

308. ŠVIESA. Lithuania, past &
present [by the editorial staff of
Šviesa] New York, N.Y., American
Lithuanian Literary Association,
1965. 188 p. maps.
DK511.L2S825 DLC; AU; CU; CLU; CtY;
CSt; CoU; DAU; FMU; GU; IC; MU;MsSM;
MeU; MtU; N; NN; NNC; NBuU; NhU;NcD;
NcU; NvU; NjP; NjR; OCl; OOxM; OClCS
PPi; RPB; TxU; TxHU; WaS.

III.2.b. MINOR WORKS

309. AKSTINAS, Bronius. Lituanija
Sovetikė. Kishinev, Kartia Moldove-
niaskė, 1972. 68 p., 8 leaves of
illus. DK511.L2A6 DLC.

310. --- Znakom'tes'. Vil'nius,
Mintis, 1975. 211 p., [29] leaves
of plates. DK511.L2A613 DLC

311. BARKAUSKAS, Antanas. The
Lithuanian countryside; past, pre-
sent, and future. Moscow, Novosti
Press Agency Pub. House, 1976. 93
p., [8] leaves of plates. illus.
DK511.L2B25 DLC

312. DORIGNY, Jean. La vie du
pere Antoine Possevin de la compag-
nie de Jesus. Où l'on voit l'histoire des importantes négociations
ausquelles il a été employé en qua-
lité de Nonce de Sa Sainteté, en Su-
ede, en Pologne, & en Moscovie, &c.
Paris, Chez Jeam Muzier, 1712. 541,
[25] p. Some information on Lithuania. BX4705.P6582D59 1712 CaAEU;
CaQMSSS; CU-A; KStMC; MdBJ.

313. GABRYS, Juozas. A sketch of
the Lithuanian nation. Paris, Lithuanian information bureau, [19-]
11 p. Balt 8319 MH; OO.

314. --- --- Paris, Impr. de la
Cour d'appel, 1911. 24 p. Published also under title: A memorandum
upon the Lithuanian nation, Paris,
1911. Brief account of the people,
their literature, history and political struggles.
ICN; InNd; ICU; MB; NN; OO; PPi;RPB;
OClIC;

315. --- --- Paris, Maretheux,
1911. 24 p. MB

316. --- --- Paris,[1912]
DK511.L2G13 1912 MiU.

317. --- --- Paris, Lithuanian information bureau [1915] 21 p.
*Q p.v.9--NN; MB.

318. LITAUEN. [Redaktoriai, A. Me-
donis, E. Zambacevičiūtė] Vilnius,
Mintis, 1974. 45 p. illus.
DK511.L2L46 DLC.

319. LITHUANIA. In The Baltic
and Caucasian states. Boston, Mass.,
1923. p. 135-166. maps.
DK46.B3 DLC; CaAEU; CaOLU; CaBViP;
CaBVaU; CoDU; CoU; CSt; CtY; CU; IEN
ICU; IU; NN; NNC; NBuU; NB; NbU; OC1
OEac; OO; OkU; OLaK; OrP; PPiU; PU-W
PPULC; RPB; TxDaM; TxU; ViU; WU; WaSp

320. LITHUANIA. [Geneva, 1939]
47 p. illus. (League of Nations. Series of publications. European conference on rural life, 12) League of
Nations. National monographs drawn
up by governments. At head of title:
... League of Nations. European conference on rural life, 1939. Official no.: C28.M.16.1939. Conf.E.V.
R.12. HD105.E8 1939a no.12 DLC;
IdU; OrU; MoU.

321. LITHUANIA. Vilnius, Mintis,
1974. 46 p. illus. DK511.L2L474
DLC.

322. LITWA. In Slownik geograficzny królewstwa polskiego i innych
krajów. Warszawa, 1880-1904. Tom 5,
p. 330-349. DK403.S53 DLC; CaBVaU;
CSt-H; ICU; IaU; KU; MiU; MH; MB; NN
NNC;

322a. --- In Slownik geograficzny... Warszawa, Wydawnictwo artys-
tyczne i filmowe, 1975. Tom 5, p.
330-349. Reprint. DK7.S46 1975
DLC; CaAEU

323. MANIUŠIS, Juozas. Sovetskaia Litva; dostizheniia i perspektivy.
Vil'nius, Mintis, 1975. 152 p., [33]
leaves of plates. col.illus.
DK511.L2M19 DLC.

324. METEL'SKIĬ, Georgiĭ Vasil'e-
vich. IAntarnyĭ bereg. Moskva,
Mysl', 1969. 203 p. illus.,maps.
DK511.K157M46 PU; DLC; GU; IU; InU;
MH; MiU; PPiU; PSt; TNJ.

325. MONFORT, Henri de. Lithua-
nie. In Problemes politiques de la
Pologne contemporaine... Paris,1931.
T.1, p. 133-144. DK418.P96 T.1
CaAEU; CoU; DAU; DCU; DLC; GEU; NN;
NBuC; OCU; PU.

326. PAWEŁ WŁODKOWIC Z BRUDZEWA,
ca.1370-ca.1435. Pisma wybrane Paw-
ła Włodkowica. Works of Paul Wladi-
miri; a selection. Wyd.1. Warszawa
Pax, 1966-1968. 3 v. On Lithuania

and Lithuanians: v.1, p.4, 99,118,
139, 145, 244.; v.2, 61-62, 104,
107, 120, 154-155, 188; v.3, 104,
115, 139-140, 146, 175, 185-186, 214.
DK425.3.P33 1966 CaAEU; CLU; CU-L;
CtY; CSt-H; DeU; DAU; DLC; IU; ICU;
MH; MH-L; MiU; MU; NN; NBuC; NcD;
NjP; OU.

327. PEČKAUSKAITĖ, Marija. Lietuvos senovės septyni paveikslai.
[The history of Lithuania]
947.5.P ICBM

328. PIROGOVA, S. Sovetskaia
Litva; ocherk o dokumental'nom fil'-
me. [Moskva] Goskinoizdat, 1952.
27 p. illus., map. (Kinoatlas Sovetskogo Soiuza)
--- --- Microfim copy (nega-
tive) Microfilm Slavic 347 AC
PN1997.P514 DLC.

329. REIMERIS, Vacys. Lietuva
broliška žemė. [Lithuania, the con-
try of brotherhood] Vilnius, Mintis,
1966. 145 p. illus., ports.
D811.R45 CtY; MH.

330. REMEIKA, Jonas. Lietuvos
praeities vaizdai. [A brief sketch
of the Lithuania's past] [Kaunas]
Spaudos Fondas [1939] [Xerox copy,
1977] 146 p. DK511.L2R45 1939a PU

331. SERAPHIM, Hans Jürgen. Lettland und Estland... Breslau, Ger.,
M. & H. Markus, 1927. p. 279-463.
(Breslau. Industrie- und Handels-
kammer Schriften, Heft 6.) Cover-
title: Die baltischen Staaten. Repr.:
Osteuropa-Institut, Breslau. Osteuropäische Länderberichte. Includes: Poralla, C. Litauen. p.403-463.
NN

332. ŠIRVYDAS, Joseph Otto. Lietuvių prabočiai Lydai. [Lydians, the
ancestors of Lithuanians] Cleveland,
Ohio, Dirva, 1918. 35 p.
947.5.Si77 PU; NN.

333. ŠLIUPAS, Jonas. Prabengtis
lietuvių tautos senovėje. So.Boston
Amerikos lietuvių tautinė sandara,
1922. 46 p. L970.1.S1 ICLJF

334. VENCLOVA, J. M. Apie senovės indus ir jų giminystę su lietu-
viais. [The kinship of old Indian
culture with Lithuania] Chicago,
Ill., [s.n.], 1975. 38 p. Summary
in English. Bibliography: p. 30-37.
DK511.L23V458 DLC.

335. WASILEWSKI, Leon. Litwa i
jei ludy. Warszawa, Skł. główny w
księg. naukowej, 1907.
949.52.W284.4 PU

III.3. NATIONAL AWAKENING

336. AUŠRINĖS KELIAIS... [Awakening...] Petrogradas, Rusų prancūzų spaustuvė, 1915. [Xerox copy, 1975] 79 p. PG8713.A8 1915a PU(Xerox)

337. BLOMBERG, Karl Johann, freiherr von. Description de la Livonie, avec une relation de l'origine, du progrès, & de la décadence de l'ordre teutonique. Des révolutions, qui sont arrivées en ce pays jusqu'à nôtre temps, avec les querres, que les Polonais, les Suedois, & les Moscovites ont eües ensemble pour cette province. On y decrit les duchez de Courlande & de Semigalle, & la province de Pilten. Enfin on y trouve le voyage de l'auteur de Livonie en Hollande l'an 1698. Avec queques remarques sur la Prusse, Brandebourg, Hanover, Hesse, & plusieurs autres cours d'Allemagne. Utrecht, G. van Poolsum, 1705. 394 p. port. Translation of An account of Livonia. DK511.L35B6 DLC; CtY; CU; IU; ICN; MH; NN; MU.

338. ČEGINSKAS, Kajetonas Julius. La renaissance nationale des Lituaniens; essai d'histoire sociologique. Thesis--University of Strasbourg. Fr.StU

339. ČEPĖNAS, Pranas. Kovos kelias į nepriklausomybę. [The struggle for independence] In Varpas (Brooklyn, N.Y.), no. 12,1973, p.40-53. See serials consulted.

340. GABRYS, Juozas. The Polish question in connexion with the Lithuanian, Ruthenian, and Jewish questins; a lecture delivered before the Paris Sociological Society. Paris, The Lithuanian Information Bureau [1915] 15 p. Reprinted from the British Review, July 1915. Balt 8319 MH; OO.

341. --- La question polonaise en relation avec la question lithuanienne, ruthène et juive; conference à la Société de sociologie de Paris, le 15 avril 1915. Paris, Impr. Chaix,1916. 12 p. (Bibliotheque des nationalités.) Extrait des Annales des nationalités, nos.7-8, 1915. Balt 8319 MH.

342. GRABOWSKY, Adolf. Die litauische Frage. In Das Neue Deutschland. Jg.6, 1917-1918, p. 225-237. See serials consulted.

343. GREENE, Victor R. For God and country; the rise of Polish and Lithuanian ethnic consciousness in America, 1860-1910. Madison, State Historical Society of Wisconsin, 1975. x, 202 p., [4] leaves of plates. illus. Bibliography: p.180-196. E184.P7G73 DLC; CaAEU

344. JURKIEWICZ, J. O litewskim ruchu narodowym w polskiej myśli politycznej w latach 1883-1914; kilka uwag krytycznych. Some critical remarks on the Lithuanian National movement in the Polish political concept from 1883-1914. In Acta Baltico-Slavica (Warszawa), v.11, 1977, p. 309-316. DK511.B25A612 DLC; CaAEU; CaOTU; CU; CtY; CLU; GU; ICU MH; MiU; NN; NNC; NNM; PU; WaU.

345. LITHUANIA; irredentist and nationalist questions in Central Europe, 1913-1939. Nendeln, Kraus Reprint, 1973. 1 v. (various pagings) illus. (Seeds of conflict. Series, 1.) In French, German, English or Polish. WaU.

346. ŁOSSOWSKI, Piotr. Litewski ruch narodowy w polskiej myśli politycznej 1883-1914. [Warszawa] Ossolineum, 1975. [Xerox copy,1976) p. [120]-157. Offprint from Polska i jej sąsiedzi. DK511.L25L65 1975a PU.

347. MATULAITIS, Kazimieras A. Lietuvių tautos išsilaisvinimas. Efforts toward Lithuanian independence. In Lietuvių Tautos Praeitis (Chicago, Ill.), kn.1, v.3, 1971, p. 37-61. Summary in English. See serials consulted.

348. PUZINAS, Jonas. Vorgeschichtsforschung und Nationalbewustsein in Litauen. Kaunas, 1935. viii, 134 p. Thesis--University of Heidelberg. DK511.L21P85 DLC.

349. RÖMERIS, Mykolas. Litwa; studyum o odrodzeniu narodu litewskiego. [By] Michał Römer. Lwow, Polskie Towarzystwo Nakładowe, 1908. [Xerox copy, 1975] 438 p. DK511.L25R6 1975 PU(Xerox)

350. SARGAS. Litwo, ojczyzno nasza... Przekład z litewskiego. Petersburg, Lietuvių Laikraštis,1906. 15 p. DK511.S24P7 1906 CaAEU; PU.

351. VAIŠNORA, Juozas. Petras Kriaučiūnas lietuvių tautinio atgimimo pradininkas Sūduvoje. [Petras Kriaučiūnas as a promoter of national awakening in Sūduva] In LKMAM, v.1, p. 117-140. See serials consulted.

352. VOLDEMARAS, Augustinas. Natsional'naia bor'ba v Velikom Kniazhestvie Litovskom v XV i XVI viekakh. [By] A.I. Vol'demar. [Graz,

Akademische Druck- und Verlagsanstalt, 1965] [Xerox copy, 1974]
p. [160-198 p. Detached from Izvestiia Otdeleniia russkago iazyka i
slovesnosti Imperatorskoĭ Akademii
nauk, XIV, 1909, 3-4. Reprint 1965.
DK511.L24V6 1965a PU.

353. YLA, Stasys. Laisvės problema. [The problem of freedom] Putnam, Conn., Immaculata Press, 1956.
246 p. JC585.Y6 DLC; CaAEU;
CaOONL; MH; OCl; OKentU; PU.

III.4. CULTURAL, INTELLECTUAL, AND SOCIAL LIFE IN GENERAL

354. BARKAUSKAS, Antanas. Kultūra ir visuomenė. [Culture and Socie-
ty] Vilnius, Mokslas, 1975. 406 p.
Bibliography: p. 393-403.
DK511.L212B37 DLC.

355. BARZDUKAS, Stasys. Lietuvis
savo tautoje, valstybėje, bendruome-
nėje; mintys tautiniam ir visuomeni-
niam ugdymui bei ugdymuisi. [The
Lithuanian in his country, state and
community...] Chicago, Ill., JAV LB
Švietimo Taryba, 1973. 258 p. illus
Added t.p.: Lithuanians- past and
present. DK511.L2B328 PU; DLC

356. BENEDICTSEN, Age Meyer. Et
folk, der vaager; kulturbileder fra
Litaven. Købenstavn, F. Hegel, 1895.
259 p. illus.
947.52.B433 PU; CtY; MnU.

357. BŪTĖNAS, Julius. Istorio-
grafo užrašai. [Notes of a histo-
riographer] Vilnius, Vaga, 1974.
374 p. PG8703.B3 DLC; PU

358. --- Literato duona. [Life of
the author] Vilnius, Vaga, 1975.
277 p. DK511.L28B88 PU; DLC; WU.

359. ELENEV, Fedor Pavlovich.
Pol'skaia tsivilizatsiia i eia vliia-
nie na zapadnuiu Rus'... S.-Peter-
burg, [Tip. V. Bezobrazova i komp.],
1863. 83 p. DK511.L2E4 DLC; WU.

360. GENZELIS, Bronius. Švietėjai
ir jų idėjos Lietuvoje XIX a. [Edu-
cators and their ideas in Lithuania
in 19th century] Vilnius, Mintis,
1972. 205 p. Summary in English
and Russian. Bibliography: p. 190-
200. DK511.L212G46 DLC; IU; OKentU
WU.

361. GOŠTAUTAS, Jonas. Ponas tei-
sėjaitis; arba, pasakojimas apie Lietuvą ir Žemaitiją. [Mr. Judge; reci-
tation about Lithuania and Žemaitija

(Samogitia). Vertė R. Jasas] Vilnius
Vaga, 1967. 128 p. (Lituanistinė
biblioteka) DK511.L212G65 PU; CtY;
CU; DLC; ICU; MiU; NN; WU.

362. GRICIUS, Augustinas. Keliai
keleliai. Iš atsiminimų. [Reminiscen-
ces] Vilnius, Vaga, 1973. 247 p.
PG8721.G635K39 DLC; IU; MB; MH; WU.

363. GUČAS, Alfonsas. Psichologi-
jos mokslo raida Lietuvoje (XIX a.
pabaiga-XX a. pradžia). [The development of psichological sciences in
Lithuania (19th-20th centuries)] Vilnius, Mintis, 1968. 204 p. facsims,
ports. Summaries in English and Russian. Bibliography: p. 174-[188].
BF108.L5G8 DLC; PU; PPULC; NN.

364. JABLONSKIS, Konstantinas.
Lietuvių kultūra ir jos veikėjai.[Li-
thuanian culture and its active men]
Vilnius, Mintis, 1973. 423 p. port.
At head of title: Lietuvos TSR Moks-
lų akademija. Istorijos institutas.
Includes texts of archive documents
in Lithuanian, Russian, Polish, and
Latin. DK511.L212J3 1973 DLC; CLU;
CSt; InU; MH; MiU; NjP; OKentU; PPiU
WU.

365. JUCEVIČIUS, Feliksas. Tauta
tikrovės ir mito žaisme. [A nation
between reality and myth] Putnam,
Conn., 1970. 175 p.
PG8749.J8T3 DLC; OKentU.

366. JUCEVIČIUS, Liudvikas Adomas.
Mokyti žemaičiai. [Educated Žemaičiai
(Samogitians)] Vilnius, Vaga, 1975.
266 p. (Lituanistinė biblioteka, 14)
DK511.L28A15 DLC.

367. JURKŪNAS, Ignas. Litauisk
kultur. [Av] Ignas Jurkunas-Schey-
nius. Stockholm, Svenska Andelsför-
laget, [1917] 86 p. illus.
DK511.L212J83 DLC; CaAEU.

368. KAPSUKAS, Vincas Lietuvos
darbininkės ir poniutės. [Ladies
and working women in Lithuania.
[n.p., Lietuvių darbininkų susivienijimas Amerikoje, 1928] 151 p. (A-
merikos darbininkų susivienijimo Amerikoj leidinys, no. 12)
HD8535.7.K3 OKentU

369. KAUPAS, Antanas. Patrimpo
laiškai. Parašė K.A.K. Shenandoah,
Pa., Žvaigždės spaustuvėje, 1907.
161 p. DK511.L713K3 InNd; PU.

370. --- --- Another edition.
Philadelphia, Pa., 1934.
891.92.K164L PU.

371. KAVOLIS, Vytautas. Lietuvio
būdas ir likimas [Lithuanian charac-

ter and fate] In Santarvė, no.9(20)
Nov. 1954, p. 320-324. See serials
consulted.

372. KUCHOWICZ, Zbigniew. Obycza-
je staropolskie XVII-XVIII wieku.
Lodz, Wydawnictwo Lodzkie, 1975.
481 p., [28] leaves of plates. ill.
Bibliography: p. 475-[482].
DK4291.K8 DLC

373. LIETUVOS TSR KULTŪROS DARBUO-
TOJŲ SUVAŽIAVIMAS, 1st, VILNA, 1969.
Pirmasis Lietuvos TSR Kultūros darbuotojų suvažiavimas. [The first
conference of the staff engaged in
the cultural activities. Sudarė E-
duardas Maurukas. Redagavo Petras
Dabulevičius] Vilnius, Mintis,1971.
248 p. DK511.L27L492 1969 DLC;
MH; PU; WU.

374. LITHUANIAN S.S.R. CENTRINĖ
STATISTIKOS VALDYBA. Narodnoe obrazovanie, nauka i kultura v Litovskoĭ
SSR. [Redaktor V.V. Grigaĭte. Vil'-
nĭus, [s.n.], 1972. 317 p. At head
of title: TSentral'noe statisticheś-
koe upravlenie pri Sovete Ministrov
Litovskoĭ SSR.
LA853.L48L53 1972 DLC

375. MIZARIENĖ, Ieva. Jaudinantys
susitikimai. [Visit to Lithuania]
Vilnius, Mintis, 1965. 122 p. illus.,
ports. DK511.L274M5 DLC

376. MOKSLO, KULTŪROS IR ŠVIETIMO
draugijos. [Lithuanian learned institutions and societieɑ. Ats. redaktorius Vytautas Merkys] Vilnius,
Mokslas, 1975. 250 p. (Iš lietuvių
kultūros istorijos, 8) On leaf pre-
ceeding t.p.: Lietuvos TSR Mokslų
akademija. Istorijos institutas.
Summaries in Russian. DK511.L212M64
DLC.

377. PASAULIO LIETUVIŲ BENDRUOME-
NĖ. Lietuva okupacijoje; pranešimai
Pasaulio lietuvių bendruomenės Seimui apie okupuotos Lietuvos gyvenimo kaikurias sritis. [Lithuania
under occupation. Reports to the Congress of World Lithuanian Community
on some aspects of life in occupied
Lithuania] New Yorkas, PLB Seimo organizacinis komitetas, 1958. 128
leaves. illus. DK511.L274P3 DLC.

378. PEČKAUSKAITĖ, Marija. Mer-
gaitės kelias. [The road which the
girl should follow] [Kirchheim-Teck,
A. Gottlieb & J. Osswald], 1948.
99 p. illus. BJ1688.L5P4 OKentU.

379. PUTVINSKIS, Vladas. Gyvenimas ir parinktieji raštai. [Life
and selected works of Vladas Putvins-
kis-Putvis] Vyr. redaktorius Alek-

sandras Marcinkevičius-Mantautas.
2. laida. Čikaga, Lietuvos Šaulių
sąjunga tremtyje, 1973. 3 v. in 1.
DK511.L28P87 1973 PU.

380. RYTOJAUS ŽMONĖS. [Men of
the future] [Sudarytojas M. Pagirys]
Vilnius, Mintis, 1966. 108 p.
HN535.7.A8R93 DLC.

381. SABALIŪNAS, Leonas. Lithua-
nia in crisis; nationalism to com-
munism, 1939-1940. Bloomington,
Ind., University Press [1972] xxi,
293 p. DK511.L27S2 PU; AAP; CaAEU
CaBVaU; CaQMM; CaOTP; CtY; CSt; CU;
CoU; DLC; FTaSU; FU; GU; IEN; ICU;
IaAS; IaU; InU; IU; KU; KyU; LU; MB
MH; MoSW; MeB; MnU; MoU; MU; MiU;NN
NBuC; NBuU; NSyU; NcD; NIC; NNC; NbU
NcGU; NcRS;NjP; NcU; NRU; OKentU;OO
OClU; OCU; OU; OrU; OrPS; OkU; PSt;
RPB; TNJ; ViU; WaU.

382. SAMAITIS, Jonas. Lithuanian
science; past and present. Translated from the Lithuanian by Olimpija Armalytė and Juozas Butkus. Vilnius, Gintaras, 1974. 106 p.,[8]
leaves of plates. illus.
AZ713.Z7L57713 DLC; PU.

383. SERGEENKOV, Mikhail Mikhaĭlovich. Gyvi palaidoti. [They are
buried alive. Zazhivo pogrebennye]
Vilnius, Mintis, 1964. 89 p.
DK511.Z9 1964s CtY

384. --- Zazhivo pogrebennye.
[Literaturnaia zapis P. Rimkus. Mos-
kva], Molodaĭa gvardiĭa, 1964. 144p.
illus. BR936.S454 DLC; IU; InU;.
MH; MdBJ; NNC; NIC; OU; WU.

385. STUDNICKI, Władysław. Stosunki społeczne i ekonomiczne na Litwie i Rusi. In Polska... Lwow, 1909.
T.2, p. 733-759.
*QR--NN.

386. VAITKŪNAS, Gytis. Ocherk
razvitiia ėsteticheskoĭ mysli v Lit-
ve. Moskva, Iskusstvo, 1972. 229p.
DK511.L212V3 DLC; PU; CaAEU:CaOTU;
CU-SB; CtY; CSt; IU; InU; MH; MiEM;
MB; MiDW; MU; NNC; NIC; NjP; NcD;NcU

387. CANCELLED.

III.5. DESCRIPTION AND TRAVEL IN
        GENERAL

388. BALTUŠIS, Juozas. Kas dainon nesudėta; kelionių įspūdžiai.
[Something that is not in the song:
impressions from the trip] Vilnius,
Valstybinė grožinės literatūros lei-

dykla, 1959. 93 p. illus.
914.75.B218 PU; OKentU

389. BARTKUS, Kasparas. Žydrai-
siais Lietuvos vandenų keliais. [On
the blue Lithuanian waterways]
Vilnius, Mintis, 1971. 84 p. illus.
DK511.L2B28 DLC.

390. ČIKAGIETĖS ĮSPŪDŽIAI KOMUNIS-
tų pavergtoj Lietuvoj. [A visit to Soviet-occupied Lithuania...] Autorė
buvo Vilniuje, Trakuose, Druskinin-
kuose, Klaipėdoje ir Palangoje.
[Chicago, Ill., Chicagos lietuvių literatūros draugijos leidinys, 1963.
95 p. map. DK511.L27C5 OKentU.

391. FRIEDERICHSEN, Maximilian
Hermann. Finland; Estland und Let-
tland; Litauen. Breslau, Ger., Hirt,
1924. 144 p. illus., maps. (Jeder-
manns Bücherei, Abt.: Erdkunde) On
Lithuania: p. 93-121.
DK511.B28F92 CLU; CU; CSt-H; CaBVaU
DLC; ICU; InU; MnU; NSyU; NhU; NNC;
OCl; OU; PU.

392. JOKUBKA, Stasys J. Tėvų
žemės įspūdžiai. [Impressions from
my homeland] Chicago, Ill., 1971.
278 p. illus. DK511.L2J6 OKentU

393. KIRVESMIES, Pentti. Kansat
kuin veljet. Matka Liettuaan, Val-
ko-Venäjälle ja Azeirbadžaniin-50
vuotta täyttävään Neuvostoliittoon.
[Brotherhood of peoples; a journey
to Lithuania, Belorussia and Azerbai-
jan...] Helsinki, Kansankulttuuri,
1972. 156 p., 8 leaves of plates.
DK29.K48 DLC.

394. KONDRATAS, Z. Pirmasis lietuvių skridimas per Atlantą. [The
first Lithuanian flight over Atlan-
tic] Vilnius, Mintis, 1969. 49 p.
illus. TL539.K65 PU; OKentU.

395. KURAITIS, Dan. Kelionė į
anapus geležinės uždangos. [Voyage
behind the Iron Curtain] Chicago,
Ill., 1959. 237 p. illus.
DK28.K85 DLC; OKentU; PU.

396. LIETUVOS DRAUGYSTĖS IR KULTŪ-
RINIŲ RYŠIŲ SU UŽSIENIU DRAUGIJA.
Lietuva šiandien. [Lithuania today]
Vilnius, Mintis, 1965. 70 p. illus.
map, ports. DK511.L2I4218 DLC.

397. --- --- Vilnius, Gintaras,
197). 111 p. illus. At head of
title: Lietuvos draugystės ir kultūrinių ryšių su užsieniu draugija.
DK511.L2I4218 1970 OKentU.

398. LITHUANIA TODAY. [Vilnius,
Mintis Pub. House, 1965, 1968] 112 p.
illus. Translation of Lietuva šian-

dien. Sponsored by the Lithuanian
Society for Friendship and Cultural
Relations with Foreign Countries.
FU.

399. MOLINARI, Gustave de. Lettres sur la russie. Nouvelle éd. en-
tièrement refondue. Paris, E. Den-
tu, 1877. 404 p. On Lithuania:
p. 13-24. DK26.M72 CaAEU; CaBVaU;
CoU; KU; ICU; MH; MiU; MiEM; NNC; OU
TxU; WU.

400. OBELIENIUS, Juozas. Lietuvos TSR vandens turistų keliai. [
Waterways for tourists in Soviet
Lithuania] Vilnius, Mintis, 1972.
210 p. DK511.L2 O21 PU; DLC.

401. SADAUSKAS, Romas. Kelionė
iš Baltašiškės į Kučiūnus. [Jour-
ney from Baltašiškė to Kučiūnai]
Vilnius, Vaga, 1973. 159 p.
DK511.L2S26 DLC; MB; NN.

402. SLAVUTINSKIĬ, Stepan Timofe-
evich. Volosti pervago moego uchas-
tka; iz otryvochnykh bospominaniĭ.
Moskva, V Univ. tip. (M. Katkov),
1879. 144 p. PG3361.S55Z523 1879
DLC.

403. ŠUMAUSKAS, Motiejus. Litva
sotsialisticheskaĭa. Vil'nius, Mintis, 1975. 158 p., [24] leaves of
plates. illus. DK511.L2S814 DLC.

404. TAURAS, Antanas. Grožis
mūsų kaime. Vilnius, Mintis, 1971.
29 p. [Beauty of our countryside]
DK511.L2T35 PU.

405. VILAINIS, A. pseud. Žmogus,
kuris amžinai keliavo; reportažai
iš kelionių Lietuvoje. [A man who
always travelled; reports on Lithuanian trips] Cicero, Ill., Knygų
leidykla Nemunas, 1950. 2 v. (paged continously) DK511.L713V71
InNd; ICLJF.

406. ŽILIUS, Jonas. Kelionė į
Europą. Kun. J. Žilinsko. New York,
N.Y., Atspauda iš Tėvynės, [191-]
52 p. plates.
*Q p.v. 167--NN(Žilinskis, Jonas)

III.6. TRAVEL GUIDES

407. AVIŽONIS, Konstantinas.
20 [i.e. Dvidešimt] kelionių po Kauno apskritį [Twenty routes through
the district of Kaunas. By] K. Avižonis, S. Kolupaila [and] Ig. Končius
Kaunas, Kauno apskrities iškylų ir
keliavimų komiteto leidinys, 1937.
110 p. 914.75.Av55 PU; CtTMF

408. BILEVIČIUS, Petras. Shau-
liiai; putevoditel'. [By] Piatras
Biliavichius. Per. s litov.] Vil'-
nius, Mintis, 1974. 63 p. illus.
DK651.S4935B5417 DLC.

409. ČIŽIŪNAS, Vaclovas. Vadovas
po Kauną ir apylinkes. [Guide
through Kaunas and its environments]
Kaunas, Spaudos Fondas, 1935. 128 p.
illus., fold.map.
DK651.K125C5 OKentU; CtY; ICBM;ICBM;
PU.

410. DAUNIENĖ, J. Kaunas; turis-
tui apie miestą. [Kaunas; a guide
for tourists] Vilnius, Mintis,
1977. 85 p., [48] leaves of plates.
At head of title: J. Daunienė, A. G
Gulbinskienė, V. Kugevičius, & A.
Semaška (sudarytojas)
DK651.K125D3 PU.

411. HANDBOOK OF CENTRAL AND EAST
Europe. A handbook and guide to Alba-
nia, Austria, Bulgaria, Czechoslova-
kia, Estonia, Finland, Greece, Hunga-
ry, Latvia, Lichtenstein, Lithuania,
Poland, Rumania, Turkey, Yugoslavia,
and to their resources. Zürich, The
Central European Times publ., 1932-.
v. illus., maps. annual.
D2.H3 DLC; CaAEU; CaBVaU; CtY; IdU;
MB; MH; NN; OCl; OClh; OClW; OU;
OrCS; OrU; PBm; PU; TU; WaS.

412. KONDRATAS, Vytautas. Veisie-
jų ežerais. [On the lakes of Veisie-
jai] Vilnius, Vaga, 1970. 84 p.,
16 leaves of illus., maps.
DK511.Y2K683 DLC; PU.

413. KONDRATENKA, B. Druskininkai
i ego okrestnosti. [Per. s litov.]
Vil'nius, Mintis, 1968. 85 p. illus.
24 leaves of illus. At head of title: B. Kondratenka, IU. IAnchiauskas.
Translation of Po Druskininkus ir a-
pylinkes. RA887.L5K617 DLC

414. --- Po Druskininkus ir apylinkes. [Through Druskininkai and
environs] Vilnius, Mintis, 1968.
144 p. illus, maps. 24 leaves of
ill. At head of title: B. Kondratenka, J. Jančiauskas.
DK651.D7K65 DLC; NN.

415. KUDABA, Česlovas and KARPA-
VIČIUS, P. Kur Nemunas teka. [Where
Nemunas flows its waters] Vilnius,
Mintis, 1970. 131 p. illus.
DK511.LŽK95 1970 CaAEU; PU.

416. MONTY, Paul. Wanderstunden
in Wilna. 2. durchgesehene Aufl.
[Wilna] Wilnaer Zeitung, 1916.
138, [6] p. front., plates, fold.
plan. 914.75.M765 PU; NN; NjP.

417. --- --- 3. duchgesehene Aufl.
[Wilna] Wilnaer Zeitung, 1918. 138,
[6] p. front., plates, fold.plan.
DK511.L26M814 CSt-H; MH.

418. PAPŠYS, Antanas. Vilnius;
turistui apie miestą. [Vilnius; a
guidebook for the tourist] Vilnius,
Mintis, 1977. 140 p., [64] leaves
of plates. DK651.V4P3 PU.

419. VAIČIŪNAS, Albinas. Lietuvos TSR turistinės bazės. [Tourist
services of the Lithuanian SSR; gui-
debook] Vilnius, Mintis, 1970.
96 p. illus.
DK511.L2V28 DLC; IU; MH; NN.

420. --- Turistskie bazy Litovskoi SSR. [Per. s litov.] Vil'nius,
Mintis, 1970. 111 p. illus. Translation of Lietuvos TSR turistinės
bazės. DK511.L2V2817 DLC; DS.

III.7. ANCIENT TRAVEL REPORTS BY
FOREIGN TRAVELLERS

421. KYBURG, Konradus, fl.14th
cent. Grovo Kyburg'o kelionė Lietu-
vona 1397 m. [K. Kyburg's journey
to Lithuania in 1397] Lietuviškai
išguldė J. Basanavičius. Plymouth,
Pa., 1900. 52 p. port. (Tėvynės
myletojų draugystė. Publications,
no. 4) G5449.07 ICN; CtTMF; NN;
PPi; PU.

422. LANCASTER (Duchy), England.
Rechnungen über Heinrich von Derby's
Preussenfahrten 1390-1391 und 1392.
Hrsg. von Hans Prutz. Leipzig, Ger.
Duncker und Humbolt, 1893. civ,226
p. *CA(Camden)--NN British Museum
entry is under Prutz, Hans.

423. VAIČIULAITIS, Antanas. Sten-
dhal in Lithuania. Translated from
Lithuanian by M. Vasiliauskas. In
Lituanus (Chicago, Ill.), no.2, v.
22, 1976, p. 29-42. See serials
consulted.

424. --- Viduramžių poetas Machaut
Lietuvoje. [The medieval poet
Guillaume de Machaut, ca.1300-1377
in Lithuania] In Židinys (Kaunas),
no.2, T.19, 1939. See serials consulted.

III.8. DESCRIPTION AND TRAVEL,
PICTORIAL WORKS

425. BALTIKUM; eine Erinnerung,
gesehen in 96 Aufnahmen. Landeskund-

liche Einführung von Erik Thomson.
Frankfurt am Main, W. Weidlich, 1963.
118 p. (chiefly illus.) map.
DK511.B28B3 DLC; CSt-H; NN; OCl; PU

426. IŠVADUOTAM KAUNUI 20 METŲ.
20 let osvozhdennomu Kaunasu. Paruošė Z. Baltuškinas, et al. Kaunas,
Šviesa, 1964. 1 v. (chiefly illus.)
DK651.K125I8 DLC; CtY; MiEM; MH;ScU

427. JUODAKIS, Vergilijus. Balys
Buračas. [Balys Buračas and his artistic photography] Vilnius, Vaga,
1971. 45 p. illus., 73 leaves of
illus. Summaries in English, German
and Russian. TR140.B87J86 DLC; IU;
ICIU; KU; MH; NN; NjP; OKentU.

428. KUDABA, Česlovas. Ignali-
nos apylinkės. [District of Ignali-
na] Vilnius, Mintis, 1975. 86 p.
(chiefly illus.)
DK511.I35K8 PU.

429. LAISVOJI MINTIS. Albumas.
Scranton, Pa., 1912- . v. illus.
ports. Preface signed by J. Šliupas.
DK511.L2L34 DLC.

430. LIANDZBERGAS, Henrikas. Rus-
nė. Dailininkas A. Dakinevičius.
Vilnius, Mintis, 1972. 1 v., 95 ill.
DK651.R85L5 PU; DLC; MB.

431. LIETUVOS FOTOGRAFIJA. [Li-
thuania in pictures. Sudarytojas
Virgilijus Juodakis. Dailininkas Alfonsas Augaitis] Vilnius, Vaga, 1969.
178, [19] p. TR650.L53 PU; DLC;MH.

432. --- [... Sudarė Julius Vaice-
kauskas] Vilnius, Vaga, 1974. 178
p. (chiefly illus.) Lithuanian, Russian, English, French, and German.
DK511.L27L42184 DLC.

433. LITVA. [Vil'nīus, Gintaras,
1970. 18] p. illus.
DK511.L2L77 DLC.

434. LITVA. FOTOKOMPOZITSIIA. Litva. Fotokompozitsiia. [Foto B. Alek-
navichiusa i dr. Stikhi E. Mezhelaī-
tisa. Moskva, Planeta, 1972] [83]p.
illus. (V bratskoī sem'e sovetskikh
narodov) Title also in Lithuanian:
Lietuva. DK511.L2L76 DLC; KU;MH.

435. MATUTIS, Anzelmas. Dainava.
Vilnius, Valstybinė Politinės ir
Mokslinės Literatūros Leidykla, 1958.
237 p. (chiefly illus.) PPiU; KyLoU

436. ORENTAITĖ, Birutė and ZAVADS-
KIS, Audrius. Lietuvos nerija. [The
Sand dunes of Lithuania. Vilnius]
Mintis, 1973. 226 p. (chiefly ill.)
Dailininkas Vilius Ambrazevičius.

Lithuanian, Russian, English, and
German. DK511.K7707 PU; DLC.

437. PUKYS, P. Klaipėda. Wil-
njus, Staatlicher Verlag für politische und wissenschaftliche Literatur,
1959. 26 p. illus.
LG2.KLA ICLJF.

438. ROMER, Helena. Wilno.
[Warszawa, etc., 1919] 40 p. plates. Slav6467.41.5 MH.

439. ŠIMKŪNAS, Romualdas. Kur ne-
tilsta paukščių daina. Vilnius,
Mintis, 1974. 47 p., 48 p. of plates. At head of title: Lietuvos
gamtos apsaugos draugija. [Where
the songs of the birds never end]
OKentU.

440. SOVETSKAIA LITVA; fotoocherk
Redaktor G. Girich. Vil'nīus, Min-
tis, 1974. [18] p. illus.
DK511.L2S64 DLC

441. STANIONIS, Vytautas and MIK-
LAŠEVIČIUS, Visvaldas. Alytus. [The
Town of Alytus.] [Alytus], Alytaus
rajono kultūros namai, 1960. 13,137
p. (chiefly illus.)
DK651.A59S7 OKentU.

442. SVEČIAI TARYBŲ LIETUVOJE.
[Visitors in Soviet Lithuania. Ch.
Levino ir J. Kacenbergo foto nuo-
traukos] Vilnius, Valstybinė grožinės literatūros leidykla, 1960.
34 p.,[86] p. of illus.
DK511.L27S96 DLC; MiEM.

443. TARYBŲ LIETUVA. [Soviet Li-
thuania] Vilnius, Mintis, 1967.
[20] p. illus.
DK511.L2T19 1967 CaAEU

444. VILNIUS. [Sudarytojas A.Me-
donis] Vilnius, Valstybinė politinės ir mokslinės literatūros leidykla, 1960. 1 v. unpaged (chiefly
illus.) List of illus. (36 p.) in
Lithuanian, Russian, Polish, German,
and English, laid in.
DK651.V4V42 DLC.

445. VILNIUS. VIL'NĪUS. Vilnius, Valstybinė politinės ir mokslinės literatūros leidykla, 1963.
1 v. (chiefly col. illus.)
DK651.V425 DLC; NN.

446. --- --- [Tsvetnoe foto
V. Tiukkelīa. Tekst I. Baravikasa.
Moskva, Progress, 1965] [48] p.
(chiefly illus.)
DK651.V4V426 DLC; MB.

447. VON MEMEL UND TRAKHENEN IN
144 Bildern. Leer (Ostfriesland),
G. Rautenberg, 1955. 1 v. (chiefly

illus.) Introd. signed: Paul Brock.
*EIB--NN.

448. YLEVIČIUS, Vytautas. Tėviš-
kė. [Homeland] [Dailininkas Rimantas Dichavičius. Vilnius] Lietuvos
kultūrinių ryšių su tautiečiais užsienyje komitetas [1971] 267 p.
(chiefly illus.) DK511.L2Y52 1971
CaAEU

IV. SERIALS

IV.1. DAILY NEWSPAPERS

449. VIENYBĖ LIETUVNINKŲ.Metas 1-
33; Vasaris 1886-Gruodis 1919. Plymouth, Pa.; Brooklyn, N.Y., 1886-1919.
35 v. Title varies: 1886-1889, Wie-
nibe Lietuwniku; 1890-1892, Vienybe
Lietuvniku; 1893-1919, Vienybė Lietu-
vninkų.
CtPAM (1897-1906); OKentU (1900-1902,
1906, 1907)

450. VILNIS. Balandžio 8, 1920-
Chicago, Ill. weekly; semiweekly;
since Sept. 1926 daily.
OKentU ([1952-1954], 1972)

IV.2. PERIODICALS

451. AIDAI; mėnesinis kultūros
žurnalas. [Echoes] Nr.1-26. München, Ger. Nr.22-26: Schwäbisch-
Gmünd] 1947-1949. [Nr.15-26, 1948-
1949: xerox copy] 4 v.
AP95.L5A43 PU

452. AKIRAČIAI; atviro žodžio
mėnraštis. Metai 1- ; Liepos mėn.
1968- . Chicago, Ill. Monthly.
OKentU(1968-1973)

453. ALGUVOS BARAS; Kempteno(Al-
gaeu) lietuvių tremtinių stovyklos
neperiodinis publicistikos ir literatūros žurnalas. Nr.1-7; May 20,
1945-1946. Kempten, Ger. Irregular. OKentU(nos.2-6; 1945-1946)

454. ATEITIS; savaitinis laikraštis, laisvamanių susivienijimo organas. September 1900-May 1901.
Pittsburgh, Pa. OKent(1900)

455. ATGARSIAI. Caracas, Vene-
cuela, 1961-1963. Bimonthly.
Mimeographed. OKentU(1961-1963,
nos.1-15)

456. AUŠRA. Spalio mėn., 1975-
Vasario mėn.16 d., 1977. [Redagavo

ir vardų rodyklę parengė Jonas Dai-
nauskas] Čikaga, Akademinės skautijos leidykla, 1977. 222 p.
AP95.L5A889 PU

457. AUŠRINĖ; lietuvių pažangio-
sios moksleivijos laikraštis. nr.1-
37; Jan.30, 1910-Dec. 1917. Vilnius.
Irregular. Dec.1919-1926 continued
to be published in Marijampolė and
Kaunas. OKent(1910-1913, v.5, no.2,
1914 (Apr.15)).

458. DAGIS; mėnesinis satyros
žurnalas. Metai 1-4; 1909-1912.
Boston, Mass.; Chicago, Ill., 1909-
1912. ICCC(1910); OKentU(1911)

459. DILGĖLĖS; literatūros, politikos ir mokslo satyriškas laikraštis. Philadelphia, Pa.; Pittsburgh,
Pa. Monthly. OKentU(1906, 1908-
1910)

460. DRAUGAS; pirmeivės lietuvių
jaunuomenės laikraštis. Nr.1-5;
gegužės 1904-1905. Bitėnai, 1904-
1905. From July 1905 continued as
Darbininkas, nos.6-9 till April 1906.
OKentU(1904)

461. GAIRĖS; meno ir literatūros
iliustruotas žurnalas. Nr.1-8; Sausis 1923-1924. Kaunas, 1923-1924.
8 nos. Bimonthly.
OKentU(nos.1-6, 1923)

462. GAIRĖS; skautų vyčių neperiodinis laikraštis. Nr.1-6; 1947-1949.
Würzburg, Ger.; Schweinfurt, Ger.,
1947-1949. Irregular.
OKentU(nos.1-5, 1947)

463. GARSAS; lietuvių Romos katalikų susivienijimo organas. Metai
1- ; gegužės 17, 1917- . Brooklyn, N.Y.; Wilkes-Barre, Pa. Weekly.
CtPAM(1918-1940); OKentU(1926-1931)

464. GIMTASIS KRAŠTAS; kultūrinių
ryšių su tautiečiais užsienyje "Tėviškės" draugijos laikraštis. Metai
1- ; vasario 2 d., 1967- . Vilnius. Weekly. Supersedes Tėvynės
Balsas. OKentU(1967-1973-)

465. JAUNIMAS; Lietuvos jaunimo
sąjungos laikraštis. 1910-1915.;
1921-birželis 1936. Vilnius; Kaunas.
Semimonthly; monthly.
OKentU(1911)

466. KANKLĖS; mėnesiniai leidiniai. [The Harp. Monthly.] No.1-56;
1917-1921. South Boston, Mass.,1917-
1921. 56 nos in 1 v. (Lietuvių
muzikos konservatorija. Lithuanian
Conservatory of Music) Edited by
Mikas Petrauskas, each number consisting of one of his compositions.
4040a.236 MB.

467. KARYS. Berlin, Ger.; Weimar, Ger., 1944-1945. Irregular.
OKentU(nos.1-5, 1944; nos.1-7,1945)

468. KŪRĖJAS; savaitinis anarchistinės krypties laikraštis. Feb.7,
1900-June 14, 1900. Chicago, Ill.,
1900. 19 nos. OKentU(1900)

469. LIETUVIAI; Reiche gyvenančių
lietuvių laikraštis. Nr.1-40; 1944-
balandžio 11, 1945. Kaunas; Berlin.
OKentU(nos.1-14, 1944; nos.1-13, 15-
17, 19-22, 1945)

470. LIETUVIS; Vokietijoje gyvenančių lietuvių dvisavaitinis laikraštis. Nr.1-6; rugpiūčio 16,1945-
lapkričio 15, 1945. Hassendorf,Ger.;
Dörverden, Ger.
OKentU(1945)

471. LIETUVIŲ GYDYTOJŲ BIULETENIS.
Chicago, Ill.
OKentU(no.4, 1961; nos.2-3, 1962; nos.
1-4, 1966; nos.1-2, 1967; nos.2-4,
1968)

472. LIETUVIŲ ŽINIOS. Nr.1-8;
Hanau, Ger. Weekly; irregular.
Mimeographed. OKentU(1945)

473. LIETUVIŲ ŽODIS. Metai 1-4;
spalio 12, 1946-kovo 1, 1949. Detmold, Ger., Baltų Centrinės Tarybos,
Lietuvių skyrius, 1946-1949.
OKentU(nos.1-9, 11, 12, 1946; nos.
1-52, 1947; nos.1-29, 31-51, 1948;
nos.1-10, 12-19, 1949)

474. LIETUVIŲ ŽURNALAS. Metai 1-
3; 1912-1914. Chicago, Ill., 1912-
1914. Monthly. Published by socialist group, mostly translations.
NN(2-3, rugs., 1913-spalio 1914)
PU(1-3; 1912-1914 incompl.)

475. LITERATŪRA; literatūros meno ir kultūros žurnalas. Kaunas,
Universitetas, 1936. [Xerox copy,
1977] Vol. 1-2; nomore published.
PG8501.L58 PU

476. LITERATŪROS LANKAI; neperiodinis poezijos, prozos ir kritikos
žodis. Buenos Aires, Argentina; Baltimore, Md., 1952-1959. 8 nos.
OKentU(1952-1959)

477. LITVA LITERATURNAĬA. Nr.1-
1966- . Vil'nĭus, Vaga. v. ill.
ports. PG8771.R1L5 DLC(1967-);
CU(1966-); CSt(1967-); CaOTU(1966-)
InU(1969); InNd; MH(1966-); MiU;
FMU; NIC(1968-); OU; TxU; WU.

478. MINTIS. Nr.1- ; 1971- .
London, [Liet. Socialdemokratų Partijos Užsienio Delegatūra] v. ill.
Some summaries in English.
DK511.L2A266 DLC

479. MOKYKLA; lietuvių mokytojų
sąjungos organas. Kovo 3(16),1909-
1915. Vilnius. Monthly.
OKentU(1909)

480. MOTERIS. Metai 1- ; 195 -
Toronto, Ont., Kanados lietuvių katalikių moterų draugija. Bimonthly.
HQ1104.M67 DLC; OKentU(1958-1963,
1965, 1968-1973)

481. MŪSŲ VILTIS. Nr.1-26; Gruodžio 24, 1945-rugsėjis 1946. Fulda,
Ger. OKentU(1945-1946); ICLJF(1945-
1946)

482. MŪSŲ VYTIS; skautiškos minties žurnalas. Metai 1- ; kovo
mėn., 1951- . Chicago, Ill., Akademinis skautų sąjudis. Monthly:
1951-1952; since 1953 bimonthly.
ICCC(nos.3-6, 1953; nos.1-6, 1954;
nos.1,3,5,6, 1955; nos.1-4, 1956);
OKentU(nos.1-1), 1951 on microfilm;
nos.1,3, 4, 6, 1958; 1961; nos.1-4,
6, 1962; no.4, 1963; nos.2-3, 5,
1965)

483. MŪSŲ ŽINIOS. 1- ; saus.2,
1972- . Chicago, Ill., Tėvai Jėzuitai Čikagoje. v. illus. biweekly. BX806.L5M85 DLC

484. NAUJAS ŽODIS. Ryga; Kaunas,
Naujo Žodžio bendrovė, 1925-1933.Semimonthly. Q57.92N234 PU(3-6; 1927-
1930) OKentU(nos.1-2; 1926)

485. NAUJASIS GYVENIMAS; religinės kultūros laikraštis. Nr.1-44;
gruodis 1945-birželis 15, 1948.
München, Ger., Lietuvių katalikų kunigų sąjunga. Semimonthly.
OKentU(1945; nos.7-9, 12, 15, 16,
1946; 1947-1948)

486. NAUJIENOS; mėnesinis žmonių
laikraštis. metai 1-3; sausis 1901-
gruodis 1903. Tilžė. OKentU(1901)
487. NAUJOJI VILTIS. 1- ;
Cleveland, Ohio.
OKentU(1970-1974; nos.1-6)

488. NEMUNAS; iliustruotas nepriklausomos kultūros žurnalas. Nr.1-
6; 1950-1951. Chicago, Ill.; Scranton, Pa. Irregular.
ICCC(nos.1-2, 1950; nos.5-6, 1951)
OKentU(nos.1-6, May 1950-June 1951
on microfilm)

489. PRANCIŠKONŲ PASAULIS; mėnesinis religinio-patriotinio turinio
laikraštis. Metai 14-18; sausis
1936-liepos 1940. Kretinga. January 1936 supersedes Šv. Pranciškaus
Varpelį (Metai 1-13) and continues
its numeration. OKentU(1936-1939)

490. PRANCŪZIJOS LIETUVIŲ ŽINIOS.
Nr.1- ; 19 . Paris. Irregular.

Mimeographed.   KentU(nos.20-22,25-
26,28-29,32-36,38-41,43-44; 1960-
1972)

491. PRANEŠĖJAS. 1- ; 196 .
Detroit, Mich. OKentU(1969-1971)

492. PROGRESAS; savaitinis laikraštis. Nr.- ; sausio 6, 1910-
lapkričio, 1910. Philadelphia, Pa.,
Atlas Trading Association, 1910.
Weekly. OKentU(1910); MePKF(Jan.
1910-June 1910)

493. RYGOS NAUJIENOS; visuomenės
literatūros, politikos ir ekonomijos laikraštis. Metai 1-7; gruodis 1909-1915. Ryga. Weekly.
OKentU(1910)

494. ŠALTINĖLIS; Lietuvos bernai-
čiams ir mergaitėms. 1906-rugpiūtis
13, 1915. Seinai. Weekly. Published as a supplement to Šaltinis. Continued in Mariampolė every two month:
December 1928-June 1940.
OKentU(1909-1910)

495. SKAUTŲ AIDAS. Metai 1-3 ;
1946-1948. Detmold, Ger.
OKentU(nos.1-5,7-8,11-12, 1946; nos.
1-2,4-8,11-12, 1947; nos.1,4, 1948)
ICCC(1946-1948)

496. ŠVIESA; akademinio jaunimo
sambūrio laikraštis. Nr.1-7; 1946-
1949. Tübingen, Ger.
OKentU(1946-1949)

497. ŠVIETIMO GAIRĖS. 1- ; gegužis 1968- . Michigan City, Ind.;
Putnam, Conn., JAV LB Švietimo Taryba. Nos.1-3 mimeographed.
OKentU(no.1, 1969; nos.2-3, 1970;
no.4, 1971)

498. TĖVIŠKĖLĖ; lietuvių vaikų
laikraštis. Metai 1-6; lapkričio
1 d., 1951-gruodis 1956. Chicago,
Ill. OKentU(1953-1956); ICCC([1953-
1956])

499. TĖVIŠKĖS AIDAI [Echoes of
homeland] 1- ; 1957- . Melbourne,
Australia, Australijos lietuvių katalikų federacija. DLC (not retained)
OKentU(no.24, 1958; nos.11,22,25,
1969; nos.2,14,16,40-50, 1970; nos.
1-3,5-12,14-16,18-19,22-23,26-30,32-
38,40-50, 1971; nos.1-9,11-26,28-37,
39-40,42-50, 1972)

500. TĖVYNĖS ATGARSIAI; Čikagos
aukštesniosios lituanistikos mokyklos
mokinių žurnalas. Nr.1- ; 195 - .
Chicago, Ill. OKentU(nos.27-35,37,
39,41-44, 1961-1966)

501. CANCELLED.

502. TIESA; a Lithuanian monthly
magazine. Pittsburgh, Pa. 1916.
no. 1-5.
* NN(1, no.4-5; Oct.-Nov. 1916)

503. TIESOS AIDAI; mėnesinis laikraštis. Nr.1-12; 1926-1928. Niaga-
ra Falls, N.Y. Monthly; irregular.
OKentU(nos.1-3,5; 1926-1927)

504. TREČIAS FRONTAS; rašytojų
aktyvistų kolektyvo literatūros ga-
zieta. Kn.1, nr.1-5; 1930-1931.
Kaunas. [Xerox copy, 1976]
PG8501.T7 PU(xerox)

505. TREMTINIŲ MOKYKLA; mėnesinis
pedagogikos žurnalas. Nr.1-6; liepos
-lapkričio 1946. Nürtingen, Ger.At-
žalyno leidykla, 1946. 6 no.
OKentU(nos.1-6, 1946)

506. TREMTIS. Metai 1-6; liepos 1950-kovo 1955. Memmingen,Ger.,
1950-1955. Weekly.
DLC([1951-1953]); ICLJF(liepos-spa-
lio, 1950)

507. VAIRAS; literatūros, dailės,
mokslo, visuomenės ir politikos laik-
raštis. Vilnius, 1914-1915. 2 v.
[Xerox copy, 1975] Incomplete: v.2,
no.23, August 8, 1915 wanting.
Contents.--v.1, no.1-17-18, Jan.5-
Dec.30, 1914.--v.2, no.1-22, Jan10-
July 25, 1915.
AP95.L5V3 PU(xerox)

508. VAIVORYKŠTĖ; literatūros ir
dailės žurnalas. Kn.1-4; 1913-1914.
Vilnius, J. Rinkevičiaus leidinys,
1913-1914. [Xerox copy, 1974]
(kn.1-4, 1913; kn.1, 1914. Complete)
PG8501.V335 PU(xerox)

509. VEIDRODIS; mėnesinis ilius-
truotas žurnalas, pašvęstas teatro
ir scenos reikalams. Nr.1-10;
Jan.-Oct., 1914. Chicago, Ill. 1v.
[Xerox copy, 1976]
PN2009.V4 PU(xerox)

510. VILTIS; tautinės krypties
laikraštis. 1- ; spalio 3, 1907-
rugsėjo 19, 1915. Vilnius.
Three times a week: Oct.3, 1907 to
Dec.1, 1913; daily: Dec.1, 1913 to
Sept.19, 1915.
OKentU(Oct.3, 1907-Apr.1, 1908)

511. ŽARIJA; Lietuvos socialdemokratų partijos savaitraštis. 1- ;
gegužis 1907-birželis 1908. Vilnius.
Weekly. Supersedes Skardas(1907.I.5
to V.23; 21 nos)
OKentU(1907-1908)

512. ŽEMĖ; Lietuvos ūkininko priedas. Metai 1- ; June 1907- .

Vilnius. Monthly: June 1907 to March 1908; semimonthly: April 1908- . OKentU(1907-1911)

513. ŽINYČIA; kvartalinis laikraštis, paskirtas apšviestesniesiems lietuviams. Tilžėje, Kaštu "Tėvynės Sargo", 1900-1902. 1 v. [Xerox copy, 1975]
AP95.L5Z5 PU(no.1-5; xerox); OKentU (1900); CtPAM(1900-1902)

514. ŽVAIGŽDĖ. Brookly, N.Y.; Shenandoah, Pa.; Philadelphia, Pa., 1901-1944. Weekly: until 1923; monthly: 1923-1926; quarterly: 1926- . ICCC(1910-1922); ICLJF(1923) CtPAM(1902-1923-) OKentU(no.1, 1931; no.2, 1933; 1935; no.3, 1936)

515. ŽVAIGŽDĖ; religinis mėnesinis žurnalas. Boston, Mass.; Chicago, Ill., Jesuit Fathers, 1943-1967. Monthly. ICCC(1943-1949;[1950]; 1951-1953;[1954-1955]; 1956; OKentU(1944-1950; 1952-1953; nos.1-4,6-12, 1954; nos.2,7, 1955; no.7, 1957; nos.1-3,5,7, 1959; nos.1-3,7-9,11, 1960; nos.2-3,5, 1961; nos.3-5,1962)

516. CANCELLED.

IV.3. ANNUALS AND OTHER PUBLICATIONS

517. ATMINIMŲ TURTAS; moksleivių metraštis, 1975-1976 mokslo metai. [Paruošimas spaudai: Regina Kučienė] Chicago, Ill., Kristijono Donelaičio Aukštesnioji lituanistinė mokykla, 1976] 112 p. E184.L7A8 PU.

518. ATŽALA; almanachas. Vilnius, Vilniaus lietuvių mokytojų katalikų leidinys, 1917.
ICCC.

519. Kanados Lietuvių Diena; metraštis. Lithuanian Day in Canada. 1- ; 1953- [Toronto, Ont., s.n.] v. illus., ports.
F1035.L5K16 CaAEU; DLC(5-); CaBVaU; CaOTU(6-)

520. LIETUVIŲ STUDENTŲ SĄJUNGA. Metraštis 1966. Chicago, Ill., 1966. 97 p. illus.
L970.4.SS ICLJF.

521. PLIENO SPARNAI; metraštis. Chicago, Ill. OKentU(no.1, 1970; nos.2-3, 1972)

522. TĖVŲ ŽEMĖS ATŽALA; Kristijono Donelaičio Aukštesniosios lituanistinės mokyklos mokinių metraštis, 1976-1977 mokslo metai. [Paruošimas spaudai D. Bindokienės. Chicago, Ill., 1977] 125 p. E184.L7T4 PU.

523. TĖVYNĖS PAŠVAISTĖ; moksleivių metraštis, 1961-1962, Maironio metai. Redagavo Mykolas Drunga, Krstina Grabauskaitė, Vytautas Nakas, Milda Pakalniškytė, Birutė Šlajutė. Metraščio globėjas Domas Velička. [Chicago, Ill.,]Čikagos aukštesnioji lituanistikos mokykla [1962] 208 p. E184.L7T42 PU.

IV.4. PUBLICATIONS OF THE UNIVERSITIES, INSTITUTIONS AND LEARNED SOCIETIES

524. BULLETIN OF BALTIC STUDIES. Tacoma, Wash.; Brooklyn, N.Y.,Association for the Advancement of Baltic Studies. Quarterly.
DK511.B25B78 DLC; MH; OKentU.

525. INSTITUTE OF LITHUANIAN STUDIES. Lituanistikos instituto 1973 metų suvažiavimo darbai. Proceedings of the Institute of Lithuanian Studies, 1973. Spaudai paruošė Rimvydas Šilbajoris. Chicago, Ill., Institute, 1975. 262 p.
DK511.L2I63 1975 CaAEU; PU.

526. INSTITUTE OF LITHUANIAN STUDIES. Lituanistikos instituto 1975 metų suvažiavimo darbai. Proceedings of the Institute of Lithuanian Studies, 1975. Chicago, Ill., The Institute, 1976. 192 p. illus.
DK511.L2I64 1976 CaAEU; PU

527. JOURNAL OF BALTIC STUDIES. v. 3- ; Spring 1972- . Brooklyn, N.Y.; Allentown, Pa., Association for the Advancement of Baltic Studies. Quarterly. Continues by vol.3, spring 1972 the Bulletin of Baltic Studies.
DK511.B25B78 DLC([3]-); AzTeS(3-); CLU(3-); CSt-H(3-); CLobS(5-);CtY(3-) CaOOCC(3-); CaOTY(4-); CU-S(3-) CaOLU(3-); FTaSU([5]-); InU(3-);ICU(3-); ICarbS([4]-); InNd(4-); MH(1-) MiMtpT([3]-); NCH(3-); NN(-);NjP(3-) NNC(3-); NhD(3-); OrU(3-); PV(3-); PBL(3-); PSt(3-); PU(3-); RPB(5-); TNJ(3-); TxHR([5]-); VtU(3-); WU(3-)

528. LIETUVIŲ TAUTOS PRAEITIS. Lithuanian historical review. Tomas 3- (9- ; 1971- . Chicago, Ill., Lietuvių istorijos draugija. v. illus. Lithuanian with summaries in English. Continues Tautos Praeitis.
DK511.L2A276 DLC; CaAEU(3-)

529. LIETUVOS ISTORIJOS METRAŠTIS. Vilnius, Lietuvos TSR Mokslų akademija, istorijos institutas.
v. illus. annual. Summaries in Russian. [Annals of Lithuanian history] DK511.L2A247 DLC; PU.

530. LIETUVOS TSR PAMINKLŲ APSAU-
GOS IR KRAŠTOTYROS DRAUGIJA. Mūsų
kalba. Vilnius. no. At head of
title: Lietuvos TSR aukštojo ir specialiojo vidurinio mokslo ministerija, Vilniaus V. Kapsuko Universitetas.
PG8501.L54a DLC(no.24, 1971-)

531. LITHUANIA. FINANSŲ MINISTE-
RIJA. Litauens wirtschaftlich-finan-
zielle Lage... 1924- . [Kaunas]
1925- . v. tables.
HC337.L5A33 DLC; PU(Jg.1924)

532. LITHUANIAN SYMPOSIUM ON
SCIENCE AND CREATIVITY, 2d., CHICAGO,
1973. Antrasis mokslo ir kurybos s
simpoziumas; paskaitų santraukos.
Abstracts of second Lithuanian sym-
posium on science and creativity.
Lithuanian and English. Chicago,
Ill., 1973. 65 p.
DK511.L2L7745 1973 CaAEU; PU

533. LITHUANIAN SYMPOSIUM ON
SCIENCE AND CREATIVITY, 2d, CHICAGO,
1973. [Programa. Program] Chicago, Ill., [Amerikos lietuvių inži-
nierių ir architektų sąjungos Čikagos skyrius] 1973. 127 p. Lithuanian and English.
E184.L7L56 PU; CaAEU.

IV.5. ALMANACS

534. JAUNIMO METŲ KALENDORIUS,
1966. Parengė St. Barzdukas. [Al-
manac for the youth year] Cleveland, Ohio., 1966. 96 p.
AY78.L5J3 PU.

535. LIETUVISZKAS AUSZROS KALENDO-
RIUS ant metų 1885... Iszleido Lietu-
vos milėtojai. Bitėnai, Kasztu
M. Jankaus ir J. Mikszo [1884].
[Xerox copy, 1978] xxviii, 72 p.
AY1039.L5L53 1884a PU(xerox)

536. LITHUANIAN ALLIANCE OF AME-
RICA. Susivienijimo Lietuvių Amerikoje kalendorius 1919 metams. [The
Lithuanian Alliance of America almanac, 1919] Sutvarkė V.K. Račkauskas. New York, N.Y., Tėvynės spauda, 1918. 224 p.
AY78.L5L52 1919 PU.

537. --- --- 1920 metams. [The
Lithuanian Alliance of America almanac 1920] Sutvarkė V.K. Račkauskas.
New York, N.Y., Tėvynės spauda, 1919.
224 p. AY78.L5L52 1920 PU.

538. METRAŠTIS 1950. [Yearbook-
almanac, 1950 with a collection of
essays] Redagavo L. Andriekus.
Kennebunk Port, Me., Tėvai Pranciško-

nai, 1949. 221 p. illus., ports.
DK511.L223M59 1950 CaAEU; MH.

539. VILNIES KALENDORIUS. Chicago, Ill. OKentU(1943-1945; 1947,
1949, 1951-1954, 1956-1957, 1959-
1961, 1963, 1965, 1971)

V. EARTH SCIENCES

V.1. GENERAL STUDIES, CONFERENCES,
ETC.

540. SAMAITIS, Jonas. Lithuanian
science; past and present. [Trans-
lated from the Lithuanian by Olimpija Armalytė and Juozas Butkus] Vilnius, Gintaras, 1974. 106 p. illus.
Q127.L5S3 PU; DLC.

541. VILNA. UNIVERSITETAS.
XX [i.e. Dvidešimtosios] Studentų
mokslinės konferencijos pranešimų
tezės: Biologija, geologija, geografija ir medicina. Tezisy dokladov
XX studencheskoĭ nauchnoĭ konferentsii: Biologiïa, eologiïa, etc. Vil-
nïus, 1967. 91 p. At head of title
Vilniaus Valstybinis V. Kapsuko universitetas. In Russian.
QH301.V448 DLC

542. VILNA. UNIVERSITETAS. GAM-
TOS MOKSLŲ FAKULTETAS. Materialy Nauchnoĭ ïubileĭnoĭ konferentsii Este-
stvennogo fakul'teta, posvïashchenn-
oĭ 50-letiïu sovetskoĭ vlasti, 19-20
oktiabrïa 1967 g. [Otv. redaktor
Ch. Kudaba] Vil'nïus, 1967. 121 p.
At head of title: Vi'nïusskiĭ gosudarstvennyĭ universitet im. V.Kap-
sukasa. QH302.V47 DLC

V.2. GEOGRAPHY

V.2.a. GENERAL STUDIES, TEXT-
BOOKS, ETC.

543. BIRŽIŠKA, Mykolas. Lietuvos
geografija; vidurinėms mokykloms vadovėlis. [Lithuanian geography...]
I. Prigimtis [pseud.] Vilnius, Lietuvių mokslo draugijos leidinys,
1918. [Xerox copy, 1976] 148 p.
DK.L2B5 1918a PU(xerox)

544. GABRYS, Juozas. Geografijos
vadovėlis skiriamas Lietuvos mokyklai, su paveikslais ir spalvuotais
žemlapiais. Žemlapius braižė A. Le-
vi ir A. Braks. [Geography textbook for the Lithuanian school...

n.p.], 1910. 77 p. illus., diagrs., maps. CaBVaU.

545. GERULAITIS, Karolis. Lietuvos TSR geografija IV klasei. 3. pataisytas leidimas. [Soviet Lithuanian geography] Kaunas, VPLL, 1957. 101 p. illus., col.maps. DK511.L2G37 1957 CaAEU.

V.2.b. CARTOGRAPHY

546. KOLUPAILA, Steponas. Lietuvos ir kaimynų žemėlapiai. [The maps of Lithuania and their neighbours] In Mūsų Žinynas (Kaunas), no. 71, 1931, 19 p. illus., ports., maps. U4.M8 DLC; NN; see also serials consulted.

546a. RUZANCOVAS-RUZANIEC, Aleksandras. Rusų karo topografijos darbai Lietuvoje XVIII ir pradžioje XIX amžių. [Russian military topographic works in Lithuania in eighteenth and the beginning of the nineteenth centuries. By] Majoras Ružancovas. In Mūsų Žinynas (Kaunas), t.2, 1922, p. 380-382. See serials consulted and also with "Naujienos" publ. house, Chicago.

547. SPEKKE, Arnolds. Baltijas jūra senajās kartēs. [The ancient maps of the Baltic sea] Stokholmā, Zelta Abele, 1959. viii, 48 p. illus., maps. GA951.S7 DLC; CtY; DS; NN; NNC; MH; OCl.

547a. TALLAT-KELPŠA, Edvardas. Lietuvos topografijos bei kartografijos darbų klausimu. [On the question of the Lithuanian topography and cartography. By] Leitenantas Tallat-Kelpša. In Mūsų Žinynas (Kaunas), t.2, 1922, p. 195- . See serials consulted and also with "Naujienos" publ. house, Chicago.

V.2.c. ATLASES AND MAPS

548. DĄBROWSKI, Feliks and NOWICKI, Edward. Mapa województwa wileńskiego. Wilno, 1928. 947.52.D113 PU.

549. GABRYS, Juozas. ...Carte ethnographique de l'Europe. Échelle moyenne 1:500,000,000. Lausanne, Librairie centrale des nationalités, 1918. [2],21 p. fold.map (in pocket) (Union des nationalités, office central, 36) Bibliography: p. [9]-21. GR573.G2 CSt-H; CSt;

CtY; DN; ICU; ICJ; MB; MH; NN; NNU-W; PU

V.3. PHYSICAL GEOGRAPHY

V.3.a. GENERAL STUDIES, TEXTBOOKS, ETC.

550. BASALYKAS, Alfonsas. Lietuvos TSR kraštovaizdis. [Landschaft of Soviet Lithuania] Vilnius, Mokslas, 1977. 237 p. GB436.L5B3 PU

V.3.b. GEOMORPHOLOGY

551. GUDELIS, Vytautas. Die Küstenentwicklung der südöstlichen Ostsee während der Spät- und Nacheiszeit. In Beiträge zur Meereskunde, Heft 24-25, 1969. See serials consulted.

552. --- Nekatorye dannye o stroenii i razvitii peresypi Kurshiu Neriia. In Akademiia Nauk SSR. Institut okeanologii. Trudy, v.10, 1954, p. 62-69. See serials consulted.

V.3.c. CLIMATOLOGY

553. GROSS, Hugo. Überblick über die Klimaentwicklung Ostpreussens seit der Eisenzeit. In Altpreussen; Vierteljahrschrift für Vor- und Frühgeschichte (Königsberg in Pr.), no.3, Jg.3, 1938. MH; see also serials consulted.

553a. KAUŠYLA, K[ęstutis]. Lietuvos klimato veiksniai. [The factors of the climate in Lithuania] In Geografinis Metraštis (Vilnius), v.2, 1959, p. 135-150. Summary in Russian and German. G1.G3135 v.2 DLC; CU; see also serials consulted.

V.3.d. HYDROGRAPHY

V.3.d.1. GENERAL STUDIES

554. KÖRNKE, B[ernhard.] Zur Entwicklung der alliuwialen Hydrographie im nordlichen Ostpreussen und in angrenzenden Litauen. In Deutsche geologische Gesellschaft, Berlin. Zeitschrift, v.82, 1930, See

serials consulted.

555. KOLUPAILA, Steponas. Die energiewirtschaftlichen Aufgaben Litauens. In World Power Conference, 2d, Berlin, 1930. Gesamtbericht. Bd.6, Sektion 9, Bericht 358, p. 75-79. TJ5.W6 DLC.

556. MIKALAUSKAS, Vladas. Okhrana podzemnykh vod Litovskoĭ SSR.[By] V.V. Mikalauskas. Vil'nius, Mokslas, 1976. 110,[2] p. illus. (Trudy Litovskiĭ nauchno-issledovatel'skiĭ institut, vyp. 30) At head of title: Upravlenie geologii pri Sovete Ministrov Litovskoĭ SSR. Summary in Lithuanian and German. Bibliography: p: 107-[111]. GB1108.L5M54 DLC.

557. VOPROSY FORMIROVANIIA RESURsov podzemnykh vod ĭuzhnoĭ Pribaltiki; sbornik stateĭ. Otv. red. V.I. Iodkazis. Vil'nius Mintis, 1974. 195 p. diagrs., maps. (Trudy. Litovskiĭ nauchno-issledovatel'skiĭ geologorazvedochnyĭ institut, vyp. 23) At head of title: Upravlenie geologii pri Sovete Ministrov Litovskoĭ SSR. Summaries and tables of contents in Lithuanian and German. GB1108.B35V65 DLC.

558. VOPROSY GIDROGEOLOGII I inzhenernoĭ geologii; sbornik stateĭ. [Redaktory: Ch. Kudaba, A. Zhedialis] Vil'nius, 19-   v. illus., fold.map. At head of title: Ministerstvo vysshego i srednego spets. obrazovaniĭa Litovskoĭ SSR. Vi'niusskiĭ gosudarstvennyĭ universitet im. Kapsukasa. Estestvennyĭ fakultet. QE33.V63 DLC; CaAEU.

V.3.d.3. RIVERS

559. BALTRUŠAITIENĖ, Irena. Pietryčių Lietuvos hidrografija: upės. [Hydrography of Southeastern Lithuania; rivers. By] J. Baltrušaitienė, J. Jablonskis, M. Lasinskas. Vilnius Mintis, 1975. 141,[3] p. fold.leaves., illus. At head of title: LTSR Mokslų akademija. Fizinių-techninių energijos problemų institutas. Summary in Russian and English. GB747.L5B34 DLC

560. BASALYKAS, A[lfonsas] Šlaitų morfogenetinės diagnostikos klausimu. [The morphogenetic diagnosis of river slopes] In Geografinis Metraštis (Vilnius), v.1, 1958, p. 177-190. tables. Summary in English and Russian. See serials consulted.

561. KOLUPAILA, Steponas. Iš Lietuvos upių tyrinėjimo istorijos. [From the history of research on Lithuanian rivers] In Kosmos (Kaunas) no.1, v.5, 1924, p. 57-61. ICCC(no.1,v.5, 1924); see also serials consulted.

562. --- Nemuno praeities pėdsakų beieškant. [Looking for the traces of the past of Nemunas] In Pėdsakai (Fulda, Ger.), vasariskovas, nr. 3-4, 1947, p. 22-27. PG8501.P42 PU; OKentU(1946-1947)

V.3.e. LIMNOLOGY

V.3.e.1. GENERAL STUDIES

563. LIETUVOS EŽERŲ HIDROBIOLOGINIAI TYRIMAI. Hydrobiological researches in the Lithuanian lakes. Summary in Russian and English. At head of title: Lietuvos TSR Mokslų akademijos Zoologijos ir parazitologijos institutas. Bibliography: p. 297-[298] QH96.25.R9L53 DLC.

563a. GALVYDYTĖ, D. Preliminariniai duomenys apie Žemaičių aukštumos limnoglacialinius baseinus ir jų terases. [Preliminary data on ice-dammed basins and their terraces in the highlands of Žemaitija] Summary in Russian and English. In Geografinis Metraštis (Vilnius), v.1, 1958, p. 297-303. See serials consulted.

V.3.e.2. LAKES

564. GIDROBIOLOGICHESKIE ISSLEDOvaniia ozer Dusia, Galstas, Shlavantas, Obialiĭa; kompleksnye issledovaniĭa Mĭatĭalĭaĭskikh ozer po Mezhdunarodnoĭ biologicheskoĭ programme. Hydrological investigations of lakes Dusia, Galstas, Šlavantas and Obelija. Vil'nius, Mokslas, 1977. 267 p. illus. At head of title: Akademiĭa nauk Litovskoĭ SSR. Institut zoologii i parazitologii. Institut botaniki. Summaries in Lithuanian and English. QH178.L5G5 DLC

565. KOLUPAILA, Steponas. Molėtų ežerai. [The lakes of Molėtai] In Girios Aidas (Chicago, Ill.), no.3-4, v.2, 1951, p. 77-83. 99.8.G44 DNAL; ICCC; ICWA; NN.

566. KONDRACKI, J[erzy. Studia nad morfologia i hydrografia poje-

zierza Brasławskiego. In Przegląd geograficzny, t.17, 1938, p.1-100. Summary in German.
G1.P7 DLC(1-4,6-18); CU(1-); DGS(6-); CaQMM; MdBJ(1-21,27-29); NN(1-); NNA(1-);

567. WRÓBLEWSKI, W[itold]. Jeziora Święciańskie: Wiszniewskie, Świrskie i Narocz. In Pamiętnik Fizyograficzny (Warszawa), v.3, 1886. See serials consulted.

V.3.e.4. BOGS

568. DREYER, Johann. Die Moore Kurlands nach ihrer geographischen Bedingtheit, ihrer Beschaffenheit, ihrem Umfange und ihrer Ausnutzugsmöglichkeit. Hrsg. mit Unterstützung der Verwaltung des Oberbefehlshaber Ost. Hamburg,Ger. L. Friederichsen, 1919. [8], 261 p. illus., fold.map. (Veröff. des Geograph. Institutes der Albertus-Universität zu Königsberg, Hft. 1) GB628.55.D7 DLC; DNAL; ICJ; ICU; MB.

V.4. ECONOMIC GEOGRAPHY

569. KAŠKELIS, Juozas. Lietuvos gintaras. [Lithuanian amber] Kaunas, Žinijos b-vés leidinys, 1932. [Xerox copy, 1977] 85 p. QE391.A5K37 1932a PU.

570. KISNĖRIUS, Jurgis. Opornyĭ razrez skvazhiny Stonishkiaĭ, Litovskoĭ SSR. IU.L. Kisnerius. Vil'nius Periodika, 1974. 201 p. illus. At head of title: Upravlenie geologii pri Sovete Ministrov Litovskoĭ SSR. Litovskiĭ nauchno-issledovatel'skiĭ geologorazvedochnyĭ institut. Biography: p. 199-201. QE276.K52 DLC

571. LENINGRAD. VSESOĬUZNYĬ NEFTĬANNO NAUCHNO-ISSLEDOVATEL'SKIĬ GEOLOGORAZVEDOCHNYĬ INSTITUT. Geologiĭa i neftegazonosnost' Pribaltiki i Belorussii; sbornik stateĭ. Leningrad, 1968. 281 p. plans., tables. (Its Trudy. Novaĭa seriĭa, vyp. 261) TN860.L372 vol.261 DLC; DI-GS.

572. MATULIONIS, Povilas. Gintaras lietuviu žemėje; populiarus gintaro tyrinėjimas mineralogijos, geologijos, pramonės ir etnografijos

žvilgsniu. [Amber in Lithuania; a popular research...] Kaunas, Varpo b-vés leidinys, 1922. [Xerox copy, 1977] 21 p. QE391.A5M3 1922a PU(xerox)

573. PIETŲ PABALTIJO PERSPEKTYvios mineralinės žaliavos. Perspektivische nutzbare Minerallen im Südbaltikum. [Atsakingas redaktorius V. Narbutas] Vilnius, 1971. 179 p. illus. (Lietuvos geologijos mokslinio tyrimo institutas. Darbai, t. 18) At head of title: Geologijos Valdyba prie Lietuvos TSR Ministrų tarybos. Summaries in Russian and German. TN36.B34P5 1971 DLC.

574. RASIKAS, R. Lietuvos ekonominė geografija. [Economic geography of Lithuania] Minsk, Baltarusijos Valstybinė leidykla, 1929. OKentU

575. RUNGE, Wilhelm. Der Bernstein in Ostpreussen; zwei Vorträge. Berlin, C.G. Lüderitzsche Verlagsbuchhandlung, 1868. 70 p. illus. 947.52.M699 PU; DI-GS; CtY; ICJ; MdBJ; MH; NN; PPG.

V.5. GEOLOGY

V.5.a. GENERAL STUDIES, CONGRESSES, AND TEXTBOOKS

576. DALINKEVIČIUS, Juozas. Geologicheskie issledovaniĭa Litvy. In Ocherki po istorii geologicheskikh znaniĭ. Moskva, 1955. vyp.3, p. 165-182. See serials consulted.

577. KUPFFER, Karl. Die natürliche Zugehörigkeit des baltischen Gebietes. In Gesellschaft für Erdkunde zu Berlin. Zeitschrift. 1930, p. 1-28. See serials consulted.

578. LIETUVOS GEOLOGŲ MOKSLINĖ KONFERENCIJA, 3d, VILNA, 1973. Lietuvos geologų III [i.e. trečios] mokslinės konferencijos medžiaga, Vilnius, 1973 m. lapkričio mėn. [Proceedings of the third conference of Lithuanian geologists] [Redagavo E. Laškovas] Vilnius, Periodika, 1973. 243 p. illus. At head of title: Geologijos valdyba prie Lietuvos TSR Ministrų tarybos. Lietuvos geologijos mokslinio tyrimo institutas. QE276.L52 1973 DLC.

579. LIETUVOS JAUNŲJŲ MOKSLININKŲ GEOLOGŲ MOKSLINĖ CONFERENCIJA, 1 ST, VILNA, 1968. Materialy Nauchnoĭ

konferentsii molodykh uchenykh geologov Litvy. Vil'nius, 1968. 84 p.
At head of title: Ministerstvo geologii SSSR. Institut geologii (Vil'-
nius). Edited by A. Grigialiene.
QE276.L53 1968   DLC; CaOTU; InU; IU;
NNC.

580.   LIETUVOS JAUNŲJŲ MOKSLININKŲ
GEOLOGŲ MOKSLINE KONFERENCIJA, 2d,
VILNA, 1968.   Materialy vtoroi nauchnoi konferentsii molodykh uchenykh
geologov Litvy. (Noiabr', 1969 g.)
Vil'nius, 1969.   94 p. At head of
title: Upravlenie geologii pri Sovete Ministrov Litovskoi SSR. Institut geologii (Vil'nius) Edited by
A. Grigialene. QE276.L532 1968 DLC.

581. REGIONAL'NAIA GEOLOGIIA PRI-
baltiki i Belorussii. [Red. kollegiia: B.L. Afanas'ev i dr.] Riga,
Zinatne, 1972. 215 p.
QE276.R4 PU; DLC; CaBVaU; InU;MoKL

V.5.b. SPECIAL STUDIES

582. DALINKEVIČIUS, Juozas. Die
Tertiärablagerungen Litauens mit Be-
rücksichtigung des mitteldevonischen
Old Red des Šventoji-Flusses, als
ihre Unterlage. Graz, 1933.
Thesis--University of Graz, Austria.
Au.GU

583. HALICKI, Bronisław. Podsta-
wowe profile czwartorzędu w dorzeczu
Niemna. In Acta Geologica Polonica
(Warszawa), zesz.1-2, T.2, 1951,
p. 6-101.   QE1.W27.3 DLC; CoU;
CoDGS; KU; NmU; NN; WyU.

584. JURGAITIS, Algirdas. Gene-
ticheskie tipy i litologiia peschano-
graviinykh otlozhenii Litovskoi SSR.
Genetic types and litology of gravel
of Lithuanian SSR. Vil'nius, Mintis
1969. 174 p. illus. (Institut geologii (Vil'nius) Trudy, vyp. 9.) At
head of title: Ministerstvo geologii
SSSR. A.A. IUrgaitis. Bibliography:
p. 167-[173]   QE276.V53 vyp. 9 DLC;
DI-GS; CaOTU; CLU.

585. KRZYWICKI, Ludwik. Posled-
niie momenty neoliticheskoi epokhi
v Litvie. Moskva, Tip. T-va I.M.
Kushnerov, 1913.
947.52.K949.4 PU.

586. LIETUVOS KVARTERINIŲ NAUDIN-
gųjų iškasenų geologijos klausimai.
Geologische Fragen über quartäre nutzbare Mineralien Litauens. [Straipsnių
rinkinys. Redagavo: V. Narbutas, A.
Jurgaitis] Vilnius, Mintis, 1972.
129 p. illus., diagrs. (Lietuvos

geologijos mokslinio tyrimo institu-
tas. Darbai, t. 19) Summaries in
Russian and German.
QE696.L72 DLC; PU.

587. MATERIALY PO STRATIGRAFII
Pribaltiki; k mezhved. stratigr. so-
veshch., Vil'nius, mai 1976 g. [Otv.
red. A.A. Grigialis] Vil'nius,
LitNIGRI, 1976. 128 p.,[14] fold.
leaves. illus. At head of title:
Upravlenie geologii pri Sovete Ministrov Litovskoi SSR. Litovskii nauchno-issledovatel'skii geologorazvedochnyi institut. Pribaltiiskaia
regional'naia mezhvedomstvennaia
stratigraficheskaia komissiia.
QE640.M37 DLC.

588. MISSUNA, A[nna] Materialy
k izucheniiu konechnykh moren Litovskogo kraia. In Materialy k poznaniiu geologicheskogo stroeniia Rossiiskoi imperii, vyp.1, 1899, p.133-
170. QE276.M28 DLC; InU; NN; see
also serials consulted.

589. --- Materialy k izucheniiu
lednikovykh otlozhenii Belorussii
i Litovskogo kraia. In Materialy
k poznaniiu geologicheskogo stroeniia Rossiiskoi imperii, vyp.1,
1902; vyp.2, 1903, p. 1-72.
QE276.M28 DLC; InU; NN; see also
serials consulted.

590. PAKUCKAS, Česlovas. Papi-
lės jūros stratigrafine apžvalga
remiantis amonitų fauna. [The review of Papilė's sea stratigraphy]
In Kaunas. Universitetas. Matematikos-Gamtos fakultetas. Darbai,
no.4, t.7, 1933, p. [445]-484. plans
tables, fold.table. Summary in German: p. 471-484. See serials consulted.

591. --- O przebiegu moren czoło-
wych ostatniego zlodowacenia północ-
nowschodniej Polski i terenów są-
siednich. In Warsaw. Instytut geologiczny. Biuletyn, no.1, 1952,
p.599-625. illus. See serials consulted.

592. PAŠKEVIČIUS, J[uozas] Cam-
brian deposits of Lithuania. Kem-
brii Litvy. In CPXXI. Vilnius,
1960. p.43-]52] See serials consulted.

593. --- The crystalline substra-
tum in the South of the East Baltic
territory. In CPXXI. Vilnius, 1960.
p. 23-[31] See serials consulted.

594. --- Eocambrian in Lithuania
and contiguous regions. In CPXXI.
Vilnius, 1960. p. 33-[41] See serials consulted.

395. --- The ordovician of Lithuania. In CPXXI. Vilnius, 1960. p. 53-[64] See serials consulted.

596. PASSENDORFER, Edward. Zarys budowy geologicznej Wilna i okolicy. In Polskie Towarzystwo Geologiczne, Kraków. Rocznik, t.16,1946, p. 53-125. *QPA--NN; CaOTU; CaOOG; CtY; DLC; NjP; NNM; see also serials consulted.

597. PERMSKAIA SISTEMA PRIBALTIKI; fauna i stratigrafiia. Pod red. P.I. Suveizdisa. Vil'nius, Mintis,1975. 305 p. (Trudy. Litovskii nauchno-issledovatel'skii geologorazvedochnyi institut, vyp. 29) At head of title: Upravlenie geologii pri Sovete Ministrov Litovskoi SSR. Summary in English. Bibliography: p.208-[218]. QE674.P49 DLC

598. PETRULIS, L. Zonal and intrazonal subterranean waters of Lithuania. Zonal'nye i intrazonal'-nye podzemnye vody Litvy. In CPXXI. Vilnius, 1960. p. 405-[414]. See serials consulted.

599. PROBLEMY SISTEMATIKI SPIRAL'-nykh nodozariid. Pod red. A.A.Gerke. Vil'nius, Mintis, 1975. 114 p.,[7] leaves of plates. illus. At head of title: Upravlenie geologii pri Sovete Ministrov Litovskoi SSR. Litovskii nauchno-issledovatel'skii geologorazvedochnyi institut. Komissiia po mikropaleontologii SSSR. Summary in English. Bibliography: p. 101-[108] QE772.P75 DLC.

600. RIMANTIENĖ, Rimutė (Jablons-kytė). Paleolit i mezolit Litvy. Vil'nius, Mintis, 1971. 203 p. with illus. At head of title: Akademiia nauk Litovskoi SSR. Institut isto-rii. R.K. Rimantene. Summary in German and Lithuanian. Bibliography: p. 178-183. GN772.L77R55 DLC; CtY; CU; ICU; InU; IEN; MH; MiEM; MiDW; NN; PPiU.

601. STAUSKAITĖ, R. Baltijos pa-jūrio kranto zonos Šventosios-Jan-tarnoe (Palvininkų) ruožo mineraloginė sudėtis. Mineralogiches-kii sostav peskov beregovoi zony Baltiiskogo moria na uchastke Shven-toii-IAntarnoe (Pal'vininkai) Summary in Russian. In Lietuvos TSR Mokslų akademija, Vilna. Darbai. Serija B, t.4(31), 1962, p. 83-106. Q4.152 DLC; see also serials consulted.

602. SUVEIZDIS, P. Permian and triassic deposits in the East Baltic area. Permskie i triasovye ot-lozheniia Pribaltiki. In CPXXI.

Vilnius, 1960. p. 93-[104]. See serials consulted.

603. --- Stratigrafiia permskikh otlozhenii Polsko-Litovskoi sinekli-zy po novym paleontologicheskim materialam. Summaries in Lithuanian and German. In Lietuvos TSR Mokslų akademija, Vilna. Geologijos ir geografijos institutas. Moksliniai pranešimai. Vilnius, 1962. sąs.1, t.14, p. 5-31. illus., map. See serials consulted.

604. TALIMAA, V. (Karajūtė) The devonian of Lithuania. Devon Litvy. In CPXXI. Vilnius, 1960. p. 79-[91]. See serials consulted.

605. TARVYDAS, R. Crystalline boulders of the last and penultimate glaciation in Lithuania. Kristalli-cheskie valuny poslednego i pred-poslednego oledenii na territorii Litovskoi SSR. In CPXXI. Vilnius, 1960. p. 215-[225]. See serials consulted.

606. VILNA. GEOLOGIJOS INSTITU-TAS. Stratigrafiia chetvertichnykh otlozhenii i paleogeografiia antro-pogena iugo-vostochnoi Litvy. [Otv. red.: A.A. Garunkshtis] Vil'nius, Mintis, 1965. 419 p. illus., diagrs., maps. (Its Trudy, vyp.2) At head of title: Gosudarstvennyi geologicheskii komitet SSSR. Ins-titut geologii (Vil'nius). Summa-ries in German and Lithuanian. See serials consulted.

V.5.e. PALEONTOLOGY, PALEOBOTANY, AND PALEOZOOLOGY

607. BODEN, K. Die Fauna der un-teren Oxford von Papilany in Litau-en. In Geologische und Paleontolo-gische Abhandlungen (Jena), N.F., Bd. 10, Heft 2, 1911, p. 125-200. See serials consulted.

608. FAUNA I STRATIGRAFIIA PALEO-zoia i mezozoia Pribaltiki i Belorus-sii; [sbornik statei] The fauna and stratigraphy of Paleozoic and Meso-zoic of Baltic and Belorussia. Pod. red. A.A. Grigialisa. Vil'nius, Min-tis, 1975. 249 p. illus. At head of title: Upravlenie geologii pri Sovete Ministrov Litovskoi SSR. Sum-maries in English. QE725.F38 DLC.

609. GROSS, Walter, geologist. Über Crossopterygier und Dipnoer aus dem baltischen Oberdevon im Zusamen-hang einer vergleichenden Untersuch-ung des Porenkanalsystems paläozoi-

scher Agnathen und Fische. Stockholm
Alquist & Wiksell, 1956. 140 p. ill.,
16 plates. (Kungl. Svenska vetenskaps-
akademien. Handlingar. 4.Serie,Bd.5,
nr. 6)   QE852.D5G87 CaAEU

610. PRANSKEVIČIUS, Antanas. Os-
trokody silura IUzhnoĭ Pribaltiki.
Vil'nius, Mintis, 1972. 279 p. ill.
(Litovskiĭ nauchno-issledovatel'skiĭ
geologorazvedochnyĭ· institut. Trudy,
vyp. 15) At head of title: Upravle-
nie geologii pri Sovete Ministrov
Litovskoĭ SSR. A.A. Pranskevichus.
Summary in Lithuanian and English.
Bibliography: p. 171-[180].
QE817.08P66 DLC.

V.7. NATURAL HISTORY

V.7.a. GENERAL STUDIES

611. BUDRYS, Rimantas. Sketches
of Lithuanian nature. [Translated
from Lithuanian by Juozas Butkus]
Vilnius, Mintis Publishers, 1974.
102 p.,[16] leaves of plates. ill.·
QH178.L5B813 DLC.

612. --- Šimtas zoologijos mįslių.
Vilnius, Vaga, 1967. 238 p. illus.
[One hundred riddles in zoology]
OKentU.

613. ISOKAS, Gediminas. Lietuvos
giriose. [In the forests of Lithua-
nia] Vilnius, Mintis, 1976. 87 p.
[24] leaves of plates.
SD217.L5I8 PU.

614. IVANAUSKAS, Tadas. Gamti-
ninko užrašai. [Notes of a botanist]
2. pataisytas ir papildytas leidimas. Vilnius, Mintis, 1974. 206
p. illus. QL50.I85 1974 DLC.

V.7.b. BOTANY

615. APALIA-ŠIDLIENĖ, Dz. Lietuvos TSR retų augalų rūšių naujos ra-
dimo vietos. [New found places of
the rare plant species in Lithuania]
In Lietuvos TSR Mokslų akademija,
Vilna. Darbai. Serija B, 1(17),
1959, p. 101-106. See serials consulted.

616. BRUNDZA, Kazys. Tipy lugov
vostochnoĭ chasti Litovskoĭ SSR.
In Botanicheskiĭ Zhurnal (Moskva),
no.1, 1958, see serials consulted.

617. DUDĖNAS, H., comp. Vaistin-
gieji augalai; katalogas. [Medici-

nal herbs; a catalogue] Sudarė H.
Dudėnas, J. Grincevičius, St. Guda-
navičius. Vilnius, Mokslas, 1976.
944 p. At head of title: Lietuvos
TSR Mokslų akademija. Botanikos institutas. Lietuvos TSR Sveikatos
apasaugos ministerijos Vyriausioji
farmacijos valdyba. Vyr. farmacijos valdybos chemijos farmacijos
fabrikas Sanitas. Text partly in
Latin, Russian, English, German, and
Polish. Summary in Russian. Bibliography: p. 935-[940]
QK99.A1D84 DLC

618. NATKEVIČAITĖ, Marija. Lietuvos augalija. Pflanzendecke Litauens. In Basalykas, A., ed. Lietuvos TSR fizinė geografija. Vilnius, 1958. v.1, p. 382-416.
GB276.L5B3 DLC; CU; CtPAM; CtTMF;
CaOTU; DI-GS; NN; NNC; PU; WaU.

619. NAUCHNAIA KONFERENTSIIA PO
ZASHCHITE RASTENIĬ, 5th, VILNIUS,
1965. Zashchita rasteniĭ ot vredi-
teleĭ, bolezneĭ i sorniakov; materialy. [Otv. red. M. Strukchinskas]
Vil'nius, Gazetno-zhurnal'noe izd-vo
1965. 185 p. At head of title: Ministerstvo sel'skogo khoziaĭstva Litovskoĭ SSR. Institut botaniki Akademii nauk. Litovskoĭ SSR.
DNAL; MH; NNBG.

620. REGEL, Konstantin. Pflanzen-
soziologische Streifzüge in Litauen.
In Botanische Jahrbücher für Syste-
matik, Pflanzengeschichte und Pflan-
zengeographie (Stuttgart, Ger.), v.
74, 1949, p. 150-172, 288-248)
QK1.B5 v.74 DLC; CaBVaU; CSt; CU;
CtY; ICJ; ICU; IU; IaSA; MH-A; MH-G;
MiU; NIC; NNC; NjP; OU; PU; WU.

621. SŁAWIŃSKI, Witold. Zielone
jeziora pod Wilnem. Wilno, Druk
Znicz, 1924. 233 p. plates, fold.
maps. (His Przyczynek do znajomoś-
ci flory okolic Wilna, 2) Bibliography: p. [215]-225.
947.52.S1 14 PU

622. SNARSKIS, Povilas. Lietuvos TSR ąžuolynai; floristiniu ir
geobotaniniu požiuriu. Redagavo
V. Butkus. Vilnius, Mintis,1972.
94 p. At head of title: LTSR Mokslų akademijos Botanikos institutas.
Lietuvos gamtos apsaugos draugija.
[The oak groves in Soviet Lithuania]
SD397.012S6 DLC; DNAL; NNBG.

V.7.c. ZOOLOGY

623. FAUNA POCHVENNYKH BESPOZVONOCH-
nykh morskogo poberezh'ia Pribaltiki.
Soil invertebrate fauna of the coas-

tal area in the East Baltic region.
[V.A. Minkiavichius, A. IAnukonis,
B.M. Kavaliauskas... et al.; Red.
kollegiia, Eitminavichiute, I.S.
(otv. red.)... et al.] AN LitSSR,
In-t zoologii i parazitologii. Vil'-
nius, Mokslas, 1976. 170 p. illus.
Summary in Lithuanian and English.
QL281.F288 DLC.

624. GLINSKII, F.A. Bieloviezhs-
kaia pushcha i zubry; ocherk. Bie-
lostock, 1899. 947.52.G494 PU.

625. LIETUVOS SPARNUOČIAI.[Birds
of Lithuania. Sudare J. Stasinas]
Vilnius, Mintis, 1973. 78 p., 16
leaves of plates. illus. At head
of title: Lietuvos gamtos apsaugos
draugija. QL690.L5L53 PU; DLC.

626. LOGMINAS, V. Kurapku veisimasis Lietuvoje. [The breeding of
the partridges in Lithuania] In
Lietuvos TSR Mokslu akademija, Vilna. Darbai. Serija B, 3(19),1959,
p. 221-227. Summary in Russian.
See serials consulted.

627. MALDŽIŪNAITĖ, S. Lietuvos
miškiniu kiauniu biologija. [The
biology of wild martens in Lithuania]
In Lietuvos TSR Mokslu akademija,
Vilna. Darbai. Serija B, 1(17),
1959, p. 189-201. illus. Summary
in Russian. See serials consulted.

628. PILECKIS, Simonas. Lietuvos
vabalai. [Beetles of Lithuania]
Vilnius, Mokslas, 1976. 241 p.
QL591.L5P5 PU.

629. PRIBALTIISKAIA ORNITOLOGICH-
ESKAIA KONFERENTSIIA, 4th, Riga,
1960. Birds of the Baltic region;
ecology and migrations... procee-
dings... Jerusalem, Israel Program
for scientific translations, 1961.
vii, 336 p. illus., maps.
QL690.B3P73 1960e DLC; A; CoFS; CU;
CaAEU(Russian ed.); CLSU; CtY-KS;
CoGrS; DI; ICU; IaU; InS; IU; ICF;
IaAS; KNK; LU; McB; MdU; MiU; MnU;
MoU; MH-Z; MtU; MU; NbU; NcD; NhU;
NhD; NjP; NBuU; OkU; TNJ; TxU; WaU.

630. PRŪSAITĖ, J[anina] Lietuvos
vilku mityba ir veisimasis. [The
nutrition and breeding of wolves in
Lithuania] In Lietuvos TSR Mokslu
akademija, Vilna. Darbai. Serija
C, 1(24), 1961, p. 177-191. Summary in Russian. See serials consulted.

631. --- Lietuvos vilku morfolo-
gine charakteristika ir ju papliti-
mas. [The morphological characteris-
tic and   expansion of wolves
in Lithuania] In Lietuvos TSR Moks-

lu akademija, Vilna. Darbai. Serija C, 1(24), 1961, p. 161-176. Summary in Russian. See serials consulted.

632. SOKAS, Juozas. Kurtinio gie-
sme. Vilnius, Vaga, 1976. 285 p.
[The song of a wild turkey]
QL49.S6 PU.

VI. THE PEOPLE

VI.1. GENERAL STUDIES, POPULATION,
       BOUNDARIES, AND THE ETHNO-
       GRAPHIC AND LINGUISTIC TER-
       RITORIES

633. BEDNARCZUK, A. On certain
aspects of gens tie and its traces
in Polish-Lithuanian borderland of
Sejny (Seinai) district. In Acta
Baltico-Slavica (Warszawa), no,9,
1976, p. 149-156. See serials consulted.

634. GELŽINIS, Martynas. Lietuviu
tautos etnines sienos vakaruose.
[The western ethnic boundaries of the
Lithuanian nation] In Karys (Brook-
lyn, N.Y.), no.5, 1972, p. 153-159.
See serials consulted.

635. HALECKI, Oskar. Geografia
polityczna ziem ruskich Polski i
Litwy 1340-1569. In Towarzystwo naukowe Warszawskie. Sprawozdania z
posiedzeń [wydziałów], t.10, 1917,
p. 5-24. See serials consulted.

636. HILDÉN, Kaarlo. Über die
sogennante ostbaltische Rasse. In
Institut international d'anthropo-
logie, 3d, session, Amsterdam, 1927.
Actes du congrès. Paris, 1928.
p. 219-223. L.Soc.42.105.70.2. for
1927 HMH-P.

637. JAŻDŻEWSKI, Konrad. Atlas
to the prehistory of the Slavs. Łódz,
1948-1949. 2 v. col.maps. (Acta
prahistorica universitatis lodzien-
sis, 1) (Łódzkie Towarzystwo naukowe, Wydz.II, Prace, nr.2) Scale of
maps 1:12oooo.
D147.J3 DLC; CaAEU; PU.

638. LEBEDKIN, M. O plemennom
sostave narodonaseleniia zapadnago
kraia Rossiiskoi imperii. In Geograficheskoe Obshchestvo SSSR. Zapiski, v.1, no.3, 1861. See serials
consulted.

639. LELEWEL, Joachim. Narody na
ziemiach słowiańskich przed powsta-
niem Polski: Joachima Lelewela w

dziejach narodowych polskich postrze-
żenia... Poznań, J.K. Żupański,1853.
lxxxii, 820 p. 947.52.L537.2 PU.

640. NATANSON-LESKI, Jan. Epoka
Stefana Batorego w dziejach granicy
wschodniej Rzeczypospolitej. Warszawa, 1930. xvi, 166 p. (Towarzystwo Naukowe Warszawskie. Rozprawy
historyczne. Tom 9, zeszyt 2)
DK511.L24N33 PU; NN.

641. --- Granica moskiewska w epoce Jagiellońskiej. In His Dzieje
granicy wschodnnej Rzeczypospolitej.
Lwow; Warszawa, 1922. (Rozprawy historyczne Towarzystwa Naukowego Warszawskiego. Tom 1, zesz. 3) A con-
tinuation of this work appeared in
1930 under title: Epoka Stefana Batorego w dziejach granicy wschodniej
Rzeczypospolitej in Rozprawy historyczne Towarzystwa Naukowego Warszawskiego. Tom 9, zesz. 2
Bw75.15 CtY; MiU; NN.

642. --- Zarys granic i podziałów
Polski najstarszej. Wrocław, Nakł.
Wrocławskiego Tow. naukowego, 1953.
393 p. fold.col.map.
*QR--NN.

643. PAKŠTAS, Kazys. Lietuvos ribų problema. [The problem of the
Lithuanian boundaries] In Lietuvių
katalikų mokslo akademija, Rome. Suvažiavimo darbai, v.3, p. 383-417.
See serials consulted.

644. PUZINAS, Jonas. Lietuvių
kilmė ir jų gyvenamieji plotai nau-
jausių tyrinėjimų šviesoje. The
origins of the Lithuanians and their
living space according to the latest
research. In Institute of Lithuanian Studies. Lituanistikos instituto 1971 metų suvažiavimo darbai.
Chicago, Ill., p.41-62. Summary in
English. DK511.L2I57 DLC; CaAEU;
InNd; MiU; NIC; NRU; PU.

645. REINHARD, M[arcel]. Histoi-
re de la population mondiale de 1700
a 1948. [Paris] Domat-Montchrestien,
1949. 794 p. illus., col.maps.
Bibliography: p. 769-783.
HB881.R4 DLC; ICU; NN; NIC; NNC;
NNUN; NcRS; NcD; NcU; MB; OU; PSt;
PU; StY; TxU; TU; ICJ.

646. SERAPHIM, Peter Heinz. Be-
völkerungsverschiebungen im baltischen Raum. In Zeitschrift für Geopolitik, v.25, no.7, July 1954, p.
405-411. D410.Z4 v.25 DLC; CLU;
CSt-H; CU; CtY; DLC; ICU; MH; MdBJ;
MiU; MnU; NN; NNA; NNC(8-); NjP;
WU; WaU.

647. SNO, Evgenii Eduardovich.

[Sbornik statei] S.-Peterburg,
O.N. Popovoi [1904] 6 pts. in 1 v.
illus. Partial contents.--[Pt.3]
Na zapadnoi okrainie. Poliaki i
Litovtsy. DK27.S56 DLC.

648. STAROWOLSKI, Szymon. Polska
albo opisanie, położenia Królewstwa
Polskiego; z języka łacinskiego
przełożył, wstępem i komentarzami
opatrzył Antoni Piskadło. Kraków,
Wydawnictwo Literackie, 1976. 249
p.,[16] leaves of plates. illus.
DK4302.5.S717 DLC

649. Le TERRITOIRE ETHNOGRAPHIQUE
de la Lithuanie. [s.l.], 1923. 13 p.
DK511.L27T4 InU; PU.

650. TETZNER, Franz Oskar. Die
Slawen in Deutschland; Beiträge zur
Volkskunde der Preussen, Litauer und
Letten, der Masuren... Braunschweig,
Ger., F. Vieweg & Sohn, 1902. xx,
520 p. illus., maps, plans.
DD78.S5T4 DLC; CaAEU; CtY; ICJ;MB;
NN; NjP; OCl; OCU; PU.

651. VARDYS, Stanley V. Brežnevo
tautybių politika ir Lietuva. [bre-
zhnev's nationality policy and Li-
thuania] In Į Laisvę (Los Angeles,
Calif.), no.61, 1974, p. 4-21. See
serials consulted.

652. VASMER, Max. Die alten Be-
völkerungsverhältnisse Russlands im
Lichte der Sprachforschung. Berlin
W. de Gruyter, 1941. 35 p. illus.
(Preussische Akademie der Wissenschaften. Vorträge und Schriften, Heft
5.) DK33.V3 DLC; MH; PU.

653. --- Beiträge zur historischen Völkerkunde Osteuropas. I.Die
Ostgrenze der baltischen Stämme. In
Akademie der Wissenschaften, Berlin.
Philosophisch-historische Klasse. Sitzungsberichte, no.24, 1932, p. 637-
666. A study based on linguistic
explanation of place names.
See serials consulted.

654. VOELKEL, Maximillian J.A.
Die heutige Verbreitung der Litauer
In Litauische Literarische Gesellschaft (Tilsit), Mitteilungen, v.2,
1883, p. 1-4. See serials consulted.

655. WARSAW. INSTYTUT BADAŃ SPRAW
NARODOŚCIOWYCH. Mapy rozsiadlenia
ludności polskiej i litewskiej na
terenie Republiki Litewskiej i na ob-
szarach północnowschodnich Rzeczypospolitej Polskiej. Skala 1:750,000.
Warszawa, The Institute, 1929. 2
fold.maps. 947.52.W263 PU; MH;NN.

656. ZAWISZA, Otton. Litwini w

Litwie. Wyd. 3., znacznie powiększo-
ne. Wilno, 1907. Bound with Dambrauskas, A. Glos litewski...
947.52.D183 PU.

657. ŻEGOTA-JANUSZAJTIS, Marian.
Strategiczne granice Polski na wschodzie. Warszawa, Nakł. Księgarni wojskowej, 1919. 8 p. Offprint from
Bellony. 947.52.Z26 PU.

658. ŻOŁTOWSKI, Adam. Border of
Europe; a study of the Polish Eas-
tern provinces. With a foreword by
Sir Ernest Barker. London, Hollis &
Carter, c1950. xvi, 348 p. Biblio-
graphy: p. 329-333.
DK416.Z6 DLC; CaAEU; PU.

VI.3. ARCHAEOLOGY

VI.3.a. GENERAL STUDIES, CONGRESSES, RESEARCH, ETC.

659. ARCHEOLOGINIAI IR ETNOGRAFI-
NIAI tyrinėjimai Lietuvoje 1968 ir
1969 m; medžiaga konferencijai,
skirtai 1968 ir 1969 m. archeologinių ir etnografinių ekspedicijų
rezultatams apsvarstyti. Vilnius,
1970 m. gegužės mėn. 14-15 d. [At-
sakingi redaktoriai: Adolfas Tautavičius, Antanas Daniliauskas] Vilnius,
1970. 153 p. [The archaeological
and ethnographical research in Lithuania, 1968 and 1969...]
GN824.L5A8 DLC; ICU; InU; CSt.

660. --- 1970 ir 1971 metais; medžiaga konferencijai, skirtai 1970
ir 1971 metų archeologinių ir etnografinių ekspedicijų rezultatams apsvarstyti. Vilnius 1972 m. gegužės
11-12 d. [Atsakingi redaktoriai:
Adolfas Tautavičius, Vitalis Morkū-
nas] Vilnius, 1972. 177 p. [Ar-
chaeological and ethnographical research in Lithuania, 1970-1971...]
GN824.L5L53 PU.

661. --- 1972-1973 m.; medžiaga
konferencijai skirtai 1972 ir 1973
metų archeologinių ir etnografinių
ekspedicijų rezultatams apsvarstyti:
Vilnius 1974 m. gegužės 28-29 d.
[Atsakingieji redaktoriai Adolfas
Tautavičius, Vitalis Morkūnas]
Vilnius, [s.n.], 1974. 206 p. ill.
At head of title: Lietuvos TSR
Mokslų akademijos Istorijos insti-
tutas. Summary in Russian.
GN824.L5A82 DLC; PU; WU.

662. BASANAVIČIUS, Jonas. Žirgas
ir vaikas; istoriškai-archeologiškas
ištyrinėjimas. [The horse and a boy;

an archaeological research] Tilžėje, Spausta rašėjo kašta, 1885.
32 p. [Xerox copy, 1971]
DK511.L21B35 1971 PU

663. BEZZENBERGER, Adalbert. Li-
tauische Gräberfelder bei Schernen,
Kr. Memel. In Altertumsgesellschaft
Prussia, Königsberg in Pr., 1892,
Bd. 17, p. 141-168. See serials con-
sulted.

664. ORDA, J. Trakų pusiasalio
pilis. [The castle on the penin-
sula of Trakai] In Lithuanian SSR.
Valstybinė architektūros paminklų
apsaugos inspekcija. Metraštis
(Vilnius), v.2, 1960, p.49-68. See
serials consulted.

665. PUZINAS, Jonas. Stand der
archäologischen Forschungen in Litauen. In Baltijas vēsturnieku konference, 1st, Riga, 1937. Runas un
referati. Riga, 1938. See serials
consulted.

666. RIMANTIENĖ, Rimutė (Jablons-
kytė). Lietuvos TSR archeologijos
atlasas. [Archaeological atlas of
the Lithuanian SSR. By] R. Rimantienė, E. Grigalavičienė, O. Bagu-
šienė. Vilnius, Mintis, 1974-1977.
3 v. and atlas, 1-3. illus. At
head of title: LTSR Mokslų akademija Istorijos institutas. Summary
in German and Russian. Bibliography: v.1, p. 223-226.
GN824.L5R55 DLC; InU; MB; NN; NjP;
PU.

667. TARASENKA, Petras. Goro-
dishcha Litvy. In Akademiia nauk
SSSR. Institut arkheologii. Kratkie soobshcheniia o dokladakh i polevykh issledovaniiakh Instituta istorii material'noi kul'tury, v.42,
1952, p. 86-91. DK30.A173 DLC;
CaOONM; MH-MU. See also serials
consulted.

VI.3.b. ACCOUNTS OF ARCHAEOLOGICAL EXCAVATIONS

668. GISEVIUS, Eduard Karl Samuel.
Die heidnischen Schlossberge in der
Umgebung des Rombinus. In Preussische Provinzial-Blätter (Königsberg
in Pr.), Bd. 22, 1837, p.97,252,444,
553; Bd.23, 1840, p.44,164,422, and
in Neue Preussische Provinzial-Blätter (Königsberg in Pr.), 3. Folge,
Bd.4, 1860, p.164. DD491.04A2 DLC
ICJ; ICRL; MH; NNUT; see also serials
consulted.

669. GUREVICH. F.D. Raginianskii
mogil'nik. In Akademiia nauk SSSR.

Institut arkheologii. Kratkie soob-
shchennia o dokladakh i polevykh issledovaniakh Instituta istorii material'noi kul'tury, v.36, 1951, p.
56-62. DK30.A173 DLC; CaOONM;
MH-P; NIC; PU;MU.

670. KULIKAUSKIENĖ, Regina(Vol-
kaitė). Pogrebal'nye pamiatniki
Litvy kontsa I.- nachala II. tysia-
cheletii nashei ery. In Akademiia
nauk SSSR. Institut arkheologii.
Kratkie soobshcheniia o dokladakh i
polevykh issledovaniakh Instituta
istorii material'noi kul'tury, v.42,
1952, p. 108-122. DK30.A173 DLC;
CaOONM; MH-MU; see also serials
consulted.

671. --- Punios piliakalnis.
[The mound of Punia] Mintis, Mintis,
1974. 84 p. illus.
DK511.L21K814 PU; DLC.

672. NAGEVIČIUS, Vladas. Die Aus-
grabungen des Walles der vorgeschich-
tlichen Befestigung (Burgberg) Apuo-
lė. In the International congress of
prehistoric and protohistoric sciences, 1st, London, 1932. Proceedings.
London, 1934. p. 302-304.
GN3.I55 1932 DLC; MH-P.

673. NAVICKAITĖ, Ona (Kuncienė)
Diržiu kapinynas. [The burial mound
of Diržiai] In Lietuvos TSR Mokslu
akademija, Vilna. Istorijos institutas. Iš lietuviu kultūros istorijos
v.2, 1959, p. 151-158. DK511.L212L5
DLC; InU; CLU; CU; ICU; KyU; NN; PU.

674. SADAUSKAITĖ, I. Kairėnu ir
Seiliūnu kapinynu radiniai. [Archaeo-
logical finds in the burial mounds
of Kairėnai and Seiliūnai] In Lietuvos TSR Mokslu akademija, Vilna.
Darbai. Serija A, 1(6), 1959, p.59-
70. See serials consulted.

675. TAUTAVIČIUS, Adolfas. Vilniaus pilies kokliai, XVI-XVII a.
[16th-17th century Dutch tiles in
the castle of Vilnius.] Vilnius,
Mintis, 1969. 47 p. (LTSR Mokslu
akademijos Istorijos institutas.
Acta historica lituanica, 4)
NE4141.L5T3 PU; ICIU; MH; PPiU.

676. --- Vilniaus pilies terito-
rijos archeologiniai kasinėjimai
[The archaeological excavations in
the area of the castle of Vilnius]
In Lithuanian SSR. Valstybinė architektūros paminklu apsaugos inspekcija. Metraštis. v.2, 1960, p.3-
48. See serials consulted.

676a. BAGDANAVIČIUS, Vytautas
Jonas. Tautos samprata ir lietuviu
individualybė; paskaitu kursas Čikagos pedagoginiam lituanistikos
institute. [Reasoning of the nation
and the individuality of Lithua-
nians] Čikaga, Autoriaus leidinys,
1977. 132 leaves. Mimeographed.
DK511.L22B14 1977 CaAEU: PU.

677. CZEKANOWSKI, Jan. Zur An-
thropologie des Baltikums. [Wyd.1.]
Wrocław [Państwowe Wydawn. Naukowe]
1957. 29 p. illus. (Polska Akademia Nauk. Zakład antropologii. Materiały i Prace antropologiczne,
nr. 27) GN585.B35C9 DLC; IU; PU.

678. ĖTNOGRAFICHESKOE KARTOGRAFI-
rovanie material'noi kul'tury narodov Pribaltiki; sbornik statei.[Otv.
redaktory V.A. Aleksandrov i N.V.
Shlygina] Moskva, Nauka, 1975.
239 p. illus. At head of title:
Akademiia nauk SSSR. Institut etnografii im. N.N. Miklukho-Maklaia.
GN585.B35E88 DLC; PU-MU.

679. ETNOGRAFINIAI TYRINĖJIMAI
Lietuvoje 1974 m.; medžiaga konferencijai skirtai 1974 m. etnografi-
niu ekspedicijų rezultatams aptarti.
Vilnius 1975 m. gruodžio 19 d. [Ats.
red. Vitalis Morkūnas] Vilnius,1975.
231 p. illus. Summaries in Russian.
[The ethnographical research in Lithuania 1974...]
DK511.L22E8 DLC; PU.

680. KRASNOV, IUrii Alekseevich.
Rannee zemledelie i zhivotnovodstvo
v lesnoi polose vostochnoi Evropy.
II. tysiacheletie do n.ė.-pervaia
polovina I. tysiacheletiia n.ė.
Moskva, Nauka, 1971. 165 p. illus.
(Materialy i issledovaniia po arkheologii SSSR, no. 174) At head
of title: Akademiia nauk SSSR. Materialy i issledovaniia po arkheologii SSSR. DK30.M42 no. 174 CaAEU
CaBVaU; CLSU; CLU; CU; CtY; DDO;DSI
MoU; NIC; PU-MU; WU; see also
serials consulted.

681. MILIUS, V[acius] Gyvuli-
ninkystė. [Husbandry] In Lietuvos
TSR Mokslu akademija, Vilna. Istorijos institutas. Lietuviu etnografijos bruožai. Vilnius, 1971.
p. 90-[109] HD725.7.L488 DLC;CtY
CaAEU; ICLJF; ICU; MH; NN; PU.

682. --- and PAVILIONYTĖ, D. ŽEM-
dirbystė. [Agriculture] In Lietuvos
TSR Mokslu akademija, Vilna. Istorijos institutas. Lietuviu etnografijos bruožai. Vilnius, 1964.

p. 49-[89]. illus. HD725.7.L488
DLC; CaAEU; CtY; ICLJF; ICU; MH;
NN; PU.

683. --- Žvejyba. [Fishing] In
Lietuvos TSR Mokslų akademija, Vilna. Istorijos institutas. Lietuvių etnografijos bruožai. Vilnius,
1964. p. 110-[125]. illus.
HD725.7.L488 DLC; CaAEU: CtY; ICLJF
ICU; MH; NN; PU.

684. PAKALNIŠKIS, Aleksandras.
Žemaičiai; etnografija. [Žemaičiai
(Samogitians); ethnography] [Chi-
cago, Ill., S. Jankus, 1977.] 164 p.
DK511.S24P3 PU.

685. REICHER, Michał. Sto lat
antropologii polskiej 1864-1964.
Osrodek wileński. Wrocław, 1968.
(Polskie Towarzystwo antropologiczne. Zakład antropologii. Materialy i Prace antropologiczne, nr.22)
572.R273 PU-Mu; IU.

686. TALKO-HRYNCEWICZ, Julian. K
antropologii narodnostei Litvy i Bie-
lorusi. In Trudy Antropologicheska-
go obshchestva pri Voenno-meditsins-
koi akademii (Leningrad) Trudy. t.1,
1894, See serials consulted.

687. TOKAREV, S.A. Litovtsy. In
His Etnografiia narodov SSSR. Moskva
1958. p. 104-113. DK33.T57 DLC;
CoU; CSt-H; CU; CtY;DS; GU; InU; KyU
MH-P; NN; NjP; NcU; NNC; NhD; NbU;
NjR; NIC; OU; RPB; TxU; ViU; WU;WaU.

687a. ŽILINSKAS, J[urgis] Baltijos jūros pakraščių gyventojų gimin-
gumas. [The congeniality of the inhabitants of the Baltic sea coast] In
Vairas (Kaunas), v. 11, 1935, p.300-
313. Mr. Kviklys (Chicago) has it.

VI.5. DEMOGRAPHY

688. KING, Gundar J. Comments
of the current state of Baltic demo-
graphic research. In Bulletin of
Baltic Studies (Tacoma, Wash.), no.4
1970, p.3-11. See serials consulted.

689. KULA, Witold. Stan i potrze-
by badań nad demografią historyczną
dawnej Polski do początku XIX wieku.
In Roczniki Dziejów społecznych i
gospodarczych (Poznan), v.13, 1951,
HC337.P7A255 DLC; CLU; CU; CSt;CtY;
KU; ICN; MB; NN; NNC; NIC; NjR; OU.

VI.6. CENSUSES, THEIR INTERPRETATION AND VITAL STATISTICS

690. JASAS, R. and TRUSKA, L.
Lietuvos didžiosios kunigaikštys-
tės gyventojų surašymas 1790 m.
Vilnius, 1972. 95 p. At head of
title: Lietuvos TSR Mokslų akademijos Centrinė biblioteka. R.Jasas
L. Truska. Perepis' naseleniia
1790 goda v Velikom Kniazhestve Litovskom. Summary in German and Russian. HA1448.L5J37 DLC

691. KOEPPEN, Petr Ivanovich.
O narodnykh perepi'iakh v Rossii.
In Geograficheskoe obshchestvo SSSR.
Zapiski, v.6, 1899, See serials
consulted.

692. ŁOWMIAŃSKI, Henryk. Popisy
wojska Wielkiego Księstwa Litewskiego w 16 wieku jako źródło do dziejów zaludnienia. In Mediaevalia,
w 50 rocznicę pracy naukowej Jana
Dąbrowskiego. Warszawa, 1960.
DK420.M4 DLC; CU; CtY; InNd; MiU;
MoU; NNC; OCl; OU; WU; WaU.

693. MAČIUIKA, Benediktas Vytenis.
Auswertung der Volkszahlungsergebnis-
se von 1970 in Sowjet Litauen. In
Acta Baltica (Königstein, Ger.),
v.11, 1970, p. 87-116. See serials
consulted.

694. REKAŠIUS, Zenonas. Gyvento-
jų kaita Lietuvoje 1940-1970 metais.
[Population changes in Soviet Lithu-
ania, 1940-1970] In Institute of
Lithuanian studies. Instituto 1971
metų suvažiavimo darbai. Chicago,
Ill., 1971. p. 177-189. Summary in
English. DK511.L2I57 DLC; CaAEU;
InNd; MiU; NIC: NRU; PU.

695. RUSSIA(1923- U.S.S.R.).
TSentral'noe statisticheskoe upravlenie. Itogi Vsesoiuznoi perepisi
naseleniia 1970 goda. Moskva, Statistika, 1972-1974. 7 v. At head
of title: TSentralnoe statisticheskoe upravlenie pri Sovete Ministrov
SSSR. Contents.--T.1. Chislennost'
naseleniia SSSR, soiuznykh i avtonomnykh respublik, kraev i oblastei
--T.2. Pol, vozrast i sostoianie v
brake naseleniia SSSR, soiuznykh i
avtonomnykh respublik, kraev i oblastei.--T.3. Uroven' obrazovaniia
naseleniia SSSR, soiuznykh i avtonomnykh respublik, kraev i oblastei.--
T.4. Natsional'nyi sostav naseleniia SSSR...--T.5. Raspredelenie naseleniia SSSR... po obshchestvennym
gruppa, istochnikam sredstv sushest-
vovaniia i otrasliam narodnogo khoziaistva.--T.6. Raspredelenie naseleniia SSSR i soiuznykh respublik
po zaniatiiam.--T.7. Migratsiia na-

seleniîa chislo i sostav semeî v
SSSR, soîuznykh i avtonomnykh res-
publikakh, kraîakh, i oblastîakh.
HA1434 1970.T77 1972   DLC; CaQMM;
CU: CSt-H; CLU; CaBVaU; GU; IEN; IU
InU; IaU; InLP; ICIU; MiU; MiDW;
MdU: MU; MB; NcU: NSyU; NjP; OkU;
PPT; PPiU; TU; TxU; TNJ; ViU;WU;
WaU.

696. ATANAITIS. Algirdas and
ADLYS, Petras.   Lietuvos TSR gyven-
tojai. [The population of Soviet
Lithuania] Vilnius, Mintis, 1973.
199 p. HA1448.L5S8   PU; CSt; CU;
DLC; InU; MH; NjP.

VI.7. LITHUANIANS ABROAD

VI.7.a. GENERAL WORKS

697. BAGDANAVIČIUS, Vytautas Jonas. Kultūrinės ir politinės problems lietuvių visuomenėje. [The
cultural and political problems in
the Lithuanian society] In Į Laisvę (Los Angeles. Calif.), no.59,
1973, p. 5-16. See serials consulted.

698. ERETAS, Juozas. Išeivijos
klausimais. [On the question of Li-
thuanoan exiles] Roma, Lietuvių katalikų mokslo akademija, 1974. 54 p.
DK511.L223E73   DLC.

699. IDEOLOGINĖ KOVA IR JAUNIMAS
Tarybų Socialistinių Respublikų Sąjungos 50-mečiui; mokslinės konferencijos medžiaga. [Ideological
struggle and the youth of USSR for
the 50th anniversary. Red. kolegija
A. Gaidys (pirmininkas)] Vilnius,
1972. 209 p. At head of title:
Lietuvos TSR Mokslų akademija. Filosofijos, teisės ir sociologijos skyrius prie Istorijos instituto. Lietuvos LKJS Centro komitetas.
DK511.L223I33   DLC; MH; NNC; PPiU;
WU.

700. JURKUS, Paulius. Lietuvių
kultūrinis gyvenimas tremtyje. [Li-
thuanian cultural life in exile] In
Metraštis 1950. Kennebunk Port,Me.
[1949] p. 185-200.
DK511.L223M59 1949 CaAEU; MH.

701. LIETUVIŲ SKAUČIŲ SESERIJA.
Lietuvių skaučių seserija; [Lietu-
vių skaučių seserijos istoriniai
bruožai. The Lithuanian girl scout
association;... historical sketch.]
[s.l., 1972] 272 p. illus.
Summary and legends in English.
HS3365.L58L53 DLC

702. LIULEVIČIUS, Vincentas. Lietuvių emigracijos priežastys. [The
reasons for Lithuanian emigration]
Čikaga, Pedagoginis lituanistikos
institutas, 1971. 31 p. illus.
JV8194.L58 DLC; MB.

703. LUKOŠEVIČIENĖ, Irena. Lietuvių socialinė veikla organizacijo-
se. [Lithuanian social activities
in their organizations] In Lietuvių
Katalikų mokslo akademija, Roma. Suvažiavimo darbai, v.8, p. 289-312.
See serials consulted.

704. LUKOŠEVIČIUS, Jonas. Reemi-
grantai. [Reemigrants] Vilnius,
Gintaras, 1971. 142 p. At head of
title: J. Lukoševičius.
DK511.L223L83 DLC; CU; IU; MH; NN;
NNC; OKentU.

705. MACEINA, Antanas. Tautos
pakaitalas ar papildas. Tremties
prasmės beieškant. [The substitute
or supplement of the nation when
searching for the meaning of exile]
In Į Laisvę (Los Angeles, Calif.),
no. 57, 1973, p. 6-27. See serials
consulted.

706. PASAULIO LIETUVIŲ BENDRUO-
MENĖ. PLB Seimo vadovas. [A guide
to the Assembly of World Lithuanian
Community] [New York, N.Y. 1958]
64 p. illus., ports. DK511.L223P3
DLC.

707. --- PLB III Seimas, New Yorke, 1968. [The Third Assembly of
the World Lithuanian Community in
New York, 1968. New York, N.Y.,
1968.] 38 p. DK511.L223P3 1968
OKentU.

708. PASAULIO LIETUVIŲ BENDRUO-
MENĖ. Seimas, 4th, Washington,1973.
Pasaulio Lietuvių Bendruomenės IV
seimas, 1973 rugpiūčio 30-rugsėjo
2, Washington, D.C. [The Fourth
Assembly of the World Lithuanian Community. Cleveland, Ohio, Pasaulio
Lietuvių Bendruomenės leidinys, 1973.
44 p. DK511.L223P35 PU.

709. VALAITIS, Jurgis. Lietuvos
politinių partijų išeivijoje dabartis ir ateitis. [The actual state
and the future of the Lithuanian political parties in exile] In Metmenys (Chicago, Ill.), no.1, 1971,
p. 18-28. See serials consulted.

710. ŽVILGSNIS Į 1969 METUS. Naujosios išeivijos dvidešimtmetis ir
švietimo, kultūros ir meno apžvalga.
[... the 20th anniversary of the
last Lithuanian imigration and a review of their cultural, educational
and art activities] In Aidai (Brooklyn, N.Y.), no.1, 1970, p.1-16.
See serials consulted.

VI.7.b. DISPLACED PERSONS

711. GAIDAMAVIČIUS, Pranas. Iš-
blokštasis žmogus; benamio likimo
perspektyvos. [The displaced person]
Augsburg, Ger., Venta, 1951. 278 p.
D809.L5G3 DLC

712. KAPAČINSKAS, Juozas. Siau-
bingos dienos; 1944-1950 metų atsiminimai. [Horrifying days; reminis-
censes, 1944-1950] Chicago, Ill.,
Lietuvių literatūros draugija, 1965.
273 p. illus. D809.G3K35 DLC.

713. KONČIUS, Juozas B. Lietuvių
tremtinių emigracija. [The emigra-
tion of Lithuanian displaced persons.]
In Metraštis 1950. Kennebunk Port,
Me., [1949] p. 202-209.
DK511.L223M59 1949 CaAEU; MH.

714. MACEINA, Antanas. Rezisten-
cija prieš tremties dvasią. [The displaced persons' resistance against
the spirit of exile] In Į Laisvę
(Brooklyn, N.Y.), no.2(39), 1954,
p.1-10. Mr. L. Kairys, Chicago,
no.1258.

715. MINGAILA, Stasys. Neapken-
čiamo žmogaus užrašai. [Notes of a
hated man. s.l., s.n., s.d.] 119 p.
OKentU.

716. NAROUCHE, Edmond. The secret
life of the political refugee. New
York, N.Y., Ventage Press, 1976.
79 p. DK511.L223N3 PU.

717. PRUNSKIS, Juozas, ed. Mano
pasaulėžiūra; kultūrininkų pasisaky-
mų rinkinys. [My personal conception
of the world...] Chicago, Ill., Lietuviškos knygos klubas, 1958. 352 p.
ports. B790.P7 DLC; CtTMF; CaAEU;
MH; NN; OKentU; PU.

718. VILAINIS, A., pseud. Amžini
šešėliai. [Perpetual shadows; reports
from the refugee camps] Chicago, Ill
Nemunas, 1953. 891.92.Si13A PU.

VI.7.c. LITHUANIANS IN UNITED STATES

719. AMERIKOS LIETUVIŲ EKONOMINIS
CENTRAS. Amerikos lietuvių ekonomi-
nio centro protokolai ir referatai,
1950-1953. [Minutes of the American
Lithuanian Economic Centre. Chicago,
Ill., 1954] 1 v. (various pagings)
Added title in English.
HS2006.L5A2 OKentU.

720. AMERIKOS LIETUVIŲ KONGRESAS,
DETROIT, 1969. Septintasis Amerikos

lietuvių kongresas, Detroite. [The
Seventh congress of American-Lithua-
nians in Detroit. Chicago, Ill., A-
merikos Lietuvių Tarybos leidinys,
1970] 131 p. illus.
HS2006.L52A2 1969 OKentU.

721. AMŽIAIS SU GIMTINE. [Always
in contact with the native land. Sudarytojas V. Kazakevičius.] Vilnius,
Vaga, 1970. 209 p., 11 leaves of
illus. "Rojaus Mizaros atminimui."
E184.L7A73 DLC; MH; NN: NjP; OKentU
PU.

722. A BRIEF RESUME OF THE HISTO-
ry of the Lithuanian Roman Catholic
Alliance of America and its people.
[Wilkes-Barre,Pa., LRK susivieniji-
mas Amerikoje, 1959.] 4 leaves.
Memeographed. IEdS.

723. BŪTĖNAS, Vladas. Pennsyl-
vanijos angliakasių Lietuva. Nuo-
traukos Algimanto Kezio. Portfolio:
Elena Bradūnaitė, Jurgis Bradūnas.
Chicago, Ill., Lithuanian Library
Press [1977] 343 p. [Lithuanian
miners in Pennsylvannia]
F158.9.L7B8 PU.

724. ČEKIENĖ, E[milija]. Amerikos lietuvių tautinė sąjunga. [Ameri-
can-Lithuanian national association]
In Naujoji Viltis (Chicago, Ill.),
no.1, 1970, p.100-110. See serials
consulted.

725. ČERNIUS, Vytautas. Akultū-
racijos klausimu. A longitudinal
acculturation study of a group of
Lithuanian refugee female. In Institute of Lithuanian Studies. Lituanistikos instituto 1975 metų suvažiavimo darbai. Chicago, Ill.,
1976. p.157-169. Summary in English. DK511.L2I64 1975 CaAEU; PU.

726. DAILIDKA, Z. Lietuvių Fondas. The Lithuanian Foundation.
In Varpas (Brookly, N.Y.), no.12,
1973, p. 55-65. See serials consulted.

727. DRAUGAS. Jungtinių Amerikos
Valstybių lietuvių senosios išeivijos istorijos gyvenimo, veiklos ir
darbų apžvalginė paroda. [An exhibition related to the history, life,
and activities of the early Lithuanian immigrant generation in the
United States] Ruošiama Draugo dienraščio 1976 m. balandžio 2-4 dienomis
[Redaktorius Bronius Kviklys] Chicago, Ill., Draugas, 1976. 64 p. ill.
Cover title: Lietuviškoji išeivija
Jungtinėse Amerikos Valstybėse.
E184.L7D72 1976 DLC.

728. FAINHAUZ, David. Lithuanians

in multi-ethnic Chicago until World
War II. Chicago, Ill., Lithuanian
Library Press and Loyola University
Press, 1977. 230 p. F550.L7F3 PU.

729. GASIŪNAS, Jonas. Mano de-
šimtmečiai Amerikoje. [My years in
America. Literatūrinis bendradarbis
A. Rudzinskas] Vilnius, Mintis,
1968. 271 p. illus.
E184.L7G3 OKentU.

730. GREENE, Victor R. The Sla-
vic community on strike; immigrant
labor in Pennsylvania anthracite.
Notre Dame, Ind., University Press,
1968. xvi, 260 p.
HD5325.M62G73 DLC; AAP; CaAEU;
CaBVaU; CaOTP; CLU; CLSU; CoU;CSt;
CSt-H; CtY; CtW; DS; DAU; FMU; FU;
FTuSU; GAT; GU; IEN; ICU; IaU; InU;
IU; KEmT; KU; KyU; LU; MH; MiU;MnU;
MoU; MU; N; NN; NNC; NSyU; NBuC;
NBuU; NIC; NcU; NjP; NjR; NcRS;NRU;
OU; OrU; OrPS; PPULC; RPB; ScU;TU;
TNJ; TxU; UU; ViU; VtU; WU; WaU.

731. CANCELLED.

732. GUDELIS, Martynas. Povilas
Mileris; biografijos bruožai. [Povi-
las Mileris; biography] Chicago,
Ill., Chicagos lietuvių literatūros
draugijos leidinys, 1973. 232 p.
illus. DK511.L28M544 DLC.

733. IŠ MŪSŲ IŠEIVIJOS DEŠIMTME-
čių; medžiaga iš Vilnies ir Laisvės
sukaktuvinių leidinių. [Decades of
our emigration; material from "Vilnis" and "Laisvė" anniversary issues
Sudarė Vilius Baltrėnas] Vilnius,
Gintaras, 1973. 192 p. illus.
E184.L7I8 DLC.

734. JACKSON, V.J. Gyvenimo ver-
petuose. [In the whirlpools of life.
By] Senas Vincas, [pseud.] Vilnius
Valstybinė grožinės literatūros lei-
dykla, 1958. 373 p. illus.
E184.L7J3 DLC.

735. JAKŠTAS, Juozas. Iškilusis
tarpsnis Amerikos lietuvių istorijoje: Dr. J. Šliūpas ir kun. A. Bur-
ba. A short segment of Lithuanian-
American history. In Lietuvių Tautos Praeitis (Chicago, Ill.), kn.2,
v.3, 1973, p. 118-133. Summary in
English. See serials consulted.

736. --- Jono Šliūpo pirmieji
žingsniai Amerikoje. Minint jo 90
metų sukaktuves nuo atvykimo į A-
meriką. The initial work of Jonas
Šliūpas in the United States. In
Lietuvių Tautos Praeitis (Chicago,
Ill.), kn.1, v.4, 1977, p. 81-96.
See serials consulted.

737. KAUPAS, Antanas. Pergyven-
tos valandos (Karvojaus laiškai),
parašė K.A.K. [The experienced hours;
reminiscences] Shenandoah, Pa.,
Žvaigždės spaustuvėje, 1906. 140 p.
*Q p.v. 1670--NN.

738. KEZYS, Algimantas. Amerikos lietuvių etninė dokumentacija.
Lithuanian Photo library. In Institute of Lithuanian Studies. Lituanistikos instituto 1975 metų suvažiavimo darbai. Chicago, Ill.,1976.
p. 171-175. Summary in English.
DK511.L2I64 1975 CaAEU; PU.

739. KUČAS, Antanas. Lithuanians
in America. Translated by Joseph Boley. Introd. by Clarence C. Walton.
So. Boston [Encyclopedia Lituanica,
1975. xiv, 349 p. illus. Bibliography: p. 335-340.
E184.L7K82 PU; DLC.

740. LIETUVIŠKOJI IŠEIVIJA Jungtinėse Amerikos Valstybėse; [paroda
skiriama Jungtinių Amerikos Valstybių 200 metų, lietuvių masinės emigracijos į Ameriką ir organizuoto
gyvenimo šimtmečiui, "Draugo" laikraščio, pradėto leisti 1909 m., o
nuo 1916 metų be pertraukos leidžia-
mo dienraščio 60 metų sukaktims paminėti. Parodą ruošia dienraštis
Draugas. Redaktorius Bronius Kviklys. Lithuanian imigrants in the
United States; 100th anniversary]
Chicago, Ill., Draugas, 1976. 64 p.
E184.L7L49 PU.

741. LITHUANIAN ALLIANCE OF AME-
RICA. Constitution and by-laws of
the Lithuanian Alliance of America.
Organized Nov.22, 1886, incorpora-
ted Nov.4, 1889. Revised and adop-
ted at the 49th regular convention,
held on July 2 to 6, 1956 incl. at
Detroit. [New York, N.Y.], 1957.
117 p. HS2007.L53A52 OKentU.

742. --- Konstitucija ir įstatai.
Susivienijimas įsteigtas lapkričio
22, 1886. Susivienijimas inkorpo-
ruotas lapkričio 4, 1889. New York,
N.Y., 1957. 100 p. At head of title:
Susivienijimas Lietuvių Amerikoje
(Lithuanian Alliance of America)
HS2008.L53A52 OKentU.

743. --- SLA 70 metų sukaktuvi-
niam 49-tam seimui; raportai ir darbai, liepos 2, 1956, Detroit, Michigan. [Reports and proceedings to the
49th Assembly of the Lithuanian Alliance of America on the occasion of its
70th anniversary in Detroit, Mich.]
New York, N.Y., Tėvynės spauda, 1956.
376 p. HS2008.L53A5 OKentU.

744. LITHUANIAN AMERICAN COMMUNI-
TY OF THE U.S.A. Jungtinių Amerikos

Valstybių Lietuvių Benruomenės įstatai ir taisyklės, 1975 m. spalio 15.
[Constitution and by-laws of the
Lithuanian American Community. Chicago, Ill., Lietuvių Bendruomenė,
1975] 55 leaves. E184.L7L532 PU.

745. LITHUANIAN AMERICAN CONGRESS,
8th, Chicago, 1974. Aštuntasis Amerikos lietuvių kongresas,[Chicagoje,
1974 m. rugsėjo 28-29 d. The Eighth
congress of American Lithuanians..]
Chicago, Ill., Amerikos lietuvių tarybos leidinys, 1975. 118 p. illus.
E184.L7L57 1974 DLC.

746. LITHUANIAN BUSINESS DIRECTO-
RY. Pittsburgh, Pa., Pittsburgho
Lietuvių vaizbos butas, 1940. 108
p. illus. L970.3Pi ICLJF.

747. A LITHUANIAN CEMETERY; St.
Casimir Lithuanian Cemetery in Chi-
cago, Ill. [Editor Algimantas Kezys]
Chicago, Ill., Lithuanian Library
Press and Loyola University Press,
1976. 247 p. illus.
NB1856.C45L5 PU; DLC.

748. THE LITHUANIANS IN AMERICA,
1651-1975; a chronology and fact
book. Compiled and edited by Algirdas M. Budreckis. Dobbs Ferry,N.Y.
Oceana Publications, 1976. vi, 174
p. (Ethnic chronology series, no.21)
Bibliography: p. 164-169.
E184.L7L58 DLC; PU.

749. LIULEVIČIUS, Vincentas. Amerikos lietuvių kultūriniai laimėji-
mai. [The cultural achievments of
the American-Lithuanians] In Aidai
(Kennebunk Port, Me.), 1963, no.2(
157), p. 67-75; no.3(158), p. 99-
105. Mr. L. Kairys, Chicago, no.340
see also serials consulted.

750. MORKUS, Albinas. "Vaduotojai" iš arti. ["Liberators" from
short distance; the story of an Lithuanian emigrant about the life in
the United States. Lietuvio emigranto atpasakojimai apie gyvenimą
JAV] Vilnius, Gintaras, 1968. 140p.
E184.L7M67 DLC.

751. PRŪSEIKA, Leonas. Atsiminimai ir dabartis. [Recollections and
the present. Chicago, Ill., 1956]
303 p. (Amerikos lietuvių darbininkų literatūros draugijos leidinys,
62) E184.L7P7 OKentU.

752. RAILA, Bronys. Bastūno mai-
štas. [Mutiny of the rover] Chicago, Ill., [Algimanto Mackaus Knygų leidimo fondas], 1977. 499 p.
DK511.L223R33 PU.

753. REIMERIS, Vacys. Užatlan-
tės laiškai; kelionės po JAV įspū-
džių mozaika. [Letters from across
Atlantic; impressions from a journey in the United States] Vilnius,
Vaga, 1974. 393 p.
E169.02.R45 PU.

754. ROUČEK, Joseph S. American
Lithuanians. In Baltic and Scandinavian countries, v.4, 1938, p. 348-
352. See serials consulted.

755. STEPONAITIS, Vytautas. Amerikiečių lietuvių kariškos aspiraci-
jos XIX amžiaus pabaigoje. Kaunas,
Valstybės spaustuvė, 1927. [Xerox
copy, 1974] 77 p. [The military
aspirations of American Lithuanians
in the 19th century]
E184.L7S7 PU.

756. SUSIVIENIJIMO LIETUVIŲ AME-
RIKOJE 90-ties metų istorija ir jos
santrauka anglų kalba, 1886-1976.
[A history of the Lithuanian Allian-
ce of America, 1886-1976] Autoriai:
Vytautas Širvydas, Antanas Diržys,
Algirdas M. Budreckis. New York,
N.Y., Susivienijimas Lietuvių Ameri-
koje, 1976. HS2008.L53S84 PU.

757. UNITED LITHUANIAN RELIEF
FUND OF AMERICA. Bendrojo Amerikos
lietuvių šalpos fondo 25 metų darbo
apžvalga. [A review of the twenty-
five years' work of the United Lithuanian Relief Fund of America.
Redagavo Domas Jasaitis. Brooklyn,
N.Y., BALF, 1970] 287 p. illus.,
ports. HS2008.U5A52 DLC; IEdS;
OKentU.

758. VAITIEKŪNAS, Vytautas. Ben-
dravimas su Lietuva. [Ties and cooperation with Lithuania. Brooklyn,
N.Y., LFB studijų biuro leidinys,
1967.] 48 p.
E184.L7V3 DLC; PU; PPULC.

759. WOLKOVICH, William Lawrence.
Bay State "blue" laws and Bimba; a
documentary study of the Anthony
Bimba trial for blasphemy and sedi-
tion in Brockton, Massachusetts,
1926. Brockton, Mass., Forum Press
[1973] 141 p. E184.L7W6 PU; AH;
CtY; DLC; IU; MB; MH; MnU-L; N; NIC;
MoSW.

760. ŽILEVIČIUS, Juozas. The Juozas Žilevičius Library of Lithuanian
Musicology. Translated by Leonardas
J. Šimutis. [Chicago, Ill., J.Žile-
vičius Library of Lithuanian Misico-
logy, 1973] 25 p.
E184.L7Z51 PU; CaAEU.

VI.7.d. LITHUANIANS IN OTHER COUNTRIES

761. ČESNULIS, Petras. Nužmogin-tieji; vilniečių golgota lenkų oku-pacijoje. [The dehumanized; the Gol-gotha for Lithuanians under the Po-lish occupation. Hamilton, Ont.], Vilniaus krašto lietuvių sąjungos leidinys, 1973. 256 p. illus., ports. Bibliography: p. 245-246. DK651.V4C45 DLC; MB.

762. DISCRIMINATION OF LITHUANI-ANS in the Belorussian SSR. In Li-tuanus (Chicago, Ill.), no.1, v.21, 1975, p. 70-74. See serials con-sulted.

763. GADON, Lubomir. Wielka emi-gracja w pierwszych latach po pows-taniu listopadowym. Wstępem po-przedził Marian Kukiel. Wyd.2. Pa-ryž, Księg. Polska, 1960. xxx,576 p. First ed. published in 1901-1902 under title: Emigracya polska. DK412.2.G3 1960 DLC; CaAEU; IU; InU; NN; MNS; PU; WaU.

764. HAMILTONO LIETUVIŲ TAUTINIŲ šokių ansamblis Gyvataras, 1950-1975. [The Lithuania folkdance en-semble "Gyvataras" of Hamilton,Ont., 1950-1975] Redaktoriai: Gediminas Breichmanas ir Vytas Beniušis. Ha-milton, Ont., Gyvataras, 1975. 104 p. illus. DK511.L223H22 1975 CaAEU

765. JOKUBKA, Jonas. Brazilijos plantacijose. [The plantations of Brazil] Vilnius, Valstybinė grožī-nės literatūros leidykla, 1962. 254 p. port. F2659.L5J6 DLC; OKentU.

766. JUCIŪTĖ, Elena. Pėdos mir-ties zonoje. [Footprints in the death zone] Brooklyn, N.Y., L.Š.S. T. Simo Kudirkos kuopa, 1974. 544 p. illus. DK511.L28J8 DLC.

767. LIETUVIŲ IMIGRACIJOS BRAZI-LIJON penkiasdešimtmetis, 1926-1976. Cinquentenário da imigração lituana do Brasil. São Paulo, [Lietuvių imigracijos Brazilijon penkiasdešimt-mečio komitetas] 1976. 207 p. F2659.L5L5 PU.

768. LITHUANIANS IN HAMILTON; to commemorate twenty fifth anniversa-ry of Lithuanian Canadian Community in Hamilton and First Lithuanian Song and Folk Dance Festival of Ca-nada. Hamiltono lietuviai: Kanados Lietuvių bendruomenės Hamiltono apylinkės 25 metų sukakčiai ir Pir-majai Kanados lietuvių dainų ir šo-kių šventei atžymėti. [Vyr. redak-torius V.P. Zubas. Hamilton, Ont.] K.L.B. Hamiltono apylinkė, 1975.

111 p. English and Lithuanian. F1059.5.H2L5 PU.

769. O BALTICO. Estonia, Le-tonia, Lituana. Rio de Janeiro, Legations of the Baltic States, 1951. 70 p. Special issue of O Baltico; orgao dos balticos do Brasil. F2659.E8B3 DLC; PU.

770. POLAND. Minorities in Poland. Lithuanian schools in the territory of Vilna and the district of Punsk-Sejny. Geneva, 1924. 1 p.l., 7 numb. leaves. Official no. C275.1924.I. Mimeo-graphed. NNUN-W.

771. SENN, Alfred.Erich. The Russian revolution in Switzerland 1914-1917. Madison, Wis., The University of Wisconsin Press,1971. xvi, 250 p. DK262.S444 DLC; CSt IaU; AAP; AU; CLSU; CtY; CU; CoU; CaBVaU; CaOTP; CLU; DAU; GAT; FTaSU; FU; GU; IU; InU; IaAS;ICU; IEN; KEmT; KU; MB; MH; MiU; MoU; MU; MnU; MoSW; MiEM; MsSM; NN;NNC NIC; NBuU; NSyU; NjR; NRU; NcU; NcD; NbU; NcGU; OC; OClU; OClW;OU OkU; OKentU; OrU; OrPS; RPB; PP; TNJ; TU; TxU; UU; ViU; WU; WaU.

772. SKARDZIS, V. Litoutsi na Belarusi. In Nash Kraĭ (Mensk), no.6-7, 1929, p. 10-25; no.8-9, 1929, p.8-22. DK511.W5A17 DLC: NN; see also, Savetskaĭa kraina, serials consulted.

773. ŠKIRPA, Kazys. Sukilimas Lietuvos suverenumui atstatyti; dokumentinė apžvalga. Uprising for the restoration of Lithuania's sovereignity. Vašingtonas, Škir-pa, 1973. [i.e. 1975] 583 p. illus. D802.L5S56 DLC; CaAEU;PU.

774. TORONTO LIETUVIŲ NAMAI, 1951-1976. [Lithuanian Home in Toronto, 1951-1976] Redagavo: Pranas Bastys, Jonas Karka, Biru-tė Strazdienė, Povilas Štuopis. Toronto, Ont.,[Toronto Lietuvių namų leidinys] 1976. 128 p. F1059.5.T68T6 PU.

775. TUMAS, Juozas. Su bėg-liais ir tremtiniais. [With the refugees. By] Vaižgantas, [pseud] Kaunas, Spindulio b-vės spaustu-vė, 1929. [Xerox copy, 1976] 270 p. (Vaižganto raštai, t.16) DK511.L223T8 1929a PU(xerox)

776. VARAŠINSKAS, Kazys. Karo sūkuriuose. [In the whirpools of the war] Vilnius, Mintis, 1970. 182 p., 8 leaves of illus. D802.L5V37 DLC; IU; MH; NNC;NjP.

777. WHITE, James D. Scottisch Lithuanians and the Russian revolution. In Journal of Baltic Studies (Brookly, N.Y.), no.1, v.6, 1975, p. 1-8. See serials consulted.

VI.7.e. LITHUANIAN RELIGIOUS ORDERS OUTSIDE LITHUANIA

778. FRANCISCANS. CUSTODY OF ST. CASIMIR. Lietuviai Pranciškonai. Lithuanian Franciscan Fathers. Kennebunk Port, Me., Franciscans,1966. [16] p. illus. Lithuanian and english. BX3650.S13F82 1966 CaAEU.

779. LIETUVOS PRANCIŠKONAI; istorijos bruožai ir paminklinio Šv. Antano vienuolyno pašventinimo iškilmių programa. Brief history of the Franciscan Fathers and dedication of the monastery in Kennebunk Port, Maine. [Boston, Mass., Darbininkas, 1947] 29 p. E184.L7L515 PU.

780. TRAKIS, Ansas, ed. Palydovas lietuviui evangelikui svetur. [Handbook for the Lithuanian protestant in exile. Bendradarbiai: Paul C. Empie, et al. Wehnen, Lietuvių evangelikų liuterionių vyriausioji bažnyčios taryba, 1952. 128 p. ill. music. BX8063.5.L57T72 DLC.

VI.7.f. PARISHES OUTSIDE LITHUANIA

781. AUŠROS VARTŲ PARAPIJA, 1950-1975; 25 metų jubiliejus. [Parisse Notre-Dame-Porte-de l'Aurore, Montreal, Que... Redagavo Jonas Narbutas] Montrealis, Aušros Vartų parapijos komiteto leidinys, 1975. 136 p. illus. BX4605.M6P373 DLC.

782. NARBUTAS, Titas. Marijos šventovės Amerikoje. [Shrines of Holy Mary in America. Putnam, Conn] Immaculata [1962] 211 p. illus. BT652.A5N38 OKentU; OCl.

783. PHILADELPHIA. ST. ANDREW'S CHURCH (Catholic) Šv. Andriejaus parapijos auksinis jubiliejus. Golden jubilee memorial edition, St.Andrew Lithuanian R.C. Church, Philadelphia, Pa. [Philadelphia, 1974] 104 p. BX4603.P52S25 PU.

784. PITTSTONO LIETUVIŲ ISTORIJA [History of Pittston, Pa., Lithuanians] Išleista minint Lietuvių Romos katalikų Šv. Kazimiero parapijos įkūrimo 50 metų sukaktį,1885-

1935. [Pittston, Pa] Šv. Kazimiero parapija, 1935. 117 p. illus. F159.L5P5 OKentU; PU.

785. ŠV.[i.e. Švento] KAZIMIERO parapija; pirmojo dešimtmečio istorija. St. Casimir's Lithuanian Roman Catholic Parish, 1959-1969. [Edited by J. Gutauskas and others] Delhi, ont., St. Casimir Parish [1970] 144 p. illus. Text in Lithuanian and English. WHi.

786. TORONTO. RESURRECTION OF OUR LORD JESUS CHRIST CHURCH. Prisikėlimo parapijos leidinys, 1956; pradinės Prisikėlimo parapijos statybos pašventinimo proga. [Laying a corner stone for the Resurrection of Our Lord Jesus Christ Church] Toronto, Ont., The Parish, 1956. 86 p. ill., ports. BX4605.T6R43 1956 CaAEU

787. UNITED STATES. BUREAU OF THE CENSUS. Census of religious bodies: 1926. Lithuanian National Catholic Church of America. Statistics, history, doctrine, and organization. Washington, D.C., GPO.1929. 6 p. incl. tables. BX4795.L5U6 1926 DLC

788. UNITED STATES. BUREAU OF THE CENSUS. Census of religious bodies 1936. Bulletin no.1-[78] prepared under the supervision of Dr. T.F. Murphy, chief statistician for religious statistics. Washington, D.C., GPO, 1939-1940. 78 v. tables. BR525.A3 1936 DLC.

789. YOUNGSTOWN, Ohio. ST. FRANCIS OF ASSISI LITHUANIAN CHURCH. Golden jubilee of St. Francis of Assisi Lithuanian Church, 1918-1968. Sunday, November 17, 1968. [Youngstown, Ohio, s.n., 1968] 1 v. (unpaged) illus. BX1418.Y6Y6 OKentU.

VII. THE STATE

VII.1. GENERAL STUDIES.

790. BURŽUAZINĖS VALSTYBINĖS TEIsinės koncepcijos, jų taikymas Lietuvoje ir kritika. [The burgeois interpretation of law and its application in Lithuania; a critical review. Red. kolegija: J. Bulavas (ats. redaktorius), V. Poškevičius ir O. Ruželytė] Vilnius, Lietuvos TSR Mokslų akademija, 1972. 200 p. At head of title: Lietuvos TSR Mokslų akademija. Filosofijos, teisės ir socio-

logijos skyrius prie Istorijos instituto. JN6745.A3B87 1918 DLC InU; OKentU; PU.

791. DIMAVIČIUS, Pranas. Die Rechtsstellung des litauischen Staatspräsidenten verglichen mit der des Reichspräsidenten; eine rechtsvergleichende Untersuchung an Hand der litauischen Verfassungen von 1 1919. Hamburg, Ger., 1949. iv,140 leaves. Thesis--University of Hamburg. Typescript. Ger.HmbU.

792. ESSEN, Wener. Litauen; ein Beitrag zu seiner.Staats- und Volksentwicklung. Die völkerrechtliche Stellung des Memellandes von Fritz Berber. Detached from Zeitschrift für Politik (Berlin), Heft 4,Bd.25, 1935. 947.52.Es78.2 PU.

--- --- also In Zeitschrift für Politik (Berlin), Heft 4, Bd.25, 1935. See serials consulted.

793. GIEDRA, Balys. Valstybė ir pilietis; visuomenės mokslo vadovėlis. [The State and the citizen...] 2. pataisyta laida. Raseiniai, S. Kadušino spaustuvė, 1930- . Includes text of the Lithuanian constitution of 1928. JN6745.A12G5 DLC.

794. GRINIUS, Kazys. Demokratiniųidėjų vystymasis Lietuvoje. [The development of democratic ideas in Lithuania] In Sėja (Chicago, Ill.), no.4, 1973, p. 9-17. See serials consulted.

795. HALECKI, Oskar. O początkach parlamentaryzmu litewskiego. In Polska Akademia Umiejętności, Kraków. Sprawozdania z czynności i posiedzeń. Tom 20, nr.8, 1915, p. 22-27. See serials consulted.

796. MAKSIMAITIS, Mindaugas. Politicheskiĭ rezhim v burzhuaznoĭ Litve v 1926-1940 gg. Vil'nĭus, Universitet, 1974. 114 p. (Uchenye zapiski vysshykh uchebnykh zavedeniĭ Litovskoĭ SSR: Pravo, T.12, vyp.2) At head of title: Politinis režimas buržuazinėje Lietuvoje... JN6745.A3 1926.M34 DLC.

VII.2. SYMBOLISM, COATS-OF-ARMS, SEALS, ETC.

797. KLIMAS, Petras. Kaip buvo nustatyta mūsų vėliava. [How was the Lithuanian Flag chosen] In Varpas (Brookly, N.Y.), no.14, 1976,

p. 21-25. See serials consulted.

798. VENCLOVA, J.M. Lietuvos vardo kilmė. [Origin of the name of Lithuania] Chicago, Ill., Chicagos lietuvių literatūros draugijos leidinys, 1972. 51 p. DK511.L23V4 OKentU.

VII.3. GOVERNMENT

VII.3.a. EXECUTIVE GOVERNMENT

799. MACKEVIČIUS, Mečys. Koalicinės vyriausybės reikšmė nepriklausomybės kovose. [The importance of coalition government during the independence Wars] In Tėvynės Sargas (Chicago, Ill.), no.1, 1970, p.68-76. See serials consulted.

VII.3.b. LEGISLATIVE GOVERNMENT, ITS HISTORY AND LEGISLATION

800. GRINIUS, Kazys. Lietuvos respublikos seimai. [Diets of the Lithuanian republic] In Sėja (Chicago, Ill.), no.1-2, 1973, p.6-10. See serials consulted.

801. IVINSKIS, Zenonas. Lietuvos Steigiamasis Seimas. [The Constituent Diet of Lithuania] In Laisvę (Los Angeles, Calif.), no.50, 1970, p. 3-25. See serials consulted.

802. JAKŠTAS, Juozas. Steigiamasis Seimas nepriklausomybės raidoje ir tautos dvasios atspindys jame. [The Constituent Diet of Lithuania] In Draugas (Chicago, Ill.), no. May 2, 1970; May 9, 1970. See serials consulted.

803. KALINKA, Waleryan. Ustawa 3 maja. Ustęp z niewydanego "Sejm" trzeciego tomu. Kraków, 1896. 60 p. MB; OCl.

804a. LAPPO, I[van] I[vanovich] Pinskiĭ seĭmik posle otrecheniĭa IAna Kazimira. In Russia. Ministerstvo Narodnogo Prosveshcheniĭa. Zhurnal, Nov.ser.chast' 25 (Feb.), 1910, p. 284-300. L451.A55 DLC;NN; see also serials consulted.

805. LAUČKA, Juozas B. Lietuvos parlamentarinė santvarka. [The Parliamentary government of Lithuania] In Tėvynės Sargas (New York, N.Y.), no.1, 1970, p. 99-123. See serials

consulted.

805a. LEONTOVICH, F[ëdor Ivano-
vich] Viecha, seĭmy i seĭmiki v Velikom Kniazhestve Litovskom. In
Russia. Ministerstvo Narodnogo Prosveshcheniĭa. Zhurnal, Nov.ser. ch.
25, Feb. 1910, p. 234-274; and
March 1910, p. 37-61. L451.A55 DLC;
NN; see also serials consulted.

806. RAČKAUSKAS, Konstantinas.
Steigiamasis Seimas ir jo dvi kons-
titucijos. [The Constituent Diet and
its two constitutions] In Tėvynės
Sargas (New York, N.Y.), no.1, 1970,
p. 124-136. See serials consulted.

807. SIDZIKAUSKAS, Vaclovas. Steigiamasis Seimas ir Lietuvos tarptautinės problemos. [The Constituent
Diet and Lithuania's international
problems] In Tėvynės Sargas (New
York, N.Y.), no.1, 1970, p. 58-67.
See serials consulted.

808. SLIWIŃSKI, Arthur. Konsty-
tucja trzeciego Maja. Warszawa,
M. Arct, 1921. 99 p. OCl.

809. ŠMULKŠTYS, L[iudas] Lietuvos Steigiamasis Seimas. [The Constituent Diet of Lithuania] In Sėja
(Chicago, Ill.), no.1-2, 1970, p.16-
26. See serials consulted.

810. SRUOGIENĖ, Vanda (Daugirdaitė) Lietuvos Steigiamasis seimas.
[The Constituent Diet of Lithuania]
New York, N.Y. [Tautos Fondas] 1975.
261 p. JN6745.A71S68 DLC; PU.

811. VAITIEKŪNAS, Vytautas. Lietuvos suverenumas Steigiamajame Sei-
me. [The soveregnity of Lithuania in
the Constituent Diet] In Aidai (Brooklyn, N.Y.), no.10, 1970, p.456-461.
See serials consulted.

812. VILIAMAS, Vladas. Steigiamasis Seimas susirenka. [The Constituent Diet in session] In Tėvynės
Sargas (New York, N.Y.), no.1, 1970,
p. 6-31. See serials consulted.

VII.3.c. PARLIAMENTARY RECORDS.

813. KONOPCZYŃSKI, W[ładysław]
Chronologja sejmów polskich, 1493-
1793. Kraków, Nakładem Polskiej
Akademii Umiejętności, 1948. In
Polska Akademia Umiejętności, Kraków. Komisja do badania historii,
filosofii w Polsce. Archivum,
nr.3, t. 16, p. 127-169. See serials consulted.

814. POLAND. SEJM, 1672(1st January) Diariussz Seymu Warszawskiego w
styczniu roku 1672. W Krakowie, Nakł.
Akademii Umiejętności, 1880. 90 p.
(Monumenta comitiorum Regni Poloniae
saeculi XVII, [1]) "Odbicie osobne
ze zbioru "Pism do wieku i spraw Jana Sobieskiego , wydania Fr. Kluczyckiego" J399.H373 DLC.

815. POLAND. SEJM, 1673. Diariusz
Seymu Warszawskiego w roku 1673, t.
z. "Pacificationis," zaczętego konti-
nuatia konfederacyi, dnia 4 stycznia,
a zakończonego jako Sejm po 8 kwietnia 1673. W Krakowie, W. Druk. Cza-
su, 1881. 70 p. (Monumenta comitiorum Regni Poloniae saeculi XVII, 3)
J399.H374 DLC.

816. POLAND. SEJM, 1701-1702.
Diariusz Sejmu walnego warszawskiego, 1701-1702. Wydał, przedm. i
przypisami opatrzył Przemysław Smo-
larek. [Wyd.1.] Warszawa, Państwowe Wydawn. Naukowe, 1962. xxv, 364
p. At head of title: Instytut Historii Polskiej Akademii Nauk. Part
of documents in Latin and German.
J399.H219 DLC; CSt; CtY; CU; IU; MH
MiDW; MiU; NN; NNC; NcD; NjP.

817. POLAND. SEJM, 1674 (1st, Ja-
nuary-February) Dwa diariusze Sey-
mów Warszawskich w r. 1674 odprawio-
nych, 1szy Conventionis od 15 stycznia do 22 lutego; 2gt Electionis od
20 kwietnia, do 9 czerwcz. W Krakowie, Nakł. Akademii Umiejętności,
1881. 71 p. (Monumenta comitiorum
Regni Poloniae saeculi XVII, 4) Odbicie osobne ze zbioru Pism do wieku
i spraw Jana Sobieskiego, wydania Fr.
Kluczyckiego. J399.H375 DLC.

VII.3.d. CONSTITUTION, ITS HISTORY
AND COMMENTARIES

818. LIETUVOS VALSTYBĖS KONSTITU-
CIJA. [The constitution of the Lithu-
anian State] In Tėvynės Sargas (New
York, N.Y.), no.1, 1970, p. 142-155.
See serials consulted.

VII.3.e. THE ADMINISTRATION OF JUSTICE
AND COURTS

819. BALTŪSIS, S. Lietuvos teis-
mai. [The courts of Lithuania] In
Sėja (Chicago, Ill.), no.1-2, 1974,
p. 19-35. See serials consulted.

819a. LAPPO, I[van] I[vanovich]
Grodskiĭ sud v Velikom Kniazhestve
Litovskom v XVI stoletiĭ. In Russia.

Ministerstvo Narodnogo Prosvescheni-
ía, Nov. ser. v.13, Jan. 1908, p.51-
113. See serials consulted.

VII.4. LAWS, STATUTES, ETC.

VII.4.a. LEGAL HISTORY AND RESEARCH

820. GRIGALIŪNAS, Stanislovas.
Die Gesetzgebung in den Verfassungen
des unabhängingen Litauens. [Heidel-
berg, Ger., 1949]. 98 leaves. Thesis
--University of Heidelberg. Typescript. Ger.HlbU.

821. VANSEVIČIUS, Stasys. Lietuvos valstybės ir teisės istorija nuo
XVI amžiaus antrosios pusės iki XVIII
amžiaus pabaigos. [History of the
Lithuanian State and law from the
16th century until the end of 18th
century] Vilnius, V. Kapsuko univr-
sitetas, 1974. 118 p.
DLC.

VII.4.b. LIETUVOS STATUTAS - LITHUA-
NIAN CODE (GRAND DUCHY):
HISTORY AND COMMENTARIES

822. DEMCHENKO, Grigoriĭ Vasil'e-
vich. Nakazanie po Litovskomu Statutu v ego trekh redaktsiĭakh (1529,
1566 i 1588 gg.); izslĭedovanie [Pe-
nalty in the three editions of the
Lithuanian statute of 1529, 1566
and 1588] Kiev, Tip. Imp. Univ. Sv.
Vladimira, 1894.
DLC-L.

823. HEJNOSZ, W. Kilka uwag o
"niewoli" w I Statucie Litewskim.
In Ehrenkreutz, Stefan, ed. Księga
pamiątkowa ku uczczeniu czterechsetnej rocznicy wydania pierwszego Statutu Litewskiego. Wilno, 1935. (Towarzystwo Przyjaciół Nauk w Wilnie.
Wydział III. Rozprawy, t.8)
DLC-L; CtY; CU; InU; MH; NN; PU.

824. KORANYI, K. O niektórych
postaniowieniach karnych Statutu
Litewskiego z roku 1529. In Ehrenkreutz, S., ed. Księga pamiątkowa
ku uczczeniu czterechsetnej rocznicy wydania pierwszego Statutu Litewskiego. Wilno, 1935. (Towarzystwo
Przyjaciół Nauk w Wilnie. Wydział
III. Rozprawy, t.8)
DLC-L; CtY; CU; InU; MH; NN; PU.

825. LAZUTKA, Stasys. I [i.e.
Pervyĭ] Litovskiĭ Statut-feodal'-
nyĭ kodeks Velikogo Kniazhestva

Litovskogo. Vil'nius, Vil'niusskiĭ
gosudarstvennyĭ universitet, 1974.
211 p. DK511.L23 PU; DLC.

826. LITHUANIA. LAWS, STATUTES,
ETC. The Lithuanian statute 1529.
Translated and ed. with an introduction and commentary by Karl von Loewe. Leiden, Brill, 1976. xiii,
206 p. (Studies in East European
history, 20)
KU.L7L82E5 1976 CaAEU; DLC-L; PU.

827. --- Statut Velikogo Kniazhes-
tva Litovskogo 1529 g. [Kraków,158]
250 p. Microfiche copy. Tumba,
Sweden, International Documentation
Center, 1970. 17 sheets. 9 x 12 cm.
IEN.

828. LOWMIAŃSKI, Henryk. Uwagi w
sprawie podłoża społecznego i gospo-
darczego unji jagiellońskiej. In
Ehrenkreutz, S., ed. Księga pamiątkowa ku uczczeniu czterechsetnej
rocznicy... Wilno, 1935. (Towarzystwo Przyjaciół Nauk w Wilnie. Wydział
III. Rozprawy, t.8)
DLC-L; CtY; CU; InU; MH; NN; PU.

829. PTASZYCKI, Stanisław. Pierw-
sze wydanie trzeciego Statutu Litewskiego i jego przeróbki. In Ehrenkreutz, S., ed. Księga pamiątkowa
ku uczczeniu czterechsetnej rocznicy
wydania pierwszego Statutu Litewskiego... Wilno, 1935. (Towarzystwo
Przyjaciół Nauk w Wilnie. Wydział
III. Rozprawy, t.8)
DLC-L; CtY; CU; InU; MH; NN; PU.

830. TAUBENSCHLAG, Rafael. Pozew
w I i II Statucie Litewskim. In
Ehrenkreutz, S., ed. Księga pamiątkowa ku uczczeniu czterchsetnej rocznicy wydania pierwszego Statutu Litewskiego... Wilno, 1935. (Towarzust-
wo Przyjaciół Nauk w Wilnie. Wydział
III. Rozprawy, t.8)
DLC-L; CtY; CU; InU; MH; NN; PU.

VII.4.c. PRIVILEGES, CONSTITUTIONS,
ETC.

831. POLAND. SEJM, 1632. Porządek na Seymie walnym elekcyey, między Warszawą á Wolą, przez opisane
Artykuły, do samego tylko aktu elekcyey należące, vchwalony y postanowiony, roku pańskiego, M.DC.XXXII.,
dnia 27, września. [s.l., 1632]
24 p. Polish and Latin.
DLC-L

832. --- , 1633. Przywileie y constitvcie sejmowe, za panowania Ie
królewskiey nći. Władisława IV., ro-

ku pańskiego M.DC.XXXIII. W Krakowie, W Druk. A. Piotrkowczuka,1633.
63,[11] p. Polish and Latin.
DLC.

833. --- , 1634. Constitvcie
Seymv walnego koronnego warszawskie-
go, dvvniedzielnego, roku pańskiego
M.DC.XXXIV. W Krakowie, W Druk. A.
Piotrkowczyka, 1634. 4,[i.e. 14],
[8] p.
DLC.

834. --- , 1635. Constitvcie
Seymv walnego koronnego warszawskiego, sześniedzielnego, roku pańskiego M.DC.XXXV. zaczętego XIV marca. W Krakowie, W Druk. A. Piotrkowczyka, 1635. 50, [7] p.
DLC.

835. --- , 1635. Constitvcie
Seymv walnego koronnego warszawskiego, roku pańskiego M.DC.XXXV.,dnia
XXI. miesiąca listopada. W Krakowie, W Druk. A. Piotrkowczyka, 1635.
12 p. DLC.

836. --- , 1637. Constitvcie
Seymv walnego koronnego warszawskie-
go, dvvniedzielnego, roku pańskiego
M.DC.XXXVII., dnia III. miesiąca
czerwca. W Krakowie, W Druk. A.
Piotrkoczyka, 1637. 12 p.
DLC.

837. --- , 1638. Constitvcie
Seymv walnego koronnego warszawskie-
go sześniedzelnego, roku pańskiego
M.DC.XXXVIII. W Krakowie, W Druk.
A. Piotrkowczyka, 1638. 56 p.
DLC.

838. --- , 1640. Vchwała Seymv
walnego koronnego, sześniedzielnego, w Warszawie, roku M.DC.XI. W
Krakowie, W. Druk. A. Piotrkowczyka,
1640. 15 p.
DLC.

839. --- , 1641. Constitvcie
Seymv walnego koronnego sześniedzielnego warszawskiego, roku pańskiego M.DC.XLI., dnia 20. miesiąca
śierpnia. W Krakowie, W Druk. A.
Piotrkowczyka, 1641. 37 p.
DLC.

840. --- , 1642. Constitvcie
y vchwała Seymu walnego koronnego
dvvniedzielnego w Warszawie, roku
M.DC.XLII., dnia XI. miesiąca lutego. W Krakowie, W Druk. A. Piotrkowczyka, 1642. 16 p.
DLC.

841. --- , 1643. Constitvcie
Seymv walnego koronnego sześcnie-
dzielnego warszawskiego, roku pańskiego M.DC.XLIII., dnia 12. miesią-

ca lutego. W Krakowie, Druk. A.
Piotrkowczyka, 1643. 26 p.
DLC.

842. --- , 1648. Porządek na Seymie walnym Elekcyey, między Warszawą
a Wolą, przez opisane Artykuły do samego tylko aktu elekcyey należące,
vchwalony y postanowiony roku pańskiego M.DC.XLVIII. dnia VI. październi-
ka. [Warszawa, Druk. Elerta, 1648]
28,[40] p. Polish and Latin.
DLC.

843. --- , 1649. Constitvcie Seymu walnego sześć niedzielnego, warszawskiego, roku pańskiego M.DC.XLIX
dnia 22 listopada. W Krakowie, W
Druk. Wdowy y Dziedziców Andrzeia
Piotrkow, 1649. 50 p.
DLC.

844. --- , 1649. Przywileie y
Constitvcie Seymowe, za panowania
Ie[go] Królewskiey Mći Iana Kazi-
mierza, roku pańskiego M.DC.XLIX.
W Krakowie, W Druk. Wdowy y Dzie-
dziców Andrzeia Piotrkow[czyka]
1649. 27 p. Polish and Latin.
DLC.

845. --- , 1650. Constitvcie y
vchwala Seymv walnego koronnego dvvniedzielnego warszawskiego, roku
panskiego M.DC.L. dnia 5 grudnia.
W Warszawie, W Druk. P. Elerta,
1650. 32 p.
DLC.

846. --- , 1652. Constitvcie Seymv walnego koronnego warszawskiego
skróconego, roku pańskiego M.DC.LII
dnia 23 lipca. W Warszawie, W.Druk.
P. Elerta, 1652. 38 p.
DLC.

847. --- , 1653. Constitvcie y
vchwała Seymv walnego koronnego dvvniedzielnego w Brzesciv Litewskim roku panskiego M.DC.LIII. dnia 24 marca odprawowanego. W Warszawie, V
Wdowy y Dziedziców Piotra Elerta,
1653. 48 p.
DLC.

848. --- , 1654. Constitvcie
Seymv walnego koronnego warszawskiego, roku pańskiego M.DC.LIV., zacze-
tego dnia 9 czerwca. W Warszawie
V Wdowy y Dziedziców Piotra Elerta,
1654. 40 p.
DLC.

849. --- , 1655. Constitvcie y
vchwała Seymv walnego koronnego dvvniedzielnego, w Warszawie, roku pańskiego M.DC.LV., dnia 19 maia odprawowanego. W Warszawie, V Wdowy
y Dziedziców Piotra Elerta, 1655.
40 p. L.C. copy imperfect. DLC.

850. --- , 1658. Constitvcie Seymv walnego ordinariynego szesćniedzielnego warszawskiego, roku panskiego M.DC.LVIII. die 10. iulij odprawuiącego się. W Warszawie wydrukowane, a dla wielu omyłek y errorow w mnieyszeniu y przydaniu w vniwersałach do grodów rozeslanych, wyrażonych, przedrukowane. W Krakowie, V Wdowy y Dziedzicow Andrzeia Piotrkowczyka, 1658. 70 p.
DLC.

851. --- ,1659. Constitvcie Seymv walnego szesćniedzielnego extraordinaryinego, przez Constitucyą przeszłego Seymu naznaczonego die XVII. martii, W Warszawie anno praesenti 1659. odprawuiącego się. W Krakowie, W Druk. Anny Teressy Wdowy Andrz. Piotr. [1659] 68,21 p.
DLC.

852. --- , 1661. Uchwała Seymu walnego koronnego szesćniedzielnego w Warszawie odprawionego, roku panskiego, M.DC.LXI. dnia 2. miesiąca maia. W Krakowie, Wdowy i Dziedziców Andrzeia Piotrkowczyka, 1661. 40 p. Summerfield D415-21 KU; DLC-L.

853. --- ,1662. Constitvcie Seymv walnego koronnego warszawskiego extraordynaryinego, roku panskiego M.DC.LXII. odprawuiącego się, vchwalone dnia 20. miesiąca lutego. W Warszawie W Druk. V Dziedzicow Piotra Elerta [1662] 28[i.e.44], 28 p. DLC.

854. --- ,1667. Constitvcie Seymv vvalnego koronnego, ex consensu totius Reipublicae, szesćniedzielnego ordynaryinego, w Warszawie roku panskiego MDCLXVII., dnia vii. miesiąca marca odprawuiącego się. W Warszawie, V Dziedziców Piotra Elerta [1667] 78[i.e. 79] p.
DLC.

855. --- ,1670. Przywileie y constitvcie Seymowe, za panowania Iego Królewskiey Mosći Michała I., roku panskiego M.DC.LXX. W Krakowie, W Druk. S. Piotrkowczyka [1670] 58 p. Polish and Latin.
DLC.

856. --- ,1673. Constitvcie Seymv walnego koronnego, ex consensv totivs Reipublicae szesć niedzielnego ordynaryinego w Warszawie roku panskiego MDCLXXIII., dnia iv. miesiąca stycznia odprawuiącego się. W Warszawie, 1673. 42, 24, [13] p.
DLC.

857. --- , 1676. Przywileie y Constitvcie Seymowe, za panowania

Iego Królewskiey Mci Jana III., roku panskiego M.DC.LXXVI. W Krakowie, W Druk. Dziedziców Krzysztofa Schedla [1676] 70, 27 p. Polish and Latin. DLC.

858. --- ,1683. Constitvcie Seymv walnego ordynaryinego sześć niedzielnego warszawskiego, roku panskiego MDCLXXXIII., die xxvii. Januarij zaczętego. W Warszawie, Drukował K.F. Schreiber [1683] 28, 20 p. Polish and Latin.
DLC.

859. --- ,1685. Constitvcie Seymv walnego ordynaryinego sześć niedzielnego warszawskiego, rokv panskiego M.DC.LXXXV., die xvi. Februarij zaczętego. W Warszawie, Drukował K.F. Schreiber [1585] 30, 13 p.
DLC.

860. --- ,1690. Constitvcye Seymv walnego ordynaryinego sześć niedzielnego warszawskiego, rokv panskiego MDCXC., dnia xvi. stycznia zaczętego. W Warszawie, W Druk. K.F. Schreibera [1690] 40, 21 p.
DLC.

861. --- ,1697. Przywileie u Constitucie Seymowe za panowania Iego Królewskiey Mci Augusta II., roku panskiego M.DC.XCVII. W Krakowie, W Druk. M.A. Schedla [1697] 17 p. DLC.

862. --- ,1699. Constytucye Seymu walnego Pacificationis warszawskiego sześćniedzielnego, zaczętego dnia xvi. miesiąca czerwca, roku panskiego M.DC.XCIX. W Warszawie W Druk. Collegij Scholarum Piarum [1699] 77 p. Polish and Latin. LC copy imperfect; pages 1-35 wanting. DLC.

863. --- ,1717. Constytucye na zakonczeniu Konfederacyi Tarnogrodzkiey y iiych konfederacyi prowincyalnych y partykularnych do niey referuiących się, tak szlacheckich iako y woyskowych koronnych y W.X.Litewskiego sub authoritate & valore Seymu Pacificationis, vigore Traktatu Warszawskiego ex consensu ordinum Reipublicae. R.P. MDCCXII. miesiąca lutego, dnia pierwszego w Warszawie postanowione. Varsaviae, Typis Collegij Scholarum Piarum [1717] [6], 80, 22, p. illus. "Traktat Warszawski, dnia trzeciego novembra 1716 roku zkonkludowany" Polish and Latin; p. [6]-52.
DLC.

VII.4.d. COLLECTIONS OF LAWS

864. BALTIC PROVINCES. LAWS, STA-
TUTES, ETC. Sbornik uzakoneniĭ i
rasporīàzheniĭ o krest'īànakh Pribaltiĭskikh guberniĭ. Sostavil i izdal
A.P. Vasilevskiĭ. Moskva, Univ.tip.,
189- . v.
DLC.

865. --- Sbornik uzakoneniĭ o
krest'īànakh Pribaltiĭskikh guberniĭ.
Sostavil V.E. Reĭtem. S.-Peterburg,
Obshchestvennaia pol'za, 1898. 3 v.
DLC.

VII.4.g. DECISIONS OF THE SUPREME
COURT AND THE STATE
CHAMBER

866. MASIULIS, B[oleslovas Jonas]
Valstybės Taryba. [The State Cham-
ber] In Teisininkų Žinios (Chicago,
Ill.), 1958, p. 2-26. See serials
consulted.

867. RUIZ DE MOROS, Pedro, 1505-
1571. Decisiones Petri Roysii Mau-
rei... de rebus in sacro auditorio
lituanico, ex appellatione judicatis
Cracoviae, 1563.
MH

868. --- --- Hac novissima omnivm
editione a M.D. Leonardo a Lege re-
cognitae, & expurgatae. Venetiis,
apvd Bartholomaevm Rvbinvm, 1572.
229 p. [Consilia-statuti collection,
v. 781]
CLU; MH-L

VII.4.i. SPECIAL TOPICS AND LEGAL
COMMENTARIES

869. BACKUS, Oswald P. Treason
as a concept and defection from Moscow to Lithuania in the sixteenth
century. In Berlin. Freie Universität. Osteuropa Institut. Forschungen zur osteuropäischen Geschi-
te (Wiesbaden, Ger.), Bd.15, 1970,
p. 117-144. See serials consulted.

870. DAINAUSKAS, Jonas. Lietuvos
D.K. įstatymai ir statutai iš 1457-
1563 metų. [The laws and statutes
of the Lithuanian Grand Duchy,1457-
1563] In Tautos Praeitis (Chicago,
Ill.), kn.2, v.2, 1965, p.81-106.
See serials consulted.

871. FINKELSTEIN, V. Litausches
internationales Privatrecht und
Stellung der Ausländer in Litauen.
In Ostrecht (Berlin), 1926, p. 729-
746. See serials consulted.

872. KISTĪAKOVSKIĬ, Aleksandr Fedorovich, ed. Prava, po kotorym su-
ditsia malorossiĭskiĭ narod...Eīà
imperatorskago... Velichestva pove-
līèniem, iz trekh knig, a imenno:
Statuta Litovskogo... v edinu knigu
svedennyīà... Kiev, v univ. tip.,
1879. 1 v. (various pagings)
DLC-L.

873. LIKAS, Albinas. Kul'tura
sudebnogo protsessa. Moskva, ĪŪrid.
lit-ra, 1971. 77 p. illus.
JN6530.P9L72 1971 CaAEU; DLC.

874. MAČYS, Vladas. Ipoteka, jos
pagrindai ir santvarka. [The Land
title, its principles, records and
organization] In Teisė (Kaunas),
no.11, p.1-34; no.12, p.1-27.
ICBM.

875. VERŽBAVIČIUS, Levas. Senoji Lietuvos šeimos teisė. Vedybų
teisė. [The family and marriage
laws in the old Lithuanian statutes]
In Teisė (Kaunas), no.18-20, p.64-
83, 26-43, 77-92.
ICBM.

VII.5. ADMINISTRATION

VII.5.b. ADMINISTRATIVE BY-LAWS,
INSTRUCTIONS, REGULATIOS
ETC.

875a. SERAPHIM, August. Kulmi-
sches und magdeburgisches Recht für
Szkudy 1572. In Tauta ir Žodis (Kaunas), v.2, 1924, p. 67-80. See serials consulted.

VII.5.c. POLICE AND SECURITY

876. LIETUVOS POLICIJA ĮSTATYMŲ
ir tvarkos tarnyboje. Buvusių policijos tarnautojų prisiminimai. [Li-
thuanian police force in service for
law and order; reminiscences of the
previous members of the police force. Redagavo Apolinaras Bagdonas.
Čikagoje, Buvusių policijos tarnautojų klubas Krivulė, 1974] 433 p..
HV8227.6.L5 PU.

VII.5.d. POLITICAL PARTIES, THEIR PLATFORMS AND PRACTICAL POLITICS

877. AMBRAZEVIČIUS, Juozas. Idealoginių grupių santykiai "Aušros" ir "Varpo" gadynėje. [The relations among the idealogical groupings during the days of "Aušra" and "Varpas"] In Krikščionybė Lietuvoje. Kaunas, 1938. BR937.L3K7 DLC; PU.

878. KASULAITIS, Algirdas Jonas. Lithuanian Christian Democracy.[Chicago, Ill., Leo XIII Fund, 1976] xxiv, 244 p. illus. Bibliography: p. 241-244. JN6745.A98K7 PU; DLC CaAEU.

879. KRIVICKAS, Vladas. The Lithuanian Populist and the agrarian question, 1918-1926. In Journal of Baltic Studies (Brooklyn, N.Y.), no. 4, v.6, 1975, p. 259-271. See serials consulted.

880. KRUPAVIČIUS, Mykolas. Krikščioniškoji demokratija. [Christian demokracy. Stuttgart, Ger., Lux, 1948] 163 p. (Tėvynės Sargo biblioteka, nr.2) (Lux leidyklos leidiniai, 6) HN373.K7 OKentU.

881. LIETUVIŲ POLITINĖS IDEOLOGIJos naujų idėjų šviesoje. [The Litthuanian political ideologies in the perspective of new ideas. By] A. Kučas, J. Daugėla, Mykolas Drunga, J. Jurkūnas, ir S. Rudys. In Varpas (Chicago, Ill.), no.10, 1970-71, p. 21-40. See serials consulted.

882. LOPAEV, Sofronii Semenovich. KLP požiūris į buržuazines partijas Lietuvoje. [The attitude of the Communist Party of Lithuanian towards bourgeois parties in Lithuania] Vilnius, Mintis, 1974. 229 p. At head of title: S. Lopaje'vas. JN6745.A98L6 PU

883. MALDEIKIS, Petras. Mykolas Krupavičius. [Chicago, Ill., Lietuvių Krikščionių Demokratų Sąjunga, 1975] 493 p. illus. Bibliography: p. 480-488. DK511.L28K76 PU.

884. PAKALKA, Jonas. Steigiamojo Seimo Lietuvos Socialdemokratų frakcija. [The Social Democratic Party of Lithuania in the Constituent Diet] In Metmenys (Chicago, Ill.), no.1, 1971, p. 69-84. A195.L5M4 DLC; OU; PU; see also serials consulted.

885. SABALIŪNAS, Leonas. Lietuvos socialdemokratija ir tautinis klausimas 1893-1904 m. Lithuanian social democracy and the national question, 1893-1904. In Institute of Lithuanian Studies. Lituanistikos instituto 1971 metų suvažiavimo darbai. Chicago, Ill., 1971. p.85-88. Summary in English. DK511.L2I57 DLC; CaAEU; InNd; MiU; NIC; NRU; PU.

886. SENN, Alfred Erich. A correspondence with Steponas Kairys. In Lituanus (Chicago, Ill.), no.1, v.21, 1975, p. 63-74. See serials consulted.

887. VALAITIS, Jurgis. Lietuvos politinių partijų išeivijoje dabartis ir ateitis. [The actual state and the future of the Lithuanian political parties in exile] In Metmenys (Chicago, Ill.), no.1, 1971, p.18-28. AP95.L5M4 DLC; OU; PU; See also serials consulted.

888. VASYS, Dalius. The Lithuanian Social Democratic Party and the revolution of 1905. In Lituanus (Chicago, Ill.), no.3, v.23, 1977, p. 14-40. See serials consulted.

889. VIKTORAS, S.A. LSDP for Lithuania's freedom. [s.l.] Lithuanian Social Democratic Party in Exile, [n.d.] 32 p. OKentU.

VII.5.f. LOCAL GOVERNMENT

890. BERSHADSKII, Sergeĭ Aleksandrovich. Retsenziĭa na sochinenie gospodina M. Liubavskago "Oblastnoe dielenie i miestnoe upravlenie Litovsko-Russkago gosudarstva ko vremeni izdaniĭa Pervago Litovskago Statuta" Sanktpeterburg, Tip. Imp. Akademii nauk, 1895. 20 p. Caption title. "Otdiel'nyĭ ottisk iz Otcheta o XXXVI prisuzhdenii nagrad gp. Uvarova. DLC-L.

891. CHODYNICKI, Henryk. Sejmiki ziem ruskich w wieku XV. Lwów, Nakł. Tow. dla Popierania nauki Polskiej, 1906. 119 p. (Studya nad historią prawa polskiego, t.3, zesz.1) JS6132.A3C5 DLC; CLU; ICU; KU; NN; MH-L.

892. WOJKOWIAK, Z. Powiat kurklewski; przyczynek do specyfiki struktury administracyjno-terrytorialnej Wielkiego Księstwa Litewskiego. In Acta Baltico-Slavica (Warszawa), v.10, 1976, p. 37-46. See serials consulted.

VII.6. ARMED FORCES

893. ALIŠAUSKAS, Kazys. Kautynės prie Valkininkų ir Rūdiškių geležinkelio ruožo 1923 m. vasario 15-23 d. [The battle along the railroad Valkininkas and Rūdiškiai, 1923] In Karys (Brooklyn, N.Y.), no.9, 1972, p. 296-299; no.10, p. 325-327. See serials consulted.

894. --- Lietuvos kariuomenės pirmosios dienos. [The first days of the Lithuanian armed forces] In Sėja (Chicago, Ill.), no.4, 1970, p. 6-12. See serials consulted.

895. 8-tas [i.e. AŠTUNTAS] PĖSTI-ninkų Kauno kunigaikščio Vaidoto pulkas; pulko penkiolikos gyvenimo metų sukakčiai paminėti, 1919-1934. [Fifteenth anniversary of the 8th Regiment of the Duke Vaidotas of Kaunas] Medžiagą rinko ir tvarkė E. Bliudnikas ir P. Nazaras. Šiauliai, 8-to pėst. Kauno Kunigaikščio Vaidoto pulko leidinys, 1934. [Xerox copy, 1977] 118 p. DK511.L27A8 1934a PU.

896. BAIPŠYS, Stasys. Žemaičiai sujudo. [The involvement of Žemaičiai (Samogitians). In Karys (Brooklyn, N.Y.), no.9, 1974, p. 333-341; no.10, p. 371-378. See serials consulted.

897. GUŽAS, Petras. Atsiminimai apie pirmąsias mūsų kariuomenės kūrimosi dienas. [Memoirs on the first days of our military forces in Vilnius] In Mūsų Žinynas (Kaunas), v.15, 1923, p. 442-454. "Naujienos" publishing house; see also serials consulted.

898. KARIUOMENĖS TEISMAS, 1919-1929. [The military tribunal, 1919-1929] Kaunas, Kariuomenės teismo leidinys, 1929. [Xerox copy, 1977] 91 p. DK511.L27K33 1929a PU.

899. LITHUANIAN SSR. VIDAUS REI-KALŲ MINISTERIJA. ARCHYVŲ SKYRIUS. Dokumenty shtaba M.I. Kutuzova,1805-1806; sbornik. Vil'nĩus, Gos. izd-vo polit. lit-ry, 1951. 338 p. illus. DK190.L5 DLC.

900. 5 [i.e. PENKTAS] DIDŽIOJO Lietuvos Kunigaikščio Kęstučio pulkas, 1919-1934. [Fifth Regiment of the Grand Duke Kęstutis of Lithuania, 1919-1934] Kaunas, 5 Pėstininkų D.L.K. Kęstučio pulko leidinys, 1934. [Xerox copy, 1977] 96 p. DK511.L27P45 1934a PU.

901. RAŠTIKIS, Stasys. Kovose

dėl Lietuvos; kario atsiminimai. [In battle for Lithuania; memoirs of a soldier] Los Angeles, Clif., Lietuvių dienos, 1956-1972. 3 v. Vol.3 has title: Įvykiai ir žmonės; iš mano užrašų. DK511.L28R3 DLC; CaAEU CSt-H; CtTMF; ICLJF; InNd; PU.

902. RUGIS, Jonas. Sibiro lietuvių batalionas, 1918-1919 m. [The Lithuanian battalion in Siberia,1918-1919] In Tautos Praeitis (Chicago, Ill.), kn.1, v.2, 1964, p. 138-142. See serials consulted.

903. ŠKIRPA, Kazys. 5 [i.e. Penkto] Pėstininkų DLK Kęstučio pulko kovos ties Seinais 1920 metais. Brooklyn, N.Y., Karys, 1971. 124 p. illus. (Raštai Lietuvos karinės istorijos, nr. 9) [The battle of the Fifth Regiment... at Seinai, 1920] DK511.L2A248 nr.9 DLC.

904. STEPONAITIS, V[ytautas] Atskiras Lietuvių batalionas Vitebske. [The separate Lithuanian Battalion in Vitebsk] In Mūsų Žinynas (Kaunas), v.2, 1922, p. 309-337. "Naujienos" Publishing House; see also serials consulted. At head of title: Kapitonas V. Steponaitis.

905. --- Bermontininkai Lietuvoje [The Bermont army forces in Lithuania] [By] Kapitonas V. Steponaitis. In Mūsų Žinynas (Kaunas), v.1, 1921, p. 76-98 p. Mr. Dainauskas, Chicago, Ill.; see also serials consulted

906. STUDIA Z DZIEJÓW POLSKIEJ historiografii wojskowej. T.1. Poznań, Wydawnictwo Naukowe Uniwersytetu im. Adama Mickiewicza, 1975-. 127 p. (Seria Historica, nr. 65) DK401.P892 DLC; MH.

907. ŽIBURKUS, Jonas. Žemaičių pulkas. [The Žemaičių (Samogitian) battalion] Vilnius, Vaga, 1969. 325 p. illus., port. DK511.L26Z5 DLC; CaAEU; OKentU; NNC; NjP.

VII.7. DIPLOMACY AND FOREIGN RE-LATIONS

VII.7.a. GENERAL STUDIES

908. DAILIDĖ, Pranas. Trumpa užsienių politikos apžvalga. [A brief outline of Lithuania's foreign policy] In Visa Lietuva. Kaunas,1932. HC337.L7A2 ICU; CSt-H.

909. DUNDULIS, Bronius. Lietuvos užsienio politika XVI amžiuje. [The

foreign policy of Lithuania in the
16th century] Vilnius, Mintis, 1971.
308 p., 17 leaves of illus. and maps.
At head of title: B. Dundulis. Summary in Russian.
DK511.L23D83 DLC; CtY; InU; MB; MH;
NNC; OKentU; WU.

910. THE GERMAN THREAT TO POLAND,
Rumania and Lithuania, and Western
counter-measures: 6 February to 11
April 1939. In Documents on international affairs, 1939-1946. London,
1951. v.1, p. 106-134.
D411.R88D 1939-46 v.1 CaAEU; see also
serials consulted.

911. GERMANY AND RUSSIA. In Documents on international affairs,
1939-1946. London, 1954. v.2, p.59-
80. D411.R8D 1939-46 v.2 CaAEU;
see also serials consulted.

912. KROSBY, Hans Peter. Finland,
Germany and the Soviet Union, 1940-
1941; the Petsamo dispute. Madison,
Wis., University of Wisconsin Press,
1968. xvii, 276 p. illus., ports.
Bibliography: p. 248-263.
D765.3.K7 DLC; CaAEU; CSt-H; DAU;
GAT; FMU; ICU; MoSW; NN; NNC; CoDuF;
CLSU; CLU; CaOTP; CtY; CaBVaU; CU;
AU; AAP;DS; DAU; FU; FTaSU; GU;InU;
IaU; IEN; IdU; KU; KyU; KEmT; LU;
MH; MU; McB; MnU; MB; MoU; N; NNR;
NBuU; NjR; NcRS; NcD; NIC; NjP; NhU
NRU; NBuC; NcGU; NcU; OU; OrCS; OkU
OrPS; OrU; PPULC; RPB; ScU; TxU; TNJ
TxFTC; TU; UU; ViU; ViBlbV; WU;

913. LEAGUE OF NATIONS. SECRETA-
RY-GENERAL, 1919-1933 (Earl of Perth)
Demande d'admission de la Lithuanie
dans la Société des Nations. Memorandum avec annexes. Application of
Lithuania for admission to the League of Nations. Memorandum with
annexes. Geneve, 1920. 15, 2, 15 p.
(numb. in duplicate) Official no.:
Document de l'assemblee 100[20-48-
100] NNUN-W.

914. LITHUANIA. UŽSIENIŲ REIKALŲ
MINISTERIJA. DEMANDE d'admission de
la Lithuanie dans la Société des Nations. Lettre en date du 12 octobre
1920. Request from Lithuania for admission to the League of Nations.
Letter, dated 12th October 1920.
[Londres. 1920] [3] leaves. At
head of title: Societe des Nations.
Official no.: Document de l'Assemblee 34 (20-48-34)
NNUN-W.

915. ŁOSSOWSKI, Piotr. Między
wojną a pokojem; niemieckie zamysły
wojenne na wschodzie w obliczu traktatu Wersalskiego, marzec-czerwiec
1919 roku. Warszawa, Książka i Wie-

dza, 1976. 353 p. illus.
DK45.G3L67 DLC.

916. PRZEZDZIECKI, Rajnold, Hra-
bia. Diplomatie et protocole a la
cour de Pologne. Paris, Éditions
Les Belles Lettres, 1934-1937. 2 v.
plates, ports., map. DK418.P76 DLC;
CU; CtY; CaBVaU; IaU; IU; InU; ICU;
MH; NN; OU; PU; WaU; CaAEU (1953-
English ed.)

917. SENN, Alfred Erich. Vaclovas Sidzikauskas on Lithuanian diplomacy in 1920's. In Lituanus (Chicago, Ill.), no.1, v.22, 1976, p.54-
64. See serials consulted.

918. --- Vaclovas Sidzikauskas on
the early years of Lithuanian diplomacy. In Lituanus (Chicago, Ill.)
no.3, v.21, p. 63-75. See serials
consulted.

919. THE U.S.S.R. Germany, and
the Western Powers; 10 March to 1st
September 1939. In Documents on
international affairs, 1939-1946.
London, 1951, v.1, p. 361-442.
D411.R88D 1939-46 v.1 CaAEU; see
also serials consulted.

920. VOLDEMARAS, Augustinas.
Raštai. [Works of A. Voldemaras. Re-
dagavo Morkus Šimkus. Chicago, Ill.]
Lietuvos atgimimo sąjudis, 1973.[i.
e. 1976] xv, 672 p.
DK511.L2V65 PU.

921. ŽEPKAITĖ, Regina. Lietuva
tarptautinės politikos labirintuose,
1918-1922.m. [Lithuania in the web
of international politics] Vilnius
Mintis, 1973. 194 p. At head of
title: Lietuvos TSR Mokslų akademija. Istorijos institutas. R. Žepkaitė. Bibliography: p. 188-[191]
DK511.L27Z45 DLC; MH; NjP; OKentU;
PU; WU.

VII.7.b. FOREIGN RELATIONS OF THE
BALTIC STATES

922. DUNSDORFS, Edgars. The Baltic dilema: the case of the De Jure
recognition of incorporation of the
Baltic States into the Soviet Union
by Australia. New York, N.Y., R.
Speller and Sons, 1975. 302 p.
JX1552.5 DLC; NN; NbU.

923. HORM, Arvo. Phases of the
Baltic political activities...with
biographical notes on Arvo Horm by
Evald Uustalu. Stockholm, Baltic
Humanitarian Association, 1973. 22p.
port. Rev. ed. of a paper original-

ly presented at the Second Conference on Baltic Studies in Scandinavia, Stockholm, 1973. DK511.B3H55 1973 DLC.

924. JUDA, Lawrence. United States' nonrecognition of the Soviet Union's annexetion of the Baltic States; politics and law. In Journal of Baltic Studies (Brooklyn, N.Y.), no.4, v.6, 1975, p. 272-290. See serials consulted.

925. KASLAS, Bronis J. The Baltic nations; the quest for regional integration and political liberty: Estonia, Latvia, Lithuania, Finland, Poland. Pittston, Pa., Euramerica Press, 1976. xiii, 319 p. maps. Bibliography: p. 303-312. DK511.B3K29 PU; DLC; CaAEU.

926. KREPP, Ednel. Security and non-agression; Baltic States and USSR treaties of non-agression. Problem of the Baltic. Stockholm, Estonian information Centre, 1973. 64p. (Problems of the Baltic, 3) JX756.1973K74 DLC; CaBVaU; CtY; CoU CSt-H; DS; FTaSU; IU; IaAS; InU; IaU MH; MnU; MnU-L; N; NjP; PPT; WaU.

927. RODGERS, Hugh I. Search for security; a study in Baltic diplomacy, 1920-1934. [Hamden, Conn.,] Archon Books, 1975. 181 p. map. DK511.B3R54 DLC; AAP; AkU; AzU; CU CaAEU; CaBVaU; CSt; CSt-H; CtW; CoU; DS; FU; FMU; GASU; GU; ICarbS; IaAS; IaU; InNd; InU; IEN; KU; MH; MoSW; MiEM; MiU; MnU; MoU; NN; NNC; NSyU; NcU; NRU; N; NjP; NvU; NjR; NmU;NdU; NSbSU; NbU; OU; OCU; OKentU; TNJ;TU; TxU; UU; ViU; WU; WaU.

928. TARULIS, Albert N. Baltic ports: Soviet claims and reality. In Baltic Review (New York, N.Y.), no. 24, 1962, p. 17-30. See serials consulted.

929. TRULSSON, Sven G. British and Swedish policies and strategies in the Baltic after the Peace of Tilsit in 1807; a study of decision-making. Lund, Gleerup, 1976. 175 p. (Bibliotheca historica Lundensis, 40) Bibliography: p. 167-175. Thesis--University of Lund. DL782.T78 DLC.

VII.7.c. INTER-RELATIONS AMONG THE
THE BALTIC STATES

930. CONFERENCE DES ETATS BALTIQUES, BULDURI, LATVIA, 1920. Minutes of the Baltic Conference at Bulduri in Latvia in 1920. Washington, D.C., Latvian Legation, 1960. 105

leaves. All documents in French; t.p. and preface only in English. DK511.B3C64 1920 DLC; CU; ICU; InU; MH-L; NN.

931. KASLAS, Bronis J. Baltijos valstybių tarpusaviai santykiai. International relations of the Baltic countries. In Institute of Lithuanian Studies. Lituanistikos instituto 1973 metų suvažiavimo darbai. Chicago, Ill., 1975. p. 25-38. Summary in English. DK511.L2I63 1975 CaAEU; PU.

932. MILOSZ, Oscar Vladislas. ... L'alliance des états baltiques. Paris, Impr. Desmoineaux & Brisset, 1919. 15 p. At head of title: O.W. de Lubicz-Milosz. Vol.of pam. CSt-H; NNC; DNW.

933. MINIOTAS, Vytautas. Atsargiai Balfas! : dokumentinė apybraiža. [Be careful, BALFAS! ; a documentary sketch] Vilnius, Mintis, 1973. 154 p. illus. E184.L7M57 DLC; MB; MH; OKentU.

934. PABALTIJO TAUTŲ SUSIARTINIMO KONGRESAS. 5th, Kaunas, 1939. Penktasis Pabaltijo tautų susiartinimo kongresas ir "Pabaltijo Savaitė" [Fifth Congress for the cooperation among the Baltic nations in Kaunas] Kaunas, 1939. 47 p. illus. (Pabaltijo tautų vienybės, Lietuvių grupės biuletenis, nr.1) DK511.B3P26 DLC.

935. SKRZYPEK, Andrzej. Związek Bałtycki; Litwa, Łotwa, Estonia i Finlandia w polityce Polski i ZSRR w latach 1919-1925. [Warszawa] Książka i Wiedza, 1972. At head of title: Polska Akademia nauk. Zakład Historii stosunków Polsko-Radzieckich. Bibliography: p. 289-300. 307 pages. DK511.B3S55 PU; DLC;CU; CaBVaU; CSt-H; ICU; InU; MH; MiU; MU; MnU; NjP; NNC; WU; WaU.

936. ŠLIŪPAS, Jonas. Lietuvių bei latvių sąjunga ir sąjungos projektas; paskaita laikyta 23 kovo 1930 m. Lietuvos universitatėje Kaune ir 6 balandžio Latvių-lietuvių vienybės draugijos valdybų susirinkime, Rygoje. [Proposal of the Latvian-Lithuanian Union by Dr. J. Šliūpas] Šiauliuose, Spaustuvė Titnagas 1930. [Xerox copy, 1977] 24 p. DK511.L2S54 1930a PU.

VII.7.d. GERMANY

VII.7.d.1. FOREIGN AND GENERAL RELATIONS

937. BAUMGART, Winfried. Deutsche Ostpolitik 1918. Von Brest-Litowsk bis zum Ende des Ersten Weltkrieg. Wien, Oldenbourg, 1966. 462 p. Bibliography: p. [385]-407-419. DD120.R8B34 1966 DLC; AAP; CaBVaU; CaAEU; CU; CU-S; CoU; CtY; CtW; CNoS CSt-H; DAU; DeU; FTaFU; FU; GU; GEU; ICU; IEN; IMS; InU; IU; IaU; KMK;LU; KyU; MH; MiDW; MiEM; MdBJ; MoSW;MaU; MCM; MnU; MoU; NN; NNC; NBuC; NBuU; NNCFR; NIC; NjP; NjR; NcD; NcU; NcGU NRU; OCl; OU; OrU; OrPS; RPB; TxU; TNJ; TxLT; TxHR; UU; ViU; WU; WaU.

938. BENCKE, Albert. Deutschland und die litauischen Probleme. In Das grössere Deutschland; Wochenschrift für deutsche Welt- und Kolonialpolitik (Weimar; Dresden, Ger.), Bd.5, Teil 1, 1918, p. 524-528. See serials consulted.

939. DEUTSCHE OSTFORSCHUNG; Ergebnisse und Aufgaben seit dem Ersten Weltkrieg, herausgegeben von Hermann Aubin, Otto Brunner, Wolfgang Kohte, Johannes Papritz... Leipzig, Ger., S. Hirzel, 1942-1943. 2 v. illus., maps. (Added t.p.: Deutschland und der Osten; Quellen und Forschungen zur Geschichte ihrer Beziehungen. Hrsg. von Hermann Aubin,Albert Brackmann, Max Hein [u.a.] ... Bd. 20, 21) DD94.D4 DLC; CaAEU;CU; CaBVaU; CSt; IaU; ICRL; MH; MdBJ; MiU; NNC; NcD; NjP; RPB; WU.

940. EULER, Heinrich. Die Aussenpolitik der Weimarer Republik, 1918-1923; vom Waffenstillstand bis zum Ruhrkonflikt. Aschaffenburg, Ger., In Commission P. Pattlech Verlag, 1957. 471 p. DD249.E8 DLC; CaBVaU CtY;;CSt; CSt-H; CLSU; CU; DS; FU; GEU; InU; ICU; LU; MH; MiU; MnU;MoU; NN; NNC; NIC; NjP; MdBJ; OkS; OrU; OOxM; OU; PSt; PPULC; RPB; ScU; TU; TxU; TxHR; WU; WaU.

941. FISCHER, Fritz. Griff nach der Weltmacht; die Krigszielpolitik des kaiserlichen Deutschland, 1914-1918. Düsseldorf, Ger., Droste, 1962. D515.F27 DLC; CaAEU; CaBVaU; CtY; CU; CSt-H; DeU; FTaSU; FU;GU; IEN; ICU; IU; IaU; KEmT; KyU; MH; MiDW; MdBJ; MiEM; MiU; MeU; MWelC; NN; NNC; NIC; NjP; NcD; NcU; NcGW; NBuU; NbU; NhU; OU;PPULC; ScU; TxU; TNJ; TU; WU; WaU.

942. FREITAG, Kurt. Raum deutscher Zukunft-Grenzland in Osten. Dresden, Ger., C. Reissner, 1933. 947.52.P949 PU.

943. GRIMM, Claus. Jahre deutscher Entscheidung im Baltikum, 1918-1919. Essen, Ger., Essenerverlags-

anstalt, 1939. xxi, 514 p. illus., ports., maps. DK511.B3G8 CaAEU; DLC; MH; MnU; NN.

944. HERZSTEIN, Robert Edwin. Adolf Hitler and the German trauma, 1913-1945; an interpretation of the Nazi phenomen. New York, N.Y., Capricorn Books, 1974. xiv, 294 p. DD247.H5H3685 DLC; AkU; CaAEU; CtY; CaBVaU; CaOTP; CSt-H; CLSU; CU; DS; GU; InU; ICarbS; InNd; IU; LU; MB; MH; MoSW; MnU; MiU; NBuU; NjP; NjR; NWM; NbU; NcRS; NmLeU; OOxM; OU; OKentU; NNU; NN; NNCoCi; PSt; TxU; TNJ; ViBlbV; WU; Wa; WaU .

945. KASLAS, Bronis J. The Lithuanian strip in Soviet-German secret diplomacy, 1939-1941. In Journal of Baltic Studies (Brooklyn, N.Y.), no.3, 1973, p. 211-225. See serials consulted.

946. --- , comp. The USSR-German aggression against Lithuania. Edited with foreword and introd. by Bronis J. Kaslas. [1st ed.] New York, N.Y., R. Speller, 1973. 543 p. illus. Bibliography: p. 507-528. DK511.L27K35 DLC; AkU; CaAEU;CaBVaU; CaOTP; CLSU; CSt-H; CoU; FU; GU; IU; IEN; InU; MB; MH; MiU; MiEM; MnU;MU; NNC; NIC; NSyU; NcD; NcU; NmU; NhU; NjP; NBuC; NvU; OCl; OU; OkU; PSt; RPB; ViU; VtU; UU; TU; TNJ; WU;WaU.

947. RIMSCHA, Hans von. Die Baltikumpolitik der Grossmächte. In Historische Zeitschrift (München,Ger) no.177, 1954, p. 281-309. See serials consulted.

948. SCHRAEDER, Hildegard. Geschichte der Pläne zur Teilung des alten polnischen Staates seit 1386. Leipzig, Ger., S. Hirzel, 1937- . illus., facsims., maps. (Deutschland und der Osten... Bd.5) Partial contents.--Teil.1. Der Teilung von 1392. DK418.S35 DLC; NN.

949. SLAVĖNAS, Julius P. Stresemann and Lithuania in the nineteen twenties. In Institute of Lithuanian studies. Lituanistikos instituto 1971 metu suvažiavimo darbai. Chicago, Ill., 1971. p. 89-103. DK511.L2I57 DLC; CaAEU; InNd; MiU; NIC; NRU; PU; and in Lituanus (Chicago, Ill.), no.4, v.18, 1972, p.5-25. See serials consulted.

VII.7.d.2. QUESTION OF KLAIPĖDA (MEMEL)

950. CONFERENCE OF AMBASSADORS, PARIS, 1923. Bericht der nach Memel entsandten Sonderkommission an die

Botschafterkonferenz... Berlin, Memelland Verlag, 1932. Bound with Brönner-Hoepfner, S. Die Leiden des Memelgebietes... 947.52.B783 PU.

951. MORROW, Ian Fitzerbert Despard. The Memel problem. In His The peace settlement in the German Polish borderlands. London, 1936. p. 419-488. D651.P7M8 CaAEU; CtY; KEmT; MB; MU; NN; NNC; NcD; NIC;OCU; OClW; OU; OrU; OrP; PSc; PBm; PHC; PU; ViU; WaS; WaU.

952. TOYNBEE, V.M. German-Lithuanian relations, 1937-1939 and the transfer of Memel to Germany, March 1939. In Survey of international affairs, 1939-1946. London, 1953, v.3, p. 357-390. D441.R88 1938 v.3 CaAEU; see also serials consulted.

953. ŽIUGŽDA, Robertas. Po diplomatijos skraiste; Klaipėdos kraštas imperialistinių valstybių planuose 1919-1924 metais. [Klaipėdos Kraštas (Memelterritory) under the yoke of diplomacy] Vilnius, Mintis, 1973. 240 p. Summary in Russian and German. Bibliography: p. 222-235. DK511.L273Z58 PU; DLC; CU; IU; MB; MH; MiU; NN; NjP; WU.

VII.7.e. POLAND

VII.7.e.1. FOREIGN AND GENERAL RELATIONS

954. DERUGA, Aleksy. Polityka wschodnia Polski wobec ziem Litwy, Białorusi i Ukrainy, 1918-1919. Warszawa, Książka i Wiedza, 1969. 330 p. (Problemy dwudziestolecia) DK440.D475 DLC; CtY; CoU; CU; FU; ICU; IU; InNd; MH; MnU; MiEM; MiU; NN; NNC; NBuC; NcU; NjP; FTaSU; KU.

955. LECZYK, Marian. Proba przezwyciężenia kryzysu w stosunkach polsko-litewskich w latach 1928-1930. In Studia z dziejów ZSRR i Europy środkowej. Warszawa, 1975. t.11, p. 151-183. See serials consulted.

956. LITHUANIA. MINISTRAS PIRMININKAS. Letter from the Prime Minister of Lithuania. Geneva, 1924. 2 leaves. Caption title. At head of title: League of Nations. Official no.: C.323.1924.VII. Protest against new acts of Polish aggression on the Lithuanian-Polish line of demarcation. NNUN-W.

957. ŁOSSOWSKI, Piotr. Litwa a wojna polsko-niemiecka 1939 r. In

Więz (Warszawa), no.10, 1971, p.95-108. AP54.W57 DLC; see also serials consulted.

958. --- Polskie ultimatum do Litwy w marcu 1938 r. widziane z placówki RP w Talinie. In Studia z dziejów ZSRR i Europy środkowej (Warszawa), t.11, 1975, p. 231-237. See serials consulted.

959. MIŠKINIS, Petras. Lietuvos ir Lenkijos santykių tarptautiniai aspektai 1919-1939. [Lithuanian-Polish foreign relations, 1919-1939.] Vilnius, Mintis, 1976. 159 p. At head of title: Lietuvos TSR Mokslų akademija. Filosofijos, teisės ir sociologijos skyrius prie Istorijos instituto. Summary in Russian. DK511.L27M55 PU; DLC.

960. PROBLEMES POLITIQUES DE LA Pologne contemporaine. Paris, Gebether et Wolf, 1931-1932. 3 v. DK418.P96 CaAEU; CoU; DLC; DCU; DAU GEU; NN; NBuC; OCU; PU.

961. ROOS, Hans. Polen und Litauen Januar bis September 1934 [and] Die litauische Affäre August 1937 bis März 1938. In His Polen und Europa; Studien zur polnischen Aussenpolitik, 1931-1939. Tübingen, 1957. p. 202-208; 305-317. DK440.M51 CaAEU CtY; CU-SC; DLC(orig.) InU; KMK; KU; MH; MoU; MoSW; NNC; NIC; OKentU; OU; OrU; ScU; TxU.

962. ŠAPOKA, Adolfas. Kultūriniai lietuvių lenkų santykiai Jogailos laikais. [Cultural relations between Lithuanians and Poles during the reign of Jogaila] In His Jogaila. Kaunas, 1935. 947.52.W797.yS PU; ICCC; OCl.

963. SUŽIEDELIS, Simas. Lietuvos lenkijos santykiai. Suvalkų sutartis. [The Lithuanian-Polish relations -Treaty of Suvalkai] In Lietuva (New York, N.Y.), nr.6, 1954, p. 81-101. See serials consulted.

964. TOYNBEE, V. M. Relations between Poland and Lithuania, 1937-1939. In Survey of international affairs, 1939-1946. London, 1953. v.3, p. 342-356. D411.R88 1938 v.3 CaAEU; see also serials consulted.

VII.7.e.2. QUESTION OF VILNIUS

965. BUDRECKIS, Algirdas. Voldemaras ir Vilniaus byla. [Voldemaras and the dispute of Vilnius] In Naujoji Viltis (Chicago, Ill.), no.6, 1973-1974, p. 45-66. See serials consulted.

966. LEAGUE OF NATIONS. COUNCIL.
Différend entre la Lithuanie et la
Pologne; rapport présenté par M. Hymans sur la conférence de Bruxelles
20 avril-3 juin 1921. Genève, 1921.
14,[2], 14 p. (numbered in duplicate) Negotiations between the dele-
gates of Poland and Lithuania, the
Belgian representative on the Council M. Hymans presiding. Official
no.: C.95.M.54.1921.VII.
NNUN-W.

967. --- Dispute between Lithuania and Poland. Provisional line of
demarcation in the neutral zone. Geneva, 1923. 2, 2 leaves. Official
no.: C.176.M.100.1923.VII. Telegram
dated Feb.22, 1923, from the acting
President of the Council to the Polish and Lithuanian Governments re-
questing them to abstain from acts of
hostility. NNUN-W.

968. --- Dispute between Poland
and Lithuania; letter dated October
30th, 1920, from M. Hymans. Geneva,
1920. 1 leaf. Official no.: 20-4-
340. Issued also in French. Note to
the Secretary-General quoting letter
from the Polish Minister at Brussels
expressing approval of the proposed
plebiscite in Vilna.
NNUN-W.

969. LEAGUE OF NATIONS. SECRETA-
RY-GENERAL, 1919-1933 (Earl of Perth)
The dispute between Poland and Lithuania; memorandum by the Secretary-General. Geneva, 1920. 5 leaves.
Official no.: 20-4-353. Includes
correspondence between the Council
Committee and the governments of Poland and Lithuania relating to a plebiscite in the Vilna region and plans
for an international force to ensure
a fair expression of opinion.
NNUN-W.

970. --- Exchange of telegrams
between the Lithuanian Government
and the Secretary-General. Geneva,
1927. 4 leaves. Official no.:
C.531.M.192.1927.VII. Contains telegrams from the Secretary-General to
the Lithuanian Prime Minister and
his replies refering to the expulsion
of Polish nationals into Lithuanian
territory (Off.no.:C.528.M.192.1927.
VII.) NNUN-W.

971. LITHUANIA. Dispute between
Lithuania and Poland. Letter from
the Lithuanian Government regarding
the resolution of the Council of February 3rd, 1923. Geneva, 1923. 10
leaves. Caption title. At head of
title: League of Nations. Official.
n.: C.218.M.125.1923.VII. Refers to
Lithuania's refusal to accept the

Council's resolution of Feb.3,1923 in
regard to the line of demarcation and
its request that the matter be sub-
mitted to the Permanent Court of International Justice (official no.:
C.161.M.85.1923.VII.)
NNUN-W.

972. LITHUANIA. MINISTRAS PIRMI-
NINKAS. Dispute between Lithuania
and Poland. Geneva, 1923. 3 leaves
Caption title. At head of title:
League of Nations. Official no.: C.
324.M.153.1923.VII. Leter, dated
Apr. 19, 1923, from the Lithuanian
Prime Minister concerning inaccura-
cies in the League's historical summary of question of the neutral zo-
nes between Poland and Lithuania (official no.: C.219.M.126.1923.VII.)
NNUN-W

973. --- Dispute between Poland
and Lithuania. Geneva, 1922. 5 leaves. Caption title. Official no.:
C.16.M.3.1922.VII. Declaration by
the Lithuanian Prime Minister before
the Constitutional Asembly, Dec.17,
1921, protesting against the election
at Vilna. NNUN-W.

974. --- Polish-Lithuanian dispute. Elections in the Vilna district.
Geneva, 1922. 2 leaves. Caption
title. At head of title: League of
Nations. Official no.: C.719.M.431.
1922.Vii. Letter dated Oct. 7, 1922,
from the Lithuanian Prime Minister
protesting against Poland's organized
elections of Vilna district.
NNUN-W.

975. --- Telegram from the Lithuanian Government. Geneva, 1927.
1 leaf. At head of title: League of
Nations. Official no.: C.528.M.192.
1927.VII. Telegram from the Lithuanian Prime Minister, concerning Poland's expulsion of undesirable Polish national into Lithuanian territory. Issued also in French.
NNUN-W.

976. LITHUANIA. UŽSIENIŲ REIKALŲ
MINISTERIJA. Différend entre la Lithuanie et la Pologne; lettre, en date du 13 septembre 1920, émanant du
chargé d'affaires de Lithuanie à Lon-
dres. Dispute between Lithuania and
Poland; letter, dated 13th September
1920 from the Lithuanian Chargé d'Affaires in London. [Londres, 1920]
[3] leaves. At head of title: Société des Nations. Official no.:20-4-
254. Appointment of Professor Voldemaras Lithuanian representative at
the forthcoming Council meeting to
discuss the Polish-Lithuanian conflict. NNUN-W.

978. --- Dispute between Lithuania and Poland. Provisional line of demarcation in the neutral zone. Geneva, 1923. 1 leaf. At head of title: League of Nations. Official no.: C.165.M.89.1923.VII. Telegram, dated Feb.18, 1923, from the Lithuanian Foreign Minister, protesting against Polish occupation of the neutral zone. NNUN-W.

979. --- --- Provisional line of demarcation in the neutral zone. Geneva, 1923. 1 leaf. At heat of title; League of Nationa. Official no.: C.175.M99.1922. [i.e.1923]VII. Telegram, dated Feb.23, 1923, from the Lithuanian Minister of Foreign Affairs protesting against the Polish advance beyond the line of demarcation. NNUN-W.

980. --- The dispute between Poland and Lithuania; communication dated 7th October, 1920, from the Lithuanian Charge d'Affaires in London. London, 1920. 1 leaf. At head of title: League of Nations. Official no.: 20-4-294. Issued also in French. Offer to submit to League arbitration. NNUN-W.

981. --- Enlargement of the Council. Letter from the Lithuanian Government. Geneva, 1926. 3 leaves. Caption title. At head of title: League of Nations. Official no.: C.182.1926. Disputes Poland's rights to admission to the Council. NNUN-W.

982. --- Polish-Lithuanian dispute. Polish prisoners detained in Lithuania. Geneva, 1922. 3 leaves. Caption title. At head of title: League of Nations. Official no.: C.192.M.106.1922.VII. Leter, dated Mar.20, 1922, from the Lithuanian Minister of Foreign affairs concerning health conditions of the Polish political prisoners at Kowno. NNUN-W.

983. LITHUANIE ET RUTHENIE BLANCHE. Varsovie, 1919. [Nendeln, Kraus Reprint, 1973] 42 p. (Seeds of conflict. Series I: Irredentist and nationalist questions in Central Europe, 1913-1939. Lithuania, no.7) Pages also numbered 172-211. NIC.

984. MES BE VILNIAUS NENURIMSIM! Lietuvos visuomene ir Vilnius. [We will never give up Vilnius...] Kaunas, Vilniui vaduoti S-ga, 1928. 52 p. Protestu telegramu rinkinys pries derybas su lenkais Karaliauciuje. L970.31.Že ICLJF; CaOONL.

985. TRECIOKAS, Albin R.V. The Polish-Lithuanian Vilna dispute before the League of Nations. New York, N.Y., 1950. iv, 169 leaves. Master thesis--Rutgers University, 1950. iv, 169 leaves. DK511.L27T7 OKentU.

986. VILNA. Le différand entre la Lithuanie at la Pologne... télégramme du Conseil municipal de Wilno à la Société des Nations. Genève, 1921. [3] leaves. Caption title. At head of title: Société des Nations. Official no.: 21-68-88. Petition stating that the town of Vilna with surrounding districts is in favor of incorporation with the Polish State. NNUN-W.

VII.7.e.3. DISCRIMINATION AGAINST LITHUANIAN RIGHTS IN THE VILNIUS REGION

987. ASTIKAS, Balys. Kruvinos tragedijos lenkams viešpataujant. [Bloodshed in the district of Vilnius during the Polish hegemony] Kaunas, Vilniaus L.J. Sąjungos Ąžuolas leidinys, 1934. [Xerox copy, 1977] 80 p. PG8721.A79L7 1934a PU.

988. ČESNULIS, Petras. Nužemintieji; vilniečiu Golgota lenku okupacijoje. [The dehumanized; the Golgotha for Lithuanians under the Polish occupation of Vilnius. Hamilton, Pnt.] Vilniaus krašto lietuviu sajungos leidinys, 1973. 250 p. DK651.V4C45 DLC; MB.

989. LITHUANIA. MINISTRAS PIRMININKAS. Lithuanian schools in the territory of Vilnius and in the district of PUNSK-Sejny... Letter from the Lithuanian Prime Minister to the Secretary General. Geneva, 1923. 1 leaf, 2-3 numb. leaves. At head of title: League of Nations. Official no.: C.779.1923.I. Mimeographed. NNUN-W.

990. THE OUTRAGE OF VILNIUS; the latest developments in the Polish-Lithuanian dispute. [Kaunas] Association for the Liberation of Vilnius [193-] 8 p. DK651.V4O8 PU.

991. POLAND. Minorities in Poland. Lithuanian schools in the territory of Vilna and the district of Punsk-Sejny. Geneva, 1924. 1 leaf, 7 num. leaves. Official no.: C.275.1924.I. Mimeographed. NNUN-W.

992. VOZKA, Jaroslaw. Polen, das

Gefängnis der Völker. Eine Übersetzung aus dem Tschechischen; mit einer Einführung von Georg Cleinow.
Berlin, Volk und Reich Verlag, 1933.
104 p.   DK415.V62 DLC.

VII.7.f. FOREIGN RELATIONS WITH RUSSIA

993. GUDELIS, Petras. Bolševikų
valdžios atsiradimas Lietuvoje 1918-
1919 metais jų pačių dokumentų šviesoje. Su Z. Ivinskio įvadu. [The
establishment of bolshevik government in Lithuania, 1918-1919 according to their documents] Londonas,
1972. 160 p. port. At head of title: Lietuvių veteranų sąjunga Ramovė. P. Gudelis. Summary in English
and German. Bibliography; p. 112.
DK511.L26G82 DLC; CaAEU.

994. HISTORY OF SOVIET FOREIGN
policy, 1917-1945; Russian text edi-
ted by B. Pomarev, A. Gromyko [and]
V. Khvostov. [Translated by David
Skvirsky] Moscow, Progress Publishrs
[1969] 497 p. DK266.I7713 DLC; CU;
CaBVaU; CaOTP; CaQMM; CtY; CU-SB;CtW;
CSt; CoDMSC; CU-SC; CaAEU; IEN; InNd;
INS; ICU; IaU; IU; KU; LU-NO; MH; MU;
MnU; MdBJ; NNC; NSyU; NmU; NcU; NjR;
OkU; OU; OrU; OrPS; RPB; TxHR; TxU;
TU; ViU; FTaSU.

995. HUNCZAK, Taras. Russian im-
perialism from Ivan the Great to the
Revolution. Introduction by Hans
Kohn. New Brunswick, N.J., Rutgers
University Press, [1974] 396 p. maps.
DK43.H86 DLC; CaBVaU; CtY; DS; FMU;
LN; MB; NcU; NBuU; OOxM; TU; Wa.
AAP; AzU; AkU; CoFS; CaOTP; CoU; F;
FU; GU; GAT; KyU; KU; IU; IEN; IaU;
MiEM; MiU; MoSW; MoWgW; MoU; MnU; MU;
N; NNC; NBuC; NNCoCi; NSyU; NjP; NjR;
NbU NRU; NcGU; NcRS; NcD; NWM; NvU;
OKentU; OCU; OU; OkU; OO; UU; ViU;
VtU; ViBlbV; TNJ; WaU.

996. JANULAITIS, Augustinas. Lietuva ir dabartinė Rusija: kas tai yra
dabartinė Rusija, kas ir kaip ją val-
do, ir ką Lietuva iš jos iki šiol tu-
rėjo ir ko gali laukti. [Lithuania
and contemporaru Russia... By] A.Ja-
nulaitis. Kaunas, A.Janulaitis,1925.
[Xerox copy, 1976] 45 p.
DK511.L27J28 1925a PU.

997. JURGĖLA, Constantine Rudyard.
Lithuania: outpost of freedom. [s.l.,
National Guard of Lithuania in Exile,
c1976] 387 p. illus. Bibliography:
p. 355-359. DK511.L27J78 DLC; PU.

998. KASLAS, Bronis. Sovietinės

Rusijos užsienio politika; Lietuvos-
SSRS 1926 metų nepuolimo sutarties
50 metų sukakties proga. [The foreign
policy of Soviet Russia and the non-
aggression treaty between Soviet U-
nion and Lithuania...] In Varpas (
Brooklyn, N.Y.), no.14, 1976, p.11-
20. See serials consulted.

999. ---, comp. The USSR-German
agression against Lithuania. Edited
with foreword and introd. by Bronis
J. Kaslas. New York, N.Y., R. Spel-
ler, 1973. 543 p. illus.
DK511.L27K35 DLC; AKU; CaAEU; CaBVaU
CSt-H; CaOTP; CLSU; FU; GU; IEN; InU;
IU; MB; MH; MiU; MnU; MiEM; MU; NNC;
NcD; NcU; NSyU; NmU; MnU; NmU; NbU;
NBuC; NjP; NvU; OCl; OkU; OU; PSt;
RPB; TNJ; TU; UU; ViU; VtU; WU;WaU.

1000. PAYNE, Pierre Stephen Robert.
and ROMANOF, Nikita. Ivan the Terri-
ble. New York, N.Y., T.Y.Crowell,
1975. viii, 502 p.
DK106.P39 1975 DLC; CaAEU.

1001. ZUTIS, J. K voprosu o litovskoĭ politike Ivana IV. In Akademiia nauk SSSR. Izvĭestiĭa. Seriĭa
istorii i filosofii, t.9, nr.2, 1952,
p. 133-144. See serials consulted.

VII.7.g. FOREIGN RELATIONS WITH OTHER COUNTRIES

1002. IVINSKIS, Zenonas. Lietuvos
ir Apaštalų Sosto santykiai amžių bėgyje (iki XVIII amžiaus galo). [The
relations between Lithuania and the
Holy See through the Ages] In LKMASD
v.4, p. 117-152. See serials consulted.

1003. KAROSAS, Viktoras. Lietuvos
ryšys su Amerika; istorinė apybraiža;
an historical sketch dedicated to the
bicentennial of the American revolution. Chicago, Ill., Devenių kultūri-
hio fondo leidinys, 1977. 176 p.
DK511.L2K32 PU.

1004. POLONS'KA-VASYLENKO, Nataliĭa
Dmytrivna. Les relations de l'Ukraine avec les États européens aux Xe -
XIIIe siècles. Paris, Éditions de
l'Est européen, 1867. 40 p. (Études
historiques et politiques)
DK508.56.P614 DLC; MU; NIC.

VII.8. TREATIES

VII.8.a. PERSONAL AND LUBLIN UNIONS THEIR HISTORY AND COMMENTA- RIES

1005. HALECKI, Oskar. Zagadnienie kulturalne w dziejach Unii Jagiellońskiej. In Przegląd Historyczny (Warszawa), t.26, 1926-1927, p. 396-408. See serials consulted.

1006. JAKŠTAS, Juozas. Liublino nijos vieta Lietuvos istorijoje.[The Union of Liublin; its place in Lithuanian history] In Lietuvių Tautos Praeitis (Chicago, Ill.), kn.1, v.3, p. 9-36. Summary in English. See serials consulted.

1007. SRUOGIENĖ, Vanda (Daugirdaitė) Liublino Unija. [The Lublin Union] In Tėvynės Sargas (New York, N.Y.), no.1, 1969, p. 81-92. See serials consulted.

VII.8.b. OTHER TREATIES

1008. DAINAUSKAS, Jonas. Kriavo akto autentiškumas. The authenticy of the Kriavas [Krewo] "Act". In Institute of Lithuanian Studies. Lituanistikos instituto 1975 metų suvažiavimo darbai. Chicago, Ill.1976. p. 51-70. Summary in English. DK511.L2I64 1975 CaAEU; PU.

1009. LITHUANIA. In Royal Institute of International affairs. Documents on international affairs. London, 1951. v.1, p. 157-159, 163-164. D411.R88D 1928 CaAEU; see also serials consulted.

1010. SIEW, Liebermann. Der Auslieferungsvertrag zwischen Litauen und den Vereinigten Staaten von America vom 9. April, 1924; ein Beitrag zum positiven Auslieferungsrecht. Berlin, W. Schulz, 1932. 176,[7] p. Inaug.-Diss.--University of Freiburg. Bibliography: p.[177-180] JX4311.S5416 DLC.

1011. WEISE, E[rich] Zur Kritik des Vertrages zwischen dem Preussischen Bund und dem König von Polen vom 6 März, 1454. In Altpreussische Forschungen (Königsberg in Pr.),v.18, 1941, p. 231-261. See serials consulted.

1012. WÓJCIK, Zbigniew. Między traktatem andruszowskim a wojną turecką; stosunki polsko-rosyjskie, 1667-1672. Warszawa, Państwowe Wydawn. Naukowe, 1968. 324 p. Summary in English. DK418.5.R9W6 DLC; CaBVaU; CaQMM; CLU; CtY; CSt; CU; IU; InU; ICU; InNd; KU; MiU; MH; NN;NjP; NBuC; NSyU; OU; WU; WaU; PU.

1013. WÓJCIK, Zbigniew. Traktat

Andruszowski 1667 roku i jego geneza. Warszawa, Państwowe Wydawn. Naukowe, 1959. 279 p. Summary in English. DK120.W6 DLC; CaBVaU; CtY;CU CSt; CoU; FMU; InU; IU; KU; MH; MiU; MiD; MH-L; NN; NNC; NIC; NjP; PPiU; PU; ViU; WU; WaU.

VII.9. THE STATE OF SOVIET LITHUANIA

VII.9.a. GENERAL WORKS

1014. GRIGAITIS, Alfonsas. Deputatas atėjo į sesiją. [An elected representative came to the session] Vilnius, Mintis, 1967. 18 p. (Deputato bibliotekėlė) JN6745.A75G7 DLC.

1015. MARGERIS, Algirdas. 150 [Šimtas penkiasdešimt] Tarybų Lietuvoje. [150 Soviets in Lithuania] Čikaga, Amerikos Lietuvių literatūros draugija, 1961. 384 p. (Its leidinys, 70) DK511.L2M3 OKentU.

VII.9.b. SOVIET CONSTITUTIONS AND THEIR COMMENTARIES

1016. KONSTITUTSIIA (osnovnoĭ zakon) SSSR. Konstitutsii (osnovnye zakony) Soĭuznykh Sovetskikh Sotsialisticheskikh Respublik. Moskva,Gos. izd-vo īurid. lit-ry, 1951. 487 p. Partial contents.--[v.] 9. Lithuanian S.S.R. Constitution. JN6515.1951A5 MWalB; DLC; NN(1954 ed.)

1017. LITHUANIAN S.S.R. CONSTITUTION. Konstitutsiia (osnovnoĭ zakon) Litovskoĭ Sovetskoĭ Sotsialisticheskoĭ Respubliki. S izmeneniami i dopolneniami, priniatymi Verkhovnym Sovetom Litovskoĭ SSR do 8. sessii chetvertogo sozyva vkliuchitel'no. Vil'nius, Gos. izd-vo polit. i nauch. lit-ry, 1958. 26 p. WU.

1018. --- Lietuvos Tarybų Socialistinės Respublikos Konstitucija (pagrindinis įstatymas) su Lietuvos TSR Aukščiausiosios Tarybos priimtais pakeitimais ir papildymais iki 8. šaukimo 8 sesijos imtinai. [Constitution of the Lithuanian SSR...] Vilnius, Mintis, 1975. 23 p. DLC-L

1019. --- Tarybų Socialistinių Respublikų Sąjungos Konstitucija (pagrindinis įstatymas). Su septintojo šaukimo RSRS Aukščiausiosios Tarybos

VII sesijoje priimtais pakeitimais ir papildymais. [Constitution of the Lithuanian SSR...] Vilnius, Mintis, 1970. 28 p.   DLC-L.

1020. RUSSIA (1923- U.S.S.R.) CONSTITUTION. LITHUANIAN. Tarybų Socialistinių Respublikų Sąjungos Konstitucija (pagrindinis įstatymas) Su septintojo šaukimo TSRS Aukščiausiosios Tarybos VII sesijoje priimtais pakeitimais ir papildymais. [Constitution of the USSR...] Vilnus, Mintis, 1970. 28 p.   DLC.

VII.9.c. SOVIET EXECUTIVE GOVERNMENT AND ADMINISTRATION

1021. LIETUVOS TSR ADMINISTRACInio-teritorinio suskirstymo žinynas. Parengė Zigmuntas Noreika ir Vincentas Stravinskas. [A handbook of territorial and administrative subdivision of the Lithuanian SSR] Vilnius, Mintis, 1974-1976. 2 v. JS6130.5.A12L49 PU; DLC.

VII.9.d. LEGISLATION AND PARLIAMENTARY RECORDS

1022. BIKELIS, Povilas. Lietuvos TSR Aukščiausioji taryba. [The Supreme Soviet of Lithuanian SSR] Vilnius, Mintis, 1976. 62 p. JN6745.A78B5 PU.

VII.9.f. SOVIET LITHUANIAN LAWS, STATUTES, ETC., AND LEGAL COMMENTARIES

1023. ANIČAS, Jonas and RIMAITIS, Juozas. Tarybiniai įstatymai apie religinius kultus ir sąžinės laisvę. [Soviet laws on religion and freedom of conscience] Vilnius, Mokslas, 1970. 79 p. BR936.A6 PU.

1024. JANKAUSKIENĖ, Valerija. Darbininkams ir tarnautojams apie darbo įstatymus. [About the Labor laws for the workers and civil servants] Vilnius, Mintis, 1971. 264 p. At head of title: V. Jankauskienė, L. Davimas. DLC

1025. LIETUVOS TSR BAUDŽIAMOJO KOdekso komentaras. [A commentary on the Soviet Lithuanian criminal procedure code. M. Apanavičius et al.] Vilnius, Mintis 1974. 422 p. DLC

1026. LIETUVOS TSR BAUDŽIAMOJO proceso kodekso komentaras. [Commentary on the code of criminal procedure in Soviet Lithuania. Ats. redaktorius M. Kazlauskas] Vilnius, Mintis, 1976. 409 p. K.L7115 PU; DLC-L.

1027. LIETUVOS TSR CIVILINIO KOdekso komentaras. [Commentary on the civil code of Soviet Lithuania. Atsakingi redaktoriai: J. Žeruolis, M. Čapskis] Vilnius, Mintis, 1976. 421 p. K.L711 PU.

1028. LIETUVOS TSR VALSTYBĖS IR teisės istorijos klausimai. [The questions of the Soviet Lithuanian State and laws] [Ats. redaktorius J. Bulavas] Vilnius, Valstybinė politinės ir mokslinės literatūros leidykla, 1960. 176 p. (Lietuvos TSR Mokslų akademija. Ekonomikos instituto darbai, t.9) DLC.

1029. LITHUANIA. LAWS, STATUTES, ETC. Lietuvos tarybų valdžios dekretai, 1918-1919; dokumentų rinkinys. [Soviet laws in Lithuania, 1918-1919; a collection of documents. Ats. redaktorius B. Vaitkevičius] Vilnius, Mintis, 1977. 166 p. DK511.L26L55 PU.

1030. LITHUANIAN S.S.R. Laws, statutes, etc. Grazhdanskiĭ kodeks Litovskoĭ Sovetskoĭ Sotsialisticheskoĭ Respubliki; ofits. tekst s izm. i dop. na 1.XII.1972 g. i s pril. postateĭno-sistematizir. materialov. Vil'niŭs, Mintis, 1973.   622 p. At head of title: Ministerstvo ĭustitsiĭ Litovskoĭ SSR. DLC

1031. --- Lietuvos Tarybų Socialistinės Respublikos Baudžiamasis kodeksas. Oficialus tekstas su pakeitimais ir papildymais 1970 m. birželio 15 d. ir su pastraipsniui susistemintos medžiagos priedu. [Soviet Lithuanian code of criminal law]. Vilnius, Mintis, 1970. 435 p. At head of title: Juridinė komisija prie Lietuvos TSR Ministrų Taryboa. DLC.

1032. --- Lietuvos Tarybų Socialistinės Respublikos Darbo įstatymų kodeksas. [Soviet Lithuanian Labour laws] Vilnius, Mintis, 1973. 150 p. At head of title: Lietuvos TSR teisingumo Ministerija. DLC.

1033. --- Lietuvos Tarybų Socialistinės Respublikos Pataisos darbų kodeksas. [The laws of Correctional

Institutions of Soviet Lithuania.]
Vilnius, Mintis, 1972. 120 p. At
head of title: Lietuvos TSR Teisingumo Ministerija.
DLC.

1034. --- Lietuvos Tarybų Socialistinės Respublikos Žemės kodeksas.
[Soviet Lithuanian land tenure law]
Vilnius, Mintis, 1971. 123 p. At
head of title: Lietuvos TSR Teisingumo Ministerija.
DLC.

1035. --- Postoíannyĭ alfavitno-
predmetnyĭ ukazatel' deĭstvuíushchikh
normatyvnykh zakonodatel'nykh aktov
Litovskoĭ SSR. Vil'niūs, Izd-vo Pre-
zidiuma Verkhovnogo Soveta Litovskoĭ
SSR, 1971. 231 p.
DLC.

1036. --- Rinkimų į Lietuvos TSR
rajonų, miestų apylinkių ir gyvenvie-
čių darbo žmonių deputatų tarybos
nuostatai, patvirtinti... 1950 m.
spalio 7 d. įsaku su pakeitimais...
ir 1963 m. sausio 8 d. įsakais. [Elec-
tio by-laws of representatives to the
Lithuanian local government] Vilnius,
Laikraščių ir žurnalų leidykla, 1963.
29 p. Law Lib. DLC; MH.

1037. --- Ugolovno-protsesual'nyĭ
kodeks Litovskoĭ Sovetskoĭ Sotsialisticheskoĭ Respubliki. Ofits. tekst
s izm. i dop. na 1.III.1972 g. i s
pril. postateĭno-sistematizir. materialov. Vil'niūs, Mintis, 1972.
562 p. At head of title: Minister-
tvo íustitsiĭ Litovskoĭ SSR.
JN6599.L3L76 1972 CaAEU; DLC.

1038. --- Ugolovnyĭ kodeks Litovskoĭ Sovetskoĭ Sotsialisticheskoĭ Respubliki. Ofits. tekst s izmeneniĭa-
mi i dop. na 10 maĭa 1971 g. i s pri-
lozheniem postateĭno-sistematiziro-
vannykh materialov. Vil'niūs, Izd.
Mintis, 1971. 538 p. At head of title: Ministerstvo íustitsiĭ Litovskoĭ SSR.
JN6599.L3L77 1971 CaAEU; CL; ICU; NcD.

1039. --- Vodnyĭ kodeks Litovskoĭ Sovetskoĭ Sotsialisticheskoĭ Respubliki. Vil'niūs, Mintis, 1973.
109 p. At head of title: Minister-
tvo íustitsiĭ Litovskoĭ SSR.
DLC.

1040. --- Zakon Litovskoĭ Sovetskoĭ Sotsialisticheskoĭ Respubliki o
raĭonnom Sovete deputatov trudíash-
chikhsíā Litovskoĭ SSR. Vil'niūs,
Mintis, 1972. 54 p.
NNC-L.

1041. --- Zemel'nyĭ kodeks Litovskoĭ Sovetskoĭ Sotsialisticheskoĭ Res-

publiki. Vil'niūs, 1971. 143 p.
At head of title: Ministerstvo íusti-
tsii Litovskoĭ SSR.
HD1165.L7L77 1971 CaAEU; CSt-H; CtY-L
DLC; DS; ICU; InU; IU; MH-L; MdU;MB;
NIC; NcD; NjP; PPiU.

1042. MARCIJONAS, A. Teisinė gamtos apsauga Lietuvos TSR. [Laws on
the protection of nature in the Lithuanian SSR] Vilnius, 1969. 70 p. At
head of title: Lietuvos TSR Aukštojo
ir specialiojo vidurinio mokslo ministerija. DLC.

1043. TARYBINĖ BAUDŽIAMOJI TEISĖ.
Bendroji dalis. [Soviet Lithuanian
criminal law. General part. Paruošė
A. Klimka, M. Apanavičius, J. Misiūnas; redagavo J. Žvirblis] Leista
naudoti vadovėliu aukštosioms teisės
mokykloms. Vilnius, Mintis, 1972.
474 p. K.T179 PU.

1044. TARYBINĖS VALSTYBĖS IR TEI-
sės pagrindai. [The foundations of
the Soviet State and law] Paruošė
K. Domaševičius et al. Vilnius, Mintis, 1967. 417 p.
JN6515 1967.T35 DLC.

VII.9.g. SOVIET LITHUANIAN FOREIGN RELATIONS

1045. BILINSKY, Yaroslav. The
background of contemporary politics
in the Baltic Republics and the Ukraine. In Conference on Baltic Studies,
3d, University of Toronto, 1972. Problems of mininations. San Jose, CA.,
1973. p. 89-122. HC243.C65 1972 DLC
CaBVaU; CaAEU; CSt; CtY; CU; GAT; IU;
ICIU; InU; ICarbS; InNd; MB; MH; MiU;
NN; NNC; NBuC; NjP; NmU; OkU; RPB;UU;
WU; WaU.

1046. POŽARSKAS, Mykolas. Lietuvos TSR bendradarbiavimas su socia-
listinėmis šalimis. [Collaboration of
Soviet Lithuania with Socialist coun-
tries] Vilnius, Mintis, 1976. 165 p.
DK511.L274P67 PU.

1047. --- Tarybų Lietuvos ir Lenkijos santykiai. [The relations between Soviet Lithuania and Socialist
Poland] Vilnius, Gintaras, 1973.
103 p., 14 leaves of illus.
DK511.L27P62 DLC.

VII.10. INTERNATIONAL LAW AND THE STATUS OF LITHUANIA

1048. PETKEVIČUS, Justinas. Die
völkerrechtliche Bedeutung der ersten

Besetzung Litauens durch die Sowjet-Union. Tübingen, 1948. 91 leaves. Thesis--University of Tübingen, 1949. Typescript. Ger.TU.

1049. PUSTA, Kaarel Robert. La statut juridique de la Mer Baltique a partir du XIX-e siècle. In Hague. Academy of International Law. Recueil des cours, v.52, 1936, p. 105-190. JX74.H3 DLC; see also serials consulted.

VIII. SOCIETY, SOCIAL STRUCTURE AND CONDITIONS

VIII.1. GENERAL STUDIES

1050. BAUER, Gerhard. Gesellschaft und Weltbild im baltischen Tradition milieu. Eine soziologisch-volkskundliche Untersuchung über die Gesellschaft und Mythologie bei den baltischen Voelkern, dargestellt anhand historischer und volkskundlicher Quellen. Heidelberg, 1972. iv,267 p. facsim. Inaug.-Diss.--Ruprecht-Karl-Universität zu Heidelberg. Bibliography: p. 239-265. NIC.

1051. DIRVELĖ, Eugenijus. Klasių kova Lietuvoje 1926 metais. [Class struggle in Lithuania, 1926] Vilnius, Valstybinė politinės ir mokslinės literatūros leidykla, 1961. 193 p. facsims. DK511.L27D5 DLC.

1052. JAKAS, Povilas. Socialinė krikščionybė. [Christianity and the social conscience. Kaunas] Akiratis, [1939.] [Xerox copy, 1977] 245 p. BT738.J3 1939a PU.

1053. KRUPAVIČIUS, Mykolas. Kunigas dvidešimtojo amžiaus visuomenėje. [A priest in the twentieth century society] Kaunas, "Šviesos" spaustuvė, 1920. [Xerox copy, 1977] 51 p. BX1912.K75 1920a PU.

1054. LIETUVOS PUBLICISTAI VALStiečių klausimu XVI a. pabaigoje-XVIII a antroje pusėje. [Lithuanian authors on the plight of the peasants in the 16th-18th centuries] Spaudai parengė Ingė Lukšaitė. Vilnius, Lietuvos TSR Mokslų akademija, 1977. HD725.7.L52 PU.

1055. MORKŪNAS, Vitalis. Nuo tamsos ligi tamsos; žemės ūkio darbinkų buitis Lietuvoje 1919-1940 m. [From dawn to dusk; the mode of life of the farm hand in Lithuania,1919-1940] Vilnius, Mokslas, 1977. 200 p.

HD1536.L5M6 PU

1056. PALTAROKAS, Kazimieras. Visuomeninis kunigo veikimas. [The activity of the priest in society] Kaune, Petronio knygynas, 1921. 96 p. HN37.C3P3 PU.

1057. RAKŪNAS, Algirdas. Klasių kova Lietuvoje 1940-1951 metais. [Class struggle in Lithuania, 1940-1950] Vilnius, Mokslas, 1976. 214 p. DK511.L27R3 PU.

VIII.2. FAMILY, MARRIAGE, AND CHILDREN

1058. ARNAŠIUS, Stasys. Motinos širdis. [Mother's heart]. Vilnius, Valstybinė politinės ir mokslinės literatūros leidykla, 1961. 85 p.ports. D802.L5A7 DLC.

1059. JAUNYSTĖ APMĄSTO GYVENIMĄ. [The youth meditate about life] Vilnius, Mintis, 1965. 138 p. HQ799.R92L53 DLC.

1060. KRIAUZA, Alb[inas] Vaikai ir jų auginimas Kupiškio apylinkėje. [Children and their upbringing in the district of Kupiškis] In Gimtasai Kraštas(Šiauliai), no.31, 1943, p. 203-235. Mr. Kviklys, Chicago, has this no.

1061. LIETUVOS VAIKAI. [Children of Lithuania] [Tekstas K. Kubilinsko, dailininkas V. Jankauskas] Vilnius, Valstybinė grožinės literatūros leidykla, 1957. [144] p. (chiefly illus) *QY--NN; CtPAM.

1062. LITHUANIAN S.S.R. CENTRINĖ STATISTIKOS VALDYBA. Zhenshchiny Litovskoĭ SSR; kratkiĭ stat. sbornik. Vil'nius, TSSU LitSSR, 1975. 113 p., 4 leaves of plates. illus. At head of title: TSSU pri Sovete Ministrov LitSSR. HQ1665.65.L56 1975 DLC.

1063. THE LITHUANIAN WOMAN. [Editor Birutė Novickis. Brookly, N.Y., Federation of Lithuanian Women's Clubs, 1968] 197 p. illus., maps, ports. HQ1665.65.L58 DLC; GU; MB; MtU; OKentU.

1064. PEČKAUSKAITĖ, Marija. Motina-auklėtoja. [Mother, the educator] [Kaunas], "Žinijos" leidinys, [1926], [Xerox copy, 1977] xvi, 176 p. LB1037.P4 1926a PU(xerox) OKentU(orig.)

1065. PETKEVIČAITĖ, Gabrielė. Apie moterų klausimą. [Women and women's

lib]. Vilniuje, M. Kukta, 1910.
15 p. Cover title.
NN.

1066. WINLOW, Anna C. Our lit-
tle Lithuanian cousin... with an introduction by Clara Vostrovsky Winlow; illustrated by John M. Foster.
Boston, L.C. Page & Co., [1926]
viii, 122 p. col. front., illus.,
plates. PZ9.W7280u DLC; MB; OCl.

VIII.3. NOBILITY, THEIR ORIGIN AND
PRIVILEGES

1067. BEMMANN, Rudolf. Die litauischen Adelsbauern und Adelsdör-
fer. In Odal; Monatschrift für Blut
und Boden (Berlin), no.1, v.11, 1942,
p. 23-29. See serials consulted.

1068. BYCHKOVA, Margarita E. Per-
vye rodoslovnye rospisi litovskikh
kniazei v Rossii. In Obshchestvo i
gosudarstvo feodal'noĭ Rossii. Sbornik stateĭ posviash. 70-letiĭu akad.
L.V. Cherepina. Moskva, 1975. p.
133-140. HN523.027 DLC.

1068a. HALECKI, Oskar. Kwestye
sporne w sprawie początków szlachty
litewskiej. In Kwartalnik Historyczny (Lwów), t.30, 1916, p. 62-72.
See serials consulted.

1069. KONARSKI, Szymon. Szlachta
kalwinska w Polsce. Z przedmową Sta-
nisława Kętrzyńskiego. Warszawa,
1936. xviii, 357 p. coats of arms.
CS874.K65 DLC; CtY; ICU; InU; MH.

1069a. LEONTOVICH, F[ëdor] I[va-
novich]. Pravosposobnost' litovsko-
russkoĭ shliakhty. In Russia. Ministerstvo Narodnogo prosveshcheniia.
Zhurnal. Novaia seriia, v.14, no.3,
March 1908, p. 53-87; v.15, no.5,
May 1908, p. 136-167; no.6, June
1908, p. 245-298; v.16, no.7, July
1908, p. 1-56; v.19, no.2, Feb. 1909,
p. 225-269; v.20. nr.3, March 1909,
p.44-88. L451.A55 DLC; ICU; NN.

1070. PIEKOSIŃSKI, F[ranciszek
Ksawery] O dynastycznem szlachty
polskiej pochodzeniu. Kraków,
Wydawn. Akademii Umiejętności, 1888.
292 p., illus. CS874.P48 DLC; CtY;
CSt; CaBVaU; MH.

1071. --- Rycerstwo polskie wie-
kow srednich. Krakow, Nakł. Akademii Umiejętnosci, 1896- . 2 v.
CR2062.P6 DLC; CtY; CDU; CU; KU; NN
NNC; PPAmP; WaU.

1072. SCHRAMM, G[ottfried, histo-
rian]. Der polnische Adel und Refor-
mation 1548-1607. Wiesbaden, Ger.,
F. Steiner, 1965. x, 380 p. (Ver-
öffentlichungen des Instituts für
Europäische Geschichte (Mainz), Bd.
36. Abt. Universalgeschichte) Bib-
liography: p. [330]-358.
DK429.S3 DLC; CtY-D; NN; OCU; PPULC;
PU; OrPS; ViU; WU; CSt; CLU; CBPac;
GU; InU; ICU; KU; KyWAT; LU; MH; MU;
MiEM; MiU; MH-AH; MiDW; MeB; MnU;
MoSW; NNC; NRU; NBuU; NcD; NcU; NjP;
NjR; NjPT; NhD; NNG; NIC; OKentU; OU
OrU; RPB; TxFTC; TxU; TNJ-R; TU; UU.

VII.4. PEASANTS, THEIR HISTORY AND
RELATIONS WITH OTHER GROUPS

1073. BALTIC PROVINCES. LAWS,
STATUTES, ETC. Sbornik uzakoneniĭ i
rasporiazheniĭ o krest'ianakh Pribaltiĭskikh guberniĭ. Sostavil i izdal
A.P. Vasilevskiĭ. Moskva, Univ.tip.,
189- . v.
DLC.

1074. BALTIC PROVINCES. LAWS,
STATUTES, ETC. Sbornik uzakoneniĭ o
krest'ianakh Pribaltiĭskikh guberniĭ.
Sostavil V.E. Reĭtern. S.-Peterburg,
Obshchestvennaia pol'za, 1898. 3 v.
DLC.

1075. DOVNAR-ZAPOL'SKII, Mitrofan
Viktorovich. Ocherki po organizatsii
zapadno-russkago krest'ianstva v XVI
viekie. Kiev, Kievskaia artel pe-
chatnago diela, 1905. 307, 167 p.
illus. HD715.D65 DLC.

1076. KATKUS, Mikalojus. Balanos
gadyne. [Age of the wooden torch]
Vilnius, Valstybine grožines literatūros leidykla, 1949. 235 p. illus.
DK511.L22K37 1949 DLC.

VIII.5. PEASANT MOVEMENTS AND
UPRISINGS

1077. JANULAITIS, Augustinas.
Valstiečių sukilimas XVIII amžiuje
Lietuvoje. [The insurrection of the
peasants in the eighteenth century in
Lithuania] Vilnius, 1910. 35 p.
947.5.J2 CtTMF.

1078. JUČAS, Mečislovas. Lietuvos
valstiečių judėjimas 1861-1914 metais.
[Peasant movement in Lithuania, 1861-
1914] Vilnius, Mokslas, 1975. 390 p.
At head of title: M. Jučas, L. Mulevičius, A. Tyla. HD725.7.J8 PU: DLC.

1079. LEONAVIČIUS, Juozas and MAK-
SIMAVIČIUS, J. Valstiečių streikas
Suvalkijoje ir Dzukijoje 1935 metais.
[Peasants' strike in Suvalkija and
Dzukija (Lithuania)]. Vilnius, Vals-
tybinė politinės ir mokslinės lite-
ratūros leidykla, 1958. 126 p. ill.
HD5397.6.A29L4 OKentU.

VIII.6. LAND TENURE

1080. MULEVIČIUS, L[eonas] Lais-
vųjų žmonių žemėvalda Lietuvoje XIX
amžiaus pabaigoje ir XX amžiaus pradžioje. 1882 m. birželio 3 d. įsta-
tymo dėl žemės išpirkimo įgyvendini-
mas. [The ownership of land by free
peasants toward the end of the 19th
and the beginning of the 20th centuries and the implementation of the
law of June 3, 1882 requiring payment
for the peasant-held land] In Lietuvos TSR Mokslų akademija, Vilna.
Darbai. Ser. A, no.1, 1963, p. 135-
164. See serials consulted.

VIII.7. SERFDOM AND SLAVERY

1081. AR DABAR YRA BAUDŽEVA.
[Do we still have slavery. Pagal len-
kišką sutaisė Parmazonas, pseud.
Adapted by S. Matulaitis from Czy
teraz niema pańszczyzny, by K.Krauz-
Kelles] Išleidė P[eterburgo] L[ie-
tuvių] S[tudentų] R[atelis] [Bitė-
nai, M. Jankaus spaust.] 1899.
[Xerox copy, 1975] 56 p.
HX315.65.A6A7 1975 PU.

1082. IVINSKIS, Zenonas. Ar Žemaičiuose Vytauto laikais buvo par-
davinėjami vergai. [Were the slaves
sold in Žemaitija (Samogitia) during
the rule of Vytautas.] In Athenaeum (Kaunas), v.1, 1931, p. 139-141.
ICCC; see also serials consulted.

1083. JUČAS, Mečislovas. Baudžiavos irimas Lietuvoje. [Disintegra-
tion of slavery in Lithuania] Vilnius, Mintis, 1972. 319 p. On verso of t.p.: Lietuvos TSR Mokslų akademijos Istorijos institutas. Bibliography: p. 308-[318]
HT807.J8 DLC; CtY; CU; ICU; InU; PU.

1084. --- Baudžiavos panaikinimas
Lietuvoje. [The abolition of serfdom
in Lithuania] In Lietuvos TSR Mokslų akademija, Vilna. Istorijos institutas. Lietuvos valstiečiai XIX
amžiuje. Vilnius, 1957. p. 83-104.
HD725.7.L5 DLC; CaAEU; CtPAM; CtY;
CU; NN; PU; PPULC.

VIII.8. LABOUR AND LABOURING CLASSES

1085. NEZABITAUSKIS, L[iudvikas]
Šeimyna ir jos būklė Žemaičiuose.
[Hired-hands and their living condi-
tions in Žemaitija (Samogitia)] In
Gimtasai Kraštas (Šiauliai), no.3-4
(7-8), 1935, p. 365-371.
ICWA; see also serials consulted.

VIII.10. ETHNIC GROUPS

1086. BLETER FUN YIDISH LITE.
Tel-Aviv, Farlag Ha-Menorah, 1974.
289 p. illus. Added t.p.: Lithuanian Jews. In English, Hebrew or
Yiddish. DS135.L5B55 DLC; MB.

1087. BLINDZ, Benjamin. Der goyrl
fun Yiddishn dokter in Lite. Tel-
Aviv, Ha-vutsoth 'yigod yivutsi Lite
Be-yisrael, 1974. 157 p. ports.
R534.A1B56 DLC.

1088. DWORZECKI, Mark. La victoi-
re du Ghetto. [Par] Marc Dvorjetski.
Traduit par Arnold Mandel. Paris,
Éditions France-Empire, 1973. 375 p.
Translation of Yerucholayim de-Lita
in kamp un umkum.
DS135.R93V5294 1973 DLC; MiU; NNJ;
NjP; OCH; PPT; TxU.

1089. FEDEROWSKI, Michał. Lud
białoruski na Rusi litewskiej; mate-
ryaly do etnografii słowiańskiej zgro-
madzone w latach 1877-1903. W Krakowie, Nakł. Akademii Umiejętności; skł.
gł. w Księg. Spólki Wydawniczej Polskiej, 1897-1903. 3 v. in 1. At
head of title: Wydawnictwo Komisyi
Antropologicznej Akademii Umiejętności w Krakowie. DK34.W5F4 DLC.

1090. GOLDHAGEN, Erich. Ethnic mi-
norities in the Soviet Union. New
York, N.Y., F.A. Praeger, 1968.
DK33.G62 DLC; AAP; AU; CaAEU; CaBVaU;
CaOTP; CLSU; CLU; CSt; CSt-H; CtY;CU;
CU-AL; CoU; CoGrS; DAU; DS; FMU; FU;
FTaSU; GU; ICU; ICJS; IaU; InU; IU;
KMK; KyU; KU; MB; MH; MeB; MiU; MnU;
MoU; MoSW; MU; N; NN; NNC; NIC; NSyU;
NBuU NcD; NcU; NcGU; NcRS; NRU; NjP;
NjR; NbU; OkU; OCU; OU; OrU; OrCS;
OrPS; OWorP; PPULC; RPB; ScU; TxU;TU;
TNJ; UU; ViU; Wa; WaU.

1091. IVINSKIS, Zenonas. Lietuva
ir žydai istorijos šviesoje. [Lithua-
nia and Jews; a historical sketch]
In Aidai (Brooklyn, N.Y.), no.10,1971,
p. 438-446; no.1-2, 1972, p. 24-30.
See serials consulted.

1092. KOESTLER, Arthur. The thirteenth tribe; the Khazar Empire and its heritage. New York, N.Y., Random House, c1976. 255 p. map. DK34.K45K59 1976 DLC; CaAEU.

1093. KRUK, Herman. Togbukh fun Vilner geto. Diary of Vilna Ghetto. Notes and explanations by Mordecai W. Bernstein. New York, N.Y., 1961. xiv, 620 p. ports., facsims. Summary in English.
D811.5.K75 DLC; CLU; CBM; CU; MB; MH; NN; NjR; OU; TxU.

1094. LEAGUE OF NATIONS. COUNCIL. Minorités en Lithuanie. Situation de la minorité polonaise en Lithuanie... Minorities in Lithuania. Situation of the Polish minority in Lithuania. Geneve, 1925. 24 p. Official no.: C.31.1925.I. "Communiqué aux membres du Conseil". Issued also in the League's Official journal, 1925, p. 581. Note of the British, Czekoslovak and Spanish representatives of the Council of the League, accompanied by the Lithuanian government's reply.
NNUN-W.

1095. LEVIN, Dov. Die Beteiligung der litauischen Juden im zweiten Weltkrieg. Acta Baltica (Königstein, Ger.), v.16, 1976, p.172-184. See serials consulted.

1096. --- Der bewafnete Widerstand baltischer Juden gegen das Nazi-Regime 1941-1945. In Acta Baltica (Königstein, Ger.), v.15, 1975, p. 166-174. See serials consulted.

1097. LEVIN, Dov. Hishtatfut Yehude Lita ba-Germanim be-Mihemet ha-'olam ha-shoniyah. Participation of the Lithuanian Jews in the Second World War. [Yerushalaim, s.n. , 1970] 2 v. Thesis--ha-Universitah ha-'ivrit. Summary in English. DS135.R93L52 DLC.

1098. --- Lohamim ve-'omdim 'al nafsham... 1941-1945. They fought back. Yerusholayim, Yad Vashem, 1974. 269, viii p., [18] leaves of plates. illus., facsims., maps. Summary in English. Bibliography: p. 233-242. DS135.L5L4 DLC.

1099. --- Participation of the Lithuanian Jews in the Second World War. In Journal of Baltic Studies (Brooklyn, N.Y.), no.4, v.6, 1975, p. 300-310. See serials consulted.

1100. RADLOFF, W. Bericht über eine Reise zu den Karaimen der westlichen Gouvernements. In Akademiia nauk SSSR. Leningrad. Bulletin de l'Académie des Sciènces de St. Pétersbourg, no.2, v.32, 1880. AS262.S34 DLC; see also serials consulted.

1101. ROBINSON, Jacob. Were the minorities treaties a failure. By Jacob Robinson, Oscar Karbach, Max M.Laserson, Neheniah Robinson [and] Marc Vichniak. New York, N.Y., Institute of Jewish affairs, 1943. xvi, 349 p. map. Bibliography: p. 269-273. JC311.R48 DLC; CaAEU; CaBVaU; ICJS; NBuU; NNUN; NcD; NjR; OkU; OrU; PBm; PPDrop; PSt; PSC.

1102. SARKIN, S. In der alter heym. In the old country. Toronto, Ont., Farlag Vochnblat, 1973. 181 p., [8] leaves of plates. illus. DS135.L5S37 vol.1 DLC.

1103. --- Zikhroynes... Memoirs; the labour movement in Lithuania and in Canada. Toronto, Ont., Farlag Vochnblat, 1973- . v. illus. DS135.L5S37 DLC.

1104. STEINBERG, Lucien. Not as a lamb; the Jews against Hitler. Translated by Marian Hunter. Farnborough, England, Saxon House, 1974. ix, 358 p. Translation of La revolte des Justes. D810.J487613 DLC; MoSW; TU; PPiU; AkU; AAP; AzU; CaBVaU; CLSU;CU; CtY; CtW; CSt; CU-SB; CNoS; CoU;CoFS; CU-S; FMU; FDaSU; IaU; IaDL; ICarbS; InU; IU; KMK; KEmT; KyU; KyLoU; LN; MH; MnU; MoU; MiEM; MU; NN; NNC; NNU NNCU-G; NSyU; NSbSU; NNCoCi; NRU; NjR NbU; NcU; NjP; NNJ; NmLcU; OCH; OkU; OU; OrPS; PPT; RPB; ScU; ScCleU; TNJ; TxBeaL; UU; ViBlbV; WU; Wa; WaU.

1105. TALKO-HRYNCEWICZ, Julian. Charakterystyka fizyczna ludności żydowskiej Litwy i Rusi. In Polska Akademia Umiejętności, Kraków. Komisya antropologiczna. Zbiór wiadomości do Antropologii Krajowej, v.16, 1892. GN2.P5822 DLC; see also serials consulted.

1106. YAD VASHEM STUDIES ON THE European Jewish catastrophe and resistance. Jerusalem, Yad Vashem, 1973. Tom 9.
DS135.E83W32 DLC.

1107. YERUSHOLAYIM DE-LITA. Jerusalem of Lithuania, illustrated and documented. Collected and arranged by Leyzer Ran. New York, N.Y. 1974. 3 v. (chiefly illus.) In English, Hebrew, Russian, and Yiddish. DS135.R93V584 PU; DLC.

VIII.11. NATIONAL MEDICINE,SOCIAL INSURANCE AND HEALTH SER-VICES

1108. ČILVINAITĖ, Mariona. Bobe-lės; kaimo akušerės. [Bobelės; the midwives of the village] In Gimta-sai Kraštas (Šiauliąi), no.3-2(7-8), 1935, p. 345-349.
ICWA.

1109. JANKAUSKAS, Stasys. Veteri-narinė medicina Nepriklausomoje Lie-tuvoje; atsiminimai. [The veterina-ry medicine in Independent Lithuania] Chicago, Ill., Lietuvių veterinari-jos draugija tremtyje, [1973] 338 p. illus. SF695.L77J36 DLC; CaBVaU; CSt-H; MiEM.

1110. KIRSNYS, Vytautas. Medici-ninė atranka ir indikacijos gydyti Lietuvos TSR kurortuose. [Medical se-lection and instruction of treatment in Soviet Lithuanian health-resorts. Vilnius, Mintis, 1969. 160 p. At head of title: V. Kirsnys, A. Kepalai-tė. Bibliography: p. 154-158.
RA887.L5K568 DLC; CaAEU.

1111. KONFERENTSIIA GIGIENISTOV I sanitarnykh vrachei Litovskoi SSR,po-sviashchennaia voprosam gigieny sela i gigieny truda, 1st, Vilna, 1966. Materialy I Konferentsii gigienistov ...Litovskoi SSR... Vilnius, 1966. 110 p. RA771.K65 1966 DLC; MBCo.

1112. KONFERENTSIIA PO VOPROSAM ISTORII MEDITSINY V PRIBALTIKE I BE-LORUSSII, VILNA AND KAUNAS, 1963. Tezisy dokladov Konferentsii istorii meditsiny v Pribaltike i Belorussii. Vilnius, 1963. 66 p.
R533.B3K6 1963c DLC; DNLM.

1113. MOKSLINĖ-PRAKTINĖ KONFEREN-CIJA KURORTOLOGIJOS IR GERONTOLOGIJOS KLAUSIMAIS, PALANGA, LITHUANIA, 1967. Kurortologijos, fizioterapijos ir ge-rontologijos klausimai; ... skirtos ...revoliucijos 50-čiui, medžiaga Palangos kurortas, 1967 m. rugpiū-čio 24-26. [On the questions of the health resorts, Spa, physiotherapy and the advanced age of people. Red. kolegija: H. Guobys, ats. redaktorius et al.] Vilnius, 1967. 389 p. Ad-ded title page and text in Russian.
DNLM.

1114. RESPUBLIKINIAI SANITARINIO ŠVIETIMO NAMAI. Saugokime vaikų sveikatą. [Lets protect the health of children]. Vilnius, Valstybinė politinės ir mokslinės literatūros leidykla, 1964. 166 p. illus.
DNLM.

VIII.12. RECREATION, GAMES, AND OLYMPIC GAMES

1115. BILAIŠYTĖ, Živilė. Žaiskim ieškojimą. [Let's play hide and seek. Čikaga, Pedagoginis institutas,1973] 40 p. PG8722.12.I35Z3 PU.

1116. LIETUVIŲ FIZINIO AUKLĖJIMO IR SPORTO SĄJUNGA. 8[i.e. Aštunto-sios] Šiaurės Amerikos lietuvių spor-tinės žaidynės: futbolas, lengvoji atletika, lauko tenisas, plaukymas. [Eighth Lithuanian games of North America: soccer, atletics, outdoor tennis and swimming. Redagavo Kęstu-tis Čerkeliūnas. New Yorke, Išleido Lietuvių fizinio auklėjimo ir sporto sąjunga, Rytų apygarda, 1958] [40 p. *Q p.v.1924--NN.

1117. LIETUVOS KREPŠINIS. [Basket-ball in Lithuania] Vilnius, Mintis, 1971. 157 p., 32 leaves of illus., ports. At head of title: A. Berta-šius and others.
GV885.8.L5L53 DLC.

1118. ŠALKAUSKIS, Stasys. Jaunuo-menės idealizmas ir modernieji šokiai. [The idealism of the young and their realism to modern dancing] Kaunas, Raidės spaustuvė, 1928. 16 p. Ats-pausdinta iš Židinio.
GV1741.S3 OKentU.

1119. SAULAITIS, Antanas. Skautų užsiėmimai; vadovėlis skautų vadovams ir skaučių vadovėms. [Handbook for the leaders of boy and girl scouts] [n.p.] LSS Skautų brolija, 1971. 342 p. illus. OKentU.

VIII.13. RESORTS, PARKS, AND SPAS

1120. KIAULEIKIS, Leonas. Palanga [Translated by V. Grodzenskis. Vil-nius, Mintis Pub. House, 1965] 36 p. illus. In English.
InNd.

1121. KIRSNYS, Vytautas. Birshto-nas. [Vil'nius, Gos. izd-vo polit. i nauch. lit-ry Litovskoi SSR, 1961] DK651.B525K517 DLC

VIII.14. ASSOCIATIONS AND SOCIETIES

VIII.14.a. ASSOCIATIONS, SOCIETIES AND FRATERNITIES

1122. ATEITININKŲ KELIU, 1911-1927

-1977; žmonės, laikai, darbai. [A history of Ateitininkai; people and achievements, 1911-1977] Red. Stasys Barzdukas. [Chicaga, Ateitis,1977] 214 p. HS1537.A84A8 PU.

1123. DAMBRAUSKAS, Aleksandras,ed. Šv. Kazimiero draugija, jos kūrimasis ir pirmųjų XXV metų veikimas,1906-1931. [The St.Casimir Society, its genesis and its activity, 1906-1931] Kaunas, 1932. 149 p. illus., ports. (Šv.Kazimiero draugijos jubiliejinis leidinys. 533) DK511.L2A27 DLC.

1124. GEČYS, Kazys. Bractwa trzeźwości w diecezji żmudzkiej w latach 1858-1864. [By] Kazimierz Gieczys. Wilno, 1935. xi, 223 p. (Studja teologiczne, 4) Summary in German. At head of title: Kazimierz Gieczys. Thesis--University of Vilnius. 947.52.G263 PU.

1125. GIMBUTAS, Jurgis. Penkios dešimtys metų Akademinei skautijai. [5oth anniversary of the Academic scouting movement] In Aidai (Brooklyn, N.Y.), no.10, 1974, p.440-446. See serials consulted.

1126. JUREVIČIUS, Juozas. Korp. Neo-Lithuania 50 metų. [50th anniversary of the fraternity Neo-Lithuania] In Naujoji Viltis (Chicago, Ill.), no.4, 1972, p. 7-11. See serials consulted.

1127. JURGĖLA, Petras. Lietuviškoji skautija. [Lithuanian scouting. Brookly, N.Y., Lietuvių Skautų Sąjunga, 1975] 824 p. HS3316.L5J8 PU; DLC.

1128. KOJELIS, Juozas. Ateitininkai Vilniuje. [Ateitininkai in Vilnius] In Ateitis (Chicago), no.7, 1970, p. 244-251. See serials consulted.

1129. LANDSBERGIS, Vytautas. Kudirkos sąjudis. Parašė Vytautas Žemkalnis. [The movement of the Kudirka followers] Melbourne, Australia, 1952. 67 p. PG8721.K8Z7 PU.

1130. LIETUVIŲ SKAUČIŲ SESERIJA. Lietuvių skaučių seserija;[Lietuvių skaučių seserijos istoriniai bruožai. The Lithuanian girl scout association; ... historical sketch] [s.l., 1972] 272 p. illus. Summary and legends in English. HS3365.L58L53 DLC.

1131. LIETUVIŲ SKAUČIŲ SESERIJA. REDAKCINĖ KOMISIJA. Skautybė lietuvaitei. [Scouting for the girls] Paruošė L.S.S. Skaučių skyriaus Redak-

cinė komisija. Chicago, Ill., L.S.S. Skaučių seserija, 1963. 349 p. ill. Bibliography; p. 334-335. HS3365.L58L54 1963 DLC.

1132. LIETUVIŲ SKAUTŲ SĄJUNGOS VADIJA. Mūsų uniformos. [Our uniforms] Išleido L.S.S. Vadija. Detmold, Ger., Aitvaras, 1946.. 23 p. illus. HS3040.L55L72 1946 CaAEU.

1133. LITHUANIAN AMERICAN COMMUNITY OF THE U.S.A. Jungtinių Amerikos Valstybių Lietuvių Bendruomenės įstatai ir taisyklės, 1975 m. spalio 15. [Constitution and by-laws of the Lithuanian American Community. Chicago, Ill., JAV Lietuvių Bendruomenė, 1975] 55 leaves. E184.L7L532 PU.

1134. THE LITHUANIAN BOY-SCOUTS ASSOCIATION IN GERMANY. Mūsų gyvenimo vaizdų albumas 30-ties metų sukakčiai nuo skautybės įkūrimo Lietuvoje paminėti... Album of the Lithuanian girl- and boy-scouts life to remember the 30th anniversary of the Lithuanian scoutism. [Detmold, Ger., The Association, 1947]. 35 p. illus. In Lithuanian, French and English. Cover title: Į taikos rytojų! A la paix! To peace! HS3040.L55L77 1947 CaAEU.

1135. RUGYTĖ, Alicija. Lietuvių istorijos d-jos 20 m. veikimo trumpa apžvalga. The Lithuanian Historical Society: overview of the last 20 years of its work and accomplishments. In Lietuvių Tautos Praeitis (Chicago, Ill.), kn.1, v.4, 1977, p. 144-148. See serials consulted.

1136. --- Lietuvių istorijos draugijai 15 metų. [15th anniversary of the Lithuanian Historical Society] In Aidai (Brookly, N.Y.), no.8, 1973, p. 374-376. See serials consulted.

1137. --- Lietuvių istorijos draugijos penkiolikmetis. The Lithuanian Historical Society, 1956-1973. In Lietuvių Tautos Praeitis (Chicago,Ill.) kn.2, v.3, 1973, p. 7-22. Summary in English. See serials consulted.

1138. Š. L. Studentų Varpo draugijos sukaktis. [The anniversary of the student association "Varpas"] In Sėja (Chicago, Ill.), no.4, 1973, p. 37-43. See serials consulted.

1139. --- Varpininkai Vokietijoje. [The Association "Varpas" in Germany] In Sėja (Chicago, Ill.), no.3, 1974, p. 46-49. See serials consulted.

1140. SALADŽIUS, Pranas. Lietuvos Šaulių Sąjungą prisimenant. [Reminiscences on the Lithuanian National Guard] In Karys (Brooklyn,N.Y.), no.7-8(189-190), 1953, p. 136; no. 9, p. 162-163; no.11, p. 199-202. Mr. L. Kairys, Chicago, no.425.

1141. SZCZESNIAK, Bolesław. The knights Hospitallers in Poland and Lithuania. 106 p. illus., map. (Studies in European history, 19) CR4731.P7S9 DLC; CtY; CoFS; DAU; ICU; MdU; MnU; ViU.
AU; CaBVaU; CaQMM; CLSU; CU-SC; CU; CNoS; CSt; CoFS; DDO; DeU; FU; GU; IaAS; IaU; ICIU; ICN; IEdS; IU; KyU; MeB; MiEM; MiU; NN; NNC; NIC; NSyU; NcD; NcU; NjP; NjR; NRU; NbU; OrPS; RPB; ScCleU; TU; TxHR; VtU.

1142. TIESOS IR MEILĖS TARNYBOJE; Lietuvių katalikių moterų draugija, 1908-1933. Redagavo Ona Beleckienė-Gaigalaitė. [... The Society of Lithuanian Catholic women, 1908-1933] Kaunas, Lietuvių katalikių moterų draugijos leidinys, 1933. [Xerox copy, 1977] 259 p. HQ1665.65.T5 1933a PU.

1143. UNITED LITHUANIAN RELIEF FUND OF AMERICA. Bendrojo Amerikos Lietuvių Šalpos Fondo 25 metų darbo apžvalga. [A review of the twenty-five year's work of the United Lithuanian Relief Fund of America. Redagavo Domas Jasaitis. Brooklyn, N.Y., BALFas, 1970] 287 p. illus., ports. HS2008.U5A52 DLC; IEdS; OKentU.

1144. VILNIUI VADUOTI SĄJUNGA. Vilniui Vaduoti Sąjungos įstatai. Kaunas, 1930. [Xerox copy, 1971] 7 p. [By-laws of the Association for Liberation of Vilnius] DK511.L27V53 1971 PU(xerox)

VIII.14.c. SECRET AND SUBVERSIVE ASSOCIATIONS

1145. BIELIŃSKI, Józef. Szubrawcy w Wilnie, 1817-1822; zarys historyczny. Wilno, Nakładem Korwina, 1910. ports., plate, fold.facsim. plate. Slav 5198.739,20 MH

1146. Z FILARECKIEGO ŚWIATA; zbiór wspomnień z lat 1816-1824. Z 24-ma ilustracjami. Wydał Henryk Mościcki. Warszawa, Instytut Wydawniczy "Bibljoteka Polska", 1924. 372 p. illus., ports. (Czasy i ludzie) Contents: Mościcki, H. Ze stosunków wileńskich w okresie, 1816-1823.--Krasiński, T. Dziennik ucznia Uniwersytetu Wileńskiego, 1816-1818. --Domeyko, I. Filareci i filomaci. --Slizień, Otto. Z pamiętnika, 1821-

1824.---Czarnocki, M. Krótka wiadomość o tajnych towarzystwach uczniów. Uniwesrsytetu Wileńskiego aż do ich rozwiązania w roku 1824.--Zan, T. Notatki pamiętnikarskie.--Masalski, E.T. Z pamiętników, 1799-1824.--Malewski, F. Dziennik więzienny. DK435.4.Z2 DLC; MH; NN; OCl; PU.

VIII.15. SOVIET LITHUANIAN SOCIETY

1147. ĖKONOMICHESKAĬA KHARAKTERIS-TIKA sfery obsluzhivaniĭa v Litovskoĭ SSR. [Otv. red. V.P. Puronas]. Vil'nĭus, Akademiĭa nauk Litovskoĭ SSR, In-t ėkonomiki, 1976. HD9986.R93L573 DLC; PU.

1148. IDEOLOGINĖ KOVA IR JAUNIMAS Tarybų Socialistinių Respublikų Sąjungos 50-mečiui; mokslinės konferencijos medžiaga. [Ideological struggle and the youth of USSR for the 50-tieth anniversary. Red. kolegija A. Gaidys (pirmininkas)] Vilnius, 1972. 209 p. At head of title: Lietuvos TSR Mokslų akademija. Filosofijos, teisės ir sociologijos skyrius prie Istorijos instituto. Lietuvos LKJS Centro komitetas. DLC.

1149. MAČIUIKA, Benediktas Vytenis. Acculturation and socialization in the Soviet Baltic republics. By Benedict V. Mačiuika. In Lituanus (Chicago, Ill.), no.4, v.18, 1972, p. 26-43. See serials consulted.

1150. --- The apparat of political socialization in Lithuania. [By] Benedict Maciuika. In Conference on Baltic Studies, 3d, University of Toronto, 1972. Problems of mininations ... San Jose, Calif., 1973. p.151-160. HC243.C65 1972 DLC; CaBVaU; CaAEU; CSt; CtY; CU; GAT; ICIU; IU; InU; ICarbS; InNd; MB; MH; MiU; NN; NNC; NBuC; NBuU; NjP; NmU; OkU; RPB; UU; WU; WaU.

1151. --- Mokslas ir mokslininkai Lietuvoje sovietinės santvarkos rėmuose. [The science and the scientists in the frame of the Soviet Lithuanian way of life] In Metmenys (Chicago, Ill.), no.20, 1970, p. 121-136. See serials consulted.

1152. --- Socialinės ir kultūrinės problemos sukolektyvintame Lietuvos kaime. Social and cultural problems in the collectivized Lithuanian countryside. In Institute of Lithuanian Studies. Lituanistikos instituto 1975 metų suvažiavimo darbai. Chicago, Ill., 1976. p. 107-122. Summary in English. DK.L2I64 1975 CaAEU; PU.

1153. --- Socialinės problemos
Sovietinėje Lietuvoje. [The social
problems in Soviet Lithuania] In
Metmenys (Chicago, Ill.), no.22, 1971
p. 97-116; no.23, p. 113-132. See
serials consulted.

1154. NUOLATINĖJE KOMISIJOJE.
[On the standing Committee]. Vilnius,
Mintis, 1967. 57 p. (Deputato biblio-
tekėlė) At head of title: L. Vaitu-
kaitis. [et al.]
JN6745.A7N8 DLC.

1155. SOVIET WEST; interplay bet-
ween nationality and social organi-
zation. Edited by Ralph S. Clem.
New York, N.Y., Praeger, 1975. xiii,
161 p. illus. (Praeger special stu-
dies in international politics and
government) JN6520.M5S656 DLC;AkU;
CaAEU; CaBVaU; CtW; CU; CSt-H; GU;
InU; ICarbS; MB; MH; MoSW; MiEM; NN;
NjR; NvU; NcU; NBuU; NRU; NcRS; NbU;
NmU; NmLcU; OOxM; OKentU; OU; PSt;
TxU; TNJ;

IX. ECONOMY

IX.1. GENERAL STUDIES

1156. BRAZAUSKAS, V[incas] East
Lithuania; an economico-geographical
essay. In CPXIX, Vilnius, 1960.
p. 383-386. See serials consulted.

1157. BUDRYS, Dzidas and BURAČAS,
Antanas. Šiuolaikinis kapitalizmas
ir buržuazinės jo teorijos; kritinė
analizė. [Current capitalism and the
bourgeois theories; critical analy-
sis] Vilnius, Mintis, 1972. 249 p.
HB501.B82 PU.

1158. DARGIS, Leonardas. Ko buvo
vertas Nepriklausomos Lietuvos ūkis.
[How good was the economy of the
Independent Lithuania.] In Naujoji
Viltis (Chicago, Ill.), no.7, 1974,
p. 67-77. See serials consulted.

1159. DOVNAR-ZAPOL'SKIĬ, Mitrofan
Viktorovich. Gosudarstvennoe kho-
zīaistvo litovskoĭ Rusi. [Kiev,19-]
cxii, 819 p.
Balt 8249.1 MH.

1160. FORSTREUTER, Kurt H[ermann.
Die ältesten Handelsrechnungen des
Deutschen Ordens in Preussen. In
Hansische Geschichtsblätter (Leipzig,
Ger.), v.74, 1956. See serials con-
sulted.

1161. GOETZ, Leopold Karl. Deutsch-
russische Handelsgeschichte des Mittelalters. Lübeck, Ger., O. Waelde,
1922. xvi, 572 p. (Quellen und Darstellungen zur hansischen Geschichte.
N.F., Bd.5)
NN; CtY; CU; IU; MH; MnU; ViU.

1162. --- Deutsch-russische Han-
delsverträge des Mittelalters. Hamburg, Ger., L. Friedrichsen & Co.,
1916. xv, 394 p. (Abhandlungen des
Hamburgischen Kolonialinstituts, Bd.
37. Reihe A. Bd.6)
HF458.G6 DLC.

1163. GRIŠKEVIČIUS, Petras. V
sem'e edinoĭ,bratskoĭ. [By] P.Gish-
kīavichīus. Vil'nīus, Mintis, 1975.
131 p., [28] leaves of plates. illus.
DK511.L274G7417 DLC.

1164. IVINSKIS, Zenonas. Die Han-
delbeziehungen Litauens mit Riga im
14. Jahrhundert. In Baltija vēsturnieku konference, 1st, Riga, 1937.
Runas un referāti. Riga, 1938. See
serials consulted.

1165. --- Lietuvių ir prūsų prekybiniai santykiai pirmoje 16 amžiaus
pusėje. [The trade relations between
Lithuania and Prussia in the early
16th century] Offprint from Židinys
(Kaunas), no.8-9, 1933.
947.52.Iv54.5 PU.

1166. KONĪUKHOVA, Tat'īana Aleksandrovna. Gosudarstvennaīa derevnīa
Litvy i reforma P.D. Kiseleva, 1840-
1857 gg.; Vilenskaīa i Kovenskaīa gubernii. [Moskva] Izd-vo Moskovskogo
universiteta, 1975. 250 p.
HD725.7.Z8V54 PU.

1167. LIETUVOS TSR MOKSLŲ AKADEMI-
JA, Vilna. ISTORIJOS INSTITUTAS.
Lietuvos gyventojų prekybiniai ryšiai
I-XIII a. [The commercial relations
of Lithuanians in the 1st to 13th
centuries. Ats. redaktorius M. Mi-
chelbertas] Vilnius, Mintis, 1972.
284 p. DK511.L21L52 PU.

1168. MAIMINAS, Jefremas. Teorijos ir tikrovė; buržuazinių ekonominių teorijų ir programų Lietuvoje
kritika, 1919-1940 m. Vilnius, Valstybinė politinės ir mokslinės literatūros leidinys, 1960. 231 p.
HC337.L5M28 DLC.

1169. MICHELBERTAS, Mykolas. Romos monetų radiniai Lietuvos TSR teritorijoje. [The finds of Roman coins
in the Lithuanian SSR territory] In
Lietuvos TSR Mokslų akademija, Vilna.
Darbai. Serija A, 1(10), 1961, p.19-
36. See serials consulted.

1170. MISIŪNAS, Romualdas J. The Šventoji project; 18th century plans for a Lithuanian port. In Journal of Baltic Studies (Brooklyn, N.Y.), no.1, v.8, p. 28-50. See serials consulted.

1171. MULEVIČIUS, Leonas. Nekotorye voprosy genezisa kapitalizma v Litve. Vil'nius, 1968. 130 p. HC337.L5M8 DLC; CU; ICU; InU; NNC; NjP.

1172. NAUSĖDAS, Kazys. Nepriklausomos Lietuvos ūkinė ir socialinė struktūra. [The economic and social structure of the Independent Lithuania] In Naujoji Viltis (Chicago, Ill.), no.5, 1973, p. 30-45. See serials consulted.

1173. ŠALČIUS, Petras. "Auszros" ir "Szwiesos" ekonomika. [Economics during the era of "Auszra" and "Szwiesa". Kaunas, Vyt. Didž. Universiteto Teisių fak., 1932.] [Xerox copy, 1976] p.[417]-449. Detached from Teisių Fakulteto darbai, t.6. HB113.A2S33 1932a PU(xerox)

1174. SMILGEVIČIUS, Jonas. Bau einer hydroelektrischen Station am Nemunas. In Lithuania. Finansų departamentas. Wirtschaftliche Informationen des Finanzdepartements der Republik Litauen (Kaunas), no.19-20, v.2, 1931. See serials consulted.

1175. --- Lietuvos elektrifikacija ir Nemuno hidroelektros stotis ties Pažaisliu. [The electrification of Lithuania and the hydroelectric power station by Pažaislis on Nemunas river] In Vairas (Kaunas), no.10, 1934, p. 320-328. ICWA.

1176. STEIN, W. Vom deutschen Kontor in Kowno. In Hansische Geschichtsblätter(Leipzig, Ger.), Bd.22 1916. See serials consulted.

1177. STUDNICKI, Władysław. Stosunki spoleczne i ekonomiczne na Litwie i Rusi. In Polska...Lwów, 1909, t.2, p. 733-759. *QR--NN.

1178. SZELĄGOWSKI, Adam. Pieniądz i przewrót cen w XVI i XVII wieku w Polsce. Lwów, Nakł. Tow. Wydawniczego, 1902. xii, 317 p. HG220.P6S9 DLC; NN.

1179. TISSOT, Louis. La signification économique et politique de Memel pour le Nord-Est européen. Paris, Société d'etudes et d'informations économique, 1938. Q 947.52T525 PU.

1180. TODD, Joan M. and EICHEL, Marijean H. A reappraisal of the prehistoric and classical amber trade in the light of new evidence. In Journal of Baltic Studies (Brooklyn, N.Y.), no.4, v.5, 1974, p. 295-314. See serials consulted.

1181. VABALAS, Aleksandras. Der Fremdenverkehr und seine wirtschaftliche Bedeutung für Litauen. Innsbruck, Austria, 1946. Thesis--University of Innsbruck. Au.InU.

1182. DAS WIRTSCHAFTSLEBEN DER RANDSTAATEN; Litauen, Lettland, Estland. Berlin, 1923. NjP.

1183. ŽEMĖ IR GAMYBA. [The soil and production. Ats. redaktorius V. Mališauskas] Vilnius, LTSR MA Ekonomikos institutas, 1977. 235 p. HD1995.65.Z39 PU.

IX.2.a. AGRICULTURE

1184. ALEKSA-ANGARIETIS, Zigmas. Agrarinis klausimas Lietuvoje. [Agrarian question in Lithuania. By Z. Angarietis. Redakcinė kolegija: R. Šarmaitis (ats. redaktorius), V. Kancevičius (sudarytojas), M. Tamošiūnas] Vilnius, Mintis, 1972. 491 p. HD725.7.A6 1972 DLC; MB; MH; MiU;NN; NNC; PU.

1185. BRIEDIS, Juozas. Die Schafhaltung in Litauen, ihre betriebswirtschaftliche Stellung und Rentabilität. Bonn, Ger., 1948. 143 leaves. Thesis--University of Bonn. Typescript. Ger.BU.

1186. INTERNATIONAL INSTITUTE OF AGRICULTURE. Le premier recensement agricole mondiale (1929-1930): Lithuanie. Rome, 1936. 51 p. (Its Bulletin, 10) S439.I65 DLC; IU; MdBJ; NN.

1187. LITHUANIA. ŽEMĖS ŪKIO RŪMAI. Žemės ūkio rūmų... metų darbų apyskaita. Berichte der Landwirtschaftskammer. Kaunas. Y9740 Ger.KIW (1929-35, t.6,1939)

1188. PAKALNIŠKIS, Kazimieras. Žemdirbių vargai ir priemonės jiems pašalinti. [Hardships of the peasants and measures taken to alleviate them. Kaunas] Ekonominės bei politinės Lietuvos žemdirbių sąjungos leidinys, 1922. [Xerox copy, 1977] 38 p. DK511.L27P26 1922a PU(xerox)

1189. TAMOŠIŪNAS, Julius. Lietuvos žemės ūkio raida ir jos problemos (kapitalizmo ir socializmo epocha). [Agriculture and its development in Lithuania during Capitalist and Soviet periods] Vilnius, Mintis, 1974. 237 p. HD1995.65.T3 PU.

1190. VASINAUSKAS, P[etras]. Žemės dirbimo būdai pagal Dotnuvos bandymų stoties 1924-1954 metų duomenys. [The methods of tilling the land according to the research data of the Dotnuva Experimental Station for the years 1924-1954] In Lietuvos TSR Mokslų akademija, Vilna. Ekonomikos institutas. Darbai, v.2, 1956, p. 73-160. See serials consulted.

1191. VENGRYS, A. Agrariniai klausimai Lietuvos marksistų raštuose 1920-1930 m. [Agrarian question in the works of the Lithuanian marxists from 1920-1930] In Lietuvos TSR Mokslų akademija, Vilna. Darbai. Serija A, 2(5), 1958, p. 3-17. See serials consulted.

1192. ŽEMĖS ŪKIO EKONOMISTO ŽINYNAS. [Handbook of agricultural economics. Bendradarbiai: J. Adomaitis et al. Sudarė R. Stasiūnas] Vilnius, Mintis, 1970. 473 p. illus. DS.

IX.2.b. AGRARIAN REFORM

1193. BAČELIS, Zenonas. Trobėsių nusikėlimas ir atlyginimas už palikimą jų vietoje. [Question of removing buildings and the compensation for leaving them on the old site]. In Žemėtvarka ir melioracija (Kaunas) no.2, 1930. See serials consulted.

1194. KAZLAUSKAS, Vytautas. Die litauische Agrarreform vom Jahre 1922 und ihre Beurteilung nach der kirchlichen Soziallehre. Thesis-- Pontifical University of Gregory, Rome. It.RG.

1195. LITHUANIAN SSR. VALSTYBINĖ ŽEMĖS ŪKIO KOMISIJA. Lietuvos TSR Valstybinės žemės ūkio komisijos protokolai, 1940 m. [Minutes of the Soviet Lithuanian Commission on agriculture of 1940] Spaudai parengė Aleksandras Jefremenka. Vilnius, Lietuvos TSR Mokslų akademija, Istorijos institutas, 1976. 227 p. HD1995.65.A3 PU.

1196. MALDUTIS, Julius. Lithuanian land reforms, 1919-1939. [New York, N.Y., Columbia University], 1967. 147 leaves. Thesis--Columbia University. Photocopy of typescript, produced by microfilm-xerography, by University Microfilms, 1973. MU; NNC.

1197. PAULIUKONIS, Pranas. Prel. Mykolas Krupavičius ir Žemės reforma. [Msgr. Mykola Krupavičius and agrarian reform] In Tėvynės Sargas (New York, N.Y.), no.1, 1969, p. 93-121; and no.1, 1972, p. 43-59. See serials consulted.

IX.3. FORESTRY

1198. LIETUVOS TSR MIŠKŲ IŠTEKLIAI IR AUGIMVIETĖS. [The forest resources in the Lithuanian SSR...] Vilnius, 1972. 298 p. maps. At head of title: Lietuvos TSR Mokslų akademijos Ekonomikos institutas. Lietuvos Žemės ūkio akademija. Lietuvos miškų ūkio mokslinio tyrimo institutas. Edited by V. Mališauskas and others. Summaries in Russian. SD217L8L49 DLC; InU.

1199. LITHUANIAN S.S.R. MIŠKŲ ŪKIO IR MIŠKO PRAMONĖS MINISTERIJA. DARBO MOKSLINIO ORGANIZAVIMO IR EKONOMINIŲ TYRIMŲ LABORATORIJA. Miško ruošos išdirbio normos ir įkainiai. Patvirtinti Lietuvos TSR Miškų ūkio ir miško pramonės ministerijos kolegijos ir Miško, poperiaus ir medžio apdirbimo pramonės darbininkų profsąjungos respublikinio komiteto prezidiumo (1969 m. kovo 17 d. posėdžio protokolas nr.11). [Production standards in the Lithuanian lumber industry] [Sudarė P. Kabašinskas ir E. Jurevičiūtė] Vilnius, Mintis,1970. 382 p. SD538.3.R9L57 DLC.

1200. MAGER, Friedrich. Der Wald in Altpreussen als Wirtschaftsraum. Köln; Böhlau, 1960. 2 v. maps. SD196.P7M3 DLC; CaAEU; CU; DA; ICU; IU; InU; LU; MH; MiU; NN; NIC; NNC; OrCS; On Lithuania: vol.1, p.38,41, 71,307; vol.2, p.49,63,81,215.

1201. MIŠKO ŽEMIŲ EKONOMINIS VERtinimas. [Economic evaluation of the wooded land. Ats. redaktorius V.Mališauskas] Vilnius, Lietuvos TSR Mokslų akademijos Ekonomikos institutas, 1975. 190 p. S599.L5M5 PU.

1202. NAUCHNAĬA KONFERENTSIĬA PO ZAKREPLENIĬŪ I OBLESENIĬŪ PESKOV, MEMEL, 1955. Voprosy zakrepleniĭa i obleseniĭa peskov; materialy Nauchnoĭ

konferentsii po zakrepleniiu i ob-
leseniiu peskov, sostoiavsheisia v g.
Klaipede v avguste 1955 g. [Redakts-
ionnaia kollegiia: A. Kvedaras i dr.]
Vil'nius, Gos. izd-vo polit. i nauchnoi lit-ry Litovskoi SSR, 1957. 250
p. illus., maps. At head of title:
Litovskii nauchno-issledovatel'skii
institut lesnogo khoziaistva. Summaries in Lithuanian.
CU.

1203. SKĖRYS, Antanas. Entwicklung und Umfang des Holzmarktes in
Litauen 1918-1940. Freiburg in Br.,
1947. vii, 160 leaves. graphs,map.
Inaug.-Diss.--University of Freiburg
in Br. Typescript.
Ger.FBrU.

IX.4. HUNTING, APIARIES, ETC

1204. BUTKEVIČIUS, I[zidorius]
Bitininkystė [Apiaries] In Lietuvos
TSR Mokslų akademija, Vilna. Isto-
rijos institutas. Lietuvių etnogra-
fijos bruožai. Vilnius, 1964. p.137-
[149]. illus.
HD725.7.L488 DLC; CaAEU; CtY; CU;
ICU; ICLJF; MH; NN; PU.

1205. KAIRIŪKŠTYTĖ-JACYNIENĖ,
H[alina] Apie bitininkystę senovės
Lietuvoje. [On the apiculture in
ancient Lithuania]. In Gimtasai
Kraštas (Šiauliai), no.31, 1943, p.
340-348. Mr. Kviklys, Chicago, has
it; see also serials consulted.

1206. TSALKIN, Veniamin Iosifovich.
K istorii zhivotnovodstva i okhoty
v vostochnoi Evrope. Moskva, AN SSSR
1962. 129 p. illus. (Materialy i
issledovaniia po arkheologii SSSR,
no. 107) At head of title: Akademiia
nauk SSSR. Materialy i issledovaniia
po arkheologii.
DK30.M42 no.107 CaAEU; CLSU; CaBVaU
CLU; CU; CtY; DDO; DSI; MoU; NIC;
PU-MU; WU.

IX.5. FISHING INDUSTRY

1207. RYBOLOVSTVO I RYBOVODSTVO
v Sievero-Zapadnom krae (Kovenskaia,
Vilenskaia i Grodnenskaia gubernii).
Otchety ekspeditsii 1904 goda, orga-
nizovannoi otdielom ikhtiologii po
porucheniiu general-gubernatora Sie-
vero-Zapadnago kraia P.D. Sviato-
polk-Mirskago. Pod red. prof. N.IU.
Zografa. Moskva, Tip. Universitetskaia, 1907. 315 p. (Russkoe Obsh-

chestvo aklimatizatsii zhivotnykh i
rastenii. Otdel ikhtiologii. Trudy,
tom 5) Summary in German
QH301.R83 DLC.

IX.6. INDUSTRY

1208. ENDZINAS, A. Drevnee proiz-
vodstvo zheleza na territorii Litvy.
In Acta Baltico-Slavica (Warszawa),
v.8, 1973, p. 21-52. See serials
consulted.

1209. LIETUVOS TSR MOKSLŲ AKADEMI-
JA, Vilna. EKONOMIKOS INSTITUTAS.
Lietuvos pramonė ikisocialistiniu lai-
kotarpiu. K. Meškauskas et al. [Li-
thuanian industry during the period
1918-1940] Vilnius, Mintis, 1976.
477 p. illus. Bibliography: p. 464-
[473] HC337.L5L462 1976 DLC; PU.

1210. NAUJOKAS, Jonas. Fabrikas
"Maistas". [Meat plant "Maistas"]
In Lietuvos Ūkis (Kaunas), no.26,1924,
p. 24-28. See serials consulted.

IX.7. COMMUNICATION AND TRANSPORT

1211. KOLUPAILA, Steponas. Mūsų
vandens keliai. [Our water-ways]
Kaunas, Skautų Aido leidinys, 1933.
[Xerox copy, 1977] 95 p.
GB1333.L5K6 1933a PU.

1212. KOSAKOVSKII, Gerasim Ivanovich. Zheleznye dorogi Litvy. Vil'-
nius, Mokslas, 1975. 248 p.
HE3139.5.K6 PU.

1213. LITHUANIA. Affaire du chemin de fer Panevėžys-Saldutiškis.
Contre-mémoire du gouvernement lithuanien. [Kaunas, Spindulio b-vė, 1938.]
82 p. MH-L.

1214. --- --- Duplique du gouvernement lithuanien. [Kaunas, Spindulio b-vė, 1938] 65 p.
MH-L.

1215. --- Exposé écrit du gouvernement de la République Lithuanienne
concernant la demande d'avis consul-
tatif adressée par le Consil de la
Société des nations à la Cour perma-
mente de justice internationale et
portant: "Les engagements internatio-
naux en vigueur obligent-ils, dans
les circonstances actuelles, la Lithuanie, et, en cas de réponse affir-
mative, dans quelles conditions, à
prendre les mesures nécessaires pour

ouvrir au trafic, ou à certaines ca-
tégories de trafic, la section de
ligne de chemin de fer Landwarow-Kai-
siadorys" Kaunas, 1931. 91 p.
947.52.L712 PU.

1216. S.P. Lietuvos pašto, tele-
grafo ir telefono ūkis, 1918-1928 m.
[The economy of Lithuanian post, te-
graph and telephone, 1918-1928] In
Lietuvos ūkis (Kaunas), no.11, 1928.
HC337.L5A16 DLC; NN.

IX.9. FINANCE

1217. BIČKAUSKAS-GĖNTVILA, Leonas.
Žemės kreditas Lietuvoje 1861-1905 m.
[Agricultural credit in Lithuania,
1861-1905). Vilnius, Mintis, 1973.
110 p. At head of title: Vilniaus
Valstybinis pedagoginis institutas.
HG2051.R92L583 PU; DLC; MH.

1218. FEDOROV, Dimitriĭ Ĭakovle-
vich. Monety Pribaltiki 13-18 stoletiĭ; opredelitel' monet. Kommenta-
rii i dopolneniĭa ĬA. Molygina. Tallin, Valgus, 1966. 421 p. illus.,
map. CJ3028.L58F2 CaAEU; CLU; CU;
CtY; DeU; DLC; ICU; InU; MH; MiU;MU;
MoSW; NIC; NjP; NcD; NSyU; NRU; OrU;
TU; ViU; WU.

1219. HOWOLDT, Gisela. Währungs-
probleme bei Staatsneubildung. Dargestellt am Beispiel der nach den
Ersten Weltkrieg 1914-1918 entstand-
en Staaten: Tschekoslovakei, Polen,
Litauen, Lettland und Estland. Hamburg, Ger., 1946. ix, 195 leaves.
Thesis--University of Hamburg. Typescript. Ger.HmbU.

1220. KARYS, Jonas K. Numizmati-
ka; žodynas, raštai. [The numismatics]
Putnam, Conn., Aukselis, 1970. viii,
340 p. illus. Bibliography: p.203-
206. CJ67.K35 DLC; MB; NN; OKentU;

1221. KIERSNOWSKI, Ryszard. Pradzieje grosza. Warszawa, Wiedza Pow-
szechna, 1975. 349 p.,[10] leaves of
plates. illus. (Biblioteka Wiedzy
Historycznej: Historia Polski)
CJ2456.K53 DLC

1222. PLATBĀRZDIS, Aleksandrs.
Coins and notes of Estonia, Latvia,
Lithuania. Stockholm, Numismatiska
bokförlaget Solna Seelig, 1968. 123 p.
illus. HG1080.2.P53 PU; CLU; CtY;
CU; DLC; IEN; MH; NN; NNC; PPULC.

1223. RAČKUS, Aleksandras M. Origin of Ruble in Lithuania and in Russia. In Numismatist (American numismatic Society. Philadelphia, Pa.),

v.47, 1934. See serials consulted.

1224. VERYHA-DEREVSKIS, Antanas
Ignas. Dvaro padūmės mokestis Užne-
munėje. [Taxation in Suvalkija (Li-
thuania). By] A.J. Veriga-Darevskis.
Kaunas, Vytauto Didžiojo Universite-
to Teisių fakulteto leidinys, 1931.
[Xerox copy, 1977] 12 p.
HJ2809.L5V4 1931a PU.

IX.10. COOPERATIVES AND COOPERATIVE
MOVEMENT

1225. BUBLYS, Vladas. Agricultural production cooperatives in independent Lithuania, 1920-1940. Summary. Das landwirtschaftliche Produk-
tions-Genossenschafswesen im unabhän-
gigen Litauen, 1920-1940. Zusammen-
fassung. London, Eng., Lithuanian
House Ltd., 1974. 80 p. Originally
published in Lithuanian , London,1972.
HD1491.L5B813 DLC; DNAL; MH; NjP;PU.

1226. R., H. Kooperacja kredyto-
wa wiejska na Litwie; stan jej obec-
ny i potrzeba reorganizacji. Kraków,
[W.L. Anczyc], 1905.
947.52.R1135 PU.

1227. ŽEMĖS ŪKIO GAMYBINĖ KOOPERA-
cija nepriklausomoje Lietuvoje, 1920-
1940. [Agricultural production cooperatives in Independent Lithuania,1920-
1940] Londonas [Nida Press], 1972.
257 p. HD1995.65.Z4 PU.

IX.11. THE ECONOMY OF SOVIET LITHUANIA

IX.11.a. GENERAL STUDIES AND ECONOMIC
PLANNING

1228. BOREIKAITĖ, Elizaveta. Socialistinės reprodukcijos tempai ir
dviejų visuomenės gamybos padalinių
santykis. [The Socialist production
intensity and the relation between
the two branches of socialized produc-
tion]. Vilnius, Mintis, 1968. 52 p.
HC336.2.B613 DLC.

1229. DARGIS, Leonardas. Sovieti-
nė statistika ir tikrovė. [The Soviet
style statistics and the reality] In
Aidai (Brooklyn, N.Y.), 1974, no.4,
p. 157-163; no.5, p. 207-216. See serials consulted.

1230. DROBNYS, Aleksandras and
ŽALKAUSKAS, Bronislavas. Penkmečio
žingsniai. [The five-years plan in
progress]. Vilnius, Mintis, 1972.

109 p. HC337.L5D72 DLC; MH.

1231. EESTI NSV TEADUSTE AKADEE-
MIA. MAJANDUSE INSTITUUT. OIGUSE
SEKTOR. Ocherki razvitii︠a︡ gosudar-
stvennosti sovetskikh pribaltii︠s︡kikh
respublik 1940-1965 gg. Tallin,Eesti
Paamat, 1965. 239 p.
JN6599.B32E3 CaOTU; CaAEU; CtY; DLC;
ICU; NNC; NcD; NjP;

1232. E︠K︡ONOMICHESKAI︠A︡ KONFEREN-
T︠S︡II︠A︡ PO STROITEL'STVU, Vilna, 1962.
E︠k︡onomika stroitel'stva v g. Vil'ni︠u︡s
materialy... [Otv. red. E. Berkmanas]
Vil'ni︠u︡s, Gospolitizdat, 1963. 118
p. Balt 8411.36 MH.

1233. E︠K︡ONOMICHESKAI︠A︡ OT︠S︡ENKA RY-
bovodnykh prudov. [Otv. redaktor V.
Malishauskas] Vil'ni︠u︡s, Institut
ekonomiki Akademii︠ ︡ nauk Litovskoi︠ ︡
SSR, 1976. 186, [3] p.
SH284.L5E6 PU.

1234. INGER, B., comp. Leedu Nõu-
ukogude Sotsialistik Vabariik. Tallinn, RK "Poliitiline Kirjandus,"
1948. 62 p. illus., map.
HC337.L5I5 DLC. [Lithuanian SSR]

1235. LENINIZMO PERGALĖ LIETUVOJE.
[The victory of Leninism in Lithuania. Red. kolegija: M. Burokevičius
(ats. red.) ir kiti] Vilnius, Mintis,
1970. 376 p., 16 leaves of illus.,
maps. HC337.L5L38 DLC; CtY; NN.

1236. LIETUVOS KOMUNISTŲ PARTIJA.
CENTRO KOMITETAS. Gerinti ekonominį
darbo žmonių švietimą; geriau organi-
zuoti socialistinį lenktyniavimą.
TSKP CK nutarimų priimtų 1971 metais,
išdėstymas. Vilnius, LKP CK leidykla, 1971. 18 p.
HC340.S6L52 1971 DLC.

1237. LIETUVOS TSR PRAMONĖS, ŽE-
mės ūkio, statybos, transporto, ryšių
komunalinio ūkio, prekybos ir buiti-
nio gyventojų aptarnavimo socialisti-
niai įsipareigojimai 1968 metų planui
ir penkmečio užduotims pirma laiko
įvykdyti. [Socialistic commitments
for the execution of the five-year
plan...by the Lithuanian SSR industry
agriculture, etc.] Vilnius, Mintis,
1968. HC337.L5L47 DLC.

1238. MANIŪSIS, Juozas. E︠k︡onomika
i kul'tura Sovetskoi︠ ︡ Litvy. Vil'ni︠u︡s,
Mintis, 1973. 135 p., 29 leaves of
illus. At head of title: I. Maniu-
shis. HC337.L5M29 DLC; CSt-H; InU;
IU; MB; NNC; NcD; NjP; PSt; PPiU;ViU;
ViBlbV.

1239. --- Soviet Lithuania; economy and culture. [Translated by V.
Grodzenskis and G. Kirvaitis] Vilnius,

Gintaras, 1973. 122 p.,[29] leaves
of plates. illus. Translation of
E︠k︡onomika i kul'tura Sovetskoi︠ ︡ Litvy. HC337.L5M2913 DLC; WU.

1240. --- Tarybų Lietuva devinta-
jame penkmetyje. [Soviet Lithuania
in the ninth five-year plan]. Vil'-
ni︠u︡s, Mintis, 1972. 74 p.
HC337.L5M32 DLC.

1241. MEŠKAUSKAS, Kazys. Lietuvos
dabartis ir ateitis. [The present
and the future of Lithuania. By]
K. Meškauskas, V. Januškevičius, V.
Puronas.. Vilnius, [s.n.], 1973. 96
p., 1 leaf of maps inserted. At
head of title: Lietuvos TSR Žinijos
draugija. HC337.L5M385 DLC; MH.

1242. POLITINĖS EKONOMIJOS PAGRIN-
dų programa politinio švietimo sistemos rateliams. [The programme of the
political economy for the groups in
political education]. Vilnius, Laikraščių ir žurnalų leidykla, 1963.
29 p. Bibliography: p. 23-[28].
HB179.L5P6 DLC.

1243. PREKYBOS IR GAMYBOS ĮMONIŲ
tiesioginiai ryšiai. [The direct relations between the industry and the
business sector] Vilnius, 1969. 123
p. HC337.L5P74 DLC; MH.

1244. PRIMENENIE METODOV OPTIMAL'-
nogo planirovanii︠a︡ narodnogo khozi︠a︡i︠ ︡-
stva respubliki. Na materialakh Lit.
SSR. Sbornik [statei︠ ︡]. Pod red. L.M.
Satunovskogo. Vil'ni︠u︡s, 1972. 178 p.
At head of title: Akademii︠a︡ nauk Li-
tovskoi︠ ︡ SSR. Institut ekonomiki.
HD84.5.P73 DLC; CU; MH; PU.

1245. RAČKAUSKAS, Kazimieras. Komunistų rupesčiai. [The worries of
communists]. Vilnius, Mintis, 1968.
63 p. HC337.L5R3 DLC.

1246. SOCIALINĖS INDUSTRINIO DARBO
problėmos; respublikinės konferencijos [medžiaga] 1973 m. vasario mėn.
1-2 d.d. Red. kolegija: R. Grigas
[et al.] [Social problems of working
conditions in the industry] Vilnius,
1973. 254 p. At head of title: Filosofijos, teisės ir sociologijos
skyrius prie Lietuvos TSR MA, Istorijos instituto.
CSt-H.

1247. ŠUMAUSKAS, Motiejus. Litva
sotsialisticheskai︠a︡. Vil'ni︠u︡s, Mintis,
1975. 158 p., [24] leaves of plates.
illus. DK511.L2S814 DLC.

1248. VILNA. UNIVERSITETAS. XX[
i.e. Dvidešimtosios] studentų mokslinės konferencijos pranešimų tezės:

Ekonomika, teisė. Tezisy dokladov XX studentskoĭ konferentsii: Ėkonomika, pravo. Vilnius, 1967. 47 p. At head of title: Vilniaus Valstybinis V. Kapsuko universitetas. In Russian. HB21.V55 DLC.

1249. ZUNDĖ. Pranas. Ekonomikos mokslas Sovietų Lietuvoje. [The science of economics in Soviet Lithuania] In Varpas (Chicago, Ill.) no.10, 1971, p. 48-60. See serials consulted.

IX.11.b. INDUSTRY AND ITS DEVELOPMENT

1250. BALASHOV, Pavel Ivanovich. Įmonė ir ekonominė reforma. [Enterprise and the reform of economy] Vilnius, Mintis, 1968. 59 p. illus. HC337.L5B34 DLC.

1251. CHARACIEJUS, Alfonsas. Ekonominė reforma lengvoje pramonėje. [Reform in the light industry] Vilnius, Mintis, 1969. 63 p. HD9735.R93L52 DLC.

1252. DARBO NAŠUMAS TARYBŲ LIETUvos pramonėje. [Labour productivity in Soviet Lithuanian industry]. Vilnius, Mintis, 1972. 247 p. At head of title: Lietuvos TSR Mokslų akademija. Ekonomikos institutas. By P. Stanikas and others. Summary in Russian. HC337.L5D36 DLC.

1253. GAMYBOS EFEKTYVUMO DIDINIMAS Lietuvos TSR pramonėje. [Growth of the industrial productivity in Soviet Lithuania. Red. kolegija: K. Meškauskas, R. Naiduškevičius, P. Stanikas (ats. redaktorius)] Vilnius, Lietuvos TSR Mokslų akademija, Ekonomikos institutas, 1974. 173 p. At head of title: Lietuvos TSR Mokslų akademijos Ekonomikos institutas. HC337.L5G33 PU; DLC.

1254. GLAGOLEVAS, V. Mekhanizatsiīa i avtomatizatsiīa truda v promyshlennosti Litovskoĭ SSR. Vil'nīus, Mintis, 1975. 60 p. HC337.L5G44 DLC.

1255. --- Technikos pažanga ir pramonės pagrindinių gamybinių fondų naudojimo efektyvumas. [Technological advance and effective use of the raw materials]. Vilnius, Mintis, 1971. 80 p. Bibliography: p.70-78. HC337.L5G45 DLC.

1256. IDZELIS, Augustine. Locational aspects of the chemical industry in Lithuania, 1960-1970. In Lituanus (Chicago, Ill.), no.4, v.19,

1973, p. 51-61. See serials consulted.

1257. KIUBERIS, Paulius. Išplėstinės reprodukcijos dėsningumai Tarybų Lietuvoje. [Laws of production in the Soviet Lithuania]. Vilnius, Mintis, 1974. 172 p. HC337.L5K48 DLC.

1258. LIETUVOS TSR MOKSLŲ AKADEMIJA, Vilna. EKONOMIKOS INSTITUTAS. Lietuvos TSR mėsos pramonės ir žemės ūkio ryšiai. [Relations between the meat industry and the agriculture industry in Soviet Lithuania. Ats. redaktorius V. Januškevičius]. Vilnius, 1975. 140 p. HD9425.L5L5 PU; DLC(title entry)

1259. LIETUVOS TSR MOKSLŲ AKADEMIJA, Vilna. STATYBOS IR ARCHITEKTŪROS INSTITUTAS. Gyvenamųjų namų sienos; vietinių medžiagų konstrukcijos mažaaukštei statybai. [Walls of dwellings; local construction materials for low buildings. Paruošė V. Barkauskas et al.] Vilnius, Valstybinė politinės ir mokslinės literatūros leidykla, 1961. 81, [3] p. illus., map. TH2231.L5 DLC; MH.

1260. LIETUVOS TEKSTILĖS PRAMONĖS MOKSLINIO TYRIMO INSTITUTAS. Mokslo darbai. 1- ; 1971- . Vilnius, Mintis. no. illus. Added title page, vol.1- : Naucho issledovatel'skie trudy. In Russian and summaries in Lithuanian. TS1300.L5 DLC.

1261. LITHUANIAN S.S.R. CENTRINĖ STATISTIKOS VALDYBA. Promyshlennost Litovskoĭ SSR. Stat. sbornik. Vil'nīus, Mintis, 1973. 418 p. At head of title: TSentral'noe statisticheskoe upravlenie pri Sovete Ministrov Litovskoĭ SSR. HC337.L5L532 1973 DLC.

1262. MAŽEIKA, Povilas A. Dabartinės Lietuvos pramonė. [The recent industry of Lithuania]. In Technikos Žodis (Chicago, Ill.), no.4, 1970, p. 17-21; no.5-6, p. 3-16; no.1, 1971, p. 2-5. See serials consulted.

1263. --- Die Entwicklung der Industrie Litauens. In Acta Baltica (Königstein, Ger.), v.9, 1969, p.177-228. See serials consulted.

1264. RUDASHEVSKIĬ, Leĭba Solomonovich. Nagliadnye sredstva glasnosti kontrolia. Vil'nīus, Mintis, 1973. 31 p. HC337.L53A87 DLC.

1265. STANKEVIČIUS, Petras. Perspektivy razvitiīa mestnoĭ promyshlennosti Litovskoĭ SSR; analiticheskiĭ obzor. P. Stankiavichius. Vil'nĭus, LitNIINTI, 1974. 39 p. (Obzornaĭa informatsiĭa) At head of title: Litovskiĭ nauchno-issledovatel'skiĭ institut nauchno-tekhnicheskoĭ informatsii i tekhniko-ėkonomicheskikh issledovanii LitNIINTI. Bibliography: p. 39. HC337.L5S73 DLC.

1266. ŪKINĖ REFORMA TARYBŲ LIETUvos pramonėje. [Reform of the Soviet Lithuanian industry. Red. kolegija: P. Stanikas (ats.red.) ir kiti] Vilnĭus, Mintis, 1970. 164 p. At head of title: Lietuvos TSR Mokslų akademija, Ekonomikos institutas. HC337.L5U44 DLC.

1267. VAITKEVIČIUS, Povilas. Razvitie elektro- i radiosvĭazi v Litve. Vil'nĭus, Mintis, 1972. 268 p. ill. Bibliography: p. 257-261. TK5101.V56 DLC; CU; NN; PU; PPiU.

1268. VYŠNIAUSKAS, Kazimieras. Materialinis skatinimas pramonės ĭmonėse (Dirbančiose naujomis planavimo ir ekonominio skatinimo sąlygomis). [The material incentive of the industrial enterprises] Vilnius, Mintis, 1969. 143 p. HF5549.5.I5V9 DLC.

1269. ŽILEVIČIUS, Rimas. Draugystės ugnis. [Gas industry in Lithuania] Vilnius, Valstybinė politinės ir mokslinės literatūros leidykla, 1962. 44 p. MH.

IX.11.c. COLLECTIVE FARMING; ITS ECONOMIC, TECHNICAL AND SOCIAL DEVELOPMENT

1270. ANDROŠIŪNIENĖ, L. Transporto naudojimas žemės ūkyje. [The transportation of the farm produce] Vilnius, Mintis, 1969. 76 p. S711.A55 DLC.

1271. GLEMŽA, Jonas. Die Landwirtschaft Sowjetlitauens 1960-1973. In Acta Baltica (Königstein, Ger.), v. 15, 1975, p. 211-279. See serials consulted.

1272. KARVELIS, Kazys. Kolūkiai ir kaimų gyvenvietės dabarties Lietuvoje. [The collective farms and the residences of today's Lithuania] In Sėja (Chicago, Ill.), no.4, 1971, p. 9-17. See serials consulted.

1273. KONDRATAS, Juozas. Tolimos pabarės. [Distant horizons... collective farm management. Bendraautoris

V. Vėteikis]. Vilnius, Vaga, 1971. 286 p., 9 leaves of illus. S562.R9K55 DLC; IU; MB; MH.

1274. LIETUVOS TSR MOKSLŲ AKADEMIJA, Vilna. BOTANIKOS INSTITUTAS. Praktiškos kovos priemonės prieš augalų ligas, kenkėjus ir piktžoles; straipsnių rinkinys. [Practical aproach to fight plant deseases, parasites and weeds. Redkolegija: J. Kriaučius et al.]. Vilnius, Valstybinė politinės ir mokslinės literatūros leidykla, 1962. 165 p. tables. At head of title: Lietuvos TSR Žemės ūkio produktų gamybos ir paruošų ministerija [ir] Lietuvos TSR Mokslų akademijos Botanikos institutas. CU.

1275. LIETUVOS TSR ĖMĖS TVARKYMO sistema. [The system of Soviet Lithuanian agriculture. By] Vytautas Geralevičius and others. Vilnius, Mintis, 1969. 524 p. S469.L5L52 DLC.

1276. LITHUANIAN SSS. VALSTYBINĖ ŽEMĖS ŪKIO KOMISIJA. Lietuvos TSR valstybinės žemės ūkio komisijos protokolai 1940m. [The minutes of the Soviet Lithuanian Commission on agriculture of 1940] Spaudai parengė Aleksandras Jefremenka. Vilnius, Istorijos institutas, 1976. 227 p. HD1995.65.A3 PU.

1277. MAČIUIKA, Benediktas Vytenis. Contemporary social problems in collectivized Lithuanian countryside. [By] Benedict V. Maciuika. In Lituanus (Chicago, Ill.), no.3, v.22, 1976, p. 5-27. See serials consulted.

1278. TAMOŠIŪNAS, Algirdas. Pagrindinių fondų ekonominio effektyvumo didinimas Lietuvos TSR tarybiniuose ūkiuose. [The increase of economic efficiency in the Soviet Lithuanian collective farming]. Vilnius, 1971. 77 p. At head of title: Lietuvos TSR Žemės ūkio ministerija. Žemės ūkio ekonomikos mokslinio tyrimo institutas. S562.L5T3 DLC.

1279. VILNA. ZEMĖS ŪKIO EKONOMIKOS MOKSLINIO TYRIMO INSTITUTAS. MOKSlinės-techninės informacijos straipsnių rinkinys. [Collection of articles and essays on pure and applied science and technology]. Vilnius, Laikraščių ir žurnalų leidykla, 1963. 72 p. S564.5.V55 DLC.

1280. ŽEMĖS ŪKIO GAMYBOS INTENSYvumas. Intensifikatsiĭa proĭzvodstva sel'skogo khozĭaĭstva. Vil'nĭus, Mintis, 1965. 92,[4] p. illus. (Kaunas. Lietuvos žemės ūkio akademija. Mokslo darbai, XII:1) Ats. redaktorius

N. Švažinskas. Summaries in Russian.
S13.K118 vol.12:1 DLC.

1281. ŽEMĖS ŪKIO GAMYBOS MECHANI-
zavimas ir automatizavimas. Mekhani-
zatsiia i avtomatizatsiia proizvods-
tva sel'skogo khoziaĭstva. [Redakci-
nė kolegija N. Švažinskas (pirmininkas) et al.]. Vilnius, Mintis,1964.
(Kaunas. Lietuvos žemės ūkio akademija. Mokslo darbai, XI:4) Lithuanian or Russian with summaries in
the other language.
S13.K118 vol.11:4 DLC.

1282. ŽEMĖS ŪKIO GAMYBOS MECHANI-
zavimas ir automatizavimas. Mekhani-
zatsiia i avtomatizatsiia proizvods-
tva sel'skogo khoziaĭstva. [Ats.re-
daktorius N. Švažinskas]. Vilnius,
Mintis, 1965. 59,[5] p. illus.
(Kaunas. Lietuvos žemės ūkio akademija. Mokslo darbai, XII:2). Summaries in Russian.
S13.K118 vol.12:2 DLC.

IX.11.d. LABOUR RESOURCES, THEIR UNIONS, INCOME, RIGHTS AND DUTIES

1283. DARBININKAS; gamyba ir lais-
valaikis. [Labouring class, production and leisure time. Red. kolegija: J. Aničas, R. Grigas, J. Galinai-
tė]. Vilnius, Mintis, 1972. 220 p.
At head of title: Lietuvos TSR Mokslų akademija. Filosofijos, teisės ir
sociologijos skyrius prie Istorijos
instituto. HD4854.D37 1972 DLC.

1284. DARBININKAS IR ĮMONĖ. [La-
bouring class and the enterprise.
Atsakingasis redaktorius R. Grigas]
Vilnius, Mintis, 1974. 319 p. At
head of title: Lietuvos TSR Mokslų
akademija. Filosofijos, teisės ir sociologijos skyrius prie Istorijos
instituto. Summary in Russian.
HD8526.5.D37 DLC.

1285. DARBO IŠTEKLIAI IR JŲ NAUDO-
jimas Tarybų Lietuvoje. [The labour
force and its use in Soviet Lithuania. Ats. redaktorius J. Skardžius]
Vilnius, Lietuvos TSR Mokslų akademijos Ekonomikos institutas, 1976.
184 p. HD5797.6.D3 PU.

1286. GINAITĖ, Sara. Tarybų Lietuvos gyventojų pajamos. [The income
of Soviet Lithuanian people]. Vilnius, Mintis, 1970. 308 p.
HC337.L53I55 PU; DS.

1287. LIETUVOS TSR GYVENTOJŲ PINI-
ginės pajamos ir jų panaudojimas.
[The income of Soviet Lithuanian people and their spending] [Ats. redaktorius J. Skardžius]. Vilnius, [s.n.]
1973. 122 p. At head of title: Lietuvos TSR Mokalų akademija. Ekonomikos institutas. HC337.L53I514 DLC;InU.

1288. NAUCHNO-TEKHNICHESKAĬA KON-
FERENTSIĬA, POSVĬASHCHENNAĬA VOPRO-
sam dvizheniĭa rabocheĭ sily, mekha-
nizatsii ucheta i analiza sostava ka-
drov v promyshlennosti, Trakai, 1965.
Tekuchest kadrov v promyshlennosti...
Otv. redaktor R. Naĭdushkevichĭus.
Vil'nĭus, 1967. 200 p. illus.
HF5549.5.T8N3 1965 DLC; MH.

X. HISTORY

X.1. BIBLIOGRAPHIES

1289. HAAF, Rudolf ten. Kurze
Bibliographie zur Geschichte des Deutschen Ordens, 1198-1561. Kitzingen
am M., Ger., H.O. Holzner, 1949. 43
p. Z6207.C55T35 DLC; CtY-D; CLU;MH;
PU.

1290. HILDEBRAND, Hermann. Otchety o razyskaniĭakh, proizvedennykh v
Rizhskikh i Revel'skom arkhivakh po
chasti russkoĭ istorii. Germ. Gil'de-
branta. Sanktpeterburg, Tip. Imp. A-
kademii nauk, 1877. 95 p. "Prilozhenie k XXIX-mu tomu Zapisok Imp. Akademii nauk, nr.3."
Z2537.H54 DLC.

1291. JABLONSKIS, Konstantinas.
1928 ir 1929 metų Lietuvos istorijos
bibliografija. [A Bibliography of Lithuania, 1928-1929] In Praeitis (Kaunas), v.1, 1930, p. 384-396.
DK511.L2P75 DLC; CaAEU; ICU(microfilm); KU; PU.

1292. --- 1930 ir 1931 metų Lietuvos istorijos bibliografija. [A
bibliography of Lithuanian history,
1930-1931]. In Praeitis(Kaunas), v.2,
p. [476]-500. DK511.L2P75 DLC;
CaAEU; ICU(microfilm); KU; PU.

1293. KLETKE, Karl. Quellenkunde
der Geschichte des preussischen Staates. Berlin, F.H. Schröder, 1858-
1861. 2 v. Z2244.P9K4 DLC; PU.

1294. MIEŽINIENĖ, A. Lietuvos TSR
istorijos bibliografiniai šaltiniai.
[Bibliographic sources of the Soviet
Lithuanian history] Vilnius, 1968.
279 leaves. Thesis--University of
Vilnius. Lith.VU.

1295. PRIŽGINTAS, V. Zenono Ivinskio darbų bibliografija. [Bibliogra-

phy of Z. Ivinskis' works] In Į
Laisvę (Los Angeles, Calif.), no.54,
1972, p. 73-78. See serials consulted.

1296. WERMKE, Ernst. Bibliogra-
phie der Geschichte von Ost- und
Westpreussen für die Jahre 1967-1970
nebst Nachträgen aus früheren Jahren.
Bearb. im Auftrag der Historischen
Kommission für ost- und westpreussi-
sche Landesforschung. Marburg (Lahn)
[Johann Gottfried Herder Institut],
1972. xii, 364 p.
DR10.W5 nr.93 PU.

1297. --- Bibliographie der Geschichte von Ost- und Westpreussen
für die Jahre 1939-1970. Bearb. im
Auftrag der Historischen Kommission
für ost- und westpreussische Landesforschung. Bonn; Bad Godesberg, Verlag Wissenschaftliches Archiv,[1974].
xv, 1153 p. Originally issued in 5
parts, 1953-1970.
Z2527.P78M47 PU; DLC; NRU.

X.2. PREHISTORY

1298. ANTONIEWICZ, J[erzy]. K
arkheologicheskomu izucheniiu drev-
nego naseleniia Pribaltiki. Issledovaniia, proizvedennye za poslednee
desiatiletie v Polskoi Narodnoi Res-
publike. In Eesti NSV Teaduste akademia. Toimetised. Uhiskonnateadus-
te seeria. Tallinn, 1957. t.6, p.
166-179. AS262.E3A2 DLC.

1299. ECKERS. Die ältesten Bewoh-
ner der Bernsteinküste in Ehst-,Liv-,
Kurland, Litauen und Preussen; eine
Skizze. Mitau, Latvia, F.Felsko,
1883. 32 p. Bound with Mittmann,F.
Führer über d.Kr. Nehr.
947.52.M699 PU.

1300. GIMBUTAS, Marija (Alseikaitė). Old Europe, 7000-3500 B.C.;the
earliest European civilization before
infiltration of Cudo-European peoples.
In Journal of Indo-European Studies
(Hattiesburg, Miss.), no.1, v.1,1973,
p. 1-20. See serials consulted.

1301. GROSS, Hugo. Die Steppen-
heidetheorie und die vorgeschichtli-
che Besiedlung Ostpreussens. In Altpreussen; vierteljahrsschrift...,
no.3-4, v.2, 1935, p. See serials
consulted.

1302. KOSTRZEWSKI, Józef. Z badań nad osadnictwem wczesnej i środkowej epoki bronzowej na ziemiach
Polskich. In Przegląd Archeologiczny, no.2, v.2, 1924, p. 161-218. See

serials consulted.

1303. KUŠNERIS (Knyševas), P. J.
Seniausios istorinės žinios apie
Pietryčių Pabaltijo tautas. Oldest
historical information about the peoples of the Southeastern Baltic territory. Translated from the Russian
by A. Tenisonas and edited by Jonas
Puzinas. In Lietuvių Tautos Praeitis (Chicago, Ill.), Bk.1, v.4, p.
117-137. See serials consulted.

1304. LELEWEL, Joachim. Narody
na ziemiach słowiańskich przed pows-
taniem Polski; Joachima Lelewela w
dziejach narodowych polskich, pos-
trzeżenia... Poznań, J. K. Żupański,
1853. lxxxii, 820 p.
947.52.L537.2 PU; BM.

1305. OKULICZ, Jerzy. Pradzieje
ziem pruskich od późnego paleolitu
do VII w.n.e. Wrocław, Zakład Narodowy im. Ossolińskich, 1973. 588 p.
(Monografie dziejów społecznych i po-
litycznych Warmii i Mazur, 1) Summary in English. GN814.P8038 PU; DLC;
ICIU; MH; MnU; MiEM; MoU; NNC; NjP.

1306. RIMANTIENĖ, Rimutė (Jablons-
kytė). Pirmieji Lietuvos gyventojai;
XI-IV tūkstantmetis pr. m.e. [The
first inhabitants of the 9th-4th centuries B.C. in Lithuania. Vilnius,
Mintis, 1972. 95 p.
DK511.L21R5 PU; MH; OKentU.

1307. ŠTURMS, Eduard. Die stein-
zeitlichen Kulturen des Baltikums.
Bonn, Ger., R.Habelt Verlag, 1970.
xxi, 298 p., 115 p. of illus. (Anti-
quitas. Reihe 3 (Serie in 4to): Abhandlungen zur Vor- und Frühgeschichte zur klassischen und provinzial-rö-
mischen Archäologie und zur Geschichte des Altertums, Bd.9)
GN776.S2S85 1970 DLC; CaAEU; CaBVaU;
CLU; CU; CtY; CSt; CoU; DDO; GU; ICU;
IU; IaU; InU; KyU; MH; MiU; MiDW;
MdBJ; MdU; MoU; MoSW; MnU; NN; NIC;
NBuU; NcD; NjP; NNC; PPiU; PSt; TxU;
ViU; WaU; WU.

X.3. GENERAL STUDIES OF THE HISTORY
OF THE BALTIC COUNTRIES

1308. ANDERSON, Edgars. Latvijas
vēsture, 1914-1920. [Latvian history
1914-1920] Stockholm, Daugava, 1967.
754 p. illus., maps, ports. On Lithuania: see index.
DK511.L178A64 CaOTU; CaAEU.

1309. Die militärische Situation
der Baltischen Staaten. In Acta Bal-

tica (Königstein, Ger.), v.8, 1968, p. 106-155. See serials consulted.

1310. --- Military policies and plans of the Baltic States on the Eve of World War II. In Lituanus (Chicago, Ill.), no.2, v.20, 1974, p. 15-34. See serials consulted.

1311. THE BALTIC. In Survey of International affairs, 1920-1923. London, 1927. p. 229-247 and Lithuania p. 215, 217.
D411.R88 1920-1923 CaAEU; see also serials consulted.

1312. CONFERENCE ON BALTIC STU-DIES, 3d, UNIVERSITY OF TORONTO,1972. Baltic history. Editors: Arvids Zie-donis, William L. Winter, Mardi Val-gemäe. Columbus, Ohio, Association for the Advancement of Baltic Studies, 1974. ii, 341 p. maps. (Publica-tions of the Association for the Ad-vancement of Baltic Studies, 5). Pa-pers presented at the 3d Conference on Baltic Studies sponsored by the Association for the Advancement of Baltic Studies at the University of Toronto, and held on May 11-14,1972, at the University of Toronto. In English or German.
DK511.B3C647 1972 DLC; CaAEU; CtY; ICarbS; NN; NjP; NmLcU; OOxM;WU;WaU.

1313. --- PROBLEMS OF MININATIONS; Baltic perspectives. Editors: Arvids Ziedonis Jr., Rein Taagepera [and] Mardi Valgemäe. San Jose, Calif., 1973. 214 p. (Publications of the Association for the Advancement of Baltic Studies)
HC243.C65 1972 DLC; CaAEU; CaBVaU; CSt; CtY; CU; GAT; ICIU; IU; InU; ICarbS; InNd; MB; MH; MiU; NN; NNC; NjP; NBuU; NBuC; NmU; OkU; RPB; UU; WU; WaU.

1314. DOUMERQUE, Émile. Une pe-tite nationalité en souffrance; les lettons; les provinces Baltiques et le pangermanisme prussien en Russie. Paris, Éditions de "Foi et Vie," 1917. iv, 150 p. illus., map.
D651.L4D6 DLC; CaBVaU; CtY; CSt-H; GU; ICJ; MH; MdBJ; NcD; ScU; WU; WaS; WaT.

1315. DUNSDORFS, Edgars. Latvi-jas vēsture, 1500-1600. [Latvian history, 1500-1600]. Stockholm,Dau-gava, 1964. 812 p. illus., facsims, maps, plans, port. At head of title: Edgars Dunsdorfs, Arnolds Spekke. Bibliography: p. 731-760. On Lithu-ania: consult index.
DK511.L173D92 CaAEU; CU; DLC; DeU; ICU; MH; MB; MiU; MnU; MiD; NN; NNC; NcU; OU; WU.

1316. --- Latvijas vēsture, 1600-1710. [Latvian history, 1600-1710] [Uppsala], Daugava, 1962. 588 p. illus., facsims., maps. On Lithuania; consult index.
DK511.L175D92 CaAEU; CtY; CU; DLC; ICU; InU; NjP; MB; MH; MiD; MnU; MiU; NN; NNC; NjP; OCl.

1317. ELKIN, Alexander. The Bal-tic States. In Survey of Interna-tional affairs, 1936-1946. London, 1958, v.3, p. 42-58.
D411.R88 1939-1946 vol.3 CaAEU; see serials consulted.

1318. ENQUIST, Per Olaf. Legio-närerna. [En roman om baltutlämnin-gen] Stockholm, Norsted, 1968. 414 p. DL658.8.E55 DLC; CU; CtY; IU; ICU; MH; NN; NIC; NcD; OkS; TNJ; TxHR.

1319. FLETCHER, William A. The British navy in the Baltic, 1918-1920; its contribution to the inde-pendence of the Baltic Nations. In Journal of Baltic Studies (Brooklyn, N.Y.), no.2, v.7, 1976, p. 134-144. See serials consulted.

1320. GORSKIĬ, Sergeĭ. Zhizn' i istoricheskoe znachenie kníazía An-dreía Mikhaĭlovicha Kurskago. Kazan', I. Dubrovin, 1858. 446 p.
DK107.K8G67 ICU; NN.

1321. HARTMANN, Waldemar. Die Bal-ten und ihre Geschichte. Berlin, F. Eher Nachf., 1942. 94 p. plates., map. (Schriftenreihe der NSDAP. Grup-pe III. Volkheid und Glaube, Bd. 7) DK511.B3H33 CaAEU; CSt-H; CU; ICRL; MH; OCU.

1322. KASLAS, Bronis J. The Bal-tic nations; the quest for regional integration and political liberty: Estonia, Latvia, Lithuania, Finland, Poland. Pittston, Pa., Euramerica Press, 1976. xiii, 319 p. maps. Bibliography: p. 303-312.
DK511.B3K29 PU; DLC; CaAEU.

1323. KENTMANN, Ruth. Livland im russisch-litauischen Konflikt; die Grundlegung seiner Neutralitätspoli-tik, 1494-1514. Marburg, Ger., 1929. Bound with Chudziński, E. Die Erobe-rung... 947.52.C473 PU.

1324. KIRBY, David. A great oppor-tunity lost? Aspects of Britisch commercial policy toward the Baltic States, 1920-1924. In Journal of Bal-tic Studies (Brooklyn, N.Y.), no.4, v.5, 1974, p. 362-378. See serials consulted.

1325. KÜNG, Andres. Vad händer i

Baltikum. Stockholm, Aldus-Bonnier, 1973. 274 p. (Aldusserien, 389) DK511.B3K78 PU; DLC; CU; CtY; InU; IU; MH.

1326. LAUTENSCHLÄGER, Karl. Plan "Catherine"; the British Baltic operation, 1940. In Journal of Baltic Studies (Brooklyn, N.Y.), no.3, v.5, 1974, p. 211-221. See serials consulted.

1327. ŁOSSOWSKI, Piotr. Kraje bałtyckie na drodze od demokracji parlamentarnej do dyktatury 1918-1934. Wrocław, Zakład Narodowy im. Ossolińskich, 1972. 303 p. DK511.B3L63 PU; CaBVaU; CLU; CSt-H; CU; DLC; ICIU; InU; IaU; MB; MH; MiU NNC; WU; WaU.

1328. LOWERY, Sidney. The Baltic States; the question of recognition of the Soviet Baltic republics... In Survey of international affairs, 19 1939-1946. London, 1955. v.6, p.245-260. D411.R88 1939-1946 v.6 CaAEU see also serials consulted.

1329. --- The Ostland. In Survey of international affairs, 1939-1946. London, 1954. v.4, p.568-575. D411.R88 1939-1946 v.4 CaAEU; see also serials consulted.

1330. MATULAITIS, Kazimieras A. Senovės skalviai (iki XIII amž.). The ancient Skalviai; a Baltic tribe] In Tautos Praeitis (Chicago, Ill.), kn.2, v.2, 1965, p. 123-142. See serials consulted.

1331. MYLLYNIEMI, Seppo. Die Neuordnung der Baltischen Länder, 1941-1944; zum nationalsozialistischen Inhalt der deutschen Besatzungspolitik. Helsinki,[Suomen historiallinen seura], 1973. 308 p. (Disertationes historicae, 2)(Historiallisia tutkimuksia, 90) D802.B3M9 PU; CaAEU; CaBVaU; CLU; CSt; CSt-H; CU-SB; DLC; InU; MiU; MoU; NcU; NjP; NBuU; TxHR; ViU; WU; WaU.

1332. PIUS II, Pope, 1405-1464. De Pruthenorum origine. In Grunau, Simonis. Preussische Chronik. Leipzig, 1889. Tomus 2, Tract.16, cap.7: Ratisponensis Dieta, p. 183-185. DD491.041P7 MdBJ; CU; MH; OCl.

1333. PUZINAS, Jonas. Baltų prekybiniai santykiai su Romos imperijos provincijomis pirmaisiais amžiais po Kristaus. Trade relations of the Balts with the Provinces of the Roman Empire during the 1st-4th centuries A. D. In Institute of Lithuanian Studies. Lituanistikos instituto 1975 metų suvažiavimo darbai. Chica-go, Ill., 1976. p.17-38. Summary in English. DK511.L2I64 1975 CaAEU; PU.

1334. RAUCH, Georg von. The Baltic States; the years of independence; Estonia, Latvia, Lithuania (1917-1940). Berkeley, Calif., University of California Press, 1974. xv, 265 p. Translation of Geschichte der Baltischen Staaten. Bibliography: p. 242-255. DK511.B3R3413 DLC; AAP; AzU; CaAEU; CaBVaU; CLSU; CU; CoFS; DAU; F; FMU; FU; ICarbS; IU; InU;InNd KEmT; MB; MH; MiU; MoSW; NNC; NNCoCi; NBuC; NBuU; NSyU; NcD; NcU; NjR; NdU; NcGU; NWM; NcRS; NvU;NmLcU; OCU; OkU; OU; OrU; PU; PSt; TxHR; TNJ; TU; UU; VtU; Wa; WaU; WU.

1335. SAPIETS-TUCKER, Maya Valda. Australia and the Baltic States,1919-1945. In Journal of Baltic Studies (Brookly, N.Y.), no.1, v.4, 1973, p. 47-56. See serials consulted.

1336. SCHAPER, Edzard Hellmuth. Aufstieg und Untergang der Baltischen Staaten. In His Untergang und Verwandlung. Zürich, 1952. p. 7-42. PT2638.A68U5 DLC; CaBVaU; IaU; MH; NN; NIC; NcU; NBuU; OkU.

1337. --- Untergang und Verwandlung; Betrachtungen und Reden. Geleitwort von Max Wehrli. Zürich,Verlag der Arche, 1952. 160 p. (Sammlung Gestalten und Wege). Partial contents.--Aufstieg und Untergang der Baltischen Staaten. Bibliographie: p. 157-160. PT2638.A68U5 DLC;CaBVaU IaU; MH; NN; NIC; NBuU; NcU; OkU.

1338. SCHIEMANN, Theodor. Russland, Polen und Livland bis ins 17. Jahrhundert. Berlin, G.Grote, 1886-1887. 2 v. illus. (Oncken, W., ed. Allgemeine Geschichte in Einzeldarstellungen. 2.Hauptabth., Th.10.) DK71.S2 MU; CaAEU; DLC; DDO; MdBJ; NjNbT; OCl; PU; PBm.

1339. SCHMIDT, Axel Johan. Dominium Maris baltici. Berlin, 1936. 76 p. maps. (Preussische Jahrbücher. Schriftenreihe, no.31.) D965.A2S349 CSt-H; CtY; MH; NN.

1340. SULLIVAN, Charles L. German Freecorps in the Baltic, 1918-1919. In Journal of Baltic Studies (Brooklyn, N.Y.), no.2, v.7, 1976, p. 124-133. DK511.B25B78 DLC; see also serials consulted.

1341. SZULC, Dominik. O znaczeniu Prus dawnych. Warszawa, W Druk. J. Klukowskiego i S.Strąbskiego, 1846. 155 p. map. 947.52.Sz76 PU.

1342. TRUMPA, Vincas. Napoleonas Baltija, Amerika; istorinės sintezės bandymas. [Napoleon, Baltic States and America; a historical synthesis]. Chicago, Ill., Algimanto Mackaus, knygų leidimo fondas, 1973. 251 p. HF1543.T73 PU; DLC; MB; OKentU.

1343. VIZULIS, Jazeps. Die baltischen Länder-Opfer sowjetischer Aggression. In Acta Baltica (Königstein, Ger.), v.8, 1968, p. 74-105. See serials consulted.

1344. WILPERT, V. von. Geschichte des Herzogtums Kurland. 3.erweiterte Auflage. Berlin-Steglitz, R.Würtz, 1917. 947.52.W688 PU.

1345. WINTER, William L. The Baltic as a common frontier of Eastern and Western Europe in the middle Ages. In Lituanus (Chicago, Ill), no.4, v.19, 1973, p.5-39. See serials consulted.

1346. --- Problems of the North-Germans and of the Hansa in the later medieval Baltic. In Bulletin of Baltic Studies (Tacoma, Wash.), no.8, v.2, 1971, p. 18-23. See serials consulted.

1347. WRANGEL, Ferdinand Ferdinandovich, Baron. Die russisch-baltische Frage. Aus dem Russischen übersetzt von A.N. St. Petersburg, H. Schmitzdorff, 1883. 61 p. GLP p.v.56, no.3--NN.

X.4. GENERAL STUDIES OF LITHUANIAN HISTORY

1348. AVIŽONIS, Konstantinas. Rinktiniai raštai. [Selected works of K. Avižonis] Roma, Lietuvių katalikų mokslo akademija, 1975- .
v. port. Vol.1 is reprinted of the 1940 ed. published by Lituanistikos instituto Lietuvos istorijos skyriaus leidinys, Kaunas. Bibliography: v.1, p. 11-35. DK511.L2A86 1975 DLC; CaAEU; DLC

1349. BATŪRA, Romas. Lietuva tautų kovoje prieš Aukso Ordą; nuo Batu antplūdžio iki mūšio prie Mėlynųjų Vandenų. [The Lithuanian struggle against the Tartars]. Vilnius, Mintis, 1975. 382 p. Summary in Russian. Bibliography: p. 317-[348] DK511.L23B3 PU; DLC.

1350. DAUKANTAS, Simanas. Raštai. [Works of S. Daukantas] Vilnius, Vaga, 1976. 2 v. illus. (Lituanistinė biblioteka, 16, 17) At head

of title. Simonas Daukantas. DK511.L2D29 1976 DLC; WU.

1351. DUCHIŃSKI, F.H. Zasady dziejów Polski, innych krajów słowiańskich i Moskwy; wyjaśnienie rzeczy co do pomnika mającego być postawionym w Nowogrodzie na pamiątkę założenia Państwa Moskiewskiego jakoby w 862 roku. Paryż, W Druk. Renou i Maulde, 18-- . v. DK414.D79 DLC.

1352. GEDGAUDAS, Česlovas. Mūsų praeities beieškant. [Looking for our ancient history. Meksiko? Del Toro spaustuvėje, 1972]. 357 p. illus. DK511.L21G4 DLC; MB.

1353. GREKOV, Igor' Borisovich. Vostochnaīa Evropa i upadok Zolotaoĭ Ordy; na rubezhe XIV-XV vv. Moskva, Nauka, 1975. 518 p. At head of titke: Akademiīa nauk SSSR. Institut slavīanovedeniīa i balkanistiki. I.B. Grekov. Bibliography: p. 488-[516]. DK90.G7 DLC; CaAEU.

1354. HRUSHEVS'KYĬ, Mykhaĭlo. Okupatsiīa ukraïns'kikh zemel' Litvoĭu i Pol'sheĭu, etc. In His Istoriīa Ukraïny-Rusy. New York, 1955. Tom 4, p. 1-496. DK508.5.H87I CaAEU; CtY; DLC; IaU; KU; NRU; OrP; RPB.

1355. --- Zagal'nyĭ pogliad na suspil'no-polïtychnu evolïutsiīu, ukraïns'kikh zemel' pid litovskim i pol's'kim rezhimom (XIV-XVII vik), In His Istoriīa Ukraïny-Rusy. New York, 1955. Tom 5, p. 1-26. DK508.5.H87I CaAEU; CtY; DLC; IaU; KU; NRU; OrP; RPB.

1356. IVINSKIS, Zenonas. Die Bedeutung des Kampfes zwischen dem lateinischen und dem griechischen Element im Grossfürstentum Litauen. In International congress of Historical Sciences, Stockholm, 1960. Rapports. D3.A2 1960d DLC; CLU; CSt-H; CSt; CLSU; CtHC; CaBVaU; CtW; DSI; DDO;IU; InNd; ICN; InU; IaU; ICU; KyU; MiU; MNS; MdBJ; MH; MiDW; MiEM; MtU; MnU; MoSCS; NN; NNC; NIC; NcU; NBSU-M;NjP; NcD; OCH; OCU; OU; OrU; OrPP; PU; PPiU; PPAmP; RPB; TxU; WaU.

1357. JAKŠTAS, Juozas. Gediminaičių dinastija Lietuvos istoriniame likime. The Gediminas dynasty in Lithuanian history. In Lietuvių Tautos Praeitis (Chicago, Ill.), kn.2, v.3, 1973, p. 23-36. Summary in English. See serials consulted.

1358. JURGĖLA, Constantine Rudyard. Lithuania; the outpost of freedom. [s.l., National Guard of Lithuania in Exile, c1976] 387 p. illus. Biblio-

graphy: p. 355-359.
DK511.L27J78 DLC; PU.

1359. KASULAITIS, Algirdas Jonas.
Lithuanian Christian democracy.
[Chicago, Ill., Leo XIII Fund, 1976]
xxiv, 244 p. illus. Bibliography:
p. 241-244.
JN6745.A98K7 PU; CaAEU; DLC.

1360. KOSMAN, M. "Podniesienie"
książąt litewskich. In Acta Baltico-Slavica (Warszawa), v.10, 1976,
p.15-36. See serials consulted.

1361. KOSMAN, Marceli. Reformacja w Wielkim Księstwie Litewskim w
świetle propagandy wyznaniowej.
Wrocław, Zakład Narodowy im. Ossolińskich, 1973. 273 p. Summary in German. At head of title: Polska Akademia Nauk. Instytut Historii.
DK511.L24K67 DLC; CSt; CU; ICU; InU
IU; MH; MU; MiEM; MiU; PPiU; PU; ViU

1362. KUTRZEBA, Stanisław. Historja ustroju Polski w zarysie. Kraków, Skład główny w księg. Gebethnera i Wolffa, 1914-1931. 4 v. Partial contents.--T.2. Litva.
JN6752.K8 DLC; CtY; CaBVaU; CoU; MH;
OCl; OU; MiU; WU. NNC(1949 ed.)

1363. LIULEVIČIUS, Vincentas.
Lietuvos senosios valstybės oficia-
lioji kalba. The official language
of the Grand Duchy of Lithuania. In
Lietuvių Tautos Praeitis (Chicago,
Ill.), kn.3, v.3, 1975, p.103-118.
See serials consulted.

1364. MASSUET, Pierre, 1698-1776.
Histoire des rois de Pologne et du
gouvernement de ce royaume. Où l'on
trouve un detail trés-circonstancié
de tout ce qui s'est passé de plus
remarquable sous le regne de Frederic Auguste, et pendant les deux
derniers interregnes, par Monsieur
M***. Amsterdam, chez F. L'Honoré,
1733.   v. On t.p. of v.3: Tome
second. Vol. 1 and part of v.2 are a
reprint of the 1698 ed. of Histoire
de Pologne et du grand-duché de Lituanie by J.G. Jolli. Cf. J.M. Qué-
rard. La France littéraire.
DK4131.J64 1733 DLC

1365. MOŚCICKI, Henryk. Pod zna-
kiem orła i pogoni; szkice historyczne. Wyd.2. zmienione... Lwów, Książnica Polska Towarzystwa Nauczycieli
szkół wyszych, 1923. 253 p. illus.
947.5.M85p 1923 IU; DLC-P4; CU; CtY;
IaU; IU; MH; NN(1915 ed.); NNC; OCH;
PU; WaU.

1366. PRZEZDZIECKI, Aleksander.
Życie domowe Jadwigi i Jagiełły z
regestrów skarbowych z lat 1388-1447.

Warszawa, 1854. 149.
DK425.P75 PU.

1367. STUDIA Z DZIEJÓW WIELKIEGO
Księstwa Litewskiego XIV-XVII wieku.
Pod redakcją Jerzego Ochmańskiego.
Poznań, 1971. 217 p. maps. At head
of title: Uniwersytet im. Adama Mickiewicza, Wydział filozoficzno-histo-
ryczny, Seria Historia. Zeszyty,
nr. 11. DK401.P892 zesz.11 DLC; MH.

1368. VANSEVIČIUS, Stasys. Lietuvos valstybės ir teisės istorija nuo
XVI amžiaus antrosios pusės iki XVIII
amžiaus pabaigos. [History of the Lithuanian State and law from the 16th
until the end of 18th centuries].
Vilnius, 1974. 118 p. At head of
title: Aukštojo ir specialiojo vidurinio mokslo ministerija. Vilniaus
V. Kapsuko Universitetas.
DLC.

1369. VILNA. UNIVERSITETAS. XVIII
[i.e. Aštuonioliktosios] Studentų
mokslinės konferencijos medžiaga: istorija ir filologija. [Materialy XVIII
Nauchnoĭ studentskoĭ konferentsii:
Istoriia i filologiia. In Lithuanian
or Russian.
D3L5V5 DLC.

1370. VOLDEMARAS, Augustinas. Raštai. [Works of A. Voldemaras. Redagavo Morkus Šimkus. Chicago, Ill.],
Lietuvos atgimimo sąjudis, 1973 [i.e.
1976]. xv, 672 p. DK511.L2V65 PU.

1371. WOJCIECHOWSKA, Maria. Polska Piastów, Polska Jagiellonów. [Poz-
nań], Druk. św. Wojciecha, 1946. 479
p. illus., ports., maps, geneal. tables. At head of title: Maria i Zygmunt Wojciechowscy.
DK420.W6 DLC; CtY; NN; NNC.

X.5. MINOR WORKS, OUTLINES, ETC.

1372. ADLERFELT, Gustaf. Histoire
militaire de Charles XII, roi de Sue-
de, depuis l'an 1700, jusqu'à la bataille de Pultowa en 1709, écrite par
ordre exprès de Sa Majesté, par mr.
Gustave Adlerfeld... On y a joint
une Rélation exacte de la bataille
de Pultowa, avec un Journal de la re-
traite du roi à Bender... Amsterdam,
J. Wetstein & G. Smith, 1740. 4 v.
port. Translated from the author's
Swedish manuscript diary by his son
Carl Maximillian Emanuel Adlerfelt.
DL735.A2   1740 DLC; CtY; ICU; ICN;
PU; PBa; PPULC; ScU.

1373. --- The military history of
Charles XII. King of Sweden, written

by the express order of his Majesty by M.G. Adlerfeld, Chamberlain to the King. To which is added an exact account of the Battle of Pultowa, with a Journal of the King's retreat to Bender. Illus. with plans of the battles and sieges. Trans. into English in 3 vols. London, Knapton, 1740. 3 v. Index to the work in vol.3, p. 285-334. Lots of information on Lithuania.
Spec.Coll. DL735.A23E5 1740 CaAEU.

1374. AKADEMIĪA NAVUK BSSR, Minsk. INSTYTUT HISTORYĪ. Belorussiīa v e-pokhu feodalizma; sbornik dokumentov i materialov. Minsk, Izd-vo Akademii nauk BSSR, 1959-1961. 3 v. DK507.5.A74 DLC; CaBVaU; CaOTU; CLU CLSU; CtY; CSt-H; CU; DDO; FMU; GU; IU; KU; MH; MiU; MU; MiEM; NN; NNC; NIC; NRU; NBC; NjP; NcD; NcU; ICU; InU; OCU; OkU; OU; PPiU; PSt; RPB; TNJ; TxHR; TxU; TU; ViU; WU; WaU.

1375. --- Historyĩa Belarusi u dokumentakh i materyialakh. Mensk, Vyd-va Akad. navuk BSSR., 1936- . v. vol.1 has added t.p.: History of White Russia in documents and materials. Vol.2 has title: Dokumenty i materiali pa historyi Belarusi; vol.3. Dokumenty i materialy po istorii Belorussii.; vol.4 iz isto-rii ustanovleniĩa Sovetskoĭ vlasti v Belorussii. DK507.A65 DLC; CLU; CU; NBC; NcU; MiU; IU; WaU.

1376. ANDERSSON, Ingvar. A history of Sweden. Translated from the swedish by Carolyn Hannay. New York, N.Y., Praeger, 1956. xxvi, 461 p. illus., ports., maps, facsims. DL648.A612 DLC; CaAEU; CoDAF; CU; GEU; MiU; MnU; MB; NcGW; OOxM; Or; PP; PBL; TU; TxU; ViU; Wy.

1377. --- Sveriges historia. 3. uppl. Stockholm, Natur och Kultur, [1950]. 502 p. illus., ports., maps. DL648.A63 DLC; CaAEU; MnU.

1378. BANNAN, Alfred J. and EDELE-NYI, Achilles, comp. Documentary history of Eastern Europe. From Sla-vic invasion before 1000 A.D. to the Czech crisis of 1968. New York,N.Y., Twayne Publishers, c1970. 392 p. DR1.B38 DLC; CaAEU; CaOTP; CLSU;CoU CoGuW; CoDuF; CBPac; FMU; FU; FTaSU; GU; ICU; InU; KyU; LN; MShM; MiU;MB; MiEM; MsU MsSM; MoSW; N; NjP; NjR; NRU; OCU; OClU; OClW; OU; OrPS; TxU; UU; ViU.

1379. BYCZKOWA, Margarita E. Le-genda o pochodzeniu wielkich książąt litewskich. Redakcje moskiewskie z końca XV i z XVI wieku. In Studia zródłoznawcze (Warszawa), tom 20,

1976, p. 183-199. Summaries in French. D13.S853 DLC; CaBVaU; CaOTU CSt; IU; ICU; MB; MH; NN; PU; WaU;WU.

1380. ERETAS, Juozas. Dvi genera-cijos mūsų krikščioniškosios kultūros tarnyboje. [Two generations in the service of our christian culture]. Roma, Lietuvių katalikų mokslo akade-mija, 1972. 54 p. Atspaudas iš LKM Akademijos Suvažiavimo Darbų, VII t. DK511.L212E45 PU.

1381. THE CAMBRIDGE HISTORY OF PO-LAND. Edited by W.F. Redaway [and others]. Cambridge, Eng., The Uni-versity Press, 1941-1950. 2 v. On Lithuania: consult indexes in both volumes. DK414.C3 DLC; CaAEU; CU; DAU; MH; MeB; MiU; MiHM; NN; NcC;NcD; NcU; NRU; NBuC; OCl; OU; OO; OCU; OClJC; OOxM; PPL; PHC; PjB; PSt; PPD; PP; PV; PPDrop; PPT; PBm; ScU; TxU; ViU.

1382. FLORINSKY, Michael T. The Southwestern Principalities and Li-thuania. In His Russia... New York, N.Y., 1953. v.1, p. 40-44. DK40.F6 1953 DLC; CaAEU; CaBVaU; CaBVa; CaBViP; CoDMS; DDO; IdU; IdB; IdPI; KyA; KyWAT; MB; MH; MiU; MtBC; MeB; MsU; MtU; NN; NIC; NcD; NcC;OCl; OClND; OU; OrAshS; OrLgE; OrP; OrSC; OrSaW; Or; OOxM; OCU; OClW; OO; ODW; OrPS; OrPR; OrStbM; OYesA; PU; PCM; PV; PPLas; PPT; PBL; PHC; PBm; PSt; PPWe; PWcS; TxU; TU; ViU; WaTC; Wa; WaE; WaSpG; WaT; WaWW; WaS; WU.

1382a --- --- New York, N.Y., Macmillan, 1960. c1953. 2 v. (xv, 1511, lxxvi p.), maps. Bibliogra-phy: p. 1482-1511. DK40.F6 1960 DLC; MH; ViU.

1383. GERUTIS, Albertas. Lietuvos kronika, 1918.II.16-1921.XII.31. [Lithuanian Chronicle...]. In Dirva (Cleveland, Ohio), nos.1-17, 1958. See serials consulted.

1384. GIEYSZTOR, Aleksander. A thousand years of Polish history, by Aleksander Gieysztor, Stanisław Her-bst [and] Bogusław Leśnodorski. [3d. ed.] Warszawa, Polonia Pub. House, 1964. 111 p. illus., maps. Trans-lation of Polskie tysiąclecie. DK415.G4813 1964 DLC; C; CLSU; CU; CU-SC; DeU; IU; IEdS; InU; KU; KMK; MH; MiDW; OrU; OrCS; UU; TxU.

1385. GOLAWSKI, Michał. Poland through the ages; an outline of Po-lish history for young readers. Eng-lish translation revised and adapted by Paul Stevenson. London, Orbis, 1971. 190 p. illus. coat of arms,

ports., maps. DK413.G6413 1971 DLC;
CtY; CU-SB; NBuU; NFQC.

1386. JAKŠTAS, Juozas. Žinios
apie Lietuvą prancūzų XIV a. autoriaus
Pilypo de Mezieres traktate. Lithuanians in the treatice "Le Songe du
vieil Pèlerin" of Philippe de Méziè-
res. In Institute of Lithuanian
Studies. Lituanistikos instituto 1975
metų suvažiavimo darbai. Chicago,Ill.,
1976. p. 41-49. Summary in English.
DK511.L2I64 1975 CaAEU; PU.

1387. JAKUBOWSKI, Jan. Dzieje
Litwy w zarysie. Warszawa, Polska
składnica pomocy szkolnych, [1921?]
57 p. (Bibljoteka składnicy, nr. 2)
DK511.L713J2 InNd; IU; PU.

1388. JANULAITIS, Augustinas.
Enėjas Silvius Piccolomini bei Jeronimas Pragiškis ir jų žinios apie
Lietuvą XIV-XV amž. [Eneius Silvius
Piccolomini and Hieronimus Pragensis
and their reports about Lithuania in
the 14th-15th centuries]. Kaunas,
1928. 63 p. (Kaunas. Universitetas.
Humanitarinių Mokslų Fakultetas. Raštai. Tom.3, sąs.5.)
BX1308.J35 1928 CaAEU; PU.

1389. JUČAS, M[ečislovas]. Nuo
Krėvos sutartics iki Liublino unijos.
[From the treaty of Kreva until Union
of Lublin]. Kaunas, Šviesa, 1970.
92 p. illus. Bibliography: p.[91-92]
DK511.L23J82 DLC; IU; MH; OKentU.

1390. KIZLYS-KIZLAITIS, A.D. Kas
žlugdė ir žlugdo lietuvių tautą?:Vin-
co Žemaičio studijos "Lietuviški vandenvardžiai ir pilkapiai nuo Vyslos
iki pat Maskvos" (1072) recenzija.
Čikaga, Kizlys-Kizlaitis, 1974. 124
p. illus. On Cover: What caused and
continues to cause the decline of the
Lithuanian nation? "Naujienų atkarpoje atspausdinta gegužės mėn. 2-21d.
1973 m., čia papildyta naujais duo-
menimis ir priedais." Summary in
English. DK511.L17K56 DLC; CaAEU.

1391. KLEPAŤSKI, P.G. Ocherki istorii Kievskoĭ zemli... Odessa, Tip.
Tekhnik, 1912- (Imperatorskiĭ Novo-
rossiĭskiĭ universitet. Zapiski isto-
riko-filologicheskago fakulteta, vyp.
5, etc.) Vol. 1.--Litovskiĭ period.
*QG--NN.

1392. KOĬALOVICH, MIKHAIL IOSIFO-
vich. Lektsii po istorii Zapadnoĭ
Rossii. Moskva, V Tip. Bakhmeteva,
1864. 303, 41 p. DK507.K58 DLC.

1393. KOPP, Max. Die Jagiellonen-
herrschaft 1386-1572. In His Polen;
seine Geschichte von den Piastenfürs-
ten bis zur Deutsch-Russisch Okkupa-

tion, 963-1939. Zürich, Europa Ver-
lag, 1940. p.13-19.
DK414.K83 CaAEU; DLC; InU; MiD; NN;
NNC; OCl.

1394. KURKIEWICZ, Władysław. Ty-
siąc lat dziejów Polski: przegląd
ważniejszych wydarzeń z historii i
kultury. Pod red. Adama Tatomira.
Wyd. 4., popr. i rozsz. Warszawa, Ludowa Spółdzielnia Wydawnicza, 1967.
675 p. maps. (Biblioteka uniwersyte-
tów ludowych i powszechnych).
DK414.K97 1967 DLC; CLU; CU;CaOOC;
CSt-H; CoU; IU; KU; MH; MiD; MU; NjP;
NN; OU; ViU; ICU.

1395. MALECZYŃSKA, Ewa. Unia Pols-
ki z Litwą i walka z agresją Zakonu
Krzyżackiego 1385-1422. Polska wobec
Czech i ziem Litewsko-Ruskich. In
Polska Akademia nauk. Instytut histo-
rii. Historia Polski. Warszawa,1958.
t.1, cz.2, p. 562-593. DK414.P83
CaAEU; CtY; CU; DLC; IU; MH; MiD; NN;
NNC; RPB; TxU.

1396. PIPES, Richard. Russia under the old regime. New York, N.Y.,
Charles Scribner's Sons, 1974. xxii,
361 p. illus. (History of civilization) DK40.P47 1974b DLC; AU; CaAEU
LN; NcU; NvU; ViBlbV; Wa.

1397. --- --- London, Weidenfeld
and Nicolson, 1974. xxii, 360 p.[24]
leaves of plates. illus. (History of
civilization) DK40.P47 DLC; CaBVaU;
CoU; InU; InNd; MdBS; MoU; MiEM; NjP;
NBuU; NNC; NcRS; PPiU; PSt; RP; TNJ;
WaU.

1398. PIUS II, Pope, 1405-1464.
Aenae Silvii Piccolomini Senensis qui
postea fuit Pius II pont. max. Opera
inedita descripsit ex codicibus chis-
ianis valgavit Josephus Cugnoni...
Roma, 1883. 1 v. (Atti della R. Accademia dei Lincei. Memorie della classe di scienze morali, storiche e fi-
lologiche. Ser.3, vol.8, p.319-686.
facsim.) De Lithuania: p. 417-419,480,
494, 584-585. AS222.R645 ser.3 vol.8
DLC; IU; ICN; MoU; MiU; MH; NcU; OCU;
OkU(microfilm); TxU.

1399. --- Europa Pii Ponti. Maxi-
mi nostrum temporum varias continens
historias. Venetiis, Otinum papien-
sem de luna, 1501. 83[i.e. 87] numb.
leaves. Rare Book Room Bp17.85 CtY;
DFo.

1400. --- De Lithuania. In His
Aeneae Silvii Piccolomini... Opera...
Roma, 1883. p. 417-419, 480, 494,
584-585. AS222.R645 ser.3 vol.8 DLC;
IU; ICU; MH; MiU; MoU; NcU; OCU; OkU
(microfilm)

1401. POLAND, THE LAND OF COPER-
NICUS. Editor-in-chief Bohdan Su-
chodolski. Wrocław, Ossolineum,1973.
231 p. illus. At head of title:
Polish academy of Sciences. Institu-
te of the History of Science and
Technology. DK425.P5813 DLC; AkU;
AzU; CaBVaU; CaOTP; CLU; CNoS; IaAS;
InU; GU; MiU; MoU; NBuU; NSyU; NcD;
NbU; NN; NIC; NmU; OU; PPT; TNJ; UU;
WU; WaU.

1402. POLONS'KA-VASILENKO, Nata-
liia Dmytrivna. Velike litovs'ko-
rus'ke kniazhivstvo. In Her Istoriia Ukraïny. Miunkhen, 1972. Tom 1,
p. 305-313. DK508.5.P57 DLC; AAP;
CaAEU; CaOTU; CLSU; CU; CU-SB; CoU;
DeU; ICIU; IEN; IU; InLP; InU; MH;
MoU; MU; NNC; NcD; NSyU; NjP; PPiU;
PSt; TxU; UU; ViU; WU; WaU.

1403. --- Velike litovs'ko-rus'-
ke kniazhivstvo v borot'bi mizh ne-
zalezhnistiu i unieiu. In Her Istoriia Ukraïny. Miunkhen, 1972. Tom 1,
p. 313-337. DK508.5.P57 DLC; AAP;
CaAEU; CaOTU; CLSU; CU; CU-SB; CoU;
DeU; ICIU; IEN; IU; InLP; InU; MH;
MoU; MU; NNC; NcD; NSyU; NjP; PPiU;
PSt; TxU; UU; ViU; WU; WaU.

1404. --- Litovs'ko-pol's'ki vid-
nosyny z tatarami. In Her Istoriia
Ukraïny. Miunkhen, 1972. Tom 1,
p. 337-346. DK508.5.P57 DLC; AAP;
CaAEU; CaOTU; CLSU; CU; CU-SB; CoU;
DeU; ICIU; IEN; IU; InLP; InU; MH;
MoU; MU; NNC; NcD; NSyU; NjP; PPiU;
PSt; TxU; UU; ViU; WU; WaU.

1405. --- Politychnyĭ lad Ukra-
ïny v litovs'ko-pol's'kiĭ dobi. In
Her Istoriia Ukraïny. Miunkhen,
1972. Tom 1, p. 346-352.
DK508.5.P57 DLC; AAP; CaAEU; CaOTU;
CLSU; CU; CU-SB; CoU; DeU; ICIU; IEN
IU; InLP; InU; MH; MoU; MU; NNC; NcD
NSyU; NjP; PPiU; PSt; TxU; UU; ViU;
WU; WaU.

1406. --- Sotsiial'nyĭ stan Ukra-
ïny v litovs'ko-pol's'kiĭ dobi. In
Her Istoriia Ukraïny. Miunkhen,1972.
Tom 1, p. 352-373. DK508.5.P57 DLC
AAP; CaAEU; CaOTU; CLSU; CU; CU-SB;
CoU; DeU; ICIU; IEN; IU; InLP; InU;
MH; MoU; MU; NNC; NcD; NSyU; NjP;
PPiU; PSt; TxU; UU; ViU; WU; WaU.

1407. --- Dukhove zhittia Ukraï-
ny v litovs'ko-pol's'kiĭ dobi. In
Her Istoriia Ukraïny. Miunkhen,1972.
Tom 1, p. 373-394. DK508.5.P57 DLC;
CaAEU; CaOTU; CLSU; CU; CU-SB; CoU;
DeU; ICIU; IEN; IU; InLP; InU; MoU;
MH; MU; NNC; NcD; NSyU; NjP; PPiU;UU;
PSt; TxU; ViU; WU; WaU.

1408. POL'SHA I RUS'; cherty obsh-
chosnosti i svoeobraziia v istoriches-
kom razvitii Rusi i Pol'shi XII-XIV
vv. [Sbornik stateĭ] Pod red. B.A.Ry-
bakova. Moskva, Nauka, 1974. 424 p.
Some articles are related to Lithu-
ania. At head of title: Akademiia
Nauk SSSR. DK71.P77 PU; AzU; CtY;
CaBVaU; CaAEU; CaOTU; DLC; GU; IEN;
ICIU;MB; MoU; MoSW; MiEM; MdU; NcD;
NcU; NjP; PPiU; RPB; TNJ; TU; ViU;
WaU.

1409. POUNDS, Norman J[ohn] G[re-
ville] Eastern Europe. Chicago, Al-
dine publishing Co., 1969. xx, 912 p.
illus., maps. DR10.P65 DLC; CaAEU;
CSt; DS; KEmT; MoSW; NjR.

1409a. --- --- Harlow, Eng., Long-
mans, 1969. xx, 912 p. illus.,maps.
HC244.P68 DLC; CaBVaU; CaQMM; CLU;
CtY; CU; DNAL; ICU; IEdS; InU; INS;
KU; MB; MiEM; MnU; MU; NcU; OrPS;ViU.

1410. QUENNERSTEDT, August Wilhelm,
ed. Karolinska kriges dagböcker jäm-
te andra samtida skrifter. Lund,
Gleerup, 1905. DL730.Q4 DLC.

1411. RAULINAITIS, Z. Prieš vi-
kingų audrą. [Before the storm of the
Vikings] [Brooklyn, N.Y.], Karys,
[1968]. 72 p. illus. (Lietuvos karinės istorijos raštai, nr.8) Cover
title. "Atspausta su papildymais iš
1966-1967 m. Kario. Pridėtas naujas
skyrius "Ginklai" (400-800 m.)."
DK511.L2A248 nr.8 DLC.

1412. RIASANOVSKY, Nicholas V.
A history of Russia. Second edition.
New York, N.Y., Oxford University
Press, 1969. 748 p. Contents.--Li-
thuanian state p. 72,88,99,111-117,
178,183; Unification of tribes and
evolution in Lithuania p. 87,146-151;
Wars with Lithuania p. 118, 148-150,
162, 167; Orthodox Church in Lithuania p. 133; Lithuania's expansion into
Russia and its effect p. 148-149; Po-
lonization of Lithuania p. 150-151;
Union of Lublin p. 150-154; Partitions
of Lithuania and Poland p. 298-299;
Statutes of Lithuania replaced by
Russian law p. 369; Emancipation of
serfs p. 411; Rebellion of 1863 p.
421; Treaty of Brest-Litovsk p. 529;
537; Litvinov protokol p. 569; mutual
assistance pact p. 573; Incorporation
into USSR p. 573, 589.
DK40.R5 1969 DLC; AU; AAP; CLU; CSt;
CoU; CoGrS; DAU; DS; FMU; FTaSU; FU;
GAT; GU; InU; ICU; IaU; IEN; IaAS;IU;
KEmT; KU; KyU; LN; MH; MnU; MiU; MiEM
MoSW; MU; N; NN; NIC; NBuC; NBuU; NbU;
NNCU-G; NjP; NjR; NcRS; NcD; NcU;NcGU
OkU; OU; OrU; OrPS; OrCS; RPB; ScU;
TNJ; TU; TxFTC; TxU; UU; ViU; ViBlbV;
WU; WaU.

1413. SHELEPIN, I. V. Kratkii̇ ocherk istorii zapadnoi̇ Russii, Litvy i Pol'shi. 2. znachitel'no dop. izd. Vil'na, Tip. A.G. Syrkina,1901. 947.52.Sh47 PU.

1414. SKIRMUNTT, Konstancja. Istorija Lietuvos trumpai apsakyta. [Lithuanian history... Translated and abridged by P. Neris] New York, N.Y. 1887. 143 p. 947.5.S CtTMF; BM.

1415. SOLOV'EV, Sergi̇ei̇ Mikhailovich. Istoriia Rossii s drevni̇ei̇shikh vremen. S.-Peterburg, Obshchestvennaia pol'za, [1894-1895]. 6 v. illus. DK40.S6 DLC; CaBVaU; NN; OrU.

1416. --- --- 2. izd. S.-Peterburg, Obshchestvennai̇a pol'za, 1896. 6 v. DK40.S62 DLC; OU.

1417. --- --- [Otv. redaktor L.V. Cherepin] Moskva, Izd-vo sots.- ekon. lit-ry, 1959- . 29 v. in 15. On recto of t.p.: Akademii̇a nauk SSSR. Institut istorii. Geographical index to all 29 volumes has page references to Lithuania. DK40.S596 DLC;AU; CaAEU; CaBVaU; CaOTU; CLSU; CtW; CtY; DeU; FU; GU; IEN; IaU; KU; KyU; LU; LNT; MH; MiD; Md; MdBJ; MNS; MiU; MnU; NN; NNC; NIC; NBC; NjP; NcU; NbU; OCU; OU; OOxM; OrU; RPB; TxHR; TxHU; VtMiM ViU; WU; WaU.

1418. TREADGOLD, Donald W. Twentieth century Russia. 4th ed. Chicago, Ill., Rand McNally, c1976. xiii, 573 p. maps. (Rand McNally history series) DK246.T65 1976 DLC.

1419. TURCHINOVICH, O. Obozri̇e̊nie istorii Bi̇elorussii s drevni̇ei̇shikh vremen. Sanktpeterburg, v Tip. E. Prat̊sa, 1857. xii, 303 p. DK507.T84 DLC; NN; WU.

1420. VARAKAUSKAS, Rokas. Pilėnų gynimas. [The defence of Pilėnai] Vilnius, Valstybinė politinės ir mokslinės literatūros leidykla, 1960. 24 p. illus. GR203.L5V3 DLC; PU.

1421. VENCLOVA, J.M. Lietuvių tautos pašaukimas. [The call of the Lithuanian nation]. Chicago, Ill., Draugo spaustuvė, 1975. 76 p. Summary in English. Bibliography: p. 68-73. DK511.L2V412 DLC; CaAEU.

1422. --- Prutėnai ir Rytų Galindai. [Prutėnai and East galindai; a Baltic tribes]. Cover title. "Atspaudas iš 1947 m. rugpiūčio 12-22 d. Naujienų." Bibliography: p. 32-39. DK511.L23V468 DLC.

1423. WESTWOOD, J. N. Endurance and endeavour; Russian history,1812-1971. London, Eng., Oxford University Press, 1973. viii, 471 p. maps. The short Oxford history of the modern world) Bibliography: p.[418]-438. DK189.W47 DLC; AAP; AzU;CaAEU CaBVaU; CaQMM; CaOTP; CSt; CLS;CU-S; CtY; CtW; CoU; CLSU; CU; CU-SB DAU; DS; DGU; FU; GAT; GU; InU; IU; INS; ICIU; IaAS; InNd; KEmT; KU; KyU; LU; MB; MH; MdU; MnU; MU; MBC; MiEM; MoU; MoSW; MiU; NN; NNC; NIC; NRU; NBuC; NNCU-G; NcD; NcU; NcRS; NcGU; NjP; NjR; NjMD; NvU; NmU; NbU; OCU; OKentU; OOxM; OO; OU; OkU; OrPS;PSt; PPiU; PPT; RPB; TNJ; TxHR; TxBeaL;UU; ViU; VtU; WU; Wa; WaU.

1424. WHITTON, Frederick Ernest. From the restoration of the monarchy to the death of Casimir IV [and] Poland under the later Jagellonic kings In His History of Poland... London, 1917. p. 38-40, 57-90. DK414.W62 CaAEU; DLC.

1425. ŽEMAITIS, Vincas. Lietuviški vandenvardžiai ir pilkapiai nuo Vyslos iki pat Maskvos; lietuvių tautos praeities fragmentai. [Lithuanian hydronyms and burial mounds from Vistula till Moscow; fragments of history. Chicago, Ill., Krumplio-Stulpino spaustuvė],1972. 63 p. illus. Summary in English. "Naujienų atkarpoje atspausdinta geg. mėn.22-birž.23 d., 1972." Bibliography: p. 57-59. DK511.L23Z39 DLC; CaAEU; InU; MB.

X.6. TEXTBOOKS

1426. ČEPĖNAS, Pranas. Naujųjų laikų Lietuvos istorija. [Current history of Lithuania. Spaudai parengti padėjo Albina Sirutytė-Čepėnienė. Chicago, Ill.], Dr. Kazio Griniaus Fondas, 1977- . v. DK511.L25C45 PU.

1427. KONČIUS, Juozas B. History of Lithuania. [By] Joseph B. Koncius. [Chicago, Ill.], Lithuanian American Community of the USA, [1972]. 142 p. Bibliography: p. 141-142. DK511.L2K682 DLC; PU; InNd.

1428. LIETUVIŲ TAUTOS IR VALSTYBĖS istorija. [History of the Lithuanian nation and the state]. Redagavo Vincentas Liulevičius. Chicago, Ill., Lietuvių bendruomenės Švietimo taryba, 1974- . v. illus. Contents.-- 1. Istorijos vadovėlis lituanistinių mokyklų IX skyriui arba V klasei.-- 2. Istorijos vadovėlis lituanistinių mokyklų X skyriui arba VI klasei. DK511.L2L413 DLC.

1429. MAIRONIS, Jonas. Lietuvos
istorija; su kunigaikščių paveikslais
ir žemėlapiu. 3.kartą atspausta ir
pataisyta. [Lithuanian history...]
Š. M-lis, [pseud.]. Petropilis, Išleista Lietuvių laikraščio pinigais,
1906. [Xerox copy, 1978] 259 p.
DK511.L2M2 1906a PU(xerox).

1430. ŠMULKŠTYS, Antanas. Lietuvos istorija. [Lithuanian history.
By] Paparonis, [pseud.]. Seinai,
Šaltinis, 1910. 142 p. illus.,ports,
maps. K5035 MB.

X.7. HISTORIOGRAPHY, CRITICISM AND REVIEWS

1431. AŚCIK, Kazimierz. Historio-
grafia w języku litewskim dotycząca
walk Litwy z Zakonem. In Acta Baltico-Slavica (Warszawa), no.9, 1976,
p.283-290. See serials consulted.

1432. DAINAUSKAS, Jonas. Lietuvos istorija naujų šaltinių šviesoje.
[Lithuanian history as reflected in
the new sources] In Tautos Praeitis
(Chicago, Ill.), kn.2, v.2, 1965,
p. 204-206. See serials consulted

1433. GERULLIS, Georg. Bretke
als Geschichtschreiber. In Archiv
für slavische Philologie (Berlin),
v.40, 1926, p. 117-163. See serials
consulted.

1434. HELLMANN, Manfred. Über ei-
nige neuere polnische Arbeiten zur
Geschichte Litauens. In Jahrbücher
für Geschichte Osteuropas. Beiheft.
(Osteuropa Institut, München), N.F.,
Bd.21, Hft.4, 1973, p. 584-606.
D1.J3 DLC; see also serials consul-
ted.

1435. IVINSKIS, Zenonas. Motiejaus K. Liubauskio mokslo darbai Lietuvos istorijos srityje. [The works
of Matvei K. Liubavskii on Lithuanian history] In Židinys (Kaunas),
no.8-9, 1933, p. 164-171.
ICWA.

1436. JAKŠTAS, Juozas. Lietuvos
aušrinė istoriografija. [Early Lithuanian historiography]. In LKMASD,
v.8, p. 221-238. See serials consulted.

1437. --- Lietuvos istorikų darbai vakarų pasaulyje. The works of
Lithuanian historians in the Western
World. In Institute of Lithuanian
Studies. Lituanistikos instituto
1971 metų suvažiavimo darbai. Chicago, Ill., 1971. p. 262-270. Summary

in English. DK511.L2I57 DLC;CaAEU;
InNd; MiU; NIC; NRU; PU.

1438. KONFERENTSIIA PO ISTOCHNIKO-
VEDCHESKIM PROBLEMAM ISTORII NARODOV
PRIBALTIKI, Riga, 1968. Tezisy dokladov i soobshchenii Konferentsii po
istochnikovedcheskim problemam istorii narodov Pribaltiki. Riga, Zinatne, 1968. 114 p. At head of title:
Akademiia nauk Latviiskoi SSR. Institut istorii.
CSt-H.

1439. PENKAUSKAS, Pranas. Lietuvos istorijos versmių leidimas. [The
publication of Lithuanian history
sources] In LKMASD, v.1, p. 359-392.
See serials consulted.

1440. PUZINAS, Jonas. Vorgeschichtsforschung und Nationalbewustsein
in Litauen [von] J. Puzinas. Kaunas,
1935. viii, 134 p. Thesis--Univer-
sity of Heidelberg.
DK511.L21P85 DLC.

1441. SLAVĖNAS, Julius P. Lietuva amerikiečių istorijos vadovėliuose.
The treatment of Lithuanian history
in American textbooks. In Institute
of Lithuanian Studies. Lituanistikos
instituto 1975 metų suvažiavimo darbai. Chicago, Ill., 1976. p. 73-77.
Summary in English.
DK511.L2I64 1975 CaAEU; PU.

1442. --- The treatment of Lithuanian history in American textbooks.
In Lithuanus (Chicago, Ill.), no.3,
v.23, 1977, p. 41-46. See serials
consulted.

1443. STANAITIS, Gediminas C.
Kodėl neparašyta Lietuvos istorija.
[Why Lithuanian history is not yet
written. Chicago, Ill., Autoriaus
leidinys], 1975. 23 p.
DK511.L2S78 1975 CaAEU.

1444. TIIUNELITE, IA. (Tijūnelytė,
J.). Al'bert Viiuk Koialovich; khro-
nist XVII v. In Acta Baltico-Slavica
(Warszawa), no.8, 1973, p. 95-108.
See serials consulted.

1445. TRUMPA, Vincas. Istorija
šiandieninėje Lietuvoje. [The teaching of History in Soviet Lithuania]
In Metmenys (Chicago, Ill.), no.20,
1970, p. 159-167. See serials consulted.

X.8. SOURCES

X.8.a. CHRONICLES

1446. HELMOLDUS, presbyter boso-
viensis, fl. 1168. Helmolda kronika
słowian [tłumaczenie Józef Matuszew-
ki]. Warszawa, PWN, 1974. 484 p.
illus. Translation of Chronica sla-
vorum. DD145.H48187 1974 DLC;PSt;
NjP.

1447. LĪETOPISEŤS RUSSKIĬ (Moskovs-
kaĭa lĩetopis'). Prigotovil k izd.
A.N. Lebedev po rukopisi, emu prinad-
lezhashcheĭ. Moskva, Univ. tip.,
1895. 189 p. "Iz Chteniĭ v Impera-
torskom Obshchestvĩe istorii i drev-
nosteĭ rossiĭskikh pri Moskovskom
universitetĩe za 1895 g."
DK1o6.L53 DLC.

1448. RUSSIA. ARKHEOGRAFICHESKA-
ĬA KOMISSIĬA. Polnoe sobranie russ-
kikh letopiseĭ, t.32: Khroniki: Li-
tovskaĭa i zhmoĭtskaĭa, i Bykhovťsa.
Letopisi: Barkulabovkaĭa, Averki i
Pantsyrnogo. Moskva, Nauka, 1975.
233 p. 947D.R922.2 t.32 PU;CaAEU.

1449. RUSSOW, Balthasar, ca.1540-
1601. Chronica der prouintz Lyfflandt, darinne vermeldet werdt, wo
dath suluige landt erstengefunden,
vnde thom christendome gebracht ys:
wol de ersten regenten des landes
gewesen sind: van dem ersten meyster
Düdesches ordens in Lyfflandt beth
vp denlesten, vnde van eines ydtli-
ken daden. Wat sick in der voranderi-
inge der lyfflendischen stende, vnd
na der tydt beth in dat negeste 1583
jar, vor seltzame vnd wünderlike ge-
scheffte im lande tho gedragen heb-
ben... beschreuen dorch Balthasar
Russowen... Thom andern mal mith
allem flyte auersehen, corrigeret,
vorbetert, vnd mith velen historien
vormehret dorch den autorem süluest.
Gedrücket tho Bart, in der förstli-
ken drückereye, dorch Andream Seit-
nern, 1584. Ed. by K.E.Napiersky.
DK511.L3S4 DLC; MH; MoU; OCl; NN.

1450. --- Livländische Chronik.
Aus dem Plattdeutschen übertragen
und mit kurzen Anmerkungen versehen
durch Eduard Pabst. Reval, F.J.Kop-
pelsen, 1845. x, 348 p.
DK511.L3R82 DLC; CtY; NN; OU.

1451. --- Chronica der Prouintz
Lyffland in erneuentem Wiederabdru-
cke, mit Wörterbuch und Namenregis-
ter versehen. Riga, N. Kymmel, 1857.
viii, 194 p. 947.52.R928 PU; NN.

1452. --- --- Nachdruck der Ausg.

Bart, Seitner, 1584. Hannover-Döh-
ren, Hirschheydt, 1967. 194 p.
DK511.L36R8 1967 DLC; CLU; DeU; LU;
MnU; MiU; MU; NNC; WU.

X.8.b. COLLECTIONS OF DOCUMENTS, IN-
DEXES TO TO DOCUMENTS, AND
THEIR DESCRIPTION

1453. ADAMUS BREMENSIS, 11th cent.
M. Adam's Geschichte der Ausbreitung
der christlichen Religion durch die
hamburgische und bremische Kirche in
dem benachbarten Norden, von Karls
der Grossen bis zu Heinrichs des IV
Zeiten... Aus dem Lateinischen übersetzt und mit erläuternden Anmerkungen begleitet von Carsten Miesegaes.
Bremen, Johann Georg Heyse, 1825.
xvi, 372 p.
MH; NNU; PLatS; PPLT.

1454. --- M. Adami Historia ecc-
lesiastica, continens religionis pro-
pagatae gesta... cura ac labore Ev-
poldi Lindenbrvch. Lvgdvni Batavo-
rvm, ex officina Plantiniana, apud
Franciscvm Raphelengivm, 1595.
6 p.l., 156,[31] p. BR854.A3 DLC;
IaU; ICN; MiU-C; MnU; NN; ViU; CaAEU(
microfilm); NcD(microfilm).

1455. AKTY, OTNOSĪASHCHIESĪA K IS-
torii ĪUzhnoĭ i Zapadnoĭ Rossii, sob-
rannye Arkheograficheskoĭu kommissĩe-
ĭu. Sanktpeterburg, V tip. P.A. Ku-
lisha, 18--. Hague, Mouton, 196-. v.
(Slavistic printings and reprintings,
178-3, 178-5) DK3.A7 DLC; CLSU;
CU-SC; IEdS; IEN; ICIU; ICU; MH;NSyU;
PPiU; TxHR.

1456. DIE BERICHTE DER GENERALPRO-
kuratoren des Deutschen Ordens an der
Kurie. Bearb. von Kurt Forstreuter.
Göttingen, Ger., Vandenhoeck und Ruprecht, 1961- . 2 v. (Veröffentlichungen der Niedersächsischen Archiv-
verwaltung, Hft. 29, etc.)
CD1373.S26A3 Hft.29 DLC.

1457. BONNELL, Ernst. Russisch-
liwländische Chronographie von der
Mitte des neunten Jahrhunderts bis
zum Jahre 1410. Im Auftrage der Kaiserlichen Akademie der Wissenschaften
hauptsächlich nach liwländischen, russischen und hansischen Quellen ver-
fasst. St.Petersburg, Eggers, 1862.
xiv, 291 p. Photo-offset. Leipzig,
Zentral-Antiquariat der Deutschen De-
mokratischen Republik, 1967.
DK511.L3B6 1967 DLC; CaAEU; CU; MH;
MiU; MU; NN(orig.ed.); PPULC; PPiU;
PU.

1458. CODEX DIPLOMATICUS MAJORIS

Poloniae documenta, et jam typis descripta, et adhuc inedita complectens annum 1400 attingentia. Editus cura Societatis literariae poznaniensis. Poznaniae, sumptibus Bibliothecae kornicensis, 1877-1908. 5 v. Added t.p. in Polish. Vol.1-4 edited by Ignacy Zakrzewski, v.5 by Franciszek Piekosiński. DK402.C6 DLC; CU; IU; ICJ; CtY; NIC; NN(v.1-3).

1459. FONTES HISTORIAE LITUANIAE. Romae, Sectio historica Academiae Lituanae catholicae scientiarum, 1971- v. illus., plates. Bibliography: v.1, pt.1, p.[xv]-xviii. DK511.L2F65 DLC; CaAEU; NjP; PU.

1460. KASLAS, Bronis J., comp. The USSR-German aggression against Lithuania. Edited with foreword and introd. by Bronis J. Kaslas. New York, N.Y., R. Speller, 1973. 543 p. illus. DK511.L27K35 DLC; AkU; CaAEU CaBVaU; CaOTP; CSt-H; CLSU; CoU; FU; GU; IEN; InU; IU; MB; MH; MU; MiU; MnU; MiEM; NNC; NIC; NSyU; NBuC; NjP NcD; NcU; NbU; NvU; NmU; OkU; OCl; OU; PSt; RPB; TNJ; TU; UU; ViU; VtU; WU; WaU.

1461. KHOROSHKEVICH, A.L. K istorii izdaniîa i izucheniîa litovskoĭ metriki. In Acta Baltico-Slavica (Warszawa), no.8, 1973, p. 69-94. See serials consulted.

1462. LITAUISCHE WEGEBERICHTE. Hrsg. von Th. Hirsch. In Scriptores Rerum Prussicarum. Leipzig, 1861-74. Bd.2, p. 664-708. DD491.04lS4 DLC; CtY; ICU; KU; MH; PU.

1463. PREUSSISCHE REGESTEN BIS ZUM Ausgange des 13. Jahrhunderts. Gesammelt und hrsg. von Max Perlbach. [Nachdruck der Ausgabe Königsberg, 1876] Hildersheim, Ger., G. Olms, 1973. xiii, iv, 400 p. DD375.P73 1973 PU.

1464. PREUSSISCHES URKUNDENBUCH; politische Abteilung... Hrsg. Unterstützung des Herrn Ministers der geistlichen Unterrichts- und Medical-Angelegenheiten von Archivrath Philipp ... in Verbindung mit Dr. Wölky. Königsberg in Pr., Hartungsche Verlagsdruckerei, 1882-1932. 2 v. in 3. DD303.P7 DLC; CaAEU(1-2,4); CaBVaU; CtY; CU; MH; NN; PU.

1465. --- Neudruck der Ausg.1909. Aalen, Scientia, 1960-1964. 5 v. in 9. CaBVaU; CtPAM; CtY; CSt; NIC.

1466. LA REPRESSIONE CULTURALE IN LITUANIA. Milano, Jaca Book, 1972. 190 p. (Archivi per la Russia e per l'Europa orientale, 6) "A cura del

Centro studi Russia cristiana." "Documentatione": p. [43]-190. BX1559.L5R5 DLC; MH; NjP.

1467. TEUTONIC KNIGHTS. Das grosse Amterbuch des Deutschen Ordens. Mit Unterstützung des Vereins für die Herstellung und Ausschmückung der Marienburg, hrsg. von Walther Ziesemer. Wiesbaden, Ger., M. Sändig,[1968]. xxiv, 991 p. Reprint of the ed. published in Danzig by A.W. Kafemann in 1921. CR4759.A44 1968 DLC; CSt;CU; CU-S; MU; NNC; NIC; NjR; OU.

X.8.c. COMMENTARIES AND INTERPRETATIONS OF SOURCE MATERIAL

1468. ARTZIKHOVSKI, Artemiĭ Vladimirovich. Miniatury Kenigsbergskoĭ letopisi. [Leningrad, Tip. "Pechatnyĭ Dvor"], 1932. 39 p. (Rossiĭskaiâ akademiîa istorii material'noĭ kul'tury, St. Peterburg. Izvestiîa, t.14, vyp.2.) *QCB--NN.

1469. BERKHOLZ, G. Der Bergmannsche Codex der livländischen Reimchronik. In Gesellschaft für Geschichte und Altertumskunde zu Riga. Mitteilungen...(Riga), v.12, 1872, p.33-71. See serials consulted.

1470. CARO, Jakob. Johannes Longinus. Ein Beitrag zur Literärgeschichte des fünfzehnten Jahrhunderts. Jena, F. Hauke, 1863. 51 p. Thesis--University of Jena. Research on the cronicle of Jan Dlugosz. *C-3 p.v. 235--NN; NIC.

1471. KUPCHINSKIĬ, O.A. O nekotorykh voprosakh datirovki srednevekovykh dokumentov na osnovennykh soderzhaniîa. In Sovetskie arkhivy (Russia (1923-USSR) Glavnoe arkhivnoe upravlenie. Moskva, nr.3, 1976, p. 79-83. CDl710.S6 DLC; AAP; CaNBFU; CLU; CSt-H; CtY; CU; FU; ICU; InLP; InU; MH; MdBJ; MiU; NIC; NjP; TNJ; WU; WaU.

1472. PERLBACH, Max. Die ältesten preussischen Annalen. In His Preussisch-polnische Studien zur Geschichte des Mittelalters. Halle, Ger., Niemeyer, 1886. Hft.2, p. 71-74. DLC-P4; ICJ; MiU; NN; OCl.

1473. PTASZYCKI, Stanisław. Wiadomość bibliograficzna o rękopisie nieświeskim kroniki Macieja Stryjkowskiego. In Pamiętnik Literacki (Warszawa), t.2, 1903, p. 220-246. See serials consulted.

1474. SEMKOWICZ, Alcksander. Kry-

tyczny rozbiór dziejów polskich Jana
Długosza do roku 1384. Kraków, Nakładem Akademii Umiejętności, 1887.
xv, 406 p. Bibliography: p.[403]-
406. WC15184 CtY; BM.

1474a. VOL'TER, E[duard] A[leksan-
drovich. Gdīe iskat' zemlīu Nal'sh-
chanskuīu Ipat'evskoī līetopisi? ;
istoriko-geograficheskaīa zametka.
In Russia. Ministerstvo Narodnogo
Prosveshcheniīa. Zhurnal (Sanktpeterburg), v. 329, May 1900, p. 195-
201. L451.A55 DLC; NN.

X.9. HISTORY BY PERIOD

X.9.a. EARLY HISTORY TO 1236

1475. HELLMANN, Manfred. Über die
Grundlagen und die Entstehung des Ordensstaates in Preussen. In Giesse-
ner Hochschulgesellschaft. Nachrichten (Giessen, Ger.), Bd.31, 1962,
p.108-126. AS182.G5 DLC; CaOTU;
CtY; CSt; CU; IU; ICU; MH; MdBJ; MiU
MdBP; MnU; MoU; NNC; NbU; PU; WU.

1476. PUZYNA, Józef Edward. Po-
czątki panstwa i dynastii litewskiej
w świetle najnowszych badań. In Nauka i Sztuka (Warszawa), nr.1, Rok 3,
1947, p. 162-170. See serials consulted.

1476a. TAUBE, M[ichael von]. Rus-
sische und litauische Fürsten an der
Düna zur Zeit der deutschen Erobe-
rung Livlands (12-13 Jh.) In Jahr-
bücher für Kultur und Geschichte der
Slaven (Breslau, Ger.), N.F., Bd.11,
Hft.3-4, 1935, p. 367-502.
CB231.A3 DLC; CSt; CU; ICU; MH; MiU
NN; NNC; OCl.

X.9.b. MINDAUGAS AND OTHER DUKES, 1236-1316.

1477. KLYMENKO, Pilip. Die Urkun-
den Mindowes für den livländischen
Orden. In Altpreussische Forschungen (Königsberg in Pr.), Bd.6, 1929.
See serials consulted.

1478. KRZYWICKI, Ludwik. W poszu-
kiwaniu grodu Mendoga. In Przegląd
Historyczny (Warszawa), v.8, 1909.
See serials consulted; also offprint
from Przegląd Historyczny, v.8, 1909
947.52.M663.yK PU.

1479. MATULAITIS, Kazimieras A.
Kronikininkų Mindaugas [Grand Duke

Mindaugas in chronicles]. In Tautos
Praeitis (Chicago, Ill.), 1964, kn.1,
v.2, p. 19-31. See serials consulted.

1480. MYKOLAITIS. Mindaugis, didysis Lietuvos kunigaikštis ir karalius. Trumpas aprašymas jo gyvenimo
ir darbų. [Mindaugas, Grand Duke of
Lithuania and the King...]. Tilžė,
1899. 58 p. Reprint from Ūkininkas.
800R7 CtTMF; NN.

1480a. PASZKIEWICZ, Henryk. Z zagadnień ustrojowych Litwy przedchrzes-
cijańskiej. Kunigasi a problem eks-
pansji litewskiej na Rusi w w. XIII.
In Kwartalnik Historyczny(Lwów),no.3,
t.44, 1930, p. 301- . See serials
consulted.

1481. URBAN, William. The Prussian
-Lithuanian frontier of 1242. In Lituanus (Chicago, Ill.), no.3, v.21,
1975, p. 5-18. See serials consulted.

1482. VENCLOVA, J.M. Mindaugo
krikštas-Lietuvos krikštas. [The ac-
ceptance of Christianity by Mindaugas.
Chicago, Ill.], JAV LB Brighton parko
apylinkės valdybos leidinys, [1972].
24 p. Bibliography: p. 23-24.
DK511.L28M568 DLC.

X.9.c. GEDIMINAS AND OTHER DUKES, 1316-1345.

1483. FORSTREUTER, Kurt Hermann.
Die Bekehrung des Litauerkönigs Gedi-
min; eine Streitfrage. In Jahrbuch
der Albertus Universität zu Königsberg in Pr. (Freiburg in Br.), v.6,
1955-1956. See serials consulted.

1484. KUČAS, Antanas. Gedimino
dinastijos kilmė. [The origin of Gediminas dynasty. By] Antanas Kučinskas.
Kaunas, Spindulio b-vės spaustuvė,
1934. [Xerox copy, 1977]. Išspausdin-
ta iš Mūsų Žinyno, nr. 107 ir 108.
24 p. DK511.L23K8 1934a PU.

1485. PASZKIEWICZ, Henryk. Z dziejów Podlasia w XIV wieku. Kwartalnik
Historyczny (Lwów), Rok 42, 1928, p.
229-245. See serials consulted.

X.9.d. ALGIRDAS, KESTUTIS AND JOGAILA 1345-1392.

1486. KELLOGG, Charlotte (Hoffman)
Jadwiga, Poland's great queen; with a
preface by Ignaz Jan Paderewski, and
an introduction by Frank H.Simonds.

New York, N.Y., Macmillan, 1931.
xxvi, 304 p. front.
DK426.K4 DLC; CaAEU; CU; MB; MH;
MiU; NN; OCU; OCl; OEac; PPGi; PPA;
PBa; PP; PPL; ViU.

1487. KUCZYŃSKI, Stefan Maria.
Sinie Wody; rzecz o wyprawie Olgier-
dowej 1362 roku. In Księga ku czci
Oskara Haleckiego... Warszawa, 1935.
p. 81-141.
NN; WU.

1488. STRZELECKA, Anna. O królo-
wej Jadwidze; studja i przyczynki.
We Lwowie, 1933. 94 p.
DK424.95.S75 PU.

X.9.e. VYTAUTAS THE GREAT, 1392-1430

1489. CHŁOPOCKA, Helena. Procesy
Polski z Zakonem Krzyżackim w XIV
wieku; studium źródłoznawcze. Poz-
nań, [Państwowe Wydawn. Naukowe],
1967. 253 p. facsims. (Poznańskie
Towarzystwo Przyjaciół Nauk. Wydział
Historii i Nauk Społecznych. Prace
Komisji Historycznej, t.23, zesz. 1)
Summary in German. Bibliography:
p. [247]-249. DK401.P895 vol.23,
pt.1 DLC; CaBVaU;CSt; InU; MU; NcD;
NBuC; NSyU; WU.

1490. GALAUNĖ, Paulius. Vytauto
portretai. [The portraits of Vytau-
tas] In Praeitis (Kaunas), t.2, 1933,
p. 72-86. DK511.L2P75 DLC; CaAEU;
ICU(microfilm); KU; PU.

1491. JONYNAS, Ignas. Vytauto
šeimyna. [The family of Vytautas].
In Praeitis (Kaunas), v.2, 1933, p.
183-244. DK511.L2P75 DLC; CaAEU;
ICU(microfilm); KU; PU.

1492. LEWICKI, Anatol. Ze study-
jów archiwalnych. Drugi Przywilej
Brzeski. In Polska Akademia Umiejętnosci, Kraków. Wydział Historyczno-
Filozoficzny. Rozprawy i Sprawozdania z Posiedzeń. Tom 24, 1889, p.
186-214. See serials consulted.

1493. PENKAUSKAS, Pranas. Vytauto Didžiojo dvasinės kultūros srityje. [The achievements of Vytautas the
Great in the area of cultural deve-
lopment]. In Athenaeum (Kaunas),
no.1, v.2, 1931, p. 1-36.
ICCC; and see also serials consulted.

X.9.e.1. BATTLE OF TANNENBER, 1410.

1494. CZERMAK, Wiktor. Grunwald.
We Lwowie, Macierz Polska, 1910.

138 p. illus. (Wydawnictwo Macierzy
Polskiej, nr. 95). Nakładem Fundacji
im. Tadeusza Kościuszki z r. 1894,
nr. 6. DK4261.C93 DLC.

1495. GABRYS, Juozas. Vytauto ir
lietuviu veiksmė didžioje karėje ir
kovoje ties Grunvaldu. (Keli praeities ruožai). Kaunas, Saliamono Banaičio spaustuvė, 1912. 85 p. illus
(Švento Kazimiero Draugijos leidinys,
nr. 113.) [The role of Vytautas and
Lithuanians in the Great War at Gün-
wald] *QYL p.v. 4--NN.

1496. ŠMULKŠTYS, Antanas. Žalgiris. Paminėjimui 500 metų jubiliejaus
kovos ties Žalgiriu. [Tanneberg; 500th
anniversary of the battle. By] Paparonis, [pseud.]. Seinai, Šaltinio
knygyno lėšomis, 1911. 55 p. illus.,
ports., maps. *Q p.v. 2602--NN.

1497. SRUOGIENĖ, Vanda (Daugirdaitė). Žalgirio mūšis; 550 metų sukakčiai atžymėti. [The battle of Tannen-
berg; a 550-tieth anniversary]. Boston, Keleivis, 1960. 24 p. illus.
947.5Sr85.3 PU; MH.

X.9.f. THE JOGAILA DYNASTY, 1430-1572

1498. BOGATYŃSKI, Władysław. Z
dziejów małżeństwa Zygmunta Augusta z
Barbarą. In Polska Akademia Umiejętności, Kraków. Wydział Historyczno-
Filozoficzny. Rozprawy, 1916. See
serials consulted.

1499. KASHPROVSKI, Yevgeni Ivanovich. Bor'ba Vasiliia III. Ivanovi-
cha s Sigismundom I. Kazimierovichem.
In Nezhin. Ukraine. Istoriko-filolo-
gicheskiĭ institut Kniazia Bezborod-
ko. Sbornik istoriko-filologicheska-
go Obschestva pri Instituti... Kiev.
Sbornik 2, 1899, p. 173-344.
*QCB--NN; BM.

1500. KOZIELSK Puzyna, Józef Edward, Fürst von. Switrigail von Litauen. Die politische Bedeutung seiner Erhebung zum Grossfürsten. Fribourg, Switzerland, St. Paulus Druke-
rei, 1914. viii, 141 p. Thesis--
Fribourg (Switzerland). Bibliography:
p. [v]-viii. DK511.L23K69 DLC; PU.

1501. MATULAITIS, Kazimieras A.
Mikalojus Radvila Juodasis, 1515-1565.
In Tautos Praeitis (Chicago, Ill.),
kn.3-4, v.2, 1967, p. 235-247. See
serials consulted.

1502. PASZKIEWICZ, Henryk. W sprawie roli politycznej Koriatowiczów na
Wołyniu i Podolu. In Ateneum Wileńs-

kie (Wilno), 1938. Criticism of the studies of J. Puzyna. Offprint. 947.52.P265.6 PU; see also serials consulted.

1503. TEKSTY LISTÓW Z LAT 1433 i 1434. In Halecki, O. Z Jana Zamoyskiego Inwentarza Archivum Koronnego. Materiały do dziejów Rusi i Litwy w 15 wieku. In Polska Akademia Umiejętności, Kraków. Komisja do Badania Historii i Filosofii w Polsce. Archivum. Rok 3, Tom 12, 1919, p. 208-218. See serials consulted.

1504. WARNKA, Stanislaus. De ducis Michaelis Glinscii contra Sigismundum Regem Poloniae et M. Ducem Lithuaniae rebellione. Berlin, 1868. Inaug.-Diss.--University of Berlin. DLC.

X.9.g. TEUTONIC KNIGHTS AND THE WARS WITH LITHUANIA 12th-15th CENTURIES

1505. AMERIKOS LIETUVIŲ DARBININKŲ LITERATŪROS DRAUGIJA. Didysis lietuvių tautos priešas; Lietuvos rašytojai apie mūsų tautos ilgaamžę kovą su vokiškaisiais grobikais. [The great enemy of our country...] Brooklyn, N.Y., Laisvės spauda, 1943. 254 p. illus., ports. (Its leidinys, 50) 891.92C Am34 PU; NN.

1506. RAMM, Boris I͡Akovlevich. Krestonosna͡ia agresi͡ia v Pribaltike i ee porazhenie. In Papstvo i Rus' v X-XV vekakh. Leningrad, 1959. p. 95-134. BX1558.R3 DLC; CaAEU; CSt CtY; CU; DDO; InU; ICU; MH; MiU; MoU NN; NNC; NIC; NcD; OrU; OkU; TxU;TU; WaU.

1507. TENBROK, Robert Hermann. A history of Germany. Translated from the German by Paul J. Dine. München, M. Hüber, 1968. 335 p. illus. Translation of Geschichte Deutschlands. DD89.T413 DLC; AU; CaBVaU; CtW; CU; CLSU; FMU; GAU; GU; IEdS; IaU; IaDL; ICU; IEN; InU; KyU; KEmT; KMK; KU;MU MeB; MShM; MnU; MiU; MiEM; NN; NNC; NIC; NBC; NjMD; NjP; NjR; NcD; NcGU; OCU; OU; OkU; PPiU; PPULC; TNJ;TxHR; TU; TxU; VіU; WU; WaU; UU.

1508. --- --- Harlow, Eng., Longmans, 1969. 335 p., 54 plates. illus., maps. DD89.T413 1969 DLC; CaQMM; CLU; CtY; IEdS; IU; DS; MiEM; MtU; MnU; NcU; NcRS.

X.9.h. LITHUANIAN-POLISH COMMONWEALTH, 1569-1795

X.9.h.1. GENERAL STUDIES

1509. CHODYNICKI, K[azimierz]. Kilka zagadnień z dziejów wewnętrznych Litwy po Unji Lubelskiej. In Pamiętnik V Powszechny Zjazd Historyków Polskich w Warszawie 28 listopada do 4 grudnia 1930. Referaty. D3.P6P65 DLC; NN; see also serials consulted.

1510. DEMBIŃSKI, Bronisław. Polska na przełomie. Warszawa, H. Altenberg 1913. xiv,[2], 575 p. facsim., port. (Biblioteka historyczna Altenberga) Description of the political situation in Europe and the state of the Polish-Lithuanian Commonwealth before partition. DK434.D4 DLC; CaAEU;CU; CoU; NN; NcD; OU; PCamA.

1511. DESFONTAINES, Pierre François Guyot. Storia delle rivoluzione della Polonia dal principio di questa monarchia fino all'ultima elezione di Stanislav Leszczynski. Venezie, [s.n.], 1737. 2 v. in 1. 947.52.D394 PU.

1512. DUNDULIS, Bronius. Švedų feodalų įsiveržimai į Lietuvą XVII-XVIII a. [Swedish raids into Lithuania in the 17th-18th centuries] DK511.L24D83 PU.

1513. FELDMAN, Józef. Polska w dobie wielkiej wojny północnej,1704-1709. Kraków, Nakł. Polskiej Akademji Umiejętności; skł.gł. w Księg. Gebethnera i Wolffa, 1925. 318 p. DK432.F44 DLC; CU; CtY; NNC.

1514. FLORIA, Borys. Wschodnia polityka magnatów litewskich w okresie pierwszego bezkrólewia. In Odrodzenie i Reformacja w Polsce (Polska Akademia nauk. Instytut historii. Warszawa), t.20, 1975, p.45-67. DK425.O3 DLC; CaOTU; CSt; CU; ICU;IU; MB; MH; MiDW; NIC; NjP; NN; PU; WU; WaU.

1515. KAMIENIECKI, Witold. Litwa a konstytucya 3-go maja. Warszawa, 1917. 947.52.P194 PU.

1516. KORZON, Tadeusz. Dzieje wojen i wojskowości w Polsce. Wyd. 2. przejrzane i uzupełnione przez autora. Kraków, Akademia Umiejętności, 1923. 3 v. illus., fold.map. DK417.K7 1923 DLC; CtY; PU; and 1912 ed. DK417.K7 1912 DLC; NN; NNC.

1517. --- Dola i niedola Jana So-

bieskiego, 1629-1674. Wydanie 2. Kraków, Nakł. Akademii Umiejętności, 1898. 3 v. map.
*QR--NN; PP.

1518. KRASZEWSKI, Józef Ignacy. Polska w czasie trzech rozbiorów, 1772-1799... Warszawa, Gebethner i Wolff, 1902-1903. 3 v. illus.,ports fold.map. DK434.K72 DLC; ICLJF; CtY; CU; InU; KU; KyU; MH; MiU; N; NN; NNC; OU; RP; ViU.

1519. KUBALA, Ludwik. Wojna Szwedcka w roku 1655 i 1656, szkiców historycznych serya 4. Lwow, H. Altenberg,[1914] vi, 495 p. illus., ports. (Biblioteka historyczna Alterberga) DL725.K8 DLC; CtY; CSt;CoU MH; NN; NNC; PSt; ScU.

1520. LACROIX, François Petit de. A review of the conditions of the principal states of Europe and the United States of America, given originally as lectures... Now first translated from the French, with notes by the translator of the Abbe Raynals letter to the National assembly of France... London, G.G.J. & J. Robinson, 1792. 2 v.
MdBJ; NNG; NcD; RPJCB.

1521. --- Verfassung der vornehmsten europäischen und der Vereinigten Staaten... Aus dem Französischen mit Berichtigungen des Übersetzers. Leipzig, Weidmannsche Buchhandlung, 1792-1803. 6 v. "Vorelesung von der polnischen Constitution. Theilung von Polen, etc." v.1, p. 191-328. JF33L14 1792 CaAEU.

1522. MANIFESTUM CONFOEDERATIONIS SENDOMIRIENSIS contra coronationem illegitimam Stanislai Leczinski. Manifest der sendomirischen Confoederation... [Tykozin, 1705] 16 p. Latin and German. Bound with Fritsch, Th. Exercitatio ivris pvblici de iure imperii. Francofvrti, 1730. JN5276.M89 1930 CaAEU.

1523. NARUSZEWICZ, Adam Stanisław, Bp., 1733-1780. Historia Jana Karola Chodkiewicza...[1560-1621]; wojewody wileńskiego, hetmana wielkiego W.X.Litewskiego. Warszawa, T. Mostowski, 1805. 2 v. (Wybór pisarzów polskich. Historya) 917.52.C459.yZi PU.

1524. --- --- Wyd. nowe Jana Nep. Bobrowicza z popiersiem Chodkiewicza. W Lipsku, Breitkopf & Haertel, 1837. 2 v. port. (Życia sławnych polaków, t.1-2.) DK430.2.C5N37 1837 CtY.

1525. --- Żywot J.K. Chodkiewicza, wojewody wileńskiego. Wydanie

Kazimierza Józefa Turowskiego. Przemyśl, M. Dzikowski, 1857-1858. 2 v. (Biblioteka Polska).
*QY--NN; MH.

1526. --- --- Kraków, Nakł. Wydawn. Biblioteki Polskiej, 1858. 2 v. in 1. DK430.2.C5N3 DLC; InU; IU; OU.

1526a. --- --- Kraków, Nakł. Wydawn. Biblioteki polskiej, 1859-1860. 2 v. 947.52.N172 PU.

1527. OGIŃSKI, Michał Kleofas. Mémoires sur la Pologne et les polonais depuis 1788 jusqu'à la fin de 1815. Paris, Ponthieu, 1826-1827. 4 v. DK435.O4 DLC; CaBVaU; CU; IaU; ICJ; InU; IU; MiU; CaAEU; NN; NIC; NWM; OCl; WaU.

1528. --- --- Pamiętniki Michała Ogińskiego... przełożone z francuskiego. Poznań, 1870-1873. 4 v. in 2. 947.52.Og44 PU.

1529. PAWIŃSKI, Adolf. Rządy sejmikowe w Polsce, 1572-1795. Na tle stosunków województw kujawskich. Warszawa, J. Berger, 1888. xiii, x, 431 p. JS6133.A8P3 DLC.

1530. POŁKOWSKI, I[gnacy], ed. Sprawy wojenne króla Stefana Batorego 1576-1586 Dyjaryjusze... Kraków, Akademia Umiejętności, 1887. xxxi, 430 p. (Akta historyczne do objaśnienia rzeczy polskich służące, t.11) *QR(AKta)--NN.

1531. RADZIWIŁŁ, Albrycht Stanisław. Memoriale rerum gestarum in Polonia, 1632-1656. Oprac.: Adam Przyboś i Roman Żelewski. Wrocław, Zakład Narodowy im. Ossolińskich, 1968-1972. 2 v. Summary in French. DK430.3.R3 PU; CaBVaU; CLU; CSt;CtY; CU; ICU; InU; InNd; DLC; MH; MU; MiU; NN; NNC; NIC; NcD; NjP; OU; TxHR;ViU; WU; WaU.

1532. ŚLIWIŃSKI, A[rthur]. Jan Sobieski. Warszawa, Wydawn. M. Arcta, 1924. 339 p. front., plates, ports, fold.maps, fold.plan. Bibliography: p. 333-336. DK431.S67 DLC; CtY; MH; NN; NNC; OCl.

1533. --- Król Władysław IV. Warszawa, M. Arct, [1925]. 222 p. front ports., plan. Bibliography: p. 221-222. DK430.3.S55 DLC; CtY; MH; NNC; NN; OCl.

1534. --- Stefan Batory. Warszawa, M. Arct, 1922. 271 p. front., ports. Bibliography: p. 267-270. DK429.5.S5 DLC; CU; MH; NN.

1535. ŠVABE, Arveds. Sigismunda Augusta Livonijas politika. [Livonian politics of Žygimantas Augustas (Sigismundus Augustus)]. In Latvijas Vēstures Instituts. Žurnāls (Riga), no.1-4, 1937. See serials consulted.

1536. TRUMPA, Vincas. Paskutiniai V. Gosiauskio metai. [The last years of V. Gosiauskis] In Lietuvos Praeitis (Kaunas), v.1, 1940. DK511.L2A233 v.1 DLC; NN; see also serials consulted.

1537. WALEWSKI, Antoni. Historia wyzwolenia Polski za Jana Kazimierza 1655-1660. Kraków, w Druk. Uniwersytetu Jagiellońskiego, 1866-1868. 2 v. Documents in French, German, Italian and Latin. DK430.5.W34 DLC(v.2.)

X.9.h.2. INSURRECTION OF 1794

1538. MORITZ, Erhard. Preussen und der Kościuszko-Aufstand, 1794; zur preussischen Polenpolitik in der Zeit der franzözischen Revolution. Berlin, Deutscher Verlag der Wissenschaften, 1968. 231 p. (Schriftenreihe des Instituts für Allgemeine Geschichte an der Humbolt-Universität, Berlin, Bd.11) Based on the author's thesis, Berlin, 1964. Bibliography: p. 199-220. DK418.5.P7M6 PU; CaBVaU; CaQMM; CLU; CFS; CtY; CoFS; CSt; CU; CU-SC; DLC; GU; ICarbS; InU; IU; LU; MH; MU;MiEM MoSW; NN; NNC; NIC; NBuU; NSyU; NjP; NcU; NcD; OU; OrU; PPULC; PPiU; PSt; TxHR; TNJ; TxU; ViU; WU.

1539. NABIELAK, Ludwik, ed. Tadeusz Kościuszko, jego odezwy, raporta uzupełnione celniejszemi aktami otnoszącemi się do powstania narodowego 1794 r. Kraków, Wyd. Centralne Biuro Wydawn. NKN., 1918. 947.52.N112 PU.

1540. --- --- Paryż, Księgarnia Luxemburgska,[1871]. DK437.A2N3 DLC; KU; NjP; OCl; PU.

1541. TRĘBICKI, Antoni. Opisanie sejmu... O rewolucji w roku 1794. Oprac. i wstępem poprzedził Jerzy Kowecki. Warszawa, Państwowy Instytut Wydawniczy, 1967. 398 p. illus. facsims., ports. DK434.T7 1967 DLC CaBVaU; CLU; CtY; CSt; CU; FU; IEN; ICU; IU; KU; MH; MiD; MiDW; MU; NNC; NSyU; NjP; NcD; OU; PU; WU; WaU.

X.9.i. LITHUANIA UNDER RUSSIAN RULE, 1795-1915

X.9.i.1. GENERAL STUDIES

1542. ANDERSON, Edgars. The Crimean War in the Baltic area. In Journal of Baltic Studies (Brooklyn, N.Y.), no.4, v.5, 1974, p. 339-361. See serials consulted.

1542a. GRUMPLOWICZ, Ladislaus[Władysław] Das russische Regime in Litauen und internationale Congress in Amsterdam. In Sozialistische Monatshefte (Berlin), Jg.8(10), Hft.8, 1904, p. 646-653. HX6.S6 1904 DLC; CSt-H; CU; ICU; IaU; MH; MdBJ; NNC; NN; NjP; WU.

1543. MOŚCICKI, Henryk. Tajny memorjał gen. gubernatora Trockiego o Litwie (1899 r.). In His Pod berłem carów. Warszawa, 1924. p. 232-242. DK434.9.M6 DLC; CaBVaU; CoU; CtY; CSt; ICU; MH; MiU; NN; OCl; OU; PU.

1544. NOL'DE, Boris Ėmmanuilovich. Baron. Die Petersburger Mission Bismarks, 1859-1862. Leipzig, R. Lamm, 1936. viii, 214 p. Translation of Peterbugskaīa missīa Bismarka. "Literatur und Dokumente" : p. 201-212. DD424.N64 DLC; CSt; MiU; MnU; NN; OClW.

1545. --- Peterburgskaīa missīa Bismarka, 1859-1862. Rossiia i Evropa v nachale tsarstvovaniīa Aleksandra II. Praha, Plamīa, 1925. 302 p. DD424.N79 CaAEU.

X.9.i.2. NAPOLEONIC WAR OF 1812

1546. BUDRECKIS, Algirdas. Lietuviai aukštieji karininkai Napoleono 1812 metų žygyje. [Lithuanian high-ranking officers in the Napoleonic Army, 1812] In Karys (Brooklyn,N.Y.) no.1, 1972, p. 16-18. See serials consulted.

1547. --- Napoleono administracinė tvarka Lietuvoje 1812 metais. [Napoleon's administrative setup in Lithuania] In Tėvynės Sargas (New York, N.Y.), no.1, 1974, p. 58-74. See serials consulted.

1548. --- Napoleono karo veiksmai Lietuvoje. [Napoleonic war activities in Lithuania] In Karys (Brooklyn, N.Y.), no.5, 1973, p.152-159; no.6, p.181-188; no.7, p.231-236; no.9, p.314-317; no.10, p.349-353. See serials consulted.

1549. SOKOLNICKI, Michał. Wojna roku 1809. Kraków, Nakł. Towarzystwa szkoły ludowej, 1910. 35 p. plates., ports., map.
DK435.S6 DLC; MH; NN.

X.9.i.3. INSURRECTION OF 1831

1550. NIEMCEWICZ, Julian Ursyn. Pamiętniki z 1830-1831 roku. Wydał Maryan Antoni Kurpiel. Kraków, Nakładem Akademii Umiejętności, 1909. 161 p. (Źródła do dziejów Polski porozbiorowych, IV)
DK435.5.N67K CaAEU; CtY; IU; MH; NNC; NcD; OU; ViU.

1551. PROTOKOLY POSEDZENIA RZĄDU Polskiego Tymczasowego w Litwie od 12 czerwca do 2 lipca 1831 r. w mieście Janowie i innych przy głównej kwaterze wojska. In Poland. Armia. Wojskowe biuro historyczne. Przegląd... Rok 2, t.3, 1930, p. 245-258. See serials consulted.

1552. ŠLEŽAS, Paulius. 1831 m. Lietuvos sukilėliv siekimai. [The goals of the Lithuanian insurgents in 1831]. In Židinys (Kaunas), no. 8-9, 1931, p. 80-81, 133-144; no. 10(82), p. 248-257.
ICCC; see also serials consulted.

1553. SLIESORIŪNAS, Feliksas. 1830-1831[i.e. Tūkstantis aštuoni šimtai trisdešimtv-tūkstantis aštuoni šimtai trisdešimt pirmv] metv sukilimas Lietuvoje. [The insurrection of 1830-1831] Vilnius, Mintis,1974. DK511.L25S55 PU; DLC; WU.

1554. SRUOGIENĖ, Vanda (Daugirdaitė). Lietuvos sukilėlė Emilija Platerytė. [The Lithuanian insurgent, Emilija Platerytė] In Karys (Brooklyn, N.Y.), no.10(1326), 1956, p.331-334. Mr. L.Kairys, Chicago, Ill., no.427; see also serials consulted.

X.9.i.4. INSURRECTION OF 1863

1555. BIRŽIŠKA, Vaclovas. Sušaudyti ir pakarti sukilėliai buv. Kauno gubernijos 1863-1864 m. [Shot and heanged to death insurgents of the former Province of Kaunas. By] Mjr. Biržiška. In Mūsv Žinynas (Kaunas), t.5, nr.15, 1923, p. 518-520. "Naujienos" Publishing House, Chicago, Ill.; see also serials consulted.

1556. CHANKOWSKI, Stanisław. Powstanie styczniowe w Augustowskiem. Warszawa, Państwowe Wydawn. Naukowe, 1972. 260 p. DK511.A84C45 PU.

1557. JAKŠTAS, Juozas. 1863[i.e. Tūkstantis aštuoni šimtai šešiasdešimt trečiv] metv sukilimas Lietuvoje. [The insurrection of 1863 in Lithuania] In Tautos Praeitis (Chicago, Ill.), kn.1, v.2, 1964, p.6-17. See serials consulted.

1558. JANULAITIS, Augustinas. Spausdintieji ir nespausdintieji 1863-1864 m. sukilimo raštai. [Published and unpublished works of the insurrection of 1863-1864] In Karo Archyvas (Kaunas), t.1, 1925, p. 207-232. D552.L5A5 DLC; see also serials consulted.

1559. KOLUMNA, Z[ygmunt] Pamiątka dla rodzin polskich. Krótkie wiadomości biograficzne o straconych na rusztowaniach, rozstrzelanych, poleglych na placu boju...1861-1866 r. Kraków, Wytłoczono w Drukarni W. Jaworskiego, 1868. 2 v. in 1. 4DKPol.9 DLC-P4; BM.

1560. ŁANIEC, Stanisław. Partyzanci żelaznych dróg roku 1863. Kolejarze i drogi żelazne w Powstaniu Styczniowym. Warszawa, Książka i Wiedza, 1974. 310 p. illus. Bibliography: p. 272-[290].
DK4378.T7L36 DLC.

1561. MICKEVIČIUS, J[uozas] 1863 metv sukilimas žemaičiuose. [The Samogitian rebelion of 1863] In Gimtasai Kraštas (Šiauliai), no.31, 1943, p. 316-331. Mr. Kviklys, Chicago has it.

1562. MILIAUSKAS, Juozas. 1863 metv sukilimą atsiminus. [Recalling the 1863 insurrection. By] Juozas Miliauskas-Miglovara. In Karo Archyvas (Kaunas), v.2, 1925, p. 45-51. Mr. Kviklys, Chicago, has it; see also serials consulted.

1563. MURAV'EV, Mikhail Nikolaevich. Chetyre zapiski grafa Murav'eva o Severo Zapadnom Krae, 1830-65. In Russkii Arkhiv (Moskva), v.11, 1885. See serials consulted.

1564. --- Zapiski grafa Murav'eva o miatezhe 1863 goda. In Russkaia Starina (Petrograd), no.12, 1882; no. 1-5, 1883; and no.6, 1884. See serials consulted.

1565. --- Zapiski ego ob upravlenii Severo-Zapadnym Kra'em i ob usmirenii v nem miatezha. In Russkaia Starina (Petrograd), no.37, 1882.

DK1.R863 DLC; see also serials consulted.

1566. SMIRNOV, Anatolii Filippo-
vich, writer on history. Sigismund
Serakovvskii. Moskva, Izd-vo Akade-
mii nauk SSSR, 1959. 134 p. illus.
(Akademiia nauk SSSR. Nauchno-popu-
liarnaia seriia) DK436.5.S5S53 DLC
CaAEU; CtY; CSt-H; ICU; InU; IU;IaU;
MH; MdBJ; NN; NNC; OU.

1567. --- Kastus' Kalinovskii.
Moskva, Izd-vo Sotsial'no-ekon.
lit-ry, 1959. 93 p. illus.,ports.
DK507.6.K3S6 DLC; CSt-H; CtY; IU;
MH; NN; NNC.

1568. TATISHCHEV, S[ergiei] S[pi-
ridonovich.] Dyplomacya rosyjska w
kwestyi polskiej 1853-1863. Warszawa, Nakład. K. Treptego, 1901. 176 p.
A translation of a series of articles published in the Russkii Viestnik. DK437.Y3 DLC; IU.

1569. VAIŠNORA, Juozas. 1863 metų sukilimas Suvalkijoje. [The insurrection of 1863 in Suvalkija] In
Tautos Praeitis (Chicago, Ill.), kn.
2, v.2, 1965, p. 1o7-122. See serials consulted.

1570. VOSSTANIE 1863 goda i RUS-
SKO-POL'SKIE revoliutsionnye sviazi
60-kh godov. Bibliograficheskii ukazatel' literatury na russkom iazyke.
Sostv. I.A. Koloeva [et al.] Moskva,
1962. 201 p. On Lithuania: p. 62-66,
102-111, 164-170.
NcU.

1571. WERESZYCKI, Henryk. Anglja
a Polska 1860-1865. Lwów, Towarzystwo Naukowe, 1934. 207 p. (Towarzystwo Naukowe we Lwowie. Wydzial II:
Historyczno-Filozoficzny. Archivum,
tom 10, zesz.3)
D1.T68 t.10 zesz.3 DLC; NN.

1572. ZAITSEV, Vladimir M[ikhailo-
vich. Sotsial'no-soslovnyi sostav
uchastnikov Vosstaniia 1863 g; na ter-
ritorii TSarstva Pol'skogo, Litvy,
Belorussii i Pravoberezhnoi Ukrainy.
Opyt statisticheskogo analiza. Moskva,
Nauka, 1973. 230 p. At head of ti-
tle: Akademiia Nauk SSSR. Institut
Slavianovedeniia i balkanistiki.
DK437.8.S6Z33 DLC.

1573. ŽIUGŽDA, Juozas. Antanas
Mackevičius. 1863-1864 metų sukilimo
reikšmė lietuvių tautos istorijoje.
[Antanas Mackevičius and the signifi-
cance of insurrection of 1863-1864 in
Lithuania] Vilnius, Mintis, 1971.
203 p. port. At head of title: Lietuvos TSR Mokslų akademija. Istorijos
institutas. DK511.L28M349 DLC; CtY;

CU; InU; NjP; PPiU; PU; WU.

X.9.i.6. INSURRECTION OF 1905 AND THE GREAT ASSEMBLY OF VILNIUS

1574. JURGINIS, Juozas. 1905 metų
įvykiai Vilniuje. [The events in Vilnius, 1905] Vilnius, Valstybinė politinės ir mokslinės literatūros
leidykla, 1958. 145 p.
DK651.V4J83 PU.

1575. MATULAITIS, Kazimieras A.
Sukilimas Sūduvoje, 1905-1906 metais.
[Insurrection of 1905-1906 in Sūduva]
In Tautos Praeitis (Chicago, Ill.),
kn.3-4, v.2, p. 257-270. See serials
consulted.

X.9.i.7. RUSSIFICATION AND TOTAL SUP- PRESSION OF THE LITHUANIAN PRESS

1576. BAGDANAVIČIUS, Vytautas Jonas. Svarbiausieji spaudos draudimo
tarpsniai. [The most important periods
of supression of the free press in Li-
thuania]. In Bagdanavičius, V.J. Kovos metai dėl savosios spaudos. Chicago, Ill.,[1957]. p.[7]-25. PN5278.
L5B3 DLC; CaAEU; CaOTU; CaOONL;
CtTMF; ICCC; ICLJF; MH; NN; OCl; PU.

1577. JAKŠTAS, Juozas. Vyskupo
M. Valančiaus memorandumas general-
gubernatoriui grafui Eduardui Trofi-
movičiui Baranovui dėl įvairių rusų
valdžios trūkdymų. Memorandum of
1866 from Bishop Valančius to the Russian Governor General. In Lietuvių
Tautos Praeitis (Chicago, Ill.), kn.
4, v.3, 1976, p. 27-32. See serials
consulted.

1578. JANCIUS, Fr.J. The book
smugglers. In The Marian (Chicago,
Ill.), no.10, v.2, 1949.
289.4.Ma ICLJF; CtTMF.

1579. KORNILOV, Ivan Petrovich.
Zadachi russkago prosveshcheniia v
jego proshlom i nastoiashchem. St.Pe-
tersburg, Tip. A.P. Lopukhina, 1902.
441 p. LA832.K665 DLC.

1580. LIETUVIŲ SPAUDOS DRAUDIMO
panaikinimo byla. [The discontinua-
tion of the total suppression of the
Lithuanian press. Spaudai parengė A.
Tyla] Vilnius, 1973. xxxi, 247 p.
At head of the title: Lietuvos TSR
Mokslų akademija. Istorijos institutas. Introduction and table of contents in Lithuanian; text in Russian.

Includes bibliographical references. PN5278.L5L48 DLC; InU; MH; PU.

1581. MAŠIOTAS, Pranas. Kai knygas draudė; įspūdžiai ir atsiminimai. [As the Lithuanian free press was totally suppressed]. 2. leidimas. Kaunas, Dirva, 1938. [Xerox copy, 1977] DK511.L25M38 1938a PU.

1582. MATUSAS, Jonas. Kunigų kova su rusų valdžia dėl tikybos ir gimtosios kalbos pradžios mokykloje. (Kauno gubernija nuo Muravjovo iki 1905 m.). [The struggle of Lithuanian clergy with the Russian government for teaching religion and Lithuanian language in the primary schools] In Tiesos Kelias Kaunas), no.5, 1930, p. 266-275. ICWA; ICCC; ICLJF; CtPAM.

1583. VAIŠNORA, Juozas. The forty years of darkness. Translated [from the Lithuanian] by Joseph Boley. [Brooklyn, N.Y.], Franciscan Press, [1975]. 59 p. PN5278.L5V313 PU;DLC.

1584. VALANČIUS, Motiejus, Bp. Maskoliams katalikus persekiojant. [The Russian persecution of catholics in Lithuania]. Surinko ir paaiškino doc. J. Tumas. [Includes: Lectures about M. Valančius by prof. J.Tumas, p.[106]-124. Paging of the reprint is that of the original book but not of the Lithuanian Historical Review] Reprint in Lietuvių Tautos Praeitis (Chicago, Ill.), bk.4, v.3, 1976, p. [56-181] See serials consulted.

X.9.k. FIRST WORLD WAR AND GERMAN OCCUPATION, 1915-1918

X.9.k.1. GENERAL STUDIES

1585. DER BOLSCHEWISMUS UND DIE baltische Front, mit Beiträgen von Kurt von Raumer [et al.] Leipzig, Ger., S. Hirzel, 1939. 104 p. maps. (Baltische Lande, Bd.4: Weltkriegs-und Nachkriegszeit, Lfg.1) DK511.B3B7 Bd.4 Lfg.1 DLC;MH; NNC.

1586. DANAHAR, David C. Lithuania through German-Polish eyes; an Austro-Hungarian State paper and the Lithuanian question, 1915-1917. In Journal of Baltic Studies (Brooklyn, N.Y.), no.1, v.4, 1973, p. 57-73. DK511.B25B78 DLC; see also serials consulted.

1587. DERUGA, Aleksy. Z dziejów ruchu rewolucyjnego na ziemiach w 1918 r. In Z dziejów stosunków Polsko-Radzieckich (Polska Akademia nauk.

Zakład historii stosunków Polsko-Radzieckick. Warszawa), t.11-12, 1975, p. 289-309. See serials consulted.

1588. GABRYS, Juozas. Lituanie et Allemagne; visées annexionistes allemandes sur la Lituanie à travers les siècles. [s.l., 1918?] Published under pseud. C. Rivas. DK511.L26R63 CSt-H.

1589. --- La Lituanie sous le joug allemand, 1915-1918; le plan annexioniste allemand en Lithuanie. 2. éd. [s.l.], 1919. Published under author's pseud.: C. Rivas. DK511.L25R61 Ed.2 CSt-H.

1590. --- --- 3. éd. Lausanne, En vente: Librairie Centrale des Nationalités, 1919. 700 p. Published under pseud. C[amille] C[harles] Rivas. 947.52.G113.5 PU; MH.

1591. KIELMANSEGG, Peter, Graf von. Deutschland und der erste Weltkrieg. Frankfurt, Ger., Athenaion, 1968. xi, 747 p. maps. (Athenaion-Bibliothek der Geschichte) D531.K45 DLC; CaAEU; CaBVaU; CLU; CLS; CoU; CoFS; CSt; CtY; CU-S; CU-SB; CU-SC; FTaSU; GASU; GU; IEN; IaU; InU; IU; MB; MH; MiEM; MiDW; MiU; MdU; MdBJ; MnU;MoU; MoSW; MU; NNC; NIC; NNCFR; NBuU;NjP; NjR; NcD; NcU; OkU; OU; OrU; OrPS; PSt; TNJ; TxHR; WU.

X.9.k.2. ACTION TAKEN FOR REESTABLISH-MENT AS AN INDEPENDENT LITHUANIAN STATE

1592. BIELINIS, Kipras. Reikalas teisingai suprasti praeitį. [It is necessary to understand correctly the past]. In Mintis (Memmingen, Ger.), March 9, 1949. CtTMF; OKentU.

1593. BIENHOLD, Marianne. Entstehung des litauischen Staates in den Jahren 1918-1919 im Spiegel deutscher Akten. Bochum, Ger., Studienverlag Dr. N. Brockmeyer, 1976. iv, 408,15, 9 p. Bibliography: p. 367-408. DK511.L26B58 1976 CaAEU; DLC; PU.

1594. CADZOW, John F. The Lithuanian question in the third state Duma. Kent, Ohio, 1972. 187 leaves. tables. Thesis--Kent State University. DK511.L25C3x OKentU.

1595. DAMBRAUSKAS, Aleksandras. Kruvina revoliucija ar ramus kultūros darbas? [By] Druskius [pseud.] [Bloody revolution or the quiet cultural work?] 2. laida. Baltimore, Pa.,

A. Ramoška, 1917. 20 p.
*Q p.v.1409--NN.

1596. HEATH, Roy E. and Senn, Alfred Erich. Edmond Privat and the Commission of the East in 1918. In Journal of Baltic Studies (Brooklyn, N.Y.), no.1, v.6, 1975, p. 9-16. See serials consulted.·

1597. SENN, Alfred Erich. The activity of Juozas Gabrys for Lithuania's independence, 1914-1920. In Lituanus (Chicago, Ill.), no.1, v.23, 1977, p. 15-22. See serials consulted.

1598. --- A conversation with Julius Bielskis. In Lituanus (Chicago, Ill.), no.4, v.21, 1975, p.37-44. See serials consulted.

1599. --- A conversation with Mykolas Biržiška. In Lituanus (Chicago, Ill.), no.2, v.21, 1975, p.55-63. See serials consulted.

X.9.ℓ. REPUBLIC OF LITHUANIA, 1918-1940

X.9.ℓ.1. GENERAL STUDIES

1600. GUDELIS, Petras. Bolševikų valdžios atsiradimas Lietuvoje 1918-1919 metais jų pačių dokumentų šviesoje. [The establishment of bolshevik government in Lithuania, 1918-1919 according to their documents] Su Z. Ivinskio įvadu. London, Eng., 1972. 160 p. port. At head of title: Lietuvių Veteranų Sąjunga Ramovė. P. Gudelis. Introduction also in English and German; summary in English and German. Bibliography: p.112. DK511.L26G82 DLC; CaAEU.

1601. JONAITIS, B. Paskutinės Nepriklausomos Lietuvos dienos. [The last days of Independent Lithuania] In Naujoji Viltis (Chicago, Ill.),no. 1, 1970, p. 5-65. See serials consulted.

1602. ŁOSSOWSKI, Piotr. Kraje Bałtyckie na drodze od demokracji parlamentarnej do dyktatury, 1918-1934. Wrocław, Zakład Narodowy im. Ossolinskich, 1972. 303 p. At head of title: Polska Akademia Nauk. Instytut Historii. Summary in German. DK511.B3L67 DLC; CaBVaU; CSt-H;CLU; CU; InU; IaU; ICIU; MB; MH; MU; MiU; NNC; NjP.

1603. PALECKIS, Justas. V dvukh mirakh. IU. Paletskis. Moskva,Izd-

vo polit. lit-ry, 1974. 524 p., [16] leaves of plates. illus. (O zhizni i o sebe) DK511.L28Ps46 DLC; CaBVaU; CaOTU; CU; CU-SB; InU; MoSW; NjP;PPiU ViU; WU.

1604. SENN, Alfred Erich. The emergence of modern Lithuania. Westport, Conn., Greenwood Press, 1975, c1959. x, 272 p. Reprint of the ed. published by Columbia University Press New York, in series: Studies of the Russian Institute, Columbia University. Bibliography: p. [241]-259. DK511.L27S4 1975 DLC; MH; ViBlbV.

1605. ŠKIRPA, Kazys. 5[i.e. Penkto] pėstininkų DLK Kęstučio pulko kovos ties Seinais 1920 metais. Brooklyn, N.Y., Karys, 1971. 124 p. illus. (Raštai Lietuvos karinės istorijos, nr. 9) [The battle of the Fifth regiment... at Seinai, 1920] DK511.L2A248 nr.9 DLC

1606. SMETONA, Antanas, Pres. Lithuania, 1874-1944. Pasakyta parašyta; kalbos ir pareiškimai 1955-1940. [It is said and written; apeeches and statements]. Sudarė Leonas Sabaliūnas. Spaudai parengė Vincas Rastenis. So. Boston, Mass., LST Korp. Neo-Lithuania filisterių kolektyvas, 1974. 350 p. Vol.1 published in Kaunas, 1935. DK511.L27S538 DLC; CaAEU; InU.

1607. STULGINSKIS, Aleksandras, Pres. Lithuania, 1885- . Selected letters of President Stulginskis. In Lituanus (Chicago, Ill.), no.3, v.17, 1971, p. 5-30. See serials consulted.

1608. ŠVOBA, Jonas. Gruodžio 17 perversmo priežasčių apžvalga. [A review of the causes for the revolt of December 17th.] In Naujoji Viltis (Chicago, Ill.), no.6, 1973-74, p.14-26. See Serials consulted.

1609. VIENUOLIS, A., pseud. Žingsniai ir žygiai; lietuvių tautos nepriklausomybės 10 metų sukaktuvėms paminėti. [...10th anniversary of Lithuania's independence] Kaunas, Vairo b-vės leidinys, [1928. Xerox copy, 1977] 208 p. (Raštai, kn.4). PG8721.V5Z5 1928a PU(xerox).

1610. ŽEPKAITĖ, Regina. Lietuva tarptautinės politikos labirintuose 1918-1922 m. [Lithuania in the web of international politics]. Vilnius, Mintis, 1973. 194 p. At head of title: Lietuvos TSR Mokslų akademija. Istorijos institutas. R. Žepkaitė. Bibliography: p. 188-[190]. DK511.L27Z45 DLC; MH; NjP; OKentU; PU; WU.

X.9.ℓ.2. THE WAR OF INDEPENDENCE, 1918-1920

1611. ALIŠAUSKAS, Kazys. Kovos dėl Lietuvos nepriklausomybės, 1918-1920. [The Lithuanian wars for independence, 1918-1920]. Redaktorius Pranas Čepėnas. Čikaga, Lietuvių veteranų sąjunga Ramovė, 1972- .
v. illus. (Lietuvių veteranų sąjungos Ramovės leidinys, nr. 5). Summary in English. Bibliography: v.1, p. 441-461. DK511.L27A65 DLC; MB; CSt-H; NN; NNC; PU.

1612. GUDELIS, Petras. Joniškėlio apskrities partizanai. [Partisans of the district Joniškėlis] Roma, [s.n.], 1975- . v. map. Partial contents.--Dalis 1. Jų organizavimas ir slaptoji veikla prieš bolševikus, 1918.XI.27-1919.III.22. DK511.L27G93 1975 CaAEU; PU.

1613. KUTRZEBA, Tadeusz. Bitwa nad Niemnem (wrzesień-pazdziernik, 1920). Warszawa, Wojskowy instytut naukowo-wydawniczy, 1926. vi, 359 p. and atlas of maps, plans. (Poland. Sztab generalny. Biuro historyczne. Studja operacyjne z historji wojen polskich 1918-1921, t.2) *QR Poland--NN; DNW.

1614. RAMOJUS, Vladas. Kritusieji už laisvę. [Those killed for freedom. By] Vladas Ramojus, [pseud.] Chicago, Ill., Lietuviškos knygos klubas, 1967-1969. 2 v. Author's real name Vladas Butėnas. DK511.L274R3 DLC; CaOTU; PU.

1615. SCHRÖDER, Otto and Heygendorff, Ralph. Die sächsischen freiwilligen Truppen in Litauen 1919. Dresden, Ger., Wilhelm und Bertha v. Baensch Stiftung, 1933. 947.52.Sch78 PU.

1616. WALIGÓRA, Bolesław. Dzieje 85-go pulku strzelców wileńskich. Warszawa, 1928. 4 p.l., 468 p. front, illus., plates, ports, diagr. DK440.W35 DLC; CU; IU; DSI; NN.

X.9.m. SECOND WORLD WAR, 1939-1945

X.9.m.1. INCORPORATION OF LITHUANIA INTO THE SOVIET UNION, 1940-1941

1617. B-čius, D., pseud. Lietuvos pavergimas Britanijos užsienių reikalų ministerijos dokumentuose. [The occupation of Lithuania in the documents of the British Foreign Office] In Metmenys (Chicago, Ill.), no.1, 1971, p. 85-107. See serials consulted.

1618. BUDRYS, Ajay. What ever happened to Lithuania. Chicago, Ill., American Lithuanian Republican League of Illinois, [1973.] [4] p.map. Reprinted from Midwest Sun-Time. DK511.L2B92 1973 CaAEU.

1619. FABRY, Philipp Walter. Die Sowjetunion und die Dritte Reich; eine dokumentierte Geschichte der deutsch-sowjetischen Beziehungen von 1933 bis 1941. Stuttgart, Ger., Seewald Verlag, 1971. 485 p. Bibliography: p. 468-477. DD120.R8F3 DLC; CaAEU; CaBVaU; CaOTY CaQMM; CLU; CtY; CSt; CSt-H; CU-SB; CU; DeU; DS; FU; GU; IaU; IU; IaAS; InU; INS; IEN; ICU; InNd; KyU; KU; LNHT; MB; MH; MU; MiDW; MiEM; MiU; MCM; MdU; MnU; MoSW; NNC; NIC; NjP; NcD; NcU; NbU; OU; OKentU; PSt; ViU; WU; WaU;

1620. GAR, Josef. Azoy iz es geshen 'in Lite; tsu der geshichte fun der sovetisher mishlaḥ 1940-1941. Tel-Aviv, Ha-Menorah, 1965. 157 p. DK511.L27G3 DLC; MH; MiU; MiDW; NNC; NN; OrPS; PPiU.

1621. GEDVILAS, Mečislovas. Lemiamas posūkis; 1940-1945 metai. Vilnius, Vaga, 1975. 388 p. [Decisive turn, 1940-1945] DK511.L27G42 PU.

1622. KANCEVIČIUS, Vytautas. 1940 [i.e. Tūkstantis devyni šimtai keturiasdešimtų] metų birželis Lietuvoje. [June 1940 in Lithuania] Vilnius, Mintis, 1973. 109 p. illus. (Lietuvos istorija). DK511.L27K3 DLC.

1623. KASLAS, Bronis J. The Lithuanian strip in Soviet-German secret diplomacy, 1939-1941. In Journal of Baltic Studies (Brooklyn, N.Y.), no. 3, 1973, p. 211-225. See serials consulted.

1624. LITHUANIA in 1939-1940; the historic turn to socialism. Edited with an introd. and comments by Vytautas Kancevičius. Vilnius, Mintis, 1976. 231 p. illus. Translation of Litva v tysiacha deviatsot tridtsat deviatom-tysiacha deviatsot sorokovom gg. DK511.L27L58 DLC.

1625. MARTÍNEZ BERSETCHE, José Pedro. Lituania martir [por] J.P. Martínez Bersetche. Ed. especial en homenaje al ler. Congreso de lituanos en América del Sur, realizado en Buenos Aires, Rep.Argentina, durante los días

2 al 5 de diciembre de 1960. Montevideo, 1960. 32 p. port. DK511.L2M2 DLC.

1626. MŪSŲ VYTIS; skautiškos minties žurnalas. Specialus numeris skirtas Lietuvių tautos didžiosios tragėdijos 25-mečio prisiminimui. [Special issue of Mūsų Vytis to commemorate the tragic occupation of Lithuania]. Chicago, Ill., 1965, no.2, p. 39-90. 947.5.M976 PU.

1627 CANCELLED.

1628. POBEDA SOTSIALISTICHESKOĬ revoliutsii v Litve... In Bor'ba za Sovetskuiu vlast' v Pribaltike. Moskva, 1967. Glava 14-16, p.479-536. DK511.B3B72 CaAEU; AAP; CaBVaU;CLU; CaOTU; CaQMM; CtY; CSt-H; DLC; DS; GU; FMU; ICU; KU; MH; MiU; MdBJ;MoSW NN; NNC; NIC; NjP; NSyU; NRU; NcD; OU; OrU; TNJ; TU; PSt; PU; RPB; ViU; WU; WaU.

1629. REMEIKIS, Thomas. The decision of the Lithuanian Government to accept the Soviet ultimatum of June 14, 1940. In Lituanus (Chicago, Ill.) no.3, v.21, 1975, p. 19-44. See serials consulted.

1630. VIZULIS, Jazeps. Die baltischen Länder; Opfer sowjetischer Aggression. In Acta Baltica (Königstein, Ger.), v.8, 1968, p. 74-105. See serials consulted.

X.9.m.2. INSURRECTION OF 1941

1631. MACKEVIČIUS, Mečys. 1941 metų sukilimas ir laikinoji Lietuvos vyriausybė mano atsiminimuose. [Insurrection of 1941 and the Provisional Government of Lithuania] In Varpas (Melrose Park, Ill.), nr.15,1977, p. 42-48. See serials consulted.

1632. ŠKIRPA, Kazys. Sukilimas Lietuvos suverenumui atstatyti; dokumentinė apžvalga. Uprising for the restoration of Lithuania's sovereignity. Vašingtonas, Škirpa, 1973. [i. e. 1975]. 583 p. illus. D802.L5S56 DLC; CaAEU; PU.

X.9.m.3. GERMAN OCCUPATION AND GUERRILLA WARFARE, 1941-1944

1633. BROWN, Zvie A. and LEVIN, Dov. Toldoteha shel mahteret. The story of one underground; the resistance of the Jews of Kovno [Kaunas,

Lithuania] in Second World War. Jerusalem, Yad Vashem, 1962. 422, xvii p. illus., ports., maps, facsims. Introduction and synopsis in English. Bibliography: p. 402-408. D802.R8B76 DLC; CLU; CtY; IEN; MWalB NN; NNC; NBuU; OU.

1634. DRUNGA, Karolis. Lithuania under Nazi occupation. In Lituanus (Chicago, Ill.), no.3, v.3, 1956, p. 3-10. See serials consulted.

1635. HEROES OF THE RESISTANCE by editors of the Army Times. New York, N.Y., Dodd, Mead Co., 1967. xviii, 133 p. "Adventures of underground fighters in Europe during World War II" D802.E9H4 DLC; CaOTP; CLU; CLSU; CtY; GAT; IaU; KyU; MB; MnU; N; NNC; NBuU; NjP; NjR; OkU; OCl; PPULC; RPB; TU; TxU; Wa.

1636. KARVELIS, Vladas. Lietuvos TSR išvadavimas iš hitlerinės okupacijos; 1944-1945. 2. pataisytas ir papildytas leidimas. [Liberation of Soviet Lithuania from Nazi occupation] Vilnius, Mintis, 1974. 168 p., [16] leaves of plates. illus., maps. Bibliography: p. 165-[167] D764.7.L5K37 1974 DLC;

1637. --- Osvobozhdenie Litovskoĭ SSR ot gitlerovskoĭ okkupatsii, 1944-1945. Vladas Karvialis. Vil'nius, Mintis, 1975. 238 p.,[17] leaves of plates. illus., maps. Bibliography: p. 236-]239]. D764.7.L5K3717 DLC.

1638. --- Osvobozhdenie Sovetskoĭ Litvy. [By] V. Karvialis. In Gitlerovskaia okkupatsia v Litve... Vil'-nius, 1966. p. 279-354. D802.L5G5 DLC; CaAEU; CaBVaS; CaBVaU CaNSHD; CaQMM; CtY; IaU; InNd; InU; ICU; IEN; IU; MH; MnU; MU; NIC; NcD; NcU; NjP; NSyU; OrU; PPiU; TU; ViU; WU; WaU.

1639. KURGANOV, M[akar Eftropeevich] Mirties akivaizdoje [Facing death. By] M. Kurganovas. Vilnius, Valstybinė politinės ir mokslinės literatūros leidykla, 1960. 156 p. illus. D805.L85K8 DLC.

1640. --- V litso smerti. Moskva, Izd-vo polit. lit-ry, 1964. 127 p. illus., ports. D805.L85K87 DLC; MH; NNC; NcD; WU.

1641. LEVIN, Dov. Die Beteiligung der litauischen Juden im zweiten Weltkrieg. In Acta Baltica (Königstein, Ger.), v.16, 1976, p. 172-184. See serials consulted.

1642. --- Der bewaffnete Widerstand baltischer Juden gegen das Nazi

Regime 1941-1945. In Acta Baltica (Königstein, Ger.), v.15, 1975, p. 166-174. See serials consulted.

1643. --- Hishtatfut Yehude Lita ba-Milhamah ba-Germanim be-Milhemet ha-'olam ha-sheniyah. Participation of the Lithuanian Jews in the Second World War. [Yerushalaim., s.n.],1970. 2 v. illus. Thesis--ha-Universitah ha--'ivrit. Summary in English. DS135.R93L52 DLC.

1644. --- Lohamim ve-'omdim 'al nafsham... 1941-1945. They fought back. Yerushalaim, Yad Vashem, 1974. 269, viii p.,[18] leaves of plates. illus., facsims., maps. Summary in English. Bibliography: p. 233-242. DS135.L5L4 DLC.

1645. --- Participation of the Lithuanian Jews in the Second World War. In Journal of Baltic Studies (Brooklyn, N.Y.), no.4, v.6, 1975, p. 300-310. See serials consulted.

1646. MASINĖS ŽUDYNĖS LIETUVOJE, 1941-1944; dokumentų rinkinys I. [Mass extermination in Lithuania; a collection of documents]. Vilnius, Mintis, 1965. 346 p. illus., facsims., maps, ports. D802.L5M3 DLC; CaAEU; CtY; CU; MH; IU; NN.

1647. MISIŪNAS, Romualdas J. Fascist tendencies in Lithuania. In Slavonic and East European Review (London, Eng.), no.110, v.48, 1970, p. 88-109. See serials consulted.

1648. MYLLYNIEMI, Seppo. Die Neuordnung der Baltischen Länder, 1941-1944; zum nationalsozialistischen Inhalt der deutschen Besatzungspolitik. Helsinki, [Suomen historiallinen seura], 1973. 308 p. (Disertationes historicae, 2) (Historiallisia tutkimuksia, 90) D802.B3M9 PU; CaAEU; CaBVaU; CLU; CU-SB; CSt; CSt-H; InU; MiU; MoU; NBuU; NjP; NcU; TxHR; ViU; WU; WaU.

1649. NACIONALISTŲ TALKA HITLERIninkams. [The nationalists helping Hitlerites. Comp. by B. Baranauskas and K. Rukšėnas]. Vilnius, Mintis, 1970. 187 p. On verso of t.p.:Lietuvos TSR Mokslų akademija. Archivinių dokumentų skelbimo redakcija. Archyvų valdyba prie LTSR Ministrų Tarybos. LTSR Centrinis valstybinis archyvas. DK511.L27N22 DLC; NN.

1650. THE OCCUPIED AND SATELITE countries in Eastern Europe; the Ostland. In Documents on International Affairs, 1939-1946. London, 1954. v.2, p. 264-291. D411.R88D 1939-46

v.2. CaAEU; see also serials consulted.

1651. OCCUPIED TERRITORIES; general. In Documents on International Affairs, 1939-1946. London, 1954. v.2. p. 188-192. D411.R88D 1939-46 v.2 CaAEU; see also serials consulted.

1652. PIRČIUPIŲ TRAGEDIJOS KALTIninkai; dokumentų rinkinys. [The guilty in the tragedy of Pirčiupiai; a collection of documents. Paruošė K. Rukšėnas] Vilnius, Mintis, 1975. D802.L5P55 PU.

1653. PO GIMTUOJU DANGUM. [Under the native sky] [Kaune, Spindulys, 1949?] 78 p. illus., ports. DK511.L274P6 DLC

1654. --- [Redaktorius V. Kubilius. Kaune?, 1964?] 78 p. illus. ports. HC337.L5P6 DLC.

1655. SINKEVIČIUS, Sigitas. Pirčiupiai; dokumentinė apybraiža. [The Village of Pirčiupiai; a documentary outline]. Vilnius, Mintis, 1974. 111 p. D802.L5S53 PU.

1656. ŠTARAS, Povilas, comp. Partizany Litvy. Lithuania's partisans. [Sostavitel' alboma i avtor teksta P. Shtaras] Vil'nius, Mintis, 1967. 46 p. D802.L5S73 DLC; TNJ.

1657. TARYBŲ LIETUVA DIDŽIAJAME TĖVYNĖS KARE. [Soviet Lithuania during the Great Patriotic War. Ats. redaktorius J. Dobrovolskas] Vilnius, Mintis, 1975. 231 p,[22] leaves of plates. illus., and atlas. Verso of t.p. Lietuvos TSR Mokslų akademijos Istorijos institutas. Partijos istorijos institutas prie Lietuvos KP-CK Marksismo-leninizmo instituto prie TSKP CK filialas. D802.L5T28 DLC.

1658. UNGER, Albert. Der Auszug der Deutschen aus Litauen. Oldenburg, Ger., F.N. Siebert, 1971. 59 p. illus., maps. DK511.L22U5 DLC;CLU; CSt; IU; MH; NNC; NjP; OKentU; TxU; WU.

1659. VICAS, J. SS tarnyboje; dokumentinis leidinys apie lietuvių apsaugos dalių įvykdytus nusikaltimus. Vilnius, Valstybinė politinės ir mokslinės literatūros leidykla, 1961. 115 p. D802.L5V45 DLC.

X.9.n. SOVIET LITHUANIA, 1945-

X.9.n.1. TREATISES AND TEXTBOOKS

1660. BUROKEVIČIUS, Mykolas. Ras-
tsvet Sovetskoĭ Litvy. Moskva, Znanie, 1965. 31 p. (Novoe v zhizni,
nauke, tekhnike. I seriia: Istoriia,
14) D410.N652 1965, no.14 DLC;
CaBVaU; MH; NcU.

1661. DIDŽIAJAM SPALIUI-50. [50th
anniversary of the October revolution]
Vilnius, Mintis, 1968. 195 p., 47
leaves of illus. 12 x 17 cm.
DK511.L27D47 DLC.

1662. GRIGOR'EV, K. Sovetskaia
Litva. Moskva, Politizdat, 1940.
58 p. "Deklaratsii Litovskogo Seĭ-
ma [21-23iiulia 1940 g.]": p. 51-58.
DK511.L27G75 DLC; IU; MH; NN.

1663. GRIŠKEVIČIUS, Petras. Lenino keliu didžiuoju. [Progressing
in footsteps of Lenin] Vilnius, Mintis, 1975. 116 p.,[28] leaves of
plates. illus. DK511.L2G75 DLC.

1664. --- V sem'e edinoĭ, brats-
koĭ. P. Grishkiavichus. Vil'nius,
Mintis, 1975. 131 p.,[28] leaves of
plates. illus. DK511.L274G7417 DLC.

1665. JURGINIS, Juozas. Lietuvos
TSR istorija; vadovėlis vidurinėms
mokykloms. [Soviet Lithuanian histo-
ry]. Kaunas, Valstybinė pedagoginės
literatūros leidykla, 1957. 173 p.
illus. DK511.L2J76 DLC; NN;PPULC.

1666. --- --- 2. leidimas. Kaunas, Valstybinė Pedagoginės literatūros leidykla, 1958. 171 p. illus.
col.maps. DK511.L2J95 1958 CaAEU;
CLU; DS.

1667. KLESTĖK, TARYBŲ LIETUVA.
Vilnius, Mintis, 1966. 276 p. illus,
fold.maps. DK511.L2K57 DLC.

1668. KLIČIUS, Jonas. Net ir žy-
dro dangaus pavydėjo. [Even the blue
sky they envied] Vilnius, Valstybinė grožinės literatūros leidykla,
1963. 381 p. plates, ports.
335.409475.K652n IEN.

1669. SHUSTIKOV, N[ikolaĭ] I[vano-
vich]. Litovskaia SSR; uchebnyĭ material. Moskva, Vysshaia partiĭnaia
shkola pri TSK KPSS, 1954. 33 p.
DK511.L2S49 DLC; MH.

1670. ŠLOVINA TARYBŲ LIETUVĄ.
[Praising Soviet Lithuania. Rinkinį
paruošė: V. Beriozovas ir A. Piroč-
kinas]. Vilnius, Mintis, 1971. 162
p., 48 leaves of illus. Some articles in Russian. Bibliography: p.121-
[162]. DK511.L27S535 DLC.

1671. SNIEČKUS, Antanas. Broliš-
koje TSRS tautų šeimoje. [In the family of USSR nations]. Vilnius, Mintis, 1972. 75 p. DK511.L274S58 DLC.

1672. --- Soviet Lithuania on the
road of prosperity. A. Sniečkus. [
Translated from the Russian; designed
by Victor Kuzyakov]. Moscow, Progress Publishers, 1974. 126 p.,[44]
leaves of plates. illus. Originally
published in Lithuanian under title:
Tarybų Lietuva-klestėjimo keliu.
DK511.L27S5613 DLC.

1673. --- Sovetskaia Litva na pu-
ti rastsveta. Vil'nius, 1970. 157
p., 31 leaves of illus.
DK511.L274S617 DLC; CaAEU; CaOTU;
CSt; CSt-H; DS; FMU; IEN; ICU; InU;
IU; MH; MnU; MU; NIC; NSyU; NjP; OU;
PSt; ViU.

1674. --- Tarybų Lietuva-klestėjimo keliu. [Soviet Lithuania on the
road of prosperity]. Vilnius, Mintis,
1970. 132 p. illus., ports.
DK511.L27S56 DLC; NN; NIC; WaU.

1675. ŠUMAUSKAS, Motiejus. Lithu-
ania; wonderful deeds ahead. London,
[Soviet Booklets], 1960. 23 p. illus.
(The Fifteen Soviet Socialist Repub-
lics today and tomorrow)
DK511.L2S8 DLC; CaAEU; CaOHM;CaSSU;
HU; MH; MnU; NIC; PPiU; TxHR; TxU;
WaU.

1676. --- La Lituanie soviétique.
[Par] Moteus Sumauskas. [Paris, J.Ri-
bot, 1961?] 32 p. illus., ports.,
map. (Coll. Études soviétiques, 143,
Supplément) DK266.A3E854 CaOOP;DS.

1677. --- Litovskaia Sovetskaia
Sotsialisticheskaia Respublika. Mos-
kva, Politizdat, 1972. 71 p. At head
of title: M.IU. Shumauskas.
DK511.L274S9 DLC; CaOTU; CtY; InU;
IU; MH; MiDW; NcD.

1678. VETLOV, I. Litva. Moskva,
Moskovskiĭ rabochiĭ, 1928. 52 p. map.
DK511.L2V414 DLC.

1679. VIENYBĖS IR DRAUGYSTĖS ŠVEN-
TĖ. [The festival of unity and frind-
ship] Vilnius, Mintis, 1973. 38 p.,
8 leaves of illus. Compiled by F.Pa-
žūsis. DK511.L2V418 DLC.

1680. WALTER, Gert. Wie Bernstein
und buntes Glas; ein Mosaik der Litauischen Sowjetrepublik. Berlin, Verlag der Nation,[1972]. 156 p. illus.
plates, map. DK511.L2W33 DLC; DS;
OKentU.

1681. ŽINIJOS DRAUGIJA. 25 let Sovetskoĭ Litve. Vil'nius, 1965. 54 p.

DK511.L274Z54 DLC.

1682. --- Soviet Lithuania's quarter century. [Vilnius, 1965] 51 p. DK511.L274Z55 DLC; InU.

X.9.n.2. CAPTIVE LITHUANIA

1683. ALANTAS, Vytautas. Romas Kalanta; gyvieji deglai Nemuno slėnyje. [Romas Kalanta; the living torches in the Nemunas Valley]. [Cleveland, Ohio, Vilties draugijos leidykla, 1976] 114 p. illus. DK511.L28K33 PU; DLC.

1684. BRAZAITIS, Juozas. Lietuvos vergijos dešimtmetis. [The tenth anniversary of slavery in in Lithuania] In Metraštis 1950. Kennebunk Port, Me., [1949]. p. 83-95. See serials consulted.

1685. FINKELSTEIN, Eitan. Old hopes and new currents in present day Lithuania. In Lituanus (Chicago, Ill.), no.3, v.23, 1977, p.47-58. See serials consulted.

1686. PASAULIO LIETUVIŲ BENDRUOMENĖ. Lietuva okupacijoje; pranešimai Pasaulio lietuvių bendruomenės Seimui apie okupuotos Lietuvos gyvenimo kaikurias sritis. [Lithuania under occupation. Reports to the Assembly of World Lithuanian Community on some aspects of life in occupied Lithuania] New Yorkas, PLB Seimo organizacinis komitetas, 1958. 128 leaves. illus. DK511.L274P3 DLC.

1687. PUZINAS, Jonas. The situation in occupied Lithuania; administration, indoctrination and russianization. In Lituanus (Chicago, Ill), no.1, v.19, 1973, p. 55-72. See serials consulted.

1688. SUPREME LITHUANIAN COMMITTEE OF LIBERATION. Lithuania. New York, N.Y., The Committee, [196-] 20 p. illus., maps. DK511.L2S96 CaAEU.

1689. UNITED STATES. SENATE. COMMITTEE ON THE JUDICIARY. Soviet political agreement and results. Staff study for the Subkommittee to investigate the Administration of the Internal security Act and other Internal Security laws of the Committee on the Judiciary, United States Senate, 84th Congress, second session. Washington, D.C., U.S. Govt. Print. Off., 1956. xiii, 63 p. (84th Cong., 2nd sess. Senate. Document no.125) JX1555.Z7U53 DLC.

1690. UNITED STATES. INFORMATION AGENCY. PRESS SERVICE. Baltic colonies of the Soviet Union. In Report on Communist colonialism and International Communism, XI (special packet) [Washington, 1956] 16 leaves. Mimeographed. HX40.U653 DLC.

1691. VAITIEKŪNAS, Vytautas. Lietuva okupacijoje. [Occupied Lithuania]. In Į Laisvę (Los Angeles, CA), no.32(69), 1963, p. 1-26. Mr. L.Kairys (Chicago) has it, no.40. See also serials consulted.

1692. THE VIOLATIONS OF HUMAN RIGHTS IN SOVIET OCCUPIED LITHUANIA; a report for 1971. Prepared by Lithuanian American Community, Inc., February 16, 1972. [Chicago, Ill., 1972]. 64 p. DK511.L274V55 PU;DLC; IEdS.

1693. ---; a report for 1972. Prepared by Lithuanian American Community, Inc., February 16, 1973. [Chicago, Ill., 1973]. 88 p. DK511.L274V56 PU; DLC.

1694. ---; a report for 1973. Prepared by Lithuanian American Community, Inc., February 16, 1974. [Chicago, Ill., 1974.] 112 p. DK511.L274V57 PU; DLC.

1695. ---; a report for 1974. Prepared by Lithuanian American Community, Inc., February 16, 1975. [Chicago, Ill., 1975] 112 p. DK511.L274V58 PU; DLC.

1696. ---; a report for 1975. Prepared by Lithuanian American Community, Inc., February 16, 1976. [Glenside, Pa., 1976] 140 p. DK511.L274V585 PU; DLC; CaAEU.

1697. ---; a report for 1976. Prepared by Lithuanian American Community,.Inc., February 16, 1977. [Glenside, Pa., 1977] 160 p. DK511.L274V587 PU.

X.9.o. COMMUNISM IN LITHUANIA

X.9.o.1. GENERAL STUDIES

1698. ADOMAVIČIŪTĖ, Stefanija. Internacionalizmas-tautų draugystės vėliava. [Internationalism-the sign of cooperation among the nations]. Vilnius, Valstybinė politinės ir mokslinės literatūros leidykla, 1963. 105 p. DK511.L274A65 DLC.

1699. BUROKEVIČIUS, Mykolas. Lietuvos KP ideologinis darbas su inteligentija 1940-1965 m. [Ideological work of the Lithuanian Communist Party with intellectuals, 1940-1965] Vilnius, Mintis, 1972. 197 p. JN6745.A98K695 PU; DLC; CtY; MH; NN; NNC; NjP.

1700. DIDYSIS SPALIS; bibliografinės ir metodinės medžiagos rinkinys. [The Great October; a bibliography... Sudarė: M. Goldas et al.] Vilnius, 1967. 213 p. Z2510.D54 DLC.

1701. GERMANTAS, pseud. Der Kommunismus, das Unglück der Menschheit. Dienstliche Übersetzung der Publikationsstelle des Preuss. Geheimen Staatsarchivs in Berlin-Dahlem. Berlin, 1938. 9 leaves (Publikationsstelle, Berlin-Dahlem. Litauische Reihe, 1) DK511.L27G4 DLC.

1702. --- Komunizmas žmonijos nelaimė. [Der Kommunismus, das Unglück der Menschheit] Kaunas, Autoriaus leidinys, 1937. [Xerox copy, 1977] 62 p. Author's real name Pranas Meškauskas. HX59.M43 1937a PU(xerox).

1703. GOLDAS, M. Leninas ir Lietuva; bibliografinė rodyklė. [Lenin and Lithuania; a bibliography] Vilnius, 1969. 71 p. Z8500.8.G585 DLC; MH.

1704. KOMUNIZMO KŪRIMO TARYBŲ LIEtuvoje teorijos ir praktikos klausimai. [The theoretical and practical questions on the establishment of communism in Soviet Lithuania. Atsakingasis redaktorius A. Jablonskis] Vilnius, Mintis, 1975. 84 p. (Ekonomika, XIII, sąs.1)(Lietuvos TSR Aukštųjų mokyklų mokslo darbai). Russian or Lithuanian with summaries in the other language. HC337.L5K64 DLC.

1705. LIETUVOS KOMUNISTŲ PARTIJA. CENTRO KOMITETAS. Nutarimai ideologiniais klausimais. [Postanovleniia po ideologicheskim voprosam]. Vilnius, LKP CK leidykla, 1971. 160 p. LA853.L48L48 DLC; NNC.

1706. --- Postanovleniia po ideologicheskim voprosam; izlozheniia postanovlenii. Vil'nius, Izd-vo TSK KP Litvy, 1972. 178 p. JN6745.A98K655 DLC.

1707. MARCELIS, Albertas. Už proletariato ir darbo valstiečių sąjungą; Lietuvos KP kova už darbininkų klasės ir darbo valstiečių sąjungą fašizmo viešpatavimo metais 1927-1940. [The struggle of the Communist Party of Lithuania for union of the labouring class and peasants, 1927-1940] Vilnius, Mintis, 1976. 365 p.

JN6745.A98K68 PU.

1708. MEŠKAUSKIENĖ, Michalina. Žvelgiu i tolius. [I am looking ahead] Vilnius, Vaga, 1969. 610 p., 13 leaves of illus. CT1218.M45A3 DLC; CtY; MB; NN; NjP; OKentU; PU.

1709. NAVICKAS, Konstantinas. Lenininės nacionalinės politikos istorinė reikšmė lietuvių tautai. [The importance of Lenin's national politics for Lithuania]. Vilnius, Valstybinė politinės ir mokslinės literatūros leidykla, 1960. 93 p. . DK511.L27N3 DLC; PU.

1710. --- The struggle of the Lithuanian people for statehood. Vilnius, Gintaras, 1971. 174 p. illus, facsims., ports. DK511.L27N317 DLC; CaBVaU; CLU; IU; ICU; InU; MH; PPiU; CtY; WU.

1711. SNIEČKUS, Antanas. Su Lenino vėliava; straipsniai, kalbos, pranešimai. [Under the flag of Lenin; articles, speeches and reports. Red. kolegija: R. Šarmaitis (pirmininkas)...et al.] Vilnius, Mintis, 1977. 2 v. DK511.L27S55 PU.

1712. SPALIO REVOLIUCIJA IR VISUOmeniniai mokslai Lietuvoje; mokslinės konferencijos medžiaga (1967 m. gruodžio 6-8 d.). [The October revolution and the social sciences in Lithuania. Ats. redaktorius M. Burokevičius]. Vilnius, 1967. Bibliography: p. 619-[644]. HX315.65.A6S6 DLC; CLU; CtY; CU;IU; ICU; MH; PU.

1713. VILNA. UNIVERSITETAS. TSKP ISTORIJOS KATEDRA. TSKP istorijos kurso seminariniai planai ir metodiniai patarimai studentams. [The advice for students and planning of seminars in the history of the Communist Party of the Soviet Union]. Redagavo: J. Bernatavičienė [et al.] Vilnius, 1969. 50 p. At head of title: Vilniaus Valstybinis V.Kapsuko universitetas. TSKP istorijos katedra. JN6598.K7V48 DLC.

1714. ŽIUGŽDA, Juozas. Tarybų Rusijos pagalba Lietuvos darbo žmonėms kovoje už tarybų valdžią 1919-1919 metais. [Help to the Lithuanian communists movement from the Soviet Union, 1918-1919]. In His Už Socialistinę Lietuvą. Vilnius, 1960. p.29-[64] Balt.8180.25 MH; CtPAM.

X.9.o.2. HISTORY OF THE COMMUNIST PARTY

1715. LIETUVOS KOMUNISTŲ PARTIJA skaičiais, 1918-1975; statistikos duomenų rinkinys. [Lithuanian Communist Party in numbers, 1918-1975. Redakcinė kolegija: P. Beresnevičius (sudarytojas), K. Surblys (ats. redaktorius), R. Šarmaitis] Vilnius, Mintis, 1976. 287 p. illus. At head of title: Partijos istorijos institutas prie Lietuvos KPCK. JN6745.A98K675 PU; DLC.

1716. LIETUVOS KOMUNISTŲ PARTIJOS istorijos apybraiža. [An outline of the Lithuanian Communist Party history. Ats. redaktorius R. Šarmaitis] Vilnius, Mintis, 1971- . v. illus, facsims., maps, ports. At head of title: v.1- : Partijos istorijos institutas prie Lietuvos KP CK. Marksismo-Leninizmo instituto prie TSKP CK filialas. JN6745.A98K67 DLC; CtY; CSt-H; ICU; MB; MH; NN; NIC; NjP; OKentU.

1717. LIETUVOS KOMUNISTŲ PARTIJOS istorijos apybraiža. Russian. Ocherki istorii Kommunisticheskoĭ partii Litvy. [Otv. redaktor R. Sharmaĭtis] Vil'nius, Mintis, 1973- . v. ill. facsims., col.maps, ports. At head of title: v.1- : Institut istorii partii pri TSK KP Litvy-filial Instituta marksisma-leninizma pri TSK KPSS JN6745.A98K6717 DLC; NcU.

X.9.o.3. REVOLUTIONISTS; THEIR PERSONAL NARRATIVES, MEMOIRES, AND REMINISCENCES

1718. ALEKSA-ANGARIETIS, Zigmas. Nepriklausomos Lietuvos kalėjimuose; arba, Baltojo teroro aukos. [The victims of the white terror in Lithuanian prisons] [By] Z. Angarietis, [pseud.]. Brooklyn, N.Y., 1922. (Amerikos lietuvių darbininkų literatūros draugijos leidinys, nr. 11). 947.5.An4 PP; PU.

1719. ARNAŠIUS, Stasys. Motinos širdis. [Mother's heart]. Vilnius, Valstybinė politinės ir mokslinės literatūros leidykla, 1961. 85 p. ports. D802.L5A7 DLC.

1720. HARĖTSKI, Maksim ĪĀnkavich. Vilenskiĭa kamunary; roman-khronike. Mensk, Belarus, 1965. 354 p. illus. PG2835.H3V5 DLC; MH.

1721. --- Vilenskie kommunary; roman-khronika. Tikhoe techenie; povest'. Perevod s belorusskogo Ageĭa Gatova. Moskva, Sov. pisatel', 1966. 286 p. PG2835.H3V517 DLC; IU; MH; NjP.

1722. --- Vilniaus komunarai.[Resistance confederates of Vilnius] [By] M. Gareckis. Vertė Alb. Žukauskas]. Vilnius, Vaga, 1965. 315 p. PG2835.H3V518 PU.

1723. JURGAITIENĖ, V. Nebuvo kada drobelių austi; atsiminimai. [There was no time to sit at home; recollections. Literatūrinis bendraautoris L. Lenkauskas] Vilnius, Valstybinė grožinės literatūros leidykla, 1963. 302 p. illus., ports. IEN; IU; MH.

1724. LIKAS, Albinas. Jie gynė Maskvą. [They defended Moscow] [Literatūrinis bendraautoris J. Baltušis] Vilnius, Vaga, 1967. 238 p. illus., ports. DK511.L28L5 DLC; CtY; IU; MH; NN.

1725. POVILAVIČIUS, Antanas. Laukė tėviškės berželiai. (Didžiojo Tėvynės karo dalyvio prisiminimai). [Reminiscences of a participant in the Great Patriotic War]. Vilnius, Vaga, 1973. 246 p. illus. D811.P638 DLC; IU; MB; MH; PU; WU.

1726. ROLNIKAITĖ, Maša. Je devais le raconter. Traduit du yiddish par l'auteur et Gaston Laroche. Préface d'Ilya Ehrenbourg. Postface du Dr. Herschel Meyer. Paris, les Éditions français réunis, 1966. 256 p. port. D810.J4R6464 DLC; CaBVaU; CtY;CSt-H; IEN; MB; NN; NNC.

1727. ŠUMAUSKAS, Motiejus. Kovų verpetuose. [Among the whirlpools of struggle]. Vilnius, Vaga, 1973. 492 p. illus. DK511.L28S84 PU; DLC; MB; WU.

1728. --- V vodovorote bor'by. M. Shumauskas. Moskva, Politizdat, 1975. 333 p., plates, port. DK511.L27S9317 DLC.

1729. VILDŽIŪNAS, Jonas and GIRČYS, Vytautas. Kova be atvangos; atsiminimai 1927-1944 metai. [The continuous struggle; reminiscences, 1927-1944. Lit. bendraautoris V. Girčys] Vilnius, Vaga, 1971. 486 p., 9 leaves of illus. DK511.L27V42 DLC; IU; NN.

1730. ŽYGIAI, APKASAI, ATAKOS; Didžiojo Tėvynės Karo dalyvių prisiminimai. [...Reminiscences of the participants in the Great Patriotic War] Vilnius, Valstybinė grožinės literatūros leidykla, 1961. 594 p. illus., ports. D811.Z77 DLC; CaAEU.

X.9.o.4. SECRET POLICE ACTIVITIES;
         GENOCIDE, DEPORTATIONS,
         AND THE FORCED LABOUR
         CAMPS

1731. BLOCH, Sidney and REDDAWAY,
P. Psychiatric terror: how Soviet
psychiatry is used to suppress dis-
sident. New York, N.Y., Basic Books,
cl977. 510 p. The title in Great
Britain: Russia's political hospital.
RC451.R9B56 DLC; CaAEU.

1732. GLIAUDYS, Jurgis. Simas.
Cleveland, Ohio, Viltis, 1971. port.
At head of title: Jurgis Gliauda.
E183.8.G55 DLC; MB.

1733. --- --- Translated from Li-
thuanian by Kęstutis Čižiūnas and J.
Žemkalnis. New York, N.Y., Manyland
Books, cl971. 120 p. port. At head
of title: Jurgis Gliauda.
E183.8.R9G5513 DLC; CaAEU; CSt;ICU;
CSt-H; NN; NIC; NjP; OKentU;PU; WU.

1734. IAKOVLEV, B[oris Aleksandro-
vich]. Kontsentratsionnye lageri
SSSR. München, 1955. 253 p. illus.,
maps. (Institut po izucheniiu istorii
i kultury SSSR. Issledovaniia i materialy. Seriia 1, vyp. 23). Summaries in English, German, and French.
Bibliography: p. 241-248.
HV8931.R8I2 DLC; CtY.

1735. KUČYS, A. Dvasinio teroro
kronika. [The chronicle of the psychiatric terror] In Varpas (Brooklyn, N.Y.), no.13, 1975, p.112-118.
See serials consulted.

1736. LITHUANIAN AMERICAN COUNCIL.
Know your enemy, Communism. [Exhibit
by Lithuanian American Council, Inc.,
U.S.A., 1970. Washington, D.C.,
1970. 82 p.] illus. Display of
photostat copies of documents, draw-
ings and photographs.
D804.R9L5 OKentU; DLC.

1737. --- --- [2d. ed. Chicago,
Ill., 1971] 96 p. illus.
DK511.L27L498 1971 DLC.

1738. PRUNSKIS, Juozas. 15 [i.e.
Penkiolika] Lietuvoje sušaudytų kunigų. [The execution of fifteen
priests in Lithuania]. Chicago, Ill.,
1942. 12 p. illus.
950.5P ICBM.

1739. RUKŠĖNAS, Algis. Day of
shame; the truth about the murderous
happenings aboard the Cutter Vigilant
during the Russian-American confron-
tation off Martha's Vineyard. New
York, N.Y., D.McKay Co. [1973]. xv,
368 p. illus. DK511.L28K87R93 1973

CaAEU; DLC; CtY; IaU; CSt-H; CoU; DS;
FU; GU; IaU; InU; IaAS; InNd; IU;KU;
MB; MH; MoU; MiEM; MiU; MoSW; MnU;MU;
N; NN; NIC; NBuC; NjP; NjR; NcD; NbU;
NmU; NvU; OkU; OU; OrU; OKentU; OOxM;
PU; TU; TxU; ULC; UU; ViU; ViBlbV;
VtU; WU; WaU; MH-L.

1740. SHUB, Anatole. Report on
the trial testimony of Simas Kudirka, Lithuanian sailor. In Lituanus
(Chicago, Ill.), no.3, v.18, 1972,
p. 7-12. See serials consulted.

1741. SPÄTH, Bernhard. Amerika-
ner verweigern politisches Asýl; die
Auslieferung des Matrosen Simas Kudirka an die Sowjets. Ulm, Süddeu-
tsche Verlagsgesellschaft, [1973].
44 p. illus. DK511.L28K875 PU;DLC.

1742. TERLECKAS, Antanas. Respect
my rights; an appeal to J.V. Andro-
pov, chief of the Soviet secret service (KGB). Prepared by The Lithuanian World Community, June 14, 1976.
[Chicago, Ill, The World Lithuanian
Community, 1976]. 35 p.
DK511.L274T45 DLC; PU.

1743. TUMAS, Juozas, 1893- .
Bolševikų kalėjimuose ir Červenės žu-
dynėse. [In the bolshevik prisons and
the massacre near Červene, Belorussia]
In Karys (Brooklyn, N.Y.), 1957: no.
2(1329), p.51-54; no.3(1330), p.86-
90; no.4(1331), p.116-119; no.5(1332),
p.151-153; no.6(1333), p.183-187; no.
7(1334), p.214-216; no.8(1335), p.254-
258; no.9(1336), p.287-291; no.10(
1337), p. 317-319. Mr. L.Kairys (Chicago) has it, no.427; see also serials
consulted.

1744. UNITED STATES. CONGRESS.
HOUSE. COMMITTEE ON FOREIGN AFFAIRS.
SUBCOMMITTEE ON STATE DEPARTMENT OR-
GANIZATION AND FOREIGN OPERATIONS.
Attempted defection by Lithuanian sea-
man Simas Kudirka. Hearings, Ninety-
first Congress, Second session. Wash-
ington, D.C., Govt.Print.Off., 1971.
247 p. ports.
KF27.F6486 1970 DLC; CaAEU; MB; NIC.

1745. --- --- Report on the hea-
rings held by the Subcommitte on De-
cember 3, 7-9, 14, 18 and 29, 1970
pursuant to H.Res.143. 91st Congress
Second session. Washington, D.C.,
Govt.Print.Off., 1971. vii, 11 p.
KF32.F669 1970 DLC; CaAEU; CLSU;
CU-AL; NIC; OClJC; OKentU;

X.9.o.5. RUSSIFICATION OF LITHUANIA

1746. GERUTIS, Albertas. Gedanken
zur sowjetischen Russifizierungspoli-

tik im Baltikum. Königstein, Ger., 1965. p. 9-35. At head of title: Institutum Balticum. Offprint from Acta Baltica(Königstein), 1965-1966. DS.

1747. HEHN, Jürgen von. Zur Entwicklung der nationalen Verhältnisse in den baltischen Sowjetrepubliken. Göttingen, Ger., Musterschmidt-Verlag, 1975. 44 p. (Historisch-politische Hefte der Ranke-Gesellschaft, Hft. 24) D6.H6 Hft. 24 DLC.

1748. NORVILAS, Algis. Lithuanian studies in bilingualism. In Journal of Baltic Studies (Brooklyn, N.Y.), no.1, v.7, 1976, p. 45-60. See serials consulted.

1749. ON THE THREAT OF LINGUISTIC assimilation. Two articles from the Lithuanian Samizdat. In Lituanus (Chicago, Ill.), no.1, v.23, 1977, p.51-62. See serials consulted.

1750. ZUBRAS, Albertas. Rusifikacija Sovietų Sąjungoje. [The russification in the Soviet Union] In Aidai (Brooklyn, N.Y.), no.2, 1973, p. 49-56. See serials consulted.

X.9.o.6. THE CHURCH AND RELIGIOUS PERSECUTION IN SOVIET LITHUANIA

1751. ANIČAS, Jonas and RIMAITIS, Juozas. Tarybiniai įstatymai apie religinius kultus ir sąžinės laisvę. [Soviet laws on religion and freedom of conscience]. Vilnius, Mokslas, 1970. 79 p. BR936.A6 PU.

1752. CHRIST BEHIND WIRE. Maspeth, Long Island, N.Y., The Lithuanian Roman Catholic Priest's League of America, c1974. 53 p. (Chronicle...no. 5) Translation of Lietuvos Katalikų Bažnyčios Kronika, no.5, 1973. BX1559.L5C48 DLC.

1753. CHRONIK DER KATHOLISCHEN KIRCHE Litauens, nr.7-9. In Acta Baltica (Königstein, Ger.), v.14, 1974, p. 9-123. See serials consulted.

1754. --- nr.13-14. In Acta Baltica (Königstein, Ger.), v.16, 1976, p. 9-93. See serials consulted.

1755. --- nr.10-12. In Acta Baltica (Königstein, Ger.), v.15, 1975, p. 9-101. See serials consulted.

1756. THE CHURCH SUFFERING. Maspeth, Long Island, N.Y., The Lithua-

nian Roman Catholic Priest's League of America, 1974. 50 p. (Chonicle of the Catholic Church in Lithuania, no.8) Translation of authentic first-hand reports from Soviet-occupied Lithuania. BX1559.L5C5 DLC.

1757. CONTONS, Albert J. Religious persecution in Lithuania-Soviet style. In Lituanus (Chicago, Ill.), no.2, v.18, 1972, p. 51-56. See serials consulted.

1758. CRONACA DELLA CHIESA CATTOlica in Lituania, no.7. In Elta Press (Roma), no.2, 1974, p.4-27. See serials consulted.

1759. --- no.8. In Elta Press (Roma), no.4, 1974, p.4-30. See serials consulted.

1760. --- no.9. In Elta Press (Roma), no.5, 1974, p. 4-28. See serials consulted.

1761. DECLARATION BY THE PRIESTS of the Catholic Church in Lithuania, dated August 1969. In Lituanus (Chicago, Ill.), no.3, v.19, 1973, p. 46-53. See serials consulted.

1762. DESECRATED SHRINES. Maspeth, N.Y., The Lithuanian Roman Catholic Priests' League of America, c1974. 62 p. (Chronicle of the Catholic Church in Lithuania, no.7) BX1559.L5D47 DLC.

1763. FREEDOM TO DIE. Maspeth, N.Y., The Lithuanian Roman Catholic Priests' League of America, 1975. 42 p. (Chronicle of the Catholic Church in Lithuania, no.9) BX1559.L5F73 DLC.

1764. GULBINAS, Konstantin P. Die neuesten Berichte und Dokumente über die Lage der Kirche in Litauen. In Acta Baltica (Königstein, Ger.), v.12, 1972, p. 45-84. See serials consulted.

1765. KAZRAGIS, Algirdas. Smurtu ir klasta. Vilnius, Mintis, 1966. 34 p. BX1559.L5K3 DLC; OKentU.

1766. KRASAUSKAS, Rapolas and GULBINAS, K. Die Lage der katholischen Kirche in Litauen. In Acta Baltica (Königstein, Ger.), v.12, 1972, p.9-44. See serials consulted.

1767. LIETUVOS KATALIKŲ BAŽNYČIOS KRONIKA; pogrindžio leidinys. [Chronicle of the Catholic Church in Lithuania. Chicago, Ill., L.K.Religinės šalpos rėmėjai, 1974- . v. illus. BX1559.L5L5 PU; CaAEU; DLC.

1768. MARTIN, André. Lituanie; terre de foix, terre de croix. Paris, Éditions Albatros, [1976]. 197 p. illus. DK511.L2M198 DLC; PU.

1769. NATIONAL AND RELIGIOUS PROtest in Lithuania. From the underground Chronicle of the Catholic Church in Lithuania. In Lituanus (Chicago, Ill.), no.2, v.20, 1974, p. 68-75.; no.3, p. 73-75; and no.4, p. 62-68. See serials consulted.

1770. NUMERO DUE DELLE CRONACA della Chiesa cattolica in Lituania. In Elta Press (Roma), no.12, 1973, p. 3-29. See serials consulted.

1771. NUMERO SEI DELLA CRONACA della Chiesa cattolica in Lituania. In Elta Press (Roma), no.9, 1973, p. 3-25. See serials consulted.

1772. PAVALKIS, Victor. The Catholic Church in the Baltic States and the Holy See, 1939-1945. In The Baltic Review (New York, N.Y.), no. 38, 1971, p. 54-64. See serials consulted.

1773. PRIMO NUMERO DELLA CRONACA della Chiesa cattolica in Lituania. In Elta Press (Roma), no.1, 1974, p. 3-28. See serials consulted.

1774. RAIŠUPIS, Matas. Dabarties kankiniai; Lietuvos vyskupų, kunigų ir tikinčiųjų kryžiaus kelias pirmoje ir antroje sovietų okupacijoje. Today's martyrs; the Calvary of the bishops, priests and people during the forst and second Soviet occupation of Lithuania. Chicago, Ill., 1972] 436 p. illus. BX1559.L5R3 PU; DLC; InNd; MB.

1775. RIMAITIS, J. Religion in Lithuania. [Translated by G. Kirvaitis. Edited by K. Smigelskis and V. Grodzenskis. Vilnius, Gintaras, 1971] 33 p. illus., maps. BR937.L3R54 DLC; CLU; CtY-D; CSt; ICIU; IU; InNd; MH; MiEM; NNC; NIC; NjP; NcD; OKentU; OU.

1776. ROSSI, Raimondo and CAMPANA, Christophoro. Lituania martire. La tragedia di un popolo e di una Chiesa. Urbania, Italy, Commissione diocezana per la Chiesa del Silenzio, 1973. 53 p. illus. BX1559.L5R65 DLC; PU.

1777. SONS, Arturs. Die aktuelle Lage der Kirche in Litauen und Lettland; Berichte und Dokumente. In Acta Baltica (Königstein, Ger.), v. 13, 1973, p. 9-39. See serials consulted.

1778. VARDYS, Stanley V. Catholicism in Lithuania. In Aspects of religion in the Soviet Union, 1917-1967. Chicago, Ill., 1971. p.379-403. BL980.R8A9 DLC; AAP; AU;CLU; CaBVaU; CaOTP; CLSU; CSt; CoU; CtY-D CtY; CBGTU; CU-L; DAU; DS; FU; FTaSU GU; IaU; IaAS; ICJS; InU; ICU; IEdS; IEG; IU; KAS; KMK; KEmT; KU; KyLxCB; KyU; LU; MH; MH-AH; MiU; MiEM; MnU; MeB; MdU; MoU; MoSW; MSohG; MNtcA; MBU-T; MU; NN; NNC; NIC; NBuU; NSyU; NjP; NjPT; NjR; NcD; NcU; NcGU;NcRS; NbU; NdU; NRU; OkU; OCIU; OO; OU;OCH OKentU; OrU; OrPS; PPULC; PPT;RP;RPB TxDaM-P; TxU; TU; UU; ViU; ViBlbV;WU Wa; WaU.

1779. WE WILL NOT. Maspeth, N.Y., The Lithuanian Roman Catholic Priests' League of America, [1975.] 39 p. (Chronicle of the Catholic Church in Lithuania, no.11) BX1559.L5W4 DLC.

X.9.o.7. ATHEISM AND THE ANTI-RELIGIOUS PROGRAMS

1780. ADOMAUSKAS, Liudas. Šventraščio paslaptys. [Secrets of the Holy Scriptures. Redagavo ir paaiškinimus paruošė P. Aksamitas] 2.pataisytas ir papildytas leidimas. Vilnius, Valstybinė politinės ir mokslinės literatūros leidykla, 1960. 173 p. BS533.A25 1960 DLC.

1781. ANIČAS, Jonas. Katalikiškasis klerikalizmas Lietuvoje 1940-44 metais. [Catholic clericalism in Lithuania, 1940-1944] Vilnius, Mintis, 1972. 253 p. At head of title: Lietuvos TSR Mokslų akademijos filosofijos, teisės ir sociologijos skyrius prie Istorijos instituto. Summaries in Latvian and Russian. BX1559.L5A5 PU.

1782. --- Socialinis politinis katalikų bažnyčios vaidmuo Lietuvoje, 1945-1952 metais. [Social and political influence of the Catholic Church in Lithuania, 1945-1952] Vilnius, 1971. 212 p. At head of title: Lietuvos TSR Mokslų akademijos filosofijos, teisės ir sociologijos skyrius prie Istorijos instituto. Summary in Russian. Bibliography: p. 101-[206] BX1775.L55A64 DLC; CtY; InU; MH; NN; OKentU; PPiU.

1783. JŪRONIENĖ, Genovaitė. Neužpirktos mišios. [Mass offering not requested] Vilnius, Mintis, 1966. 87 p. BL2780.J82 OKentU.

1784. LAURINAITIS, Stasys. Jų Dievas. [Their God]. Vilnius, Valstybinė politinės ir mokslinės literatūros leidykla, 1962. 42 p. illus., ports.

BX1775.L55L3 DLC; OKentU.

1785. MACEINA, Antanas. Sowjetische Ethik und Christentum; zum Verständnis des Kommunistischen Menschen. Witten, Ger, Eckhart-Verlag, 1969. 203 p. Based on lectures presented at the Evangelische Akademie Westfalen, Arbeitskreis Bochum, 1962-1965. BJ1390.M22 DLC; GU; MH-AH; MoSW; NjPT; NcD; PPiU; PSt; ViU; WU.

1786. NIUNKA, Vladas. Nuo Vatikano Pirmojo iki Vatikano Antrojo. [From the first until the second Vatican Council]. Vilnius, Valstybinė politinės ir mokslinės literatūros leidykla, 1963. 89 p. BX1767.N5 DLC;

1787. RAGAUSKAS, Jonas. Stupaĭte, messa okonchena! Avtorizovannyĭ sovremennyĭ perevod s litovskogo F. Dektora i I. Rudasa]. Moskva, Gos. izd-vo polit. lit-ry, 1961. 310 p. illus. BX1559.L5R37 DLC; FMU; IU; MH; NN; NNC.

1788. RELIGIJOS IR ATEIZMO KLAUSIMAI. [The questions on religion and atheism. Redagavo P. Aksamitas] Vilnius, Valstybinė politinės ir mokslinės literatūros leidykla, 1963. 366 p. R119.6365 MH.

1789. ŠEŠTOKAS, Konstantinas. Kas išganys liaudį? [Who will save the people?]. Pirmoji dalis:Ar prietariškasis tikėjimas bei tikyba išganys liaudį? Chicago, Ill., Spauda Lietuvių žurnalo, 1912. 208 p. BL80.S4 OKentU.

1790. VALADKA, Mykolas. Popiežiai ir Lietuva; kodėl slepiama istorinė tiesa. [Popes and Lithuania...] Scranton, Pa., 1954. 244 p. BX1559.L5V3 OKentU.

1791. VILNA. LIETUVOS TSR ATEIZMO MUZIEJUS. Religinės kovos ir erezijos Lietuvoje. [Religious struggles and heresies in Lithuania. Red. komisija: P. Aksamitas (pirmininkas), J. Jurginis, A. Martinonis]. Vilnius, Mintis, 1977. 109 p. BR1050.L5V5 PU.

1792. ŽMONĖS IR RELIGIJA. [People and religion. Ats. redaktorius Kazys Grigas] Vilnius, Vaga, 1977. 234 p PG8709.Z55 PU.

X.10. UNDERGROUND MOVEMENT AND RESISTANCE AGAINST THE INCORPORATION INTO THE SOVIET UNION

1793. CHIENAS, M[enašas]. Sterviatniki s chuzhoĭ storony. [Perevod s litovskogo E. Efros. By M. Khienas, K. Shmigel'skis i Ė. Uldukis]. Vil'nius, Gos. izd-vo khudozh. lit-ry Litovskoĭ SSR, 1961. 303 p. illus. At head of title: M. Chienas, K. Shmigel'skis, Ė. Uldukis. Translation of Vanagai iš anapus. DK511.L27C4557 DLC.

1794. --- Vanagai iš anapus; dokumentinė apybraiža. [Hawks from abroad. By] M. Chienas, K. Šmigelskis [ir] Ė. Uldukis. Vilnius, Valstybinė grožinės literatūros leidykla, 1960. 275 p. illus. DK511.L27C455 OKentU; MH.

1795. --- --- 2. laida. Vilnius, Valstybinė grožinės literatūros leidykla, 1961. 273 p. illus. DK511.L27C455 1961 DLC; OCl.

1796. DAUMANTAS, Juozas, pseud. Fighters for freedom; Lithuanian partisans versus the U.S.S.R., 1944-1947. Translated from the Lithuanian by E.J. Harrison and Manyland Books. New York, N.Y., Manyland Books, c1975. 254 p., [4] leaves of plates. illus. Translation of Partizanai už geležinės uždangos. D802.L5D313 DLC; PU.

1797. MIKUCKIS, Juozas. Šioje ir anoje pusėje. [On this and the other side. Redaktorė A. Petruševičienė] Vilnius, Mintis, 1974. 147 p. PG8721.M46Z PU.

1798. NEMATOMASIS FRONTAS. [The invisible front. Sudarytojas A. Viršulis]. Vilnius, Mintis, 1967. 212 p. illus. HV8224.N45 DLC.

1799. ROSITZKE, Harry August. The CIA's secret operations; espionage, counterspionage, and covert action. New York, N.Y., Reader's Digest Press, 1977. xxx, 286 p. JK468.16.R67 DLC; CaAEU.

X.11. LIBERATION ACTIVITIES OUTSIDE LITHUANIA

1800. AUDĖNAS, Juozas. Žmogaus teisės VLIKo darbuose. [Human rights as discussed at the Supreme Lithuanian Committee of Liberation]. In Varpas (Melrose Park, Ill.), nr.15, 1977, p. 17-28. See serials consulted.

1801. BALTIC COMMITTEE IN SCANDINAVIA. The Baltic States, 1940-1972; documentary background and survey of developments, presented to the European Security and Cooperation Conference. [2nd. ed.] Stockholm, Baltic Committee in Scandinavia, 1972. 120 p. Bibliography: p. 118-[121]. DK511.B3B283 1972 DLC; CaBVaU;DNIH; CaOTP; CSt-H; IaAS; InU; IU; MnU; MU NjP; OrU; PPT; WU.

1802. BALTIC FEDERATION IN CANADA. We accuse the Soviet Union and her leaders. Toronto, Ont., Baltic Federation, 196- . 1 v. Bound with Baltic States Freedom Council. Manifesto. New York, N.Y.,[196-]. DK.B3B18 CaAEU.

1803. BALTIC STATES FREEDOM COUNCIL. The Baltic countries; Soviet colonies in the heart of Europe.New York, N.Y., The Council, 196- . [8] p. illus., map. DK511.B3B197 CaAEU.

1804. --- Manifesto; the twenty-fifth anniversary of Soviet aggression against the Baltic States. By Free Estonians, Latvians and Lithuanians. New York, N.Y., The Council, [196- .] 3 leaves. Bound with Baltic Federation in Canada. We accuse the Soviet Union and her leaders. Toronto, Ont., [196- .].

1805. HORM, Arvo. Phases of the Baltic political activities... with biographical notes on Arvo Horm by Evald Uustatu. Stockholm, Baltic Humanitarian Association, 1973. 22 p. DK511.B3H55 1973 DLC.

1806. KARO KURSTYTOJŲ KESLAI IR manevrai; straipsnių rinkinys. [Intentions and plots of the war-mongers; collection of articles. Redaktorius L. Šarpis] Vilnius, Valstybinė politinės ir mokslinės literatūros leidykla, 1962. 151 p. D344.K474 DLC.

1807. KOJELIS, Juozas. VLIKo reorganizavimas; pasisakymai Vl. Juodeikio, J. Kuprionio, P. Pamataičio, A. Razmos ir P. Raulinaičio. [The reorganization of the Supreme Lithuanian Committee of Liberation...] In Į Laisvę (Los Angeles, Calif.), no. 60, 1974, p. 75-94. See serials consulted.

1808. KRIVICKAS, Domas. Lithuania's struggle against agression and subjugation. In Audėnas, J., ed. Twenty years' struggle for freedom of Lithuania. New York, 1963. p.118-146. DK511.L27T84 CaBVaU; CaOOP; CaQMM; CaOTP; InNd; MH; N; NN; NNC; PP; OCl; OClW; OrU; PP; PPiU; PU.

1809. KRUPAVIČIUS, Mykolas. Šiandieninė lietuvių tautos kova už laisvę. [The present struggle of the Lithuanian nation for freedom] In Metraštis 1950. Kennebunk Port, Me., [1949] p. 97-108. DK511.L223M59 1949 CaAEU; MH; see also serials consulted.

1810. LIULEVIČIUS, Vincentas. Išeivija Lietuvos atkūrimo darbe. [The exiles in the activities for an independent Lithuania]. Čikaga, Pedagoginis lituanistikos institutas, 1971. 66 p. illus. Bibliography: p.61-63. DK511.L223L58 DLC; ICLJF.

1811. LUŠYS, Stasys. The origin of the Supreme Committee for Liberation of Lithuania. In Audėnas, J.ed. Twenty years' struggle for freedom of Lithuania. New York, 1963. p.25-39. DK511.L27T84 CaBVaU; CaOOP; CaOTP; CaQMM; InNd; MH; N; NN; NNC; OCl;OrU; OClW; PP; PPiU; PU.

1812. MACEINA, Antanas. Būsimoji mūsų veikla, jos kryptys, uždaviniai ir būdai. [Our future activity, its direction, means and ways] In Į Laisvę (Los Angeles, Calif.), no.61, 1974, p. 22-44. See serials consulted.

1813. MIKUCKIS, Juozas. Šioje ir anoje pusėje. [On this and the other side. Redaktorė A. Petruševičienė] Vilnius, Mintis, 1974. 147 p. PG8721.M46Z PU.

1814. MORKUS, Albinas. "Vaduotojai" iš arti; lietuvio emigranto atpasakojimai apie gyvenimą JAV. "Liberators" from near; the story of a Lithuanian emigrant about the life in the United States] Vilnius, Gintaras, 1968. 140 p. E184.L7M67 DLC.

1815. NAINYS, Bronius. Tauta ir išeivija laisvės kovoje. [The nation and the exiles in the struggle for freedom of Lithuania] In Į Laisvę (Los Angeles, Calif.), no.50, 1970, p.28-37. See serials consulted.

1816. NEMICKAS, Bronius. Lietuvos išlaisvinimo politinės veiklos apžvalga. [A review of the political activities for an independent Lithuania] In Naujoji Viltis (Chicago, Ill.),no. 1, 1970, p. 115-122. See serials consulted.

1817. ŠIDLAUSKAS, K[azys]. Supreme Committee for Liberation of Lithuania as representative of Lithuanian national interests. In Audėnas, J., ed. Twenty years' struggle for freedom of Lithuania. New York, 1963. p. 93-117. DK511.L27T84 CaBVaU; CaOOP; CaOTP; CaQMM; InNd; MH; N; NN; NNC; OCl; OClW; OrU; PP; PPiU; PU.

1818. SUPREME LITHUANIAN COMMITTEE

OF LIBERATION. VLIKo grupių komisijos pranešimas. Tų grupių atstovų 1958 m. gegužės 10 d. pasitarimui (New York) apie pastangas įtraukti ir VLIKą bendram Lietuvos laisvinimo darbui jame nedalyvaujančias grupes. [The report of the Group Commission of the Supreme Lithuanian Committee of Liberation] Cleveland, Ohio, Išleido Cleveland Lietuvių demokratinių grupių Prezidiumas, 1958. 80 p.   OKentU.

X.12. LOCAL HISTORY

X.12.a. CITIES

X.12.a.1. KAUNAS

1819. ABRAMAUSKAS, Stasys. Kaunas. [The city of Kaunas, its suburbs and environs. By] S. Abramauskas, V. Černeckis, A. Gulbinskienė. [Vilnius, Mintis, 1968] 237 p. illus. Balt.8619.2 MH.

1820. BALTUŠNIKAS, Zenonas. Kaunas. [Translated by M. Ginsburgas. Edited by A. Medonis and V. Grodzenskis] Vilnius, Gintaras, 1973. 40 p. illus.   DK651.K125B3513 DLC; MH.

1821. BALTUŠNIKAS, Zenonas. Kaunas. Zenonas Baltushnikas. [Per. s litov.].   Izd. 2-e, ispr. Vil'niūs, Mintis, 1974. 63 p. DK651.K125B3517 1974 DLC.

1822. KEŽINAITIS, Petras. Kauno apylinkėse. [Kaunas and its environs] Vilnius, Valstybinė politinės ir mokslinės literatūros leidykla, 1958. 126 p. illus.   LG2KAU ICLJF.

X.12.a.2. VILNIUS

1823. FRANK, Joseph. Pamiętniki d-ra Józefa Franka, profesora Uniwersytetu Wileńskiego. Z francuskiego przetłumaczył, wstęppem i uwagami opatrzył Władysław Zahorski. Wilno, Kurjer Litewski, 1913. 3 v. in 1. DK651.V4F7 PU.

1824. JAKŠTAS, Juozas. Vilnius lietuvių tautos įr valstybės branduolys. Vilnius, the nucleus of the Lithuanian nation. In Lietuvių Tautos Praeitis (Chicago, Ill.), kn.3, v.3, p. 119-130. See serials consulted.

1825. JANKEVIČIENĖ, A[lgė] Nekoto-

rye sooruzheniĩa Vil'niũsa XVI veka. In Arkhitekturnoe Nasledstvo (Moskva) t.17, 1964; See serials consulted.

1826. PUZINAS, Jonas. Vilnius 650 metų sukaktis miesto ar Gedimino sostinės? The 650th anniversary of Vilnius; as a city or as Gediminas' capital? In Institute of Lithuanian Studies. Lituanistikos instituto 1973 metų suvažiavimo darbai. Chicago, Ill., 1975. p. 9-24. Summary in English. DK511.L2I63 1975 CaAEU; PU.

1827. VILNA. [Gorodovoe polozhenie 1785 g.]. Mieskie postanowienie. Vilna, 1796. MH.

1828. VILNA. Russia (City). Otchet goroda Vil'na za 1863- . Vil'na.   v.   HJ4055.V5A3 DLC.

1829. VILNA. VYKDOMASIS KOMITETAS. Vilniaus miesto vykdomojo komiteto posėdžių protokolai 1940-1941 m. [City of Vilnius Councils minutes of meetings for 1940-1941]. Spaudai parengė Vanda Ragaišienė. Vilnius, LTSRMAII, 1975. 137 p. (Acta historica Lituanica, 10) DK651.V4A5 PU; DLC.

1830. VILNIAUS MIESTO ISTORIJA nuo Spalio revoliucijos iki dabartinių dienų. [History of the City of Vilnius from October revolution up to this day. Redakcinė kolegija: H.Šadžius, R. Žepkaitė, J. Žiugžda, vyriausiasis redaktorius]. Vilnius, Lietuvos TSR Mokslų akademija, Istorijos institutas; Leidykla Mintis,1972. 331 p. illus., ports. Summary in Russian.   DK651.V4V415 PU; CLU; CU; DLC; InU; MiU; NNC; NjP; OClW; OKentU PPiU.

1831. VILNIUI 650 METŲ; straipsnių rinkinys. [The 650th anniversary of Vilnius; collection of articles. Red. kolegija: Mečislovas Jučas, Henrikas Šadžius, Bronius Vaitkevičius (ats. redaktorius] Vilnius, Lietuvos TSR Mokslų akademijos Istorijos institutas, 1976. 159 p. DK651.V4V45 PU; DLC.

1832. ŽILYS, Povilas. Kaip lenkai 1920 m. liepos mėn. užleido Vilnių Rusams ir atidavė lietuviams. Polish withdrowal from Vilnius in July of 1920 and the return of the Lithuanian army[into the city] In Lietuvių Tautos Praeitis (Chicago, Ill.), kn.2, v.3, 1973, p. 82-91. Summary in English. See serials consulted.

X.12.a.3. OTHER CITIES

1833. ANYKŠČIAI. [The Town of A-nykščiai. Parengė Anykščių kraštotyrininkai. Vilnius, Mintis, 1971] 111 p. illus., diagrams.
DK511.A58A5 PU; DLC; IU; MB; MH.

1834. BALTAKEVIČIUS, Juozas, ed. Lietuvos miestai; bendri istorijos bruožai. [Lithuanian cities; a brief history] Šiauliai, "Mūsų Momento" leidinys, 1932. [Xerox copy, 1975] 288 p. DK511.L2B325 PU.

1835. BILEVIČIUS, Petras. Šiauliai. [The City of Šiauliai]. Vilnius, Mintis, 1972. 142 p.
DK651.S5B5 PU.

1836. BITINAITĖ, Vilhelmina and TREČIOKAS, E. Biržai. [The Town of Biržai]. Vilnius, Mintis, 1971. 44 p., 16 leaves of illus.
DK651.B52B58 DLC; IU; MB; MH.

1837. BUDRAITIS, Petras. Joniškis. [The Town of Joniškis]. Vilnius, Mintis, 1973. 93 p.
DK651.J65B8 PU; DLC.

1838. DUBINGIAI. [The Town of Dubingiai] [Redakcinė komisija:... Stasys Skredenis (pirmininkas)] Vilnius, Vaga, 1971. 408 p. illus. At head of title: Lietuvos TSR Paminklų apsaugos ir kraštotyros draugija.
DK651.D75D83 DLC; PU.

1839. ERETAS, Juozas. Rėzos gimtinė Karvaičiai ir jų poetai. [Karvaičiai, the birthplace of Rheza, and its poets]. In Athenaeum (Kaunas), v.9, 1938, p. 153-186. See serials consulted.

1839a. FIJAŁEK, Jan. Dorsuniszki [The Town of Darsuniškiai]. In Kwartalnik Historyczny (Lwów), no.3, v. 44, 1930, p. 333-340. See serials consulted.

1840. LIETUVOS TSR PAMINKLŲ APSAUGOS IR KRAŠTOTYROS DRAUGIJA. Kernavė [The Town of Kernavė]. Red. komisija: V. Milius (pirmininkas) ir kiti. Vilnius, Vaga, v.t.p. 434 p. illus. On verso of t.p.: Lietuvos TSR Paminklų apsaugos ir Kraštotyros draugija. Summaries in English.
DK651.K35L5 PU; DLC.

1841. KRIVICKAS, Sigitas. Palanga. [The Town of Palanga]. Vilnius, Mintis, 1970. 60 p.
DK651.P21K7 PU.

1842. LAURAITIS, Vincas. Žemaičių Kalvarija. [The Town of Žemaičių

Kalvarija]. 2.leidimas. Vilnius, Valstybinė politinės ir mokslinės literatūros leidykla, 1961. 26 p.
DK651.Z45L3 1961 DLC.

1843. MATUSAS, Jonas. Šiluva seniausiais laikais. [The Town of Šiluva in the most ancient times]. In Aidai (Kennebunk Port, Me), no.4(149) 1962, p. 178. Mr. L.Kairys (Chicago) has it as no.339; see also serials consulted.

1844. MISIŪNAS, Romualdas J. The Šventojis project: 18th century plans for a Lithuanian port. In Journal of Baltic Studies (Brooklyn, N.Y.), no.1 v.8, p. 28-50. See serials consulted.

1845. N. V. Rokiškio miestas prieš karą ir po karo. [The Town of Rokiškis before and after the First World War. By N.V.] In Savivaldybė (Kaunas), no.8, 1932. JS6130.5.A1S3 DLC; CtPAM; see also serials consulted.

1846. NAUDUŽAS, Julius. Šiaulių miesto archeologiniai paminklai.[Archaeological monuments of the City of Šiauliai]. In Lietuvos TSR Mokslų akademija, Vilna. Istorijos institutas. Iš lietuvių kultūros istorijos, v.2, 1959, p. 177-187.
DK511.L212L5 DLC; CLU; CU; InU; KyU; NN; NNC; PU; PPiU.

1847. PAKALNIŠKIS, Aleksandras. Plungė. [The Town of Plungė] In Lietuvių Tautos Praeitis (Chicago, Ill.), kn.3, v.3, p. 131-146. See serials consulted.

1848. PETRONIS, Julijonas. Ukmergė. [The Town of Ukmergė]. Vilnius, Mintis, 1976. 70 p.,[32] leaves of plates. DK651.U55P PU; DLC.

1849. PLESKUS, Stanislovas. Alytus. [The Town of Alytus]. Vilnius, Mintis, 1973. 59 p., 32 leaves of illus. DK651.A59P PU; DLC; MB; MH.

1850. PONEVIEZH. In Pamiatnaia knizhka Kovenskoi gubernii. Kovno, 1898, p. 88-108. DK511.K55P32 DLC.

1851. PUZINAS, Jonas. Iš Šiaulių miesto istorijos. [From the history of Šiauliai]. In Savivaldybė (Kaunas) Metai 7, 1929, no.2, p.6-14; no3, p.9-17; no.4, p.6-13; no.5, p.11-19; no. 7, p.3-9; no.9, p.8-13. JS6130.5.A1S3 DLC; see also serials consulted.

1852. ROZGA, Leopoldas. Skuodas. [The Town of Skuodas]. Vilnius, Mintis, 1976. 45 p. DK651.S6R6 PU.

1853. SKODŽIUS, Petras. Biržietiška mozaika; publicistika. [The mozaic of Biržai...] Vilnius, Mintis, 1976. 131 p. DK651.B528S55 PU.

1854. ŠULCAITĖ, O. Istorijos puslapius verčiant. [Looking through the pages of history]. Vilnius,1971. 315 p. illus. At head of title: Lietuvos K.P. Šiaulių Miesto Komitetas. Lietuvos TSR Paminklų apsaugos ir kraštotyros draugijos Šiaulių miesto skyrius. NNC.

1855. RŪGYTĖ, Alicija, ed. Švėkšna. [The Town of Švėkšna]. Čikaga, Švėkšniškių draugija, 1974. xiv, 528 p. illus., facsims., ports. Summary in English. DK651.S83R8 PU; DLC.

1856. TREČIAKAUSKAS, Kęstutis. Kėdainiai. [The Town of Kėdainiai] Vilnius, Mintis, 1974. 111 p. DK651.K25T PU.

1857. USPENSKIĬ, Vladimir Petrovich. Litovskie pogranichnye gorodki: Seluk, Goryshin i drugie... Tver', Izd. Tverskoĭ uchen. arkhivnoĭ kommissii, Tip. Gubernskago pravleniĩa, 1892. 34 p. map. DK511.S3B19 ICU.

1858. WOJCIECHOWSKI, Jarosław. Stary zamek w Grodnie. Warszawa, Skł. główny, Kasa im. Mianowskiego, 1938. 66 p. illus., plans. Paged also [119]-142, [229]-270. Reprints from Biuletyn Historii Sztuki i Kultury, rok 6. Q947.52W826 PU.

1859. ŽERVYNŲ KAIMAS.[The Village of Žervynai] Bendra redakcija Kazio Šešelgio. Vilnius, Periodika, 1974. 47, 108 p. illus. (Lietuvių liaudies architektūros paminklai, 1). At head of title: Lietuvos TSR Aukštojo ir Specialiojo vidurinio mokslo ministerija. Vilniaus inžinierinis statybos institutas. Summaries in English German and Russian. NA1197.Z47Z47 PU; DLC.

X.12.b. REGIONS, DISTRICTS, ETC.

1860. PICHEL, Charles Louis Thourot. Samogitia; the unknown in history. Wilkes-Barre, Pa., Maltese Cross Press, [1975]. 320 p. illus. Bibliography: p. 311-315. DK511.L2P5 PU; DLC.

1861. PUZINAS, Jonas. Švekšnos kraštas Baltijos pajūrio archeologinių tyrinėjimų šviesoje. [The Švekšna region in the light of archaeological research on the Baltic coast. Chicago, Ill., Lietuvių istorijos

draugija, 1975. p.7-102. Offprint from Lietuvių Tautos Praeitis, kn.3 (11), v.3, DK511.S89P8 PU; see also serials consulted.

1862. ŠNEIDERIS, E[milis]. Liškiavos senovė. [The past of Liškiava] In Gimtasai Kraštas (Šiauliai), no. 3-4, 1934, p. 167-174; no.1(5), 1935, p. 199-203. Leidėjas:Šiaulių Krašt.Dr. ICWA.

1863. TOTORAITIS, Jonas. Būdingieji Sūduvos arba Užnemunės istorijos bruožai.[Brief sketch of Sūduva's history] In LKMASD, no.2,1973, p. 259-282. See serials consulted

1864. VANSEVIČIUS, Stasys. Teisinis rėžimas Vilniaus krašte 1920-39 metais. [Legal authority in the district of Vilnius, 1920-1939]. Vilnius, Mintis, 1973. 72 p. DK511.V4V3 PU.

1865. VENCLOVA, J. M. Suduvia, jotvingiai, dainuviai; pietų lietuviai [and] apie Suduvą bendrai. [Suduviai, jotvingiai (Yatwyags), dainuviai, the Southern Lithuanians] Chicago, Ill., Lietuvių literatūros draugijos leidinys, 1974. 71 p. Bibliography: p. 58-71. DK511.L23V47 DLC; CaAEU.

1866. ŽILĖNAS, Algimantas. Zarasų kraštas. [Zarasai region] Vilnius, Mintis, 1973. 127 p. illus. DK511.Z365Z5 PU; DLC; MH; OKentU.

X.12.c. TERRITORY OF MEMEL (Klaipėdos Kraštas)

X.12.c.1. GENERAL STUDIES

1867. BRUOŽIS, Ansas. Mažosios Lietuvos politikos veidrodis. [The political situation of Lithuania Minor. By] A.B. Klaipėdiškis, [pseud.]. Kaunas, K.A.M. Karo mokslo skyrius,1923. [Xerox copy, 1977]. 4, 182, 6 p. DD491.O45B7 1923a PU.

1868. HUBATSCH, Walter. Das Memelland und das Problem der Minderheiten. In Die deutschen Ostgebiete zur Zeit der Weimarer Republik. Graz, Austria, 1966. (Studien zum Deutschtum im Osten) DD732.2.S78 Hft.3 DLC; CtY; CU; ICU; MH; MeU; NN; NIC; NBuU; NcD.

1869. KIRCHE IM MEMELLAND. Hrsg. von Ew. Presseverband für Deutschland. Berlin, 1935. 35 p. 947.52K633 PU.

1870. MILKOVAITIS, K. Klaipėdos kraštas ir jo ekonominė bei kultūrinė reikšmė Lietuvai. [Klaipėdos Kraštas (The Territory of Memel) and its importance for Lithuania] In Karys (Brooklyn, N.Y.), no.1, 1972, p. 1-7. See serials consulted.

1871. VOLKSBUND FÜR DAS DEUTSCHTUM IM AUSLAND, Berlin. Memelland. 2. verb. Auflage. Berlin, 1932. 947.52.V886 PU.

1872. WALTER, Eginhard. Das Memelgebiet Bevölkerung und Wirtschaft eines Grenzlandes. Königsberg in Pr. Institut für osteuropäische Wirtschaft, 1939. 141 p. tables. *TAH--NN; DLC-Pr.; MH; NN.

1873. WEISE, Julius. Herzog Erich von Braunschweig der letzte Komtur des Deutsch Ordens zu Memel. Königsberg in Pr., Ostpreussische Druck und Verlagsanstalt, 1908. 947.52.Eri3.yW PU.

1874. ŽIUGŽDA, Po diplomatijos skraiste; Klaipėdos kraštas imperialistinių valstybių planuose, 1919-1924 metais. [Under the diplomatic cover; Klaipėdos Kraštas (The Memel Territory) in the plans of the imperialistic countries in 1919-1924] Vilnius, Mintis, 1973. 240 p. Summary in German and Russian. Bibliography: p. 222-235. DK511.L273Z58 PU; DLC; IU; CU; MH; MiU; MB; NN; NjP; WU.

X.12.c.2. AUTONOMY, STATUTE, LAWS, STATUTES, ETC., AND THEIR INTERPRETATION

1875. HAGUE. PERMANENT COURT OF INTERNATIONAL JUSTICE. Hagos tribunolo sprendimas Klaipėdos byloje. [Interpretation of The Statute of the Memel Territory. Perspausdinta iš Užsienių Reikalų Ministerijos leidinio. Kaunas], 1932. [Xerox copy, 1977]. 43 p. DK511.L273H3 1932a PU(xerox).

1876. --- ...Interprétation du Statut du territoire de Memel... Interpretation of the Statute of the Memel territory. Leyden, A.W. Sijthoff [1932] 70, 4-70 p. ([Publications] Sér. A-B, Arrêts, ordonnances et avis consultatifs, fasc. no.49) Judgement of August 11th, 1932, XXVth session. Paged in duplicate; French and English on opposite pages. JX1971.A6 ser.A-B no.49 DLC; CLU; CaSSU; CSt-H; FU; HU; ICN; IEN; MH; MnU; NN; NcD; NbU; PPiU; TxDaM; WaU.

1877. --- ...Interpretation of the statute of the Memel territory. Judgments of June 24th and August 11th, 1932. (Series A-B., fascicule nos.47 and 49) Leyden, A.W. Sijthoff [1932] 656 (i.e. 725) p. (Its [Publications] Ser C. Pleadings, oral statements and documents...no. 59). Added t.p. in French. Paged in part in duplicate; French and English on opposite pages. JX1971.5.A6 ser.C no.59 DLC; CaAEU; ICN; MnU; NbU; OrU.

1878. PETKEVIČIUS, Tadas. Klaipėdos krašto statuto vykdymo priežiūra. [The supervision of the implementation of the Statute of Klaipėdos Kraštas (The Memel Territory)]. Kaunas, Spindulio b-ės spaustuvė, 1932. 21 p. (Vytauto Didžiojo Universiteto Teisių fakulteto darbai, t.6, kn.14) At head of title: Le contrôle d'exécution du Statut du Territoire de Memel. MH; ICU; see also serials consulted.

X.12.d. LITHUANIA MINOR AND EAST PRUSSIA

X.12.d.1. GENERAL STUDIES

1879. ARNOLD, Udo. Studien zur preussischen Historiographie des XVI Jahrhunderts. Bonn, Ger.,[Kotaprintdruck Universität Bonn], 1967. 259 p. illus., facsims. Inaug.-Diss.-- Bonn University. DD86.A75 CaAEU; CSt; CtY; DLC; ICU; IU; ICN; InU;NjP; WU.

1880. BUDRYS, Stasys. Pergalės monumentas Kaliningrade. Vilnius,Vaga, 1965. xxvii,[31] p. illus. [The monument of victory in Kaliningrad (Königsberg in Pr.)]. At head of title: St. Budrys. Introduction and legends in Russian (10 p.) inserted. DD901.K8B75 DLC; MH.

1881. GAUSE, Fritz. Die Russen in Ostpreussen, 1914-1915. Königsberg in Pr.. Gräfe und Unzer, 1931. 425 p. plates., ports., fold.map, facsims. D552.P7G3 DLC; CtY; CSt-H; ICN; NN.

1882. HAAF, Rudolf ten. Deutschordensstaat und Deutschordensballeien; Untersuchungen über... vom XIII bis zum XVI Jahrhundert. Göttingen, Ger., Musterschmidt Verlag, 1951. 124 p. (Göttinger Bausteine zur Geschichtswissenschaft, Hft.5) CR4765.H25 DLC; CtY; InU; MH; MiU; NIC; OCU.

1883. HERING, Ernst. Der Deutsche

Ritterorden. Leipzig, Ger., W.Gold-
mann,[c1943]. 310 p. plates, map.
CR4765.H54 DLC; CaAEU; CoU; CLU;CSt;
GU; ICU; MH.   CU; CtY.

1884. HUMBOLT, Wilhelm, Freiherr
von. Schulpläne des Jahres 1809;
der Königsberger und der Litauische
Schulplan. Über die innere und äus-
sere Organization der höheren wissen-
schaftlichen Anstalten in Berlin 1810
"Studienbehelf für Übungen der Erzie-
hungswissenschaftlichen Seminars".
Hamburg, Ger., Universität, 1946. 16
p. (Studienbehelfe zu den Vorlesun-
gen, nr.3).   LA775.B5H8 DLC.

1885. KENKEL, Horst. Familienna-
men im nördlichen Ostpreussen; Herkunft, Wandel und Wechsel. In Altpreussische Geschlechterkunde; Fami-
lienarchiv (Hamburg), Jg.18, 1971,
Hft.4-6, p. 317-323. CS670.A45 DLC;
see also serials consulted.

1886. KIRRINNIS, Herbert. Tilsit,
die Grenzstadt im deutschen Osten.
Tilsit, Druck und Verlag Sturmverlag,
[1935]. 212 p. illus., maps., plans,
diagrs., tables.
NN.

1887. KÖHLER, Gustav. Der zweite
grosse Aufstand der Preussen gegen
den deutschen Orden 1260-1274. In
His Entwicklung des Kriegswissens...
in der Ritterzeit. Breslau, Ger.,
1886. Bd.2, p. 1-91.
CU; ICN; KU; MiU; MdBJ; MB; MeB; NIC;
OClW.

1888. KROLLMANN, Christian Anton
Christoph. Die Entstehung der Stadt
Königsberg. Königsberg in Pr.;Ber-
lin, Ost-Europa Verlag, 1939. 3 p.l.,
28 p. illus., facsims.
DD901.K8A2 Bd.1 DLC.

1889. LITHUANIA MINOR; a collection of studies on her history and
ethmography. Edited by Martin Bra-
kas. New York, [Lithuanian Research
Institute, [1976]. 304 p. English,
German and Lithuanian.
DK511.L2L57 PU; CaAEU; DLC.

1890. LUBENOW, Hedwig. Kaisertum
und Papstum im Widerstreit bei der
Gründung des Deutschordenstaates in
Preussen. In Geschichte in Wissen-
schaft und Unterricht (Verband der
Geschichtslehrer Deutschlands).
Stuttgart, Ger., Jg.23, 1972, p. 193-
211. Dl.G66 DLC; CaBVaU; CaOKQ;
CaOLU; CaOTU; CLSU; SLU; CoU; CSt;
CU; GEU; IaU; ICU; InNd; IU; KyU; MH;
MdBJ; MiDW; MiU; MnU; MoU; NN; NNC;
NIC; NjR; OrU; PPiU; PU; TxHR; WaU;
WU.

1891. MASCHKE, Erich. Preussen.
Das Werden eines deutschen Stammes-
namens. In Ostdeutsche Wissenschaft
(München, Ger.), Bd.2, 1956,p.116-156.
See serials consulted.

1892. PERLBACH, Max, comp. Quel-
len-Beiträge zur Geschichte der Stadt
Königsberg im Mittelalter. Wiesbaden,
Ger., M. Sändig,[1969]. vi, 214 p.
Reprint of the ed. published in Göt-
tingen by R. Reppmüller in 1878.
DD901.K8P4 1969 DLC; CLU; CU; CtY;
ICU; IaU; INS; MoSW; MU; MiU; NSyU;
NNC; OrU.

1893. POCIECHA, Władysław. Die
Entstehungsgeschichte der preussischen
Huldigung 1467-1525. (Geneza hołdu
pruskiego). Dienstliche Uebersetzung
der Publikationsstelle des Preuss.
Geheimen Staatsarchivs in Berlin-Dah-
lem, ausgeführt von Horst G. Ost.
Berlin, 1937. 143 leaves. (Germany.
Publikationstelle Berlin-Dahlem. Pol-
nische Reihe. Bücher und grössere
Aufsätze, nr.95).
DD491.O57P615 DLC.

1894. --- Geneza hołdu prusskie-
go 1467-1524. Gdynia, Kasa im. Mianowskiego, 1937. iv, 146 p. (Wydawnictwo Instytutu Bałtyckiego).
*QO p.v.143---NN; CtY.

1895. SCHOEPS, Hans Joachim.
Preussen; Geschichte eines Staates.
5. Aufl. Berlin, Propyläen Verlag,
[1967, c1966]. 422 p. maps. Infor-
mation on ancient Prussia: p. 13-[18]
DD347.S36 1967 CaAEU; CaBVaU; CLU;CU;
CSt; CtY; CtW; CAL; CU-S; DAU; DeU;
DLC; FTaSU; GU; InU; IU; IEN;KU; LU;
MB; MH; MnU; MdU; MoU; MoSW; MtU;MU;
NN; NNC; NIC; NBuU; NjP; NjR; NcD;NcU
NLD; NbPol; OkS; OO; OU; PPULC; S;ScU
TxHR; TxLT; TxU; TNJ; TU; ViU; WU.

1896. THIELEN, Peter Gerrit. Die
Verwaltung des Ordensstaates Preussen
vornehmlich im XV Jahrhundert. Köln,
Ger., Böhlau, 1965. viii, 196 p.
(Ostmitteleuropa in Vergangenheit und
Gegenwart, 11).   CR4765.T5 DLC;CLU;
CaAEU; CaBVaU; CaQMM; CSt; CtY; CtW;
CFS; CU; DeU; GEU; IaU; InU; IU;LNHT;
MB; MH; MnU; MiU; MeWC; MoSW; MiEM;
NN; NNC; NjP; NcD; OU; PPiU; PU; TU;
TxU; UU; WU.

1897. TOMAS-TAMAŠAUSKAS, Henrikas.
Lietuviškasis pamarys; Pakalnės (Lan-
kos) ir Labguvos apskritys su ju vie-
tovardžiais ir schematiniu žemėlapiu.
[Lithuanian sea shores; Pakalnė and
Labguva regions with their place names and the map. Chicago, Ill.], Chicagos Lietuvių literatūros draugijos
leidinys, 1975. 336 p. DD491.O435T6
PU; DLC.

1898. TSCHACKERT, Paul, ed. Urkundenbuch zur Reformationsgeschichte des Herzogthums Preussen. Leipzig, Ger., S. Hirzel, 1890. 3 v.
(Publikationen aus den K. Preussisch-
en Staatsarchiven, Bd. 43-45.)
943.1.DP956 Bd.43-45 PU; CBPai;
CtY-D; IEN; LU-NO; MH-AH; MiU; MiDW;
MU; NNC; NcU; OU; OrU; TNJ-R;

1898a. --- --- Neudruck der Ausg.
1890. Osnabrück, Ger., Zelle, 1965.
     v. (Publikationen aus den K.
preussischen Staatsarchiven, Bd.43).
BR358.P7T72 DLC.

1899. VOTA, J., pseud. Der Untergang des Ordenstaates Preussen und
die Entstehung der preussischen Kö-
nigswürde; aus den Quellen dargestellt
von Dr. J. Vota. Mainz, Ger., Kirch-
heim & Co., 1911. xxiv, 608 p.
"Gedrückte Literatur": p. [xxi]-xxiv.
DD491.O56V6 DLC; NN.

X.12.d.2. COLONIZATION OF LITHUANIAN
LANDS

1900. KAMENETSKY, Ihor. Secret
Nazi plans for Eastern Europe; a study of Lebensraum policies. New York,
N.Y., Bookman Associates, 1961. 263
p. On Lithuanians and Lithuania,
its colonization, cultural and educational policy, germanization, proper-
ty confiscation and Lithuanian underground: p. 34,62-63,90-91,94,112-113,
150 and 203. DK802.P6K22 DLC;CaAEU;
AU; CLU; CtY; CSt-H; DS; FTaSU; IaU;
IEN; ICU; MB; MH; MiU; NNC; NIC; NjR;
NcU; OClW; ScU; TNJ; WU.

1901. RIECKENBERG, H. Die Scha-
tullsiedlung in Preussen bis zum Jahre 1714. In Altpreussische Forschungen (Königsberg in Pr.), v.16, 1939.
See serials consulted.

1902. ROUSELLE, M. Das Siedlungs-
werk des Deutschen Ordens im Lande
Gerdauen. In Altpreussische Forschungen (Königsberg in Pr.), v.6, 1929.
See serials consulted.

1903. WILKE, E. Die Ursachen der
preussischen Bauern- und Bürgerun-
ruhen 1525. In Altpreussische Forschungen (Königsberg in Pr.), v.7,
1930. See serials consulted.

1904. WOJCIECHOWSKI, Zygmunt. The
territorial development of Prussia
in relation to the Polish homelands.
Toruń, Poland, The Baltic Institute,
1936. 78 p. illus., maps. (The
Baltic pocket library)
DD350.W6 DLC.

X.12.e. YATWYAGS (Sudovians)

1905. KAMIŃSKI, A. Materiały do
bibliografii archeologicznej Jaćwierzy od I do XIII w. In Materiały
Starożytne. Warszawa, 1956. tom 1,
p. 193-273. DK409.M3 DLC; see also
serials consulted.

X.13. PERSONAL NARRATIVES

1906. ANYSAS, Martynas. Atsiminimai iš Klaipėdos Krašto 1933-1939 m.
[Recollections of the Klaipėdos Kraštas (Memel Territory), 1933-1939] In
Lietuvių Tautos Praeitis (Chicago,
Ill.), kn.2, v.3, 1973, p.92-117.See
serials consulted.

1907. AUGUSTAITIS, Jonas. V.Var-
dys ir Šova apie Raštikio atsimini-
mus. [V.Vardys and Šova about the memoirs of Raštikis]. Chicago, Ill.,
Autoriaus leidinys, 1975. 36 p. Cover title. Reprinted from "Naujienos"
Oct.15-Nov.9, 1974.
DK511.L28R22A92 1975 CaAEU.

1908. BALČIŪNAS, Juozas. Dangus
debesyse; autoriaus išgyvenimai 1918-
1919 metais. [Heaven in the clouds;
the experiences by the author in 1918-
1919. London], Nida,[c1967]. 325 p.
CSf; CaAEU; MiD; OCl.

1909. BIELINIS, Kipras. Gana to
jungo. [It's enough of that yoke].
New Yorkas, Išleista Kipro Bielinio
ir Amerikos lietuvių socialdemokratų
sąjungos literatūros fondo lėšomis,
1971. 492 p. DK511.L28B46 PU; DLC;
OKentU.

1910. BIRONTAS, Adolfas. Vardan
teisybės; trys atsakymai mane puolu-
siems priešams. [For the sake of
truth...] [s.l., s.n., 195-]. 31 p.
DK511.L27B54 DLC.

1911. BUTKUS, Juozas. Žemės lips-
na. [By] Butkų Juzė, [pseud.]. Berlin, Ger., "Gega", [192-]. 128 p.
Hvc46U21B97 CtY; PPULC; PU.

1912. DAMBRAUSKAS, Aleksandras.
Mano užrašai. [My notes. By] Adomas
Jakštas, [pseud.]. In Mūsų Senovė
(Kaunas), 1921, p. 398-406; 1922, p.
796-807. ICCC; see also serials con-
sulted.

1913. DEMERECKIS, Jonas. Savanorio ir kontržvalgibininko atsiminimai.
Chicaga, Demereckis, 1976. 200 p.
illus. [Memoirs of a volunteer sol-
dier and counterintelligence agent].

DK511.L27D45 DLC.

1914. DOVYDĖNAS, Liudas. We will conquer the world. New York, N.Y., [Romuva], 1971. 219 p.
DK511.L27D6513 PU; InNd.

1915. FELIŃSKA, Ewa. Revelations of Siberia. By a banished lady. Ed. by Col. Lach Szyrma... London, Eng., Colburn and Co., 1852. 2 v.
DK755.F31 1852 DLC; CtY; CU; MH; MiU; NjP; PPL; WaU; CY(1853 ed.); ViU(1854 ed.).

1916. JANUŠKIS, Jonas. Atsitiktinio kareivio užrašai. [Notes of a warrior]. Bostonas, 1970. 127 p.
DK511.L28J36 PU.

1917. JUCIŪTĖ, Elena. Pėdos mirties zonoje. [Footprints in the death zone]. Brooklyn, N.Y., Š.S.T.Simo Kudirkos kuopos komitetas, 1974. 544 p. illus. DK511.L28J8 DLC.

1918. JUODVALKIS, Jonas. Mano dienos; atsiminimai. [My days; reminiscences]. Red. Kviklys. Chicago, Ill., A. Kairys, 1973. 112 p.
DK511.L28J85 PU.

1919. KARDELIS, Jonas. Atsiminimai. [Reminiscences]. In Sėja (Chicago, Ill.), 1970, no.1-2, p.46-49; no.3, p.41-43; no.4, p.41-45; 1971, no.1-2, p.54-59; no.4, p.43-44; 1972, no.1-2, p.65-66; 1973, no.1-2, p.68-69; no.3, p.58-60; no.4, p.56-59; 1974, no.1-2, p.71-74. See serials consulted.

1920. KOŁACZKOWSKI, Julian. Wspomnienia. Kraków, 1898-1901. 5 v.
Slav.5685.37 MH(v.2-5).

1921. KOSSAKOWSKI, Józef, Bp. Pamiętniki 1738-1788. Wydał Adam Darowski. Warszawa, Gebethner i Wolff, 1891. port.
MH.

1922. KRUPAVIČIUS, Mykolas. Atsiminimai. [Recollections. Chicago, Ill.], Lietuviškos knygos klubas, [1972]. 363 p. illus.
DK511.L28K75 PU; DLC; InU; MB; NjP; OCl.

1923. LELIS, Petras. Lietuvos keliu; 1910-1973 metai. [The Lithuanian road, 1910-1973] DK511.L28L44 PU; CaAEU.

1924. LUKAŠEVIČIUS, Henrikas. Vienas mažas gyvenimas; linksmi ir liūdni autobiografiniai apdūmojimai. Čikaga, Akademinės skautijos leidykla, 1975. 192 p. [..pleasant and sad autobiographical recollections]

DK511.L28L85 PU.

1925. MARTUS, Andrius M. Lietuvoje Europos karės metu. [During the First World War in Lithuania]. Worcester, Mass., M. Paltanavičius,1916. [Xerox copy, 1975]. 77 p. illus., ports. DK511.L26M35 1916a PU(xerox); MiD(orig.); RP(orig.)

1926. MATULIONIS, Jonas. Neramios dienos. [Unpredictable days; reminiscences]. Toronto, Ont., Litho-Art, 1975. 579 p. illus.
DK511.L27M34 PU; DLC; CaAEU.

1927. MEYSZTOWICZ, Walerian. Poszło z dymem; gawędy o czasach i ludziach. London, Eng., Polska Fundacja Kulturalna, 1973-1974. 2 v. illus., facsims. DK413.M49 DLC; CLU; InU; MH; MiU; NN; NNC; NBuU; WU; WaU.

1928. MICKOLEIT, Kurt. Aus der Jugendzeit. Berlin, 1911. 247 p. At head of title: A.K.T. Tielo [pseud] 834.M5830a IU; InU.

1929. MILAŠIUS, Bronius. Žvilgsnis atgal. [Recollections. Redagavo ir kalbą taisė Juozas Kralikauskas] Hamilton, Ont., 1964. 173 p.
DK511.L28M54 PU.

1930. NIEMOJEWSKI, Stanisław, 1560-1620. Pamiętniki ... 1606-1608. Lwów, Nakładem Zakładu im. Ossolinśkich, 1899. xxxii, 336 p. ports.
WD3289 CtY; MH; NN; NNC.

1931. NIESSEL, Henri Albert. Vokiečių išsikraustymas iš Baltijos kraštų; memuarai. [The evacuation of Baltic States by the German armies] Iš prancūzų kalbos vertė Jurgis Griška. Kaunas, Sakalas, 1938. 188 p. Translation of L'évacuation des pays baltiques par les Allemands.
947.5N2 CtTMF; OCl; PU.

1932. NIMTZ-WENDLANDT, Wanda, ed. Erzählgut der Kurischen Nehrung; ein Buch der Erinnerung. Marburg, Ger., Elwert, 1961. 198 p. (Schriften der Volkskunde-Archivs, Marburg, 9).
398C.M382 Bd.9 PU.

1933. OŽELIENĖ, Sofija. Dienų vitražai. [The changing days; reminiscences] Chicago, Ill., 1974. 380 p.
D802.L5094 DLC; PU.

1934. PAKALNIŠKIS, Aleksandras. Metai praeityj; prisiminimai. [The years behind; reminiscences]. Čikaga, Išleido Stasys Jankus, 1976. 295 p.
DK511.L27P26 DLC; PU.

1935. PAUŽUOLIS, Juozapas. Paskutinė rinktinė; atsiminimai iš II-jo

pasaulinio karo laikų. [The last unit
; reminiscences from the Second World
War] [s.l., s.n], 1972. 45 p.
DK511.L27P37 PU.

1936. PETRUITIS, Jonas. Mūsų žygiai. [Our campaigns]. Kaunas, 1935-
1937. 2 v. 2nd edition has the title: Laisvę ginant; mūsų žygiai (publ.
1952-53). 947.52P7 CtTMF.

1937. PLESKEVIČIUS, Petras. Mes
nešėmė laisvę; Lietuvos nepriklausomybės kovų savanorio kūrėjo atsiminimai. [We carried the freedom; recollections from the Lithuanian inde-
pendance wars. Hamilton, Ont.],Rūta,
[1961] 139 p. illus., fold.map.
DK511.L27P53 DLC; CtTMF; MiD; PPULC;
PU.

1938. POCZOBUT-ODLANICKI, Jan.Wła-
dysław. Pamiętnik 1640-1684. Warszawa, M. Ziemkiewicz, J.I., Kraszewski, 1877. 212 p. Tom 3.
*QR--NN.

1939. POŽĖLA, Vladas. Jaunystės
atsiminimai. [Recollections from the
past] Redagavo Pranas Čepėnas. [Lon-
don, Eng., Nida], 1971. 335, iv p.
port. Išleido Amerikos lietuvių socialdemokratų sąjunga, literatūros
fondas. DK511.L28P69 PU; DLC.

1940. PUŠINIS, Bronius. Raštai:
atsiminimai, straipsniai, laiškai.
[Works: reminiscences, essays and
letters. Redakcinė komisija: A.Gri-
gaitytė (sudarytoja), R. Šarmaitis,
M. Tamošiūnas (ats. redaktorius)].
Vilnius, Mintis, 1973. 294 p.
HX315.65.A6P8 1973 PU; DLC; MH; NN;
NNC; WU.

1941. RAILA, Bronys. Versmės ir
verpetai; akimirksnių kronikos.
[Springwells and whirlpools; events
of the day in the twinkling of an
eye]. Chicago, Ill., B. ir A. Bud-
ginų leidinys, [1970]. 351 p. port.
OC1.

1942. RAŠTIKIS, Stasys. Kovose
dėl Lietuvos; kario atsiminimai. [In
the battle for Lithuania; memoirs of
a soldier]. Los Angeles, Calif., Lietuvių Dienos, 1956-1972. 3 v. Vol.3
has title: Įvykiai ir žmonės; iš mano užrašų. DK511.L28R3 DLC; CaAEU;
CSt-H; CtTMF; ICLJF; InNd; PU.

1943. RYLIŠKIS, Andrius. Fragmentai iš praeities miglų; atsiminimai.
[Fragments from the nebuleous past;
reminiscences] Chicago, Ill., [s.n.]
1974- . v. DK511.L27R92 DLC.

1944. Sabaliauskienė Rožė. Prie
Merkio mano kaimas; atsiminimai.[My

village upon the river Merkys. Bendraautoris J. Aidulis]. Vilnius, Vaga, 1972. 281 p. DK511.L28S227 DLC.

1945. STIKLIUS, Pranas. Mano ru-
dens derlius. [Harvest of my autumn.
Literatūrinis bendraautoris Robertas
Keturakis] Vilnius, Vaga, 1971. 321
p. illus. DK511.L2S717 DLC; IU;MB;
MH; NN; OKentU; PU.

1946. STROLIA, Juozas. Lietuvos
Vyčio pėdsakais; 1940-1945 m. atsiminimai ir įspūdžiai. [Reminiscences
from 1940-1945]. Chicago, Ill., Chicagos lietuvių literatūros draugijos
leidinys, 1969. 176 p. port.
ML410.S935A3 DLC.

1947. TALKO-HRYNCEWICZ, Julian.
Z przeżytych dni 1850-1908. Warszawa, Skład glowny: Dom Książki Polskiej, 1930. port and plates.
GN21.T3A3 DLC;MH.

1948. TUMĖNAS, Wanda (Mingaila).
Mano atsiminimai. [My recollections]
Chicago, Ill., The Author, 1957].
174 p. illus., ports.
RA989.L5T8 DLC; ICLJF; PU.

1949. UNTULIS, Matas. Nuo perkūno iki bazilikos. [By] Laisvūnas,
[pseud.]. Kaunas, Laisvamanių eti-
nės kultūros draugijos leidinys,1938.
103 p. DK511.L28J32 PU.

1950. VALAITIS, Jonas. Praeities
apybraižos (1900-1950). [Sketches of
the past, 1900-1950. Chicago, Ill.],
K.Valaitis, [1974]. 288 p.
DK511.L28V33 PU.

1951. VASILIAUSKAS, Pranciškus.
Mano sielos atgarsiai. [Echoes of my
soul. By] Meškuitis, [pseud.] [s.l.,
s.n.[, 1943. 249 p. WU.

1952. --- Tėvynės ilgesyje. [s.l.,
s.n.], 1947. 212 p. WU.

1953. VITKUS, Juozas. 1863 metų
sukilimas lietuvoje; prisiminimai.
[The insurrection of 1863 in Lithuania; memoirs. Kaunas, Raidės spaus-
tuvė], 1933. [Xerox copy, 1977]. 23 p.
DK511.L25V57 1933a PU.

1954. VSEZARUBEZHNOE OB"EDINENIE
VILENTSEV. Na sluzhbe otechestva.
[Otv. red. V.I. Shailitskii]. San
Frantsisko, 1963. 527 p. illus.
U604.V5V8 DLC; KU; MH; NN; NNC; WaU.

1955. YLA, Stasys. A priest in
Stutthof; human experiences in the
world of the subhuman. Authorized
translation from the Lithuanian by
the Manyland Books and by Nola M.Zo-

barskas. Introd. by Charles Angoff.
New York, N.Y., Manyland Books, c1971.
xvi, 294 p. illus. D805.G3Y5513
DLC; IU; MB; MH; MU; NIC; NjP; NcD;
OKentU; OU; WU.

1956. ZAN, Tomasz. Z wygnania;
dziennik...z lat 1824-1832. Z autografu wydała Marja Dunajówna. Wilno, Nakł. Tow. Przyjaciół Nauk, 1929.
iii, 231 p. (Towarzystwo Przyjaciół
Nauk w Wilnie. Wydział I. Rozprawy
i materiały, tom 2, zeszyt 4.)
*QPA--NN.

1957. ZOKAS, Antanas. Nuo Duby-
sos iki La Platos; atsiminimai. [From
Dubysa until La Plata; reminiscences]
Vilnius, Vaga, 1972. 264 p., 13 lea-
ves of illus. F2659.L5Z64 DLC;CtY;
IU; MB; MH; NN; PU.

XI. PHILOSOPHY

1958. BALVOČIUS, Jonas. Šiapus
ir anapus grabo. Parašė J. Gerutis,
[pseud.].[On this and other side...]
Chicago, Ill., Spauda ir kaštais "Kataliko", 1903. 185 p. OCl.

1959. BIRALO, Al'bert Afanas'evich.
Filosofskaia i obshchestvennaia mysl'
v Belorussii i Litve v kontse XVII-
seredine XVIII vv. Minsk, Izd-vo
BGU, 1971. 179 p. B4757.B57 PU;CU;
CU-SB; CaOTU; CtY; CSt; CaAEU; CaQMM;
ICIU; ICU; IU; MH; MiDW; MiEM; MdBJ;
MB; MiU; MdU; MU; NN; NNC; NIC;NSyU;
NcU; NcD; OU; OrU; TxU; WaU.

1960. DAMBRAUSKAS, Aleksandras.
Augščiausias gėris. [The supreme
good] Kaunas, Šv. Kazimiero, 1937.
189 p. OCl.

1961. --- Kultūros viešpatija.
[The domain of culture]. Parašė A.
Jakštas, [pseud.] Kaunas, Šviesos
spaustuvė, 1919. 23 p. PU.

1962. --- Mokslas ir tikėjimas;
populiarių apologiškų straipsnių
rinkinys. [Science and religion...]
Įvadą parašė J.E. Vysk., P.Bučys.
[s.l.], "Žinijos", 1930. 400 p.
OCl.

1963. FILOSOFIJOS ISTORIJOS CHRES-
tomatija: Antika. [The history of
philosophy: Antiquity. Sudarytojas
Bronius Genzelis. Ats. redaktoriai:
J. Mažiulienė, A. Rybelis]. Vilnius,
Mintis, 1977. 508 p.
B108.F5 PU.

1964. GAIDAMAVIČIUS, Pranas. Mil-
žinas, didvyris, šventasis; žmogiško-

sios pilnaties vizija. [The Giant,
the heroe, the holy: a vision of the
complete man]. Brooklyn, N.Y., Tėvų
Pranciškonų leidinys, 1954. 246 p.
BD232.G26 DLC; OKentU.

1965. --- Didysis nerimas; žvilgsnis ieškojančion žmogaus širdin.
[The great perplexity of searching
man's soul]. Putnam, Conn., Immaculata, 1961. 297 p. illus. Preface
in English. Bibliography: p.285-294.
BX2350.2.G3 DLC; OKentU; PU.

1966. GIRNIUS, Juozas. Laisvė ir
būtis; Karl Jasperso egzistencinė me-
tafizika. [Freedom and existance;
Carl Jaspers' existential metaphysics]
Brooklyn, N.Y., Aidų leidinys, [1953]
151 p. B3279.J34G5 OKentU.

1967. GRAUSLYS, Alfonsas. Ieškau
tavo veido; rodyklės ieškojimo keliuose. [Guidelines for the searching
man] Chicago, Ill., Lietuviškos knygos klubas, 1971. 296 p. OCl.

1968. GRINIUS, Jonas. Grožis ir
menas; estetikos pagrindai. [Beauty
and art; the foundations of aesthe-
tics] Kaunas, V.D. Universiteto Teologijos-filosofijos fakulteto leidinys, 1938. 352 p.
BH39.G75 PU.

1969. GRUODIS, Stasys. Krikščio-
niškos dorovės mokslas. [Christian
morality]. 2. laida. Stuttgart,Ger.
[Lux], 1947. 175 p.
BX2350.G78 1947 OKentU.

1970. JUCEVIČIUS, Feliksas. Mintis dialektiniame žaisme; [filosofi-
jos sampratos raida.[Thoughts in dia-
lectic interplay; a development of
philosophical reasoning]. [Montreal,
Que.], 1977. 273 p. BD28.J8 PU.

1971. KUZMICKAS, Bronius. Šiuolai-
kinė katalikiškoji filosofija; kritinė apybraiža. [Contemporary catholic
philosophy; a critical outline]
Vilnius, Mintis, 1976. 207 p.
BX176.2.K85 PU.

1972. MACEINA, Antanas. Didysis
inkvizitorius. [Der Grossinquisitor]
Weilheim Teck, Ger., Atžalynas, 1946.
192 p. PG3325.B73M5 OKentU.

1973. --- --- 2. papildyta laida.
[Kirchheim Teck, Ger., Venta], 1950.
221 p. (Cor inquietum; studijos Die-
vo ir žmogaus santykiams nušviesti,1)
PG3325.B73M5 1950 DLC; CtY; MH;OKentU;
OCl.

1974. --- Das Geheimnis der Bosheit; Versuch einer Geschichtstheolo-
gie des Widersachers Christi als Deu-

tung der Erzählung vom Antichrist Solowjews. Freiburg, in Br., Herder, [1955]. viii 236 p. BT985.M3 DLC; CtY-D; CLSU; DCU; FMU; MiU.

1975. --- Der Grossinquisitor; geschichtsphilosophische Deutung der Legende Dostojewskijs. Mit einem Nachwort von Wladimir Szylkarski: Messianismus und Apokalyptik bei Dostojewskij und Solowjew. Heidelberg, Ger., F.H. Kerle, 1952. 340 p. PG3328.Z6M2 DLC; CLSU; CSt; CtY; CU; FMU; FTaSU; ICU; MoU; NN; NNC; NIC; NcD; PU.

1976. --- Jobo drama; žmogiškosios būties apmąstymas. [A drama of Job; a deliberation of the existence of Man. Schweinfurt, Ger., Venta, 1950. 240 p. (His Cor inquietum; studijos Dievo ir žmogaus santykiams nušviesti, 3) BS1415.M23 DLC;ICU; MB; MH; OKentU; OCl; PU.

1977. --- Kultūros filosofijos įvadas. [An introduction to the cultural philosophy]. Kaunas, V.D. Universiteto Teologijos-filosofijos fakulteto leidinys, 1936. 225 p. OCl.

1978. --- Niekšybės paslaptis; Antikristas istorijoje pagal V. Solovjovo pasakojimą. [Das Geheimnis der Bosheit;... Brooklyn, N.Y., Ateitininkų federacija], 1964. 294 p. BT985.M32 DLC; MiD; OClCS; PPULC.

1979. --- Socialinis teisingumas; kapitalizmo žlugimas ir naujos santvarkos socialiniai principai. [Social justice, the destruction of capitalism and the social principals of the new order. Kaunas], Sakalas, [1938]. OCl.

1980. PLEČKAITIS, Romanas. Feodalizmo laikotarpio filosofija Lietuvoje; filosofija Lietuvos mokyklose XVI-XVIII amžiais. [The philosophy in Lithuania during the time of feodalism; the philosophy in Lithuanian schools during the 16th-18th centuries] Vilnius, Mintis, 1975- . v. B4742.P55 PU.

1981. PRUNSKIS, Juozas. Mokslas ir religija. [Science and religion] Los Angeles, Calif., Lietuvių Dienos, [1964]. 141 p. ports. BT1220.P74 OKentU.

1982. ŠALKAUSKIS, Stasys. Filosofijos įvadas. [An introduction to philosophy] Kaunas, Šviesa, 1928. Atspausta iš filosofijos laikraščio "Logos". BD26.S35 OKentU.

1983. SERAPINAS, Rapolas, comp.

and tr. Ties grožio vertybėmis: Platonas, Nietze, Goethe, Geigeris,Wölflinas, Focillonas, Walzelis, Neumanas, Plotinas, Schilleris, Lessingas, Croce. [About value of beauty: Plato, Nietsche, Goethe...] Peržiūrėjo ir pagrindinę įvado dalį parašė Vosylius Sezemanas. Kaune, Sakalo leidykla, [1944]. 509 p. BH28.L5S4 PU.

1984. SKAISGIRIS, Rimantas. Šiuolaikinės buržuazinės filosofijos pagrindinės kryptys; kritinė apybraiža. [The basic trends of the contemporary bourgeois philosophy; a critical review] Vilnius, Mintis, 1971. 221 p. B804.S573 DLC; PU.

1985. STOROST, Wilhelm. Apsišvietimas. [Acculturation; the process of becoming adapted to new cultural patterns. By] Vidūnas, [pseud.]. Tilžê, Rûta, 1908. 891.92St78 PU

1986. --- Gimdimo slêpiniai. [The mystery of creation]. 3., taisîtas leidimas. Tilžêj, Rûta, 1921. 101 p. BP565.S82 1921 DLC.

1987. --- Sâmonê; sâmoningumas ir nesâmoningumas: žwilgsniai î gîvenimo esmê. [Consciousness; a look into the essence of existence. By] Vidûnas, [pseud.]. Tilžê, Rûta, 1936. 199 p. BF311.S69 DLC; PU.

1988. --- Slêpiningoji žmogaus didîbê. [Mysterious qualities of a human being]. 2. leidimas. Tilžê, Rûta, 1921. 61 p. BP565.S83 1921 DLC; PU.

1989. --- Tauresnio žmoniškumo užtekêjimas. [The rise of dignified benevolence. By] Vidûnas, [pseud.]. Detmold, Ger., 1948. 891.92St78K PU.

1990. --- Visumos sâranga. [The composition of the universe]. 2. leidimas. [By] Vidûnas, [pseud.] Tilžê, Rûta, 1921. 31 p. BP565.S835 1921 DLC; PU.

1991. --- Žmonijos kelias. [The way of mankind. By] Vidûnas, [pseud.] Tilžê, Rûta, 1908. 891.92St78 PU.

1992. --- --- Tilžê, Rûta, 1914. 891.92St78L PU.

1993. SUŠINSKAS, Alfonsas. Šviesos ir šešėliai. [The light and shadows. By] Alfa Sušinskas. Redagavo Titas Narbutas. [Brooklyn, N.Y., Alfos Sušinsko raštams centro komitetas, 1973. BJ1668.L5 PU.

1994. VYČINAS, Vincentas. Earth and Gods; an introduction to the philosophy of Martin Heidegger. The Ha-

gue, Nijhoff, 1961. xii, 328 p.
B3279.H49V9 DLC; AU; CaOKQ; CaQMU:
CBPaC; CLU; CFS; CtY; CtW; CtCA; CU;
CoU; CSaT; CCC; CLSU; FMU; FTaSU; FU;
GU; GEU; IW; IaU; IEG; ICMcC; InRenS
IU; ICU; IMunS; KyLoS; KyNaT; KyLxCB
Ky; LU; MB; MH; MBU-T; MiDW; MBtS;
MiU; MoSW; McU; MnU; MWelC; NN; NNC;
NIC; NRU; NcD; NcU; NjP; NjMD; NjPT;
O; OkU; OkS; OU; ODW; OOxM; OClCS;
OCA; ORU; PPiU; PU; RPB; ScU; TxDaM
TxU; TxHR; WU; WaU.

1995. --- --- The Hague, M. Nijhoff, 1969. xii, 328 p.
OWorP; ViU.

1996. --- Greatness and philosophy; an inquiry into Western Thought.
The Hague, M. Nijhoff, 1966 [1967].
xi, 297 p.   B72.V6 DLC; IaU; ICU;
NcU; OkEG; OrU; TxHR; WaU.

1997. --- Our cultural agony.
The Hague, M. Nijhoff, 1973. x,203 p.
CB428.V9 DLC.

1998. --- Search for Gods. The
Hague, M. Nijhoff, 1972.[1973].
x, 286 p.   BD450.V9 DLC.

1999. ZUMERIS, Bronius. Dabarties
sutemose; žvilgsnis į mūsų laikotarpio žaizdas ir skaudulius. [In the
twilights of today; a glance at our
sufferings and woonds of the past]
Chicago, Ill., Lietuviškos knygos
klubas, 1967. 187 p.
BV4509.L5Z82 PU; PPULC.

XII. RELIGION

XII.1. CATHOLIC CHURCH

XII.1.a. GENERAL STUDIES

2000. ANDZIULYTĖ-RUGINIENĖ, Marija.
Die Gründung des Bistums Samaiten.
Fribourg, Switzerland, 1923. 100 p.
Inaug.-Diss.--University of Fribourg.
Swz.FU.

2001. ARKIVYSKUPAS MEČISLOVAS REI-
NYS. [Archbishop M. Reinys. Chicago,
Ill.], Lietuvių krikščionių demokra-
tų sąjunga,[1977] 245 p.
BX4705.R43A7 PU.

2002. GORSKI, Tadeusz. Paskutinis
Vilniaus Vyskupas Jurgis Matulaitis-
Matulevičius, 1918-1925. The last
Bishop of Vilnius Jurgis Matulaitis-
Matulevičius, 1918-1925. In Lictuvių
Tautos Praeitis (Chicago, Ill.), kn.
1, v.4, p. 97-104. See serials consul-
ted.

2003. HALECKI, Oskar. From Flo-
rence to Brest, 1439-1596. New York,
N.Y., Fordham University Press, 1958.
444 p. On Lithuania: p. 19,23,44,55,
56,129,133,142,149,173,190,314,419.
BX830.1596.H3 1958 DLC; AU; CtY;DCU;
CaAEU; CaBVaU; CSt; DCU; GEU-T; ICU;
InRenS; InU; IU; KU; MH; MoSW; MiU;
MtU; NN; NNC; NB; NjR; NcD; NcU; NIC;
NhD; OCU; OO; PV; Plm; ScU; TxU;TxDaM
WaU.

2003a. --- 2d ed. Hamden, Conn.,
Archon Books, 1968. 456 p.
BX830. 1596.H3 1968 DLC; AAP; CaOTP;
CtY; CoU; CLU; CtY-D; GU; FU; FMU;IU;
InU; ICU; IaU; IaAS; ICMcC; InStme;
KAS; KW; KyU; MB; MH; MiEM; MnU; MoU;
MoSW; MU; NIC; NBuU; NjPT; NjR; NbU;
OkU; OU; OCIU; OrCS; OrU; RPB; UU;
ViU.

2004. IVINSKIS, Zenonas. Die Be-
deutung des Kampfes zwischen dem la-
teinischen und dem griechischen Ele-
ment im Grossfürstentum Litauen. In
International Congress of Historical
sciences, 11th, Stockholm, 1960. Rap-
ports. D3.A2 1960d DLC; CaBVaU;CLU;
CSt-H; CSt; CLSU; CtHC; CtW; DDO;DSI;
IaU; ICN; ICU; InNd; InU; IU; KyU;MH;
MiU; MNS; MdBJ; MiDW; MiEM; MtU; MnU;
MoSCS; NN; NNC; NIC; NBSU-M; NjP;NcD;
NcU; OU; OCH; OCU; OrU; PU; OrPR;PPiU
PPAmP; RPB; TxU; WaU.

2005. JATULIS, Paulius. Kardinolo
Jurgio Radvilo veikla lietuvių tarpe.
[The activity of Cardinal J. Radvila
among the Lithuanians] In LKMASD,
v.7, p. 235-267. See serials consulted.

2006. JURGINIS, Juozas. Pagonybės
ir krikščionybės santykiai Lietuvoje.
[The relations between paganism and
christianity in Lithuania] Vilnius,
Mintis, 1976. 126 p. BL945.J8 PU.

2007. --- Pasmerkimas; pasakojimas apie Kazimierą Liščinski. [Con-
demnation; story about K. Liščinskis]
BL2790.L9J81 PU.

2008. --- The reasons for the belated dissemination of Christianity
in the Baltics [by] J. Jurginis.
Moscow, Nauka Pub. House, Central
Dept. of oriental Literature, 1970.
11 p. At head of title: XIII International Congress of Historical Sciences, Moscow, August 16-23, 1970. Bibliography: p. 11-[12].
PPiU.

2009. KATOLITSIZM V SSSR I SOVRE-
mennost'. Materialy nauchnoĭ konferentsii, sostoĭavsheĭ v g. Shauliaĭ
17-18 dekabrĭa 1969 g. [Otv. red. I.
Anichas. Vil'nĭus, 1971. 245 p.

At head of title: Akademiĩa nauk Litovskoĭ SSR. Otdel filosofii, prava i sotsiologii pri Institute istorii. Shĩauliãiskiĭ pedagogicheskiĭ
institut im. K. Preikshasa. Bibliography: p. 231-[245].
BX1765.2.K36 PU; CtY; CU; DLC; InU.

2010. KOSMAN, Marceli. Drogi za-
niku pogaństwa u Bałtów. Wrocław,
Zakład Narodowy im. Ossolińskich,
1976. BL945.K6 PU.

2011. MARTIN, André. Lithuanie;
terre de foix, terre de croix. Paris, Éditions Albatros, [1976]. 197
p. illus. DK511.L2M198 DLC; PU.

2012. MATULAITIS, Kazimieras A.
Vakarų ir Rytų Bažnyčių Unija ir kan-
kinys Juozapatas Kuncevičius. Saint
Juozapatas Kuncevičius and the Union
of the Eastern and the Western Church.
In Lietuvių Tautos Praeitis (Chicago,
Ill.), kn.2, v.3, 1973, p. 37-52.
Summary in English. See serials con-
sulted.

2013. MATULEVIČIUS, Jurgis, Bp.
In service of the Church. The servant of God George Matulaitis-Matulewicz; biographical sketch and Spiritual diary. [by] Vincenzo Cusumano.
Chicago, Ill., [Lithuanian Catholic
Press, 1974]. 145 p. illus. "The
original edition of In the service
of the Church was published in Italian in 1963 by Ancora, Milan, Italy,
under the title: Innamorato della
Chiesa." InNd.

2014. PAKARKLIS, Povilas. Popiežiai ir lietuvių tauta. [Popes and
the Lithuanian nation]. Richmond
Hill, N.Y., Laisvė, 1950. 255 p.
Amerikos lietuvių darbininkų literatūros draugijos leidinys, no.57)
BX1559.L5P282 OKentU.

2015. PANUCEVIČ, Vacłaŭ. 375[i.
e. Trysta semdzesĩat pĩatyĩa] uhodki
Bierasciejskaj vunii, 1596-1971; referat čytany ŭ Biełaruskim nacyjanal-
na-relehijnym centru ŭ Chicago, 11
šniežnĩã 1971 h. Chicago, Ill.,1972.
140 p. port. Added title page: The
Brest Union, 1596-1971. White Russian in Latin alphabet. Bibliography: p. 129-136.
BX4711.622.P36 DLC.

2016. RAMM, Boris ĨAkovlevich.
Katolicheskaĩa ekspansiĩa v Pribal-
tike v pervoĭ chetverti XIV v. In
Papstvo i Rus' v X-XV vekakh. Lenin-
grad, 1959. p. 180-190.
BX1559.R3 DLC; CaAEU; CSt; CtY; CU;
DDO; InU; ICU; MH; MiU; MoU; NN; NNC;
NIC; NcD; OkU; OrU; TxU; TU; WaU.

2017. --- Papstvo i Litovsko-Rus-
skoe gosudarstvo pri Gedimine. In
Papstvo i Rus' v X-XV vekakh. Lenin-
grad, 1959. p. 190-208.
BX1558.R3 DLC; CaAEU; CSt; CtY; CU;
DDO; InU; ICU; MH; MiU; MoU; NN; NNC;
NIC; NcD; OkU; OrU; TxU; TU; WaU.

2018. --- Papstvo i Rus' v X-XV
vekakh. Leningrad, Izd-vo Akademii
nauk SSSR, Leningradskoe otd-nie,
1959. 282 p. At head of title: Akademiĩa nauk SSSR. Muzeĭ istorii re-
ligiĭ i ateizma. Bibliography: p.
[246]-264. BX1588.R3 DLC; CaAEU;
CSt; CtY; CU; DDO; InU; IU; ICŲ; MH;
MiU; MoU; NN; NNC; NIC; NcD; OkU;OrU;
TxU; TU; WaU.

2019. LA REPRESIONE CULTURALE IN
LITUANIA. Milano, Jaca Book, 1972.
190 p. A cura del Centro studi Russia cristiana. BX1559.L5R5 DLC.

2020. RIMAITIS, J. Religion in
Lithuania. [Translated by G. Kirvai-
tis. Edited by K. Smigelskis and V.
Grodzenskis. Vilnius, Gintaras,1971]
33 p. illus., maps.
BR937.L3R54 DLC; CLU; CtY-D; CSt;IU;
ICIU; InNd; MiEM; NNC; NIC; NjP; NcD;
OU; OKentU;

2021. STRÖM, Åke V. and BIEZAIS,
Haralds. Germanische und baltische
Religion. Stuttgart, Ger., Kahlham-
mer, 1975. 391 p. (Die Religion der
Menschheit, Bd.19:1)
BL860.S75 PU; DLC.

2022. VAIŠNORA, Juozas. Marijos
garbinimas Lietuvoje. [The The Virgin
Mary cultus in Lithuania] Rome,1958.
444 p. illus. (Lietuvių katalikų
Mokslų akademija, Rome. Leidinys,nr.5)
Bibliography: p. [409]-417.
BT645.V2 ICU; DCU; OCl.

2023. YLA, Stasys. Dievas sutemose; religiniai lūžiai lietuvių gyve-
nime. [God in the twilight; religious
rifts in the life of Lithuanians.
Totonto, Ont., Tėviškės Žiburiai,
1964] 391 p. BR1050.L5Y43 OKentU.

XII.1.b. HISTORY OF THE CATHOLIC
CHURCH IN LITHUANIA

2024. BRIZGYS, Vincentas. Katalikų
Bažnyčia Lietuvoje; pirmoje rusų okupacijoje 1940-1941 metais., vokiečių
okupacijoje 1941-1944 m.(trumpa apžvalga) [Catholic Church in Lithuania
during the Soviet and German occupa-
tions, 1940-1941 and 1941-1944].
Chicago, Ill., 1977. 192 p.
BX1559.L5B7 PU.

2025. JAKŠTAS, Juozas. Vyskupo
M. Valančiaus memorandumas general-
gubernatoriui grafui Eduardui Trofi-
movičiui Bararanovui dėl įvairių rusų valdžios trukdymo. Memorandum of
1866 from Bishop Valančius to the
Russian Governor General. In Lietuvių Tautos Praeitis (Chicago, Ill.),
Bk.4, v.3, 1976, p. 27-32. See serials consulted.

2026. JATULIS, Paulius. Vyskupas
Motiejus Valančius; nauja medžiaga
iš Vatikano archyvo: laiškai 1850-
1868. New materials from the Vatican archives written between 1850
and 1868, dealing with Bishop Valančius. In Lietuvių Tautos Praeitis
(Chicago, Ill.), Bk.4, v.3, 1976, p.
33-55. See serials consulted.

2027. VALANČIUS, Motiejus, Bp.
Maskoliams katalikus persekiojant.
[The Russian persecution of catholics
in Lithuania] Surinko ir paaiškino
doc. J.Tumas. [Includes: lectures a-
bout M. Valančius by prof. J. Tumas:
p. [106]-124] In Lietuvių Tautos
Praeitis (Chicago, Ill.), Bk.4, v.3,
1976, p. [56-181]. See serials consulted.

XII.1.c. RELIGIOUS ORDERS

2028. GIDŽIŪNAS, Viktoras. De vi-
ta et apostolatu fratrum minorum ob-
servantium in Lituania saec. XV et
XVI. Brooklyn, N.Y., 1976. 134 p.
Extractum ex Archivum Franciscanum
Historicum, 68 (1975)-69 (1976).
BX3645.L5G53 PU; CaAEU.

2029. --- Pranciškonų įnašas į
lietuvių tautos kultūrą. [The contribution of Franciscan Fathers to the
Lithuanian culture] In Metraštis
1950. Kennebunk Port, Me., [1949]
p. 111-118. See serials consulted.

2030. --- Trečiasis Šv. Pranciškaus ordinas. [The Third Order of
St. Francis] Brooklyn, N.Y., [Tre-
čiojo ordino Šv. Kazimiero provinci-
ja], 1971. 286 p.
BX3651.G52 PU; CaAEU.

2031. LIETUVOS PRANCIŠKONAI; istorijos bruožai ir paminklinio Šv. Antano vienuolyno pašventinimo iškilmių proga. Brief history of the Franciscan Fathers and dedication of the
monastery, Kennebunk Port, Maine.
[Boston, Mass., Darbininkas, 1947]
29 p. E184.L7L515 PU.

2032. MATULAITIS, Kazimieras A.
Kamalduliai Lietuvoje. [The religi-

ous Order Kamalduliai in Lithuania]
In Tautos Praeitis (Chicago, Ill.),
kn.3-4, v.2, 1967, p. 249-256. See
serials consulted.

2033. RABIKAUSKAS, Paulius. Pirmieji Jėzuitai Vilniuje ir pirmieji
lietuviai jėzuitai. [The first Jesu-
its in Vilnius and the first Lithuanian Jesuits] In KLMAM. v.5, p.301-
337. See serials consulted.

2034. VAIŠNORA, Juozas. Bandymas
įvesti Nekaltai Pradėtosios ordiną
Lietuvos-Lenkijos valstybėje. [An
attempt to establish the Imaculate
Conception Order in the Lithuanian-
Polish state] In Lietuvių Katalikų
mokslo akademija, Roma. Metraštis,
v.2, p. 265-289. See serials consulted.

2035. VYTELL, Virginia Marie.
Praise the Lord, all you nations; Lithuania's historical and cultural development from a background for the
life story of Rev. Alphonsus Maria,
CP, missionary and founder of the
Poor Sisters of Jesus Crucified and
of the Sorrowful Mother. Eimhurst
[i.e. Elmhurst] Pa., Sisters of Jesus
Crucified and the Sorrowful Mother,
c1976. 351 p. illus. Passionists
in Lithuania.
BX4705.A5554V95 DLC; PU.

XII.1.d. PARISHES AND THEIR HISTORY

2036. JANKUS, L. Šiluva; L. Jankaus, buv. ministranto Šiluvoj prisiminimai. [Reminiscences of L. Jankus
from Town of Šiluva] Brooklyn, N.Y.,
[Franciscan Fathers Press], 1968. 55
p. illus. OKentU.

2037. OCHMAŃSKI, Jerzy. Biskups-
two wileńskie w średniowieczu; ustroj
i uposażenie. Poznań, [Wydawn. Uniwersytetu im. A. Mickiewicza], 1972.
118 p. (Uniwersytet im. Adama Mickiewicz w Poznaniu. Wydział Filosoficzno-
Historyczny. Seria: Historia, nr.55)
BX1559.V503 PU.

2038. TOTORAITIS, Jonas. Vygrių ir
Seinų vyskupijų steigimas. [The founding of the dioceses of Vygriai and
Seinai] In Šaltinis (Marijampolė),
no.12, 1926. See serials consulted.

XII.2. PROTESTANT CHURCH; GENERAL
STUDIES AND HISTORY

2039. ARBUSOW, Leonid. Wolter von
Plettenberg und der Untergang des
Deutschen Ordens in Preussen. Eine

Studie aus der Reformationszeit Livlands. Leipzig, Ger., Verein für Reformationsgeschichte, 1919. 85 p. (Schriften des Vereins für Reformationsgeschichte, nr. 131) BR300.V65 nr.131 MU; CaAEU; CU; DLC ICMcC; MH-AH; MoSCS; NN; NNUT; NmU; NcD; OCU; OU; PPLUC; PPLT.

2040. FIJAŁEK, Jan. Ks. Jan Tortyłowicz-Batocki; pierwszy ewngelik na Żmudzi i apostoł luterski na Litwie prusskiej. In Reformacja w Polsce (Warszawa), v.1. See serials consulted.

2041. GUDAITIS, Kristupas. Lietuviai evangelikai. [Lithuanian protestants. Rodney, Ont.], Rūta, [1956] 434 p. illus., ports. BX4854.L5G8 DLC.

2042. --- Lietuvos liuteronai ir reformatai laikų bėgyje. [The Lutherans and the members of the reformed Church in Lithuania through the Ages] In Mūsų Sparnai (Chicago, Ill.), no. 8-9, 1955. See serials consulted.

2043. JØRGENSEN, Kai Eduard Jordt. Ökumenische Bestrebungen unter den polnischen Protestanten bis zum Jahre 1645. København, I kommission hos Nyt Nordisk Forlag, 1942. 410 p. Thesis--University of Copenhagen. Bibliography: p. [404]-407. BX4854.P7J6 DLC; CU; IaU; IU; ICU; MH; MH-AH; NN; NNUT; NIC; NjP; OU; PPLT; ViHarEM.

2044. KAHLE, Wilhelm. Aufsätze zur Entwicklung der ewangelischen Gemeinden in Russland. Leiden, E.J. Brill, 1962. xvi, 267 p. map. (Oekumenische Studien, 4). Literaturverzeichnis: p. [250]-258. CaBVaU; DCU; GEU-T; ICU; MH-AH; MU; NN; NIC; NNUT; NBuC; NjPT; NcD. CSt; CLU; CtY; CtHC; CU; D; DEU; DLC IU; IEG; InNd; ICU; KU; MiDW; MiEM; MiU; MoU; NNC; NjMD; NjP; NHU;OrU;OU R; TNJ; TxU; TxHR; WaU.

2045. KOSMAN, Marceli. Reformacja i kontrreformacja w Wielkim Księstwie Litewskim w świetle propagandy wyznaniowej. Wrocław, Zakład Narodowy im. Ossolińskich, 1973. 273 p. At head of title: Polska akademia Nauk. Instytut istorii. Summary in German. DK511.L24K67 DLC; CSt; CU; ICU; InU; IU; MH; MiEM; MiU; MU; PU; PPiU; ViU.

2046. KRASIŃSKI, Walerjan Skorobohaty. Historical sketch of the rise, progress, and decline of the reformation in Poland and of the influence which the Scriptural doctrines have exercised on that country in litera-ry, moral, and political respects,by Count Valerian Krasinski... London, Eng., Printed for the author and sold by Messrs. Murray [etc.] 1838-1840. 2 v. Includes some information on Reformation in Lithuania. BR420.P7K8 DLC; CtY; CU; CaAEU;ICU; MiU; NN; MdBJ; NjNbs PP; PPM; WE.

2047. LUBIENIECKI, Stanisław. Stanislai Lubieniecii Historia reformationis Polonicae. Prefacione instruxit Henricus Barycz. Warszawa, PWN, 1971. xxxvi, 332 p. (Biblioteka pisarzy reformacyjnych, nr.9) Reprint of the 1685 ed. BR420.P7L8 1971 DLC.

2048. ŠAPOKA, Adolfas. Jeronimas Pragiškis ir jo kelionė Lietuvon. [Hieronymus Pragensis and his voyage to Lithuania] In Praeitis (Kaunas), v.2, 1933, p. 252-290. DK511.L2P75 DLC; CaAEU; ICU(microfilm); KU; PU.

2049. STUDNICKI, Wacław Gizbert. Zarys historyczny Wileńskiego kośc. ew.-ref. i jego biblioteki. Z dodaniem przedruku H. Merczynga ze "Zwiastuna ewangelickiego" o czterokrotnem zburzeniu zboru wileńskiego. W Wilnie, Nakł. Tow. Miłośników Historji Reformacji Polskiej, 1932. 31 p. BX9480.L5S7 PU.

2049a. SZLUPAS, John. Lithuania and its Ancient Calvinistic Churches. In Princeton Theological Review (Princeton, N.J.), v.5, 1907, p. 242-280. Brl.P6 DLC; CSt; CtY; DeWI; ICU:ICN ICP; ICT; GEU; MoSC; MH-AH;MdBJ;MiD; NN; NNC; NNG; NIC; NcD; NjP; NjR;OC; OCl; OO; OU; OWC; PPi; PPT; PPC;RPB; TNV; TxSS; VRT; WHi.

XII.3. OTHER CHURCHES

2050. BUČYS, Petras, Bp. Rusai stačiatikiai Lietuvoje. Vysk. Petras Bučys, M.I.C. [Russian orthodox and old rites Church in Lithuania] In Athenaeum (Kaunas), t.7, sąs.1, p.65-136. Mr. Kviklys (Chicago) has it; see also serials consulted.

2051. --- --- In Lietuvių Katalikų mokslo akademija, Rome. Suvažiavimo darbai, v.2, p. 125-142. See serials consulted.

2052. KRAKHKOVSKIĬ, IUlian Fomich. Pravoslavnyia sviatyni goroda Vilna v XIV-XVIII vv. In Arkheologicheskiĭ s"ezd, 9th, Vilna, 1893. Trudy, t.2, 1897. DK30.A75 1893 v.2 DLC; CU;MH; NN; NNC; NjP; OrU.

2053. ŠIDLAUSKAS, Domas. Visuo-
mybė; naujos tyros tikybos mokslas,
dorovė, apeigos ir organizacija.[Com-
mon religion...By] Visuomio, [pseud.]
Kaunas, 1926. 219 p. illus., port.
947.52Si13 PU.

XIII. CULTURE

XIII.1. GENERAL STUDIES

2054. CONFERENCE ON BALTIC STUDIES.
1st, University of Maryland, 1968.
Summary of proceedings. Edited by
Ivar Ivask. Tacoma, Wash., 1969.
x, 128 p. DK511.B25C6 1968a PU;CU;
CaAEU; CaBVaU; CaOTP; CLU; CtY; DLC;
GU; ICarbS; InU; MH; MoU; MeB; NNC;
NIC; NjR; NbU; OU; OKentU; OkU; OrPS;
OrU; WU.

2055. CONFERENCE ON BALTIC STUDIES.
2d, San Jose State College, 1970.
Summary of proceedings. Edited by
Rimvydas Šilbajoris, Arvids Ziedonis,
Jr. [and] Edgar Anderson. Norman,
Okla., 1971.[c1972] 232 p. illus.
(Publications of the Association for
the Advancement of Baltic Studies,2)
DK511.B25C6 1970 DLC; CaAEU; CaOTP;
InU; InNd; ICarbS; NjP; PSt; WU.

2056. CONFERENCE ON BALTIC STUDIES.
4th, University of Illinois at Chicago Circle, 1974. Summaries of papers.
Brooklyn, N.Y., Association for the
Advancement of Baltic Studies, 1974.
80 p. (Publication of the Association for the Advancement of Baltic
Studies, 4) DK511.B25C74 1974 CaAEU.

2057. GRINIUS, Jonas. Literature
and the arts in captive Lithuania. In
Vardys, V.S., ed. Lithuania under
the Soviets. New York, 1965. p.197-
213. DK511.L27V35 DLC; AzU; CaAEU;
CaOTU; CaSSU; CtY; CSt; CSt-H; CU;IU;
ICU; IaU; IEN; InU; KU; MH; MnU; MoU;
NN; NNC; NIC; NBuU; NjP; NjR; NcD;
NhU; OCl; OClW; OrU; PPiU; PU; RPB;
TxU; ViU; WU; WaU.

2058. LIAUDIES TALENTAI. Narodnye
talenty. [Sudarė O. Kreivytė. Atsa-
kingas redaktorius S. Sverdiolas.Dai-
lininkė L. Pučkoriūtė. Kaunas, 1969]
47 p., 234 plates. On leaf facing
t.p.: Lietuvos TSR Kultūros ministerija. Liaudies Meno Rūmai. Lithuanian and Russian. English, German
and French summaries.
MH.

2059. LIETUVOS TSR KULTŪROS DAR-
BUOTOJŲ SUVAŽIAVIMAS. 1st, Vilna,1969.
Pirmasis Lietuvos TSR Kultūros dar-

buotojų suvažiavimas. [Conference of
Lithuanian cultural activities perso-
nnel. Sudarė Eduardas Maurukas. Redagavo Petras Dabulevičius] Vilnius,
Mintis, 1971. 248 p. DK511.L27L492
1969 PU; DLC; MH; WU.

2060. [LITHUANIAN STUDIES; essays
by Alfred Senn, Antanas Klimas, Vincas Krėvė, and Antanas Vaičiulaitis.
Eleven offprints and three pamphlets]
1 v. Contents.--1. Senn, Alfred. Ostpreussens Vorgeschichte sprachlich be-
leuchtet. Reprinted from The Germa-
nic Review, v.15, no.1, 1940. 19 p.
--2. Senn, Alfred. Notes on religious folklore in Lithuania. From Slavic Studies published by Cornell University Press, Ithaca, N.Y. p.[162]-
179.--3. Senn, Alfred. On the sources of a Lithuanian tale. A reprint
published as a chapter of Corona,1941.
p. [8]-22.--4. Senn, Alfred. On the
degree of kinship between Slavic and
Baltic. An offprint from The Slavic
and East European Review, v.20, 1941,
p. 251-265.--5. Senn, Alfred. The
Lithuanian language; a characteriza-
tion. Chicago, 1942. 49 p.--6. Vaičiulaitis, Antanas. Outline history
of Lithuanian literature. Chicago,
Ill., 1942. 54 p.--7. Senn, Alfred.
The historical development of the Lithuanian vocabulary. Reprinted from
the Quarterly Bulletin of the Polish
Institute of Arts and Science in Ame-
rica, 1943. 24 p.--8. Senn, Alfred.
The Standard Lithuanian in the making.
An Offprint from The Slavonic and East
European Review, v. 22, 1944. p.102-
116.--9. Krėvė, Vincas. Gilshe (trans-
lated under supervision of Alfred
Senn) An offprint from The American
Slavic and East European Review, v.6,
nos. 16-17, 1947, p. [102]-115.--1o.
Senn, Alfred. The relationships of
Baltic and Slavic. Reprinted from
Ancient Indo-European dialects; Pro-
ceedings of the Conference on Indo-
European linguistics... 1963. University of California Press, 1966. p.
[139]-151 p.--11. Senn, Alfred. Nachwort zum Wörterbuch der litauischen
Schriftsprache. Sonderdruck aus Senn-
Salys. Wörterbuch der litauischen
Schriftsprache, Bd.5, p. 561-565. Heidelberg, 1968.--12. Senn, Alfred.
Paronomasie im Litauischen. Sonderdruck aus Orbis Scriptus; Festschrift
für Dmitrij Tschiževskij zum 7o Ge-
burtstag. München, 1966. p.[717]-721.
--13. Klimas, Antanas. Baltic, Ger-
manic and Slavic. Offprint from Donum Balticum. Stockholm, 1970. p.
[263]-269. DK511.L2L58 PU.

2061. MYKOLAS LIETUVIS, 16th cent.
Apie totorių lietuvių ir maskvėnų pa-
pročius; dešimt įvairaus istorinio tu-

rinio fragmentų. [About the customs of Lithuanians, Russians and Tartars] [Vertė Ig. Jonynas] Vilnius, Vaga, 1966. 135 p. facsims. (Lituanistinė biblioteka) Includes original t.p.: De moribus tartarorum, lituanorum et moschorum. Basileae, 1615. Lithuanian and Latin.
DK511.L22M9 1966 DLC; CaAEU; CSt; ICU; PU.

2062. PRAETORIUS, Matthäus. Deliciae Prussicae oder Preussische Schaubühne. Hrsg. von William Pierson. Berlin, Duncker, 1871. 152 p. xv, OCl; OClW.

2063. ŽVILGSNIS Į 1969 METUS. Naujosios išeivijos dvidešimtmetis ir švietimo, kultūros ir meno apžvalga. [...the 20th anniversary of the last Lithuanian imigration and a review of their educational and cultural activities] In Aidai (Brooklyn, N.Y.), no.1, 1970, p. 1-16.See serials consulted.

XIII.2. PRIMITIVE RELIGION AND MYTHOLOGY

2064. BATYR, A. Skazaniia o litovskom gromoverzhtsie Perkunie. In Moscow. Universitet. Izvestiia, no,9, 1871, p. 443-462.
CLU; CU; KU; ViU.

2065. GIMBUTAS, Marija (Alseikaitė). Senoji lietuvių religija. [The ancient Lithuanian religion] In Aidai (Kennebunk Port, Me.), no.1(57), 1953, p. 4-12. Mr. K. Kairys (Chicao) has it; see also serials consulted.

2066. --- The gods and goddesses of Old Europe: 7000 to 3500 BC myths legends and cult images. Berkeley, Calif., University of California Press, 1974. 303 p. illus., maps. Bibliography: p. 257-268.
GN803.G55 1974b DLC; CaAEU; CaBVaU; CLSU; CU; CBGTU; CoU; CSt; AAP; AzU; DAU; F; FU; FMU; GAT; IaU; IaAS; IU; InU; ICU; KyU; MB; MoWgT; MoSW; MoU; MnU; N; NNC; NIC; NBuC; NBuU; NSyU; NRU; NjPT; NjR; NcD; NcU; NcGU; NcRS NjP; NbU; NvU; OkU; OKentU; OCU; OrU OOxM; OrPS; PSt; TNJ; TU; UU; VtU; ViBlbV; WaU.

2067. --- Perkūnas; the Thunder God of the Balts and the Slavs. In The Journal of Indo-European Studies (Hattiesburg, Miss.), no.4, v.1, 1973 p. 466-477. See serials consulted.

2068. GRIENBERGER, Theodor R. von.

Die Baltica des Libellus Lasicki. Untersuchungen zur litauischen Mythologie. In Archiv für Slavische Philologie (Berlin), v.18, 1896, p.1-86. PG1.A67 CaAEU(microfiche); see also serials consulted.

2069. MACCULLOCH, John Arnott. Celtic [mythology] by John Arnott Macculloch... Slavic [mythology] by Jan Máchal.. with a chapter on Baltic mythology by the editor L.H. Gray. Boston, Mass., Marshall Jones Co., 1918. x, 398 p., [40] plates. (The mythology of all races, v.3). Bibliography: p. [363]-398.
BL25.M99 v.3 NIC; DLC; NN; CU; FTaSU KU-M; IdU-SB; IdB; MB; MH-AH; MiU;NN; NcC; NcD; OOxM; OCl; OCU; ODW; OrSaW; OrPR; OrPR; OrP; ViU; WaTC.

2070. MELETIUS, Joannes. Dereligione et sacrificiis veterum Borussorum, epistola... ad Georgium Sabinum. In Chytraeus, David, 1531-1600. Davidis Chrytraei oratio de statu ecclesiarum... in Graecia, Asia, Boëmia, etc., epistolae Constantinopolitanae et aliae... quibus... Francofurti, A. Wecheli, 1583.
MH; MdBP.

2071. MEULEN, Reinder van der. De Godsdienst der Heidense Balten en Slaven. Bearn, Hollandia-drukkerij, 1913. (Groote godsdiensten, Ser.2, no.10) OCl.

2072. STELLA, Erasmus. De Borussiae antiquitatibus libri duo. Hrsg. von Theodor Hirsch. Basileae, I.Frobenius, 1518. 38 p. A German chronicler who described the religion and history of Ancient Prussians.
DD377.S8 ICU; ICN; MB; MH.

2073. STRÖM, Åke V. and BIEZAIS, Haralds. Germanische und Baltische Religion. Stuttgart, Ger., Kahlhammer, 1975. 391 p.
BL860.S75 PU; DLC.

XIII.3. ANCIENT FOLK CULTURE

XIII.3.a. GENERAL AND MISCELLANEOUS STUDIES

2074. BAGDANAVIČIUS, Vytautas Jonas. Cultural wellsprings of folktales. Translated from the Lithuanian by Jeronimas Zemkalnis. New York, N.Y., Manyland Books, [1970] viii, 196 p. Bibliography: p. 194-196. GR20.B313 DLC; CaAEU; AzU; CU; CLSU; CLU; ICN; InNd; InU; IU; KU;MB; MU; NjP; NcD; OCl; OrU; RPB; ViBlhV.

2075. BALYS, Jonas. Tautosakos rinkėjo vadovas. Kaunas, Lietuvių tautosakos archyvo leidinys, 1936. 79 p. [Handbook for the collector of folklore] Bound with Dovydaitis, J. Tautosakos rinkėjo darbas. Kaunas, 1929. GR203.L5B33 PU; MH.

2076. --- --- 2. laida. Kaunas, Lituanistikos instituto Lietuvių tautosakos archyvo leidinys, 1940. [Xerox copy, 1976]. GR203.L5B33 1940a PU.

2076a. BARTSCH, Christian. Über das litauische Märchen. In Litauische Literarische Gesellschaft, Tilzit. Mitteilungen, v.1, 1883, p. 395-396. PG8503.L7 DLC; CtY; ICU; MH; NN; NjP; OClW; MiU.

2077. BRADŪNAS, Elena. "If you kill a snake, the sun will cry", Folktale type 425-M; a study in Oicotype and Folk belief. In Lituanus (Chicago, Ill.), no.1, v.21,1975, p. 5-44. See serials consulted.

2078. GERULIS, Petras. Rutelė mūsų dainose. [Rue in Lithuanian folk songs]. Kaunas, 1932. 28 p. 891.92H G329 PU(xerox)

2079. GIMBUTAS, Marija (Alseikaitė). Liaudies meno šaknys [The roots of the folk art]. In Aidai (München, Ger.), no.14, 1948, p. 210-215. Mr. L. Kairys (Chicago) has it as no. 2992; see also serials consulted.

2080. HARMJANZ, Heinrich. Die deutsche Feuersegen und deren Varianten in Nord- und Osteuropa. Helsinki, Suomalainen tiedeakatemia, 1932. 192 p. facsims. Inaug.-Diss. --University of Königsberg in Pr. GR1.F55 no.103 DLC; MiU; OCl; OU;PU.

2081. KARPIUS, Kazys S. Kas slepiasi už žmonių pasakų. Gamtos veiksmė ir žmonių pažiūros į tai... by K. Karpavičius. Cleveland, Ohio, Spauda ir lėšos Dirvos, 1918. 148 p. front(port.), illus., map. [What is behind the narrative folklore; the nature and the opinion of the people] *QY--NN.

2082. KOKARE, E. Paralleli v latyshskikh, litovskikh i prusskikh poslovitsakh i pogovorkakh. In Fol'klor Baltskikh Narodov, 1968, p.227-278. map. GR203.L3F6 CaAEU; CaOTU DLC; ICU; NjP; PPiU; PU; WaU.

2083. KRĖVĖ-MICKEVIČIUS, Vincas. Aitvaras liaudies padavimuose. [Goblin in the folk legend... Vinjetę piešė K. Šimonis]. Kaunas, Spindulio b-vė, 1933. 156 p. illus.

(Kaunas. Universitetas. Humanitarinių mokslų fakulteto leidinys). At head of title: V. Krėvė. GR203.L5M61 ICU; CU; MH; NN;

2084. KRIVICKIENĖ, Gražina. Žvilgsnis į gyvųjų ir mirusiųjų santykius lietuvių tautosakoje. Relationship between the living and the dead in Lithuanian folklore. In Institute of Lithuanian studies. Lituanistikos instituto 1973 metų suvažiavimo darbai. Chicago, Ill., 1975. p.247-262. Summary in English. DK511.L2I63 1975 CaAEU; PU.

2085. LIETUVIŲ TAUTOSAKOS STILIUS IR ŽANRAI. [The style of the Lithuanian folk literature. Redakcinė kolegija: Ambr. Jonynas (ats. redaktorius) ir kiti] Vilnius, Vaga, 1971. 506 p. (Literatūra ir Kalba, 11). At head of title: Lietuvos TSR Mokslų akademija. Lietuvių kalbos ir literatūros institutas. Summaries in Russian, German, English and French. PG8709.L49 DLC; ICIU; WU.

2086. LUDOWOŚĆ DAWNIEJ I DZIŚ; studia folklorystyczne pod. red. Ryszarda Górskiego, Juliana Krzyżanowskiego. Wrocław, Zakład Narodowy im. Ossolińskich, 1973. 291 p. illus. At head of title: Polska Akademia Nauk. Instytut Badań Literackich. PG513.L8 DLC; ViU; WaU.

2087. MEULEN, Reinder van der. Gamtos palyginimai lietuvių dainose ir raudose. [The comparison of nature in Lithuanian folksongs and the songs of lamentation]. Vilnius, Žaibo spaustuvė, 1919. 106. WU.

2088. SHEIN, Pavel Vasil'evich, comp. Materialy dlia izucheniia byta i iazyka russkogo naseleniia Sievero-Zapadnogo Kraia. S.-Peterburg, Tip. Imp. Akademii nauk, 1887-1903. 2 v. in 3. Running title: Bielorusskii sbornik. PG2834.8.S543 CaAEU(t.2, pt.1); DLC; NN.

2089. VOL'TER, Ėduard Aleksandrovich. Romantische-sagenhafte Motive des litauischen Volksliedes. Von E. Wolter. In Litauische Literarische Gesellschaft, Tilsit. Mitteilungen, v.4, 1894, p. 64-69. See serials consulted.

XIII.3.b. FOLKLORE

XIII.3.b.1. BIBLIOGRAPHIES

2090. KERBELYTĖ, Bronislava. Lietuvių liaudies padavimų katalogas. Katalog litovskikh narodnykh predanii. The catalogue of Lithuanian local folk-legends. Vilnius, , 1973. 129 p. At head of title: Lietuvos TSR Mokslų akademija, Lietuvių kalbos ir literatūros institutas. GR203.L5K48 PU; DLC.

2091. LIETUVOS TSR MOKSLŲ AKADEMIJA. Llietuvių liaudies dainų katalogas; darbo dainos, kalendorinių apeigų dainos. [A catalogue of Lithuanian folksongs; work songs and of calendar rites. Edited by] Vanda Misevičienė. Vilnius, Vaga, 1972. 337 p. WU.

XIII.3.b.2. GENERAL COLLECTIONS

2092. SCHLEICHER, August, ed. & tr. Litauische Märchen, Sprichworte, Rätsel und Lieder. Gesammelt und übers. von August Schleicher. [Nachdruck der Ausgabe Weimar 1857] Hildesheim, Ger., G. Olms, 1975. ix, 244 p. music. Reprint of the 1857 ed. published by H. Böhlau, Weimar. GR203.L5S37 1975 PU; DLC(title entry).

XIII.3.b.3. NARRATIVE FOLKLORE

2093. BALYS, Jonas, ed. Lietuvių liaudies sakmės. I. [Lithuanian folk legends] Kaunas [Lietuvių tautosakos archyvas] 1940. [Xerox copy, 1976] 2 v. (xxvi, 448 p.). Fabula obscena: p. 424-448. GR203.L5B32 1940a PU.

2094. --- Lietuvių sąmojus; liaudies anekdotai. [Lithuanian witticism; folk anecdotes, funny stories, and jokes]. Kaunas, Sakalas, 1937. [Xerox copy, 1976] 255 p. GR203.L5B325 1937a PU(xerox).

2095. BASANAVIČIUS, Jonas. Lietuviškos pasakos yvairios. [Various Lithuanian folktales] Kaunas, Švyturys, 1928. 2 v. WU.

2095a. BASSANAVITIUS, J. Oškabalun myslei. [Riddles of Oškabaliai] In Litauische Literarische Gesellschaft, Tilsit. Mitteilungen, v.2, 1928, 1887, p. 189-198 (19-28). See serials consulted.

2096. CICĖNAS, Jeronimas. Daugeliškių burtai. [Magic of Daugeliškiai] Vilnius, 1934. 49.92C483 PU

2097. DAUKANTAS, Simanas. S.Daukanto rinkimo patarlės. [A collection of 300 proverbs which were originally published in his "Abeciela lijtuwiu-kalnienu ir žiamajtiu kalbos.." Petropile, 1842 . p. 47-56 and reprinted in] Tauta ir Žodis (Kaunas), kn.1, 1923, p. 322-327. PG8501.T3 DLC; CaAEU; CU; ICU; ICCC; MH; NN; NNC; PU; WU.

2098. GIEDRAITIS, Antanas. Tautos pasakos. [Folktales]. Iliustravo K. Šimonis. vol.1, fasc.1. Jurbarkas, [s.n.], 1928. 76 p. WU.

2099. --- --- 2.leidinys. Kaunas, Spaudos Fondas, 1930. 176 p. WU.

2100. GRIGAS, Kazys. Lietuvių patarlės; lyginamasis tyrinėjimas. [Lithuanian proverbs; comparative study] Vilnius, Vaga, 1976. 321 p. At head of title: Lietuvos TSR Mokslų akademija, Lietuvių kalbos ir literatūros institutas. PN6505.L5G72 PU.

2101. KRĖVĖ-MICKEVIČIUS, Vincas. Dainavos šalies senų žmonių padavimai. [Legends of ancient people in the distric of Dainava]. Vilnius, M.Kuktos spaustuvė, 1912. 158 p. MB; OCl.

2102. --- --- Iliustravo A. Galdikas. Kaunas, Švyturys, 1921. 152 p. plates. Hvc48.K87 CtY; MH; WU.

2103. --- --- [another edition] Kaunas, 1928. 1 v. (His Raštai. Kaunas, 1921-1930. vol.9.) RP.

2104. --- --- [Another edition]. Vilnius, Vaga, 1970. 215 p. PG8721.K7D2 1970 DLC; NN.

2105. --- Gilšė; dzūkų legenda. Bobulės vargai. [Legends] Vilnius, M. Kukta, 1909. 42 p. (Vilties išleidimas, nr. 17) CtY; OCl.

2106. --- Gilshe. [...legend. Translated from the Lithuanian under the supervision of Alfred Senn] Menasha, Wis., 1947. p. 102-115. An offprint from the American Slavic and East European Review, v.6, nos.15-17, May 1947. PU; see also Slavic Review (Menasha, Wis.), v.6, 1947. D377.A1A5 CaAEU; CLU; CU; CaBVaU; CtY; CaOLU; CaOTU; CaMWU; DLC; ICU; IEN; IU; IaU; InU; MH; MdBJ; MiU; NN; NNC; NIC; NcD; NjP; OU; PU; WaS; WaU; WU.

2107. --- Milžinkapis. [A legend from the district of Dainava]. Vilnius, M. Kukta, 1912. 36 p. Hvc48.K86 CtY.

2108. --- --- [Another edition].

Chicago, Ill., Tėviškėlė, 1955. 19
p. illus.   PG8721.K7M5   C.

2109. --- Sutemose; pasakos ir
dainos. [At dusk of the evening; story telling and folk songs] Kaunas,
Švyturio b-vė, 1921. 247 p. At
head of title: V. Krėvė.
PG8721.K9S96 1921   ICU; CtY.

2110. --- Užkeikta merga; Dainavos šalies padavimas. [Bewitched woman; a legend from the district of
Dainava]   OCl.

2111. LIETUVIŠKOS PASAKOS: [iš
Jono Basanavičiaus rinkinių vikams paruošė Jonas Stukas. 2. papildytas
leidimas] Vilnius, Vaga, 1974. 286
p. [Lithuanian folk tales; selected
from the collection of J. Basanavičius... 2nd enlarged ed.]
GR203.L5L51   PU.

2112. LIETUVOS TSR Mokslų akade-
mija. Pasakos, sakmės, oracijos.
[Folktales, legends, etc.] Surinko
Mečislovas Davainis-Silvestraitis.
Vilnius, Vaga, 1973. 455 p.   WU.

2113. LOJEWSKI, Erich von. Die
Menelhexe; Sagen und wundersame Ge-
schichten aus Ostpreussen. [Illus.
Adolf Lehnert]. Rendsburg, Ger., M.
Möller, 1956. 103 p. illus.
CtY; MH; NN; NIC.

2114. PUIKŪNAS, Jonas Mingirdas,
comp. & ed. Lietuvių smulkioji tau-
tosaka: mįslės; minklių, mįslių šim-
tagyslių rinkinys-šiupinys. [Lithua-
nian folklore; riddles...] Surinko
ir užrašė Jonas Mingirdas Puikūnas.
[Los Angeles, Calif., Bonnie Press],
1971. 173 p. PN6377.L5P8   PU; DLC.

2115. SLANČIAUSKAS, Matas, comp.
Šiaurės Lietuvos pasakos. [Tales
from Northern Lithuania. Parengė
Norbertas Vėlius ir Ada Seselskytė.
Redagavo Kostas Aleksynas]. Vilnius,
Vaga, 1974. 449 p. illus. At head
of title: Lietuvos TSR Mokslų akade-
mija, Lietuvių kalbos ir literatūros
institutas. Summary in Russian and
English.   GR203.L5S56   PU; DLC.

2116. --- Šiaurės Lietuvos sakmės ir anekdotai. [Legends and funny
stories of Northern Lithuania. Parengė Norbertas Vėlius ir Ada Seselskytė. Redagavo Kostas Aleksynas].
Vilnius, Vaga, 1975. 396 p.
GR203.L5S57   PU; DLC; WU.

2117. SVAZ ČESKOSLOVENSKO-SOVETS-
KÉHO PŘATELSTVI. Vyber z rozprávok
národov Litovskej, Lotyšskej a Estón-
skej SSR. Bratislava, 1958. 63 p.

GR203.L5S8   DLC.

2117a. TETZNER, Franz Oskar. Lock-
und Scheuchrufe bei Litauern und Deutschen. In Globus (Braunschweig,Ger.)
no.6, Bd.84, 1903, p. 87-89.
Gl.G57   DLC; CU; CaOG; ICU; IU; MH;
MnU; NIC; NN; NNC; NhD; NjP; OClW.

2117b. --- Zur litauischen Sprich-
wörterpoesie. In Globus (Braunschweig, Ger.), no.4, Bd. 93, 1908, p.
63-65. Gl.G57 DLC; CU; CaOG; ICU;
IU; MH; MnU; NIC; NN; NNC; NhD; NjP;
OClW.

2117c. --- Zur Sprichwörterkunde
bei Deutschen und Litauern. In Globus (Braunschweig, Ger.), no.4, v.84,
1903, p. 61-63. Gl.G57 DLC; CU; IU;
CaOG; ICU; MH; MnU; NIC; NN; NNC;NhD;
NjP; OClW.

2118. VĖLIUS, Norbertas. Mitinės
lietuvių sakmių būtybės; laimės, lau-
mės, aitvarai, kaukai, raganos, bur-
tininkai, vilktakiai. [Mythological
beings in Lithuanian legends: fairies
goblins, witches and others]. Vilnius.
333 p.   GR203.L5V4   PU.

2118a. WOLTER, Eduard. Litauische
Zauberformeln und Besprechungen. In
Litauische Literarische Gesellschaft,
Tilsit. Mittleilungen (Heidelberg,
Ger.), v.2, 1887, p. 301-306. See
serials consulted.

2119. ZAHORSKI, W[ładysław]. Podania i legendy Wilenskie. Wilno,
Nakładem i drukiem J. Zawadzkiego,
1925.   491.922Zal6   PU; NN; OCl.

2120. ŽILIUS, Jonas. Gelionas ir
kurkas. Padavimus surinko Jonila,
[pseud.] [Legends...] Klaipėda,
spaudė Ryto bendrovė, 1929. 46 p.
491.922Z67.2   PU.

2121. ZOBARSKAS, STEPAS, COMP.
and ed. Lithuanian folk tales. Ill.
by Ada Korsakaittė. [Brooklyn, N.Y.]
G.J. Rickard, [1958]. 200 p. illus.
Bibliography: p. 191-200. GR203.L5Z6
DLC; CLU; CaAEU; CU; CtPAM; CaOTP;IU;
ICU; KU; NbU; PP; PPiU; PU.

XIII.3.b.4. FOLKSONGS

2122. BALYS, Jonas, comp. Lietuvių dainos Amerikoje. Antrasis rinkinys: Lyrinės, meilės, papročių,
darbo, švenčių ir pramogų dainos. Lithuanian folksongs in America. Second collection: lyric songs of love,
customs, work, feasts and entertain-
ments. Collected and edited by Dr.

Jonas Balys. Silver Springs, Md.,
Lithuanian Folklore Publishers, 1977.
342 p., 12 p. of plates. (Lietuvių
tautosakos lobynas, 6).
M1668.7.B20 CaAEU; DLC.

2123. --- Retos dainos-gražuolės.
[The rare beautiful songs.] In Aidai
(Kennebunk Port, Me.), no.8(42),1952,
p. 348-353. See serials consulted.

2124. --- , comp. Šimtas liaudies baladžių. [One hundred folk ba-
lads]. Iliustravo D. Tarabildienė.
Vilnius, LTSR Valstybinė leidykla,
1941. [Xerox copy, 1976]. 203 p.
PG8715B35 1941a PU.

2125. --- Über die litauischen
Volksbalanden. In Acta Ethnologica
(Copenhagen), no.2-3, 1938, p. 73-99.
CU; ICF; ICU; MH; MH-P; MnU; NN;PPT;
PPAP.

2126. BARTSCH, Christian. Dainų
balsai. Melodien litauischer Volks-
lieder. Walluf bei Wiesbaden, M.
Sändig, 1972. 2 v. in 1. Reprint
of the Heidelberg 1886-1889 ed. published by C. Winter.
M1766.L4D3 CaOTU; MH; NN.

2127. BIRUTĖS DAINOS; parinktos
dainelės vartojimui Lietuvos jaunuo-
menei. 2. laida. Tilžėje, "Birutės"
leidinys, 1914. 48 p.
PG8715.B5 1940a PU.

2128. ČIURLIONYTĖ, Jadvyga. Litovskoe narodnoe pessenoje tvorchestvo. Vilnius, 1966. 325 p. music.
ML3681.L6C58 1966 CaAEY; CtY.

2129. JAKIMAITIENĖ, P. Lietuvių
liaudies baladės. [Lithuanian folk
ballads] In Literatūra ir Kalba
(Vilnius), v.9, 1968, p. 297-[350].
Summary in Russian.
PG8503.L6 DLC; CaAEU; CLU; CtY;InU;
IU; ICU; KyU; NN; OClW; PU; WU.

2130. KAZLAUSKIENĖ, Bronė. Vestuvinės dainos jaunojo pusėje.[Wed-
ding songs at the bridegroom's home]
Vilnius, Vaga, 1977. 285 p.
PG8715.K36 PU.

2131. --- Vestuvinės dainos jaunosios pusėje. [Wedding songs at the
bride's home]. Vilnius, Vaga, 1976.
463 p. PG8715.K35 PU.

2132. KRASZEWSKI, Józef Ignacy.
Dajny; pieśni litewskie. [Edited by]
Mykolas Biržiška. Vilnius, Wydawnic-
two "Głosu Litwy", 1919. 49 p. WU.

2133. LIAUDIES DAINOS; tinkamos
deklamacijoms...[Folksongs suitable
for recitation]. South Boston, Mass,

Išleidimas "Laisvės", 1912. 48 p.
*Q p.v.172--NN.

2134. PATERSON, Adrian, tr. Old
Lithuanian songs... Introduction by
Martin Lings. Kaunas, Pribačis,1939.
xxiv, 95 p. PG8771.E3P3 DLC; CtY;
KU; NN; NNC; NIC; NjP; PPiU; PU.

2135. PEACOCK, Kenneth. A garland
of rue; Lithuanian folksongs of love
and betrothal. Collected and edited
by Kenneth Peacock. Musical trans-
cription by the author. Song texts
transcribed and translated by Danutė
Rautinš. Ottawa, Ont., Canadian Centre for Folk Culture Studies, 1972.
viii, 60 p., and 4 phonodiscs (8 s.
LP 33 1/3 rpm. ML3693.L5P4 PU; CtY
CaOTP; InU; InNd; MU; NcD.

2136. ŽVINGILAS, Antanas, comp.
Naujausios ir visokios dainos. [Most
recent and other songs]. So.Boston,
Mass., "Keleivio", 1907. [Xerox co-
py, 1976]. 124 p. PG8715.Z9 1907a
PU.

XIII.3.c. FOLK MUSIC, FOLK DANCES,
AND FOLK FESTIVALS

2137. AUGUSTAITYTĖ-VAIČIŪNIENĖ,
Juzė. Tautinių šokių švenčių takais.
[Lithuanian folk dances and its his-
tory]. Chicago, Ill., Chicagos lietuvių literatūros draugijos leidinys,
1969. 100 p. illus.
GV1688.L5A8 PU; CaOONL.

2138. BREICHMANIENĖ, Genovaitė.
Didžiuokimės mūsų tautiniais šokiais.
[Let us be proud of our folk dances]
In Varpas (Chicago, Ill.), no.11,
1972, p. 53-61. See serials consul-
ted.

2139. 25 [i.e. Dvidešimt penkeri]
dainos metai; nusipelnęs respublikos
kolektyvas-Vilniaus Valstybinio V.
Kapsuko vardo universiteto Akademinis
choras. [25th anniversary of the
Vilnius University Choir. Leidinį
sudarė T. Ramanauskaitė-Pažūsienė et
al. Meninis redaktorius A. Jurėnas]
Vilnius, Vaga, 1965. 71 p. illus.,
facsims., map, ports.
ML302.8.V542U54 DLC; IU; MH.

2140. JUNGTINIŲ AMERIKOS VALSTY-
BIŲ IR KANADOS LIETUVIŲ TAUTINIŲ ŠO-
KIŲ ŠVENTĖS KOMITETAS. Jungtinių
Amerikos Valstybių ir Kanados lietuvių II-osios tautinių šokių šventės
repertuaras jauniesiems. [Repertoire
for the second Lithuanian folk-dance
festival in U.S.A.] Chicago, Ill.,
Komitetas, 1963. 24 p. diagrs.,

music. GV1688.L5J95 1963 CaAEU.

2141. KAZLAUSKIENĖ, Bronė. Vestuvinės dainos jaunojo pusėje. [Wed-
ding songs at the bridegroom's home]
Vilnius, Vaga, 1977. 285 p.
PG8715.K36 PU.

2142. --- Vestuvinės dainos jaunosios pusėje. [Wedding songs at the
bride's home]. Vilnius, Vaga, 1976.
463 p. PG8715.K35 PU.

2143. LITHUANIAN FOLK DANCE FESTI-
VAL. 5th, Chicago, Ill., 1976.
Laisvojo pasaulio lietuvių penktoji
tautinių šokių šventė. [Fifth Lithu-
anian folk dance festival in the
Free World]. Ruošia JAV Lietuvių
Bendruomenė 1976 m. rugsėjo mėn. 5 d.
International Amfiteatre Chicago,
Illinois. [Redagavo Danutė Bindokie-
nė. Chicago, Ill., Penktosios tau-
tinių šokių šventės komitetas,1976].
158 p. Lithuanian and English.
E184.L7L525 1976. PU.

2144. MŪSŲ ŠOKIAI. [Our folk dan-
ces]. Chicago, Ill., Jungtinių Amerikos Valstybių ir Kanados Lietuvių
II-sios Tautinių šokių šventės Komitetas, 1962. 261 p. illus. Edited by Petras Petruitis.
GV1688.L5P49 CaAEU; IEdS.

2145. PEACOCK, Kenneth. A survey
of ethnic folkmusic across Western
Canada. [Ottawa], 1963. 13 p. (National Museum of Canada. Department
of Northern Affairs and National Resources. Anthropology papers no.5)
E78.C2A23 no.5 DLC; CaAEU; CtY;
CaOON; MeB; MH-P; MU; IEdS; MB; NNC;
UU; WaU.

2146. SMITH, Gertrude Madeira. Lithuanian dances as danced by representatives of that nationality, where
they have colonized in Chicago. Des-
criptions by Helen Rich Shipps. Music
arranged [for pianoforte] by Gertrude
Madeira Smith. Chicago, Ill., Clay-
ton F. Summy Co., 1914. [2], 5 p.
4040a.160 MB.

XIII.3.d. MANNERS AND CUSTOMS

2147. AUGUSTAITIS, Dainė. Litau-
isches Brauchtum im Jahreslauf; von
Allerseelen bis zum Georgstag. In
Munich. Universität. Seminar für
slavische Philologie. Aus der Geis-
teswelt der Slawen. München, Ger.,
1967. p. 248-256. PG13.M96 CaAEU;
CaBVaU; CLU; CtY; CLU; CoU; CSt; CU;
CU-S; CU-SB; GU; IU; ICU; InU; MB;MH
MoU; MoSW; MdU; MiU; MiEM; NNC; NRU;

NcU; NjP; NbU; OrU; TxU; TU; ViU; WU;
WaU.

2148. ČEPIENĖ, Irena. Lietuvių
liaudies vestuvių veikėjai. [The participants in Lithuanian wedding fes-
tivities]. Vilnius, Mokslas, 1977.
125, [2] p. GT2771.L5C4 PU.

2149. KRIAUZA, ALB[inas]. Šis tas
apie kupiškėnų jaunimo pramogas. [
Something about the social activities
of the youth of Kupiškis.]. In Gimtasai Kraštas (Šiauliai), no.31,1943,
p. 246-251. Mr. B. Kviklys, Chicago, has it; see also serials consulted.

2150. PIUS, Helen. Lithuanian
Christmas tree ornaments. [By] Helen
Pius and Frank Zapolis. Chicago, Ill.
Zapolis, 1969. 12 p. illus.
GT4985.P69 1969 CaAEU.

XIII.3.e. MATERIAL CULTURE

XIII.3.e.1. NATIONAL COSTUMES,WEAVING, ORNAMENTS, ETC.

2151. ANTONIEWICZ, Włodzimierz.
Les plus anciens vestiges de l'homme
en Pologne du nord-est en Lithuanie;
[by] Prof. Dr. Vladimir Antoniewicz.
In The International congress for
prehistoric and protohistoric sciences. 1st, London, 1932. Proceedings.
London, 1934. p. 88-89.
GN3.I55 1932 DLC; MH-P.

2152. BERNOTIENĖ, Stasė. Lietuvių
liaudies moterų drabužiai XVIII-a.pab.
-XX a. pr. [The National costumes of
the Lithuanian women in 18th-20th
centuries]. Vilnius, Mintis, 1974.
xvi, 277 p. (Chiefly illus.) Summary
in Russian. GT1330.L5B4 PU; OU.

2153. DRABUŽIAI. Odezhda. [Suda-
rė ir parengė J. Balčikonis... etal.]
Vilnius, Vaga, 1974. 346 p., (chief-
ly illus.) (Lietuvių liaudies menas).
Lithuanian and Russian.
GT1051.L5D72 DLC; CLU.

2154. HAHM, Konrad. Ostpreussische Bauernteppiche. Im Auftrage des
Deutschen Vereins für Kunstwissan-
schaft. Jena, E. Diederich, 1937.
115 p. illus. (maps., facsim., diagr)
i.e. 45 plates. (Forschungen zur
deutschen Kunstgeschichte, Bd. 21)
Schriftenverzeichnis: p. 112-113.
CtY.

2155. ŠVAŽIENĖ, Marija (Kondracky-
tė). Marija Švažienė. [Teksto autorė

Laima Cieškaitė] Vilnius, Vaga,1973.
[8] p.,[16] leaves of plates. ill.
(Šiuolaikiniai lietuvių dailininkai)
Lithuanian, Russian and English.
NK3071.L5S9 PU; DLC.

2156. SZTUKA LUDOWA NA LITWIE I
Białej Rusi; typy ludowe. In Wieś
Ilustrowana (Warszawa), Rok 4, no.9,
1913. Q947.52W637 PU.

2157. TAMOŠAITIENĖ, Anastazija.
Mergaičių darbeliai. [Handicraft for
the girls]. Kaunas, JŪR sąjungos
leidinys, 1937. NK9171.L5T31 PU.

2158. --- Mezgimas. [Knitting.
Kaunas], Žemės ūkio rūmų leidinys,
[1935]. 64 p. TT820.T3 PU.

2159. TAMOŠAITIS, Antanas. Audi-
mas. [Weaving. Kaunas], Žemės ūkio
rūmų leidinys, [1933]. 48 p.
NK8856.T33 PU.

2160. --- Staltiesės. [Table-
cloths. Kaunas], Žemės ūkio rūmų
leidinys, 1935. 7 p., [35] leaves
of plates. NK8856.T34 PU.

XIII.3.e.2. FOLK ART, WOOD CARVING, CROSSES, ETC.

2161. BALTRĖNIENĖ, Marija. Lietuvių liaudies muzikos instrumentai;
mokymo priemonė. [Lithuanian folk
music instruments]. Vilnius, Valstybinis pedagoginis institutas,1972.
79 p. ML511.L5B3 PU.

2162. BALTRUŠAITIS, Jurgis. Ele-
ments de l'art populaire lituanien.
In Studi Baltici (Roma), v.10, 1969,
p. 1-42. See serials consulted.

2163. DAUGIRDIENĖ, Halina (Mačiu-
lytė). Taupioji virėja [The economic cook; a cookbook]. Brockton, MA.,
P.M. Juras, 1951. 157 p.
TX725.D325 DLC; MiD.

2164. GRINIUS, Jonas. Lietuvių
kryžiai ir koplytėlės. [Lithuanian
crosses and shrines]. In KLMAM,
v.5, p. 1-182. See serials consulted.

2165. KUDIRKA, Juozas. Lietuvos
puodžiai ir puodai. [Lithuanian pot-
ters and pottery]. Vilnius, Mintis,
1973. 116 p. At head of title: Lietuvos TSR Mokslų akademija, Istorijos institutas. Summary in Russian.
TP803.L5K83 PU; DLC; InU.

2166. KUŠNERIS (Knyševas), P.J.
Apie medinius antkapius ir kai ku-

riuos laidojimo paminklus pietryčių
pabalčio teritorijoje. Wooden grave-
marks and other burial monuments in
the southeastern Baltic territory.
[Translated from the Russian by A.Te-
nison and edited by Dr. Jurgis Gim-
butas]. In Lietuvių Tautos Praeitis
(Chicago, Ill.), Bk.1, v.4, 1977, p.
105-116. See serials consulted.

2167. LIETUVOS GASPADINĖ; arba pa-
mokinimai kaip prigulinčiai suvarto-
ti Dievo dovanas. Parašė Žmona,
[pseud.]. [Lithuanian cookery...].Til-
žėje, Išleido P. Mikolainis. [19--].
80 p. illus. NNR.

2168. LITHUANIAN COOKERY. Comp.
by Izabėlė Sinkevičiūtė; [translated
by Laima Kurpis]. Brooklyn, N.Y.,
Darbininkas, 1976. 316 p. illus.
TX723.5.L8L57 DLC.

2169. MICHELSONIENĖ, M. Nauja val-
gių knyga; su tarptautine virtuve, su
stalo etiketu ir kitomis informacijo-
mis. [New cookbook; includes international cooking, etiquette and other
information] [Boston, Mass.], 1954.
641.59475 M CaOTP.

2170. PILSUDSKI, Bronisław. Krzy-
że litewskie... Krakow, 1922.
709.475P648 PU.

2171. ZAWADZKA Wincentyna A.L.
Kucharka Litewska. Zawierająca: przepisy gruntowne i jasne sporządzenia
rozmaitych potraw. Chicago, W. Dynie-
wicz, 1896. 455, 15 p.
TX725.Z3 DLC.

XIII.4. LANGUAGE

XIII.4.a. BIBLIOGRAPHIES AND GUIDES TO LITHUANIAN LANGUAGE

2172. DAMBRIŪNAS, Leonardas. JAV
kalbininkų lituanistų darbų apžvalga.
[A survey of works of U.S. linguists
on Lithuanian language]. In Institute of Lithuanian Studies. Lituanis-
tikostikos instituto suvažiavimo darbai (Chicago, Ill.), 1971. p.254-261.
Summary in English. DK511.L2I57 DLC
CaAEU; InNd; MiU; NIC; NRU; PU.

2173. LIETUVOS TSR MOKSLŲ AKADEMI-
JA, Vilna. CENTRINĖ BIBLIOTEKA. Lietuvių kalbotyra, 1965-1968. Bibliografinė rodyklė. Litovskoe iazyko-
znanie, 1965-1968; bibliograficheskiǐ
ukazatel'. Vilnius, 1971. 244 p.
At head of title: Lietuvos TSR Mokslų akademijos Centrinė biblioteka.
Lietuvių kalbos ir literatūros insti-

tutas. O.Kriukelienė ir E. Stanevi-
čienė. Lithuanian and Russian.
Z7044.6.L4L52 DLC; AzU; CLU; MiU;
MiDW; MH; NN; NIC; OKentU; PU; TxU

2174. --- --- [Lithuanian linguistics, 1969-1972; a bibliography].
Vilnius, 1977. Z7044.6.L4L5 PU.

2175. MODERN LANGUAGE ASSOCIATION
OF America. MLA international bibliography of books and articles on
the modern languages and literatures,
1919 25-   . New York, N.Y., New
York University Press, 1964-   .
annual. Reprint of the Annual bibliography (1921 55 called American
bibliography) issued in each vol.,be-
ginning with that for 1922, of the
association's publications (PMLA).
Lithuanian linguistics: p. 1958,
p.356; 1959, p.412-413; 1960, p.350-
351; 1961, p.386-387; 1962, p.341-
342; 1963, p.354; 1964, p.314-315;
1965, p.353-354; 1966, p.376, 378-379;
1967, p.600-602; 1968, p.
vol.3: 1969, p.78-79; 1970, p.62-64;
1971, p.63-65; 1972, p.91-92; 1973,
p.88-90; 1974, p.84-86; 1975, p.77-78.
1976, p. 96-97.
Lithuanian literature: 1957, p.363;
1958, p.334-335; 1959, p.241; 1960,
p.360; 1961, p.398-399; 1962, p.354;
1963, p.363-364; 1964, p.323-324;
1965, p.367; 1966, p.395-396; 1967,
p.898-900; 1968, p.   ; vol.2:
1969, p.230; 1970, p.219-222; 1971,
230-232; 1972, p.246-248; 1973, p.
264-267; 1974, p.273-277; 1975,p.257-
250; 1976, p.267-272;
Lithuanian bibliography and general:
1957, p.348-349; 1958, p.320; 1959,
p.405; 1960, p.345; 1961, p.379;1962,
p.343; 1963, p.360-361; 1964, p.321;
1965, p.363; 1966, p.389-390; 1967,
p.895-896; 1968, p.
Folklore: 1957, p.364; 1958, p.336;
1962, p.355; 1963, p.374; 1964,p.333;
1965, p. 381; 1966, p.412; 1967, p.
929.
Z7006.M64 DLC; AAP; AU; AzU; CaAEU;
CaBVaU; CaOPAL; CaOTU; CaOTV; CaQMU;
CLSU; CLU(1956-);CoD(1963-); CoU;CSt;
CtY(1963-); CU(1963-); CU-Riv(1963-)
FTaSU(1921 25-1969-); GASU(1963-);
GDS(1969-); GU(1963-); IaAS(1963-);
IaU(1966-); ICU(1963-); InLP(1964-);
InTI(1966-); IU(1963-);KU; KMK;KyU(
1963-); LU; MH; MeB; MBU(1957-);MCM(
1963-); MdBJ(1963-); MNS(1957-); MSU;
MSSU; MnU(1963-); MiU; MWalB(1963-);
MWelC(1963-); NB(1963-); NN; NBuU;
NbU(1964-); NcD; NcU(1963-); NhD(
1963-); NNU(1963-); NBuT; NRU(1963-);
OU; OCU; OCl(1963-); OkS(1963-);OCLW;
OClCS; OSW(1969-); OOxM; ViBlbV(1921-
25-); ViU; RP; PU.

2176. DIE OSTEUROPÄISCHEN LITERA-
turen und slawischen Sprachen von A.

Bezzenberger, A. Brückner [u.a.].
Berlin; Leipzig, B.G. Teubner, 1908.
viii, 396 p. Partial contents.--V.
Die litauisch-lettischen Literaturen.
CB5.K8 DLC; CaBVaU; CaOTU; CU; CSt;
GoU; GU; DDO; IaU; ICJ; ICN; MiU;NIC;
NcD; NcU; OCl; OCH; OrU; PPLT; PU;TU;
PBm; WaU.

XIII.4.b. INDO-EUROPEAN, PRUSSIAN AND BALTIC LANGUAGES

2177. ANDERSEN, Henning. The Dative of subordination in Baltic and
Slavic. In Baltic Linguistics (University Park, Pa.), 1970, p. 1-9.
PG8002.B3 DLC; see also serials
consulted.

2178. ANGELUS, Oskar. Über das Ab-
sterben der baltischen Mundarten. In
Acta Baltica (Königstein, Ger.), v.15,
1975, p. 155-165. See serials consulted.

2179. ANTKOWSKI, Ferdynand. La
chronologie de la monophtongaison des
diphtongues dans les langues indo-eu-
ropéennes. Poznań, PWN, 1956. 53 p.
(Poznańskie Towarzystwo Przyjaciół Nauk. Wydział Filologiczno-filozoficz-
ny. Prace Komisji Filologicznej,16:4)
Pages also numbered: 154-203.
P599.A63 1956 CaAEU; CaBVaU; CtY;CLU;
DLC; ICU; InU; MH; MiDW; MnU; NN;NIC;
NcD; NjP; PU; RPB; TxU.

2180. BAMMESBERGER, Alfred. Abs-
traktbildungen in den baltischen
Sprachen. Göttingen, Ger., Vandenhoeck & Ruprecht, [1973]. 157 p.
(Ergänzungshefte zur Zeitschrift für
vergleichende Sprachforschung auf
dem Gebiet der indogermanischen Sprachen, nr.22). PG8049.B3 1973 PU;
DLC; CaAEU; CLU; ICN; InU; MnU; NIC;
NjP; NcD; NcU; OCU; PU; ViU; WU.

2181. BALTIĬSKIE ÎAZYKI I IKH VZA-
imnosvîazi so slavîanskimi, finno-
ugorskimi i germanskimi îazykami; tezisy dokladov nauchnoĭ konferenͭsii,
posvîashchennoĭ 100-letiîu so dnîa
rozhdeniîa akd. ÎA. Endzelina. [Otv.
redaktor R. ÎA. Grabis]. Riga, Zinatne, 1973. 130 p. PG8001.B28 PU;WU;
DLC.

2182. BALTO-SLAVÎANSKIE ISSLEDOVA-
niîa. [Otv. redaktor T.M. Sudnik].
Moskva, Nauka, 1974. 263 p. illus.
At head of title: Akademiîa Nauk SSSR
Institut Slavîanovedeniîa i balkanis-
tiki. PG8018.B28 PU; CU-SB; DLC;MU.

2183. BALTO-SLAVÎANSKIĬ SBORNIK.
[Otv. red. V.N. Toporov]. Moskva,

Nauka, 1972. 423 p. PG8018.B3 PU;
CaBVaU; CaOTU; CaQMM; CtY; CU-SB;CU;
DLC; IU; ICIU; MB; MH; MiEM; MiDW;
MiU; MnU; MU; NNC; NIC; NjP; NcD;OrU
PPiU; TxU; TNJ; UU; WU.

2184. BALTŲ IR SLAVŲ KALBŲ RYŠIAI.
[Relation between Baltic and Slavic
languages. Atsak. redaktorius: K.
Morkūnas]. Vilnius, Mintis, 1968.
205 p. (Lietuvių kalbotyros klausimai, 10) At head of title: Lietuvos
TSR Mokslų akademija. Lietuvių kalbos ir literatūros institutas. Summaries in German and Russian.
PG8501.L5 no.10 DLC; WU.

2185. BALTŲ KALBŲ VEIKSMAŽODŽIO
tyrinėjimai. Issledovaniia po baltiĭs-
komu glagolu. Red. kolegija: A. Sabaliauskas (ats.redaktorius)]. Vilnius, Mintis, 1973. 262 p. (Lietuvių kalbotyros klausimai, 14). At
head of title: Lietuvos TSR Mokslų
akademija. Lietuvių kalbos ir literatūros institutas. English, German,
Latvian, Lithuanian, or Russian. Summaries in English, Lithuanian or Russian. PG8501.L5 no.14 DLC; MiU; NjP;
WU.

2186. BEDNARCZUK, Leszek. Finno-
Ugric loans in Baltic. In Journal
of Baltic Studies (Brooklyn, N.Y.),
no.2, v.8, 1977, p. 99-104. See
serials consulted.

2187. BURWELL, Michael. The voca-
lic phonemes of the old Prussian Elbing vocabulary. In Baltic Linguistics (University Park, Pa.), 1970.
p. 11-21. PG8002.B3 DLC; See also
serials consulted.

2188. CHEKMAN, V.N. Ob otrazhe-
nii indo-evropeĭskikh slogovykh plav-
nykh v balto-slavianskom iazykovom
areale. In Acta Baltico-Slavica(Warszawa), v.9, 1976, p. 15-26. See
serials consulted.

2189. CONFERENCE ON BALTIC STUDIES,
3d, University of Toronto, 1972. Baltic literature and linguistics. Editors: Arvids Ziedonis, Jr. [and others]
Columbus, Ohio, Association for the
Advancement of Baltic Studies, 1973.
iii, 251 p. (Publications of the Association for the Advancement of Baltic Studies, 4). Selected papers
from the conference sponsored by the
Association for the Advancement of
Baltic Studies and the University of
Toronto. PG8001.C65 1972 DLC;CSt;
CaAEU; CU; ICIU; ICarbS; MnU-A; NBuC;
NNU; NbU; OOxM; OrU; VtU; WU; WaU.

2190. DONUM BALTICUM. To professor
Christian S. Stang on the occasion
of his seventieth birthday, 15 March

1970. Ed. Velta Rūķe-Draviņa. Stock-
holm, Almquist & Wiksell, 1970. xiv,
598 p. illus. In English, French,
German, Latvian, Lithuanian or Rus-
sian. PG8002.D6 DLC; CaAEU;CaBVaU;
CaQMM; CLU; CtY; CU-SB; ICU; ICIU;IU;
InU; InNd; IaU; LU; MH; MnU; MU; NNC;
NN; NIC; NjP; NbU; NcU; OU; PSt; PU;
TxU; ViU; WU; WaU.

2191. ECKERT, Rainer. Baltische
Studien. Mit einem Geleitwort von Ru-
dolf Fischer und einer Bibliographie
von Rainer Eckert und Frido Mětšk.
Berlin, Akademie-Verlag, 1971. 102
p. (Sitzungsberichte der Sächsischen
Akademie der Wissenschaften zu Leip-
zig. Philologisch-Historische Klasse
Bd.115, Hft.5). Bibliography: p.[75]-
98. AS182.S213 Bd.115 Hft 5 DLC;
CoU; CtY; CLU; FU; GU; ICIU; InU;IaU;
MH; MU; NBuU; NjP; PPiU; ViU; CaBVaU;
CaQMM.

2192. ENDZELĪNS, Jānis. Compara-
tive phonology and morphology of the
Baltic languages. Translated by Wil-
liam R. Schmalstig and Benjamiņš Jē-
gers. The Hague, Mouton, 1971 [1972]
357 p. (Slavic printing and reprin-
ting, v.85). PG8018.E513 1972 DLC;
AzU; CaAEU; CaBVaU; CLSU; CSt; CtY;
CU; CU-S; CU-SB; CU-SC; CoU; CoFS;
CtW; CNoS; FU; FTaSU; GU; ICU; ICIU;
IaU; InU; IU; IEdS; InNd; KyU; KyLoU;
LNHT; MH; MCM; MoU; MdU; MnU; MiU;MU;
NN; NNC; NIC; NSyU; NjP; NjR; NmU;
NbU; NRU; NcU; OU; OrU; PSt; PPiU;PU;
RPB; ViU; VtU; ViBlbV; TxHR; WaU.

2193. FRAENKEL, Ernst. Zur baltoslavischen Sprachgeschichte und Gram-
matik. In Archiv für slavische Philologie (Berlin), v.39, 1925, p. 69-
92. See serials consulted.

2194. GERULLIS, Georg. Baltica.
In Archiv für Slavische Philologie
(Berlin), v.39, 1925, p. 44-69. See
serials consulted.

2195. --- Herkunft der Dative
Sing. der i-Stämme im Baltischen. In
Archiv für Slavische Philologie (Berlin), v.38, 1923, p. 55-82. See serials consulted.

2196. GUDAVIČIUS, Aloyzas. Leksi-
ko-semanticheskaia gruppa zritel'nogo
vospriiatiia v russkom i litovskom
iazykakh (opyt semanticheskoĭ tipolo-
gii). Vil'nius, Vil'niusskiĭ gos.
universitet, 1970. 20 p. Avtoreferat dissertatsii na soiskanie uchenoĭ stepeni kandidata filologicheskikh nauk. PG8667.G8 PU.

2197. ILLICH-SVITYCH, Vladislav
Markovich. Indoevropeiskie aktsen-
tuatsionnye paradigmy imen v Baltiĭs-

kom. In His Imennaĭa aktsentuatsiĭa v baltiĭskom i slavĭanskom... Moskva, 1963. Chast 1, p. 1-88. This chapter deals mostly with the accentuation of Lithuanian language. PG8032.I4 DLC; CaAEU; CaBVaU; CaOTU; CtY; CSt; CoU; CU-S; CLU; FMU; GU;IU; InU; ICU; InNd; KU; MH; NN; NRU; NIC; NjP; NcD; NcU; NNC; OU; OrU; PPiU;PU; RPB; TxU; ViU; WU.

2198. JĒGERS, Benjamiņš. Einige baltische und slavische Verwandte der Zippe von lit. dirbti. In Studi Baltici (Roma), v.10, 1969, p.63-112. See serials consulted.

2199. KILIUS, J., comp. Lesebuch für Philologen. Vilnius, 1969. 397 p. P73.K5 DLC.

2200. KLIMAS, Antanas. Baltic and Slavic revisited. In Lituanus (Chicago, Ill.), no.1, v.19, 1973, p. 7-26. See serials consulted.

2201. --- Baltų ir slavų kalbų santykių tyrinėjimai, 1970-1975. Research on the problem of the relationship between Baltic and Slavic, 1970-1975. In Institute of Lithuanian Studies. Lituanistikos instituto 1975 metų suvažiavimo darbai. Chicago, Ill., 1976. p. 141-149. Summary in English. DK511.L2I64 1975 CaAEU; PU.

2202. --- Some questions concerning the relationship of Baltic and Slavic. In International Congress of Linguists. Proceedings. 1928. See serials consulted.

2203. KUDIRKIENĖ, Lilija. Obraz i znachenie glagol'noĭ frazeologii litovskogo i latyshskogo ĭazykov. Vil'nĭus, Vil'nĭusskiĭ gos. universitet, 1976. 41 p. Avtoreferat dissertatsii na soiskanie uchenoĭ stepeni kandidata filologicheskikh nauk. PG8641.K8 PU.

2204. LATVIJAS PADOMJU SOCIALISKĀS REPUBLIKAS ZINĀTŅU AKADĒMIJA. VALODAS UN LITERATŪRAS INSTITŪTS. Rakstu krājums veltījums akadēmiķim... profesoram Jānim Endzelīnam viņa 85 dzīves un 65 darba gadu atcerei.[Festschrift for prof. Jānis Endzelīn on his 85th birthday anniversary and 65 years of his scientific activity] Riga, 1959. 375 p. port. Text in Latvian, Russian, English, German, etc. 491.804L365r NSyU; CLU; CtY; CU; MiU; NN; PU.

2205. LEVIN, Jules F. The Slavic element in the Old Prussian Elbing vocabulary. Berkeley, Calif., University of California Press, 1974.

xiv, 110 p. (University of California publications in linguistics, v.77) P25.C25 v.77 PU;CaAEU; CaBVaU; CLSU; CoU; DLC; IaU; INS; IU; OkU; OrPS; PSt; ViU; WaU.

2206. LEWY, Ernst. Kleine Schriften. Berlin, Akademie-Verlag, 1961. xv, 759 p. port. (Deutsche Akademie der Wissenschaften zu Berlin. Veröffentlichungen der sprachwissenschaftlichen Kommission, Bd.1). About Old Prussian language in II Abteilung: Indogermanisches p. 200-349. P27.L67 CaAEU.

2207. MAZHĬULIS, V. K voprosu o vzaimnykh otnosheniĭakh baltiĭskikh ĭazykov. In Acta Baltico-Slavica (Warszawa), no.9, 1976, p. 65-70. See serials consulted.

2208. MEULEN, Reinder van der. Oudpruisisch mixkai. Amsterdam,Noord-Hollandsche Uitgevers maatschappij, 1943. 12 p. (Mededeelingen der Nederlandsche Akademie van Wetenschappen. Afdeeling letterkunde. Nieuwe reeks, deel 6, no.2). OCl.

2209. NEPOKUPNYĬ, Anatoliĭ Petrovich. Balto-severnoslavĭanskie ĭazykovye svĭazi. Vil'nĭus, Vil'nĭusskiĭ gos. universitet, 1975. 59 p. Avtoreferat dissertatsii na soiskanie uchenoĭ stepeni doktora filologicheskikh nauk. PG8096.A1N41 PU.

2209a. --- --- Kiev, Nauk. Dumka, 1976. 224 p. maps. At head of title: Akademiĭa nauk Ukrains'koĭ SSR. Institut ĭazykovedeniĭa im. A.A.Potebni. Bibliography: p. 199-[217]. PG8018.N4 DLC.

2210. NESSELMANN, Georg Heinrich Ferdinand. Forschungen auf dem Gebiete der preussischen Sprache. Königsberg in Pr., A. Rosbach, 1870-71. 3 v. Offprints from Altpreussische Monatschrift, Bd.7, Hft.4; Bd.8, Hft. 1 and 8. 491.91N37.3 PU; NjP; see also serial: DD491.O4A3 DLC; IU; MH; MH-Z; NNC; NjP.

2211. PALMAITIS, Lētas. Istoriĭa lichnykh mestoimeniĭ v baltiĭskikh ĭazykah. Vil'nĭus, Vil'nĭusskiĭ gos. universitet, 1975. 26 p. Avtoreferat dissertatsii na soiskanie uchenoĭ stepeni kandidata filologicheskikh nauk. PG8059.P3 PU.

2212. PORZEZIŃSKI, Wiktor. Die baltisch-slavische Sprachgemeinschaft. In Rocznik Słowistyczny. Revue slavistique (Kraków), v.14, 1911, p.1-26. PG1.R6 DLC; CaBVaU; CaOTU; CtY;CSt; ICU; MH; NcD; NIC; NjP; OClW; PPiU; TU; WU.

2213. RŪKE-DRAVIŅA, Velta. Initial consonant combinations in Lithuanian and Latvian. In Donum Balticum. Uppsala, 1970. p. 429-440. See serials consulted.

2213a. SCHMALSTIEG, William R[iegel], Jr. The East Baltic accusative plural. In Lingua (Haarlem, Netherlands), no.4, v.16, 1966, p.377-382. P9.L47 DLC; see also serials consulted.

2214. --- Keli tocharu ir baltu kalbu panašumai. Some similarities between Tokkarian and the Baltic languages. In Institute of Lithuanian Studies. Lituanistikos instituto 1973 metu suvažiavimo darbai. Chicago, Ill., 1975. p. 207-212. Summary in English. DK511.L2I63 1975 CaAEU; PU.

2215. --- An Old Prussian grammar; the phonology and morphology of the three catechisms. University Park, Pa., Pennsylvania State University Press, 1974. PG8204.S3 PU;AkU; AAP; AzU; CaBVaU; CLSU; CoFS; CtY; CoU; FU; GU; IaU; ICarbS; InU; IU;KU; KyU; LU; MH; MiU; MB; MoU; MoSW;NSyU; NN; NNC; NNU; NjR; NcGU; NRU; NvU; NmU; OkU; OKentU; OCU; OU; OOxM; OrU; TNJ; TU; TxU; ViU; VtU; WU; WaU.

2216. --- Priebalsiu palatizacija prieš priešakinius balsius Baltu kalbose, specialiai atsižvelgiant i Prūsu kalbą. Palatization of consonants before front vowels in the Baltic languages, with special reference to Old Prussian. In Institute of Lithuanian Studies. Lituanistikos instituto 1975 metu suvažiavimo darbai. Chicago, Ill., 1976. p. 135-139. Summary in English. DK511.L2I64 1975. CaAEU; PU.

2217. --- Several studies on Old Prussian. In Institute of Lithuanian Studies. Lituanistikos instituto 1973 metu suvažiavimo darbai. Chicago, Ill., 1975. p.v.3, p.153-170. DK511.L2I63 1973 CaAEU; PU.

2218. --- Studies in Old Prussian; a critical review of the relevant literature in the field since 1945. University Park, Pa., Pennsylvania State University Press, 1976. ix, 420 p. PG8202.S3 PU.

2219. --- Tokharian and Baltic. In Lituanus (Chicago, Ill.), no.3, v.20, 1974, p. 5-11. See serials consulted.

2220. SENN, Alfred. Slavic and Baltic linguistic relations. In Donum Balticum. Uppsala, 1970. p.485-

494. See serials consulted.

2221. VRACIU, A. Izuchenie balto-slavianskikh îazykovykh otnoshenii v Rumynii. Les études des rapports linguistiques Balto-Slaves en Roumanie. In Acta Baltico-Slavica (Warszawa), v.10, 1976, p. 59-88. See serials consulted.

2222. --- Die Stellung der baltischen Sprachen im Rahmen des Indo-Germanischen; unter besonderer Berücksichtigung der alten baltoslavischen Sprachbeziehungen. In Acta Baltico-Slavica (Warszawa),v.11, 1977, p.109-166. See serials consulted.

2223. WARREN, Cowgil. The normative plural and present singular of the active participles in Baltic. In Baltic Linguistics (University Park, Pa.,) 1970, p. 23-37. PG8002.B3 DLC; see also serials consulted.

2224. WATKINS, Calvert. Remarks on Baltic verb inflexion. In Baltic Linguistics (University Park, Pa.), 1970, p. 165-170. See serials consulted.

2224a. WIJK, Nicolaas van. Zum altpreussischen Imperativ und zum litauischen Permissiv. In Indogermanische Forschungen (Berlin), v.47,1929, p. 161-168. See serials consulted.

2224b. --- Zum baltischen und litauischen Akzentverschiebungsgesetz. In Indogermanische Forschungen (Berlin), v.40, 1922, p. 1-40. See serials consulted.

XIII.4.c. HISTORY AND RESEARCH

2225. AŠMANTAS, Andrius. Iš romantiškosios i mokslinę kalbotyrą Lietuvoje. [The transition from romantic toward the scientific linguistics in Lithuania] In LKMASD (Rome), v.3, p. 219-233. See serials consulted.

2226. BASANAVIČIUS, Jonas. Prie historijos musun rašybos. [The history of our orthography]. Parašė J.Basanavitius. Tilžėje, Spaustuvėje O. v. Mauderodes, 1899. [Xerox copy, 1974]. 17 p. PG8545.B3 PU.

2227. CHEKMAN, V.K. K proiskhozhdeniîu litovskogo akan'îa. Some remarks on Lithuanian "akanye." In Acta Baltico-Slavica (Warszawa), v.11, 1977, p. 167-192. See serials consulted.

2228. DAMBRIŪNAS, Leonardas. Bendrinės lietuvių kalbos raida per pastarąjį penkiasdešimtmetį. The trends in standard Lithuanian during the last 50 years. In Institute of Lithuanian Studies. Lituanistikos instituto 1975 metų suvažiavimo darbai. Chicago, Ill., 1976. p. 149-155. Summary in English. DK511.L2I64 1975 CaAEU; PU.

2229. --- The state of linguistics in Soviet Lithuania. In Baltic Linguistics (University Park, Pa.), 1970, p. 39-46. See serials consulted.

2230. DONUM BALTICUM. To professor Christian S. Stang on the occasion of his seventieth birthday, 15 March 1970. Ed. by Velta Rūķe-Draviņa. Stockholm, Almquist & Wiksell, 1970. xiv, 598 p. illus. In English, French, German, Latvian, Lithuanian or Russian. PG8002.D6 DLC; CaAEU; CaBVaU; CaQMM; CLU; CtY; CU-SB; ICU; IaU; ICIU; InU; IU; InNd; LU; MH; MnU; MU; NN; NNC; NIC; NjP; NcU; NhU; OU; PSt; PU; TxU ViU; WU; WaU.

2231. DROTVINAS, Vincentas. Lietuvių kalbos tyrinėjimų tarybiniais metais apžvalga; mokymo priemonė studentams. [The Lithuanian language research during the Soviet period; a review] Vilnius, 1972. 100 p. At head of title: Lietuvos TSR Aukštojo ir specialiojo vidurinio mokslo ministerija. Vilniaus valstybinis pedagoginis institutas. Lietuvių kalbos katedra. PG8524.D76 DLC.

2232. FORD, Gordon Buell, Jr. Some remarks about Jonas Kruopas' 1947 edition of Martynas Mažvydas' Cathechism of 1547. In Lituanus (Chicago, Ill.), no.2, v.18, 1972, p.34-44. See serials consulted.

2233. --- Some remarks about Simonas Vaišnoras' Žemčiūga teologiška or Margarita theologica, "Theological Pearl" of the year 1600. In Lituanus (Chicago, Ill.), no.2, v.18, 1972, p. 27-33. See serials consulted.

2234. --- Some remarks about the Wolfenbuttel Lithuanian Postile manuscript of the year 1573. In Baltic Linguistics (University Park, Pa.), 1970. p. 67-69. See serials consulted.

2235. GAILIŪNAS, Pranas. Lietuvių kalbos dėstymo metodika savikontrolės pratimai; programuoto mokymo priemonė. [The method to teach Lithuanian language...] Vilnius, 1973. 224 p. At head of title: Vilniaus V.

Kapsuko Universitetas. Lietuvių kalbos katedra. P. Gailiūnas. PG8519.G3 DLC.

2236. GENIUSHENE, Ė. Sh. Litovskie "sub"ektnye" vozvratnye glagoly v sopostavlenii s russkimi. Lithuanian "Subjective" reflexive verbs and their Russian equivalents. In Acta Baltico-Slavica (Warszawa), v.10, 1976, p. 219-234. See serials consulted.

2237. HAMP, Eric P. Lithuanian ugnis, Slavic ogn (ogon'). In Baltic Linguistics (University Park, Pa.), 1970. p. 75-79. See serials consulted.

2238. JĒGERS, Benjamiņš. Zum Etymologie von lit. kaulyti "zudringlich betteln, feilschen" und lett. kaulet "ds." In Donum Balticum. Uppsala, 1970. p. 211-221. See serials consulted.

2239. JONIKAS, Petras. Lietuvių bendrinės rašomosios kalbos kūrimasis antroje XIX a. pusėje. [The formation of written standard Lithuanian in the second half of the nineteenth century]. Čikaga, Pedagoginis lituanistikos institutas. 1972. xi, 334 p. At head of title: Pedagoginis lituanistikos institutas. PG8525.J61 PU; CU; DLC; ICIU; InU; MB; NIC.

2240. --- Tarmės ir bendrinė rašyba. [The dialects and the standard orthography]. In Donum Balticum. Uppsala, 1970. p.230-240. See serials consulted.

2241. KAD PAMOKA BŪTŲ ĮDOMI; iš lietuvių kalbos ir literatūros mokytojų darbo patirties. [To make the lesson interesting; from the teaching experience of Lithuanian language and literature. Sudarė ir redagavo: V. Diržinskienė ir K. Margevičius] Vilnius, Laikraščių ir žurnalų leidykla, 1965. 110 p. PG8519.K3 DLC.

2242. KLIMAS, Antanas. Generatyvinė kalbotyra ir lietuvių kalba. Generative grammar and the Lithuanian language. In Institute of Lithuanian Studies. Lituanistikos instituto 1973 metų suvažiavimo darbai. Chicago, Ill., 1975. p. 175-187. Summary in English. DK511.L2I63 1973 CaAEU PU.

2243. --- Some attempts to inventory Lithuanian phonemes. In Baltic Linguistics (University Park, Pa.), 1970, p. 93-102. See serials consulted.

2244. KOEPPEN, Petr Ivanovich. O proiskhozhdenii iazyka i literatury

litovskikh narodov. S.-Peterburg,
1827. 106 p. (His Materialy dlīa
istorii prosvīeshchenīīa v Rossii,
t.3) Z2491.A1K7 DLC.

2245. KOT, Stanisław. Un gesuita
Boemo, patrocinatore delle lingue na-
zionali slave e la sua attività in
Polonia e Lituania. In Ricerche slavistiche (Roma), t.3, 1954. See
serials consulted.

2246. LEBEDYS, Jurgis. Lietuvių
kalba XVII-XVIII a. viešajame gyve-
nime. [Lithuanian language in the
public life of the 17th-18th centuries in Lithuania. Sudarytoja V.Za-
borskaitė] Vilnius, Mokslas, 1976.
276 p. PG8525.L4 PU.

2247. LIETUVIŲ KALBOS GRAMATIKOS
TYRINĖJIMAI. [The research on Lithuanian grammar. Ats. redaktorius V.
Ambrazas] Vilnius, Mintis, 1969.
280 p. (Lietuvių kalbotyros klausimai, 11). At head of title: Lietuvos TSR Mokslų akademija. Lietuvių
kalbos ir literatūros institutas.
PG8501.L5 no.11 DLC; CtY; CU;CaBVaU;
InU; MH; NjP; OU.

2248. LIETUVOS TSR MOKSLŲ AKADEMI-
JA, Vilna. LIETUVIŲ KALBOS IR LITE-
RATŪROS INSTITUTAS. Lietuvių kalbos
ir literatūros institutas; Lietuvos
TSR Mokslų akademija, Lietuvių kal-
bos ir literatūros institutas. [The
Institute of Lithuanian language and
literature... Parengė A. Seselskytė]
Vilnius, Mintis, 1973. 77 p.,[4]
leaves of plates. illus. Bibliogra-
phy: p. 53-74. PG8519.L5 1973 DLC;
InU; PU.

2249. LINGIS, Juozas. Išnykę ir
pasikeitę socialinės reikšmės žodžiai
lietuvių kalboje. [The vanished and
changed words of the social meaning
in Lithuanian] In Donum Balticum.Up-
psala, 1970. p. 290-302. See serials
consulted.

2250. MIRONAS, Ričardas. Kalbos
mokslo pagrindai. [Outline of lingus-
tics]. Mokymo priemonė studentams
neakivaizdininkams. Vilnius, 1971.
119 p. At head of title: Lietuvos
TSR Aukštojo ir specialiojo mokslo
ministerija. Vilniaus Valstybinis V.
Kapsuko universitetas. PG8523.M5 DLC.

2251. --- Kalbos įvadas; mokymo
priemonė aukštosioms mokykloms. [An
outline of linguistics...] Vilnius,
1969. 105 p. At head of title:
Lietuvos TSR aukšt. ir spec. vidur.
mokslo ministerija. P106.M55 PU.

2252. MOKYTOJO LITUANISTO DARBO
klausimai. Iš šeštųjų respublikinių
pedagoginių skaitymų sudarė L. Gedvilas ir R. Norkevičienė. [The problems
of the teacher of Lithuanian language
and literature] Kaunas, Šviesa, 1968.
143 p. PG8519.M6 DLC.

2253. NORKUS, Jonas. Kalbos daly-
kai. [Linguistics]. Kaunas, Spaudos
Fondas, 1932. 95 p. 491.92N1 CtTMF.

2254. OLEKIENĖ, O. Glagol'no-imen-
nye predlozhnye slovosochetanīīa s
vremennym znacheniem v sovremennom litovskom literaturnom īazyke i ikh so-
otvetstvīīa v russkom (na materiale
slovosochetaniī s vinitel'nym padezhe)
Vil'nīus, Vil'nīusskiī gos. universitet, 1970. 2o p. Avtoreferat disser-
tat͡sii na soiskanie uchenoĭ stepeni
kandidata filologicheskikh nauk.
PG8617.05 PU.

2255. PALIONIS, Jonas. Lietuvių
literatūrinės kalbos istorijos įvadas;
mokymo priemonė LTSR aukštųjų mokyklų
studentams lituanistams. [A historical outline of the Lithuanian literary language]. 2., pataisytas bei iš-
plėstas leidimas. Vilnius,[Vilniaus
universiteto leidybinis skyrius],1976.
64 p. PG8525.P31 1976 PU; DLC.

2256. PIROČKINAS, Arnoldas. Prie
bendrinės kalbos ištakų; J. Jablonskio gyvenimas ir darbai 1860-1904 m.
[J.Jablonskis his life and works,1860-
1904]. Vilnius, Mokslas, 1977. 226 p.
PG8517.J3P52 PU.

2257. REKLAITIS, Janine (Kanauka).
Lietuvių kalbos kitimas bendros indo-
europiečių kalbų raidos šviesoje.
Diachronic change in Lithuanian in relation to the general development of
Indo-European languages. In Institute of Lithuanian Studies. Lituanistikos instituto 1973 metų suvažiavimo darbai. Chicago, Ill., 1975. p.
197-205. Summary in English.
DK511.L2I63 1975 CaAEU; PU.

2258. --- Theory of analogical
change: application to Lithuanian.
[Stanford, Calif.], 1971. Thesis
(Ph.D.)--Stanford University, 1972.
CSt; CaAEU(xerox); InU.

2259. RUHIG, Philipp. Meletema,
e re ipsa, autoribus variis atq. ex-
perientia, sistens linguam lituani-
cam, suasu doctrina excellentissi-
morum quorundam autorum luci publi-
cae datum a Philipo Ruhigio. Inster-
b[urg], Prusso, ecclesiae Walterke-
mensis in districtu Insterburgensis
pastore germanico-lituanico. Anno
quo lituanus gaudens inactus fuit
Biblia prima. [i.e. 1735]. Reproduced
in 1977 by xerography from the original manuscript owned by K.Varnelis,

Chicago, Ill.. [57] leaves.
PG8522.R8 1735a PU.

2260. SABALIAUSKAS, Algirdas. No-
ted scholars of the Lithuanian language; biographical sketches. Translated by William R. Schmalstieg and
Ruth Armentrout. Published jointly
by Akademinės Skautijos leidykla and
Dept. of Slavic languages, Pennsyl-
vannia State University. Chicago,
Ill.; Philadelphia, Pa., 1973. 168 p.
Translation of Žodžiai atgyja, Vilnius, 1967.   OU; PSt.

2261. --- Šimtas kalbos mislių.
[A Hundred riddles in linguistics.
Vidutiniam ir vyresniam mokykliniam
amžiui. Ill.: R. Palčiauskas]. Vil-
nius, Vaga, 1970. 248 p. illus.
PG8523.S3 DLC; ICIU; NjP.

2262. --- Žodžiai atgyja; pasakojimas apie lietuviško žodžio tyrinė-
tojus. [A story about the researchers
of the Lithuanian language] Vilnius,
Vaga, 1967. 202 p. ports.
ICU.

2263. --- Žodžiai pasakoja. [Words
are telling. Vidutinio ir vyresnio-
jo mokyklinio amžiaus vaikams]. Vilnius, Vaga, 1965. 138,[2] p. illus.
(Noriu žinoti) ICIU; ICU.

2264. SALYS, Antanas. Kalbotyra
mokslinių tyrimų dėstyme. [Linguis-
tics among the scientific research]
In LKMASD, v.2, p. 217-256. See serials consulted.

2265. SCHMALSTIEG, William Riegel.
Jonas Kazlauskas' contribution to Li-
thuanian linguistics. In Lituanus(
Chicago, Ill.), no.1, v.18, p.5-14.
See serials consulted.

2266. SKARDŽIUS, Pranas. J.Kaz-
lausko "Lietuvių kalbos istorinė gramatika". [J. Kazlauskas' Lithuanian
historical grammar]. In Institute
of Lithuanian Studies. Lituanistikos
instituto 1973 metų suvažiavimo darbai. Chicago, Ill., 1975. p.269-280.
Summary in English. DK511.L2I63
1975 CaAEU; PU.

2267. --- Lietuvių kalba ir jų
senovinė kultūra. [The Lithuanian
language and its ancient culture] In
Aidai (München, Ger.), no.8, 1947,
p. 345-348. Mr. Liudas Kairys in
Chicago has it; see also serials consulted.

2268. --- Lietuvių kalba, jos su-
sidarymas ir raida. [Lithuanian language, its structure and evolution].
In Tremties Metai (Tübingen, Ger.),
1947, p. 417-442. PG8713.T721 InNd;

CaAEU; CaOTP; CtY; CtTMF; DLC; MiD;
NN; PU.

2269. --- Martynas Mažvydas ir jo
vaidmuo lietuvių bendrinės kalbos istorijoje. [M. Mažvydas and his role
in the history of the standard Lithuanian language]. In Aidai (München,
Ger.), no.4, 1947, p. 198-200.
Mr. Liudas Kairys in Chicago, Ill.,
has it as no. 2787; see also serials
consulted.

2270. SKLIUTAUSKAS, Jokūbas. Iš
armėniško sąsiuvinio. [Comparative
study of Armenian and Lithuanian].
Vilnius, Mintis, 1968. 150 p. illus.
MH.

2271. SPROGIS, Ivan Iakovlevich(Ja-
nis). Litovskiĭ iazyk v pamiatnikakh
iuridicheskoĭ pis'mennosti. S.-Peter-
burg, 1896. Reprint from Izviestiĭa
Imperatorskoĭ Akademii Nauk, 1896, serial, t.4, no.4, p. [415]-420.
491.922Sp95 PU.

2272. VANAGAS, A. K voprosu o lat-
viazhskikh Iazykovykh reliktakh v Litve. In Acta Baltico-Slavica (Warszawa), no.9, 1976, p.71-88. See serials
consulted.

2273. VENCLOVA, J.M. Sudaviai,
jotvingiai, dainuviai; piety lietuviai. Apie Suduvą bendrai. [Sudovians
Yatwyags and dainuviai, the Southern
Lithuanians...]. Chicago, Ill., Lietuvių literatūros draugijos leidinys,
1974. 71 p. At head of title:J.Venc-
lova. Bibliography: p. 58-71.
DK511.L23V47 DLC; CaAEU.

2274. ZINKEVIČIUS, Zigmas. Kalbotyros pradmenis. [Introduction into
linguistics]. Kaunas, Šviesa, 1969.
101 p. illus., facsims., ports.
P106.Z5 DLC; CaBVaU; PU.

2275. --- W sprawie kontaktów ję-
zykowych litewsko-polskich w Wilnie
w XVII wieku. In Acta Baltico-Slavica (Warszawa), no.9, 1976, p.125-132.
See serials consulted.

2276. ŽMONĖS IR KALBA. [People and
language. Sudarė Bronys Savukynas].
Vilnius, Mokslas, 1977. 239 p.
PG8523.Z55 PU.

2277. ŽODŽIAI IR ŽMONĖS.[Words and
people. Sudarė Bronys Savukynas].
Vilnius, Mintis, 1974. 221 p. illus.,
ports. At head of title: LTSR Paminklų apsaugos ir kraštotyros draugija.
Kalbos komisija. PG8524.Z6 DLC; PU.

XIII.4.d. OLD TEXTS

2278. ALEKNAVIČIUS, Kajetonas.
Pasakos, pritikimaj, weselos ir gies-
mes. Par K. Olechnowicziu sudieri-
nimays lietuwiszkay paraszitos. Wilniui, Drukarnioi iszspaustos pinigays
A. Dworca, 1861. [Xerox copy, 1977]
144[i.e. 146] p.
PG8721.A46P3 1861a PU(xerox).

2279. ANTONIEWICZ, Karol Bołoz.
Szwentdienis darbas; arba, Skajtimaj
szwentosi dienosi del brolu letuwiu,
iszguldita isz linkiszka letuwiszkaj
par K.P.W. [Viksvą]. Wilniuji, Kasztu ir spaustuwioji J. Zawadzkie,1862.
[Xerox copy, 1975]. 278 p.
BV4839.P6A5 1862a PU(xerox).

2280. BRETKŪNAS, Jonas. Postilla;
tatai esti, Trumpas ir prastas isch-
guldimas Euangeliu, sakamuiu Baszni-
czoi Krikschczioniszkoie... [Sermons]
Karaliaucziuie, 1591.[Xerox copy,
1972] BV4254.L5B7 1972 PU(xerox).

2281. IMITATIO CHRISTI. Tamószaus
isz Kempés kéturos knygéles apie pa-
sekimmą Kristaus prásto draugbrolio
lietuwiszkay iszwerstos ir iszdruk-
kawotos mete 1830. Tiléje, Prie dru-
kkawótojo E. Pusto, [1830]. 284 p.
Bonaparte Collection no. 13442 ICN.

2282. KELIOS EWANGELISZKOS GIES-
meles isz tuleropu knygeliu surinktos. Heidekrug, O. Sekunna,[190-]
891.920K968 PU.

2283. KIALETAS ŽODŽIU APLINK SZKA-
pleriu mukos Pono Jezuso. Wilniuje,
Kasztu ir spaustuwieje J. Zawadskia,
1861. 44 p. BX2310.S3K5 PU.

2284. KUŠELIAUSKAS, Serafinas Laurynas. Szkala pavargeliu siratų ir
apie daugel kitų naudingų žinių.
Tilžéje, 1904.[Xerox copy, 1971].
109 p. PG8721.K85S9 1971 PU(xerox)

2285. LUTHER, Martin. The old
Lithuanian catechism of Martynas Maž-
vydas(1547). Edited and translated
by Gordon B. Ford, Jr. Assen, Van
Gorcum, 1971. xvi, 104 p.
PG8525.L85 1971 PU; CaOTU.

2286. MAŽVYDAS, Martynas. Pirmoji
lietuviška knyga. [The first book in
the Lithuanian language. Įvadiniai
straipsniai K.Korsako ir M.Ročkos.
Tekstą ir komentarus paruošė M.Ročka]
Vilnius, Vaga, 1974. 345 p.
BX8070.M39 1974 PU.

2287. --- Pirmosios lietuviškos
knygos autorius, jo mirties 400 metų
sukakčiai paminėti. [The author of

the first Lithuanian book...]. Chicago, Ill., Pedagoginis Lituanistikos
institutas, 1963. 1 v. Includes
facsimile of "...first known Lithuanian book, published in 1547."
CU.

2288. PETKEVIČIUS, Merkelis,d.1608.
Polski z litewskim katechism, albo,
Krótkie wiedno mieysce zebranie wia-
ry y powinnośći krześćiańskiey z pas-
terstwem zborowym y domowym, z mod-
litwami, psalmami y piosnkami...
W Wilnie, Nakł. ego mśći panna M.Piet-
kiewicza, pisarza ziemskiego wileńskiego, 1598. Reprint. [Kaunas, 1939]
1 v. BX9429.P6P5 InU(1939 ed.).

2289. --- 1598 metų Merkelio Pet-
kevičiaus katekizmas. 2.leidimas,
fotografuotinis. Kaunas, 1939. 1 v.
(various pagings)(Švietimo ministerijos Knygų leidimo komisijos leidinys, 506). Original title: Polski z
litewskim katechizm...wydany nakładem Malchera Pietkiewicza w Wilnie,
1598. Includes psalms, prayers,hymns
and ritual of the Reformed Church.
Text in Polish and Lithuanian.
MH.

2290. UHLENBECK, Christian Corne-
lius, ed. Die drei catechismen in
altpreussischen Sprache, nach Nesselmann's Ausgabe neu hrsg. und mit Anmerkungen versehen ... Leiden, Blan-
kenburg, 1889. 491.91Uh63 PU.

2291. VARNAS, Jonas. Siejamoses
paszaro-žoles... Wilniuy, Spaustuwieje, J. Zawadzkia, 1854. 23 p.
Bonaparte Collection no. 13472 ICN.

XIII.4.e. PHONETICS, ACCENT, AND ACCENTUATION

2292. BUCH, Tamara. Lithuanian
phonology in Christian Donelaitis.
[Translated from the Polish manuscript
by Alfred Buch and coworkers. Tel-
Aviv, 1974] 58,[3] leaves. Reproduced from typescript. PG8540.B8 PU.

2293. DARDEN, Bill J. Accent in
the Lithuanian noun declension. In
Baltic Linguistics (University Park,
Pa.), 1970. p.47-52. See serials
consulted.

2294. FORTUNATOV, Filip Fedorovich.
Lektsii po fonetike. In Lund,Sweden.
Universitet. Slaviska Institutet.
Årsbok (Lund), 1957 58, p.[5]-63. See
serials consulted.

2295. --- Zur vergleichenden Be-
tonungslehre der lituslavischen Sprachen. In Archiv für Slavische Philo-

logie, Berlin), v.4, 1880, p.575-589. See serials consulted.

2296. GAILIŪNAS, Pranas. Kirčiuokime taisyklingai; mokymo priemonė. [Let's stress correctly; teaching guide]. Vilnius, 1970. 83 p. PG8544.G25 DLC.

2297. HEESCHEN, Claus. Einführung in die Grundprobleme der generativen Phonologie mit besonderer Berücksichtigung der litauischen Phonologie. Bonn, Ger., 1968. 285 p. On spine: Generative Phonologie. Inaug. -Diss.--University of Bonn. Bibliography: p. 5-9. P217.H35 DLC.

2298. KURYŁOWICZ, Jerzy. Intonation et morphologie en lituanien. In Studi Baltici (Roma), no.7, 1940, p. 37-87. *ZAN-*Q70--NN(film reproduction); see also serials consulted.

2299. MATERIALY KOLLOKVIUMA LABOratorii éksperimental'noĭ fonetiki i psikhologii rechi. Pod red. V.A. Artemova i B.I.Svetsevichiusa. Vil'niūs, Vil'niusskiĭ gos. pedagog. in-t, Laboratoriia éksperimental'noĭ fonetiki i psikhologii rechi, 19--. v. illus. At head of title: Ministerstvo vysshego i srednego spetsial'nogo obrazovaniia Litovskoĭ SSR. Vil'niusskiĭ gosudarstvennyĭ pedagogicheskiĭ institut. Laboratoriia éksperimental'noĭ fonetiki psikhologii rechi. Added title pages in English and Lithuanian. Summaries in English and Lithuanian. PG8541.M3 DLC; MH; PU.

2300. MIKALAUSKAITĖ, Elzbieta. Lietuvių kalbos fonetikos darbai. [Phonetics of the Lithuanian language]. Vilnius, Mokslas, 1975. 247 p. illus. At head of title: Lietuvos TSR Aukštojo ir specialiojo vidurinio mokslo ministerija. Vilniaus Valstybinis pedagoginis institutas. Lietuvių kalbos katedra. PG8541.M5 1975 DLC.

2301. MUSTEIKIS, Kazimieras. Sopostavitel'naia morfologiia russkogo i litovskogo iazykov.[Posobie dlia vyzov respubliki po spetsial'nostiam: rus. iaz. i literatura litov. iaz. i literatura i zhurnalistika]. Vil'niūs, Mintis, 1972. At head of title: K. Musteikis. PG8529.M8 DLC; CSt; CU; InU; IU; InLP; MB; MH; ICU; MiU; MiDW; MnU; MU; NNC; NIC; NjP; WU.

2302. ROBINSON, David F. The Phonology of Slavic loanwords in Lithuanian. In Journal of Baltic Studies (Brooklyn, N.Y.), no.2, v.4, 1973, p. 127-129. See serials consulted.

2303. SCHNITZER, Marc L. The du-

ration of the long vowels as a perceptual cue in Lithuanian. In Lituanus (Chicago, Ill.), no.1, v.18,1972, p. 58-72. See serials consulted.

2304. ZINKEVIČIUS, Zigmas. Iš lietuvių istorinės akcentologijos; 1605 m. katekizmo kirčiavimas. [Historical accentuation in Lithuanian; the accentuation of the 1605 ed. of cathecism] Vilnius, [Vilniaus universiteto Leidybinis skyrius], 1975. 95 p. At head of title: LTSR Aukštojo ir specialiojo vidurinio mokslo ministerija. PG8544.Z5 PU; DLC.

XIII.4.f. GRAMMAR

XIII.4.f.1. GENERAL STUDIES, TEXTBOOKS, AND EXERCISES

2305. DĖJUS, Titas. Lietuvių kalbos gramatika III klasei. [Lithuanian grammar...]. Kaunas, Valstybinė pedagoginės literatūros leidykla, 1958. 89 p. PG8535.D42 1958 OKentU.

2306. DĖJUS, Titas and MACEIKIENĖ, S. Lietuvių kalbos gramatika IV klasei. 5.leidimas. [Lithuanian grammar] Kaunas, Valstybinė pedagoginės literatūros leidykla, 1956. 110 p. At head of title: T. Dėjus ir S. Maceikienė. PG8535.D4 1956 OKentU.

2307. GAILIŪNAS, Pranas and ŽIUGŽDA, Juozas. Lietuvių kalbos gramatika. [Lithuanian grammar. 3-sis leidimas.] Kaunas, Šviesa, 19--. v. Partial contents.--2 dalis. Sintaksė. PG8613.G3 DLC; CaAEU; PU.

2308. GAILIŪNAS, Pranas. Skyryba; skaitmeniniai pratimai. [Punctuation; exercises]. Vilnius, 1971. 43,[3] p. At head of title: Lietuvos TSR Aukštojo ir specialiojo vidurinio mokslo ministerija. Vilniaus Valstybinis V. Kapsuko universitetas. Lietuvių kalbos katedra. P. Gailiūnas. PG8643.G3 DLC; WU.

2309. GRAŽBYLYS, Petras, pseud. Senasis lietuviškas kalbomokslys (gramatika) su lietuviškai-rusiškai-lenkišku tam tikru žodynu... [Lithuanian grammar with Lithuanian-Russian-Polish dictionary]. Kaunas, Spaustuvė Sakalausko, 1905. [6, 3]-127 p. At head of title: P-as Gra-lys. 491.92R500 ICJ.

2310. KALBOS PRAKTIKOS PATARIMAI. [Advice and exercises for the Lithuanian language. Sudarė Aldonas Pupkis. Vyr redaktorius Zigmas Zinkevi-

čius]. Vilnius, Mokslas, 1976. 381
p. PG8645.K29 PU.

2311. KAPLANAS, Jokūbas and DAM-
BRIŪNAS, Leonardas. Lietuvių kalbos
gramatika VI-jam pradinės mokyklos
skyriui. Kaunas, 1938- . v.
At head of title: J. Kaplanas ir L.
Dambrauskas. PG8533.K3 OKentU.

2312. LABUTIS, Vitas. Žodžių junginių problemos; mokymo priemonė. [
Problems of arranging sentences; a
textbook]. Vilnius, Vilniaus universiteto Leidybinis skyrius], 1976. 92
p. PG8617.L3 PU.

2313. LIETUVOS TSR MOKSLŲ AKADE-
MIJA, Vilna. LIETUVIŲ KALBOS IR LI-
TERATŪROS INSTITUTAS. Lietuvių kal-
bos gramatika. [Lithuanian grammar.
Vyr. redaktorius K. Ulvydas]. Vil-
nius, Mintis, 1965-1976. 3 v. Bib-
liographical references included in
"Sutrumpinimai": v.1, p.[731]-[743].
Contents.--l. t. Fonetika ir morfo-
logija(daiktavardis, budvardis, skai-
tvardis, įvardis).--2.t. continua-
tion.--3.t. Sintaksė.
PG8533.L5 1965 DLC; CaAEU; CaBVaU;
CaOTU; CLU; CtY; CSt; CU; InU; ICU;
IU; MH; NN; NNC; NBuU.

XIII.4.f.2. READERS, PHRASE BOOKS AND ORTHOGRAPHY

2314. ABETSELE ZHEMAĬTISHKAĬ-LIE-
tuvishka. [Zhemoĭtsko-litovskiĭ bukvar'], ishdota par isakima IO Miles-
tas Viriausioia Reditoia Shiaures-va-
karo shalies M. N.Murav'eva. Vil'-
nius, Spaustuvee A. Kirkora, 1864.
[Xerox copy, 1976] 42 p. This is
one of the Lithuanian books printed
in Cyrillic during the period of the
prohibition of the Lithuanian press,
1864-1904. PG8537.A25 1864a PU.

2315. ALEKNAVIČIUS, Kajetonas.
Elementarius; arba, Lengwus mokslas
skaytit raszto szwento. Letuwiszkay
del wayku lietuwniku par kunigu K.
Olechnowicziu ape reykału moksło ir
wieżliwu apsiėjimu kalbiasieys para-
szitas. Wilniui, Pinigays raszito-
jaus iszspaustas, 1858. [Xerox copy,
1977]. 70 p. [Childrens' reader].
PG8537.A55 1858a PU.

2316. ANGLIŠKI PASIKALBĖJIMAI.
2. kirčiuota ir papildyta laida. [s.l.,
s.d.]. 79 p. [Phrase book].
MiD.

2317. BOCZKAUSKAS, F.W.S. Priei-
giausias mokslas angliszko liežuwio
be pagialbos kito. 2.iždawimas.

[English-Lithuanian self-instructor]
Mahanoy City, Pa., D.T. Boczkauskas,
1904. [Xerox copy, 1975]. 235 p.
PE1129.L6B3 1904a PU(xerox).

2318. BRAZYTĖ-BINDOKIENĖ, Danutė,
comp. Lietuvių literatūros skaitymai; aukštesniajai lituanistinei mokyklai. [Reader of Lithuanian literature for The High School of Lithuanian Studies. Chicago, Ill., [Kr.
Donelaičio Aukštesnioji lituanistinė
mokykla,] 1976. 587 p. At head of
title: Danutė Bindokienė.
PG8537.B7 PU.

2319. BUDGINIENĖ, A. Darbas su at-
siliekančiaisiais iš lietuvių kalbos
rašybos. [Work with the students who
fall behind in written Lithuanian
language]. Vilnius, Periodika,1973.
61 p. At head of title: Lietuvos
TSR Ministrų Tarybos Valstybinis profesinio techninio mokymo kabinetas.
Respublikinis mokymo metodikos kabinetas. PG8519.B8 DLC.

2320. BUKVARS ZHEMAĬTISHKAĬ-RUSISH-
kasis. Bukvar' Zhmudsko-russkiĭ, pa-
rashitas pagal mokima nu V.Zolotova
padota, ishgul'ditas par Iona Krechin-
ski. Kovna, Tip. Sh. Sokolovskago,
1865. 88 p. PG8537.B8 1865a PU.

2321. ČENIENĖ, Jovita, comp.
Skaitiniai VI klasei. [Reader]. Sudarė J. Čenienė ir V. Eidukaitis. 5.lei-
dimas. Kaunas, Valstybinė pedagoginės literatūros leidykla, 1957. 212
p. illus. PG8537.C42 1957 OKentU.

2322. --- --- 4. leidimas. Kaunas, Valstybinė pedagoginės literatūros leidykla, 1956. 253 p. illus.
PG8537.C42 1956 OKentU.

2323. --- Skaitiniai V klasei.
[Reader]. Sudarė J. Čenienė ir V.
Eidukaitis. 4. leidimas. Kaunas,
Valstybinė pedagoginės literatūros
leidykla, 1956. 191 p. illus.
PG8537.C4 1956 OKentU.

2324. --- --- 5.leidimas. Kaunas,
Valstybinė pedagoginės literatūros
leidykla, 1957. 191 p. ports.
PG8537.C4 1957. OKentU.

2325. DOMIJONAITIS, Juozapas.
Skaitymo pradžiamokslis. [Primary
Reader] Sutaisė J. Domijonaitis. Da-
lis II. Chicago, Ill., Draugas Pub.
Co.,[1915]. 76 p. illus.
PG8713.D669 InNd; ICJ; OKentU.

2326. GABRYS, Juozas. Skaitymo
knyga, mažiems ir dideliems; išrink-
tieji raštai... Tilžėje, Jagomastas,
1908. OCl. [Children's reader...]

2327. JAKUČIONIS, A. Praktiška rašymo skaitymo metodika; kompleksinis mokymas. [Practical method of writing and reading...]. Kaunas, Mokytojų knygyno "Šviesa"leidinys,1934. 78, 13 p. WC13359 CtY.

2328. JANSONIENĖ, Natalija. English-Lithuanian phrase-book. Anglų-Lietuvių pasikalbėjimų knygelė. [Vilnius, Mintis, 1969] 181 p. PG85 PG8539.J35 DLC; CaAEU.

2329. K, D.S. Rankvedis prancuzų kalbos. [Handbook of French language]. Sutaisė D.S.K.... Worcester, Mass., Spauda ir Turtas "Amer. Lietuvio," 1918. 110 p. 491.9292 ICJ; ICN.

2330. KADŽYTĖ, Liuda. Rašybos mokymas V-VIII klasėse; lietuvių kalbos dėstymo metodika. [Teaching spelling from Grade 5 to Grade 8]. Leista naudoti mokymo priemone respublikos aukštosiose mokyklose. Vilnius, Mintis, 1966. 190,[2] p. LB1577.L5K3 DLC.

2331. KAMANTAUSKAS, Viktoras. Anglų kalbos gramatika. [An English language grammar]. Weilheim-Teck, Ger., Atžalynas, 1947. 120 p. PE1129.S79K3 DLC.

2332. LAUKIS, Joseph. How to write letters in English and Lithuanian languages; a comprehensive and practical guide to correspondence. Showing the structure, composition, formalities and uses of the various kinds of letters, notes and cards. Kaip rašyti laiškus lietuviškoje ir angliškoje kalbose... Suredagavo J. Laukis. Chicago, Ill., Spauda "Lietuvos", 1911. 293 p. PE1129.S79L3 DLC; ICJ; NN.

2333. --- Rankvedis angliškos kalbos, praktiškas būdas išsimokinimui angliškos kalbos pačiam per save be pagalbos mokytojaus...[Handbook of English language; a practical method to learn English alone without aid of a teacher]. Chicago, Ill., Spauda "Lietuvos," 1906. 310 p. PE1129.L6L3 DLC; MB; NB; NN; OC1;PU.

2334. --- --- [Another edition]. 4. pataisytas spaudimas. Chicago,Ill, "Lietuva", 1912. 310 p. PE1129.S79L4 1912 DLC; NN; PU.

2335. LAZAUSKAS, Juozas. Rašybos reforma ir gyvenimas. [The reform of orthography and life]. In Mokykla ir Gyvenimas (Kaunas), no.6-9, 1934. Offprint. 491.922B964 PU.

2336. LIETUVIŲ KALBOS RAŠYBA IR skyryba. [The orthography and punctuation in Lithuanian. Ats. redaktorė A. Valeckienė] Vilnius, Mokslas,1976. 390 p. At head of title: Lietuvos TSR Mokslų akademija. Lietuvių kalbos ir literatūros institutas. PG8545.L5 PU; DLC.

2337. MARCIŃSKI, Maciej Franciszek. Grammatyka litewsko-polska. Gramatika arba spasabas iszsimokinimo lenkiszkos kalbos. Warszawa, Drukarnioje kunigų Missionoriu pas Szwenta Kriżiu, 1861. 152 p. 3286.39 MH.

2338. MEDŽIAGA GIMTOSIOS KALBOS ugdymui ir aplinkos pažinimui; papildomai prie knygos "Mūsų mažiesiems." [Materials to foster the native language... Sudarė L. Karpavičienė]. Vilnius, 1966. PG8713.M4 DLC.

2339. MILUKAS, Antanas. Lietuviška chrestomatija. [Lithuanian reader] Parengė kun. A. Milukas. Išleista kaštais "Susivienymo Lietuvių Amerikoje", Shenandoah, Pa., V.J. Stagaro spaustuvė, 1901. 176 p. 891.928M3 CtTMF; NN.

2340. MURKA, Jonas. Mažasis lietuvių kalbos vadovėlis III pradžios mokyklos skyriui. [A Lithuanian language reader...]. 3.leidimas. Kaunas, Spaudos Fondas, 1931. 128 p. illus. PG8537.M8 1931 OKentU.

2341. PLAČAS, Juozas, comp. Gintaras. Lithuanistinių mokyklų aštuntajam skyriui. [Amber; a reader for the Lithuanian schools...]. Chicago, Ill., JAV LB Kultūros Fondas, 1961. 255 p. illus., music, ports. PG8537.P69 1961 CaAEU; PU.

2342. SCHLEICHER, August, ed. & tr. Litauisches Lesebuch und Glossar. Prag, Calve, 1857. 351 p. WU.

2343. SENN, Alfred. Kleine litauische Sprachlehre. Nachdr. d. Ausg. Heidelberg 1929. Hildesheim, Ger.; New York, N.Y., Olms,[1974]. xi,304 p. Original ed. published by J.Groos. PG8531.S45 1974 DLC; CaAEU; MH.

2344. STAŠAITIENĖ, V. Russko-litovskiĭ razgovornik. Rusisky-lietuviškų pasikalbėjimų knygelė. 3.Leilimas. Vilnius, Mintis, 1968. 325 p. PG8539.S7 1968 DLC; CaAEU.

2345. VAIKŲ SKAITYMĖLIAI SU LIETUvos žemėlapėliu. [Reader for children with the map of Lithuania]. Vilnius, "Vilniaus Žinių," 1905. 259 p. fold. map. Rvc24V19 CtY.

2346. VARGO MOKYKLAI. [Reader: Vargo Mokykla]. Leidimas antrasis.

Vilnius, Švyturio, 1919-1921. 2 v.
170 p. (Būrelio mokytojų rinkinys
Kalbos mokslo reikalui, 1)
PG8713.V426 InNd; CtTMF; PU; WU.

2347. --- --- 4.leidimas. Kaunas, Švyturio b-vė, 1922.
Hvc24Jll CtY; WU.

XIII.4.f.3. MORPHOLOGY

2348. AMBRAZAS, Vytautas. Lietuvių kalbos dalyvių atributyvinė-pre-
dikatyvinė vartosena. [The attribu-
tive-predicative use of Lithuanian
participles]. In Lietuvos TSR Mokslų akademija, Vilna. Lietuvių kalbos ir literatūros institutas. Lietuvių kalbos morfologinė sandara
ir jos raida.. Vilnius, 1964. p.47-
79. PG8501.L5 v.7 DLC;CLU; CtY;
CU; ICU; InU; IU; MH; NN; PU. WaU.

2349. BALDAUF, Lucia. Über die
Pronominalform des Adjektivs im litauischen Prädikat. In Donum Balticum. Uppsala, 1970. p. 30-37. See
serials consylted.

2350. DAMBRIŪNAS, Leonardas. Kelios pastabos dėl lietuvių kalbos dalyvių sistemos ir reikšmės. Some remarks on system and meaning of Lithuanian participles. In Institute of
Lithuanian Studies. Lituanistikos
instituto 1973 metų suvažiavimo darbai. Chicago, Ill., 1975. p.189-196.
Summary in English.
DK511.L2I63 1975 CaAEU; PU.

2350a. --- Verbal aspects in Lithuanian. In Lingua Posnaniensis(Poznan), v.7, 1958, p. 253-262. As offprint 491.92.D183.3 PU; see also
serials consulted.

2351. FORD, Gordon B[uell], Jr.
The old Lithuanian third person im-
perative ink(IO. In Baltic Linguistics (University Park, Pa.), 1970.
p.71-74. See serials consulted.

2352. --- The origin of the Lithuanian first person singular opta-
tive. In Donum Balticum. Uppsala,
1970. p. 124-127. See serials consulted.

2353. GENIŪSHENE, Ė. SH. Tranzi-
tivnye refleksivy v litovskom îazyke.
Transitive reflexive verbs in Lithuanian. In Acta Baltico-Slavica (Warszawa), v.11, 1977, p. 193-210. See
serials consulted.

2354. JAKAITIENĖ, Evalda, LAIGONAI-
TĖ, Adėlė and PAULAUSKIENĖ, Aldona.

Lietuvių kalbos morfologija; vadovėlis respublikos aukštųjų mokyklų lietuvių kalbos ir literatūros specialy-
bei. [Lithuanian morphology; a text
book...] Vilnius, Mokslas, 1976. 282
p. PG8559.J3 PU.

2355. JAKAITIENĖ,E[valda]. Veiksma-
žodžių daryba; priesagų vediniai. [
Verb formation...]. Vilnius, V.Kap-
suko Universitetas, 1973. 66 p. At
head of title: Lietuvos TSR Aukštojo
ir specialiojo vidurinio mokslo ministerija. Vilniaus V. Kapsuko universitetas. Lietuvių kalbos katedra.
PG8597.J34 DLC; PU.

2356. JAŠINSKAITĖ, Irena. Lietuvių kalbos ištiktukai. [Lithuanian
language interjections]. Vilnius,
Mintis, 1975. 117 p. PG8609.J3 DLC.

2357. KLIMAS, Antanas. Studies on
word formation in Lithuanian. In Lituanus (Chicago, Ill.), no.3, v.20,
1974, p. 49-72. See serials consulted.

2358. KNIŪKŠTA, Pranas. Imena pri-
lagatel'nye s sufiksom -inis i ikh
grammaticheskie sinonimy v sovremennom litovskom îazyke. Vil'-
nîus, Vil'nîusskiĭ gos. universitet,
1971. Avtoreferat dissertatsii na soiskanie uchenoĭ stepeni kandidata filologicheskikh nauk. PG8577.K55 PU.

2359. --- Priesagos -inis būd-
vardžiai; daryba, reikšmės, gramati-
niai sinonimai. [Adjectives with suf-
fix -inis word-formation, meaning and
grammatical synonims]. Vilnius, Mokslas, 1976. 219 p. At head of title:
Lietuvos TSR Mokslų akademija. Lietuvių kalbos ir literatūros institutas.
Summary in Russian. PG8577.K56 PU;
DLC.

2360. PISANI, V. A proposito di
etimologia lituana; questioni di me-
todo e prospettive storiche. In Studi Baltici (Roma), 1969, v.10, p.43-
63. See serials consulted.

2361. PROSDOCIMI, A.L. Lituano
ežeras, latino egeria. In Studi Baltici (Roma), v.10, 1969, p. 130-142.
See serials consulted.

2362. SKARDŽIUS, Pranas. Prielink-
snis su ir jo vartojimas. [Preposi-
tion su and its use] In Gimtoji Kalba (Kaunas), 1939, p. 100-106.
PG8509.G54 PU; ICCC.

2363. ŠLIŽIENĖ, N. Apie sudurti-
nes atliktines veiksmažodžio laikų ir
nuosakų formas lietuvių literatūrie-
je kalboje. [The forms of the com-
pound tenses and moods of the verbs

in the Lithuanian literary language].
In Lietuvos TSR Mokslų akademija,
Vilna. Lietuvių kalbos ir literatūros institutas. Lietuvių kalbos morfologinė sandara ir jos raida. Vilnius, 1964. p. 81-95. (Kalbotyros
klausimai, 7). PG8501.L5 v.7 DLC;
CU; CLU; CtY; ICU; InU IU; MH; NN;
PU; WaU.

2364. ŠUKYS, Jonas. Taisyklingai
vartokime linksnius. [Let's use cases
to the rule]. Kaunas, Šviesa, 1976,
158 p. PG8575.S9 DLC.

2365. URBUTIS, Vincas. Daiktavar-
džių daryba. [Formation of the nouns]
In Lietuvos TSR Mokslų akademija,
Vilna. Lietuvių kalbos ir literatūros
institutas. Lietuvių kalbos gramati-
ka. Vilnius, 1965. v.1, p. 251-473.
PG8533.L5 v.1 DLC; CaAEU; CaBVaU;CU;
CaOTU; CLU; CtY; CSt; ICU; InU; IU;
MH; NN; NNC; NBuU.

2366. --- Slovoobrazovanie imen
sushchestvitel'nykh v sovremennom
litovskom iazyke. Vil'nius, Vil'niusskii gos. universitet, 1971. 31 p.
Avtoreferat dissertatsii na soiskanie uchenoi stepeni doktora filologicheskikh nauk. PG8571.U7 PU.

2367. VALECKIENĖ, Adėlė. Būdvar-
džių daryba. [The formation of ad-
jectives]. In Lietuvos TSR Mokslų
akademija, Vilna. Lietuvių kalbos ir
literatūros institutas. Lietuvių
kalbos gramatika. Vilnius, 1965.
v.1, p. 550-603. PG8533.L5 v.1 DLC;
CaAEU; CaBVaU; CaOTU; CLU; CtY; CSt;
CU; ICU; InU; IU;MH; NN; NNC; NBuU.

2367a. WIJK, Nicolaas van. Das litauische langvokalische Präteritum.
In Indogermanische Forschungen (Berlin), Bd.34, p. 367-383 (1914-1915).
See serials consulted.

2368. --- Die litauischen Quanti-
tätsoppositionen. In Indogermanische Forschungen (Berlin), Bd.58,
1941. P501.I4 DLC; AAP;CaBVaU;FU;
FTaSU; ICoU; KyU; LU; MB; MiU; NSyU;
NN; NRU; PBm; PPT; TxHR; TxLT; ViU;
WvU; see also serials consulted.

2369. --- Die pronominalen Ades-
sivformen des Altlitauischen. In
Archivum Philologicum (Kaunas), v.4,
1933. See serials consulted.

2370. ŽODŽIŲ FORMOS IR JŲ VARTOSE-
NA. [Word forms and their usage. Ats.
redaktorė Valeckienė]. Vilnius,
Mintis, 1974. 326 p. (Lietuvių kalbotyros klausimai, 15). At head of
title: Lietuvos TSR Mokslų akademija.
Lietuvių kalbos ir literatūros institutas. Summaries in Russian.

PG8524.Z65 DLC.

XIII.4.f.4. SYNTAX

2371. DOBROVOLSKIS, Bronius and
GEDVILAS, Leonas. Preliminarinis sin-
taksės ir skyrybos mokymas. B. Dobrovolskis, L. Gedvilas.[Preliminary
teaching of syntax and punctuation]
Kaunas, Šviesa, 1974. 220 p. (Pedagogikos darbai, 6). At head of title: Lietuvos TSR Švietimo ministerija. Pedagogikos mokslinio tyrimo
institutas. PG8613.D6 DLC.

2372. KALINAUSKAS, Bronius. Lietuvių kalbos žodžių junginių sintaksė;
mokymo priemonė. [Syntax of word con-
junction in Lithuanian]. Vilnius,
Valstybinis pedagoginis institutas,
1972. 185 p. At head of title: Lietuvos TSR Aukštojo ir specialiojo vidurinio mokslo ministerija. Vilnius
Valstybinis pedagoginis institutas.
Bibliography: p. 178-180.
PG8625.K3 DLC.

2373. PIROČKINAS, Arnoldas. Pri-
duriamosios konstrukcijos dabartinė-
je lietuvių literatūrinėje kalboje;
mokymo priemonė studentams lituanistams. [Dangling constructions in the
present Lithuanian literary language]
Vilnius, 1969. 72 p.
PG8625.P5 DLC; MH.

XIII.4.f.5. GRAMMATICAL USAGE BY
PARTICULAR AUTHORS

2374. BŪTĖNAS, Petras. A. Jakšto
poetinis žodynas. [The poetical vocabulary of A.Jakštas]. In LKMASD, v.
3, p. 260-312. See serials consulted.

2375. GRINIUS, Kazys. D-ro Vinco
Kudirkos raštų žodynas. [The dictio-
nary of V. Kudirka works]. Kaunas,
Varpas, 1924. 29 p. WU.

2376. HOFMANN, Erich. Das Halb-
partizip in Daukšas Postille. In
Donum Balticum. Uppsala, 1970. p.
198-205. See serials consulted.

2377. JONIKAS, Petras. Žemaitė ir
bendrinė kalba. [Žemaitė and the
standard Lithuanian language]. In
Lituanistikos Darbai (Chicago, Ill.),
v.3, 1973, p. 135-142. See serials
consulted.

2378. KUDZINOWSKI, Czesław. Inekssłownik do "Daukšos Postilė". Poznań,[Wydawn. Naukowe Uniwersytetu im. Adama Mickiewicza, 1977. 2 v. PG8674.K8 PU.

2379. SALYS, Antanas. Martyno Mažvydo raštų kalba. [The language of Martynas Mažvydas]. In Metmenys (Chicago, Ill.), no.25, 1973, p.3-14. See serials consulted.

2380. VAIČIULAITIS, Antanas. Vyskupo Motiejaus Valančiaus raštų stilius. The stylistic qualities of the works of Bishop Motiejus Valančius. In Institute of Lithuanian Studies. Lituanistikos instituto 1975 metų suvažiavimo darbai. Chicago, Ill. 1976. p. 79-89. Summary in English. See serials consulted.

2381. ŽULYS, Vladas. Leksika sochinenii Ionasa Rezy. [By] V.Zhulis. Vil'nīus, Vil'nīusskii gos. universitet, 1970. 14 p. Avtoreferat dissertatsii na soiskanie uchenoi stepeni kandidata filologicheskikh nauk. PG8661.Z8 PU.

XIII.4.g. STYLE, COMPOSITION, ETC.

2382. BARAUSKAITĖ, Janina. Stilistika imeni sushchestvitel'nogo v sovremennom litovskom iazyke. Vil'nīus, Vil'nīusskii gosudarstvennyi universitet, 1971. 26 p. Avtoreferat dissertatsii na soiskanie uchenoi stepeni kandidata filologicheskikh nauk. PG8571.B3 PU.

2383. GIRDZIJAUSKAS, J. Lietuvių eilėdara. [Lithuanian versification] Vilnius, Lietuvos TSR Aukštojo ir specialiojo vidurinio mokslo ministerija, 1967. 53 p. WU.

2384. PIKČILINGIS, Juozas. Kas yra stilius. [What is style.]. Vilnius, Vaga, 1971. 209 p. PG8637.P51 PU; ICIU.

2385. --- Lietuvių kalbos stilistika. [The stylistic qualities of the Lithuanian language]. Vadovėlis respublikos aukštųjų mokyklų lietuvių kalbos ir literatūros bei žurnalistikos specialybėms. Vilnius,Mintis, 1971-1975- . v. PG8637.P5 PU; CtY; DLC; WU.

2386. RAMONAITĖ, Valerija. Epitetai. Palyginimai. Mokymo priemonė studentams. Šiauliai, 1972. 35 p. PG8641.R3 PU.

2387. STILISTIKA IR LITERATŪRA MOKYKLOJE; iš septintųjų Respubliki-

nių pedagoginių skaitymų. [Stylistics and literature in the school... Sudarė R. Norkevičienė ir A. Šoblinskas] Kaunas, Šviesa, 1969. 43 p. (Mokytojo bibliotekėlė). PG8519.S7 DLC.

2388. VOSYLYTĖ, Klementina. Sravnitel'nue frazeologizmy litovskogo iazyka. Vil'nīus, Vil'nīusskii gos. universitet, 1973. 42 p. Avtoreferat. At head of title: Klementina Vosilite. PG8673.V6 PU.

XIII.4.h. ONOMASTICS; PERSONAL NAMES, ETC.

2389. BUCH, Tamara and JONIKAS, Petras. Die litauischen Flurnamen der Umgegend von Seinai und Suvalkai. Bonn, Ger., Baltisches Forschungsinstitut, 1971. 83-103 p. (Commentationes Balticae, 14/15:2). Offprint:MH; see also serials consulted.

2390. FALK, Knut Olaf. O metodach slavizacji litewskich nazw osobowych i miejscowych; o genezie i rozpowszechnienie nazw na -ance. In Lund. Universitet. Slaviska institutet. Språkliga bidrag. Meddelenden från seminarierna för Slaviska språk..., t.5, nr.22: Miscellanea polonica, 1966, p. 1-16. See serials consulted.

2391. --- Ze studiów nad hydronimią Suwalską: Jeglówek, Jegleweczek, Jegliniec. In Lund. Universitet. Slaviska institutet. Språkliga bidrag. Meddelenden...t.5, nr.22: Miscellanea polonica, 1966, p. 52-61. See serials consulted.

2392. --- Ze studiów nad nazwami jezior Suwalskich: Okmin, Okminek oraz inne dublety hydronimiczne. In Lund. Universitet. Slaviska institut. Språkliga bidrag. Meddelenden... t.5, nr.22: Miscellanea polonica, 1966, p. 26-42. See serials consulted.

2393. FRÖLICH, Gustav. Flussnamen in Ostpreussen. In Zeitschrift der Altertumsgesellschaft, Insterburg, v.19, 1930. CtY; MH; NjP.

2394. HALICKA, Irena. Nazwy miejscowe środkowej i zachodniej Białostoczyzny, dzierżawcze, patronimiczne i rodzinne. Warszawa, PWN, 1976. 239 p. (Rozprawy i monografie, nr.9) PG6576.H3 DLC.

2395. HOFMANN, Erich. Zum ausdrücken der Landwirtschaft in Litauischen. In Die Sprache (Wien), v.7, 1974, p. 123-130. See serials consulted.

2396. JĒGERS, Benjamiņš. Remarks on some Baltic names of tools of the type Lithuanian kaltas-chisel. In Baltic Linguistics (University Park, Pa.), 1970, p. 81-86. See serials consulted.

2397. JONIKAS, Petras. Lietuvos studentų pavardės XV-XVIII amž. Europos universitetuose. [The names of the Lithuanian students in the European universities in 15th-18th centuries]. In Lituanistikos Darbai (Chicago, Ill.), v.3, 1973, p. 201-215. See serials consulted.

2398. KIZLYS-KIZLAITIS, A.D. Kas žlugdė ir žlugdo lietuvių tautą. ; Vinco Žemaičio studijos "Lietuviški vandenvardžiai ir pilkapiai nuo Vyslos iki pat Maskvos"(1972) recenzija. What caused and continues to cause the decline of the Lithuanian nation. Čikaga, Kizlys-Kizlaitis, 1974. 124 p. illus. Summary and table of contents in English. Reprint from "Naujienos" May 2-21, 1973. DK511.L17K56 DLC; CaAEU.

2399. KONDRATIUK, M. Mikrotoponimy litewskie od důgnas, karklynas, vidůgiris w gwarach polskich i bialoruskich Bialostoczyzny. In Acta Baltico-Slavica (Warszawa), no.9,1976, p. 219-224. See serials consulted.

2400. KRAHE, Hans. Baltische Ortsnamen westlich der Weichsel. In Altpreussen; Vierteljahrsschrift (Königsberg), v.8, 1943. See serials consulted.

2401. KUZNETSOV, IŪliĭ Petrovich. Drevniíà dvuosnovnyíà lichnyíà imena u litovtsev, ikh sostav i proiskhozhdenie. S.-Peterburg, Tip. S.N. Khudekova, 1896. 20 p. At head of title: IŪ. P. Kyznetsov. "Otdiel'nyĭ ottisk iz Zhivoĭ Stariny, vyp.1, 1896 g." CS2880.K89 DLC.

2402. LEWY, Ernst. Die altpreussische Personennamen. Inaug.-Diss. --University of Breslau, 1904. 72 p. 491.9.F493 PU; CtY; ICRL; MH; MiU.

2403. NEPOKUPNYĬ, A[natoliĭ Petrovich]. Baltiĭskaia i balto-slavianskaia geograficheskaia terminologiia Belorussii i Ukrainy. In Acta Baltico-Slavica (Warszawa), no.9,1976, p. 99-124. See serials consulted.

2404. PRINZ, Jürgen. Die Slavisierung baltischer und Baltisierung slavischer Ortsnamen im Gebiet des ehemaligen Gouvernements Suwalki. Wiesbaden, Ger., Otto Harrassowitz, 1968. 320 p. map. (Veröffentlichungen der Abteilung für slavische Spra-

chen und Literaturen des Osteuropa-Instituts, Slavisches Seminar, an der Freien Universität Berlin, Bd.34) PG303.P95 CaAEU; CtY; CSt; GU; ICU; InU; INS; LU; MH; MiU; MiDW; MiEM; MnU; MU; NNC; NIC; NSyU; NjP; NcD;NcU; OU; OrU; PPiU; RPB; WaU.

2405. SAFAREWICZ, Jan. Polskie imiona osobowe pochodzenia litewskiego. In Język Polski (Kraków), v.30, 1950. See serials consulted.

2406. SENN, Alfred. Der heutige Stand der Erforschung litauischer Gewässernamen und davon abgeleiteten Ortsnamen. In Akademie der Wissenschaften, Münich. Kommission für Ortsnamenforschung. Studia Onomastica Monascensia, v.4, 1961. See serials consulted.

2407. SKARDŽIUS, Pranas. Lietuvių vandenvardžiai su "nt"; jų daryba, kilmė ir reikšmė. [Lithuanian hydronyms with "nt" and their formatipn...] In Lituanistikos Darbai (Chicago,Ill.) v.3, 1973, p. 9-70. See serials consulted.

2408. VARDAI IR ŽODŽIAI. [Names and words. Sudarė Bronius Savukynas] Vilnius, Mintis, 1971. 244 p. illus. At head of title: LTSR Paminklų apsaugos ir kraštotyros draugija. Lietuvių kalbos sekcija. PG8523.V37 PU; DLC; InU; NjP; OKentU; WU.

2409. ŽEMAITIS, Vincas. Lietuviški vandenvardžiai ir pilkapiai nuo Vyslos iki pat maskvos; lietuvių tautos praeities fragmentai. Lithuanian hydronyms and burial mounds from Vistula to Moscow. [Chicago, Ill., Krumplino-Stulpino spaustuvė, 1972]. 63 p. illus. DK511.L23Z39 DLC; CaAEU; InU; MB.

2410. ZINKEVIČIUS, Zigmas. Lietuvių antroponimika; Vilniaus lietuvių asmenvardžiai XVII a. pradžioje. [Lithuanian anthroponimy; ...]. Vilnius Mokslas, 1977. PG8662.Z5 PU.

XIII.4.i. FOREIGN ELEMENTS IN THE LITHUANIAN LANGUAGE

2411. KOLBUSZEWSKI, Stanisław F. Nowe prace w badaniach nad pożyczkami fińskimi w językach Baltyckich. In Acta Baltico-Slavica (Warszawa), v.8, 1973, p. 145-150. See serials consulted.

2412. PAŽŪSIS, Lionginas. Foneticheskaíà i morfologicheskaíà integratsíà angliĭskikh zaimstvovaniĭ v

litovskom Íazyke Severnoĭ Ameriki.
Vil'nĭus, Vil'nĭusskiĭ gos. universitet, 1971. 19 p. Avtoreferat dissertatsii na soiskanie uchenoĭ stepeni kandidata filologicheskikh nauk. PG8664.E5P3 PU.

XIII.4.k. DICTIONARIES AND LEXICO-
graphy

2413. AMBRASAS, Kazys Juozas.
Leksiniai lietuvių kalbos substitu-
tai. [Lexical substitutes in Lithuanian language]. Vilnius, Vilniaus
universitetas, Leidybinis skyrius,
1976. 106 p. PG8617A55 PU.

2414. --- Nekotorye voprosy sub-
stitutsiĭ litovskogo ĭazyka; v sopostavlenii s angliĭskim v perevod-
cheskom aspekte. Vil'nĭus, Vil'nĭusskiĭ universitet, 1972. 24 p. Avtoreferat dissertatsii na soiskanie
nauchnoĭ stepeni kandidata filologicheskikh nauk. PG8650.A5 PU.

2415. HOFMANN, Erich. Zur litauischen Lexikographie. In Zeitschrift
für vergleichende Sprachforschung...
(Berlin), v.88, p. 291-298. See serials consulted.

2416. IŠ LIETUVIŲ LEKSIKOLOGIJOS
ir leksikografijos. [From the Lithuanian lexicology and lexicography.
Red. kolegija: K. Morkūnas (Ats.red.)
ir kiti]. Vilnius, Mintis, 1970.
206 p. (Lietuvių kalbotyros klausimai, 12). At head of title: Lietuvos TSR Mokslų akademija. Lietuvių
kalbos ir literatūros institutas.
Summaries in Russian. Includes bibliographical references.
PG8501.L5 no.12 DLC; WU.

2417. LEKSIKOS TYRINĖJIMAI, [Lexi-
cological research; collection of
articles. Red. kolegija: J.Kruopas
(ats.red.) ir kiti]. Vilnius, Mintis, 1972. 227 p. (Lietuvių kalbotyros klausimai, 13). At head of
title: Lietuvos TSR Mokslų akademija
Lietuvių kalbos ir literatūros institutas. Summaries in Russian.
PG8501.L5 no.13 DLC; NjP; WU.

2418. LIETUVIŲ TERMINOLOGIJA,
[Lithuanian terms and phrases. Ats.
redaktorius J.Kruopas]. Vilnius,
Mokslas, 1975. 270 p. (Lietuvių kal-
botyros klausimai, 16).
PG8501.L5 no.16 DLC.

2419. SKARDŽIUS, Pranas. Etimolo-
ginio lietuvių kalbos žodyno problemos. Problems of etymological dictionary of the Lithuanian language.

In Institute of Lithuanian Studies.
Lituanistikos instituto 1971 metų su-
važiavimo darbai. Chicago, Ill.,1971.
p. 121-128. Summary in English.
DK511.L2I57 DLC; CaAEU; InNd; MiU;
NIC; NRU; PU.

2420. --- Lietuviški tarptauti-
nių žodžių atitikmenys. [Lithuanian
equivalents of International words].
Čikaga, Pedagoginis lituanistikos
institutas, 1973. 100 p.
PG8664.A3S5 PU; DLC; InNd.

XIII.4. . DIALECTOLOGY: PROVINCIA-
LISMS, ETC.

2421. BARANAUSKAS, Antanas, Bp.,
1835-1902, comp. Litauische Mundarten. Unveränd. Neudruck der Ausg.
von 1920-1922. Niederwalluf bei
Wiebaden, Ger., M. Sändig, 1971. 2
v. At head of title: Sächsische For-
schungsinstitute in Leipzig, Forschungsinstitut für Indogermanistik.
Contents.--Bd.1. Texte. hrsg. von
F.Specht.--Bd.2. Grammatische Ein-
leitung mit lexikalischem Anhang. Bearb. von F. Specht.
PG8688.B37 1971 DLC; NIC; PU.

2422. GRINAVECKIENĖ, Elena. Prie-
balsių minkštėjimo ryšys su galūnių
trumpėjimu Stegvilių tarmėje. [The
connection between the softening of
the consonants and the shortening of
the endings in the dialect of Steg-
vilai]. In Lietuvių kalbotyros klausimai (Vilnius), v.4, 1961, p. 167-
183. PG8501.L5 v.4 DLC; CaAEU; CtY;
CLU; CU; ICU; InU; MH; NN; PU.

2423. --- Prieveiksmiai su forma-
tu -(i)ai šiaurės vakarų aukštaičių
tarmėse. [Adverbs with -(i)ai in the
dialects of the North-West Aukštai-
čiai]. In Lietuvos TSR Mokslų akademija, Vilna. Lietuvių kalbos ir
literatūros institutas. Lietuvių
kalbos morfologinė sandara ir jos raida. Vilnius, 1964. p. 179-186.
PG8501.L5 v.7 DLC; CLU; CtY; CU;ICU;
InU; IU; MH; NN; PU.

2424. GRINAVECKIS, Vladas. Žemaičių tarmių istorija; fonetika. [His-
tory of the Žemaičiai(Samogitian)
dialects...] Vilnius, Mintis, 1973.
370 p. PG8688.G7 DLC; CU; InU; MB;
MiU; OKentU; WU.

2425. KARDELYTĖ, Jadvyga. Gervė-
čių tarmė; fonetika ir morfologija.
[Dialect of Gervėčiai...]. Vilnius,
Mintis, 1975. 143 p.
PG8693.K3 PU; DLC.

2426. OTRĘBSKI, Jan Szczepan. Le dialecte lituanien nord-est de la paroisse de Twerecz. In Polska akademia umiejętności, Kraków. Bulletin international de l'Academie des sciences de Cracovie. Classe de Philologie.... 1929, p. 67-79. See serials consulted.

2427. SENKUS, J[uozas]. Kai kurie ryškesnieji linksnių vartojimo atvejai pazanavykio Kapsų tarmėje. [Some examples of the usage of the cases in the Pazanavykių-Kapsų dialect]. In Lietuvos TSR Mokslų akademija, Vilna. Darbai. Serija A, 2(7), p. 177-189, 1959. Mr. B. Kviklys, Chicago, has it; see also serials consulted.

2428. --- Prielinksnių vartojimas bei svarbesniosios jų reikšmės kapsų ir zanavykų tarmėse. [The usage of prepositions and their more important meanings in Kapsų-Zanavykų dialects]. In Lietuvos TSR Mokslų akademija, Vilna. Darbai. Serija A, no.1(8), 1960, p. 125-150. See serials consulted.

2429. SUDNIK, T.M. Dialekty litovsko-slavi͡anskogo pogranich'i͡a; ocherki fonologicheskikh sistem. Moskva, Nauka, 1975. 229 p.,[4] fold. leaves. illus. At head of title: Akademii͡a nauk SSSR. Institut slavi͡anovedenii͡a i balkanistiki. PG2834.1.S85 DLC.

2430. ŠUTŲ ŠNEKTOS TEKSTAI. [Texts of the Šutų dialect] [Redakcinė komisija:... A.Girdenis (pirmininkas)...]. Vilnius, Lietuvos TSR Aukštojo ir specialiojo vidurinio mokslo ministerijos Leidybinė redakcinė taryba, 1977. 124 p. PG8693.S8S8 PU.

2431. URNEVIČIŪTĖ, Žaneta. Oppozit͡sii͡a tverdykh i mi͡agkikh soglasnykh i ee razvitie v aukshtaĭtskikh dialektakh litovskogo i͡azyka. Vil'ni͡us, Vil'ni͡usskiĭ gos. universitet, 1970. 17 p. Avtoreferat dissertat͡sii na soiskanie uchenoĭ stepeni kandidata filologicheskikh nauk. PG8688.U7 PU.

2432. VITKAUSKAS, Vytautas. Morfofonematicheskie dialektizmy v govorach zhemaitov dunininkov. Vil'ni͡us, Vil'ni͡usskiĭ gos. universitet, 1974. 42 p. Avtoreferat dissertat͡sii na soiskanie uchenoĭ stepeni kandidata filologicheskikh nauk. PG8693.S3V5 PU.

2432a. WOLTER, E. Zur litauische Dialektkunde. I: Die Litauer im Kreise Slonim (Slanimas). Gouv.Grodno

(Gardinas); II: Zur Kunde der Wilnaer litauischen Dialekte. In Litauische Litterarische Gesellschaft, Tilsit. Mitteilungen (Heidelberg, Ger.) Bd.4, 1899, p. 166-187. See serials consulted.

XIII.5. LITERATURE

XIII.5.a. BIBLIOGRAPHIES

2433. BUFIENĖ, Teklė. Lietuvos TSR rašytojai, literatūrinių premijų laureatai; rekomenduojamosios literatūros rodyklė. [The writers of Soviet Lithuania who received the literary awards; recomended bibliography]. Vilnius, 1969. 187 p. ports. Z2537.B93 DLC; MH; NNC; PU.

2434. DAGYTĖ, Emilija. Tarybų Lietuvos rašytojai; biografinis žodynas. [Soviet Lithuanian authors; biography. Žodyno autorė Emilija Dagytė ir Danutė Straukaitė. Redaktorius Viktoras Beržinis] Vilnius, Vaga, 1975. 190 p.,[4] leaves of plates. ports. PG8709.D3 DLC; PU.

2435. JUREVIČIŪTĖ, I[rena] and JUODPALYTĖ, Genovaitė. Grožinė literatūra, 1961-1970; katalogas: Literatūra, dailė, muzika. [Belles lettres of 1961-1970; a catalogue: literature art and music].Vilnius, Vaga, 1972. 542 p. Z2537.J87 DLC; MB; WU; PU.

2436. KEBLIENĖ, Stefa. Tarybinių tautų rašytojai lietuvių kalba, 1940-1970; bio-bibliografija. [Soviet Lithuanian authors in Lithuanian language; a bio-bibliography]. Vilnius, Lietuvos TSR valstybinė respublikinė biblioteka, 1973. 415 p. At head of title: Lietuvos TSR Valstybinė respublikinė biblioteka. Z2537.K41 PU; DLC; WU; PU.

2437. KUCHARZEWSKI, Jan. Czasopiśmiennictwo polskie wieku XIX w Królestwie, na Litwie i Rusi oraz na emigracyi; zarys bibliograficzno-historyczny... Warszawa, Gebethner i Wolff, 1911. 121 p. Repr.: Przegląd Narodowy. *QO p.v.p.12, no.2-- NN.

2438. LEVICKAITĖ, Danutė. Lietuvių rašytojai vaikams (proza). [Lithuanian authors of childrens literature]. Vilnius, Lietuvos TSR Valstybinė respublikinė biblioteka, Vaikų literatūros skyrius, 1972. 112 p. Z2537.L4 PU.

2439. LIETUVOS TSR MOKSLŲ AKADEMI-

JA, Vilna. LIETUVIŲ KALBOS IR LITE-
RATŪROS INSTITUTAS. Lietuvių literatūros mokslas ir kritika, 1971-1973;
bibliografinė rodyklė. [Lithuanian
literature and criticism, 1971-1973;
a bibliography. Sudarė Eugenijus
Stancikas. Redagavo Jonas Vosylius].
Vilnius, Vaga, 1976. 428 p. Sequel
to: Tarybinis lietuvių literatūros
mokslas ir kritika apie literatūrinį
palikimą and Tarybinė lietuvių literatūra ir kritika. Z2537.L517 PU.

2440. --- Tarybinis lietuvių literatūros mokslas ir kritika apie
literatūrinį palikimą, 1959-1970;
bibliografinė rodyklė. [Soviet Lithuanian literature and criticism, 1959-
1970; a bibliography. Sudarė Eugenijus Stancikas. Redagavo Jonas Vo-
sylius]. Vilnius, Vaga, 1975. 430 p.
Z2537.L516 PU.

2441. LITAUISCHE LITERATUR.
Tilsit, 1912. In Allgemeine Litauische Rundschau (Tilsit), Jahrg.3,
1912, p. 30-32. *QYA--NN(3).

2442. ŠIUPŠINSKIENĖ, Klara. Pje-
sės; bibliografinė rodyklė, 1945-1970.
[Drama; a bibliography, 1945-1970].
Vilnius, Lietuvos TSR Valstybinė res-
publikinė biblioteka, 1972. 179 p.
Z2537.S57 PU.

2443. STANCIKAS, Eugenijus. Cancelled.

XIII.5.b. HISTORY AND CRITICISM

XIII.5.b.1. TREATISES, ESSAYS, AND SPECIAL TOPICS

2444. ALANTAS, Vytautas. Lietuvio rašytojo misija tremtyje. [The
mission of the Lithuanian writer in
exile]. In Naujoji Viltis (Chicago,
Ill.), no.4, 1972, p. 20-29. See
serials consulted.

2445. AMBRAZEVIČIUS, Juozas. Naujosios lietuvių literatūros idėjinės
ir forminės linkmės. [The new ideolo-
gical and form trends in Lithuanian
literature]. In LKMASD, v.2, 1973,
p. 233-246. See serials consulted.

2446. AREŠKA, Vitas. Tradicija
ir ieškojimai. [Tradition and search
for something new]. Vilnius, Vaga,
1973. 411. PG8709.A7 PU; DLC; WU.

2447. AUGULYTĖ, Vida and ČERNIUS,
Rimas, and MASILIONIS, Juozas. Lietuvių literatūra; trumpas lietuvių
literatūros kursas su chrestomatija

aukštesniosios lituanistinės mokyklos
aštuntajai klasei. [Lithuanian literature; an autline...] Čikaga, JAV
Lietuvių bendruomenės Švietimo taryba, 1977. 376 p. At head of title:
V. Augulytė, R. Černius, J. Masilionis. PG8703.A8 PU.

2448. BALTARAGIS, Andrius. Vincas
Krėvė Lietuvoje; jo sovietinio trak-
tavimo raida 1940-1965. [V. Krėvė in
Lithuania and Soviet interpretation
of his works, 1940-1965]. In Metmenys (Chicago, Ill.), no.10, 1965, p.
61-82. See serials consulted.

2449. BALTRŪNAS, Aleksas. Keliai -
artimi ir tolimi; apybraižos, esės,
literatūros kritika. [...outlines,
essays and literary criticism]. Vilnius, Vaga, 1977. 213 p.
PG8701.B3 PU.

2450. BASANAVIČIUS, Jonas. Rinktiniai raštai. [Selected works of J.
Basanavičius. Paruošė D. Krištopai-
tė]. Vilnius, Vaga, 1970. xxiv,
1036 p. illus., facsims., ports.(Lituanistinė biblioteka)
PG8703.B32 1970 DLC; InU; InNd; MiU;
NN.

2451. BIRŽIŠKA, Mykolas. Mūsų
raštų istorija. II dalis: 1864-1904.
2. leidimas. [History of our literature, 1864-1904] Kaunas, Švyturio
bendrovė, 1925. 144 p. WU.

2452. BRAŽĖNAS, Petras. Ties dešimčių riba. Vilnius, Vaga, 1974.
269,[2] p. PG8701.B7 PU.

2453. BŪTĖNAS, Julius. Istoriogra-
fo užrašai. [Notes of a historiogra-
pher]. Vilnius, Vaga, 1974. 374 p.
PG8703.B8 DLC; PU.

2454. --- Literato duona. [Life
of the author]. Vilnius, Vaga, 1975.
277 p. DK511.L28B88 PU; DLC; WU.

2455. CIPLIJAUSKAITĖ, Birutė. Old
themes experienced anew in recent Lithuanian poetry. In Journal of Baltic Studies (Brooklyn, N.Y.), no.2/3,
v.6, 1975, p. 190-197. See serials
consulted.

2456. ČIURLIONIENĖ, Sofija (Kyman-
taitė), ed. Lietuvių literatūros istorijos konspekto chrestomatija. [An
outline of the history of Lithuanian
literature]. Voronežas, Russia,1918.
86 p. WU.

2457. DEVOTO, Giacomo. Le letterature dei paesi baltici:Finlandia,
Estonia, Lettonia, Lituania. Nuova
edizione aggiornata. Firenze, Sanso-
ni; Milano, Accademia, 1969. 570 p.

(Le letterature del mondo, 26). Published in 1957 under title: Storia delle letterature baltiche. Partial contents.---La letteratura lituana, di A.Senn. Bibliography: p. 529-536. PH302.D4 1969 DLC; CtY; IU; NcD;NjP.

2458. --- Storia delle letterature baltiche. Milano, Nuova accadeia, 1957. 430 p. col.map. (Thesaurus litterarum. Sezione 1: Storia delle letterature di tutto il mondo). "Nota bibliografica relativa alla letteratura lituana": p. 427-428. CLU;CSt; CU; InU; MH; NN; NjP; NcD; PU; TNJ.

2459. GALINIS, V[ytautas]. Literatūra, dabartis, žmogus. [Literature and man in the present]. Vilnius, Vaga, 1966. PN779.L6G3 DLC; CtY; MH; NN; PU.

2460. --- Naujos kryptys lietuvių literatūroje; nuo simbolistų iki trečiafrontininkų. [The new trends in Lithuanian literature...]. Vilnius, Vaga, 1974. 497 p. PG8709.G32 PU; DLC; NjP.

2461. --- Novye napravleniîa v litovskoî literature 1917-1932. Vil'nîus, Vil'nîusskiî gos. universitet, 1971. 37 p. Avtoreferat dissertatsii na soiskanie uchenoî stepeni doktora filologicheskikh nauk. PG8709.G325 PU.

2462. GINEITIS, Leonas. Klasicizmo problema lietuvių literatūroje. [On the problem of classicism in the Lithuanian literature]. Vilnius, Vaga, 1972. 315 p. At head of title: Lietuvos TSR Mokslų akademija. Lietuvių kalbos ir literatūros institutas. PG8709.G5 PU; DLC; CtY;IU;InU; MH; NNC; OKentU; PPiU; PU; WU.

2463. GISEVIUS, Eduard Karl Samuel. Der literarische Nachlass. Tilsit, 1881. 491.922G448 PU.

2464. GLIAUDYS, Jurgis. Bandymas atrasti mūsų prozos esmę. [An attempt to discover the essence of our prose] In Naujoji Viltis (Chicago, Ill.), no.1, 1970, p. 66-80. See serials consulted.

2465. GRAŽYTĖ-MAZILIAUSKIENĖ, Ilona. Herojus lietuvių prozoje. The heroe in contemporary Lithuanian prose]. In Institute of Lithuanian Studies. Lituanistikos instituto 1971 metų suvažiavimo darbai. Chicago, Ill., 1971. p. 149-159. DK511.L2I62 1971 CaAEU; DLC; ICBM; InNd; MiU; NIC; NRU; PU; WU.

2466. GRINIUS, Jonas. Veidai ir problemos lietuvių literatūroje. [Faces and problems in Lithuanian literature]. Roma, Lietuvių katalikų mokslo akademija, 1973-1977. 2 v. At head of title, v.1- : Lietuvių katalikų mokslo akademija. PG8701.G7 DLC; NN; PU.

2467. GUDAITIS, Leonas. Pervyî litovskiî literaturnyî zhurnal "Vaîvorikshte", 1913-1914. Vil'nîus, Vil'nîusskiî gos. universitet, 1975. 22 p. Avtoreferat dissertatsii na soiskanie uchenoî stepeni kandidata filologicheskikh nauk. PG8501.V335G8 PU.

2468. --- Platėjantys akiračiai; lietuvių literatūrinė spauda 1904-1917 metais. Vilnius, Vaga, 1977. 440 p. [Publications of Lithuanian literature 1904-1917] PG8709.G8 PU

2469. JASENAS, Eliane. Prosper Mérimée and Lithuania. In Journal of Baltic Studies (Brooklyn, N.Y.), n.2, v.8, p. 150-161. See serials consulted.

2470. JOSADĖ, J[okūbas]. Knyga ir tikrovė. [The Book and reality]. Vilnius, Valstybinė grožinės literatūros leidykla, 1961. 203 p. PG8703.J6 DLC; MH; PU.

2471. KORSAKAS, Kostas. Puškino poveikis lietuvių literatūrai. [Pushkin's influence on Lithuanian literature]. Vilnius, Valstybinė politinės ir mokslinės literatūros leidykla, 1949. 34 p. PG3335.7.L5K6 PU.

2472. --- Rašytojai ir knygos; trečia kritikos knyga. [Writers and books; third book of literary criticism. By K. Korsakas-Radžvilas. Kaunas], Spaudos Fondas, 1940. [Xerox copy, 1974]. PG8701.K61 PU.

2473. KORSAKIENĖ, Halina. Susitikimaî; įspūdžiai ir mintys. [...impressions and ideas]. Vilnius, Vaga, 1977. 379 p. PG8709.K68 PU.

2474. LANKUTIS, Jonas. Lietuvių dramaturgijos raida. [The development of Lithuanian drama]. Vilnius, Vaga, 1974. 441 p. illus. At head of title: Lietuvos TSR Mokslų akademija. Lietuvių kalbos ir literatūros institutas. Summary in Russian. Table of contents also in English. PG8709.L24 DLC; PU; CaAEU; NjP.

2475. LEBEDYS, Jurgis. Lituanistikos baruose. [In the field of Lithuanian linguistics and literature. Paruošė J. Girdzijauskas]. Vilnius, Vaga, 1972. 2 v., 11 leaves of illus. Includes bibliographical references.

Contents.--t.1. Studijos ir straip-
sniai.--t.2. Recenzijos, paskaitos.
PG8701.L4 DLC; CLU; CtY; CU; ICU; IU
InU; MH; MiU; NNC; NjP; OKentU; PU;
TxU; WU.

2476. --- Senoji lietuvių lite-
ratūra. [Older Lithuanian literature]
[Paruošė J. Girdzijauskas]. Vilnius,
Mokslas, 1977. 361 p.
PG8703.L4 PU.

2477. LENINAS LIETUVIŲ LITERATŪ-
roje. [Lenin in Lithuanian literatu-
re]. Vilnius, Vaga, 1970. 407 p.
PG8709.L4 DLC; CU; InU; MH; NNC: PU.

2478. LIETUVIŲ POETIKOS TYRINĖJI-
MAI. [Research of Lithuanian poetry.
Ats. redaktorius Ambr. Jonynas].
Vilnius, Vaga, 1974. 493 p. (Litera-
tūra ir kalba, 8). At head of title;
Lietuvos TSR Mokslų akademija. Lietu-
vių kalbos ir literatūros institutas.
Lithuanian and Russian.
PG8709.L485 DLC.

2479. LIETUVOS TSR MOKSLŲ AKADEMI-
JA, Vilna. LIETUVIŲ LITERATŪROS INS-
TITUTAS. Puškinas ir lietuvių literatūra. [Pushkin and Lithuanian lite-
rature]. Redagavo K. Korsakas. Vilnius, Valstybinė grožinės literatūros leidykla, 1950. 147 p. illus.
PG3355.7.L5L5 PU; DLC.

2480. LINGIS, Juozas. Kompendium
i äldre litauisk litteraturhistoria.
[Utg.av] Stockholms universitet, Slaviska institutionen, baltiska språk.
Stockholm, 1973. ii, 95 leaves,[7]
leaves of plates. illus.
PG8703.L5 DLC; MH; PU.

2481. LOEBER, Dietrich A. Baltic
authors under Soviet law; regular
publishing and Samizdat. In Conference on Baltic Studies, 3d, University of Toronto, 1972. Problems of
mininations... San Jose, Calif.1973.
p. 175-192. HC243.C65 1972 DLC;
CaAEU; CaBVaU; CtY; CSt; CU; GAT; IU;
ICIU; InU; ICarbS; InNd; MB; MH; MiU;
NN; NNC; NBuC; NBuU; NjP; NmU; OkU;
RPB; UU; WaU; WU.

2482. MACIŪNAS, Vincas. Lietuviškoji "marseljetė". [The Lithuanian
"Marseillaise". In Literatūra (Chicago, Ill.), kn.2, 1954.
Balt.9601.258.5 MH; PU; WU; see also
offprint: 891.92B2295.yM PU.

2483. MARTINAITIS, Marcelijus. Po-
ezija ir žodis. [Poetry and the word]
Vilnius, Vaga, 1977. 245 p.
PG8709.M33 PU.

2484. MASIONIENĖ, Birutė. Lev
Tolstoi i Litva 1887-1940. Vil'nius,
Vil'niusskii gos. universitet, 1971.

15 p. Avtoreferat dissertatsii na
soiskanie uchenoi stepeni kandidata
filologicheskikh nauk.
PG3409.7.L5M3 PU.

2485. MATULIS, Anatole C. The Bal-
tic-Lithuanian culture in German literature; a retrospective and pros-
pective view. In Journal of Baltic
Studies (Brooklyn, N.Y.), no.2, v.4,
1973, p. 135-142. See serials consulted.

2486. --- Alexander Solzhenitsyn
and the Baltic peoples. In Journal
of Baltic Studies (Brooklyn, N.Y.),
no.2, v.3, 1972, p. 124-132. See
serials consulted.

2487. MIŠKINIS, Motiejus. Lietuvių literatūra. 1.dalis. [Lithuanian
literature. Part 1. Kaunas], Spaudos Fondas, 1939. [Xerox copy,1977].
358 p. No more published.
PG8703.M55 1939a PU.

2488. NASTOPKA, Kęstutis. Lietuvių ir latvių literatūrų ryšiai. [Ties
of Lithuanian and Latvian literature]
Vilnius, Vaga, 1971. 413 p.
PG8709.N35 PU.

2489. NAUJOKAITIS, Pranas. Lietu-
vių literatūros istorija. [History of
Lithuanian literature]. Brooklyn,N.Y.,
JAV LB Kultūros Fondas, 1973-1976. 4 v.
Partial contents.--t.1. Nuo Mažvydo
iki Maironio.
PG8703.N35 DLC; WU.

2490. --- Lietuvių tautinę samo-
nę ugdžiusi literatūra. [The literature which has influenced the Lithuanian national consciousness]. In Tėvynės Sargas (New York, N.Y.), no.1,
1970, p.45-54. See serials consulted.

2491. NORKUS, Jonas, ed. Lietuvių
literatūros nagrinėjimai. [Analysis
of Lithuanian literature]. Parinko
mokyklai J. Norkus. Kaunas, Spaudos
Fondas, 1928. 294 p. Collection of
articles. OCl; PU.

2492. PETRAS CVIRKA LITERATŪROS
moksle ir kritikoje. [P. Cvirka literary man and critic. Sudarė Rimantė
Umbrasaitė] Vilnius, Vaga, 1977.
353 p. PG8721.C8Z8 PU.

2493. POLSKII ROMANTIZM I BALTIIS-
kie literatury. Vil'nius, Mintis,
1973. 42 p. WU.

2494. PRANSKUS, Bronius. Laikas
ir literatūra. [The time and literature. Sudarė B. Preskienis ir A.
Sprindis. Red. komisija: J.Bielinis
et al.]. Vilnius, Vaga, 1973. 489 p.
PG8701.P7 PU; DLC; WU.

2495. PRONCKUS, E., comp. Kristi-
jono Donelaičio jubiliejiniai metai.
[The jubilee year of K. Donelaitis].
Sudarė E. Pronckus ir J. Petronis.
Redakcinė komisija: K. Doveika et al.
Vilnius, Vaga, 1965. 245 p. illus.,
facsim., ports. Summary in Russian,
German and English.
PG8721.D7 DLC; CtY; IU; MH; PU.

2496. RAILA, Bronys. Paguoda.
[Consolation. London, Eng.], Nida,
1974-1975. 3 v. (His Akimirksnių
kronikos, 4)(Nidos knygų klubo leidinys, nr. 91) PG8701.R3 PU; DLC.

2497. RIŠKUS, Jonas. Lietuvių literatūros vadovėlis IX klasei. [Text-
book of Lithuanian literature for
the Grade 9. 2.leidimas]. Kaunas,
Šviesa, 1971. 278 p. illus.
PG8703.R5 1971 DLC; MB; PU.

2498. SENOSIOS LIETUVIŲ LITERATŪ-
ros baruose. [In the field of old Lithuanian literature. Sudarė J. Zin-
kus]. Vilnius, 1971. 222 p. illus.
At head of title: LTSR Aukštojo ir
specialiojo vidurinio mokslo ministerija. Vilniaus V. Kapsuko universitetas. Lietuvių literatūros katedra.
PG8701.S4 DLC; MH; NNC; OKentU; PU;
WU.

2499. ŠEPKUS, Lionginas. Lietuvių literatūros vadovėlis XI klasei.
[Textbook of Lithuanian literature
for the Grade 11. 6.leidimas]. Kaunas, Šviesa, 1968. 318 p. illus.
PG8703.S4 1968 DLC; PU.

2500. ŠEŠPLAUKIS, Alfonsas. Sha-
kespearian traits in Lithuanian literature. In Lituanus (Chicago, Ill.),
no.3, v.16, 1970, p. 5-33. See serials consulted.

2501. --- Lithuanians in Upton
Sinclair's "The Jungle". In Lituanus (Chicago, Ill.), no.2, v.23,
1977, p. 24-31. See serials consulted.

2502. --- , comp. Nemarioji žemė;
Lietuva pasaulinės poezijos posmuose.
Antologija. [... Lithuania in World
poetry; anthology]. Sudarė Alfonsas
Tyruolis, [pseud.]. Boston, Mass.
Lietuvių enciklopedijos leidykla,
1970. 176 p. PN6109.L5S4 DLC;InNd;
MB.

2503. SIDERAVIČIUS, Rimantas.
Aleksandras Puškinas ir Lietuva. [A.
Pushkin and Lithuania]. Vilnius, Va-
ga, 1976. 301 p. PG3355.7.L5S49 PU.

2504. --- Tvorchestvo Pushkina v
Litve. Vil'nius, Vil'niusskii gos.
universitet, 1972. 16 p. Avtoreferat dissertatsii na soiskanie uchenoi

stepeni kandidata filologicheskikh
nauk. PG3355.7.L5S5 PU.

2505. ŠILBAJORIS, Rimvydas. Notes
on Lithuanian poetry. In Lituanus
(Chicago, Ill.), no.2, v.19, 1973,
p. 5-15. See serials consulted.

2506. ŠIMKUS, Jonas. Apie literatūrą. [About literature]. Vilnius,
Vaga, 1956. 380 p. 891.92HSi44 PU.

2507. --- Apie žmones, įvykius ir
save; dienoraščiai, laiškai, atsiminimai. [About people, happenings and
myself; diaries, letters and recollections. Paruošė K. Doveika]. Vilnius,
Vaga, 1971. 538 p.
PG8721.S48Z5 PU; DLC; NNC.

2508. SLUCKIS, Mykolas. Nachalo
vsekh nachal; stat'i, literaturnye
portrety. M.Slutskis. Per. s litov.
B. Zalesskoi. Moskva, Sov. pisatel',
1975. 316 p. illus. PG8703.S57 DLC
WU.

2509. SPALIS, R[omualdas], pseud.
Jaunimas mūsų literatūroje. [Youth in
our literature]. In Varpas (Brooklyn, N.Y.), no11, 1972, p. 111-120.
Serials consulted.

2510. STOBERSKI, Zygmunt. Historia literatury litewskiej; zarys.
Wrocław, Zakład Narodowy im. Ossolińskich, 1974. 231 p. illus., facsims.,
ports. PG8703.S8 CaAEU; DLC; IU;
MiDW; NNC; PU; ViU; WU; WaU.

2511. STUDNICKI, Wacław Gizbert.
Mickiewicz and his country. [Trans-
lated from Polish by Thomas J. Wosi-
kowski. Chicago, Ill., 1955.]. 7 p.
illus. PG7158.M5Z9287 DLC.

2512. UŽKALNIS, Petras. Nuo Rudaki iki Donelaičio. [From Rudaki until Donelaitis]. Vilnius, Vilniaus
universitetas, 1969-1972. 2 v.
PN849.R9U93 PU; CU; ICU; InU; IU;
DLC; MiU; OKentU.

2513. VAIČIULAITIS, Antanas. Li-
thuanian literature. In New Catholic
Encyclopedia. New York, 1967. v.8,
p. 845-850. BX841.N53 v.8 CaAEU;AAP;
CtY-D; CBPaC; CMenSP; CSaT; CoU; DAU;
DPU; DSI; FTaSU; GAT; GU; IaU; IdU;
ICU; IEG; IEN; KEmT; KU; KyLxCB; KyU;
LU; MB; MeB; MiU; MnU; MoU; MsSM;MtU;
N; NNC; NSyU; NcD; NNMM; NjPT; NbU;
OO; OCH; OKentU; OCl; ODW; OOxM; OrU;
OrPS; OrStbM; PPULC; PU; ScU; SBGTU;
TU; Wa.

2514. VALIUKĖNAS, Dalija J. Jurgis Baltrušaitis and William Blake;
a brief comparison. In Lituanus (
Chicago, Ill.), no.1, v.20, 1974,

p. 58-76. See serials consulted.

2515. --- Jurgis Baltrušaitis ir William Blake; tarp mistikos ir humanizmo. Jurgis Baltrušaitis and William Blake: between misticism and humanism. In Institute of Lithuanian Studies. Lituanistikos instituto 1973 metų suvažiavimo darbai. Chicago, Ill., 1975. p. 147-162. Summary in English. DK511.L2I63 1975 CaAEU; PU.

2516. VENCLOVA, Antanas. Apie gyvenimą ir rašytojo darbą; kritikos straipsniai. [The life and the author; a collection of articles. Sudarė V. Galinis]. Vilnius, Vaga, 1976. 682 p. PG8701.V41 PU.

2517. --- Jaunystės atradimas. [Discovery of the adolescence]. Vilnius, Vaga, 1970. 642 p., 25 leaves of illus. PG9721.V4J3 1970 DLC;IU; ICIU.

2518. --- V poiskakh molodosti; vospominaniĩa. Moskva, Sov. pisatel', 1969. 376 p. illus. At head of title: Antanas Ventslova. PG8721.V4J317 DLC; CSt; CU; IU; MH; NN; NIC; NjP.

2519. ZALATORIUS, Albertas. Lietuvių apsakymo raida ir poetika.[The development of Lithuanian prose and poetry]. Vilnius, Vaga, 1971. 362 p. At head of title: Lietuvos TSR Mokslų akademija. Lietuvių kalbos ir Literatūros institutas. PG8709.Z5 PU; CLU; DLC; IU; NjP; PPiU; PU; OU; WU.

2520. ŽIRGULYS, Aleksandras. Literatūros keliuose; memuarinės-biografinės apybraižos. [In the literary field; biographical sketches]. DK511.L28A185 PU.

XIII.5.b.2. BY PERIOD TO 1944

2521. PRANSKUS, Bronius. Devynioliktojo amžiaus lietuvių poezija. [Lithuanian poetry of the 19th century]. In His Lietuvių poezija XIX amžiaus. Vilnius, 1955. p.5-[26]. 891.921P ICCC; CtPAM; ICLJF; NN.

2522. RIŠKUS, Jonas and UMBRASAS, Kazys. Literatura litewska: literatura XIV-XVII w.; literatura drugiej polowy XIX w. In Literatura dla klasy IX. By E. Kuosaitė-Jašinskienė, M. Remberg, M. Nielžwiecka, J. Riškus, K. Umbrasas [and] L.Walkūnas. Kaunas, Šviesa, 1968. p. 175-[240]. PN507.L77 CaAEU.

2523. TUMAS, Juozas. Tremtiniai,
romantininkai. [The exiles, novelists] [By] Vaižgantas, [pseud.]. Kaune, Hum. mokslų fakulteto leidinys, 1929. [Xerox copy, 1976]. 324 p. (Vaižganto raštai, t.11) PG8701.T83 1929a PU(xerox).

2425. --- Beletristai. [By] Vaižgantas,[pseud.]. Kaune, Hum. mokslų fakulteto leidinys, 1929. [Xerox copy, 1975]. 318 p. (Vaižganto raštai, t.13). PG8703.T76 1929a PU.

2525. VYKINTAS, Stepas. Naujosios mūsų literatūros keliai. [The trends of our contemporary literature]. In Kemežys, V., ed. Lietuva 1918-1938. Kaunas, 1938. 947.52L625 PU; CtTMF ICLJF; ICCC.

XIII.5.b.3. THE SOVIET PERIOD

2526. AMBRASAS, Kazys. Kritikos etiudai. [Reviews of Lithuanian literature]. Vilnius, Vaga, 1976. 669 p. PG8701.A55 PU.

2527. --- Pažangioji lietuvių kritika. [The advanced Lithuanian criticism]. Vilnius, Vaga, 1966. 359 p. At head of title: K. Ambrasas. Bibliography: p. 304-[345]. PG8703.A54 DLC; CtY; IU; ICIU; MH; NN.

2528. BALTAKIS, Algimantas. Poetų cechas; pastabos apie šiuolaikinę lietuvių poeziją. [The poets; comments on contemporary Lithuanian poetry]. Vilnius, Vaga, 1975. 489 p. PG8709.B33 PU.

2529. BUČYS, Algimantas. Romanas ir dabartis; lietuvių tarybinio romano raida iki 1970 m. (Žanro problemos). [Novel and the present time; development of the Soviet Lithuanian novel up to 1970]. Vilnius, Vaga, 1973. 430 p. Bibliography: p. 423-[427]. PG8709.B8 PU; DLC; InU; IU; NjP. WU.

2530. BŪTĖNAS, Julius. Lietuvių literatūros vadovėlis vidurinėms mokykloms. [Lithuanian literature; a textbook...]. Kaunas, Valstybinė pedagoginės literatūros leidykla,1957- PG8701.B82 OKentU; WU.

2531. DOVEIKA, Kostas. Lietuvių rašytojai Didžiajame Tėvynės kare. [The Lithuanian authors in the Great Patriotic War]. Vilnius, Vaga, 1967. 326 p. illus. PG8709.D6 DLC; CtY; CU; IU; MiEM; MH; NN; NjP; PU.

2532. GRICIUS, Augustinas. Laiko dvasia. Kaunas, Valstybinė grožinės literatūros leidykla, 1946. 217 p.   891.92G873L PU; DLC; WU.

2533. JURAŠIENĖ, Aušra Marija. The problem of creative artistic expression in contemporary Lithuania. In Lituanus (Chicago, Ill.), no.3, v. 22, 1976, p.48. See serials consulted.

2534. KELERTAS, Violeta. Language in contemporary Lithuanian narrative. In Lituanus (Chicago, Ill.), no.4, v.23, 1977, p. 33-44. See serials consulted.

2535. KUBILIUS, Vytautas. Literatura i zhizn'. In Sovetskaīa Litva; almanakh (Vilnius), kn.11, 1965, p. 107-119. PG8771.R1S6 DLC; CtY; CU; MH; NNC; PU.

2536. LANKUTIS, Jonas. Panorama litovskoī sovetskoī literatury. Ionas Lankutis. Vil'nīus, Vaga, 1975. 138 p.   PG8703.L33 DLC; WU.

2537. --- Panorama of Soviet Lithuanian literature. [Translated by V. Vladyko]. Vilnius, Vaga, 1975. 122 p.   PG8703.L313 DLC; WU.

2538. LIETUVIŠKO ŽODŽIO ATGARSIAI; rusų tarybinė kritika apie lietuvių literatūrą. [...Soviet Russian criticism of Lithuanian literature. Vertimas į lietuvių kalbą. Sudarė Stasys Lipskis]. Vilnius, Vaga, 1976. 500 p.   PG8701.L5 PU.

2539. LIETUVIŲ LITERATŪRINIAI RYŠiai ir sąveikos; straipsniai, recenzijos, apžvalgos, archyvinė medžiaga. [Connections and influences on Lithuanian literature; articles, reviews, etc. Ats. red. K. Doveika]. Vilnius, Vaga, 1969. 526 p. (Literatūra ir Kalba, 10). At head of title: Lietuvos TSR Mokslų akademija. Lietuvių kalbos ir literatūros institutas. Contributions in Lithuanian and Russian. MH.

2540. LIETUVOS TSR MOKSLŲ AKADEMIJA, Vilna. LIETUVIŲ KALBOS IR LITERATŪROS INSTITUTAS. Lietuvių literatūros kritika. [Critical review of Lithuanian literature. Redagavo K. Korsakas, K. Doveika]. Vilnius, Vaga, 1971-1972. 2 v. PG8709.L53 PU; CaBVaU; CSt; CU; DLC; ICIU; IU; MB; MH; MiU; NN; NNC; NIC; NjP; OKentU; OU; PPiU; PU; WU.

2541. LINKEVIČIUS, Jonas. Sovetskaīa litovskaīa detskaīa poēziīa, 1940-1970 gg. Vil'nīus, Vil'nīusskiī gos. universitet, 1971. 24 p. Avtoreferat disertatsii na soiskanie u-chenoī stepeni kandidata filologicheskikh nauk. PN1009.L5L52 PU.

2542. --- Vaikų poezijos dešimtmečiai; tarybinės lietuvių vaikų poezijos ištakos, formavimasis ir raida. [Decades of children literature; the development of the Soviet Lithuanian children's literature]. Vilnius, Vaga, 1972. 306 p. PN1009.L5L53 PU; DLC; MH.

2543. LIPSKIS, Stasys. Dialogas su herojumi; penki apmąstymai apie literatūrą ir gyvenimą. [Dialogue with the hero; five deliberations about literature and life]. Vilnius, Vaga, 1972. 113 p. PG8701.L56 PU; MH.

2544. --- Litovskaīa literatura 1975; spravochnik. Vil'nīus, Vaga, 1977. 142 p.,[8] leaves of plates. illus. PG8703.L56 DLC; PU.

2545. --- ŠIUOLAIKINĖS APYSAKOS horizontai; etiudai apie 1960-1975 metų lietuvių tarybinę apysaką. [The horizons of contemporary short stories; a study about the Soviet Lithuanian short story for the years 1960-1975]. PG8709.L54 PU.

2546. MACIJAUSKIENĖ, Marija. Nematomas tiltas. [Invisible ties]. Vilnius, Mintis, 1976. 123 p. PG8701.M3 PU.

2547. OZEROV, Lev Adol'fovich. Žvelgiant į saulę. Knyga apie lietuvių poeziją ir dar kai ką. [About Lithuanian poets and their poetry...]. Vilnius, Vaga, 1969. 200 p. At head of title: Levas Ozerovas. PG8709.Op DLC; CaAEU.

2548. ROSTOVAITĖ, Tatjana. Heroika ir svajonė; apie lietuvių tarybinę poeziją. [Heroism and dreams; about Soviet Lithuanian poetry]. Vilnius, Vaga, 1976. 264 p. PG8709.R6 PU.

2549. ŠILBAJORIS, Rimvydas. Experiments with style in Soviet Lithuanian prose. In Journal of Baltic Studies (Brooklyn, N.Y.), no.2/3, v. 6, 1975, p. 198-203. See serials consulted.

2550. --- Forbidden thoughts, permitted voices; poets in Lithuania and in the Leningrad underground. In Lituanus (Chicago, Ill.), no.4, v.23, 1977, p. 45-53. See serials consulted.

2551. ŠIUOLAIKINĖS KRITIKOS PROBlemos. [Current problems of criticism. Ats. redaktorius: J. Stepšys]. Vilnius, Vaga, 1975. 449 p. At head of title: LTSR Mokslo akademija. Lietu-

vių kalbos ir literatūros institutas.
LTSR Rašytojų sąjungos literatūros
kritikos komisija.
PG8709.S52 PU; DLC; WU.

2552. ŠIUOLAIKINĖS POEZIJOS PROB-
lemos. [Problems of contemporary Lithuanian poetry. Sudarė V. Daujoty-
tė]. Vilnius, Vaga, 1977. 413 p.
PG8709.S54 PU.

2553. TARYBINĖ LIETUVIŲ LITERATŪ-
RA. [Soviet Lithuanian literature
for the 11th Grade]. Kaunas, Šviesa,
1969- v. port. (Mokinio biblioteka). PG8713.T3 DLC.

2554. TARYBŲ LIETUVOS RAŠYTOJAI.
[Authors of Soviet Lithuania; auto-
biographies]. Red. komisija: Juozas
Baltušis (pirmininkas), Jonas Lanku-
tis, Alfonsas Maldonis. Sudarė A.
Mickienė ir A. Paraščiakas]. Vil-
nius, Vaga, 1977. 2 v.
PG8701.T32 1977 PU.

2555. TORNAU, J[urgis]. Romano
autoriaus rūpesčiai. [Concern of the
authors in prose]. Vilnius, Vaga,
1966. 218 p. Rvc38T633 CtY; MH;
MiEM.

2556. TRIMONIS, Rytis. Atakuojan-
čio laiko lyrika; pokario metų tarybinės lietuvių lyrikos raida (1945-
1954). [Poetry of the agressive period; Soviet Lithuanian poetry and
its trends, 1945-1954]. Vilnius,Va-
ga, 1976. PG8709.T73 PU; DLC.

2557. --- Litovskaía sovetskaía
lirika poslevoennykh let 1945-1954
g.g. Vil'nius, Vil'níusskíí gos.
universitet, 1972. 14 p. Avtoreferat disertatsii na soiskanie uchenoí
stepeni... PG8709.T72 PU.

2558. VAŠKELIS, Bronius. The as-
sertion of ethnic identity via myth
and folklore in Soviet Lithuanian literature. In Lituanus (Chicago, IlL)
no.2, v.19, 1973, p. 16-27. See serials consulted.

2559. --- The motif and anxiety
in the contemporary short story of
Lithuania. In Journal of Baltic Studies (Brooklyn, N.Y.), no.2/3, v.6,
1975, p. 162-169. See serials consulted.

2560. --- Nerimaujantis žmogus
šiandieninėje Lietuvos smulkioje prozoje. [The motif of anxiety in the
contemporary short story of Lithua-
nia]. In Metmenys (Chicago, Ill.),
no.28, 1974, p. 154-174. See serials
consulted.

2561. --- Pokario partizanai sovietinėje lietuvių literatūroje.[The

active partizans after the war in the
Soviet Lithuanian literature]. In
Metmenys (Chicago, Ill.), no.19, 1970,
p. 101-117. See serials consulted.

2562. ZABORSKAITĖ, Vanda. Eilėraščio menas. [Art of poetry]. Antras papildytas leidimas. Vilnius,Va-
ga, 1970. 366 p. PN1049.L5Z3 DLC;
MB; NjP; PU.

XIII.5.b.4. LITHUANIAN LITERATURE
ABROAD

2563. AUGUSTINAVIČIENĖ, Aldona.
Laisvė mūsų poezijoje. [Freedom in our
poetry]. In Varpas (Chicago, Ill.),
no.10, 1970-1971, p. 143-148. See
serials consulted.

2564. BALDUS, Alexander. Die heutige Dichtung der baltischen Völker;
die litauische Dichtung. In Begegnung (Köln, Ger.), no.15-16, Aug.1957,
v.12, p. 251-255; no.17, Sept.1957,
p. 267-270. See serials consulted.

2565. GRAŽYTĖ-MAZILIAUSKIENĖ, Ilona. Nauji keliai išeivijos literatūroje. [New trends in the Lithuanian
literature in exile]. In Metmenys (
Chicago, Ill.), no.21, 1971, p. 152-
160. See serials consulted.

2566. NAUJOKAITIS, Pranas. Lietuvių literatūra svetur. [Lithuanian literature in exile]. In Tėvynės Sargas (New York, N.Y.), no.1, 1969, p.
139-157. See serials consulted.

2567. OSTRAUSKAS, Kostas. Rašytojas ir egzilis. [The author and exile]
In Metmenys (Chicago, Ill.), no.27,
1974, p. 10-36. See serials consulted.

2568. REIKALAS, Kęstas. Prozos
dominuojama 1971 m. literatūra. [Do-
mination of prose in Lithuanian literature in 1971]. In Metmenys (Chicago, Ill.), no.23, 1972, p. 173-190.
See serials consulted.

2569. --- Tomais gausūs septinias-
dešimtieji. [Lithuanian literature in
exile, 1970]. In Metmenys (Chicago,
Ill.), no.21, 1971, p. 173-189. See
serials consulted.

2570. --- 1972-ji romano metai išeivijos literatūroje. [The 1972 as a
year of novel in Lithuanian literature in exile]. In Metmenys (Chicago,
Ill.), no.25, 1973, p.175-182. See
serials consulted.

2571. ---Žvilgsnis į 1969 metų

egzilės literatūrą. [A look at the
Lithuanian literature in exile for
1969]. In Metmenys (Chicago, Ill.),
no.19, 1970, p. 169-184. See serials
consulted.

2572. ŠILBAJORIS, Rimvydas. The
experience of exile in Lithuanian literature. In Lituanus (Chicago, Ill)
no.1, v.18, 1972, p. 48-57. See serials consulted.

2573. --- An intellectuals encoun-
ter with nature; modern trends in Lithuanian poetry. In Lituanus (Chicago, Ill.), no.2, v.20, 1974, p.5-14.
See serials consulted.

XIII.5.b.5. LIFE AND WORKS OF INDIVI-
DUAL AUTHORS

2574. AISTIS, Jonas. Kanauninkas
Juozas Tumas-Vaižgantas. [Monsignor
Juozas Tumas-Vaižgantas, his life and
works]. In LKMASD, v.8, p. 37-50.
See serials consulted.

2575. ALANTAS, Vytautas. Deiman-
čiukų sėjėjas ir rinkėjas (Vaižgantas). [Vaižgantas, the brilliant
writer]. In Naujoji Viltis (Chicago,
Ill.), no.1, 1970, p. 81-93. See serials consulted.

2576. AMBRAZEVIČIUS, Juozas. Jakšto ir Vaižganto jungas. [The works of
Jakštas and Vaižgantas]. In LKMASD,
v.3, p. 234-242. See serials consulted.

2577. --- Maironio vieta lietuvių religinėj literatūroj. [The place
of Maironis in Lithuanian religious
literature]. In LKMASD, v.1, p. 333-
348. See serials consulted.

2578. AREŠKA, Vitas. Salomėja Nėris. [Kaunas, Šviesa, 1974]. 185 p.
PG8721.N4Z6 PU.

2579. BIRŽIŠKA, Mykolas. Donelaičio gyvenimas ir raštai su kalbos pa-
aiškinimais.[Donelaitis, his life
and works]. Kaunas, Švyturio b-vė,
1921. 2 v. WU.

2580. BLEKAITIS, Jurgis. Henriko
Radausko poezija. The poetry of Hen-
rikas Radauskas. In Institute of Li-
thuanian Studies. Lituanistikos ins-
tituto 1971 metų suvažiavimo darbai.
Chicago, Ill., 1971. p. 129-148.
Summary in English. DK511.L2I57 DLC;
CaAEU; InNd; MiU; NIC; NRU; PU.

2581. BUKELIENĖ, Elena. Jonas Avyžius; kūrybos bruožai. [Jonas Avyžius

and his creative traits]. Vilnius,
Vaga, 1975. PG8721.A85Z63 PU;DLC.

2582. ČESNULEVIČIŪTĖ, Petrė. Vincas Krėvė. [Vincas Krėvė-Mickevičius,
his life and works. Kaunas, Šviesa,
1976] 86 p. PG8721.K7Z65 PU.

2583. GALINIS, Vytautas. Petro
Cvirkos apsakymai. [Short stories of
Petras Cvirka]. Vilnius, Valstybinė
grožinės literatūros leidykla, 1954.
365 p. PG8721.C3Z66 PU.

2584. GIRA, Liudas. Kun. Tumo-
Vaižganto gyvenimas ir darbai. [Rev.
Tumas-Vaižgantas, his life and works]
Kaunas, Pažangos b-vės leidinys,1930.
[Xerox copy, 1977]. 64 p.
PG8721.T77Z7 1930a PU(xerox).

2585. GRAŽYTĖ-MAZILIAUSKIENĖ, Ilona. The naked eye; some aspects of
the prose of Mykolas Sluckis. In Lituanus (Chicago, Ill.), no.2, v.22,
1976, p. 47-58. See serials consulted.

2586. --- Variations on the theme
of dehumanization in the short stories
of Juozas Aputis. In Books Abroad
(Norman, Okla), no.4, v.47, 1973, p.
695-701. See serials consulted.

2587. GRINIUS, Jonas. Juozo Gru-
šo dramaturgija. [Drama works of Juozas Grušas]. In Aidai (Brooklyn,N.Y.)
no.9, 1971, p. 396-405. See serials
consulted.

2588. KAČIULIS, Justinas. Vytautas Montvila. [Vytautas Montvila,his
life and works]. Vilnius, Vaga, 1977.
317 p. PG8721.M56Z74 PU.

2589. KEBLYS, Kęstutis. Vaizduo-
jamojo požiūrio metodika Škėmos ir
Sluckio romanuose. Methodology of
presentation: The author's vantage
point in the novels of Škėma and Sluckis. In Institute of Lithuanian Studies. Lituanistikos instituto 1975
metų suvažiavimo darbai. Chicago,
Ill., 1976. p. 99-106. Summary in
English. DK511.L2I64 1975 CaAEU;PU.

2590. KUBILIUS, Vytautas. Teofilis Tilvytis. Vilnius, Valstybinė
grožinės literatūros leidykla, 1956.
156 p. illus. PG8721.T55Z73 OKentU.

2591. KUZMICKAS, Vincas. Kazys
Binkis; gyvenimo ir kūrybos apybrai-
ža. [Kazys Binkis, his life and works]
Kaunas, Šviesa, 1977. 140 p.
PG8721.B5Z7 PU.

2592. LANKUTIS, Jonas. Eduardo
Mieželaičio poezija. [Poetry of E.
Mieželaitis]. 2.papildytas leidimas.

Vilnius, Vaga, 1971. 219 p.
PG8721.M45Z7 1971 PU; DLC; IU;MH;NN.

2593. --- Justino Marcinkevičiaus draminė trilogija. [J. Marcinkevičius and his drama works]. Vilnius, Vaga, 1977. 222 p. PG8721.M35Z75 PU.

2594. --- Vincas Mykolaitis-Putinas; kritiko-biograficheskiĭ ocherk. Moskva, Sovetskiĭ pisatel', 1967. 163 p. WU.

2595. --- Vinco Mykolaičio-Putino kūryba. [Creative works of V. Mykolaitis-Putinas]. Vilnius, Vaga, 1973. 350 p. WU.

2596. MACIŪNAS, Vincas. Motiejus Valančius, Liudas Rėza, Juozas Tumas-Vaižgantas and Jurgis Savickis. Chicago, Ill., 1976. 63 leaves. PG8703.M15 1976 CaAEU(xerox).

2597. --- Pilypo Ruigio rankraštis anų laikų rėmuose. Chicago, Ill. 1977. 15 leaves. Reprinted from Draugas (Chicago, Ill.), no.107,113, 125 and 130. [Manuscript of P. Ruigis as in his time]. PG8703.M16 1977 CaAEU(xerox).

2598. MOCKŪNAS, Liūtas. M.Sluckis per daug apsaugotam uoste. [M.Sluckis is in a much too sheltered port] In Metmenys (Chicago, Ill.), no.24, 1972, p. 177-185. See serials consulted.

2599. NAUJOKAITIS, Pranas. Tragiškos epochos veidas Bernardo Brazdžionio poezijoje. [The presentation of Lithuania's tragedy in the poetry of Bernardas Brazdžionis]. In Tėvynės Sargas (New York, N.Y.), no.1, 1972, p.93-105. See serials consulted.

2600. NERAMIOS ŠVIESOS PASAULIAI; knyga apie dramaturgą Juozą Grušą. [... a book about J. Grušas, the dramatist]. Parengė Algis Samulionis. Vilnius, Vaga, 1976. 245 p. PG8721.G7Z8 PU.

2601. POMARENKO, Lidiia A. Eduardas Miezhelaitis. Kiev, Dnipro,1960. 92 p. WU.

2602. SALVATORI, Giuseppe. Figure del risorgimento letterario lituano; Vincas Krėvė-Mickevičius. Roma, 1932. In Studi Baltici (Roma), t.2, 1932, p. [23]-34. See serials consulted.

2603. ŠILBAJORIS, Rimvydas. Icchokas Meras: keturi romanai. Four novels by Icchokas Meras. In Institute of Lithuanian Studies. Lituanis-

tikos instituto 1975 metų suvažiavimo darbai. Chicago, Ill., 1976. p. 91-98. Summary in English. DK511.L2I64 1975 CaAEU; PU.

2604. --- Pastabos apie Donelaičio "Metų" struktūrą. [Notes on the structure of Donelaitis' "Metai"].In LKMASD, v.8, p. 189-198. See serials consulted.

2605. --- The "Reminiscences" of Jonas Mekas; poetic form and rooted sorrow. In Journal of Baltic Studies (Brooklyn, N.Y.), no.4, v.4, 1973, p. 327-334. See serials consulted.

2606. --- Sigita Geda, magician and minstrel. In Books Abroad (Norman, Okla.), no.4, v.47, 1973, p.701-707. See serials consulted.

2607. --- Some structural principles in the theater of Kostas Ostrauskas. In Lituanistikos darbai (Chicago, Ill.), v.3, 1973, p.173-197.See serials consulted.

2608. --- Struktūros ir dimensijos Tomo Venclovos poezijoje. Structures and dimensions in the poetry of Tomas Venclova. In Institute of Lithuanian Studies. Lituanistikos instituto 1973 metų suvažiavimo darbai. Chicago, Ill., 1975. p. 163-173. Summary in English. DK511.L2I63 1975 CaAEU; PU.

2609. --- Šviesa ir spalvos Juditos Vaičiūnaitės poezijoje. [The light and colours in the poetry of Judita Vaičiūnaitė]. In Metmenys (Chicago, Ill.), no.22, 1971, p.5-23. See serials consulted.

2610. SKRUPSKELIS, Viktoria. Alfonsas Nyka-Niliūnas; a poet of qualities. In Books Abroad (Norman, Okla.), no.4, v.47, 1973, p.708-715. See serials consulted.

2611. --- Dviejų polių trauka. Alfonso Nykos-Niliūno poezija perskaičius. [The poetry of A. Čipkus - Nyka-Niliūnas, pseud.]. In Aidai Brooklyn, N.Y.), no.8, 1970, p. 348-357. See serials consulted.

2612. STRIOGAITĖ, Dalė Jadvyga. Proza K. Boruty; problema romantizma. [By] Dalė IAdviga Strėgaitė. Vil'nius, Vil'niusskiĭ gos. universitet, 1976. 24 p. Avtoreferat dissertatsii na soiskanie uchenoĭ stepeni kandidata filologicheskikh nauk. PG8721.B6Z8 PU.

2613. TRUMPA, Vincas. J. Tumas-Vaižgantas; gyvenimo kritikas. [J.Tumas-Vaižgantas; a critic of life].

In Metmenys (Chicago, Ill.), no.21, 1971, p. 78-96. See serials consulted.

2614. TUMAS, Juozas. Antanas Baranauskas, 1835-1902. [Lectures on Lithuanian literature; Antanas Baranauskas. By] Vaižgantas, [pseud.]. Kaunas, [s.n.], 1924. 117 p. PG8721.B325T83 1975 PU(xerox of 1924 ed.); CtTMF(orig.); WU(orig.).

2615. --- L. Ivinskis...[Lectures on Lithuanian literature; Laurynas Ivinskis. By] Vaižgantas, [pseud.]. Kaunas, Valstybės spaustuvė, 1924. [Xerox copy, 1975]. 67 p. PG8721.I85T8 1975 PU(xerox); WU(original).

2616. --- Lietuvių literatūros draudžiamojo laiko paskaitos: Antanas Vienažindys, Antanas Kriščiukaitis, Martynas Jankus, Ksaveras Sakalauskas. [Lectures on Lithuanian literature: A. Vienažindys, A. Kriščiukaitis, M. Jankus, K. Sakalauskas. By] Vaižgantas, [pseud.]. Kaunas, Valstybės spaustuvė, 1925.[Xerox copy, 1977]. 175 p. PG8709.T8 1925a PU(xerox).

2617. UMBRASAS, Kazys. Žemaitė; biografija ir kūrybos ištakos. [Žemaitė (Julija Žymantienė); a biography and creative writings. Parengė: C. Galinis, V.Kubilius, R. Mikšytė]. Vilnius, Vaga, 1975. 317 p. PG8721.Z9Z9 PU; DLC.

2618. VAŠKELIS, Bronius. Jurgio Baltrušaičio kolizijos, kelyje į lietuvių literatūrą. [The difficulties for Jurgis Baltrušaitis in his change over to Lithuanian literature]. In Metmenys (Chicago, Ill.), no.26, 1973, p.67-89. See serials consulted.

2619. --- Iš Jurgio Baltrušaičio kūrybos palikimo. [From the literary estate of Jurgis Baltušaitis]. In Lituanistikos Darbai (Chicago, Ill.), v.3, 1973, p. 233-247. See serials consulted.

2620. WILLEKE, Audronė B. Socialist realism and the psychological novels of Alf. Bieliauskas. In Journal of Baltic Studies(Brooklyn, N.Y.), no.4, v.8, p. 294-300. See serials consulted.

2621. ZDANYS, Jonas. The applied aestheticism of Henrikas Radauskas. In Lituanus (Chicago, Ill.), no.1,v. 23, 1977, p. 23-42. See serials consulted.

2622. ZĖKAITĖ, Janina. A. Vienuolio kūryba iki 1917 metų. [The crea-

tive works of A. Vienuolis before 1917]. Vilnius, Valstybinė grožinės literatūros leidykla, 1957. 495 p. facsims. (Literatūra ir Kalba, 2). (Lietuvos TSR Mokslų akademijos Lietuvių kalbos ir literatūros darbai, t.2). ICIU.

XIII.5.c. BELLES LETTRES

XIII.5.c.1. ANTHOLOGY, COLLECTIONS, ETC.

2623. ATMINIMŲ PAUKŠČIAI; lietuvių poetų dedikuoti eilėraščiai. Sudarė Vanda Šatkuvienė. Vilnius, Vaga, 1976. 79 p. PG8715.A78 PU.

2624. AUŠTA RYTAS, AUŠTA NAUJAS... iš XIX a. pabaigos- XX a. pradžios revoliucinės demokratinės lietuvių poezijos. [Revolutionary poetry from 19th-20th centuries. Paruošė Dalia Gargasaitė]. Vilnius, Vaga, 1977. 381 p. PG8715.A8 PU.

2625. BALTUTIS-Dulkė, Klemensas, ed. Septyni: Stasys Būdavas, Klemensas Dulkė, Mykolas Linkevičius, Alė Sidabraitė, Vytautas Sirijos-Gira, Stepas Zobarskas, Kazys Župka. Kaunas, Sakalo b-vė, 1933. 103 p. 891.921B ICCC.

2626. ČIA PRIĖJO KINDZIULIS; antrą kartą. [..Lithuanian anecdotes, wit and humor. Red. J. Bulota. Dailininkas R. Palčiauskas]. Vilnius,[s.n.], 1973. 158 p. illus. At head of title: Lietuvos TSR žurnalistų sąjunga. PN6267.L5C5 DLC.

2627. DRAUGAI; apsakymų rinkinys. [Collection of short stories]. Vilnius, Tiesos leidykla, 1952. 157 p. PG8719.D7 DLC.

2628. EMIGRANTO DALIA; lietuvių beletristikos rinkinys. [Anthology]. [Sudarė V. Kazakevičius; red. komis. J.Baltušis (pirm.)...et al.]. Vilnius, Vaga, 1973. 413 p. Bibliography: p. 409-[410]. PG8719.E6 DLC;Wa.

2629. GAUČYS, Povilas. Pietų kryžiaus padangėje; Lotynų Amerikos rašytojų novelių antologija. [Anthology of novels]. Sudarė Povilas Gaučys. [Chicago, Ill.], Lietuviškos knygos klubas, [1951]. 480 p. map. PQ7087.L5G3 OKentU.

2630. GYVAJAI LIETUVAI. Liudas Gira, Salomėja Nėris, Antanas Venclova, Kostas Korsakas, Jonas Šimkus, Eduardas Mieželaitis. [Anthology].

Moskva, 1942.   891.92G976A PU.

2631. IŠ TARYBINĖS LIETUVIŲ POE-
zijos. [Soviet Lithuanian poetry].
Sudaryta pagal Lietuvos TSR Švietimo ministerijos programą. Kaunas,
Valstybinė pedagoginės literatūros
leidykla, 1957. 186 p. (Mokinio biblioteka). PG8715.I8 OKentU.

2631a. IŠSISUPUS PLAČIAI; eilėraščiai. [Sudarė Donata Linčiuvienė].
[Poetry of places]. Vilnius, Vaga,
1974. 324 p. illus.
PG8715.I8 DLC; WU.

2632. JONYNAS, Antanas. Pernykš-
tis sniegas; satyra ir humoras. [By]
Antanas Jonynas [and] Kostas Kubilinskas. [Lithuanian wit and humor].
Vilnius, Valstybinė grožinės literatūros leidykla, 1957. 164 p.
NB.

2633. KOVOS KELIAIS. [Surinko ir
paruošė B. Pranskus]. Vilnius, Valstybinė grožinės literatūros leidykla,
1961. 390 p.   891.92C K848 PU.

2634. KOVŲ PUSLAPIAI; [šioje kny-
goje surinkti karo meto lietuvių rašytojų, poetų ir publicistų būdin-
giausi kūriniai. Redakcinė komisija:
E.Mieželaitis (pirm.)...et al.   A
collection of literary works of Lithuanian authors written during the
Second World War]. Vilnius, Vaga,
1974. 622 p.,[20] leaves of plates.
illus. D802.L5K595 DLC.

2635. LENINUI, STALINUI MŪSŲ DAINA.
[Redakcinė komisija: Teofilis Tilvytis et al. Vilniuje], Valstybinė
grožinės literatūros leidykla, 1952.
PG8715.L35 DLC.

2636. LIETUVIŲ POEZIJA IŠEIVIJOJE,
1945-1971. [Lithuanian poetry in exile, 1945-1971]. Redagavo Kazys Bradūnas. Chicago, Ill., Ateitis, 1971.
671 p. (Literatūros serija, nr.5).
Bibliography: p. [640]-644.
PG8715.L52 DLC; InNd; MB; NN.

2637. NEKLAUSKIT MEILĖS VARDO. [
Sudarė Dalia Montvilienė]. Vilnius,
Vaga, 1970. 240 p. PG8715.N4 PU;
DLC; IU; MB; MH; NjP.

2638. NUOŠIRDUMAS. [Universiteto
Literatų būrelio kūrybos rinkinėlis]
Vilnius, 1967. 109 p. At head of
title: LTSR Aukštojo ir spec. mokslo
ministerija. Vilniaus Valstybinio
V.Kapsuko v. universiteto Literatų
būrelis. PG8713.N8 DLC.

2639. PETRULIS, Juozas, comp.
"Aušros" poezija; įvadas ir tekstai.
Kaunas,[S.Jeselevičiaus spaustuvė],

1928. [Xerox copy, 1977]. 100 p.
PG8715.P45 1928a PU(xerox).

2640. POEZIJOS PAVASARIS. [The
spring of poetry; selected works for
1965. Ats. red. Vacys Reimeris].Vil-
nius, Vaga, 1965. 186 p. illus.,
ports. PG8715.R4 DLC; IEN; IU; FU;
NN.

2641. --- [Eilėraščių rinkinys.
Ats. red. J. Marcinkevičius. Dail. B.
Leonavičius]. Vilnius, Vaga, 1968.
279 p. illus. and phonodisc (2 s.
7 in. 33 rpm.). PG8715.P6 DLC;CaAEU;
CtY; OKentU; PSt; PU.

2642. --- [Atsakingasis redaktorius J. Marcinkevičius. Dailininkas
A.Kazakauskas]. Vilnius, Vaga, 1969.
205 p. illus. PG8715.P62 DLC; MH;
CaAEU; OKentU; PU.

2643. --- [Red. komisija: ...A.
Jonynas (pirm.) ir kiti. Dailininkas
V. Bačėnas]. Vilnius, Vaga, 1970.
PG8715.P62 1970 DLC; MB.

2644. --- [Red. komisija: Eugenijus Matuzevičius (pirm.). Dailininkas
Vytautas Valius]. Vilnius, Vaga,1971.
249 p. illus. PG8715.P63 1971x
OKentU; PU.

2645. --- [Red. komisija: ...J.
Macevičius (pirmininkas) ... et al.;
dailininkas, K.Dockus]. Vilnius Vaga, 1974. 222 p. illus., ports.
PG8715.P63 DLC; OKentU; PU.

2646. PRANSKUS, Bronius. Lietuvių
literatūros chrestomatija. Dalis 1- .
[The chrestomathy of Lithuanian lite-
rature]. Minskas, Baltarusijos valstybinė leidykla, Nacionalinis sekto-
rius, 1933- .   v.   Contents.--
t.1. Proletariniai-revolucinė literatūra.   *QY--NN.

2647. ŠALMAS IR PIENĖ; eilėraščiai
apie didįjį tėvynės karą. [Sudarė R.
Umbrasaitė]. Vilnius, Vaga, 1975.
483 p. PG8715.S3 PU; MH.

2648. ŠIMUKONIENĖ, Gražina, comp.
Su daina. New York, N.Y., 1967. 351
p. PG8715.S55 PU; PPULC.

2649. SPALIO ŽVAIGŽDĖS; eilėraščiai. [Sudarė Rytis Trimonis. Vilnius, Vaga, 1977]. 351 p.
PG8715.S77 PU.

2650. TAUTOS VAINIKAS; puikiausia
eilių-dainų ir deklamacijų knygelė.
Cleveland, Spauda Dirvos, 19--.   v.
PG8715.T3 DLC.

2651. TERRA AUSTRALIS; AUSTRALIJOS
lietuvių poezijos rinkinys. Redagavo

Juozas Almis Jūragis. Sydney, Australia, Mintis, 1972. 157 p.
PG8750.A8T4 PU.

2652. TĖVYNĖ MANA; eilėraščiai. [Sudarė R.Umbrasaitė]. Vilnius, Vaga, 1976. 358 p. PG8715.T4 PU.

2653. TILTAI IR TUNELIAI. [Sąmojų poezijos rinkinys. Brooklyn, N.Y., Ateitis, 1969] 125 p. (Literatūros serija, nr. 2). At head of title:Remigijus Bičiūnas et al.
ICIU; OU; OKentU.

2654. TRETIEJI VAINIKAI; lietuvių poezija išeivijoje, 1944-1974. Redagavo: Paulius Jurkus, Anatolijus Kairys, Pranas Naujokaitis. Chicago, Ill., Dialogas, 1975. 288 p.
PG8715.T7 PU; DLC.

2655. VARPAI; literatūros almanachas 1943. [Redaktorius K. Jankauskas. Šiauliai], Šiaulių meno ir mokslo centras, 1943.[Xerox copy, 1976] 328 p. PG8713.V3 1943a PU(xerox).

2656. VILNIAUS MŪRAI, [Sudarė S.Budrytė ir L.Sauka; dailininkas V.Kalinauskas]. Vilnius, Vaga, 1973. 262 p. illus. Poems. PG8715.V5 DLC; PU.

XIII.5.c.2. COLLECTED AND SELECTED WORKS

2657. AISTIS, Jonas. Dievai ir smūtkeliai. [By] J.Kossu-Aleksandravičius. Kaunas, Sakalas, 1935.[Xerox copy, 1976]. 288 p.
PG8721.A4D5 1935a PU(xerox).

2658. AKISTATOJ SU PAVOJUM; apybraižos, apsakymai, apysakos. Vilnius, Vaga, 1976. 389 p.
HV8227.6.A5 PU.

2659. ANDZIULAITIS-KALNĖNAS, Juozas. Raštai. [Red. komisija: K.Korsakas (pirm.) ir kiti. Paruošė K.Nastopka]. Vilnius, Vaga, 1971. 401 p. (Lituanistinė biblioteka, 9).
PG8701.A5 1971 DLC; CtY; IU; MB;MH; NN; OKentU; PU.

2660. AUDRONAŠA-SUCHOCKIS, Vladas. Saulėta diena; rinktinė. Vilnius,Vaga, 1974. 349 p. illus., port.
PG8721.A83S2 DLC; PU; WU.

2661. AVYŽIUS, Jonas. Didžiojo užutekio gyventojai. Vilnius, Valstybinė grožinės literatūros leidykla, 1963. 100 p. illus. Jaunesniojo ir vidutinio mokyklinio amžiaus vaikams.
OKentU.

2662. AŽUKALNIS, Valerijonas. Raštai lietuviški. [Paruošė J.Girdzijauskas]. Vilnius, Vaga, 1968. 364 p. facsims. (Lituanistinė biblioteka).
PG8721.A92 1968 PU; CaAEU; CU-S; DLC; ICU; MB; MH; NN; NjP; OKentU; OU;PSt; PPULC;

2663. BALTAKIS, Algimantas. Upės ir tiltai; rinktinė. Vilnius, Vaga, 1976. 614 p. PG8722.12.A4U6 PU.

2664. BALTUŠIS, Juozas. Gieda gaideliai; dramos ir feljetonai. Vilnius, Vaga, 1975. 403 p.
PG8721.B32G5 DLC; PU.

2665. --- Kas dainon nesudėta;kelionių įspūdžiai. Vilnius, Vaga,1976. 437 p. PG8721.B32K3 PU; OKentU(ed. 1959).

2666. --- Nežvyruotu vieškeliu; apsakymų rinktinė. Vilnius, Vaga, 1971. 449 p. PG8721.B32N4 PU; DLC; MH; NNC; WU.

2667.--Raštai. Vilnius, 1957-4 v. 891.92B2185 PU.

2668. --- Raštai. Penki tomai. Vilnius, Vaga, 1969- . 5 v.
PG8721.B32 DLC; PU.

2669. --- Su kuo valgyta druska. Vilnius, Vaga, 1973-1976. 2 v.
PG8721.B32S8 PU; DLC; MH.

2670. BAUŽA, Aleksandras. Kur mėlynas dangus; apsakymų rinktinė. Vilnius, Vaga, 1971. 363 p. PG8721.B37 K8 PU; DLC; IU; MB; MH; NN; NNC;NjP.

2671. BILIŪNAS, Antanas. Rinktinė. Vilnius, Vaga, 1974. 245 p. illus. PG8721.B46A6 1974 PU; DLC.

2672. BILIŪNAS, Jonas. Raštai. Tilsit, Ger., Biliūnienė, 1913. 144 p. WU.

2673. BINKIS, Kazys. Raštai. [Sudarė ir paaiškinimus parašė Vytautas Galinis]. Vilnius, Vaga, 1973. 2 v. PG8721.B5 1973 PU; DLC.

2674. BIRŽIŠKA, Vaclovas. Eilės ir proza. [By] Smutkelis, [pseud.]. Voronežas, Russia, Lietuvos reikalų komisariato Kultūros ir švietimo skyrius, 1918.[Xerox copy, 1973]. 35 p.
PG8721.B52E5 1973 PU(xerox).

2675. BORUTA, Kazys. Drauge su draugais. [Raštai], 10. [Sudarė ir paaiškinimus parašė V.Vilnonytė]. Vilnius, Vaga, 1976. 413 p.
PG8721.B6D7 PU.

2676. --- Saulės parnešti išėjo.

[Sudarė ir paaiškinimus parašė V.Vilnonytė]. Vilnius, Vaga, 1973. PG8721.B6S3 PU; DLC; NjP; WU.

2677. BRAZDŽIONIS, Bernardas. Pietų vėjelis. [Piešiniai Povilo Osmolskio. Brooklyn, N.Y., 1952. By] Vytė Nemunėlis, [pseud.]. 24 p. ill. (Jaunimo skaitymai). 891.92B739Pi PU.

2678. --- Po tėvynės dangum. Žodžiai Vytės Nemunėlio, [pseud.]. Paveikslai Vytauto Augustino. [Brooklyn, N.Y., Vaga, 1952]. [30] p. ill. 891.92B739Po PU; PPULC.

2679. BUTKUS, Juozas. Rinktinė. [Sudarė J.Būtėnas]. Vilnius, Valstybinė grožinės literatūros leidykla, 1962. 206 p. facsim., ports. PG8721.B83R5 1962 DLC.

2680. DĖNAS, Vytautas. Ir mirdami kovojo. Vilnius, Mintis, 1967. 111 p. PG8722.14.E5I7 DLC; IU; MH.

2681. DONELAITIS, Kristijonas. Raštai. [Redakcinė komisija: K.Korsakas(pirmininkas), K.Doveika, L.Gineitis, J.Kabelka, K.Ulvydas]. Vilnius, Vaga, 1977. 599 p. PG8721.D7 1977 PU.

2682. --- Raštai. M.Biržiška, [ed.]. Kaunas; Vilnius, Švyturio b-vė, 1921. 88 p. WU.

2683. DRILINGA, Antanas. Monologų knyga. [Iliustracijos L.Paškauskaitės]. Vilnius, Vaga, 1971. 93 p. illus. PG8722.14.R5M6 PU; MH.

2684. GUSTAITIS, Antanas. Saulės šermenys. Dailininkas V.Vizgirda. Chicago, Ill., Išleido Algimanto Mackaus knygų leidimo fondas, 1973. 111 p. illus. PG8721.G85S2 DLC;InNd; InU.

2685. JAKUBĖNAS, Kazys. Bundanti žemė. Rinktinė. [Dailininkas R.Dichavičius]. Vilnius, Vaga, 1972. 319 p. illus. PG8721.J25B8 1972 DLC; IU; MB; NN; PU; WU.

2686. JASILIONIS, Stasys. Žodžiai iš širdies. [Redakcinė komisija: V. Mazuriūnas et al. Surinko A.Vaivutskas]. Vilnius, Valstybinė grožinės literatūros leidykla, 1961. 462 p. illus., ports. PG8721.J37Z3 1961 DLC; CtY; MH; OKentU.

2687. JASIUKAITIS, Konstantinas. Raštai. [Sudarė ir paaiškinimus parašė B.Pranskus]. Vilnius, Valstybinė grožinės literatūros leidykla, 1959. 2 v. illus., ports. CtY.

2688. JONYNAS, Antanas. Juokingos

epitafijos. Misterija; eiliuotos satyros ir humoro rinktinė. Vilnius, Vaga, 1975. 189 p. PG8722.2.O5J8 PU.

2689. JUCEVIČIUS, Liudvikas Adomas. Raštai. Vilnius, Valstybinė grožinės literatūros leidykla, 1959. 678 p. facsims. On leaf proceeding t.p.: Iš literatūrinio palikimo. CtY; CtPAM; DLC; NN; WU.

2690. JUNČAS-KUČINSKAS, Mykolas. Raštai. [Sudarytojas R. Čepas. Ats. redaktorius R. Maliukevičius]. Vilnius, Mintis, 1976. 190 p. DK511.L28J83 PU.

2691. KARIBUTAS, Juozas. Kelionė aplink pasaulį; kelionių įspūdžiai. Los Angeles, Calif., 1974. 423 p. G440K35 PU; InNd.

2692. KRATULIS, Algirdas. Patentas nr.2383319. Vilnius, Mintis,1966. 22 p. (Mokslo naujienos visiems, 29) PG8722.21.R3P3 DLC.

2693. KRISTALPONIS, A. Visas turtelis--šimtinė; atvirom akim bandyti svetingi kraštai. Chicago, Ill.,1971. 239 p. port. PG8749.K74V5 DLC.

2694. KUBILINSKAS, Kostas. [Raštai. Sudarė ir paaiškinimus parašė Sigita Papečkienė]. Vilnius, Vaga, 1972. 2 v. illus. Poems. PG8722.21.U2 1972 PU; CtY.

2695. LANDSBERGIS, Gabrielius. Raštai. [Paruošė A.Žirgulys]. Vilnius, Vaga, 1972. 322 p. illus. At head of title: Gabrielius Landsbergis-Žemkalnis. PG8721.L31 1972 PU; DLC; CtY; MB; MH; NN; NNC; OKentU; WU.

2696. LEMBERTAS, Pranas. Tau, sesute; gyvenimas, kuryba, prisiminimai. [n.p.], 1969. 269 p. illus.,ports. PG8749.L4T3 1969 DLC; OKentU.

2697. LIOBYTĖ, Aldona. Kuršiukas. Penkių dalių pasaka apie meilę. Vilnius, Vaga, 1971. 84 p. illus., music. PG8721.L5K8 DLC.

2698. LIŪDŽIUS, Juozas. Raštai, straipsniai, atsiminimai. Selected works, memoirs. [Redagavo Jonas Valaitis. Chicago, Ill., Chicagos Lietuvių literatūros draugija, 1961]. 246 p. 891.92L743 PU; DLC-L; MH.

2699. MACEVIČIUS, Bronius. Čia ošia pušys; rinktinė. Vilnius,Vaga, 1975. 314 p. PG8722.23.A3C5 PU.

2700. MERKYTĖ, Aleksandra. Žingsniuojančiai jaunatvei. [Surinko ir paaiškinimus parašė B.Pranskus]. Vilnius, Valstybinė grožinės literatūros leidykla, 1961. 206 p. illus. PG8721.M4Z38 DLC; PU.

2701. MIKUCKIS, Juozas. Derliaus vainikas; ·eilėraščiai. Didvyriai; sceninis fragmentas. Selima Chalija; legenda. London, Eng., Nida, 1964. 359 p. ·port. (Nidos knygų klubo leidinys, nr. 47). PG8721.M46D4 OKentU.

2702. MONTVILA, Vytautas. Raštai. [Redakcinė komisija: V.Reimeris, V. Kubilius]. Vilnius, Valstybinė grožinės literatūros leidykla, 1955. 891.92M765 PU.

2703. MOZŪRIŪNAS, Vladas. Raštai. [Sudarė, paaiškinimus parašė Ramona Dambrauskaitė]. Vilnius, Vaga, 1971. 2 v. illus. PG8721.M6 1971 PU; DLC; IU; MH; NN; NNC; OKentU.

2704. MYKOLAITIS, Vincas. V.Mykolaitis-Putinas. 4.leidimas. Kaunas, Valstybinė pedagoginės literatūros leidykla, 1960. 186 p. (Mokinio biblioteka). PG8721.M9A6 1960 DLC.

2705. PAKALNIS, Antanas. Silpnybė; humoro ir satyros rinktinė. [Dailininkas Andrius Cvirka]. Vilnius, Vaga, 1972. 358 p. illus. MH.

2706. PALECKIS, Justas. Kelionių knyga. Vilnius, Vaga, 19--. 395 p. 45 p. of illus. G464.P34 OKentU.

2707. --- Meksikoje. Vilnius,Vaga, 1964. 195 p. illus. F1216.P3 OKentU.

2708. PAŠKAUSKAS, Jurgis. Pietų Amerikoj; kelionės įspūdžiai. Parašė ir savo lėšomis išleido Jurgis Paškauskas. Chicago, Ill., Draugas, 1938. 94 p. illus. E2223.P3 OKentU.

2709. PAUKŠTELIS, Juozas. Kelionė po Užkaukazę. [Pjesės: Audra ateina, Vaiduokliai, Asmeninis reikalas] Vilnius, Vaga, 1973. 363 p. PG8721.P37K4 1973 PU; MH.

2710. PEČKAUSKAITĖ, Marija. Irkos tragedija; novelės vaizdeliai, drama "Pančiai." [Sename dvare; apysakos]. Vilnius, Vaga, 1969. 2 v. illus. PG8721.P4A6 1969 DLC; CaAEU; CtY;MB.

2711. PIETARIS, Vincas. Rinktiniai raštai. [Paruošė V. Kuzmickas] Vilnius, Vaga, 1973. 709 p. illus. (Lituanistinė biblioteka, 13). PG8721.P5A6 1973 PU; DLC.

2712. PUTVINSKIS, Vladas. Gyvenimas ir parinktieji raštai. Vyr. redaktorius Aleksandras Marcinkevičius-Mantautas. 2.laida. Čikaga, Lietuvos Šaulių sąjunga tremtyje, 1973.

3 v. in 1. DK511.L28P87 1973 PU.

2713. RAČKAUSKAS, Vladas Karolis. Rinktinė. [Redaktorė A.Ubeikaitė]. Vilnius, Valstybinė grožinės literatūros leidykla, 1957. 311 p. port. CtY; CLU.

2714. REGRATIS, Artūras, pseud. Artūras Regratis ir jo raštai. Brooklyn, N.Y., Laisvė, 1927. 176 p. illus. (Amerikos lietuvių proletarų Meno sąjungos leidinys, 11). PG8721.R38R32 OKentU.

2715. --- Raštai. [Surinko ir paaiškinimus parašė B.Pranskus. Redakcinė komisija V.Kubilius, V.Reimeris ir R.Sartaitis]. Vilnius, Valstybinė grožinės literatūros leidykla, 1962. 281 p. illus., ports., facsims. PG8721.R38R3 DLC; MH; PU.

2716. ROSTOVAITĖ, Tatjana. Šventė; rinktinė. Vilnius, Vaga, 1976. 367 p. WU.

2717. SAUDARGIENĖ, Vlada R. Tolimų kraštų miražai. [By] Ava Saudargienė. London, Eng., Nida, 1976. 342 p. G464.S38 PU.

2718. SAVICKIS, Jurgis. Truputis Afrikos. [By] Rimošius, [pseud.]. 491.922Sa94T PU.

2719. ŠIKŠNYS, Marcelinas. Sparnai; rinktinė. Vilnius, Vaga, 1973. 287 p. ill. PG8721.S46S6 1973´ PU; DLC; IU; WU.

2720. SKLIUTAUSKAS, Jokūbas. Estiškos akvarelės. Vilnius, Mintis, 1975. 254 p. DK511.E53S55 PU.

2721. --- Riteris iš Sakartvelo. Vilnius, Mintis, 1972. DK511.G3S56 PU.

2722. SKRIPKA, Vytautas. Jūros klėtys. [Dailininkas M.Vilutis]. Vilnius, Vaga, 1972. 56 p. illus. PG8722.29.K7J8 DLC; MH.

2723. SMELSTORIUS, J[onas] B., comp. Sielos balsai, eilės, dainos ir balados su paveikslais. Sutaisė J.B. Smelstorius. So.Boston, Mass., Keleivio spaustuvė, 1913. 221 p. PN6109.L5S58 OKentU; NN; NjP; OCl; PU; PP; RP; RPB.

2724. STRAZDAS, Antanas. Parinktieji raštai mokyklai. [Spaudai paruošė J.Petrulis, K.Korsakas-Radžvilas. Kaunas, 1938]. 192 p. PG8721.S75 1938 PU.

2725. SUŠINSKAS, Alfonsas. Jaunystės maršas; knuga jauniesiems jaunuoju gyvenimo keliu. Antrasis pataisytas ir papildytas tremties leidimas. [Brooklyn, N.Y., Spaudė Tėvų Pranciškonų spaustuvė, 1956]. 260 p. CB113.L5S8 1956 OKentU.

2726. TREINYS, Pranas. Ragana, pelė ir Faustas; teatrinis romanas, apsakymai. [Dailininkė N.Kryževičiūtė-Jurgelionienė]. Vilnius, Vaga, 1971. 259 p. illus. PG8722.3.R4R3 PU; DLC; OKentU.

2727. VALANČIUS, Motiejus, Bp. Raštai. [Tekstą paruošė B.Vanagienė. Įvadas ir paaiškinimai V.Vanago ir V.Merkio]. Vilnius, Vaga, 1972. 2 v. illus. (Lituanistinė biblioteka, 11-12). PG8721.V327 1972 PU; CtY; MH.

2728. VALIŪNAS, Silvestras. Ant marių krašto. [Paruošė Regina Mikšytė]. Vilnius, Vaga, 1976. 239 p. PG8721.V329A8 PU.

2729. VENCLOVA, Antanas. Šalys ir žmonės. Vilnius, Vaga, 1972. 355 p. illus. PG8721.V4S32 PU; DLC; WU.

2730. --- Šiaurės sidabras. Vilnius, Valstybinė grožinės literatūros leidykla, 1962. 183 p. DL305.V4 DLC; PU.

2731. VĖŽYS, Rimas. Raidės laiko griaučiuose. Chicago, Ill., Algimanto Mackaus knygų leidimo fondas,1969. 93 p. PG8749.V44R3 DLC; InU; IcIU; MH; OCl.

2732. VILKUTAITIS, Antanas. Rinktiniai raštai. [By] Keturakis, [pseud.]. [Paruošė Vincas Kuzmickas]. Vilnius, Vaga, 1976. 190 p. (Lituanistinė biblioteka, 18). PG8721.V525A6 1976 PU.

2733. VITKAUSKAS, Arėjas. Už tėvynę; eilės ir apysakos iš kovų už Lietuvos nepriklausomybę metų 1919-1921. Independence, Mo., Cagey Historicals, 1975. 64 p. illus. Reprint of the 1926 ed., published in Kaunas. PG8721.V84U99 1975 CaAEU DLC.

2734. VYTIS-VRUBLEVIČIUS, Bruno. Lietuviai legijonieriai Vietname. [By] Vytis, [pseud.]. Toronto, Ont., 1968. 86 p. DS550.V93 PU;PPULC.

2735. ŽYMANTIENĖ, Julija (Beniuševičiūtė). Žemaitės raštai karės metu. [By] Žemaitė, [pseud.]. So.Boston, Mass., Lietuvos šelpimo fondo leidinys, 1917. 126 p. illus. PG8721.Z9 1917 DLC; CtY; CtTMF; MH; OCl; OKentU; PU; WaS.

XIII.5.c.3. PROSE

2736. ALANTAS, Vytautas. Amžinasis lietuvis; romanas. [London,Eng., Nida], 1972. 412 p. (Nidos knygų klubo leidinys, nr.84). PG8721.A45A5 PU; DLC; OkU; OKentU.

2737. --- Atspindžiai ūkanose; novelės. So.Boston, Mass., Lietuvių Enciklopedijos leidykla, 1976. 379 p. PG8721.A45A8 PU.

2738. Šventaragis; istorinis romanas. Cleveland, Ohio, Viltis, 1972-1974. 2 v. PG8721.A45S9 PU; DLC.

2739. ALEKSA, O[svaldas] and MISEVIČIUS, V[Vytautas]. Vidurnakčio sargybiniai. [Apsakymai. Dailininkas K. Ramonas]. Vilnius, Mintis, 1968. 124 p. illus. PG8722.1.L4V5 DLC

2740. ALMENAS, Kazys. Sauja skatikų; premijuotas romanas. Chicago,Ill. Draugo spaustuvė, 1977. 249 p. PG8749.A4S3 PU.

2741. --- Šienapiūtė; romanas. Vilnius, Vaga, 1970. 491 p. PG8749. A4S5 DLC; IU; MH; MB; NN; NjP;OKentU PU.

2742. ANDRIUŠIS, Pulgis. Anoj pusėj ežero; lyrinės apysakos. Nördlingen, Ger., Sudavija, 1947. 84 p. WU.

2743. --- Siuntinėlis iš Amerikos. Antroji tremties humoro knyga. Donauwörth, Sudavija, 1947. 96 p. WU.

2744. --- Vabalų vestuvės. Piešiniai Osmolskio. Schweinfurt, Ger., Tėviškės Garsas, 1948. 30 p. 891.92An26V PU; PPULC.

2745. APUTIS, Juozas. Horizonte bėga šernai. Novelės. Vilnius, Vaga, 1970. 175 p. PG8722.1.P8H6 DLC; NN; NNC; NjP.

2746. --- Rugsėjo paukščiai; novelės. Vilnius, Vaga, 1967. PG8722.1.P8R8 DLC; IU; MH.

2747. --- Sugrįžimas vakarėjančiais laukais; novelės. Vilnius, Vaga, 1977. 283 p. PG8722.1.P8S8 PU.

2748. --- Žydi bičių duona; apsakymai. Vilnius, Valstybinė grožinės literatūros leidykla, 1963. 53 p. port. PG8722.1.P8Z49 DLC; IU; MH.

2749. AVYŽIUS, J[onas]. Išsivadavimas. Vilnius, Valstybinė grožinės literatūros leidykla, 1951. 84 p. PG8721.A85I8 DLC.

2750. --- Kaimas kryžkelėje; romanas. 3-as leidimas. Vilnius, Vaga, 1970. 507 p.
PG8721.A85K3 1970 DLC; NN; NjP.

2751. --- Sodybų tuštėjimo metas; romanas. 2. leidimas. Vilnius, Vaga, 1973. 612 p. MB.

2752. --- Žmogus lieka žmogum; apsakymai ir apysakos. Vilnius, Vaga, 1975. 505 p.
PG8721.A85Z35 1975 DLC; PU.

2753. --- Žmogus ir įvykiai. Vilnius, Valstybinė grožinės literatūros leidykla, 1954. 146 p.
*QY--NN.

2754. BAGDONAVIČIUS, Kazys. Vargas dėl ploto. Vilnius, Vaga, 1973. 175 p. illus. Dailininkas A. Cvirka.
PG8722.12.A33V3 PU; MH.

2755. BALAŠEVIČIUS, Banguolis. Agentas ir robotas; fantastinė apysaka. Vilnius, Vaga, 1973. 237 p.
PG8722.12.A36A4 PU.

2756. BALČIŪNAS, Juozas. Karnavalo aikštėje; novelės. [By] Juozas Švaistas, [pseud.]. London, Eng., Nida, 1972. 284 p. PG8721.B27K3 PU; InU.

2757. --- Šilkinė suknelė; apysakos. Kaunas, 1927. At head of title: J. Švaistas, [pseud.]. RP; OCl.

2758. BALIONIENĖ, Emilija. Palaukių vasara. Vilnius, Vaga, 1967. 57 p. Short stories. NN.

2759. --- Prieblandos balanda; apsakymai. Vilnius, Vaga, 1972. 129 p. PG8722.12.A38P7 PU; MH.

2760. BALTRŪNAS, Aleksas. Šviesos gimimas; apsakymai. Vilnius, Vaga, 1974. 124 p. PG8721.B28S9 PU;DLC; WU.

2761. --- Tolimi keliai; apysaka. 2. pataisytas leidimas. Vilnius, Vaga, 1973. 421 p.
PG8721.B28T6 1973 DLC; MH; NN; WU.

2762. --- Traukiniai išeina iš pirmo kelio. Vilnius, Vaga, 1975. 359 p. PG8721.B28T7 PU; DLC.

2763. BALTUŠIS, Juozas. Abišalė; apsakymai. Vilnius, Vaga, 1974. 325 p. PG8721.B32A64 DLC; PU.

2764. BALTUŠNIKAS, Romualdas. Gegužio nakties vėjas; apsakymai. Vilnius, Vaga, 1977. 125 p.
PG8722.12.A46G4 PU.

2765. --- Sugrįžtantis šauksmas.

[Iliustravo B.Uogintas]. Vilnius, Vaga, 1969. 131 p. illus.
PG8722.12.A46S9 DLC; NjP.

2766. BALVOČIUS, Jonas. Jonukas Karklynas eina Lietuvos pažintų. Parašė Prietelis, [pseud.]. Shenandoah Pa., Lietuvių katalikiszkos bendrijos spaustuvėje, 1903. 47 p.
891.92.B219J PU; PPULC.

2767. --- Kunigo giminė. Parašė J. Gerutis, [pseud.]. Shenandoah, Pa., Kasztu A.Miluko, 1906. 68 p.
891.92B219K PU; PPULC.

2768. --- Paklydėliai. 2.leidimas. Parašė J.Gerutis,[pseud.]. Brooklyn, N.Y., Žvaigždės skyrius, 1915. 891.92.B219P PU; PPULC.

2769. BANAITIS, Juozas. Kelias į kalną. Vilnius, Vaga, 1970. 351 p.
PG8722.12.A5K4 DLC; CaOTU; IU; MB; MH; NNC; NjP; OKentU; PU.

2770. BARANAUSKAS, Albinas. Rudenys ir pavasariai; arba, Užplynių Pultinevičius namie ir svetur. Chicago, Ill., Lietuviškos knygos klubas, 1975-1976. 2 v. PG8721.B324R8 PU.

2771. BARONAS, Aloyzas. Abraomas ir sūnus; premijuotas romanas. Chicago, Ill., Lietuviškos knygos klubas, 1973. 206 p.
PG8721.B34A2 PU; DLC; InU.

2772. --- Šilko tinklai; pasakojimai. Chicago, Ill., Ateitis,1974. 184 p. (Literatūros serija, nr.9). PG8721.B34S5 PU; DLC.

2773. --- Vėjas lekia lyguma; romanas. 2. papildyta laida. Chicago, Ill., Lietuvos atgimimo sąjudis,1973. 188 p. (Laisvosios Lietuvos knygų leidyklos leidinys, nr.5). OU.

2774. BAUŽA, Aleksandras. Išeities taškas; apsakymai. Vilnius,Valstybinė grožinės literatūros leidykla, 1963. 153 p. PG8721.B37I8 DLC.

2775. BIELIAUSKAS, Alfonsas. Išdrožti sapnai. Vilnius, Vaga, 1973. 312 p. PG8701.B5 PU.

2776. --- Ji mylėjo Paulį; romanas. Vilnius, Vaga, 1976. 297 p.
PG8721.B43J5 PU.

2777. --- -tada, kai lijo; romanas. Vilnius, Vaga, 1977. 452 p.
PG8721.B43T3 PU.

2778. --- Siūbavo jovarai; apsakymai. Vilnius, Vaga, 1972. 243 p.
PG8721.B45S5 PU; DLC; IU; WU.

2779. BILIŪNAS, Jonas. Laimės žiburys. Vilnius, Vaga, 1976. 79 p. WU.

2780. --- Liūdna pasaka. Vilnius, Vaga, 1973. 279 p. PG8721.B47A6 1973 PU.

2781. BISTRICKAS, Stasys. Eiliniai žmonės; apybraižos. Vilnius, Valstybinė politinės ir mokslinės literatūros leidykla, 1957. 60 p. PG8721.B62A6 1957 CaAEU.

2782. BOCZKAUSKAS, T.D. Vaidelota; apisaka isz pirmutinės pusės trilikto szimtmeczio, iszimta isz Lietuviszku užlieku. Mahanoy City, Pa., Boczkauskas, 1907. 177 p. illus. GR203.L5B6 OKentU; WU.

2783. BORUTA, Kazys. Dangus griūva. Jurgio Paketurio klajonės. [Paaiškinimus parašė V.Vilnonytė]. Vilnius, Vaga, 1972. 442 p. (His Rinktiniai raštai, 5). PG8721.B6D3 1972 PU; MH; NNC.

2784. --- Mediniai stebuklai;arba, Dievadirbio Vinco Dovinės gyvenimas ir darbai. 2.leidimas. Vilnius, Vaga, 1971. 241 p. PG8721.B6M4 1971 CaOTU; PU; DLC; MH; WU.

2785. --- Neramūs arimai. [Sudarė ir paaiškinimus parašė V.Vilnonytė. Redakcinė komisija: J.Baltušis (pirmininkas), ir kiti.] Vilnius,Vaga, 1970. 440 p. illus. PG8721.B6N4 1970 DLC; CaOTU; IU;MB; MH; NN; NNC.

2786. --- Skambėkit vėtroje, beržai. [Sudarė ir paaiškinimus parašė V.Vilnonytė]. Vilnius, Vaga, 1975. 437 p. (His Raštai, 9). PG8721.B6S5 PU.

2787. --- Sunkūs paminklai. [Paaiškinimus parašė V.Vilnonytė]. Vilnius, Vaga, 1972. 356 p. (His Rinktiniai raštai, 4). PG8721.B6S8 1972 PU; MH; NNC.

2788. BRAZAUSKAS, Viktoras. Antrą kart gimę; apysaka ir apsakymai. Vilnius, Vaga, 1976. 205 p. PG8722.12.R29A5 PU.

2789. BRAZYTĖ-BINDOKIENĖ, Danutė. Baltosios pelytės kelionė į mėnulį. [Viršelis ir iliustracijos Elenos Brazytės. Chicago, Ill.], Lietuviškos knygos klubas,[1966]. 58 p. ill. MB.

2790. --- Parkas anapus gatvės. Chicago, Ill., JAV LB Švietimo taryba, 1973. 157 p. PZ90.L5B74 DLC;MB.

2791. --- Viena pasaulyje; romanas. Chicago, Ill., Lietuviškos knygos klubas, 1971. 241 p. PG8749.B7V5 PU; OCl.

2792. BUBNYS, Vytautas. Alkana žemė; romanas. Vilnius, Vaga, 1971. 397 p. illus. PG8722.12.U2A5 PU;DLC; MB; NNC.

2792a. --- Alkana žemė, Po vasaros dangum, Nesėtų rugių žydėjimas; trilogija. Vilnius, Vaga, 1977. 692 p. PG8722.2.U2A6 PU.

2793. --- Baltas vėjas; apysakos ir apsakymai [jaunesniam ir vidutiniam mokykliniam amžiui]. Vilnius, Vaga, 1974. 276 p. PG8722.12.U2B2 PU; DLC.

2794. --- Nesėtų rugių žydėjimas; romanas. Vilnius, Vaga, 1976. 517 p. PG8722.12.U2N4 PU.

2795. --- Po vasaros dangum; romanas. Vilnius, Vaga, 1973. 443 p. PG8722.12.U2P6 PU.

2796. BŪDAVAS, Stasius. Europietė. London, Eng., Nida, 1976. 173 p. PG8721.B81E8 PU.

2797. --- Širdys ir gėlės; apysakos. Kaunas, 1932. OCl.

2798. BUDRYS, Rimantas. Audra, pušis ir mano aviliai; novelės. Vilnius, Vaga, 1967. 79 p. PG8721.B814A9 DLC.

2799. --- Erškėtis prie kelio;novelės ir impresijos. Vilnius, Vaga, 1972. 89 p. PG8721.B814E7 PU; DLC; IU; MH; OKentU.

2800. --- Liepsnelė-saulės spindulys. Girios novelių romanas. Vilnius, Vaga, 1969. 373 p. PG8721.B814L5 DLC; CaAEU; MB; MH.

2801. BULOTA, Juozas. Atbulas išradimas; humoreskos, feljetonai, pamfletai. Vilnius, Vaga, 1974. 110 p. PG8722.12.U55A8 PU.

2802. ČEKUOLIS, A. Tylos takais. [Piešiniai A. Skliutauskaitės]. Vilnius, Valstybinė grožinės literatūros leidykla, 1960. 195 p. illus. G464.C38 OKentU.

2803. CINZAS, Eduardas. Brolio Mykolo gatvė. Chicago, Ill., Algimanto Mackaus knygų leidimo fondas, 1972. 306 p. PG8749.C5B7 DLC;InU; MB; OU; OKentU.

2804. --- Raudonojo arklio vasa-

ra; romanas. Chicago, Ill., Algimanto Mackaus knygų leidimo fondas,1975.
312 p.   PG8749.C5R3 DLC.

2805. CVIRKA, Petras. Ąžuolas;
apsakymai. [Dailininkas J.Kuzminskis]
Vilnius, Vaga, 1974. 381 p. illus.
PG8721.C8A88 1974 DLC; WU.

2806. --- Frank Kruk; arba, Gra-
borius Pranas Krukelis. Kaunas,Sa-
kalas, 1934.[Xerox copy, 1978].
2 v. PG8721.C8F7 1934a PU(xerox).

2807. --- Kasdienės istorijos;
apsakymai. [Iliustravo A.Makūnaitė].
Vilnius, Vaga, 1969. 147 p. illus.
PG8721.C8K3 1969 DLC; OKentU.

2808. --- Meisteris ir sūnūs; romanas. Vilnius, Vaga, 1976. 286 p.
PG8721.C8M4 1976 PU.

2809. --- Žemė maitintoja. Vil-
nius, Vaga, 1971. 250 p.
PG8721.C8Z4 1971 CaOTU; DLC; IEN;IU;
ICIU; MB; MH; NN; NNC.

2810. DAMBRAUSKAS, Aleksandras.
Nakties matymai; vaizdeliai iš arti-
mos praeities... Kaunas, S.Banaičio
spaustuvė, 1906. 32 p.   CtY.

2811. --- Svetimos gėlės; pasako-
jimai-mažmožiai. Kaunas; Vilnius,
1923. 158 p. At head of title:
A. Jakštas, [pseud.].   OCl.

2813. DAUTARTAS, Vladas. Auksinio
lino vaišės; apysakos. Vilnius, Vaga, 1976. 301 p.   WU.

2813. --- Ieškau mylimo veido;
apsakymų rinktinė. Vilnius, Vaga,
1977. 404 p. PG8722.14.A8I4 PU.

2814. --- Miškinukas ir senelis;
apsakymai.[Iliustravo Edmundas Žiau-
beris]. Vilnius, Vaga, 1971. 125 p.
PG8722.14.A8M5 PU; DLC.

2815. --- Paskui vaivorykštę; apsakymai. Vilnius, Vaga, 1974. 204 p.
PG8722.14A8P3 DLC; WU.

2816. --- Pokalbis su upokšniu;
novelių rinktinė. Vilnius, Vaga,
1971. 417 p. illus.
PG8722.14.A8P6 CaOTU; DLC; IU; MB;MH;
 NN; NNC.

2817. --- Prakeikimo vartai; apysaka. [Iliustravo Kastytis Skromanas]
2.leidimas. Vilnius, Vaga, 1974.
209 p. illus.   PG8722.14.A8P7 1974
DLC; WU.

2818. DIDŽIULYTĖ-MOŠINSKIENĖ, Halina. Ošiančios pušys. Chicago,Ill.,
Lietuviškos knygos klubas, 1968.

177 p.   PG8749.D5 DLC; OKentU.

2819. DIKONIS. Mužikų vaikai.
Vilkaviškis,[s.n.], 1931. 103 p. WU.

2820. DIRGĖLA, Povilas and DIRGĖ-
LA, Petras. Pasimatymai; apysakos.
182 p. PG8722.14.I7P3 DLC;MB;MH;NN.

2821. DIRGĖLA, Povilas and DIRGĖ-
LA, Petras. Šalavijų kalnas; roma-
nas. Vilnius, Vaga, 1977. 370 p.
PG8722.14.I7S3 PU.

2822. DIRGĖLA, Povilas. Žaibai
gęsta rudenį; [apysakų ir apsakymų
rinkinys]. Vilnius, Vaga, 1971. 367
p. port. PG8722.14.I7Z3 CaOTU;DLC;
IU; MB; MH; OU; PU; NN.

2823. DOVYDAITIS, Jonas. Dideli
įvykiai Naujamiestyje. Vilnius,Vals-
tybinė grožinės literatūros leidykla,
1956.   891.92D754D PU; CtY.

2824. --- Draugai iki mirties.
Kaunas, Valstybinė grožinės literatū-
ros leidykla, 1947. 94 p.
*Q p.v.1389--NN.

2825. DOVYDAITIS, Jonas. Keistos
vestuvės. Vilnius, Vaga, 1972. 448
p. PG8722.14.09K4 DLC;IU;NN;NNC;WU.

2826. --- Pavojingi keliai. Vilnius, Valstybinė grožinės literatūros leidykla, 1956. 325 p.   IU.

2827. --- Pavojų ieškotojai; romanas. Vilnius, Vaga, 1973. 386 p.
PG8722.14.09P3 DLC; MB; MH; WU.

2828. --- Perkūno žirgai; romanas.
Vilnius, Vaga, 1975. 518 p.
PG8722.14.09P4 DLC.

2829. --- Skaudi šviesa. Žydrieji
ežerai; romanai. 2.leidimas. Vilnius, Vaga, 1977. 522 p.
PG8722.14.09S58 1977 PU.

2830. DOVYDĖNAS, Liudas. Cenzūros
leista; Didžiajam Vilniaus seimui atminti. Kaunas, 1931. 205 p.   OCl.

2831. --- Naktys Karališkiuose;
apysaka. Chicago, Ill., Terra, 1955.
168 p. illus.   891.92D755N PU;OCl.

2832. --- Tūkstantis ir viena vasara; romanas. Detroit, Mich., L.Vis-
mantas, C.J.Walls, 1954. 1 v.
*QY--NN; PU.

2833. ELINAS, Mejeris. Per vieną
naktį. Vilnius, Valstybinė grožinės
literatūros leidykla, 1963. 240 p.
PG8722.15.L5P4 DLC.

2834. ENSKAITIS, Pranas. Rūtos ir

lelijos; skautiški apsakymai. [Hamilton, Ont., 1976] 135 p.
PG8721.E55R8 PU.

2835. FRANKIENĖ-VAITKEVIČIENĖ, Vanda. Užburtos kanklės; pasakojimai apie senovę. [Čikaga, Laiškai Lietuviams, 1971]. 166 p.
PG8721.F7U9 PU.

2836. GAILIUS, Jonas, pseud. Susitikimas; apysaka. New York, N.Y., 1951. Real name; Jonas Kuzmickis. 891.92.K969S PU; OCl.

2837. --- Gundymai; apysaka. Parašė Jonas Gailius, [pseud.]. Buenos Aires, Argentina, "Laiko" leidinys, 1957. 143 p. Real name: Jonas Kuzmickis. 891.92.K969G PU; OCl.

2838. --- Kaip jis ją nužudė. [Caracas, 1954]. 127 p. Real name: Jonas Kuzmickis. PG8721.G3K3 DLC.

2839. --- Kartuvės. Parašė Jonas Gailius, [pseud.]. Rodney, Ont., Rūta, 1951. 103 p. Real name: Jonas Kuzmickis. 891.92.K969K PU; OCl; DLC-P4(4 PG Lith.103).

2840. GAISRYS, Juozas. Gyvenimo žingsniai. Vilnius, Valstybinė politinės ir mokslinės literatūros leidykla, 1960. 245 p. illus.
PG8721.G33G9 1960 DLC.

2841. GALINDAS, Raimondas. Žvaigždės negęsta; apsakymai. Vilnius, Vaga, 1965. 61 p. PG8722.17.A4Z41 DLC.

2842. GIEDRA, Vincas. Eina į miška medžiai. [Dailininkė N. Meškauskaitė]. Vilnius, Vaga, 1971. 104 p. PG8722.17.I43E5 PU; DLC; MH; NNC; OKentU.

2843. --- Užkeikti namai; romanas. [Dailininkas A. Kubilius]. Vilnius, Vaga, 1967. 269 p. front.
PG8722.32.I5U9 OKentU.

2844. GIEDRAITIS, Antanas. Aišvydo pasakos. [By] Antanas Giedrius, [pseud.]. Iliustracijos Onos Baužienės. [Chicago, Ill., Lietuviškos knygos klubas, 1971]. 140 p.
PG8721.G47A5 PU; DLC.

2845. --- Murklys; apysaka. Boston, Mass., Išlaido "Keleivio" leidykla, 1962. 130 p. illus. At head of title: Author's pseud. A.Giedrius.
GR203.L5G52 OKentU.

2846. --- Smilgos; apsakymai. London, Eng., Nida Press, 1969. 205 p. (Nidos knygų klubo leidinys, nr. 74) At head of title: A.Giedrius.
PG8721.G46S5 DLC;MB; MnU.

2847. GIRDZIJAUSKAS, Vytautas. Trys moterys ir vienas vyras. Vilnius, Vaga, 1971. 240 p.
PG8721.G47A5 PU; MB; MH; NNC.

2848. --- Žmonės man buvo geri; romans. Vilnius, Vaga, 1973. 261 p.
PG8722.17.I68Z4 DLC; MH.

2849. GLIAUDYS, Jurgis. Brėkšnės našta; romanas. Chicago, Ill., Lietuviškos knygos klubas, 1972. 384 p. At head of title: Jurgis Gliauda.
PG8749.G6B7 DLC; PU.

2850. --- Liepsnos ir apmaudo ąsočiai. Chicago, Ill., Lietuviškos knygos klubas, 1969. 304 p.
PG8749.G6L5 DLC; MB; OCl.

2851. --- Sunkiausiu keliu; romanas. Chicago, Ill., Dr.Kazio Griniaus fondo keidinys, 1973 [1972]. 251 p. At head of title: Jurgis Gliauda.
PG8749.G6S9 1973 DLC; OKentU.

2852. --- Taikos Rytas; novelių rinkinys. London, Eng., Nida, 1972. 229 p. (Nidos knygų klubo leidinys, nr.83) At head of title: Jurgis Gliauda. PG9749.G6T3 DLC; MB; OU.

2853. GLINSKIS, Juozas. Verdenes. Vilnius, Vaga, 1967. 63 p. NN.

2854. GRICIUS, Augustinas. Tėvų tėvai; apsakymai. Vilnius, Vaga,1972. 323 p. PG8721.G635T4 DLC; IU; NN; OKentU; PU; WU.

2855. --- Vyrai, nesijuokit! Vilnius, Vaga, 1969. 425 p. PG8721.G635V9 DLC; IU; MB; MH; NN; OKentU.

2856. GRUŠAS, Juozas. Karjeristai; romanas. Vilnius, Vaga, 1971. 288 p. PG8721.G7K3 1971 PU; MH; MB.

2857. --- Laimingasis--tai aš. Vilnius, Vaga, 1973. 295 p. PG8721.G7L3 DLC; IU; MB; MH; OKentU; WU.

2858. GRYBAS, Vladas. Išeinu su saule. [Sudarė ir spaudai paruošė Rytis Trimonis]. Vilnius, Vaga,1977. 668 p. PG8721.G75I8 PU.

2859. GUDAITIS-GUZEVIČIUS, Aleksandras. Broliai; romanas. 3.leidimas. Vilnius, Vaga, 1977. 2 v. PG8721.G8B7 1977 PU.

2860. GURAUSKIS, Juozas. Apsakymai. Vilnius, Valstybinė grožinės literatūros leidykla, 1963. PG8721.G84A83 1963 DLC; NN.

2861. --- Rudens vėjas. [Paruošė

Vincas Kuzmickas]. Vilnius, Vaga, 1975. 292 p. PG8721.G84R8 PU.

2862. GUSTAITIS, Algirdas. Tarp Šveicarijos ir Danijos. Nördlingen, Ger., 1946. 96 p. WU.

2863. GUTAUSKAS, Leonardas. Ištrūko mano žirgai. Vilnius, Valstybinė grožinės literatūros leidykla, 1961. 58 p. illus. PG8721.G9I8 DLC.

2864. IGNATAVIČIUS, Eugenijus. Pradalgių tyla. Vilnius, Vaga, 1971. 178 p. PG8722.19.G5P7 DLC; MB; MH; NN; NNC; PU.

2865. --- Sekmadienio pieva. Vilnius, Vaga, 1966. 58 p. (Pirmoji knyga) PG8722.19.G5S4 DLC.

2866. INČIŪRA, Kazys. Fatima burtininkė. Kaunas, Vairas, 1929. 223 p. OCl.

2867. JACINEVIČIUS, Leonidas. Miestas didelis--mažas. Vilnius, Vaga, 1966. 69 p. (Pirmoji knyga) PG8722.2.A3M5 DLC.

2868. --- Rūgštynių laukas; apysakos. Vilnius, Vaga, 1968. 227 p. PG8722.2.A3R8 DLC; NN.

2869. JANAVIČIUS, Vytautas. Nevykelio užrašai. Iliustravo Eva Kubos. Sydney, Australia, H. Šalkauskas, 1975. 109 p. PG8722.2.A56N4 PU.

2870. JANKAUSKAS, Kazys. Jaunystė prie traukinio; romanas iš geležinkeliečių gyvenimo. Kaunas, Sakalas, 1936. [Xerox copy, 1977]. 262 p. T.p. and p. 45-46 wanting. PG8721.J27J3 1936a PU.

2871. --- Krito kaštonai. Vilnius, Valstybinė grožinės literatūros leidykla, 1959. 429 p. PG8721.J27K7 DLC; CLU; PU.

2872. JANKUS, Jurgis. Ir nebepasimatėm; pasakojimai. Chicago, Ill., Lietuviškos knygos klubas, 1977. 343 p. PG8749.J3I7 PU.

2873. --- Užkandis; pasakojimai. Brooklyn, N.Y., Ateitis, 1973. 219 p. (Literatūros serija, nr.7) PG8749.J3U9 DLC; InNd; MB; OKentU.

2874. JASINSKAS, Vladas. Ramonas pakėlė ginklą... Dokumentinė apybraiža. Vilnius, Mintis, 1967. 149 p. PG8722.2.A8R3 DLC; IU; MiEM; NN.

2875. --- Šūviai sauleteky. Vilnius, Valstybinė grožinės literatūros leidykla, 1961. 133 p.

PG8722.2.A8S8 DLC.

2876. JASIUKAITIS, Konstantinas. Griuvėsiuose. Boston, Mass., 1913. 891.92J314G PU.

2877. JUOZĖNAS, L. Pirmoji nuodėmė; feljetonai. Vilnius, Valstybinė grožinės literatūros leidykla, 1963. 98 p. PG8722.2.U6P5 DLC; MH.

2878. KAIRYS, Anatolijus. Ištikimoji žolė; romanas. Chicago, Ill., Lietuvos Atgimimo Sąjudis, 1971. 254 p. (Laisvosios Lietuvos knygų leidykla. Leidinys, nr.2) PG8721.K2I8 PU; DLC.

2879. KAPNYS, Stasys. Viešnagė kaime; apsakymai, pjesės, eilėraščiai. Vilnius, Vaga, 1975. 389 p. PG8721.K24V5 DLC; PU.

2880. KAREIVIS, J.D., pseud. Dvejopas galas. Kaunas, S. Banaičio spaustuvė, 1913. 31 p. (Šv. Kazimiero draugijos leidinys, nr.145). PG8721.K26D8 DLC.

2881. KARPIUS, Kazys S. Alpis, Kęstučio išlaisvintojas; istorinė apysaka. Cleveland, Ohio, Dirva, 1942. 288 p. At head of title: Kazimieras karpavičius. 891.92K149A PU;ICCC;WU.

2882. --- [Autoriaus pataisyta 2. laida. Cleveland, Ohio], Viltis, 1971. 227 p. PG8749.K3A5 1971 PU; OCl.

2883. KAŠAUSKAS, Raimondas. Motociklininkai; apysakos. Vilnius,Vaga, 1973. 292 p. PG8722.21.A715M6 DLC; NN.

2884. --- Suaugusiųjų žaidimai; apsakymai ir apysakos. Vilnius, Vaga, 1969. 310 p. PG8722.21.A7S8 PU; DLC; NjP.

2885. KASPERUNAS, Georgiĭ Vladimirovich. Kur veda keliai. Vilnius, Mintis, 1969. 153 p. PG8722.21.A77K8 DLC.

2886. KATILIŠKIS, Marius. Apsakymai. Chicago, Ill., Algimanto Mackaus knygų leidimo fondas, 1975. 253 p. PG8721.K29A8 PU; DLC.

2887. KAUKAS, Kostas. Milžinų sąspyriai; humoreskos, feljetonai,satyriniai apsakymai. [Dailininkas A. Cvirka]. Vilnius, Vaga, 1975. 219 p. illus. PG8722.21.A8M5 DLC.

2888. KAVALIŪNAS, Vacys. Aidai ir šešėliai; premijuotas romanas. Chicago, Ill., Lietuviškos knygos klubas, 1972. 234 p. PG8749.K38A7 DLC;PU.

2889. KAVALIŪNAS, Vacys. Hestera; romanas. Chicago. Ill., Lietuviškos knygos klubas, 1974. 221 p. PG8749.K38H4 DLC.

2890. --- Kalnų giesmė; premijuotas romanas. Chicago, Ill., Lietuviškos knygos klubas, 1963. 201 p. PG8722.21.A9K3 DLC; CaAEU;CtTMF;CtY; CaOONL; MB; PU.

2891. KAZANAVIČIENĖ, Aldona. Pajūrio pasakos. [Paruošė Jonas Stukas] Vilnius, Vaga, 1976. 291 p. PG8721.K35P3 1976 PU.

2892. KELIUOTIS, Juozas. Svajonės ir siaubas. Kaunas,[s.n.], 1940. 318 p. PG8721.K44S9 PU; CtTMF.

2893. KEMEŽAITĖ, Birutė. Sudiev! Aš išeinu...; romanas. Chicago, Ill., Laisvosios Lietuvos knygų leidykla, 1971. 295 p. PG8749.K43S8 PU;CaOTP.

2894. KESIŪNAS, Povilas. Tarp žalsvų palapinių; romanas. Chicago, Ill., 1953. 292 p. PG8721.K48T3 DLC; MB; MH; OCl; PU.

2895. KETURAKIS, Robertas. Saulabroliai. [Dailininkė E. Kučaitė]. Vilnius, Vaga, 1969. 111 p. illus. PG8721.K5S18 DLC; PU.

2896. KIAULEIKIS, Leonas. Be kaukės; feljetonai. [Iliustracijos Igno Martinaičio. Vilnius, Valstybinė grožinės literatūros leidykla, 1963. 115 p. illus. PG8722.21.I2B4 DLC; IU.

2897. --- Pražūtinga profesija. [Dailininkas S. Krasauskas]. Vilnius, Vaga, 1970. 151 p. illus. PG8722.21.I2P7 PU; DLC; IU; MB; MH; NN.

2898. --- Viskas iš dūmų. Vilnius, Vaga, 1967. 149 p. illus. PG8722.21.I2V5 DLC.

2899. KIELA, Kazys. Karvės oda. Vilnius, Vaga, 1970. 198 p. PG8722.21.I3K3 DLC; IU; MH; NN;NjP; PU.

2900. KLAJŪNAS, Jonas, pseud. Vištų karalija. [s.l., s.n.], 1944. 57 p. WU.

2901. KLIMAS, Ramūnas. Atostogos po Aukštaitijos pilnatimi; apsakymai ir apysakos. Vilnius, Vaga, 1976. 213 p. PG8722.21.L5A8 PU.

2902. --- Paukščių lesinimo šventė. Vilnius, Vaga, 1971. 92 p. (Pirmoji knyga) MH.

2903. KOCHANSKAS, Aleksandras. Neramios naktys. Vilnius, Mintis,1969. 94 p. PG8722.21.03N4 DLC.

2904. KRALIKAUSKAS, Juozas. Martynas Mažvydas Vilniuje; premijuotas romanas. Chicago, Ill., Lietuviškos knygos klubas, 1976. 307 p. PG8721.K65M3 PU.

2905. --- Tautvila; romanas. Chicago, Ill., Lietuviškos knygos klubas, 1973. 205 p. PG8721.K65T3 PU; DLC.

2906. --- Vaišvilkas; romanas. Chicago, Ill., Lietuviškos knygos klubas, 1971. 234 p. PG8721.K65V3 PU; DLC.

2907. KRĖVĖ-MICKEVIČIUS, Vincas. Dainavos šalies senų žmonių padavimai. 5. laida. Schweinfurt, Ger., [Išleido "Tėviškės" knygų leidykla], 1948. 221. p. PG8721.K7D2 1948 DLC;CaOTP; PU; WU.

2908. --- [Another edition]. Iliustravo S. Valiuvienė]. Kaunas, VGLL, 1957. 252 p. illus. PG8721.K7D2 1957 DLC; CaAEU; CaOTP; OKentU; PU.

2909. --- Raganius; prieškarinių laikų sodžiaus gyvenimo šešėliai. 3.leidimas. Nördlingen, Ger., Sudavijos leidykla, 1948. 192 p. OCl; WU.

2910. --- Žentas. Vilnius, Valstybinė grožinės literatūros leidykla, 1956. 170 p. At head of title: Vincas Krėvė. PG8721.K7Z4x OKentU;MH.

2911. KRIŠČIUKAITIS, Antanas. Brička. Iliustravo A.Kučas. Aišbė, [pseud.]. Kaunas, Valstybinė grožinės literatūros leidykla, 1947. 36 p. WU.

2912. --- --- [Another edition]. Medžio raižiniai A. Kučo. Vilnius, Valstybinė grožinės literatūros leidykla, 1964. 33 p. illus. PG8721.K744B7 DLC; WU.

2913. --- Kas teisybė, tai ne melas. Aišbė, [pseud.]. Vilnius, J. Zavadskis, 1905. 64 p. WU.

2914. --- --- "Aiszbės",[pseud.]. Szeszios pataisytos ir naujai atspaudytos apysakėlės. Tilžėje, Spauda M. Jankaus. PG8721.K744K3 1974 PU(xerox); DLC.

2915. --- ---; rinktinė. Vilnius, Vaga, 1974. 271 p. At head of title; A. Kriščiukaitis-Aišbė. PG8721.K744K3 1974 DLC.

2916. KUBILINSKAS, Kostas. Žalios pusnys. Vilnius, Vaga, 1972. 318 p. illus., ports. (Kostas Kubilinskas, 2). PG8722.21.U2Z2 1972 DLC; MB; MH; NNC; OKentU; WU.

2917. KUDIRKA, Vincas. Laisvos valandos. [Paruošė Aldona Vaitiekū- nienė]. Vilnius, Vaga, 1976. PG8721.K8 PU.

2918. LANKAUSKAS, Romualdas. Aki- mirka ir amžinybė; novelių rinktinė. Vilnius, Vaga, 1976. PG8721.L315A5 PU; WU.

2919. --- Džiaso vežimas; apysa- ka, novelės. Vilnius, Vaga, 1971. 149 p. PG8721.L315D9 DLC; MB; MH; NNC; OKentU; PU.

2920. --- Netikėtų išsipildymų valanda; romanas. Vilnius, Vaga, 1975. 257 p. PG8721.L315N4 PU;DLC.

2921. --- Prisiminimai po vidu- nakčio; romanas. Vilnius, Vaga,1977. 142 p. PG8721.L315P7 PU.

2922. --- Šmėkla; apysaka ir no- velės. Vilnius, Vaga, 1974. 237 p. PG8721.L315S52 PU; DLC.

2923. --- Tą šaltą žiemą; roma- nas. Atspindžiai jūros veidrody; a- pysaka. Vilnius, Vaga, 1972. 238 p. PG8721.L315T3 PU; MH; OKentU.

2924. LAPIENIS, Ignas. Senelės laivas; pasakojimai, padavimai, le- gendos. Vilnius, Valstybinė groži- nės literatūros leidykla, 1960. 105 p. illus. PG8721.L33S4 DLC.

2925. LASTAS, Adomas. Lietuvos knygnešio likimas; pergyvenimų apy- saka. K. Šimonio piešiniai. Šiau- liai, "Kultūros" b-vės leidinys,1925. [Xerox copy, 1977]. 52 p. PG8721.L335L5 1925a PU(xerox); WU.

2926. --- Saulėta pasakėlė. Le- lija; senovės lietuvių mytas. Vetra; didžiojo karo ūpas. Adomas Juodasai, [pseud.]. Marijampolė, 1920. 891.92L335 PU(film)

2927. LASTAUSKIENĖ, Marija (Iva- nauskaitė). Auka; apysaka. Vilniu- je, "Vilties" išleidimas, 1907.[Xe- rox copy, 1977]. 72 p. PG8721.L34A8 1907a PU(xerox); CtY.

2928. --- Radybos; apysaka. Įva- do žodį parašė Liudas Gira. Kaunas, "Sakalo" b-vės leidinys, 1930.[Xe- rox copy, 1977]. 163 p. At head of title: M. Lastauskienė-Lazdynų Pelė- da. p. 157-158 wanting. PG8721.L34R3 1930a PU(xerox); OCl.

2929. --- Šiaurės sostinėje; apy- saka. Lazdynų Pelėda, [pseud.]. Vil- nius, Vaga, 1972. 212 p. PG8721.L34S5 PU.

2930. --- Upės dovana; apsakymė- liai. Kaunas, Valstybinė grožinės literatūros leidykla, 1946. 64 p. PG8721.L34U6 DLC.

2931. LAUCEVIČIUS, Bronius. Antras krikštas; šių laikų apysaka. Parašė Br. Vargšas, [pseud.]. Chicago, Ill., 1907. 83 p. *QYN p.v. 379, no.4. NN.

2932. LAURINAVIČIUS, Povilas. Be druskos...; romanas. Chicago, Ill., Chicagos lietuvių literatūros draugi- jos leidinys, 1968. 404 p. port. PG8749.L39B4 DLC; OKentU; PU; PPULC.

2933. LESKAITIS, Stasys. Spūdai. Kaunas, Sakalas, 1937.[Xerox copy, 1975]. 180 p. At head of title: Sta- sys Ivošiškis. PG8721.L46S6 1975 PU.

2934. LUKAŠEVIČIUS, Henrikas. Li- kimo žaismas; romanas. Chicago, Ill., Lietuviškos knygos klubas, 1953. 231 p. PG8721.L8L5 DLC; CaOONL; PU; ICIU.

2935. LUKINSKAS, Romualdas. Gam- tos klaida; apsakymai. Vilnius, Va- ga, 1964. 125 p. PG8722.22.U4G3 DLC

2936. --- Mėlynas laukas; apysa- kos ir apsakymai. Vilnius, Vaga,1971. 619 p. PG8722.22.U4M4 PU; DLC; IU; MB; MH.

2937. MACIJAUSKAS, Jonas. Saulė leidžias, saulė teka; atsiminimai. Literatūrinis bendraautoris P. Marge- vičius. Vilvius, Valstybinė grožinės literatūros leidykla, 1961. 285 p. illus. DK511.L28M3 DLC.

2938. MACIJAUSKIENĖ, Marija. Gy- venimo akimirkos. Vilnius, Mintis, 1968. 94 p. PG8722.23.A29G9 CaAEU.

2939. MAČIUKEVIČIUS, Jonas. Bu- čiuoju šalį; romanas. Vilnius, Vaga, 1976. 246 p. PG8722.23.A295B8 PU.

2940. --- Laikrodžiai nesustoja; apysaka, vyresniam mokykliniam amžiui. [Il. N. Kryževičiūtė-Jurgelionienė]. 2. leidimas. Vilnius, Vaga, 1974.. 213 p. illus. PG8722.23.A295L3 1974 DLC.

2941. --- Rojaus kampelis; apysa- ka. Vilnius, Vaga, 1971. 251 p. PG8722.23.A295R5 PU; DLC; IU; MH; OKentU.

2942. --- Trys pirštai; apysaka.

Vilnius, Vaga, 1973. 186 p.
PG3722.23.A295T7 PU; DLC.

2943. MAČIULIS, Jonas. Augo die-
medis; apsakymai apie Petro Cvirkos
vaikystę. 2. papildytas leidimas.
Vilnius, Vaga, 1976. 221 p.
PG8722.23.A297A8 1976 PU.

2944. MANE JUS JAUSITE DARBE, KO-
VOJ. [Redakcinė komisija: Kostas Kor-
sakas, Alfonsas Maldonis, Eduardas
Mieželaitis. Sudarė Arvydas Valionis]
Vilnius, Vaga, 1976. 313 p.
PG8721.N4Z8 PU.

2945. MARCINKEVIČIUS, Antanas.
Nuo Lazduonos į Donbasą. Vilnius,
Vaga, 1967. 122 p.
PG8721.M336N8 DLC.

2946. MARCINKEVIČIUS, Jonas. Kario pasakojimai. Vilnius, Vaga,1975.
150 p. PG8721.M34K3 PU.

2947. MARGERIS, Algirdas. Saulės
rūstybė. Chicago, Ill., Naujienų
spauda, 1955. 311 p.
PG8749.M3S3 OKentU.

2948. MARKEVIČIUS, Anelius. Grum-
tynės įlankoje; novelės. Vilnius,
Vaga, 1972. 188 p.
PG8721.M355G7 PU; DLC; IU; MH.

2949. --- Juokas vidurnakty; novelių rinktinė. Vilnius, Vaga, 1974.
437 p. PG8721.M355J8 PU; MH.

2950. MARTINKUS, Vytautas. Akmenys; romanas. Vilnius, Vaga, 1972.
314 p. PG8722.23.A72A5 PU; DLC;MH;
NNC.

2951. --- Rotušės laikrodžio va-
gis; apsakymai. Vilnius, Vaga, 1974.
234 p. PG8722.23.A72R PU; DLC.

2952. MARUKAS, K., pseud. Kam pa-
tekės saulė; romanas. 2. laida.
Vilnius, Vaga, 1971. 373 p.
PG3721.M36K3 1971 DLC; IU; MH.

2953. --- O mūsų tiek mažai; romanas. Vilnius, Vaga, 1973. 301 p.
PG8721.M36 O PU; DLC; MH; OKentU;WU.

2954. MELNIKAS, Petras. Debesys
ir properšos. Chicago, Ill., Lietuviškos knygos klubas, 1977. 292 p.
PG8749.M42D4 PU.

2955. MERAS, Itskhokas. Lygiosios trunka akimirką; romanas. Vilnius, Valstybinė grožinės literatūros leidykla, 1963. 301 p.
PG8722.23.E7L9 DLC; MH; NN.

2956. --- ---. Ant ko laikosi pasaulis. Vilnius, Vaga, 1968. 306 p.

PG8722.23.E7L9 1968 DLC.

2957. --- Mėnulio savaitė; romanas. Vilnius, Vaga, 1971. 193 p.
PG8722.23.E7M4 DLC; MB; MH.

2958. --- Striptizas; arba, Pary-
žius-Roma-Paryžius. Southfield, Mich.
Ateitis, 1976. 227 p.
PG8722.23.E7S7 PU.

2959. --- Žemė visada gyva; novelės. Vilnius, Valstybinė grožinės
literatūros leidykla, 1963. 146 p.
PG8722.23.E7Z4 DLC; PU.

2960. MIKELINSKAS, Jonas. Genys
yra margas...; romanas. Vilnius, Vaga, 1976. 291 p.
PG8722.23.I35G4 PU.

2961. --- Rugpiūčio naktį; apsakymų rinktinė. Vilnius, Vaga, 1971.
377 p. PG8722.23.I35R8 PU; DLC; IU;
MH; MB.

2962. --- Vandens nešėja; romanas.
Antras leidimas. Vilnius, Vaga, 1972.
300 p. NN.

2963. --- Žvaigždžių dulkės; apysakos ir apsakymai. Vilnius, Vaga,
1975. 445 p. PG8722.23.I35Z45 DLC;
PU.

2964. MIKULĖNAITĖ, Ema. Pirmasis
meilės laiškas; apsakymai. Vilnius,
Vaga, 1972. 130 p.
PG8722.23.I38P PU; MH.

2965. MILIŪNAS, Viktoras. Juoda
upė; apsakymai. Vilnius, Vaga, 1970.
270 p. PG8721.M47J8 DLC; NN; NNC;
NjP; OKentU; PU.

2966. --- Vestuvės "Paryžiuje";
apsakymai. Vilnius, Vaga, 1973. 326
p. PG8721.M47V PU; DLC; WU.

2967. MINGĖLA, Vladas. Medinis
Dievas. Detroitas, 1974. 246 p.
PG8721.M49M4 PU.

2968. MINIOTAS, Vladas. Žvėjai iš-
plaukia į jūrą. Vilnius, Mintis,
1966. 76 p. PG8722.23.I5Z9 DLC;NN.

2969. MISEVIČIUS, Vytautas. Čiči-
nskas; apysaka. Kaunas, Šviesa, 1968.
96 p. illus. PG8722.23.I72C5 DLC;
IU; MH.

2970. MIŠKINIS, Antanas. Žaliaduo-
nių gegužė; pasakojimai. Vilnius,Va-
ga, 1977. 274 p.
PG8721.M53Z3 PU.

2971. MIZARA, Rojus. Kelias
į laimę; apysaka. Richmond Hill,N.Y.

Laisvė, 1950. 368 p.
PG8749.M5K4 OKentU.

2972. --- Povilas Jurka. Mortos
divorsas. Kelias į laimę. Romanai.
[Dailininkas K. Dockus]. Vilnius,
Vaga, 1973. 573 p. illus.
PG8749.M57P6 1973 DLC; MB; MH;OKentU
WU.

2973. MORKUS, Albinas. Laukinių
Vakarų madona; rinktinė. Vilnius,Va-
ga, 1970. 294 p.
PG8722.23.07L38 DLC; NN.

2974. MUSTEIKIS, Antanas. Kiau-
ros rieškučios; romanas. Chicago,
Ill., Lietuviškos knygos klubas,1972.
259 p. PG8749.M8K5 DLC; OCl; PU.

2975. MYKOLAITIS, Vincas. Altorių
šešėly; romanas. Trijose dalyse. Chicago, Ill., Išleido Literatūros megėjų burelis,[n.d.]. 631 p. At head
of title: V.Mykolaitis-Putinas.
PG8721.M9A67 OKentU.

2976. --- --- 5.leidimas. Vilnius, Vaga, 1971. 613 p. At head
of title: V. Mykolaitis-Putinas.
PG8721.M9A67 1971 PU.

2977. --- Krizė; romanas. Kaunas,
Sakalas, 1937.[Xerox copy, 1976].
33o p. PG8721.M9K7 1937a PU(xerox)
At head of title: V.Mykolaitis-Putinas.

2978. --- Sukilėliai; kovų dėl
žemės ir laisvės vaizdai, 1861-1864.
Vilnius, Vaga, 1973. 615 p. At
head of title: V. Mykolaitis-Putinas.
Contents.--1. Gana to jungo.--2. Ginklai. PG8721.M9S8 1973 PU; DLC; MB
MH; WU.

2979. NARAŠKEVIČIUS, Petras. Di-
delio miesto gatvė; apysaka. Vilnius,
Vaga, 1969. 117 p. illus.
PG8722.24.A68D5 DLC.

2980. NAUJOKAITIS, Pranas. Maži
žingsniai; pasakojimai jaunimui.
[Brooklyn, N.Y., Išleido Lietuvių
Bendruomenės New Yorko Apygarda],
1960. 119 p. illus. OKentU.

2981. --- Pasisėjau žalią rūtą;
romanas. Brooklyn, N.Y., Darbininkas, 1972. 232 p.
PG8721.N35P3 PU; OKentU.

2982. NENDRĖ, O. Antroji banga;
romanas. Chicago, Ill., 1970. 202p.
PG8749.N4A8 DLC; MB.

2983. NORBUTAS, Vytautas. Skor-
piono ženklas; fantastiniai apsakymai. Iliustravo Alfonsas Augaitis.
Vilnius, Vaga, 1972. 188 p.
PG8722.24.07S5 PU; DLC.

2984. ORINTAITĖ, Petronėlė. Erelių
kuorai; romanas. Cleveland, Ohio,
Viltis, 1976. 384 p.
PG8721.07E7 PU.

2985. --- Iš sostinės; apysakos.
Kaunas, 1932.[Xerox copy, 1977]. 160
p. PG8721.07I81932a PU.

2986. --- Liepalotų medynuose.
London, Eng., Nida, 1971. 216 p.
(Nidos knygų klubo leidinys, nr.82)
OU.

2987. PAKALNIS, Antanas. Inteli-
gentų klubas. Vilnius, Vaga, 1970.
127 p. NNC.

2988. CANCELLED.

2989. PAKALNIŠKIS, Aleksandras.
Mes grįžtama; jauno žmogaus dienoraštis. [Čikaga, S. Jankus, 1974]. 367
p. DK511.L28P32 PU.

2990. PAUKŠTELIS, Juozas. Čia mūsų namai; romanas(III). Vilnius, Vaga, 1970. 486 p.
PG8721.P37C5 1970 OKentU.

2991. --- CANCELLED.

2992. --- Kaimynai; romanas. Vilnius, Vaga, 1966. 252 p.
PG8721.P37K3 1966 OKentU.

2993. --- Netekėk saulele! Roma-
nas. Vilnius, Vaga, 1974. 333 p.
"Romana II" of the author's trilogy.
Sequel: Jaunystė. PG8721P37N4 1974
DLC.

2994. PAŽĖRAITĖ, Karolė. Anapilio
papėdėje; romanas. Chicago, Ill.,
Lietuviškos knygos klubas, 1971. 286
p. PG8721.P38A82 DLC; PU.

2995. --- Liktūnas; romanas. Eich-
stätt-Rebdorf, Ger., Suduva, 1948.
198 p. WU.

2996. PEČKAUSKAITĖ, Marija. Apysakėlės. Shenandoah, Pa., Žvaigždės
spaustuvėje, 1907. 69 p. PU.

2997. --- Adomienė; gyvenimo pie-
šinėlis. Vilniuje, M. Kuktos spaustuvė, 1908. 24 p. ("Vilties" išleidimas, nr.9) At head of title: Šatrijos Ragana, pseud.
891.92P336Ad PU; CtY.

2998. --- Dėl tėvynės. Parašė
Šatrijos Ragana, [pseud.]. Kaune,Sa-
liamono Banaičio spaustuvė, 1907. 35
p. Hvc48P341 CtY; OCl.

2999. --- Į šviesą. Vilnius, Vaga, 1974. 190 p. At head of title:
Šatrijos Ragana. PG8721.P4A6 1974 PU.

3000. PETKEVIČIUS, Vytautas. Apie
duoną, meilę ir šautuvą; romanas.
2. pataisytas leidimas. Vilnius, Vaga, 1974. 588 p.
PG8722.26.E8A8 1974 DLC.

3001. --- Baltas šešėlis; apsakymai. Vilnius, Vaga, 1970. 246 p.
8722.26.E8B3 DLC; NN; OKentU.

3002. --- Ko klykia gervės; apysaka. [Vidutiniam mokykliniam amžiui]
Iliustravo E. Žiauberis. 2-as leidimas. Vilnius, Vaga, 1973. 309 p.
illus. PG8722.26.E8K6 1973 DLC.

3003. --- Visi prieš vieną; apsakymai dideliems, mažiems ir milži-
nams. Vilnius, Vaga, 1976. 177 p.
PG8722.26.E8V5 PU.

3004. PIKTURNA, Ignas. Jūrų vėjai; apsakymai. Vilnius, Vaga, 1975.
PG8721.P55J82 PU.

3005. --- Rasa. Vilnius, Vaga,
1968. 262 p. ICIU.

3006. --- Šiandien jūra graži;
apsakymai. Vilnius, Valstybinė grožinės literatūros leidykla, 1960.
187 p. illus. PG8721.P55S5 DLC.

3007. PLAČENIS, Kazys. Pulkim ant
kelių...; romanas iš kun. Antano
Strazdo gyvenimo. 2. laida. Brook-
lynn, N.Y., 1958-1966. 2 v.
891.92P682P PU; CtTMF(v.1); OKentU.

3008. POCIUS, Algirdas. Ištirpę
migloje; apsakymai. Vilnius, Vaga,
1972. 185 p. PG8721.P6I8 PU; DLC;
IU; NN.

3009. --- Randai medyje; apsakymų rinktinė. Vilnius, Vaga, 1968.
362 p. illus. PPULC.

3010. Tik du sūnūs; apsakymai.
Vilnius, Vaga, 1966. 133 p.
PG8721.P6T5 DLC; MH; NNR; NN.

3011. POLIS, Algimantas. Tik vie-
na naktis; apsakymai ir apysaka.
Vilnius, Vaga, 1971. 154 p.
PG8722.26.O5T5 PU; DLC.

3012. Polis, Algirdas. Jūros dulkės. Vilnius, Valstybinė grožinės
literatūros leidykla, 1961. 57 p.
illus. PG8721.P64J8 DLC.

3013. POŽĖRA, Juozas. Atsisvei-
kinimas su šiaure. Vilnius, Mintis,
1972. 248 p. DK771.C4P65 DLC;NN.

3014. --- Auksas. Dvi apysakos.
[Dailininkas A. Švabas]. Vilnius,
Vaga, 1971. 252 p. illus.
PG8722.26.O9A96 DLC;IU;MB;MH;PU.

3015. --- Baltos saulės diena;me-
džiotojo užrašai. [Dailininkas A. Ta-
rabilda]. Vilnius, Mintis, 1966.
162 p. illus.
PG8722.26.O9B3 DLC; MoSW; NN.

3016. --- Man vaidenasi arkliai;
apysakos. Vilnius, Vaga, 1977. 393 p.
PG8722.26.O9A6 1977 PU.

3017. --- Mano teismas; romanas.
Vilnius, Vaga, 1968. 235 p.
PG8722.26.O9M33 DLC; PPULC; OKentU.

3018. --- Mano vienintelis rūpestis. Vilnius, Vaga, 1967. 261 p.
PG8722.26.O9M35 DLC.

3019. --- Meškos mokslai. Vilnius, Vaga, 1969. 84 p. illus.
PZ90.L5P6 DLC.

3020. --- Šiaurės eskizai. [Dail.
I. Katinienė]. Vilnius, Mintis, 1969.
140 p. illus.
PG8722.26.O9S5 DLC.

3021. PRAČKAUSKAITĖ, Cecilija. Ku-
mečio duktė; apysaka. [Literatūrinis
bendraautoris: P. Margevičius]. Vilnius, Valstybinė grožinės literatūros
leidykla, 1960. 292 p. illus.
PG8721P67K8 1960 DLC; PU.

3022. PŠIBILIAUSKIENĖ, Sofija (Ivanauskaitė). Stebuklingoji tošelė.
[Vyresniam mokykliniam amžiui. Iliustravo K. Juodikaitis]. Vilnius, Vaga, 1972. 243 p. illus. At head of
title: Lazdynų Pelėda.
PG8721.P7S8 1972 DLC; WU.

3023. PUIDA, Kazys. Geležinis vil-
kas; romanas. Kaunas, Krivulė, 1927.
[Xerox copy, 1977]. 256 p.
PG8721.P84G4 1927a PU(xerox); WU(orig)

3024. PŪKELEVIČIŪTĖ, Birutė. Naujųjų metų istorija; romanas. Chicago, Ill., Lietuviškos knygos klubas,
1974. 183 p. PG8749.P8N3 DLC.

3025. RAGAUSKIENĖ, R. (Aidukaitė).
Skaraidykit kaip paukštės. Vilnius,
Vaga, 1965. 286 p. At head of title:
R. Aidukaitė-Ragauskienė.
PG8722.28.A36S56 DLC; IU; MH.

3026. RALYS, Jeronimas. Rykštės.
[s.l.], Škotijos Šviesos draugystė,
1902.[Xerox copy, 1975.] 24 p. At
head of title: Nežinomas, [pseud.].
PG8721.R29R9 PU.

3027. RAMANAUSKAS, Antanas. Lie-
tuvos vaizdeliai. [Brooklyn, N.Y.,
Knygos megėjų klubas, 1962]. 100 p.
PG8749.R31L5 PU; CaOONL.

3028. RAMONAS, Vincas. Dulkės raudonam saulėleidy. 2.papildytas leidimas. Chicago, Ill., JAV LB Švietimo taryba, 1976. 399 p. PG8721.R3D8 1976 PU.

3029. --- Kryžiai; romanas. [Tübingen, Ger.], Patria, 1948. 318 p. PG8721.R3K7 1948 OKentU.

3030. RASA, Rėnė, pseud. Meilė trikampyje. Chicago, Ill., Lietuviškos knygos klubas, 1967. 219 p. Real name: Regina Raslavičienė. PG8722.28.A79M3 CaAEU; CaOONL.

3031. RIMKEVIČIUS, Vytautas. Girėnai. Vilnius, Vaga, 1971. 276 p. illus. PG8722.28.I58G48 DLC; IU; MB; MH.

3032. --- Kaimo kronikos. [Dail. V. Kalinauskas]. Vilnius, Vaga, 1967. 349 p. illus. PG8722.28.I58K3 DLC; MH; NN.

3033. --- Nuosavas velnias. Vilnius, Vaga, 1970. 349 p. illus. PG8722.28.I58N8 DLC; PU.

3034. RIMKUS, Petras. Abejingumas. Vilnius, Mintis, 1967. 92 p. PG8722.28.I59A63 DLC.

3035. RODA, Donatas. Nuotykinga kelionė; pamfletas. Vilnius, Vaga, 1974. 166 p. PG8722.28.O3N8 PU.

3036. RŪTA, Alė, pseud. Laiškas jaunystei; beletristika. [Brooklyn, N.Y., Pranciškonų spaustuvė], 1977. 131 p. PG8721.R82L3 PU.

3037. --- Po Angelų sparnais;novelės. London, Eng., Nida Press, 1973. 192 p. (Nidos knygų klubo leidinys, nr.89) PG8749.R8P6 DLC; MB; PU.

3038. --- Prisikėlimas; romanas. London, Eng., Nida Press, 1968. 205 p. (Nidos knygų klubo leidinys, nr. 68). PG8749.R8P74 DLC; OKentU.

3039. SABALIAUSKAS, Adolfas. Kada rožės žydžia. Žalios Rūtos [pseud.] atausta tautos pasaka. Helsinkai, Suomių literatūros draugijos spaustuvė, 1917.[Xerox copy, 1977]. 76 p. PG8721.S3K3 1917a PU.

3040. SADAUSKAS, Romas. Mažas girios dienoraštis. Vilnius, Vaga, 1976. 238 p. PG8722.29.A29M3 PU.

3041. SADŪNAS, Jonas. Broliai Kilimoniai. Vilnius, Mintis, 1973. 91 p. PG8722.29.A3B7 DLC; OKentU.

3042. SAJA, Kazys. Po to, kai

jie pavirto medžiais; apysakos, apsakymai, pasakos. Vilnius, Vaga,1976. 414 p. PG8722.29.A38P6 PU.

3043. ŠALTENIS, Saulius. Atostogos. Vilnius, Vaga, 1966. 73 p. (Pirmoji knyga). PG8722.29.A43A9 DLC.

3044. --- Riešutų duona; apysakos. Vilnius, Vaga, 1972. 176 p. illus. PG8722.29.A43R5 PU; DLC; IU; OKentU.

3045. ŠAVELIS, Rimantas. Dievo avinėlis; romanas. Vilnius, Vaga, 1974. 374 p. PG8722.29.A9D5 PU;MB.

3046. SAVICKIS, Jurgis. Šventadienio sonetai. Berlynas, 1922. 144 p. PG8721.S37S84 OKentU; CtY; OCl; OCU; PU.

3047. --- Ties aukštu sostu. Kaunas, 1928. [Xerox copy, 1976]. 236 p. PG8721.S37T5 1928a PU(xerox);OCl(orig)

3048. ŠIMKUS, Jonas. Naujo kelio pradžia. [Redakcinė komisija: A. Venclova (pirm.). Vilnius, Vaga, 1970. 466 p., 4 leaves of illus. PG8721.S48N3 DLC; CtY; NjP.

3049. --- Prie krintančio vandens; apysaka ir apsakymai. Vilnius, Vaga, 1976. 262 p. PG8721.S48P7 PU;DLC.

3050. SIMONAITYTĖ, Ieva. Aukštųjų Šimonių likimas. Vilnius, Vaga, 1966. 326 p. illus. PG8721.S5A9 OKentU.

3051. --- --- ; romanas. Vilnius, Vaga, 1973. 337 p. PG8721.S5A9 1973 PU.

3052. --- --- Vilnius, Vaga,1976. 335 p. WU.

3053. --- Paskutinė Kūnelio kelionė; romanas. Vilnius, Vaga, 1971. 271 p. PG8721.S5P29 PU; DLC; CaAEU; IU; MB; MH; NN.

3054. --- Pikčiurnienė; apysaka. 4.leidimas. Vilnius, Vaga, 1975. 304 p. PG8721.S5P5 1975 DLC.

3055. --- Vilius Karalius; romanas. 1.tomas. Kaunas, Švietimo ministerijos Knygų leidimo komisijos leidinys, 1939. 445 p. No more published in this edition. PG8721.S5V5 PU.

3056. SIMUKAS IR MAGDUTĖ, tikras atsitikimas. Chicago, Ill., Lėšomis ir spauda "Lietuvis", 1913. 28 p. *QYN p.v.379, no.8--NN.

3057. SIRIJOS GIRA, Vytautas. Atlanto idilės; romanas. Vilnius, Vaga, 1973. 278 p. PG8721.S52A8 PU;MH.

3058. --- Bėgimas nuo šešėlio; romanas. Vilnius, Vaga, 1975. 325 p. PG8721.S52B4 PU; WU.

3059. --- Buenos Aires. Voratinkliai draikės be vėjo; romanai. Vilnius, Vaga, 1976. 518 p. PG8721.S52B79 1976 PU.

3060. --- Raudonmedžio rojus; romanas. Vilnius, Vaga, 1972. 374 p. PG8721.S52R3 PU; MB; MH.

3061. --- Štai ir viskas. Atlanto idilės; romanai. Vilnius, Vaga, 1977. 459 p. PG8721.S52S7 1977 PU.

3062. --- Susitikimas su Brunhilda; apsakymai ir apysakos. Vilnius, Vaga, 1971. 216 p. PG8721.S53B3 DLC; CaOTU; MB; NjP; PU.

3063. SKIRKA, Antanas. Kur bėga Šešupė; pasakojimai ir legendos. [Belmore, Australia], 1964. 132 p. PG8721.S525K8 PU; OKentU.

3064. ŠKLIARAS, B. Raudona šviesa. Vilnius, Mintis, 1971. 92 p. At head of title: B.Škliaras, R.Žarėnas. PG8722.29.K53R3 DLC.

3065. SKODŽIUS, Petras. Atsiiknojusi lentelė; satyra ir humoras. Vilnius, Valstybinė grožinės literatūros leidykla, 1959. 197 p. illus. PG8721.S54A92 DLC.

3066. --- Didysis susivienijimas; satyrinė apysaka. Vilnius, Valstybinė grožinės literatūros leidykla,1963. 208 p. illus. PG8722.29K6D5 DLC.

3067. --- Meilės paslaptys; humoras su trupučiuku satyros. [Iliustracijos J. Varno]. Vilnius, Vaga,1968. 165 p. illus. PG8722.29.K6M4 DLC.

3068. --- Sunku būti moterimi; novelės. Vilnius, Vaga, 1973. 158 p. PG8722.29.K6S9 DLC; IU.

3069. SKRIPKAUSKAS, Antanas. Savanoriai aria; romanas. Kaunas, Karvelio ir Rinkevičiaus prekybos namų leidinys, 1936.[Xerox copy, 1977]. 197 p. PG8721.S526S3 1936a PU(xerox)

3070-3073 CANCELLED.

3074. SLUCKIS, Mykolas. Aš vėl matau vėliavą; rinktiniai apsakymai vaikams. [Iliustravo K. Juodikaitis] 345 p. illus. PG8721.S56A75 DLC;WU.

3075. --- Išdaigos ir likimai. Dailininkas St. Krasauskas. Vilnius, Vaga, 1964. 263 p. IEN; MH;OKentU.

3076. --- Kvietimas šokiui vidurnaktį; apysakos ir romanas. Vilnius, Vaga, 1977. 392 p. PG8721.S56K9 PU.

3077. --- Laiptai į dangų; romanas. Vilnius, Valstybinė grožinės literatūros leidykla, 1964. 450 p. PG8722.29.L8L3 DLC; NN; PU.

3078. --- --- 2.leidimas. Vilnius, Vaga, 1970. 376 p. PG8722.29.L8L3 1970 DLC; IU; MB; MH; NjP; OKentU.

3079. --- Merginų sekmadienis; apsakymai ir apysakos. [Dailininkas A. Každailis]. Vilnius, Vaga, 1971. 425 p. illus. PG8721.S56M4 DLC; PU.

3080. --- Nedidelė avarija; apysakos. Vilnius, Vaga, 1976. 522 p. PG8721.S56N4 PU; DLC; WU.

3081. --- Saulė vakarop; romanas. Vilnius, Vaga, 1976. 429 p. PG8721.S55S3 PU.

3082. --- Svetimos aistros; apysaka. 2.leidimas. Vilnius, Vaga, 1975. 341 p. PG8721.S56S9 1975 PU;MH.

3083. --- Vėjų pagairėje; novelės. Vilnius, Valstybinė grožinės literatūros leidykla, 1958. 315 p. IU; OKentU.

3084. SMALSTYS, Jurgis. Vasaros rytas. Vilnius, "Naujosios Gadynės" išdavimas, 1906.[Xerox copy, 1975]. 16 p. PG8721.S58V3 PU(xerox).

3085. ŠMULKŠTYS, Vaikų balius. Chicago, Ill., Draugas, 1928. 47 p. At head of title: Paparonis, [pseud.] OCl.

3086. SPALIS, Romualdas, pseud. Gatvės berniuko nuotykiai; apysaka jaunimui ir senimui. [Memmingen,Ger., Tremtis, 1952]. 508 p. IU;OCl; PU.

3087. --- --- Chicago, Ill., Vyduno fondas, 1969. [2. pataisytoji laida. Iliustracijos Alg. Trinkūno]. 527 p. illus. PG8721.S64G3 1969 DLC; MB.

3088. SPRINDIS, Adolfas. Senelė nori mirti. Vilnius, Vaga, 1970. 153 p. PG8722.29.P7S4 PU; NjP.

3089. STANEVIČIUS, Simonas. Pasakėčios. [Edited by] J. Lebedys. Vilnius, Valstybinė grožinės literatūros leidykla, 1948. 49 p. WU.

3090. STAUGAITIS, Justinas. Tiesiu keliu; apysaka iš mūsų atgimimo

laikų. Kaunas, Šv. Kazimiero draugija, 1934-1935. 3 v. (Šv. Kazimiero draugijos leidinys, nr.612,620,
624). At head of title; J. Gintautas, [pseud.].
PG8721.S69T5 OKentU; WU.

3091. STOROST, Wilhelm. Kaimo
didvīris; apīsakaitė. Tilžė, 1914.
At head of title: Vīdūnas, [pseud.].
891.92St78K PU.

3092. STRIUPAS, Romas. Žmogus
žmogui. Kaunas, Naujoji Kuryba,1924.
178 p. WU.

3093. TAMUOLIS, Eduardas. Susi-
kertančios linijos; apysaka. Vilnius,
Vaga, 1968. 218 p.
PG8722.3A4S9 DLC; OKentU.

3094. TARASENKA, Petras. Pabėgi-
mas. [Vidutiniam ir vyresniam mokykliniam amžiui. Iliustravo V. Jankaus-
kas]. 2.leidimas. Vilnius, Vaga,
1972. 243 p. illus.
PG8721.T35P3 1972 DLC; PU.

3095. TARULIS, Petras, pseud.
Žirgekiai padebesiais; apysakos.
Nördlingen, Ger., Sūdavija, 1948.
149 p. WU.

3096. TAUTKAITĖ, Eugenija. Pir-
mieji; apysaka. 2.leidimas. Vilnius,
Vaga, 1977. 232 p.
PG8721.T37P5 1977 PU.

3097. TOLIUŠIS, Juozas. 13-ji
laida; pasakojimų pynė jaunimui.
Chicago, Ill., JAV LB Švietimo tarybos leidinys. 254 p. PG8722.305 PU.

3098. TOMARIENĖ, Sonė. Saulės
vestuvės; pasakos. [Iliustravo Vlada Stančikaitė. Chicago, Ill., H.
Tomaras, 1957]. 126 p. illus.
PG8749.T6S3 DLC; MB.

3099. TREINYS, Pranas. Tėvai ir
krikštatėviai; sakmių romanas. [Dai-
lininkas V. Ambrazevičius]. Vilnius,
Vaga, 1972. 408 p.
PG8722.3.R4T4 PU; DLC; MB.

3100. TULPĖ, P., pseud. Kalnų
dvasia ir kitos novelės. [1.dalis].
Freiburgas, 1946. 206 p. illus.
PG8721.T76K3 DLC; CtTMF.

3101. --- Tilto sargas. [s.l.],
Povilo Abelkio Lietuviškų knygų lei-
dykla, 1949. 151 p.
PG8721.T76T5 OKentU.

3102. TULYS, Antanas. Paskutinis
pasimatymas; apsakymų rinkinys. Vilnius, Vaga, 1976. 197 p.
PG8749.T8P3 PU.

3103. TUMAS, Juozas. Dėdės ir dėdienės. Nebylys. Rimai ir Nerimai.
Apysakos. Vilnius, Vaga, 1974. 231
p. At head of title: Vaižgantas, [
pseud.]. PG8721.T77A6 1974 PU.

3104. --- Galicijoje, Amerikoje,
Prancūzijoje, Italijoje. Kaunas,
Spindulio b-vės spaustuvė, 1931.[Xe-
rox copy, 1976]. 301 p. (Vaižganto
raštai, 17). PG8721.T77G3 1931a PU.

3105. --- Vaizdeliai. Tilžėje,
1902. 60 p. At head of title: Vaižgantas, [pseud.]. PG8721.D87V4 PU.

3106. --- Valiulio pasaka. [Vidu-
tiniam ir vyresniam mokykliniam amžiui. Iliustravo B. Demkutė. Vilnius,
Vaga, 1969. 240 p. illus.
PG8721.T77V3 1969 DLC.

3107. TUMĖNAS, Justinas. Dėdė;
arba, Ainių kančios, Justino Tumėno;
su Vandos Mingailytės studija. Bern,
Switzerland, M. Drechsel, 1914. 136
p. PG8721.T8 DLC; NN; PU(xerox);WU.

3108. ULDUKIS, E[dvardas]. Su šau-
tuvu ir plūgu; dokumentinė apysaka.
Vilnius, Vaga, 1966. 257 p. At head
of title: E. Uldukis, V. Gailiūnas.
PG8722.31.L4S8 DLC; NN.

3109. UMBRASAS, Kazys. Kairionys;
apysakos. Vilnius, Vaga, 1976. 429
p. PG8721.U55K3 PU; DLC.

3110. URBONAS, Vydmantas. Pašaukimas. Vilnius, Mintis, 1968. 151 p.
PG8722.31.R2P3 DLC.

3111. --- Saulėti horizontai. Vilnius, Mintis, 1966. 156 p. illus.
PG8722.31.R2S3 DLC.

3112. --- Žemės balsas. Vilnius,
Mintis, 1965. 86 p.
PG8722.31.R2Z2 DLC.

3113. URNEVIČIŪTĖ, Dalia. Našlės
rūtos; apysakos. Vilnius, Vaga,1972.
205 p. PG8722.31.R6N28 DLC; IU; MH.

3114. --- Septyni slėniai. Vilnius, Vaga, 1965. 75 p. illus.
PG8722.31.R6S4 PU; IU; MH.

3115. VABALAS, A. Tarpumiškių le-
genda. Vilnius, Valstybinė politinės ir mokslinės literatūros leidykla, 1963. 74 p. PG8722.32.A2T3 DLC.

3116. VAIČIULAITIS, Antanas. Auk-
sinė kurpelė; pasakų rinktinė. [Dai-
lininkas V.K. Jonynas. Nördlingen,
Ger.], Venta, 1957. 244 p. illus.
PG8721.V3A9 DLC; CtY; NN; OCl; PU.

3117. --- Vakaras sargo namely.

Čikaga, [J. Karvelis], 1976. 165 p.
PG8721.V3V28 DLC; PU.

3118. VAILIONIS, Vladas. Likimo
audrose; romanas. London, Eng., Nida,
1976. 344 p. PG8749.V29L5 PU.

3119. VAITKUS, Mykolas. Auštant;
romanas. Kaunas, Sakalas, 1939- .
[Xerox copy, 1977]: PG8721.V322.A8
1939a PU(xerox, v.1)

3120. VAITUKAITIS, Leonas. Be pa-
liaubų; romanas. Vilnius, Valstybinė grožinės literatūros leidykla,
1963. 318 p. port.
PG8722.32.A58B4 DLC; MH; NN.

3121. VALAITIS, Jonas. Jaunamar-
tė. Čikaga, [Autoriaus leidinys],
1976. 126 p. PG8721.V325J3 PU.

3122. VALOTKA, Eugenijus. Urvinis
žmogus; humoreskos. Dailininkas Alfonsas Augaitis. Vilnius, Vaga,1972.
137 p. illus. PG8722.32.A6U7 PU;MH.

3123. VALUCKAS, Andrius. Nemuno
sūnūs; romanas. [Chicago, Ill., Autoriaus leidinys, 1955]. 2 v.
PG8749.V33N4 DLC; NN; OCl; PU.

3124. VANAGAITĖ-PETERSONIENĖ, Stasė. Nulaužta šaka; trijų vaizdelių
pynė. Chicago, Ill., 1964. 81 p.
PG8721.V35N8 DLC.

3125. VARGOVAIKIS, pseud. Vien-
turtis. Vilnius, J. Zavadzkio spaustuvė, 1911. 59 p. (Lietuvos Ūkininko
išleidimas, nr.26).
*QYN p.v.372, no.9--NN.

3126. VASERIS, Pranas. Girių sar-
gai; apysakos. Melbourne, Australia,
[P.Vaseris], 1973. 210 p.
PG8721.V36G5 PU.

3127. VENCLOVA, Antanas. Draugystė; įžanga į subrendusį amžių. Romanas. [Naujas leidimas]. Vilnius, Vaga,1966. 416 p. illus.
PG8721.V4D7 DLC; IU; MH.

3128. --- "Džiunglės"; gyva knyga. [Vilnius, 1965]. 11 p. illus.
Offprint from Pergalė, 1965, no.6,
p.158-168. InU.

3129. --- Epochos vėjas; straipsniai apie literatūrą. Vilnius, Vaga,
1975. 563 p. PG8701.V42 1975 PU.

3130. --- Gimimo diena; romanas.
2.leidimas. Vilnius, Valstybinė
grožinės literatūros leidykla, 1960.
619 p. illus. PG8721.V4G5 1960 DLC.

3131. --- Mirtis Lisabonoj; rinktiniai apsakymai. [Ilius. St.Krasaus-

ko]. Vilnius, Vaga, 1967. 523 p.
illus. PG8721.V4M5 OKentU; MH.

3132. --- Pavasario upė. [Medžio
raižiniai A. Makūnaitės]. Vilnius,
Vaga, 1964. 469 p. illus.
PG8721.V4P3 1964 OKentU; ICIU; IU;MH

3133. CANCELLED.

3134. VENCLOVA, Antanas. Vidurio
vėtra. Vilnius, Vaga, 1971. 671 p.
illus., 16 leaves of illus.
PG8721.V4V5 1971 DLC; OKentU; WU.

3135. VETEIKIS, Vyt[autas]. Dangus visuomet žydras. Vilnius, Valstybinė grožinės literatūros leidykla,
1962. 291 p. PG8721.V46D3 DLC.

3136. VIENUOLIS, A., pseud. Padavimai ir legendos. [Iliustravo Albina Makūnaitė]. Vilnius, Vaga, 1971.
148 p. PG8721.V5P25 1971 PU; DLC;NN;
WaU.

3137. --- Prieš dieną. Kryžkelės.
Romanai. Vilnius, Vaga, 1971. 497
p. At head of title: Antanas Vienuolis. PG8721.V5P7 1971 DLC; MB;NjP.

3138. VIJEIKIS, Vladas. Saigūnas;
istorinė apysaka. Iliustracijos autoriaus. [Chicago, Ill., Tėviškėlė],
1976. 156 p. PG8749.V49S3 PU.

3139. VILIMAITĖ, Bitė. Grūdų mies-
telis. Vilnius, Vaga, 1966. 53 p.
(Pirmoji knyga). PG8722.32.I4G7 DLC.

3140. --- Obelų sunki našta; apysaka ir apsakymai. Vilnius, Vaga,
1975. 102 p. PG8721.32.I4O2 DLC.

3141. VITAITIS, Stasys E. Gyvenimo purve; romanas. Vilnius, Vaga,
1977. 377 p. PG8749.V55G9 1977 PU.

3142. VOLERTAS, Vytautas. Praga-
ro vyresnysis; premijuotas romanas.
Chicago, Ill, Lietuviškos knygos klubas, 1971. 273 p. PG8749.V6P7 PU;MB.

3143. ZABIELA, benediktas. Klaida; romanas. Melbourne, Australia,
Autoriaus leidinys, 1965. 232 p.
891.92Z12K PU.

3144. ZALECKIS, Leonas. Seklumos.
Vilnius, Vaga, 1971. 65 p. (Pirmoji
knyga). PG8722.36.A5S4 PU; MH.

3145. ZEIKUS, Liudas. Laiptai į
tolumas; romanas. Viršelis A.Galdi-
ko. Chicago, Ill., Draugo spaustuvė,
1954. 241 p. PG8749.Z4L3 DLC;OCl;
PU.

3146. ŽILINSKAITĖ, Vytautė. Humo-

reskos. [Dailininkas Alfonsas Augaitis]. Vilnius, Vaga, 1971. 150 p.
PG8722.36.I4H8   PU; MH.

3147. --- Karuselėje. Vilnius, Vaga, 1970. 309 p. illus. NjP.

3148. --- Mano neapykanta stipresnė. [Dokumentinė apysaka]. Vilnius, Vaga, 1964. 226 p. illus.
PG8722.36.I4M33 DLC; IU; MH.

3149. --- --- [Another edition]. [Iliustravo Ed. Jurėnas]. 2.leidimas. Vilnius, Vaga, 1970. 288 p. illus.
PG8722.36.I4M33 1970 DLC.

3150. --- --- 3.leidimas. Vilnius, Vaga, 1977. 261 p.
PG8722.36.I4M33 1977 PU.

3151. --- Paradoksai; humoras ir satyra. Vilnius, Vaga, 1974. 135 p.
PG8722.36.I4P3 PU.

3152. ŽILIONIS, Vincas. Atsisakom nuo senojo svieto; romanas. Vilnius, Vaga, 1975. 564 p. MH.

3153. --- Būdviečių mokykla; romanas ir apsakymai. Vilnius, Vaga, 1976. 278 p.
PG8721.Z49B8 1976 PU; WU.

3154. ŽITINSKAS, Romualdas. Mūsų nerimo keliai; apysaka. Vilnius, Vaga, 1972. 237 p. PG8722.36.I8M8 PU; DLC; IU; MH; NNC; NjP.

3155. ŽLABYS, Juozas. Gyvenimo novelės. Kaunas, Sakalas, 1940. [Xerox copy, 1977]. 178 p.
PG8721.Z55G9 1940a PU(xerox).

3156. ŽMUIDZINAS, Jonas. Runcė ir Dandierinas. London, Eng., Nida, 1969. 110 p. (Nidos knygų klubo leidinys, nr.73). PG8722.36.M8R8 DLC; OKentU; PU.

3157. ZOBARSKAS, Stepas. Menesienos sėja. [2.laida]. New York, N.Y., [195-]. 72 p. 891.92Z78D PU.

3158. ŽUKAUSKAS, Albinas. Geri akmenys. Vilnius, Vaga, 1973. 351 p. PG8722.36.U4G4 DLC; MB; MH; OKentU.

3159. --- Sangrąžos. [Benamė meilė]. Vilnius, Vaga, 1973. 520 p.
PG8722.36.U4S2 DLC; OKentU; PU.

3160. --- Sunkus džiaugsmas. [Dailininkas A. Švažas]. Vilnius,Vaga, 1969. 387 p. illus.
PG8722.36.U4S9 DLC; NjP; OKentU; PU.

3161. ZURBA, Algimantas. Keistuolių miestas; apsakymai ir apysakos.

Vilnius, Vaga, 1973. 262 p.
PG8722.36.U7K4 PU; MH.

3162. --- Šimtadienis; romanas. Vilnius, Vaga, 1975. 303 p.
PG8722.36.U7S5 PU.

3163. ŽVIRDAUSKAS, Vitas. Vandenyno druska. Vilnius, Vaga, 1968. 142 p. PG8722.36.V5V3 DLC;NN;ICIU.

3164. ŽYMANTIENĖ, Julija (Beniuševičiūtė). Kent kaltas, kent nekaltas. Vilnius, 1907. 39 p. (Lietuvos Ūkininko priedas, išleidimas, nr.9). At head of title: Žemaitė . 891.93Š2 CtTMF; NN.

3165. --- Kunigo naudą vėjai gaudo. Stebuklai. Vilnius, 1914. 42 p. At head of title: Žemaitė. 891.93Ž2 CtTMF.

3165a --- Kunigo naudą vėjai gaudo. Nuo audros palindus. Kelionė į Šidlavą. Kaunas, Valstybinė grožinės literatūros leidykla, 1946. 88 p. *ZQ-218--NN.

XIII.5.c.4. DRAMA

3166. ADOMĖNAS, Vincas. Užvis sunkiausia; keturių veiksmų komedija. Vilnius, Valstybinė grožinės literatūros leidykla, 1960. 109 p. 891.92Ad754 PU; PPULC.

3167. ALANTAS, Vytautas. Dramos veikalai; Aukštadvaris, Buhalterijos klaida. Dillingen, Ger., Mūsų Kelias, 1947. 127 p. WU.

3168. BIČIŪNAS, Vytautas. Paskerdę milijonai; [drama]. Kaunas,1928. [Xerox copy, 1977]. 137 p.
PG8721.B42P3 1928a PU(xerox).

3169. --- Varnalėšos; 3-jų veiksmų piršlybos. Kaunas, Vilkolakis, 1931. [Xerox copy, 1977]. 60 p.
PG8721.B42V3 1931a PU(xerox).

3170. --- Žalgiris; 5-ių veiksmų istoriška drama. Kaunas, Vytauto Didžiojo komiteto leidinys, 1932. [Xerox copy, 1977]. 195 p.
PG8721.B42Z3 1932a PU(xerox).

3171. BRAZIULEVIČIUS, Vladas. Augila nebrendila; vieno veiksmo komedija. [Kaunas, Varpas, 1936]. 63 p. (Liaudies teatras, br.1). On cover: Sakalas. PG8721.B7A8 OKentU.

3172. CANCELLED.

3173. BUTKUS, Juozas. Palaidūnas;

dviveiksmis kaimo gyvenimo vaizdelis.
Šiauliai, 1925. 27 p. At head of
title: Butkų Juzė.
PG8721.B83P3 PU.

3174. BUTRIMAS, Edmundas. Tėvų
kaltė; dvi dramos. Nördlingen, Ger.,
Sūdavija, 1947. 175 p. WU.

3175. DAUGIRDAS, Tadas. Girkal-
nio užgavėnės; vienaveiksmis paveiks-
las su dainomis ir šokiais. Biržai,
M. Yčo ir bendrovės spaustuvėje,
1913.[Xerox copy, 1977]. 32 p.
Includes also: T.Daugirdas. Tėtė pa-
kliuvo, p.[17]-26 and W.Perzyński,
Idealis gyventojas, p.[27]-32.
PG8721.D34G5 1913a PU.

3176. DAUGUVIETIS, Borisas. Žal-
dokynė, trijų veiksmų pjesė. [Kaune]
Valstybinė grožinės literatūros leidykla, [1947]. 131 p.
891.92D269Z PU; DLC.

3177. FROMAS, Aleksandras. Vai-
dilutė; arba, Žemaičių krikštas;
penkių veiksmų šešių paveikslų istorijos drama. Riga, 1910. 80 p.
At head of title: A. Gužutis.
PG8721.F7V3 PU.

3178. GLINSKIS, Juozas. Grasos
namai; trijų veiksmų drama. Vilnius, Vaga, 1971. 71 p.
PG8722.17.L5G7 PU.

3179. --- Po svarstyklių ženklu;
drama. Vilnius, Vaga, 1977. 56 p.
PG8722.17.L5P6 PU.

3180. GRICIUS, Augustinas. Dramos. Augustinas Gricius; [šmaikšti
dramaturgo plunksna J. Lankutis; paaiškinimai A. Samulionis]. Vilnius,
Vaga, 1974. 626 p. Contents.--Pa-
langa.--Božegraika.--Ponaitis.--Idė-
jiškas pagrindas.--Radijo Jomarkas.
--Gyveno ponas Pšepadalskis.--Išva-
karės.--Karšta vasara.--Sėja ir piū-
tis.--Buvo buvo, kaip nebuvo.
PG8721.G635D7 1974 DLC; WU.

3181. --- Karšta vasara; pjesės.
Vilnius, Valstybinė grožinės litera-
tūros leidykla, 1955. 210 p.
PG8721.G635K3 OKentU.

3182. GRUŠAS, Juozas. Adomo Brunzos paslaptis. [Zigmantas Sierakaus-
kas]. Vilnius, Vaga, 1967. 158 p.
Contents.--Adomo Brunzos paslaptis;
dviejų dalių drama.--Zigmantas Sie-
rakauskas; keturių veiksmų drama.
PG8721.G7A7 DLC; IU; MH; PU.

3183. --- Švitrigaila; dramos.
Vilnius, Vaga, 1976. 467 p.
PG8721.G7S9 PU.

3184. --- Žmogus be veido; dvi
dramos. Vilnius, Vaga, 1970. 203 p.
PG8721.G7Z4 DLC; IU; MB; MH.

3185. IŠNAROS; trijų aktų komedija. Parašė Padaužų dramos skyrius.
[s.l., s.n.], 1941. 49 p.
PG8749.I8P PU.

3186. JACINEVIČIUS, Leonidas.
N kilometre; dviejų dalių pjesė.Vil-
nius, Vaga, 1977. 60 p.
PG8722.2.A3N2 PU.

3187. JASIUKAITIS, Konstantinas.
Vieno akto opera Šienapiūtė. Kaunas.
OCl.

3188. Kairys, Anatolijus. Trys
komedijos: Ku-Kū, Didysis penktadie-
nis, Rūtos ir bijūnai. Chicago, Ill.,
Dialogas, 1975. 224 p.
PG8721.K2T7 PU; CaAEU.

3189. KRĖVĖ-MICKEVIČIUS, Vincas.
Likimo kelias; misterija. 1-2 dalis.
Kaunas, 1926-1929. 2 v. (His Raštai.
Kaunas, 1921-1930. v.7-8. RP.

3190. KRIŠČIUKAITIS, Antanas. Avi-
nėlis nekaltasis; 4 veiksmų komedija.
Kaunas, 1921. At head of title:
Aišbė, [pseud.]. 891.92T832Li PU.

3191. LANDSBERGIS, Algirdas. Vėjas gluosniuose. Gluosniai vėjuje;
du stebuklingi vaidinimai. Chicago,
Ill., Algimanto Mackaus knygų leidimo fondas, 1973. 126 p.
PG8721.L3V4 PU; DLC; OKentU.

3192. LAUCEVIČIUS, Bronius. Jono
širdis; drama 5-se veikmėse. Parašė
Br. Vargšas, [pseud.]. Chicago, Ill.
Spauda ir lėšomis "Kataliko", 1911.
66 p. *QYN--NN(Vargšas, Br., pseud]

3193. --- Lizdas naminio liūto;
drama trijose veikmėse. Parašė Br.
Vargšas, [pseud.]. Chicago, Ill.,
"Lietuvis", 1913. 30 p.
*QYI p.v.3, no.7--NN(Vargšas,Br.,
pseud.).

3194. --- Milijonai vandenyl;
drama 3-se veikmėse. Parašė Br. Vargšas, [pseud.]. Chicago, Ill., Turtų
"Lietuvos", 1909. 32 p.
PG8749.L37M5 DLC; PU.

3195. ---Penktas prisakymas; drama vienoje veikmėje. Parašė Br.Varg-
šas, [pseud.]. Philadelphia, Pa.,
1912. 23 p. PG8721.L348P42 PU.

3196. --- Pirmieji žingsniai;
drama 4-se veikmėse. Parašė Br.Varg-
šas, [pseud.]. Chicago, Ill., Spauda "Lietuvos", 1909. 50 p.
PG8721.L348P5 PU; NN(Vargšas,Br.)

3197. --- Saliamono sapnas; vieno veiksmo drama. Parašė Br. Vargšas, [pseud.]. Chicago, Ill., M.G. Valaskas, 1917. 23 p.
PG8721.L348S3 1917 PU.

3198. --- Spąstai; vieno akto farsas. Parašė Br. Vargšas, [pseud.] Chicago, Ill., Spauda Naujienų,[s.d.] 22 p. PG8721.L36S7 DLC.

3199. LAURINČIUKAS, Albertas. Vidutinė moteris; trijų veiksmų pjesė. Vilnius, Vaga, 1971. 96 p.
PG8722.22.A9V5 PU; DLC; NNC.

3200. LYDINIS, pseud. Replėse; 3-jų veiksmų drama. Kaunas, Vilniui Vaduoti Sąjunga, 1938. 95 p. WU.

3201. MARCINKEVIČIUS, Juozas. Čičinska; dramatizuota trijų dalių poema su prologu ir epilogu. Vilnius, Vaga, 1976. 129 p.
PG8722.23.A66C5 PU.

3202. MARCINKEVIČIUS, Justinas. Katedra; 10-ties giesmių drama. Vilnius, Vaga, 1971. 154 p. [Dailininkas V. Kalinauskas].
PG8721.M35K3 PU; DLC; CaAEU; NNC.

3203. --- Mindaugas; dviejų dalių drama-poema. Vilnius, Vaga, 1970. 119 p. illus.
PG8721.M35M5 1970 OKentU; DLC.

3204. MATJOŠAITIS, Stasys. Varpininkai; 4 veiksmų drama. Vilnius, "Ruch" spaustuvė, 1924.[Xerox copy, 1975]. 32 p. At head of title:Esmaitis, [pseud.].
PG8721.M367V3 1924a PU(xerox).

3205. NAGORNOSKIS, Vincas. Doros sargas; vaizdelis iš baudžiavos laikų. Drama trijuose aktuose. Worcester, Mass., Spauda "Amerikos Lietuvio", 1921.[Xerox copy, 1975]. 90 p. PG8749.N32D6 1921a PU(xerox).

3206. --- Pileniečiai; istoriška tragedija penkiuose aktuose, aštuoniuose atidengimuose. Shenandoah, pa., Spauda ir turtu "Darbininkų Vilties", 1908.[Xerox copy, 1975]. PG8749.N32P5 1908a PU(xerox).

3207. OSTRAUSKAS, Kostas. Kvartetas; dramos. Chicago, Ill.,[Algimanto Mackaus knygų leidimo fondas], 1971. 170 p. PG8749.O8K9 PU; DLC; ICU; InU; MB; OKentU.

3208. PAUKŠTELIS, Juozas. Užgrobtoj žemėj; 5 veiksmų drama. Kaunas, "Žinijos" bendrovės leidinys, 1931. [Xerox copy, 1977]. 152 p. PG8721.P37U9 1931a PU(xerox)

3209. PETKEVIČAITĖ, Gabrielė and ŽYMANTIENĖ, Julija (Beniuševičiūtė). Parduotoji laimė; 4 veiksmų drama. Vilnius, J. Zavadzkis, 1905. 48 p. At head of title: Dvi Moteri,[pseud.] WU.

3210. RIMKEVIČIUS, Vytautas. 27 [i.d. Dvidešimt septynios] išpažintys. Vilnius, Vaga, 1975. 283. PG8722.28.I5D9 PU.

3211. --- Girių kirtėjai. Vilnius, Vaga, 1970. 85 p.
PG8722.28.I58G5 DLC; IU; MB; MH.

3212. SAJA, Kazys. Abstinentas. Trys komedijos. Vilnius, 1970. loo p. Published by the Liaudies Meno Rūmai of Lietuvos TSR Kultūros ministerija. Contents.--Vadinas gyvenu.--Abstinentas.--Palangos liūtas.
PG8722.29.A38A7 DLC; MH.

3213. --- Devynbėdžiai; dviejų dalių muzikinė pasaka. Vilnius,Vaga, 1974. 109 p. PG8722.29.A38D4 DLC

3214. --- Dilgėlių šilkas; tragikomiška Tomo Adomonio savaitė su divertismentais. Vilnius, Vaga, 1972. 94 p. PG8722.29.A38D5 PU; DLC; IU; MH; OKentU.

3215. --- Mamutų medžioklė; 2-jų dalių komedija-groteskas. Vilnius, Vaga, 1969. 93 p.
PG8722.29.A38M3 DLC; IU; MH; OKentU.

3216. --- Mediniai balandžiai; dviejų dalių drama. Vilnius, Vaga, 1977. 78 p. PG8722.29.A38M4 PU.

3217. --- Šventežeris; trijų veiksmų pjesė. Vilnius, Vaga, 1971. 88 p. PG8722.29.A38S9 PU; DLC; NN;NjP; OKentU; OU.

3218. SAMULEVIČIUS, Raimundas. Aidas. Dvylika scenų su dainelėmis. Vilnius, Vaga, 1969. 98 p. PG8722.29.A48A7 DLC; IU; MH.

3219. --- Pasiklydęs tarp žvaigždžių; pjesė. Vilnius, Vaga, 1966. 88 p. PG8722.29.A48P3 DLC.

3220. ŠIMUTIS, Leonardas. Į tėvynę; dviejų aktų vaizdas. Chicago, Ill., Draugas, 1928.[Xerox copy,1928. [Xerox copy, 1976]. 47 p. PG8749.S54I2 1928a PU(xerox).

3221. SKLIUTAUSKAS, Jokūbas. Raganų dauba. Daktaras Asklepijus. Dvi vienaveiksmės pjesės. Vilnius, Vaga, 1974. 75 p.
PG8722.29.K55R3 PU; MH.

3222. ŠLIBURYS, Jonas. Emigracija;

iš darbininkų gyvenimo paveikslėlis.
Brooklyn, N.Y., Spauda "Vienybės Lie-
tuvninkų", 1908. 47 p.
PG8749.S57E5 PU.

3223. ŠMULKŠTYS, Antanas. Ponas
ir mužikas; drama penkiuose aktuose.
Pagal Aleksandrą Gužutį parašė Paparonis, [pseud.]. Seinai, Lenkaičio
...spaustuvėje, 1910. 891.92Sm94P
PU.

3224. STEPULIONYTĖ, Juzė. Iszga-
ma; drama II-se aktuose. Laida II,
pertaisyta. Chicago, Ill., Turtu
ir spauda "Kataliko", 1904.[Xerox
copy, 1976]. 24 p. At head of title: J.S. PG8721.S693I8 1904a PU.

3225. STOROST, Wilhelm. Laimės
atošvaista; penkiū veiksmū tragaidē
su atvarta ir užvarta. Tilžē, Rūta,
1934. 132 p. At head of title: Vīdūnas. PG8721.S7L3 DLC.

3226. --- Mūsū laimējimas; myste-
rija. Tilžē, 1913. At head of
title: Vīdūnas. 891.92St78M PU.

3227. --- Numānē; vienveiksmē
komēdija. Tilžēje, Rūta, 1911. 30
p. At head of title: Vīdūnas.
PG8721.S7N8 DLC.

3228. --- Pasaulio gaisras; penkiū veiksmū tragaidē su ļeiga ir iš-
eiga. Tilžē, Rūta, 1928. At head
of title: Vīdūnas. 891.922St78 PU.

3229. --- Piktoji gudrībē; myste-
rija. Tilžē, Rūta, 1908. At head
of title: Vīdūnas. PG8721.S7P5 DLC:
PU.

3230. --- Probotšiūn šešēliai;
dramātiška aidija trijose dālīse.
Tilžēje, V. Storost, 1908. 182 p.
illus. At head of title: Vīdūnas.
PG8721.S7P7 DLC; OKentU.

3231. TAUTKAITĖ, Eugenija. Pradžia; 4 veiksmų pjesė saviveiklai.
Vilnius, Valstybinė grožinės literatūros leidykla, 1955. 63 p.
891.92T149P PU.

3232. URNEVIČIŪTĖ, Dalia. Pago-
nė; pjesės. Vilnius, Vaga, 1975.
305 p. PG8722.31.R6P3 PU; MH.

3233. --- Tēvuko žaislai. Tylu-
va - 2 km. Vilnius, Vaga, 1968.
202 p. PG8722.31.R6T4 PU;MH;MB;
OKentU.

3234. VAIČIŪNAS, Petras. Dramos
ir komedijos. Vilnius, Vaga, 1971.
2 v. PG8721.V32A19 PU; DLC; MH;NN;
NNC; WU.

3235. --- Pražydo nuvytusios gėlės; 3 veiksmų, 4 paveikslų pjesė.
Kaunas, Švyturio bendrovės leidinys,
1923. 35 p. (Teatro biblioteka,nr.6)
PG8721.V32P7 DLC; OKentU; PU.

3236. VYTURĖLIS, pseud. Žiemos
ledai; 3-jų veiksmų dabarties sodie-
čių gyvenimo dramos vaizdelis. Tilžē, E. Jagomasto ("Lituanijos") spau-
stuvē, 1913.[Xerox copy, 1977]. 48 p.
PG8721.V9Z3 1913a PU(xerox).

3237. ŽALPYS, Jonas. Du broliu;
penkių atidengimų drama iš lietuvių
gyvenimo Amerikoje. Ketvirtas aktas
skolintas iš Alex. Bisono. Boston,
Mass., "Keleivio" spauda ir lėšomis,
1916.[Xerox copy, 1976]. 60 p. At
head of title: J.J. Zolp.
PG8749.Z3D8 1916a PU(xerox).

3238. ŽYMANTIENĖ, Julija (Beniuševičiūtė). Apsiriko; 2-jų aktų komedija. Vilnius, J. Zavadzkio, 1912.
131 p. At head of title: Žemaitė,
[pseud.]. WU.

XIII.5.c.5. POETRY

3239. AISTIS, Jonas. Eilėraščiai.
Kaunas, Piūvis, 1932.[Xerox copy,
1977]. 112 p. At head of title: J.
Kossu-Aleksandravičius.
PG8721A5E5 1932a PU(xerox).

3240. --- Poezija. Kaunas, Sakalas, 1940.[Xerox copy, 1977]. 378 p.
At head of title: J. Kuosa Aleksandriškis. PG8721.A4P6 1940a PU(xerox)

3241. ALEKNAVIČIUS, Kajetonas.
Kikilis laibakojis. [Paruošė J. Pily-
paitis]. Vilnius, Vaga, 1971. 234
p. PG8721.A46K5 1971 PU; DLC; MB;
NN; NNC; OKentU.

3242. ALIONIS, Algirdas. Paukš-
tukų medis. Vilnius, Vaga, 1970.
5o p. (Pirmoji knyga).
PG8722.1.L5P3 DLC.

3243. ALIŠAS, Venancijus, pseud.
São Bento varpai; lyrika. Kaunas,
Sakalas, 1938.[Xerox copy, 1974].
95 p. Author's real name: Aleksandras Arminas. PG8721.A74S3 1974 PU.

3244. AMBRASAS, Arvydas. Žemė,
nepalik mūsų; eilėraščiai. [Paruošė
M. Martinaitis]. Vilnius, Vaga,
1974. 63 p. (Pirmoji knyga; 74).
MH.

3245. ANDRIEKUS, Leonardas. Po
Dievo antspaudais; Vytauto Didžiojo
godos. Iliustravo Telesforas Valius.

New Yorkas, [Pranciškonų spaustuvė],
1969. 106 p. illus.
PG9119.A5P6 DLC; OKentU.

3246. --- Už vasaros vartų; lyrika. Iliustravo Telesforas Valius.
New Yorkas,[Pranciškonai], 1976.
79 p. PG8749.A5U9 PU; DLC.

3247. ANGLICKIS, Stasys. Suvirpa
žemės pilnatis; eilėraščiai. Vilnius,
Vaga, 1975. 125 p. PG8721.A58S8 PU.

3248. --- Žemė ir želmenys; rinktinė. Vilnius, Vaga, 1972. 243 p.
PG8721.A58Z25 DLC; MB; NN; PU.

3249. ASTRAUSKAS, Gediminas. Ki-
bernetija. [Dailininkas R. Palčiaus-
kas]. Vilnius, Vaga, 1972. 84 p.
PG8721.A8K5 DLC; PU.

3250. --- Nemėgstu odžių. Vilnius, Valstybinė grožinės literatūros leidykla, 1961. 77 p. illus.
PG8721.A8N4 DLC.

3251. --- Širdis ir šaukštas.
Vilnius, Vaga, 1967. 92 p. illus.
PG8721.A8S5 DLC.

3252. AUGUSTAITYTĖ-VAIČIŪNIENĖ,
Juzė. Ant aukuro laiptų. Chicago,
Ill., Terra, 1961. 112 p.
891.92Au45A PU.

3253. --- Rūpestis. Čikaga,
J. Karvelis, 1970. 128 p.
PG8721.A83R8 PU.

3254. --- Skeveldros. Schweinfurt, Ger., L. Vismantas, 1946.
103 p. PPULC; PPU; PU; DLC-P4
4 PG-Lith.68.

3255. --- Su baltu nuometu.
Marijampolė, 1931. 891.92Au45F PU;
WU.

3256. --- Žvaigždėtos naktys.
Chicago, Ill., [Chicagos skautinin-
kės], 1952. 891.92Au45Z PU

3257. BABICKAS, Petras. Svetimoj
padangėj. Buenos Aires, Argentina,
1947. [Xerox copy, 1976]. 63 p.
PG8721.B2S9 1947a PU(xerox).

3258. --- Toli nuo tėvynės.
[s.l., s.n.[, 1945. 32 p.
PG8721.B2T6 DLC.

3259. --- ---; [eilėraščiai].
2., papildytas leidimas. Roma,1946.
105 p. port. PG8721.B2T6 1946 DLC.

3260. BALIUKONYTĖ, Onė. Laukinės vaivorykštės. Vilnius, Vaga,
1971. 75 p. PG8722.12.A35L3 DLC;
IU; MH; NjP; OU; OKentU; PU.

3261. BALTAKIS, Algimantas. Aki-
mirkos. [Dailininkė L. Paškauskaitė].
Vilnius, Vaga, 1970. 151 p. illus.
PG8722.12.A4A76 DLC; IU; MH; NN;NjP
NNC.

3262. --- Duona ir debesys; ly-
rika. [Dailininkė Lili Paškauskaitė].
Vilnius, Vaga, 1973. 151 p.
PG8722.12.A4D8 PU; MH.

3263. --- Keliaujantis kalnas;
eilėraščiai. [Dailininkas Vl. Žilius]
Vilnius, Vaga, 1967. 124 p. illus.
PG8722.12.A4K4 DLC.

3264. --- Stebuklinga žolė; eilėraščiai. [Vytauto Jurkūno (jaunesniojo) medžio raižiniai]. Vilnius,
Vaga, 1971. 421 p. illus.
PG8722.12.A4S75 PU; DLC; MB;MH; WU.

3265. BARONAS, Aloyzas. Alijo-
šiaus lapai; humoristiniai eilėraščiai. Įvadą parašė Antanas Gustaitis.
Chicago, Ill., Lietuviškos knygos
klubas, 1975. 87 p. At head of title: Dr.S. Aliūnas, [pseud.].
PG8721.B34A53 PU; CaOTP.

3266. BAUŽINSKAITĖ-KAIRIENĖ, Aldona. Detalės; eilėraščiai. [Brook-
lyn, N.Y., 1968]. 72 p.
PG8749.B38D4 PU; PPULC; RPB.

3267. BERNOTAS, Albinas. Sleks-
tis. [Dailininkas R. Tarabilda]. 98
p. illus. PG8722.12.E7S55 DLC; MB;
PU.

3268. BINKIS, Kazys. Lyrika. Vilnius, Vaga, 1972. [Iliustravo V.Ži-
lius]. 125 p. PG8721.B5A17 1972 PU;
DLC; MH; IU.

3269. --- Poezija. [Red. komisija T. Tilvytis et al.]. Vilnius,
Valstybinė grožinės literatūros leidykla, 1949. xxiii, 536 p.

3270 --- --- Iliustracijos Domi-
celės ir Arūno Tarabildų. Vilnius,
Valstybinė grožinės literatūros leidykla, 1963. 286 p.
Microfilm 29657PG DLC; MH.

3271. --- 100 [i.e. Šimtas] pavasarių; arba, Pavasario linksmybės ir
sielvartai ir kiti apdūmojimai šio
laiko nuotykiai pritaikinti ir bent
kiek naujoviškai parašyti per Kazimierą Binkį. Kauna, Kaštu P.Stik-
liaus, 1926.[Xerox copy, 1977]. 45 p.
PG8721.B5S5 1926a PU(xerox).

3272. BLOŽĖ, Vytautas. Dainos;
rinktinė. Vilnius, Vaga, 1976. 356
p. PG8722.12.L6D3 PU.

3273. --- Poezija; rinktinė.

Vilnius, Vaga, 1974. 300 p.
PG8722.12.L6A6 1974 DLC; WU.

3274. --- Žemės gėlės; eilėraščiai. Vilnius, Vaga, 1971. 68 p.
PG8722.12.L6Z4 PU; DLC; IU; MB;MH.

3275. BOGUTAITĖ, Vitalija. Po
vasaros; eilėraščiai. [Southfield,
Mich.], Ateitis, [1976]. 71 p.
PG8749.B62P6 PU.

3276. BORIKAS, S. Šilalės baladė. Vilnius, Mintis, 1968. 121 p.
PG8721.B56S5 DLC.

3277. BORUTA, Kazys. Kryžių Lietuva. [Kaunas], Spaudos Fondas,
[1940]. [Xerox copy, 1977]. 110 p.
PG8721.B6K7 1940a PU(xerox).

3278. BRADŪNAS, Kazys. Alkana
kelionė. Čikaga,[Ateitis], 1976.
115 p. PG8749.B67A55 PU.

3279. --- Pokalbiai su karalium,
anno Domini 1323-1973. Čikaga, M.
Morkūnas, 1973. 69 p. illus.
PG8749.B67P6 PU; DLC; InNd; MB;
OKentU.

3280. --- Svetimoji duona; eilėraščiai. München, Ger., Aidai, 1945.
95 p. WU.

3281. BRAZAUSKAS, Viktoras. Vasaros muzikantai. Vilnius, Vaga,
1970. 89 p. (Pirmoji knyga)
PG8722.12.R3V3 DLC; MB; MH; NN.

3282. BRAZDŽIONIS, Bernardas.
Kunigaikščių miestas. Kaunas, Saka-
las, 1939. [Xerox copy, 1977]. 126p.
PG8721.B7K8 1939a PU(xerox).

3283. --- Ženklai ir stebuklai;
eilėraščiai. Kaunas, Sakalas, 1936.
[Xerox copy, 1977]. 94 p.
PG8721.B7Z4 1936a PU(xerox).

3284. BRAZINSKAS, Algirdas. Už
mylimą Baltiją; eilėraščiai. [New
York, N.Y.], Amerikos Lietuvių Tautinės sąjungos Richmond Hill skyrius
1973. 32 p. PG8722.12.R3U9 PU.

3285. BREIMERIS, Feliksas. Skam-
bantis laikas. 2., papildyta laida.
Chicago, Ill., 1977. 69 p.
PG8721.B72S PU.

3286. BUCEVIČIENĖ, Stasė. Žiburys tamsoj žybėjo; eilėraščiai. Vilnius, Vaga, 1975. 74 p.
PG8722.12.U23Z5 PU.

3287. BŪDVYTIS, Pranas V. Ištre-
mimo keliais; pirmieji bandymai
1901-1919. Kaunas, Jagomasto spaustuvė "Lituania" Tilžėje, 1921. [Xe-

rox copy, 1877]. At head of title:
Pr.V. Būdvytis Svyrūnėlis.
PG8721.B815I8 1921a PU(xerox).

3288. BUIVYDAITĖ, Bronė. Skudu-
čiai. Panevežys, 1933.[Xerox copy,
1977]. 116 p. PG8721.B816S5 1933a
PU.

3289. BUKONTAS, Alfonsas. Mėnulio
takas; eilėraščiai. Vilnius, Vaga,
1977. 63 p. PG8722.12.U38M4 PU.

3290. --- Piešiniai ant vandens;
eilėraščiai. Vilnius, Vaga, 1972.
74 p. PG8722.12.U38P5 DLC; MH; PU;
OKentU.

3291. --- Slenkančios kopos. Vilnius, Vaga, 1967. 50 p. NN.

3292. BYRAS, Antanas. Minčių tru-
pinys; eilėraščių rinkinys. Parašė
Palanta, [pseud.]. Toronto, Ont.,
Kanados lietuvių literatūros draugi-
jos Centro komitetas, 1961. 80 p.
PG8749.B9M5 OKentU.

3293. CHURGINAS, Aleksys. Sankry-
ža; eilėraščiai. [Dailininkas A. Žvi-
lius]. Vilnius, Vaga, 1974. 102 p.
illus. PG8721.C45S2 DLC.

3294. --- Saulės taku. [Kaunas],
Valstybinė grožinės literatūros leidykla, 1947. 116 p. DLC-P4; NN.

3295. --- Sietuvas. Vilnius, Vaga, 1973. 112 p.
PG8721.C45S5 DLC; IU; MB; MH; WU.

3296. ČIPKUS, Alfonsas. Vyno ste-
buklas; eilėraščiai. Chicago, Ill.,
Išleido Algimanto Mackaus Knygų leidimo fondas, 1974. 76 p. At head of
title: Alfonsas Nyka-Niliūnas.
PG8721.C48V9 DLC.

3297. DABULSKIS, Aleksas. Basas
pegasas. Vilnius, Vaga, 1977. 72 p.
PG8722.14.A2B3 PU.

3298. DABULSKIS, Aleksas. Nulia-
da. [Satyriniai eilėraščiai. Dailininkas J. Varnas]. Vilnius, Vaga,
1972. 79 p. illus.
PG8722.4.A2N8 DLC; MH.

3299. DAMBRAUSKAS, Aleksandras.
Rudens aidai; eilės. 2.leidinys.
Kaunas, Šviesa, 1920. At head of
title: Adomas Jakštas. WU.

3300. DANDIERINAS, Runcė. Šilkai
ir vilkai; dainos vietinės ir sovietinės. [Iliustracijos P. Osmolskio.
Brooklyn, N.Y., B. Pavabalys,[1950].
62 p. illus. Real name: Leonardas
Žitkevičius. PG8721.D3S5 DLC; MiD.

3301. DAUTARTAS, Vladas. Jis--ka-
pitonas Pramuštgalvis, Vilnius, Vaga, 1970. 89 p. illus.
PG8722.14.A8J5 DLC.

3302. DEGUTYTĖ, Janina. Prieblan-
dų sodai; eilėraščiai. [Dailininkas
Vytautas Valius]. Vilnius, Vaga,
1974. 98 p. illus.
PG8722.14.E35P7 DLC; WU.

3303. --- Šviečia sniegas. Vilnius, Vaga, 1970. 71 p. illus.
PG8722.14.E35S9 PU; MH; NjP.

3304. DONELAITIS, Kristijonas.
Das Jahr in vier Gesängen. Übertragen von L.G.Rhesa. Königsberg in Pr.
1818. 162 p. It contains also the
first edition of his Metai in Lithuanian ed. by L.G.Rhesa.
Balt. 9645.19.100 MH.

3305. --- Metai. [Edited by J.
Ambrazevičius; illus. by V.K. Jony-
nas]. Kaunas, Spindulys, 1941. 206
p. WU.

3306. DREVINIS, Paulius. Kryžke-
lė kelių plačių. Vilnius, Vaga,1966.
118 p. PG8722.14.R46K7 DLC; NN.

3307. --- Tėviškės eglės. Vil-
nius, Vaga, 1971. 68 p.
PG8722.14.R46T4 DLC; MH; NN; NjP;
OKentU.

3308. DRILINGA, Antanas. Šiluma;
eilėraščiai. Vilnius, Vaga, 1968.
127 p. illus. PG8722.14.R5S5 DLC;
NN; OKentU.

3309. --- Žolės spalva; rinktinė.
Vilnius, Vaga, 1975. 249 p.
PG8722.14.R5Z4 DLC.

3310. GAIDAMAVIČIUS, Zigmas. Gė-
lynas. Kaunas, Valstybinė grožinės
literatūros leidykla, 1948. 156 p
facsims., port.
PG8721.G28G4 1948 DLC.

3311. GEDA, Sigitas. Mėnulio
žiedai. Vilnius, Vaga, 1977. 142 p.
PG8722.17.E3M4 PU.

3312. --- Pėdos. Vilnius, Vaga,
1966. 53 p. (Pirmoji knyga).
PG8722.17.E3P4 DLC;PU.

3313. --- Strazdas; poema. Vil-
nius, Vaga, 1967. 52 p. illus.
PG8722.17.E3S7 DLC; IU; MH; OKentU;
NN.

3314. GENYTĖ-ŠMAIŽIENĖ, Viktorija.
Gyvenimas ir darbai; eilėraščiai.
[Brooklyn, N.Y., J. Šmaižys], 1973.
96 p. illus.
PG8749.G4G9 1973 DLC; MB.

3315. GIEDRA, Vincas. Skaidrioji
versmė; eilėraščiai. Vilnius, Valstybinė grožinės literatūros leidykla,
1961. 100 p. PG8722.17.I4S58 OKentU.

3316. --- Vingiai; eilėraščiai
ir poemos. Vilnius, Vaga, 1975. 96p.
PG8722.17.I43V5 PU.

3317. GIRKONTAITĖ, Ramutė. Riks-
mas. Vilnius, Vaga, 1969. 44 p.
8722.17.I7R5 DLC; MH; OKentU.

3318. GRAIČIŪNAS, Jonas. Pėdų es-
tampai. Vilnius, Vaga, 1966.
PG8721.G615P4 DLC; NN.

3319. --- Saulėlydžio freskos.
Vilnius, Vaga, 1973. 134 p.
PG8721.G615S PU.

3320. --- Vilniaus kotraforsai.
Vilnius, Vaga, 1976. 121 p.
PG8721.G615V5 PU.

3321. GRAŽYS, Remigijus. Per gel-
tonas kalvas; eilėraščiai. [Dailinin-
kas D. Kuzminskis]. Vilnius, Vaga,
1973. 54 p. illus.
PG8722.17.R3P4 DLC; MH; NN.

3322. GRICIUS, Alfonsas. Pažadin-
ti sfinksai; lyrika. Los Angeles,
Calif., Lietuvių Dienos, 1961. 47 p.
PG8721.G63P3 DLC; IU; OCl; OO; PU.

3323. --- Tropikų elegijos; lyrika. Adelaide, Australia, [Išleido
"Australijos Lietuvis"], 1953. 61 p.
illus. GP8721.G63T7 DLC.

3324. --- Žemė ir žmogus; sonetai. Würzburg, Ger., [Žalgiris],
1947. 55 p. 891.92G872Z PU.

3325. GRYBAS, Vladas. Įkvėpimas.
Vilnius, Vaga, 1976. 93 p.
PG8721.G75I5 PU.

3326. Taikos vardu; eilėraščiai.
[Vilniuje[, Valstybinė grožinės li-
teratūros leidykla, 1952. 126 p.
PG8721.G75T3 DLC.

3327. --- Žemės atgimimo šventė-
je. Vilnius, Vaga, 1968. 263 p.
illus. PG8721.G75Z3 DLC; PSt.

3328. GURNEVIČIUS, Vladas. Vėjo
malūnai; epigramos. Vilnius, Vaga,
1975. 108 p. PG8722.17.U7V4 PU.

3329. GUSTAITIS, Motiejus. Meilė;
poema. Chicago, Ill., Spauda "Kataliko", 1914. 24 p.
891.92G976M PU; CaOONL; WU.

3330. --- Sielos akordai. Jaros-
lavlis, 1917. [Xerox copy, 1977].
64 p. PG8721.G86S5 1917a PU(xerox).

3331. --- Tėvynės ašaros. 2.laida. Erškėčių taku. 1.laida. Piešiniai V. Bičiūno. Jaroslavlyje, Spaustuvė E. Lipkis, 1916. 64 p. 891.92G976T PU.

3332. GUTAUSKAS, Leonardas. Vartai po diemedžiu; eilėraščiai. Vilnius, Vaga, 1976. 110 p. PG8721.G9V3 PU.

3333. INČIŪRA, Kazys. Su jaunyste; pirmoji eilėraščių ir dainų knyga. Kaunas, 1928. [Xerox copy, 1977] 128 p. PG8721.I5S8 1928a PU.

3334. JAKŠTAS, Jonas. Balti vidudieniai; eilėraščiai. Vilnius,Vaga, 1964. 97 p. PG8722.2.A55B3 DLC

3335. --- Prisiminimai be datų; eilėraščiai. [Dailininkas E. Katilius]. PG8722.2.A55P7 PU; DLC; IU; WU.

3336. --- Žalsvieji žirginiai; eilėraščiai. [Vilnius, Valstybinė grožinės literatūros leidykla, 1960] 78 p. illus. PG8721.J24Z2 DLC.

3337. JANONIS, Julius. Eilėraščiai. Kaunas, Šviesa, 1967. 53 p. (Mokinio biblioteka) PG8721.J3E36 OKentU.

3338. --- Pūslėtosioms rankoms; [eilėraščiai. Dailininkas V. Galdikas]. Vilnius, Vaga, 1973. 226 p. illus. PG8721.J3P8 1973 DLC.

3339. JANUŠYTĖ, Liūnė. Pirmosios dienos. Kaunas, Valstybinė grožinės literatūros leidykla, 1948. 891.92J289P PU.

3340. JASILIONIS, Stasys. Pavasarių godos; eilių rinkinys. [s.l.], Išleido Dienraštis Laisvė, 1948. 256 p. PG8721.J37P3 OKentU.

3341. JASIUKAITYTĖ, Vidmantė. Ugnis, kurią reikia pereiti. Vilnius, Vaga, 1976. 77 p. PG8722.2.A75 PU.

3342. JOKIMAITIS, Gediminas. ... su naktim kalbėsiu. Vilnius,Vaga, 1971. 83 p. PG8722.2.O4S8 PU; MH.

3343. --- Vandenų muzika. Vilnius, Vaga, 1969. 41 p. PG8722.2.O45V3 DLC; OKentU.

3344. JONAUSKAS, Mečys. Darbų vardai; eilėraščiai. Vilnius, Vaga, 1977. 110 p. PG8722.2.O49D3 PU.

3345. JONIKAS, Petras. Lydėjau viešnią vėtroje; eilių rinktinė.

[New York, N.Y., 1968]. 168 p. PG8721.J62L9 PU; OKentU.

3346. JONYNAS, Antanas. Metai kaip strazdas; eilėraščiai. Vilnius, Vaga, 1977. 92 p. PG8722.2.O51M4 PU

3347. --- Pasiryžimo metas; eilėraščiai. Vilnius, Vaga, 1973. 159 p. PG8722.205P28 DLC.

3348. --- --- 2.papildytas leidimas. Vilnius, Vaga, 1977. 186 p. PG8722.2.O5P3 PU.

3349. --- Žmogaus širdis, kareivio širdis; rinktinė lyrika. [Dailininkas Stasys Krasauskas]. Vilnius, Vaga, 1974. 405 p. illus. PG8722.205Z4 DLC; WU.

3350. JŪRA, Klemensas. Krivio lėmimas; baladės. Fröseburg, Ger., [Lithuania], 1946. [Xerox copy,1977]. 79 p. At head of title: Rimas, [pseud.]. PG8721.J73K7 1946a PU.

3351. JURGELIONIS, Kleofas. Glūdiliūdi. [Paruošė A. Rabačiauskaitė]. Vilnius, Vaga, 1971. 266 p., 5 leaves of illus. At head of title: Kleopas Jurgelionis. PG8721.J75G5 1971 DLC; NN; NNC; PU.

3352. JURKUS, Paulius. Juodvarniai; pasaka-poema. [Piešiniai autoriaus]. Brooklyn, N.Y., "Darbinko" laikraštis, 1975. 200 p. PG8721.J8J8 PU.

3353. KAIRYS, Anatolijus. Karūna; istorinė trilogija-poema. Devyni veiksmai, dvidešimt septyni paveikslai, prologas ir epilogas. Mindaugo epocha 1237-1268. Chicago, Ill., Dialogas, 1974. 318 p. PG8721.K2K3 PU; DLC; OKentU.

3354. KARIUS, Vytautas. Tylos veidrodis;[eilėraščiai]. Vilnius,Vaga, 1972. 139 p. PG8722.21.A7T9 DLC; MH.

3355. KARČIAUSKAS, Mykolas. Klevo medus. Vilnius, Vaga, 1972. 59 p. PG8722.21.A71K6 PU.

3356. --- Žvirgždės poema; poema. Vilnius, Vaga, 1976. 68 p. PG8722.21.A71Z9 PU.

3357. KAROSAS, Vytautas. Poilsis ant laiptų; poezija. [Chicago, Ill.] 1969. 88 p. port. PG8749.K26P6 1969 DLC; MB; OKentU;PU

3358. KARVELYTĖ, Ada. Ne tie varpai; lyrika. [Brooklyn, N.Y., Darbininkas], 1972. 64 p. PG8749.K29N4 DLC; OKentU.

3359. KAZOKAS, V. Sapnų pėdomis; eilėraščiai. [Chicago, Ill., M.Morkūnas,] 1953. 62 p. PG8721.K3S3 DLC; OKentU; PU.

3360. KEIDOŠIUS, Petras. Ji vėl su manimi; eilėraščiai. Vilnius, Vaga, 1974. 117 p. PG8722.21.E5J5 PU.

3361. KETURAKIS, Robertas. Atspindžiai; eilėraščiai. Vilnius, Vaga, 1974. 110 p. PG8721.K5A8 PU.

3362. KIRŠA, Faustas. Aidų aidučiai. Kaunas, 1921. 891.92K635A PU.

3363. --- Giesmės. Kaunas, Alkas, 1934.[Xerox copy, 1976]. 231 p. PG8721.K57G5.1934a PU.

3364. --- Palikimas; eilėraščiai, nebaigti eilėraščiai, Aidų aidužiai, Pelenai III ir IV, Pabėgeliai, užrašai ir kt. Leidinį spaudai parengė Stasys Santvaras. [Boston, Mass.], Lietuvių enciklopedijos leidykla, [1972]. 318 p. PG8721.K57P3 PU;DLC.

3365. --- Pelenai. Antroji knyga. [Kaunas], Sakalas, [1938]. [Xerox copy, 1974]. 59 p. PG8721.K57P4 1974. PU.

3366. --- Rimgaudo žygis; poema. Kaunas, ["Spindulio"spaustuvė],1930. [Xerox copy, 1977]. 44 p. PG8721.K57R5 1930a PU.

3367. KISIELIUS, Romualdas. Pirmoji sėja. New York, N.Y., 1960. 41 p. 891.92K644P PU; CtTMF.

3368. KONDROTAS, Saulius Tomas. Pasaulis be ribų. Vilnius, Vaga, 1977. 100 p. PG8722.21.053P3 PU.

3369. KONTRIMAITĖ, Marytė. Kristalų atskalos. Vilnius, Vaga, 1971. 53 p. (Pirmoji knyga). PG8722.21.055K7 PU; MH.

3370. KOZULIS, Pranas. Dulkės ežere. Toronto, Ont., 1950. 62 p. 891.92K949D PU; DLC-P4.

3371. KRIPAITIS, Edmundas. Akimirkos. Vilnius, Vaga, 1969. 85 p. (Pirmoji knyga). PG8722.21.R5A8 DLC; MH; OKentU.

3372. KUBILINSKAS, Kostas. Lygumos dainuoja; lyrika. Vilnius, Vaga, 1964. 319 p. port. PG8722.21.U2L9 DLC; IU; MH.

3373. KUMPIKEVIČIŪTĖ, Viktorija. Vasara laukuos; lyrika. [Kaunas], Šv.Kazimiero d-ja, [1939].[Xerox copy, 1976]. 55 p. PG8721.K83V3 PU.

3374. KUNDROTAS, Juozas. Gilios medžių šaknys. Vilnius, Mintis,1975. 79 p.,[4] leaves of plates. illus. PG8722.21.U5G5 DLC.

3375. --- Marytė Melnikaitė. Vilnius, Mintis, 1968. 83 p. illus. PG8722.21.U5M3 DLC.

3376. LAPAŠINSKAS, J[onas]. Jaunystės daina; eilėraščiai. Vilnius, Valstybinė grožinės literatūros leidykla, 1953. 62 p. PG8721.L32J3 DLC

3377. --- Žemė ilgisi meilės; eilėraščiai. Vilnius, Vaga, 1968. 117 p. PG8721.L32Z4 PU; DLC; NN.

3378. LASTAS, Adomas. Auksinės varpos; eilių rinkinys, 1-ji knyga. [Marijampolė, Autoriaus leidinys], 1921.[Xerox copy, 1977]. 160 p. PG8721.L335A8 1921a PU.

3379. MAČERNIS, Vytautas. Vizijos; pomirtinė poezijos knyga. [Sudarė Vytautas Saulius. Iliustracijos V. Aleksandravičiaus.] Roma, Centrinis Lietuvių Komitetas Italijoje, 1947. 79 p. WU.

3380. --- Žmogaus apnuoginta širdis. Vilnius, Vaga, 1970. 291 p., 5 leaves of illus. PG8721.M24Z3 1970 DLC; ICIU; IU; MB; MH; NjP; OKentU; PU.

3381. MACEVIČIUS, Juozas. Atošvaistės; rinktinė. Vilnius, Vaga, 1971. 305 p. PG8722.23.A27A8 CaOTU; DLC; IU; MB; MH; NN; NNC; NjP; PU.

3382. --- Distancija; eilėraščiai. Vilnius, Vaga, 1972. 102 p. illus. PG8722.23.A27D5 PU; MH.

3383. --- Mano poezija; eilėraščiai. Vilnius, Valstybinė grožinės literatūros leidykla, 1963. 106 p. PG8722.23.A27M3 DLC.

3384. --- Šauksmas; eilėraščiai. Vilnius, Vaga, 1975. 99 p. WU.

3385. MAČIUIKA, Vytautas. Negludinti akmenys; eilėraščiai. Vilnius, Vaga, 1965. 47 p. port. PG8722.23.A29N4 DLC.

3386. MAČIUKEVIČIUS, Jonas. Kraujo analizė. Vilnius, Vaga, 1969. 94 p. PG8722.23.A295K7 DLC; IU; MH.

3387. MACKEVIČIUS, Bronius. Grįžtančios gervės. Vilnius, Vaga, 1973. PG8722.23.A3G7 PU; MH.

3388. --- Žygiais matuojame širdis. Vilnius, Valstybinė grožinės

literatūros leidykla, 1962. 107 p.
PG8722.Z3A3Z48 DLC; MH.

3389. MACKUS, Algimantas. Chapel
B. Chicago, Ill., [Algimanto Mackaus vargo knygų leidimo fondas],1965.
63 p. PG8749.M27C5 DLC; CLU; MH.

3390. --- Elegijos. Chicago,
Ill., 1959. 48 p. At head of title;
Algimantas Pagėgis, [pseud.].
891.92M214E PU.

3391. --- Jo yra žemė; eilėraščiai. Chicago, Ill., 1959. 91 p.
illus. PG8742.M3 DLC; MH; PU.

3392. --- Neornamentuotos kalbos
generacijos, ir Augintiniai. Chicago,
Ill., 1962. 891.92M219N PU.

3393. --- Poezija. [Redakcinė
komisija: Algimantas Baltakis, Alfonsas Maldonis, Vacys Reimeris]. Vilnius, Vaga, 1972. [Dailininkas A.
Smilingis]. 168 p.
PG8749.M27 1972 PU; DLC; MH; NN;
OKentU.

3394. Maironis, Jonas. Baladės.
Iliustravo Pranas Lapė. [Paaiškini-
mai: Juozas Brazaitis]. Woodhaven,
N.Y., Romuva, [1966]. 90 p. illus.
PG8721.M3A58 DLC; InU; OKentU; PU.

3395. --- Raseinių Magdė; poema-
tas. 3.leidimas. Kaunas, Aušra,
1921. 31 p. WU.

3396. MALDONIS, Alfonsas. Kelionė; rinktinė lyrika. Vilnius, Vaga,
1975. 373 p. PG8722.23.A5K4 PU;WU.

3397. --- Pėdsakai; eilėraščiai.
[Dailininkas V. Valius]. Vilnius,
Vaga, 1971. 103 p. illus.
PG8721.M33P4 DLC; NNC; OKentU; WU.

3398. --- Vandens ženklai; eilėraščiai. [Dailininkas V. Kalinaus-
kas]. Vilnius, Vaga, 1969. 99 p.
illus. PG8721.M33V3 DLC.

3399. MARCINKEVIČIUS, Juozas. Rudens šalys. Vilnius, Vaga, 1969.
67 p. PG9049.23.A67R8 DLC; IU; MH;
PU.

3400. MARCINKEVIČIUS, Justinas.
Baladė apie Ievą. Lino raižiniai
A. Makūnaitės. Vilnius, Vaga, 1965.
28 p. illus.,PG9721.M35B3 DLC;MH.

3401. --- Eilėraščiai. Mažosios
poemos. Vilnius, Vaga, 1975. 402 p.
PG8721.M35E5 PU; WU.

3402. --- Mažvydas; trijų dalių
giesmė. Vilnius, Vaga, 1977. 149 p.
PG8721.M35M3 PU.

3403. --- Poemos. [Dailininkė L.J.
J. Paškauskaitė]. Vilnius, Vaga,
1972. 2 v. illus. PG8721.M35P6 PU;
CaAEU; DLC; OKentU; WU.

3404. --- Sena abėcėlė; eilėraš-
čiai. [Dailininkė. L. Paškauskaitė].
Vilnius, Vaga, 1969. 348 p. illus.
PG8721.M35S4 DLC; NN.

3405. --- Šešios poemos; Pradžios
poema, Ugnies poema, Meilės poema,
Heroica, **Devyni** broliai, Homo sum.
[Dailininkas S. Krasauskas]. 123 p.
PG8721.M35A17 1973 PU; DLC; MB; MH.

3406. MARTINAITIS, Marcelijus.
Akių tamsoj, širdies šviesoj; eilė-
raščiai. [Dailininkas Vladislovas
Žilius]. Vilnius, Vaga, 1974. 86 p.
PG8722.23.A7A8 DLC.

3407. --- Balandžio sniegas; eilėraščiai. Vilnius, Valstybinė grožinės literatūros leidykla, 1962. 45
p. port. PG8722.23.A7B3 DLC.

3408. --- Debesų lieptais. Vilnius, Vaga, 1966. 78 p. illus.
PG8722.23.A7D4 PU; DLC; IU; MB; MH.

3409. --- Kukučio baladės. Vilnius, Vaga, 1977. 85 p.
PG8722.23.A7K8 PU.

3410. --- Saulės grąža. [Daili-
ninkas Vl. Žilius]. Vilnius, Vaga,
1969. 78 p. illus. PG8722.23.A7S2
DLC; OKentU.

3411. MARTINKUS, Vytautas. Lote-
rija. Vilnius, Vaga, 1969. 87 p.
(Pirmoji knyga). PG8722.23.A7L6
OKentU; MH.

3412. MASIONIS, Antanas. Kelias;
eilėraščiai. Vilnius. Vaga, 1974.
62 p. PG8722.23.A8K4 DLC.

3413. --- Vardan dienovidžio.
Vilnius, Vaga, 1970. 52 p. (Pirmoji
knyga). PG8722.23.A8V3 DLC;MB;MH.

3414. MATUZEVIČIUS, Eugenijus.
Paukščių takas; eilėraščiai. Vilnius,
Vaga, 1970. 111 p. illus.
PG8721.M37P3 DLC; IU; NNC; NjP; MH;
OKentU.

3415. MEKAS, Jonas. Jonas Mekas.
[Poezija. Dailininkas V. Valius].
Vilnius, Vaga, 1971. 227 p. illus.
PG8749.M4A6 1971 DLC; MH;NNC;OKentU.

3416. MICIŪTĖ, Ona. Pirmoji šake-
lė. [Iliustravo Eduardas Jurėnas].
Vilnius, Vaga, 1972. 176 p.
PG8722.23.I25P5 PU.

3417. --- Slėnių paukščiai; [eilėraščiai. Dailininkas R. Dichavičius]. Vilnius, Vaga, 1971. 176 p. illus. PG8722.23.I25S5 DLC; IU;MB; MH; PU.

3418. MIEŽELAITIS, Eduardas. Aleliumai. Vilnius, Vaga, 1974. 561 p. PG8721.M45A49 PU; DLC.

3419. --- Antakalnio barokas. Vilnius, Vaga, 1971. 298 p. PG8721.M45A53 PU; DLC; WU.

3420. --- Aviaskizai. Vilnius, Vaga, 1975. 586 p. PG8721.M45A98 DLC.

3421. --- Čia Lietuva; poetinė publicistika. [Papildytas leidimas]. Vilnius, Vaga, 1974. 549 p. PG8721.M45C5 1974 PU; DLC.

3422. --- Dainos dienoraštis. [Iliustravo Laima Barisaitė. Vilnius Vaga, 1973]. 126 p. PG8721.M45D3 PU; DLC.

3423. --- Gintaro paukštė. Bloknotai. [Dailininkas V. Žilius]. Vilnius, Vaga, 1972. PG8721.M45G5 PU; DLC; IU; MB; NNC.

3424. --- Kontrapunktas. Vilnius, Vaga, 1975. 495 p. PG8721.M45K6 1975 PU.

3425. --- Mano lakštingala. Vilnius, Valstybinė grožinės literatūros leidykla, 1956. 367 p. illus., port. *QY--NN.

3426. --- Montažai. Vilnius,Vaga, 1969. 396 p. PG8721.M45M6 DLC; IU.

3427. --- Pantomima. Vilnius,Vaga, 1976. 658 p. PG8721.M45P3 PU.

3428. --- Tekstai. Vilnius, Vaga, 1977. 570 p. PG8721.M45T4 PU.

3429. Žmogus; [eilėraščiai. Medžio raižiniai S. Krasausko]. 4.leidimas. Vilnius, Vaga, 1971. 118 p. illus. PG8721.M45Z35 DLC; WU.

3430. --- Monodrama. Vilnius,Vaga, 1976. 614 p. PG8721.M45M59 PU.

3431. MIKAILAITĖ, Ona. Šiapus jūros; lyrika. [Putnam, Conn., Nekaltai Pradėtosios Marijos Seserys],1976. 62 p. PG8749.M52S5 PU.

3432. MIKUCKIS, Juozas. Didvyriai ir smulkmenos. Ryga, 1915. 891.92M584D PU.

3433. --- Lyrika; rinktinė. [Su-

darė Vytautas Kazakevičius]. Vilnius, Vaga, 1975. 167 p. PG8721.M46L91 PU.

3434. MIKUTA, Algimantas. Ašmenys. Vilnius, 1970. 81 p. PG8722.23.I4A7 PU; MH; OU.

3435. --- Šiandien piešime žaibus; eilėraščiai. [Dailininkas Br. Leonavičius]. Vilnius, Vaga, 1973. 94 p. PG8722.23.I4S5 PU; DLC.

3436. MIŠKINIS, Antanas. Dienoraštis, 1965-1971. Devintoji poezijos knyga. Vilnius, Vaga, 1972. 126 p. PG8721.M53D5 PU; DLC; MB; NN;OKentU; WU.

3437. --- Iš drobių rašto; rinktinė. Vilnius, Vaga, 1975. 246 p. PG8721.M53I8 PU.

3438. MONTVILA, Vytautas. Eilėraščio šūvis; [eilėraščiai. Iliustravo R. Gibavičius]. Vilnius, Vaga, 1975. 264 p. illus. PG8721.M56E35 1975 DLC.

3439. --- Žiburiai. Iliustravo Kastytis Juodikaitis. Vilnius,Vaga, 1973. 52 p. PG8721.M56Z3 PU.

3440. MOZŪRIŪNAS, Vladas. Varpos iš laukų. Vilnius, Valstybinė grožinės literatūros leidykla, 1958. 891.92M879V PU.

3441. MYKOLAITIS, Vincas. Poezija. Vilnius, Vaga, 1973. 2 v. PG8721.M9A17 1973 DLC; NN; WU.

3442. --- Rūščios dienos. [Redagavo Domas Velička. Čikaga, Pedagoginis lituanistikos institutas,1972]. 49 p. At head of title: V.Mykolaitis -Putinas. PG8721.M9R8 1972 PU;DLC.

3443. --- Tarp dviejų aušrų.Kaunas,[Sakalas], 1927.[Xerox copy,1977] 101 p. PG8721.M9T3 1927a PU.

3444. NASVYTYTĖ, Aldona Irena. Vėjo dainos. [Chicago, Ill., s.n., s.d.]. 50 p. PG8721.V3V4 OKentU.

3445. NAUJOKAITIS, Pranas. Akmens širdis; elegijos. [Brooklyn,N.Y. Ateitis], 1960. 104 p. OKentU.

3446. --- Auksiniai rageliai; lyrika. [Chicago, Ill.], Lietuviškos knygos klubas, [1968]. 64 p. PG8721.N35A9 DLC.

3447. NEKROŠIUS, Juozas. Kaštonai ir kaktusai; eilėraščiai. [Dailininkė N. Kryževičiūtė-Jurgelionienė]. Vilnius, Vaga, 1970. 102 p. illus.

PG8722.24.E4K3 DLC; MB; MH; NjP;
NNC; OKentU; PU.

3448. NERIMA, Narutė. Relikvijos;
lyriniai natiurmortai. [Los Angeles,
Calif.], Lietuvių Dienos, [1964].
71 p. PG8749.N44R4 DLC; OKentU.

3449. NĖRIS, Salomėja. Mama! Kur
tu. [Iliustravo Kastytis Juodikaitis]
Vilnius, Vaga, 1971. [36] p.
PG8721.N4M3 PU.

3450. --- Poezija. Vilnius,Vaga,
1972. 2 v. PG8721.N4P 1972 PU.

3451. --- Širdis mana - audrų daina. [Medžio raižiniai Albinos Makū-
naitės]. Vilnius, Vaga, 1974. 476 p.
PG8721.N4S5 PU.

3452. ONAITIS, Vytautas. Nerimo
pasakos; eilėraščiai. Vilnius, Vaga,
1971. 186 p. PG8722.25.N3N4 PU;DLC;
MB; MH; IU.

3453. ORINTAITĖ, Petronėlė. Šuli-
nys sodyboj; lyrika. Iliustravo Mikas
Šileikis. Čikago, 1950. 96 p. ill.
PG8721.O7S8 DLC; WU.

3454. PABIJŪNAS, Algimantas. Juo-
ko ašaros; [satyriniai eilėraščiai].
Dailininkas J. Varnas. Vilnius,Va-
ga, 1973. 117 p. illus.
PG8722.26.A2J8 PU; DLC.

3455. --- Kepurė dega; satyriniai
eilėraščiai. Vilnius, Valstybinė
grožinės literatūros leidykla, 1961.
93 p. illus. PG8722.26.A2K4 DLC.

3456. --- Šimtas perkūnsargių;
satyriniai eilėraščiai. [Dailininkas
S. Krasauskas]. Vilnius, Vaga,1967.
90 p. PG8722.26.A2S55 PU.

3457. PALČINSKAITĖ, Violeta.
Aikštės. Vilnius, Vaga, 1965. 74 p.
illus. PG8721.P27A7 DLC.

3458. PALECKIS, Justas. Metų
vieškeliais, 1917-1972; eilėraščiai.
[Dailininkas P. Rauduvė]. Vilnius,
Vaga, 1973. 334 p. illus.
PG8721.P3M4 DLC; IU; WU.

3459. --- Tūkstantis žingsnelių.
Medžio raižiniai J. Kuzminskio. Vil-
nius, Vaga, 1970. 141 p. illus.
PG8721.P3T8 DLC; NN; OKentU.

3460. PALILIONIS, Petras. Atolas.
Vilnius, Vaga, 1972. 55 p.
PG8722.26.A56A8 PU.

3461. PAROJUS, Juozas. Į laisvę
ir mėnulį, 1918-1968. New York,N.Y.,
[Spausdino Vagos spaustuvė], 1968.
75 p. PG8721.P35I2 PU; OKentU.

3462. --- Partizanų akys. New
York, N.Y., 1965. 89 p. PG8721.P35P3
PU.

3463. PATACKAS, Gintaras. Atleisk
už audrą. Vilnius, Vaga, 1976. 61 p.
PG8722.26.A78A8 PU

3464. PAUTIENIŪTĖ, Teresė. Lyg
nebūtų rytojaus; eilėraščiai. [Chi-
cago, Ill.], Ateitis,[1975]. 75 p.
PG8722.26.A83L9 PU.

3465. PETRUKAITIS, Pijus. Tran-
šėjų vingiuose. Vilnius, Vaga,1966.
94 p. port. PG8721.P453T7 DLC.

3466. PUIŠYTĖ, Aldona. Žalvario
raktas. Vilnius, Vaga, 1970. 50 p.
(Pirmoji knyga) PG8722.26.U4Z24 DLC;
MB; MH.

3467. RADZEVIČIUS, Bronius. Balsai iš tylos. Vilnius, Vaga, 1970.
PG8722.28.A34B3 DLC; MH; NN.

3468. RADŽIUS, Aleksandras. Baltas mėnulio miestas; eilėraščiai.
Čikaga, [M. Morkūnas], 1975. 72 p.
illus. PG8749.R26B3 PU; DLC.

3469. --- Paukščių takas; eilėraščiai. [Hollywood, Calif.], Lietuvių Dienos, [1961]. 47 p.
PG8749.R26P3 DLC; OCl; PU.

3470. RAŠČIUS, Pranas. Miško šu-
linys; eilėraščiai. Vilnius, Vaga,
1972. 134 p. PG8722.28.A8M5 PU;
DLC; MB; NN; OKentU.

3471. --- Pirštai tarp durų; satyriniai eilėraščiai. Vilnius, Vaga,
1966. 96 p. illus. PG8722.28.A8P5
DLC; IU; MH.

3472. --- Trauklapiai; eilėraščiai. Vilnius, Vaga, 1974. [Daili-
ninkas R.Palčiauskas]. 213 p.
PG8722.28.A8T7 PU; DLC.

3473. RATNIKAS, Jonas. SPARNAI;
eilėraščiai. Vilnius, Valstybinė
grožinės literatūros leidykla, 1962.
58 p. port. PG8722.28.A9S6 DLC;MH.

3474. REIMERIS, Vacys. Eisenos.
[Dailininkas E. Katilius]. Vilnius,
Vaga, 1970. 324 p. illus.
PG8721.R4E35 DLC; IU; NjP; PU.

3475. --- Vėjo vynas. Vilnius,
Vaga, 1976. 184 p. PG8721.R4V4 PU.

3476. ROSTOVAITĖ, Tatjana. Ugnis
ir vanduo. Vilnius, Vaga, 1970. 127
p. PG8722.28.O78U4 DLC; MB;MH;NjP.
IU.

3477. --- Tarp jūros marių. Vil-

nius, Vaga, 1966. 129 p.
PG8722.28.078T3 DLC.

3478. RUDOKAS, Vytautas. Pušų
vargonai. Sonetų knyga. Vilnius,Va-
ga, 1972. 88 p. PG8722.28.U3P8 DLC;
WU.

3479. RUDOKAS, Vytautas. Žolės
džiaugsmas ir liūdesys. Vilnius,Va-
ga, 1970. 99 p. PG8722.28.U3Z4 DLC
IU; NN; PU.

3480. RUKŠA, Balys. Ugnies par-
davėjas; poezija. [Iliustravo Viktoras Bričkus]. Tonto, Ont.,[Baltija],
1952. 95 p. 891.92R857U PU;ICCC.

3481. RUTKŪNAS, Benediktas. Mė-
lyna diena; eilėraščiai. [Putnam,Conn.
Immaculata Press], 1967. 96 p.
PG8721.R83M4 PU; OKentU.

3482. --- Sparnus man meta paukštės. Ketvirta lyrikos knyga. Weilheim-Teck, Ger., Atžalynas, 1947.
158 p. illus. At head of title:
Benys Rutkūnas. PG8721.R85S6 OKentU;
WU.

3483. SAGATAS, Petras. Plauk mano laiveli; eilėraščiai. [Chicago,
ill.,] 1962. 111 p. illus.
PG8749.S3P5 DLC; NN; OKentU.

3484. --- Sauleleidžio spindu-
liuose; eiliuoti kūrinėliai. [Jono
Tričio viršelis ir vinjetės]. Chicago, Ill., 1957. 96 p. illus.
PG8749.S3S35 DLC; NN; PU.

3485. SAKALAS, Juozas. Saulėte-
kio skrydis. [München, Ger.], 1966.
166 p. PG8722.29.A4S3 DLC; WaU.

3486. ŠAKYTĖ, Stasė. Alkana žemė;
eilėraščiai. Brooklyn, N.Y., Ateitis, 1967. 72 p. 891.92Sa294 PU;
OKentU; PPULC; RPB.

3487. ŠALTENIS, Saulius. Duokiš-
kis. Vilnius, Vaga, 1977. 63 p.
PG8722.29.A43D8 PU.

3488. SAUKAITYTĖ, Dalia. Rugpiūčio žemuogės; poezija. Vilnius, Vaga, 1972. 51 p. (Pirmoji knyga, 72)
PG8722.29.A8R8 DLC; MH.

3489. SAULAITIS, Marija. Kai mes
nutylam. Putnam, Conn., Immaculata
Press, 1967. 83 p. PG8749.S35K3 PU.

3490. ŠAVELIS, Rimantas. Palei
žalią krantą. Vilnius, Vaga, 1970.
90 p. (Pirmoji knyga).
PG8722.29.A9P3 DLC; MB; MH; NN.

3491. SEALEY, Danguolė. Kai tu
arti manęs; eilėraščiai. [Los Ange-

les, Calif., Lietuvių Dienos, 1965.
38 p. PG8749.S4K3 DLC.

3492. --- Laiškai Dievui; eilėraščiai. [Brooklyn, N.Y.], Ateitis,
[1970]. 72 p. (Literatūros serija,
nr.4). PG8749.S4L3 DLC.

3493. --- Pakeliui į emmaus; ei-
lėraščiai. Danguolė Sadūnaitė [i.e.
Danguolė Sealey]. Putnam, Conn.,Iš-
leido Nek. Pr. Šv. M. Marijos Seserų
Kongregacija, 1974. 95 p.
PG8749.S4P3 DLC.

3494. ŠEIŽYS, Mykolas. Dainos-dai-
nelės; eilių rinkinys. Kaunas, S.Ba-
naičio spaustuvė, 1909. (Šv. Kazimiero draugijos leidinys, nr.71).
At head of title. M. Dagilėlis, [
pseud.]. 891.92Se47Da PU.

3495. --- Dainos ir sakmės.
Tilžė, "Tėvynės Sargas", 1903. At
head of title: M.Dagilėlis.
891.92Se47D PU

3496. SELELIONIS, Eduardas. Sąži-
nė; poema. Vilnius, Valstybinė grožinės literatūros leidykls, 1960.
133 p. illus. PG8721.S39S2 DLC.

3497. ŠEMERYS, Salys. Granata
krūtinėj; rinktinė. Vilnius, Vaga,
1969. 119 p. port. PG8722.29.E4G7
DLC; NjP.

3498. --- --- Kaunas, Keturių Vėjų leidinys, 1924.[Xerox copy, 1975].
30 p. PG8721.S38G7 1975 PU.

3499. ŠEŠPLAUKIS, Alfonsas. Die-
medžio paunksmėje; sonetai. [West
Bridgford, Eng.], Šaltinis, 1974. 35
p. At head of title: Alfonsas Tyruolis,[pseud.]. PG8721.S4D5 PU; DLC.

3500. --- Kelionė; eilėraščiai.
Chicago, Ill., Lietuvių katalikų
spaudos draugija, 1950. 127 p. ill.
At head of title: A. Tyruolis,[pseud.]
PG8721.S4K4 OKentU; DLC-P4; MB; MH;
NNC; PU.

3501. ŠIMKUS, Alfredas. Vidudie-
nių potvyniai. Vilnius, Vaga, 1972.
49 p. (Pirmoji knyga). PG8722.29.I53
V5 PU; MH.

3502. SIMS-ČERNECKYTĖ, Marija.
Ant kryžkelių senų; eilėraščiai. 2.,
papildyta laida. Redagavo Vyt. Alantas. [Cleveland, Ohio, 1971[. 296 p.
PG8722.29.I57A8 1971 DLC; OKentU.

3503. ŠIOŽINYS, Jonas. Baltos
langinės; eilėraščiai. Vilnius,Vaga,
1973. 85 p. PG8722.29.I58B3 DLC.

3504. --- Rogių kelias; rinktinė.

Vilnius, Vaga, 1976. 141 p.
PG8721.S515R6 PU.

3505. ŠIRVYS, Paulius. Ilgėsysta giesmė; rinktinė. [Dailininkas Petras Rauduvė]. Vilnius, Vaga, 1972. 238 p. illus. MB.

3506. --- Ir nusinešė saulę miškai. Vilnius, Vaga, 1969. 73 p. PG8722.29.I7I7 PU.

3507. SKABEIKA, Leonas. Vidurnakčių aikštėse. [Leidinį parengė ir paaiškinimus parašė A. Sluckaitė. Vilnius], Vaga, [1964]. 261 p. ill., facsims., ports. PG8721.S526V5 DLC.

3508. SKINKYS, Algirdas. Medžių pėdos. [Sudarė ir paaiškinimus parašė Martynas Vainilaitis]. Vilnius, Vaga, 1972. 167 p. PG8722.29.K5M4 PU; DLC; MB; NN.

3508a. SKUČAITĖ, Ramutė. Apeisim ežerą. Vilnius, Vaga, 1977. 78 p. PG8722.29.K8A8 PU.

3508b. --- Keliai ir pakelės; eilėraščiai. Vilnius, Vaga, 1969. 74 p. PG8722.29.K8K4 DLC; IU; OKentU; MH.

3508c. --- Pusiausvyra; eilėraščiai. Vilnius, Vaga, 1972. 77 p. PG8722.29.K8P8 PU; MH.

3508d. --- Žydintis speigas; eilėraščiai. Vilnius, Vaga, 1965. 65 p. port. PG8722.29.K8Z9 DLC.

3509. ŠLAITAS, Vladas. Pro vyšnių sodą; eilėraščiai. [Chicago, Ill.], Ateitis,[1973]. 68 p. (Literatūros serija, nr.6). PG8722.29.L3P7 PU; DLC; MB;OKentU.

3510. --- Žmogiškosios psalmės; eilėraščiai. Detmold, Ger.,[Pradalgė], 1949. 110 p. illus. PG8722.29.L3Z35 DLC.

3511. ŠMULKŠTYS, Antanas. Eilių rinkinys. Kaunas, "Aušros" knygynas, 1921. 127 p. At head of title: Paparonis, [pseud.]. 891.92P517E PU; OCl.

3512. ŠNAPŠTYS, Juozas. Volungė; eilės, pirmieji bandymai. Tilžėje, J. Schoenke, 1906. [Xerox copy,1975]. 96 p. PG8721.S59V6 1906a PU(xerox) At head of title: Margalis,[pseud.].

3513. --- Volungė ir vieversėlis. Kaunas, S. Banaičio spaustuvė, 1907. [Xerox copy, 1976]. 174 p. At head of title: Margalis,[pseud.]. PG8721.S59V62 1907a PU (Xerox).

3514. SPUDAS, Vaidotas. Mėlynos pušys; eilėraščiai. Vilnius, Valstybinė grožinės literatūros leidykla, 1963. 77 p. port. PG8722.29.P8M4 DLC; IU.

3515. --- Susitikt tave norėčiau vėlei. [Paruošė A. Bernotas, G. Suveizdienė]. Vilnius, Vaga, 1974. 325 p. PG8722.29.P8S8 PU.

3516. SRUOGA, Balys. Giesmė apie Gediminą. Grafika Viktoro Petravičiaus M. Dobužinskio viršelis ir iliustracijos. Kaunas, Sakalas, 1933. 61 p. 891.922Sr85 PU

3517. STIKLIUS, Kostas. Graži dovanėlė Lietuvos artojams; eilės. Chicago, Ill., Turtu ir spauda "Kataliko", 1909. 21. At head of title: K. Stiklelis. *Q p.v.2590--NN.

3518. --- Keplos kančios; eilės. Chicago, Ill., Spauda "Lietuvos", 1909. 28 p. PG8721.S695K4 PU.

3519. STONIS, Vincas. Ašarėlės; eilėraščiai. Kaunas, Ateitininkų sušišelpimo fondo leidinys, 1924. 118 p. WU.

3520. --- Lyrika; rinktinė. Vilnius, Vaga, 1970. 163 p. port. PG8722.29.T6L9 DLC; ICIU; MB; NN; NNC; NjP; OKentU.

3521. STRAZDAS, Antanas. Giesmė apie siratas. Red. komisija Just.Marcinkevičius (pirm.)...[et al.]. Paruošė V. Vanagas. Vilnius, Vaga, 1974. 101 p.,[3] leaves of plates. illus. (Poezijos biblioteka Nersmės) PG8721.S75G5 1974 DLC; PU.

3522. --- Pasaulinės ir dvasinės giesmės. [Spaudai paruošė J. Petrulis, K. Korsakas-Radžvilas. Kaunas, [Spaudos Fondas, 1938].[Xerox copy, 1977]. 247 p. PG8721.S75P 1938a PU.

3523. STRAZDAS, Steponas. Eilėraščių rinkinys. Boston, Mass., M. Strazdienė, 1965. 159 p. illus. PG8749.S73E PU; OKentU.

3524. STRIELKŪNAS, Jonas. Raudoni šermukšniai. Vilnius, Vaga,1966. 38 p. (Pirmoji knyga). PG8722.29.T7R3 DLC; PU.

3525. --- Vėjas rugiuos. Dailininkas A. Každailis. Vilnius, Vaga, 1971. 96 p. illus. PG8722.29.T7V4 DLC; IU; NNC; PU.

3526. ŠULCAITĖ, Vilija. Laukinės vynuogės. Dailininkė Rita Rozytė. Vilnius, Vaga, 1973. 102 p. PG8722.29. U4L3 PU; MH.

3527. --- Raudonas sniegas. Vilnius, Vaga, 1967. 92 p.
PG8722.29.U4R3 DLC; NN; OKentU.

3528. --- Sauja kmynų. [Dailininkė E. Kriaučiūnaitė]. Vilnius,Vaga, 1970. 99 p. illus. PG8722.29.U4S3 DLC; NN.

3529. --- Volungė jaučia lietų; eilėraščiai. Vilnius, Vaga, 1974. 117 p. PG8722.29.U4V6 PU; DLC.

3530. SUTEMA, Liūnė, pseud. Nebėra nieko svetimo. Chicago, Ill., Gintaras, 1962. 60 p. 891.92K157N PU.

3531. ŠVABAITĖ, Julija. Septyni saulės patekėjimai; eilėraščiai. Chicago, Ill., Ateitis,[1974]. 80 p. PG8749.S9S4 PU; OKentU. At head of title: Švabaitė-Gylienė.

3532. --- Vynuogės ir kaktusai. Chicago, Ill., Lietuviškos knygos klubas, [1963]. 96 p. PG8749.S9V9 DLC; CaOONL; MB; OCl; PU.

3533. ŠVAIKUS, Laimutis. Gyvastis. [Bridgford, Eng.], Šaltinis, [1973]. 96 p. PG8722.29.S8G9 PU.

3534. TENISONAITĖ, Zenta. Pavasaris ir aš; eilėraščiai. [London, Eng., Nida Press, 1973]. 47 p. PG8722.3.E5P3 PU; DLC.

3535. --- Šviesos iliuzijos; eilėraščiai. [London, Eng., Nida Press, 1975]. 55 p. PG8722.3.R5S9 PU.

3536. TILVYTIS, Jurgis. Rūtų saujelė parašė A. Žalvarnis, [pseud.]. Kaunas, Išleista J. Sabaliaucko,1912. [Xerox copy, 1975]. 16 p. PG8721T54R8 1912a PU.

3537. TILVYTIS, Teofilis. Artojėliai; pirmoji ir antroji dalis. [Kaunas], Spaudos Fondas,[1940].[Xerox copy, 1977]. 55 p. PG8721.T55A7 1940a PU.

3538. --- Daina gyvybės kaina. [Dailininkas S. Rozinas]. Vilnius, Valstybinė grožinės literatūros leidykla, 1962. 100 p. illus. MH;NN.

3539. --- Deja, dar pasitaiko. [Piešiniai Igno Martinaičio]. Vilnius, Vaga, 1964. 109 p. illus. MH.

3540. --- Gimtieji akmenys; eilėraščiai. Vilnius, Vaga, 1977. 308 p. PG8721.T55G5 PU.

3541. --- Laukai laukeliai; lyrikos rinktinė. [Dailininkas Petras Rauduvė]. Vilnius, Vaga, 1974. 374 p. illus. PG8721T55L3 PU; DLC.

3542. --- Skiedros; satyrinė ir humoristinė poezija. [Parengė Jonas Pilypaitis]. Vilnius, Vaga, 1976. 366 p. PG8721.T55S55 PU.

3543. --- Trejos devynerios; satyriniai eilėraščiai. [Dailininkas S. Krasauskas]. Vilnius, Vaga,1972. 470 p. illus. PG8721.T55T7 PU;DLC.

3544. --- Žemė grįžta namo; poemos. [Parengė Jonas Pilypaitis]. Vilnius, Vaga, 1975. 475 p. PG8721.T55Z4 PU.

3545. TUMIENĖ, Elena. Karaliai ir šventieji; eilės. Los Angeles, Calif. [Lietuvių Dienos], 1957. 80 p. ill. PG8749.T82K3 DLC; CaAEU; PU.

3546. TYSLIAVA, Juozas. Nemuno rankose; poezijos rinktinė. Kaunas, Varpo bendrovės leidinys, 1924. 78 p. PG8722.3.Y73N4 DLC; ICCC.

3547. --- Tolyn. Kaunas, P. Stiklius, 1926. [Xerox copy, 1974]. 59 p. PG8721.T92T6 PU.

3548. ULDUKIS, Edvardas. Aštuntasis "Divonio" jūreivis. Vilnius, Vaga, 1977. 104 p. PG8722.31.L35A7 PU.

3549. URBONAS, Mykolas J. 150 [i. e. Šimtas penkiasdešimt] religinio turinio leilėraščių. Parašė ir išleido M.J. Urbonas. DuBois, Pa., 1963. 91 p. ports. PG8749.U69S5 PU; OKentU.

3550. URBONAVIČIUS, Kazimieras. Jono Kmito eilės. Boston, Mass.,Lietuvių prekybos bendrovė,[s.d.]. 191 p. At head of title: Jonas Kmitas, [pseud.]. OKentU.

3551. VAIČAITIS, Pranas. Lėkite, dainos. [Paruošė Albertas Zalatorius] Vilnius, Vaga, 1975. 424 p. PG8721.V29L4 PU; WU.

3552. VAIČIŪNAITĖ, Judita. Klajoklė saulė. Vilnius, Vaga, 1974. 255 p. PG8722.32.A5K5 PU.

3553. --- Pakartojimai; eilėraščiai. Dailininkas R. Gibavičius.Vilnius, Vaga, 1971. 135 p. illus. PG8722.32.A5P25 DLC; IU; MH; PU.

3554. VAIČIŪNAS, Petras. Iš tolių beribių; rinktinė. [Dailininkas V.Kalinauskas]. Vilnius, Vaga, 1973. 303 p. illus. PG8721.V32I8 PU;MB.

3555. VAINILAITIS, Martynas. Vyturiai palydi plūgą. Vilnius, Valstybinė grožinės literatūros leidykla, 37 p. port. PG8722.32.A52V9 DLC;PU.

3556. VAITKUS, Mykolas. Liepsne-
lės; eilės. Kaunas, Išleido A. Petronio knygynas, [1921]. 157 p.
PG8721.V322L5 1921a PU(xerox);OKentU
(orig.).

3557. VALAITIS, Leonardas. Kel-
mai ir kelmučiai;[satyriniai eilėraščiai. [Dailininkas J. Varnas]. Vilnius, Vaga, 1973. ·114 p. illus.
PG8722.32.A6K4 DLC.

3558. VALAITIS, Viktoras. Žygyje.
Vilnius, Valstybinė grožinės litera-
tūros leidykla, 1953. 71 p. illus.
PG8721.V325Z48 DLC.

3559. VĖGĖLIS, Jonas. Visgailis.
[Putnam, Conn., Immaculata Press],
1963. 242 p. illus. PG8749.V4V5
DLC; CaOTU; ICU; MnU; OClW; OKentU;
PU.

3560. VENCLOVA, Antanas. Beržai
vėtroje. Kaunas, 1930. OCl.

3561. --- Vakarinė žvaigždė.Vil-
nius, Vaga, 1971. 2o6 p.
PG8721.V4V3 PU; DLC; NNC; NjP; NN.

3562. VENCLOVA, Tomas. Kalbos
ženklas; eilėraščiai. Vilnius, Vaga, 1972. 62 p. PG8722.32.E5K3 PU;
DLC; MH; OKentU.

3563. VENYS, Antanas. Geležiniai
žiedai. [Chicago, Ill.], Nemunas,
[1955]. 60 p. PG8721.V4G4 DLC;PU.

3564. VERBA, Algirdas. Pakelės
žalumos; eilėraščiai. Vilnius,Vaga,
1977. 69 p. PG8722.32.E68P3 PU.

3565. VEŠČIŪNAITĖ, Aldona. Žodžiai kaip salos. [Chicago, Ill.,
Algimanto Mackaus Knygų leidimo fondas, 1976]. 64 p. PG8749.V44Z6 PU.

3566. VILKELIS, Jonas. Gyvenimo
sūkuriai; rinktiniai eilėraščiai.
New York, N.Y., Lietuvių meno sąjunga, 1956. 124 p. PG8749.V5G9 PU.

3567. VISKOŠKA, Jonas. Gyvybė;
kantata, ir kitos trumpos poemos.
Chicago, Ill., "Lietuvos", 1907. 41
p. *QYI p.v.3--NN.

3568. VITKAUSKAS, Arėjas. Spindu-
liai ir šešėliai; eilės. Jersey City, N.J., World-wide News Bureau,
1975. 64 p. Reprint of the 1926 ed.
PG8721.V84S75 1926a CaAEU; PU.

3569. ZAKIENĖ, Danutė. Saulė že-
mę apkabina; eilėraščiai. Vilnius,
Valstybinė grožinės literatūros leidykla, 1962. 34 p. port.
PG8722.36.A4S3 DLC.

3570. ŽALINKEVIČAITĖ, Elena. Eskizai. Kaunas, "Spindulio" b-vės
spaustuvė, 1930. [Xerox copy, 1977].
80 p. At head of title: Alė Sidabraitė,[pseud.]. PG8721.Z34E 1930a
PU.

3571. ŽUKAUSKAS, Albinas. Atabra-
dai. Vilnius, Vaga, 1976. 187 p.
PG8722.36.U4A85 PU; MH.

3572. --- Atodangos; eilėraščiai.
Vilnius, Vaga, 1971. 163 p.
PG8722.36.U4A9 PU; DLC; IU; MH;OKentU

XIII.5.c.6. TRANSLATIONS INTO FOREIGN
LANGUAGES

3573. AUS LITAUISCHER DICHTUNG.
[Translated by] Horst Engert. Dut-
sche Nachdichtungen. 2. verm. und
veränderte Auflage. Kaunas; Leipzig,
Ostverlag der Buchhandlung Pribačis,
1938. 112 p. WU.

3574. AVYŽIUS, Jonas. Derevnîa na
pereput'e; roman. Perevod s litovskogo V. Chepaĭtisa. Moskva, Sovetskiĭ pisatel', 1966. 496 p. illus.,
port. PG8721.A85K37 DLC; CSt; MH;
NjP; NcD; OU.

3575. --- --- Per. s litov. V.Che-
paĭtisa. [Poslesl. I. Lankutisa.
Ill. A. Makunaĭte]. Moskva, "Izvestiia", 1969. 463 p., 8 leaves of
plates. (Biblioteka "Piat'desiat let
sovetskogo romana). At head of title; Ionas Avizhîus. PG8721.A85K37
1969 PU; DLC; IaU; IU; MH; NIC; TNJ.

3576. --- La grande saignée; ro-
man. Traduit de la version russe et
de l'original lituanien par Mireille
Lukosevicius. [Moscou], Editions du
Progrès, [1976]. 614 p.
PG8721.A85S614 PU.

3577. --- The lost home; a novel.
[Translated by Olga Shartse]. Moscow, Progress Publishers, 1974. 544
p. illus. (Progress, Soviet authors
library) Translation of Sodybų tuštėjimo metas. CtY.

3578. --- Poterîannyĭ krov; roman. Perevod s litovskogo Virgili-
ĭusa Chepaĭtisa. Moskva, Sov. Pisatel', 1974. 557 p. illus. At head
of title: Ionas Avizhîus.
PG8721.A85P6 DLC; IaU.

3579. --- Reka i berega; povesti
i rasskazy. Perevod s litovskogo.
Moskva, Sovetskiĭ pisatel', 1960.
536 p. MH.

3580. --- Stekliannia gora; roman. [Avtoriz. perevod s litovskogo V. Chepaĭtisa]. Vil'nius, Goslitizdat, 1964. 432 p. Translation of Į stiklo kalną. At head of title: Ionas Avizhius. MH.

3581. BALDAUF, Lucia, tr. & ed. Litauische Lyrik; eine Anthologie litauisch-deutsch. Ausgewählt und übersetzt von Lucia Baldauf. München, Ger., W. Fink, 1972. 306 p. PG8715.B3 PU; DLC; CtY; CSt; FU;GU; MB; MiDW; MiU; MdU; NjP; NNC; PPiU; PSt; TxU; ViU; WU.

3582. BALTAKIS, Algimantas. Peshaia ptitsa; izbrannoe. Vil'nius, Vaga, 1969. 270 p. PG8722.12.A4P417 DLC; NNC.

3583. --- Podzemnye reki; stikhotvoreniia. Vstupit. stat'ia V. Guseva. Moskva, Khudozh. lit-ra,1975. 253 p. WU.

3584. BALTUŠIS, Juozas. Prodani lita; roman u novelakh. Pereklad z litovs'koi. Kyiv, Dnipro, 1972. 263 p. port. Translation of Parduotos vasaros. PG8721.B197P2U3 1972 CaAEU.

3585. --- Prodannye gody; roman v novellakh. Pereveli s litovskogo K. Kela i Z. Fedorova. Vil'nius,Vaga, 1974. 712 p. illus. At head of title: Iuozas Baltushis. PG8721.B32P317 PU; MH.

3586. BARANAUSKAS, Antanas. Anikshchiaiskii bor. [Perevod s litovskogo Nikolaia Tikhonova. Graviury na dereve I.M. Kuzminskisa]. Vil'nius, Vaga, 1976. 58 p. PG8721.B325A817 1976 PU.

3587. --- The forest of Anykščiai. The original Lithuanian text with the English verse-translation by Nadas Rastenis. Introd. and editing by Juozas Tininis. 2d. ed. [Los Angeles, Calif.], Lithuanian Days, 1970. 61 p. Translation of Anykščių šilelis. PG8721.B325A8 DLC; CaAEU; MH; NcU; OU; OKentU.

3588. BARONAS, Aloyzas. Mana sieva? Mans dēls?; romāns. No lietuvju valodas tulkojis Zarinu Jānis. New York, N.Y., Grāmatu Draugs, 1975. 187 p. At head of title: Aloizs Barons. Translation of Menesiena. CaOTP.

3589. --- Paaudžu mezglos; romāns. No lietuviešu valodas tulkojis Zarinu Jānis. [Brooklyn, N.Y.], Grāmatu Draugs, 1974. 189 p. At head of title: Aloizs Barons. Translation of

Abraomas ir sūnus. MB.

3590. --- The third woman; a novel. Authorized translation from the Lithuanian by Nola M. Zobarskas. Introd. by Charles Angoff. New York, N.Y., Manyland Books, 1968. 169 p. PZ4.B2656Th DLC; CU; CSt; CaAEU;MB; MH; MiU; ICU; IEN; NN; NcU; OU; PU; PPULC.

3591. BAUŽA, Aleksandras. Dvoe na naberezhnoi. [Povesti i novelly]. Perevel s litovskogo avtor. Vil'nius, Vaga, 1972. 245 p. At head of title: Aleksandras Bauzha. PG8721.B37D9 DLC CaOTU; IU; MB; MH; NjP; OU; PU; WU.

3592. --- Ogni na doroge; rasskazy. Perevod s litovskogo avtora. Moskva, Sovetskii pisatel', 1963. 165 p. illus. PG8721.B3704 DLC;NNC;NjR

3593. BIELIAUSKAS, Alfonsas. Kaunasskii roman. Perevod s litovskogo F. Dektora. Moskva, Sov. pisatel', 1967. 323 p. PG8721.B43K317 DLC; IU; MH.

3594. --- --- [Another edition]. Avtorizovannyi perevod s litovskogo F. Dektora. Moskva, Izvestiia, 1968. 238 p. illus. (Biblioteka Piat'desiat let sovetskogo romana) PG8721.B43K317 1968 DLC; CaAEU;CaOTU IaU; InU; NIC; NjP; OU.

3595. --- --- [and] MY eshche vstretimsia, Vil'ma. Tsvetut rozy alye. Romany. Avtoriz. per. s litov. F.Dektora. [Il. D.S. Mukhin]. Moskva,Sov. pisatel', 1973. 656 p. illus. At head of title: Al'fonsas Beliauskas. PG8721.B43A56 1973 DLC.

3596. --- My eshche vstretimsia, Vil'ma; roman. Moskva, Sovetskii pisatel', 1965. 272 p. At head of title: Al'fonsas Beliauskas. WU.

3597. --- Tsvetut rozy alye; roman. [Perevod s litovskogo F. Dektora.] Vil'nius, Gos. izd-vo khudozh. lit-ry Litovskoi SSR, 1960. 479 p. At head of title: Al'fonsas Beliauskas. PG8721.B43T8 DLC; MH.

3598. BILEVIČIUS, Ėlijas. Den' za dnem; ocherk zhizni odnogo pokoleniia. Vil'nius, Vaga, 1973. 290 p. At head of title: Ėliias Biliavichius [and] Iurii Polev. MH.

3599. BORUTA, Kazys. Die Mühle des Baltaragis. Aus dem Russischen übers. von Lieselotte Remané. Mit Ill. von Sigrid Huss. Berlin, Rütten & Loening, 1970. 295 p. illus. PG8721.B6B35 DLC; InNd.

3600. BUBNYS, Vytautas. Berezy na vetru. Zhazhdushchaia zemlia. Povest' i roman. Perevod s litovskogo V. Chepaitisa. Moskva, Sovetskii pisatel', 1972. 367 p. illus. At head of title: V. Bubnis. PG8722.12.U2B4 PU; DLC; IU; MB; MH; NjP.

3601. --- Tri dnia v avguste; roman. Per. s litov. V. Chepaitisa, il. E. Zhiauberis. Moskva, Sov. pisatel', 1974. 277 p. illus. At head of title: Vitautas Bubnis. PG8722.12.U2T7 DLC.

3602. BUDRYS, Rimantas. Prozrachnye vetry; roman, povest', rasskazy. Avtoriz. per. s litov. [Khudozh. A. I. Kazakauskas]. Moskva, Sov. pisatel', 1975. 566 p. illus. At head of title: Rimantas Budris. PG8721.B814A57 1975 DLC.

3603. CONFRONTATIONS WITH TYRANNY; six Baltic plays with introductory essays. Edited by Alfreds Straumanis. Prospect Heights, Ill., Waveland Press,[1977]. 363 p. PN1621.C65 PU.

3604. DAUTARTAS, Vladas. Plyvut oblaka. Povesti i rasskazy. Avtoriz. per. s litov. G. Kanovichusa i D. Epshteinaite. [Il. R.V. Dikhavichus]. Moskva, Sov. pisatel', 1973. 288 p. illus. PG8722.14.A8P5 DLC;MH; NjP.

3605. DEGUTYTE, Janina. Golubye delty. Perevod s litovskogo. Moskva, Sovetskii pisatel', 1971. 152 p. WU.

3606. DONELAITIS, Kristijonas. Rocni doby. [Translated by] Hana Jachova. Praha, [s.n.], 1960. 122 p. WU.

3607. DOVYDAITIS, Jonas. Golubye ozera; roman. Perevod s litovskogo Violetta Dombrovskaia. Vil'nius, Vaga, 1973. 277 p. At head of title: Ionas Dovidaitis. MH.

3608. DOVYDENAS, Liudas. Brali Domeikas; ar, Lietuvas valsts 1936 g. premiju godalgots romans. No lietuvju valodas tulkojis Kazis Duncis. Riga, Valters un Rapa, 1937. 210 p. *QYN--NN; OCl.

3609. --- The Brothers Domeika; a novel in the English translation by Milton Stark. South Boston,Mass., Lithuanian Encyclopedia Press, 1976. 237 p. Translation of Broliai Domeikos. PZ3.D7517Br DLC.

3610. DRILINGA, Antanas. Antanas Drilinga;[izbrannaia lirika.] Moskva, Molodaia gvardiia, 1966. 31 p. (Bibliotechka izbrannoi liriki) PG8722.14.R5A7 DLC.

3611. GRICIUS, Augustinas. Liudi; rasskazy. Per. s litovskogo.[Illus. I.V. TSarevich]. Moskva, Sovetskii pisatel', 1962. 204 p. illus. MH; NNC.

3612. --- Zharkoe leto. (Razbitaia vaza). P'esa v 4 deistviiakh, 5 kartinakh. [Perevod s litovskogo E. Mal'tsasa i V. Grodzenskisa]. Moskva, Iskusstvo, 1957. 111 p. illus. At head of title: A. Gritsius. PG8721.G635K37 DLC.

3613. GRUSAS, Juozas. Kar'eristy; roman. [Predisl. I. Lankutisa. Avtoriz. per. s litov. B. Vladimirov]. 248 p. illus. At head of title: IUozas Grushas. PG8721.G7K317 DLC.

3614. --- Taina Adomasa Brundzy; p'esy. Per. s litov. [Il. V.IU. Kaminauskas]. Moskva, Sov. pisatel', 1972. 406 p. illus. At head of title: IUozas Grushas. PG8721.G7T3 DLC; InU; ICIU; MH; NjP.

3615. DER HEXENSCHLITTEN; litauische Märchen. Illustrationen, Horst Hussel. Aus dem Litauischen von Irene Brewing. Nachdichtungen, Ilse Tschörtner]. 2. Aufl. Berlin, Verlag Volk und Welt, 1975. 166 p. ill. PZ34.H48 1975 DLC; PU.

3616. JASINSKAS, Jonas. A kiss in the dark, by J. Jasmin,[pseud.]. Translated from the Lithuanian by Milton Stark. Chicago, Ill., International Press,[1954]. 150 p. PZ4.J38Ki DLC; NN.

3617. JONYNAS, Antanas. Posledniaia vecheria;[satir. povest'].[Per. S. Vasil'ev, ill., E. Kriauchiunaite] Vil'nius, Vaga, 1970. 155 p. illus. PG8722.2.O5P317 DLC; MH; WU.

3618. --- Rozhdenie poeta; stikhi. Per. s litovskogo Larisy Vasil'evoi. Moskva, Sov. pisatel', 1974. 175 p. illus. At head of title:Antanas Ioninas. MH.

3619. KAIRYS, Anatolijus. Curriculum vitae; a comical tragedy in two acts. [From the Lithuanian translated by A. Milukas. Hollywood,Calif. 1971]. 87 p. illus. PG8721.K2C813 PU; OCl.

3620. KISINAS, Izidorius, ed. Lietuviu literaturos antologija (hebraju kalba) 1.knyga. Kaunas, 1931. 143 p. PG8713.K53 PU.

3621. KORSAKAS, Kostas. Stikhi.
Vil'nius, Vaga, 1976. 347 p. WU.

3622. KRĖVĖ-MICKEVIČIUS, Vincas.
Koldun. Rasskazy i povest'. Perevod
A. Bauzhi i I. Kaplanasa. Moskva,
Goslitizdat, 1963. 376 p.
891.92K889R PU; IaU; IU; NNC; OU.

3623. --- Predaniia Dainavskoĭ
stariny. Perevod s litovskogo A.Pol-
nika. [Vstup. stat'ia IA. Lankutisa]
Moskva, Khudozhestvennaia literatura, 1973. 253 p. illus. At head
of title: Vintsa Kreve.
PG8721.K7D217 1973 PU; DLC; MH; NN;
NjP; ViU.

3624. LAURINČIUKAS, Albertas.
Sredniaia amerikanka; p'esa v trekh
deĭstviiakh s prologom. Perevod s
litovskogo A. Berman. P'esa otredaktirovana i napravlena dlia raspost-
raneniia Upr. teatrov Ministerstva
kul'tury SSSR. Otv. redaktor M. Medvedeva. Moskva, Otdel raspostrane-
niia dramaticheskikh proizvedeniĭ
VUOAP, 1971. 75 leaves. At head of
title: Al'bertas Laurinchukas.
PG8722.22.A9S7 DLC.

3625. LITOVSKIE POETY XX VEKA.
[Sbornik]. Vstup. stat'ia, sostav-
lenie i primechaniia V. Galinisa.
Red. poeticheskikh perevodov N.L.
Brauna i L.A. Ozerova. [Leningrad],
Sovetskiĭ pisatel', Leningradskoe
otd-nie, 1971. 590 p. PG8771.R3L5
DLC; CaOTU; CtY; IU; ICU; CU; CLSU;
FMU; InU; MH; MnU; MiU; MiDW; NN;NNC
NcD; NhU;NjP; OU; PU; RPB; PSt; TxU;
WU.

3626. MACEVIČIUS, Juozas. Distan-
tsiia; stikhi. Moskva, Sov. pisatel',
1976. 120 p. WU.

3627. MACEVIČIUS, Juozas. Veter
v litso; stikhi. Perevod s litovskogo Germana Valikova. Moskva, Sov.
pisatel', 1972. 118 p. port.
PG8722.23.A27A57 1972 DLC; THJ.

3628. MACIJAUSKAS, Jonas. Rodina
zovet. Literaturnaia obrabotka IU.
Butenasa. [Sokr. perevod s litovskogo V. L'vova]. Moskva, Voen. izd-vo,
1960. 318 p. illus. PG8721.M25R6
DLC.

3629. MACIUKEVIČIUS, Jonas. Chasy ne ostanavlivaiutsia; povest'. Perevel s litovskogo Feliks Dektor. [
Moskva, Molodaia gvardiia, 1971].
222 p. At head of title: Ionas Ma-
chiukevichius. PG8722.23.A295C5 PU;
CaOTU; DLC; IU; MB; MH; NjP.

3630. MACKEVIČIUS, Bronius. Bes-
pokoinye ptitsy; stikhi. Per. s li-

tovskogo Viacheslava Kuznetsova. Moskva, Sov. pisatel', 1973. 126 p.
port. MH. At head of title; Bronius
Matskiavichius.
3631. MALDONIS, Alfonsas. Aprel'-
skie razlivy. [Perevody]. Vil'nius,
Vaga, 1973. 230 p. MH.

3632. --- Stikhi. Perevod s litovskogo. Moskva, Khudozhestvennaia
literatura, 1971. 190 p. illus.,
port. PG8721.M33A55 1971 CaOTU;MH.

3633. --- Vysokie noty; stikhi.
Perevod s litovskogo. Moskva, Sov.
pisatel', 1963. 78 p. NN; IU; MH.

3634. MARCINKEVIČIUS, Justinas.
Auf der Erde geht ein Vogel. [Hrsg.
und mit einem Nachwort versehen von
Leonhard Kossuth, nachgedichtet von
Heinz Czechowski et al. 1.Aufl.].
Berlin, Volk und Welt, 1969. 181 p.
facsim. PG8721.M35A9 DLC.

3635. --- Die Fichte, die gelacht
hat. [Aus dem Russ. von Ingeborg
Schröder. Berlin, Aufbau-Verl.1970].
128 p. PG8721.M35P8715 DLC.

3636. --- Krov' i pepel. Stena.
Mindaugas. Poėmy. Perevod s litov.
A. Mezhirova. [Predisl. V. Otneva.
Il. S. Krasauskas]. Moskva, Khudozh.
lit., 1973. 351 p. illus.
PG8721.M35K717 1973 DLC; TNJ.

3637. --- Mindaugas; drama-poėma
v dvukh chastiakh. Perevel s litovskogo Aleksandr Mezhirov. Vil'nius,
Vaga, 1973. 150 p. At head of title: IUstinas Martsinkiavichius.
PG8721.M35M517 PU; MH.

3638. --- Sosna kotoraia smeialas'. Moskva, Izvestiia, 1967. 376
p. Includes M. Sluckis, Lestnitsa v
nebo. At head of title: IUstinas
Martsinkiavichius. WU.

3639. --- Stena; poėma goroda.
[Per. s litov. A. Mezhirov. Ill. S.
Krasauskas]. Vil'nius, Vaga, 1968.
126 p. illus. At head of title:
IUstinas Martsinkiavichius.
PG8721.M35S517 DLC; IU; OU.

3640. --- --- [Another edition].
[Per. s litov. A. Mezhirov. Ill. S.
Krasauskas]. Moskva, Mol. gvardiia,
1969]. 88 p. illus. PG8721.M35S517
1969 DLC.

3641. MARKEVIČIUS, Anelius. Bal-
tiiskiĭ ėtiud; rasskazy. Moskva,Sov.
pisatel', 1974. 271 p. port. At
head of title: Anelius Markiavichius.
PG8721.M355A57 1974 DLC.

3642. MARUKAS, K., pseud. Dlia ko-

go vzoĭdet solnt͡se. Perevela s litovskogo H. Shaforenko. Vil'nĭus,Va-
ga, 1976. 229 p. PG8721.M36K317
1976 DLC.

3643. --- Proshchaĭ, Brazilka;[
povest'. Per. s litov. A. Berman].
Vil'nĭus, Vaga, 1969. 447 p.
PG8721.M36Z217 DLC; CU; NjP.

3644. MATUZEVIČIUS, Eugenijus.
Lunnyĭ bereg; stikhi. Perevel s litovskogo Lev Ozerov. Moskva, Sovetskiĭ pisatel', 1972. 159 p. At head
od title: Éugeniĭus Matuziavichĭus.
PG8721.M37L8 PU; MH.

3645. MERAS, Itskhokas. 'Al mah
ha-'olam 'omed. Tel-Aviv, Ha-Kibuts
ha-meuḥad, 734[1973]. 153 p. (Sif-
riyat shevut) Translation of Ant ko
laikosi pasaulis. PG8722.23.E7A816
DLC; CLU; MH; NN; NjP.

3646. --- Na chem derzhits͡ia mir;
roman-balada. Nich'͡ia dlit͡s͡ia mgno-
ven'e; roman. Avtorizovannyĭ perevod
s litovskogo Feliksa Dektora. Moskva, Khudozh. lit-ra, 1966. 301 p.
illus. PG8722.23.E7N3 DLC; MH;NcD;
OU; OKentU.

3647. --- La partie n'est jamais
nulle (deux nouvelles) [par] Icchokas
Meras. Moscou, Progrès, 1969. 270 p.
Translation of the Russian version
of Lygiosios trunka akimirka, and
Ant ko laikosi pasaulis. Contents.--
La partie n'est jamais nulle.--Sur
quoi repose le monde.
PG8722.23.E7L914 DLC; CtY; MH.

3648. --- Die Mondwoche. [Aus dem
Litauischen von Irene Brewing. 1.
Aufl.]. Berlin, Verlag Kultur und
Fortschritt, 1968. 187 p.
PG8722.23.E7M415 CaOWtU; DLC; IEN;
MoSW; OkU; WU.

3649. --- Remis für Sekunden [von]
Icchokas Meras. [Aus dem Litauischen
von Irene Brewing. Wien], Die Buch-
gemeinde, 1967. 177 p.
PG8722.23.E7L915 DLC; WU.

3650. --- --- [und] Worauf ruht
die Welt. 2 Romane. [von] Icchokas
Meras. [Aus dem Litauischen übers.
von Irene Brewing.]. [Hamburg; Düssel-
dorf], Claassen, [1969]. 324 p.
PG8722.23.E7L915 1969 DLC;MoSW;WU.

3651. --- Worauf ruht die Welt.
[Von] Icchokas Meras. [Aus dem Litauischen von Irene Brewing]. Berlin,
Verlag Kultur und Fortschritt, 1967.
157 p. Translation of Ant ko laikosi pasaulis. PG8722.23.E7A815 DLC;
IEN; IU; MH; OkU.

3652 MIEŽELAITIS, Eduardas. Che-
lovek;[stikhi]. Per. s litov. Moskva,
Khudozh. lit., 1971. 94 p. (Biblio-
teka proizvedeniĭ, udostoennykh Le-
ninskoĭ premii) At head of title:
Éduardas Mezhelaĭtis. Translation of
Žmogus. PG8721.M45Z357 1971 DLC;
NjP; OU; PU; WU.

3653. --- Kontrapunkt. Liriches-
kai͡a proza. Avtorizovannyĭ perevod s
litovskogo]. Moskva, Izvestii͡a, 1972.
447 p. PG8721.M45K6 PU; CaOTU; CtY;
CU; DLC; IU; IaU; InU; MB; MH; MiDW;
NNC; NjP; WU.

3654. --- Liricheskie étĭudy. [
Per. s litov. Ill.: É. Neizvestnyĭ.]
Moskva,,Mol. gvardii͡a, 1969. 256 p.
illus. PG8721.M45L917 DLC; CaOTU;
CFS; IU; ICU; MB; MH; MdU; MiDW; NN;
NNC; NIC; NjP; PSt; WU.

3655. --- Der Mensch. Gedichtzyk-
lus. [Die Interlinearübersetzung be-
sorgte Irene Brewing. Nachgedichtet von H. Czechowski. [Mit Holzsch-
nitten von Stasis Krasauskas]. Berlin, Verlag Kultur und Fortschritt,
1967. 116 p. PG8721.M45Z355 DLC.

3656. --- Mikropoémy. [Perevod na
russkoĭ i͡azyk]. Moskva, Sov. pisatel', 1975. 255 p. illus. At head
of title: Éduardas Mezhelaĭtis.
PG8721.M45A57 1975 DLC.

3657. --- Nochnye babochki. Mo-
nolog. [Avtoriz. per. s litov. B.Za-
lesskoĭ i dr. Ill.: V. Medvedev. Moskva, Sov. pisatel', 1969. 400 p.
illus., port. At head of title: Éduardas Mezhelaĭtis.
PG8721.M45N317 DLC; MB; WU.

3658. MIKELINSKAS, Jonas. My, li͡u-
di; roman. [Perevela s litovskogo
B. Zalesskai͡a]. Vil'nĭus, Vaga,1966.
340 p. At head of title: I. Mikelinskas. MH; IU.

3659. --- My, li͡udi! - A chasy
idut; roman. Per. s litov. [Vstupit.
stat'i͡a É. Vetrovoĭ]. Moskva, Khudozh. lit., 1969. 424 p. illus.,
port. At head of title: Ĭonas Mikelinskas. PG8722.23.I35M9 DLC;CaOTU;
IU; MH.

3660. --- Und die Uhr geht wei-
ter. Roman. [Aus dem Russischen übers.
von Lieselotte Remané]. Berlin; Weimar, Aufbau-Verl., 1969. 206 p.
PG8722.23.I350215 DLC.

3661. MIKONIS, Antas. Balà, Roman
aus dem Litauischen. Leipzig; Berlin,
Lühe Verlag, 1943. 362 p.
PT2625.I546B3 DLC; CSt; CtY; CoU; IaU
MB; NN; NNC; TxU; ViU.

3662. MILIŪNAS, Viktoras. Bereg
tot i bereg ētot; rasskazy. [Avtori-
zovannyĭ perevod s litovskogo B. Za-
lcsskoĭ i G. Garasimova. [Moskva,
Sovetskiĭ pisatel', 1970]. 264 p.
illus. PG8721.M47B4 PU; CaOTU;DLC;
IU; MB; MH; NN; NjP.

3663. --- Svad'ba v "Parizhe";
rasskazy. Avtoriz. per. s litov. B.
Zalesskoĭ i G. Garasimova. [Il.: I.
Z. Leviant]. Moskva, Sov. pisatel',
1973. 280 p. illus. PG8721.M47S9
DLC; CaOTU; MH; NjP.

3664. MOĪA LITVA;[sbornik dlīa
khudozhestvennoĭ samodīatel'nosti.
Sudarytoja G. Mareckaitė]. Vil'nīus,
Dvorets narodnogo tvorchestva Lit.
SSR, 1972. 87 p. On title page: Mi-
nisterstvo kul'tury Litovskoĭ SSR.
PG8771.R1M6 DLC.

3665. MONTVILA, Vytautas. [Stikhi.
Sost. i per. s litovskogo L. Ozerov.
Red. kollegīa: V.M. Inber i dr.]
Moskva Goslitizdat, 1962. 254 p.
port. (Biblioteka Sovetskoĭ Poēzii)
MH.

3666. NAD SINIM NEMANOM; sbornik
rasskazov. [Red. V.J. Jazvickas].
Moskva, OGIZ, 1944. 123 p. WU.

3667. NAREČIONIS, Romualdas. Sen-
timental'naīa istorīa; drama v trekh
deĭstviiakh. Perevod s litovskogo I.
Kaplanasa. P'esa otredaktirovana i
napravlena dlīa rasspostranenīia Upr.
teatrov Ministerstva kul'tury SSSR.
Otv. redaktor M. Medvedeva. Moskva,
Otdel rasspostranenīia dramaticheskikh
proizvedeniĭ VUOAP, 1971. 71 p.
At head of title: Romual'das Nareche-
nis. Translation of Sentimentali istorija. PG8722.24.A7S417 DLC.

3668. NĖRIS, Salomėja. Biała
ścieżka. Wybrał Zygmunt Stoberski.
Wyd.1. [Warszawa], Państwowy Instytut Wydawn., 1963. MB.

3669. --- Lirika. Perevod s litovskogo. [Moskva, Khudozh. lit.,
1871]. 229 p. port. PG8721.N4A55
1971 CaOTU; DLC; IU; MB; MH; NjP;
OU; WU.

3670. --- Stikhi. Per. s litovskogo. Sost. A. Maldonis. Vstup. sta-
t'īa A. Ventslovy. Moskva, Goslitizdat, 1961. 238 p. port. (Biblioteka Sovetskoĭ poēzii) MH; NN.

3671. --- U rodnika. [Per. s li-
tovskogo pod red. D. Samoĭlova].
Vil'nius, Vaga, 1967. 140 p. illus.
At head of title: Salomeia Neris.
CaOTU; IU; MH; NN.

3672. ÖLLER, Ragnar, tr. & ed.
Litauiska noveller, ett urval av modern litauisk novellkonst. Till
svenska av Ragnar Öller och Nils Boh-
man. [Stockholm], Vepe Förlag,1940.
240 p. *QY--NN. Includes:
Biliūnas, Krėvė, Vienuolis, Šeinius,
Savickis, Cvirka and Orintaitė.
*QY--NN.

3672a. PAKALNIS, Antanas. Klub
inteligentov. Vil'nīus, Vaga, 1971.
319 p. WU.

3673. PALČINSKAITĖ, Violeta. ĪA
dogonīaīu leto; skazka v dvukh deĭst-
viīakh. Perevod s litovskogo i
stsenicheskaīa red. L'va Ustinova.
P'esa otredaktirovana i napravlena
dlīa rasspostranenīia Upr. teatrov Ministerstva kul'tury SSSR. Otv. redaktor V. Komissarova. Moskva, Otdel
rasspostranenīia dramaticheskikh proizvedeniĭ VUOAP, 1971. 58 leaves.At
head of title: Violetta Pal'chinskaĭte. PG8722.26.A54I2 DLC.

3674. PALECKIS, Justas. Na zhiz-
nennom puti; stikhotvorenīia. Per s
litov. [Vstupit. stat'īa L. Ozerova].
Moskva, Khudozh. lit., 1969. 199 p.
PG8721.P3V6 1969 DLC; NIC.

3675. --- Zhizn' nachinaetsīa;
vospominanīia, passkazy, ocherki.
[Moskva], Profizdat, 1970. 264 p.
port. PG8721.P3G8917 DLC; CaOTU;IU;
MH.

3675a. PAUKŠTELIS, Juozas.ĪUnost'.
[Per. s litovskogo G. Kanovicha].
Vil'nīus, Goslitizdat, 1961. 333 p.
MH; OU; NNC.

3676. --- Zdes' nash dom; roman.
[Avtoriz. per. s litov. B. Zalesskoĭ
i G. Gerasimova. Ill.: Ė. ĪUrenas].
Vil'nīus, Vaga, 1971. 320 p. illus.
At head of title: ĪUozas Paukshtīa-
lis.' Translation of Čia mūsų namai.
PG8721.P37C517 DLC; IU; MB; MH; NjP
TxU.

3677. PEČKAUSKAITĖ, Marija. Irki-
na tragedīia; rasskazy i povest'.
[V starom pomest'e]. Perevela s litovskogo Dalīa Ėpshteĭnaĭte. Vil'-
nīus, Vaga, 1972. 237 p. At head
of title: Shatrīės Ragana, [pseud.]
PG8721.P4I72 PU.

3678. PETKEVIČIUS, Vytautas. O
khlebe, līubvi i vintovke; roman.Per.
s litov. N. Shaforenko. [Il.: R.V.
Dikhavichius]. Moskva, Sov. pisatel',
1972. 495 p. illus. At head of title: V. Petkīavichīus.
PG8722.26.E8A817 DLC; CU; MB; MH;
NjP; OU; PU.

3679. PIEŚNI I GWIAZDY; litewskie wiersze wybrane. Wybór, wstęp i opracowanie: Leopold Lewin i Zygmunt Stoberski. [Warszawa], Państwowy Instytut Wydawniczy, [1971]. 227 p. PG8772.P6P5 PU.

3680. POCIUS, Algirdas. Dvoe v gorodke; rasskazy. [Per. s litovskogo D. Ėpshteĭnaĭte, I.Kaplanas i E. Mal'tsas]. Vil'nius, Vaga, 1969. 310 p. At head of title: Al'girdas Potsius. MH.

3681. --- Po pereput'iam proĭdennym; rasskazy. Per. s litovskogo I. Kaplanasa. Moskva, Sov. pisatel', 1966. 171 p. At head of title: Al'girdas Potsius. IU; MH.

3682. --- Vkus tmina; rasskazy. Perevod s litovskogo. Moskva, Khudozh. lit-ra, 1974. 221 p. illus. At head of title: Al'girdas Potsius. PG8721.P6A57 1974 DLC.

3683. POŠKA, Dionyzas. Der Muschik Schemaitens und Litauens. Nachdichtung von Hermann Buddensieg. München, Ger., W. Fink, 1967. 19 p. Translation of Mužikas Žemaičių ir Lietuvos. PG8721.P66M815 DLC; NRU; WU.

3684. POŽĖRA, Juozas. Mnie chudiatsia koni; povesti, rasskazy, ocherki. Avtoriz. per. s litov. F.Dektora. [Il. B.N. Chuprygin]. Moskva, Sov. pisatel', 1974. 422 p. port. At head of title: IUozas Pozhera. PG8722.26.09M5 DLC.

3685. --- Moi sud; povest'. [Avtorizovannyĭ perevod s litovskogo Feliksa Dektora]. Moskva, molodaia gvardiia, 1972. 174 p. At head of title: IUozas Pozhera. PG8722.26.09M3317 PU; CaOTU; CU-S; DLC; IU; MB; MH; NjP.

3686. --- Net u menia drugoĭ pechali; ocherki. [Perevod s litovskogo F. Dektora. Moskva, Sovetskiĭ pisatel', 1970]. 439 p. At head of title: IU. Pozhera. PG8722.26.09N4 DLC; IU; MH; NjP; OU; PU.

3687. REIMERIS, Vacys. Tvoe teplo; stikhi. Perevod s litovskogo. Moskva, Sovetskiĭ pisatel', 1961. 111 p. MH.

3688. RIMKEVIČIUS, Vytautas. Plyvushchaia zemlia. Perevel s litovskogo Grigoriĭ Kanovich. Vil'nius,Vaga, 1973. 388 p. At head of title: Vitautas Rimkiavichius. PG8722.28.I58P5 PU; MH.

3689. RUDOKAS, Vytautas. Proseka k solntsu; stikhi. Perevod s litov. V. Kornilova. [Ill.: N.A. Zarin]. Moskva, Sov. pisatel', 1969. 79 p. illus. PG8722.28.U3P717 DLC; IU; NNC.

3690. ŠIMKUS, Vladas. Ul'i; stikhi. Per. s litovskogo Vladimira Kornilova i Leonida Milia. Moskva, Sov. pisatel', 1973. 103 p. illus. At head of title: Vladas Shimkus. MH.

3691. --- Zemlia vas liubit; stikhotvoreniia. [Avtoriz. per. s litovskogo Georgiia Gerasimova]. Moskva, Sov. pisatel', 1963. 107 p. illus. IU; MH. At head of title: Vladas Shimkus.

3692. SIMONAITYTĖ, Ieva. Poslednee puteshestvie Kunialisa; roman. Avtorizovannyĭ perevod s litovskogo V. Chepaĭtisa. Moskva, Sov. pisatel', 1974. 285 p. port. At head of title: Eva Simonaĭtite. PG8721.S5P2517 DLC.

3693. --- Sud'ba Shimonisov; roman. [Perevel s litovskogo V. Chepaĭtis]. Vil'nius, Vaga, 1966. 375 p. PG8721.S5A917 DLC; IU; MH; NN; OU.

3694. SIRIJOS-GIRA, Vytautas. Buenos-Aires; roman. Perevod s litovskogo E. Mal'tsasa. Moskva, Sovetskiĭ pisatel', 1958. 190 p. illus. PG8721.S52B8 DLC; NIC.

3695. SITORAHOI LITVA. Dushanbe, Irfon, 1969. 115 p. PG8772.T3S5 DLC.

3696. SLUCKIS, Mykolas. Adamovo iabloko; roman. [Avtoriz. per. s litovskogo E. Kutorgi. Ill. A. Gaigaliuka. Moskva, Mol. gvardiia, 1969. 350 p. illus. At head of title: Mikolas Slutskis. Translation of Adomo obuolys. PG8721.S56A6417 DLC; IEN; KU; MH; NjP; OU.

3697. --- Lestnitsa v nebo. [And] IUstinas Mrtsinkiavichius: Sosna, kotoraia smeialas'. Moskva, Izvestiia, 1967. 374 p. illus. PG8722.29.L8L3129 1967 CaAEU; IaU; MH; WU.

3698. --- --- [Avtoriz. per. s litovskogo E. Kutorgi. Vstupit. stat', ia A. Buchisa]. Moskva, Khudozh. lit., 1969. 279 p. illus. At head of title: Mikolas Slutskis. Translation of Laiptai į dangų. PG8721.S56L317 1969 DLC; NN.

3699. --- Lestnitsa v nebo. Zhazhda. Chuzhye strasti. [Romany. Il.: A. Gangaliuka]. Moskva, Mol. gvardiia, 1973. 632 p., 9 leaves of illus.

At head of title: Mikolas Slutskis. PG8722.29.L8L317 DLC; NjP.

3700. --- Ode an ein Schwein. [Aus dem Russischen und Litauischen übers. von Irene Brewing, Charlotte Kossuth und Herbert Wotte. Hrsg. von Charlotte Kossuth. 1.Aufl.]. Leipzig, P. Reclam, 1970. 183 p. (Reclams Universal-Bibliothek, Bd.262) PG8721.S56A47 DLC.

3701.---Odnim chudom men'she; rasskazy. [Avtoriz. per. s litovskogo G. Kanovicha. Illius. L. Puchkoriūte]. Vil'nīus, Goslitizdat Litovskoĭ SSR, 1962. 506 p. illus. At head of title: Mikolas Slutskis. MH; NcD.

3702. --- Rasskazu. Avtorizovannyĭ perevod s litovskogo I. Kaplanasa. Moskva, Sovetskiĭ pisatel',1960. 280 p. CSt.

3703. --- TSena botinok; rasskazy. Per. s litovskogo. Moskva, Pravda, 1966. 45 p. (Biblioteka Ogonek, nr.24) At head of title: Mikolas Slutskis. MH; CLU.

3704. --- Uvertiūra i tri deĭstviia; rasskazy. Per. s litovskogo. [Khud. S. Krasauskas]. Moskva, Khudozh. lit-ra, 1965. 343 p. illus. IU; MH; MiU. At head of title: Mikolas Slutskis.

3705. --- Volshebnaia chernil'nitsa; povest' v neobyknovennykh prikliucheniiakh i razmyshleniiakh Kolobka i Kolyshka. [Perevod s litovskogo F. Dektora]. Vil'nius, Vaga, 1967. 202 p. illus. At head of title: Mikolas Slutskis. PG8721.S56V6 DLC; MiDW.

3706. SRUOGA, Balys. V teni ispolina; dramy. [Poslesl. I. Lankutisa. Per. s litov. Ill.: A. Grubavichius]. Vil'nius, Vaga, 1968. 617 p. illus. PG8721.S68V2 1968 DLC; IU; MH; NIC; NN.

3707. STOBERSKI, Zygmunt, comp. Tam gdzie malwy lśnią czerwone; antologia literatury litewskiej. [Wyd.1. Warszawa], Państwowe Wydawn. Naukowe, [1973]. 254 p. illus. PG8772.P6S8 DLC; CLU; CSt; CU; ICU; IU; MiU; ViU; WU; WaU.

3708. STRAZDAS, Antanas. Pesni. [Perevod s litovskogo D. Brodskiĭ i IA. Sashin. Ill.: I. Kostylev]. Moskva, Goslitizdat, 1958. 94 p. illus. CU.

3709. TENISONAITĖ, Zenta, comp. & tr. Een steen heeft geen hart; bloomlezing uit de hedendaagse litouse poezie. Met een inleiding van Antanas Vaičiulaitis. [Oudenaarde, Orion, 1971]. 83 p. PG8772.F5T4 PU; DLC.

3710. TILVYTIS, Teofilis. Izbrannoe. Perevody s litovskogo. Moskva, Gos. izd-vo khudozh. lit-ry, 1951. 247 p. port. PG8721.T55A57 DLC.

3711. --- Poêmy. Moskva, Gos. izd-vo khudozh. lit-ry, 1958. 254 p. port. IEN; LU-NO; NN.

3712. TUMAS, Juozas. Sin at Easter, and other stories. Translated from the Lithuanian by Danguolė Sealey [and others]. Biographical outline by Antanas Vaičiulaitis. Edited by Nola M. Zobarskas. Introd. by Charles Angoff. New York, N.Y., Manyland Books, [c1971]. xv,131 p. port. At head of title: Vaižgantas, [pseud.]. Contents.--Sin at Easter. --Rimas and Nerimas.--The Misfit.-- Aleksiukas' father and mother. PG3.T8315Si3 DLC; FTaSU; GU; IaU; ICU; MU; NBuU; NIC; NcD; NjR; OU; ViU; WU.

3713. URNEVIČIŪTĖ, Dalia. Nazyvai menia mater'iu; drama v dvukh chastiakh s prologom. Perevod s litovskogo F. Dektora. Otvetstvennyĭ redaktor V. Komissarova. Moskva, Otdel rasprostraneniia dramaticheskikh proizvedeniĭ VUOAP, 1965. 75 leaves. PG8722.31.R6N3 DLC.

3714. --- Zatish'e - 2 km; drama v 2-kh ch. Avtoriz. per. s litov. F. Dektora. Moskva, Iskusstvo, 1973. 64 p. (Segodnia na stsene) PG8722.31.R6T917 1973 DLC.

3715. VAIČIŪNAITĖ, Judita. Stikhi. Per. litovskogo. Moskva, Molodaia gvardiia, 1964. 72 p. illus. At head of title: IUdita Vaichiūnaĭte. IU; MH.

3716. VENCLOVA, Antanas. Buria v polden'; dokumental'naia povest'. Moskva, Sov. pisatel', 1971. 480 p. At head of title: Antanas Ventslova. WU.

3717. --- Den' rozhdeniia; roman. Avtoriz. per. s litovskogo V. Chepaĭtisa. Moskva, Goslitizdat, 1962. 341 p. port. At head of title: Antanas Ventslova. MH; MnU.

3718. --- Lirika. [Perevel s litovskogo Leonid Mil']. Vil'nius,Vaga, 1970. 146 p. illus. At head of title: Antanas Ventslova. PG8721.V4A58 1970 DLC; IU; CU; NIC.

3719. --- Rodnoe nebo; stikhi.
Per. s litovskogo. Moskva, Gos. izd
-vo khudozh. lit-ry, 1944. 46 p. At
head of title: Antanas Ventslova.
PG8771.R9V4 DLC.

3720. --- Serebro severa. [Pere-
vod s litovskogo V. Chepaĭtisa].
Moskva, Sovetskiĭ pisatel', 1973.
153 p. illus. At head of title: A.
Ventslova.   DL305.V417 DLC.

3721. --- Ty znaesh' kraĭ; ital-
ianskie stikhi.   Perevel s litovskogo Leonid Mil'. Moskva, Pravda,1965.
30 p. (Biblioteka Ogonek, 22) MH.
At head of title: Antanas Ventslova.
MH.

3722. --- Vecherniaia zvezda;
stikhi. Per. s litov. L. Milia. Moskva, Sov. pisatel', 1972. 175 p.
illus., port. At head pf title:An-
tanas Vetslova. PG8721.V4V317 1972
DLC; NjP.

3722a. --- Vesenniaia reka; povest'. Avtorizovannyĭ perevod s litovskogo V. Chepaĭtisa. Moskava,Sov.
pisatel', 1967. 347 p. illus. At
head of title: Antanas Ventslova.
PG8721.V4Z517 DLC; IU; MH; OU; PPiU;
TNJ.

3723. VIENA JŪRA. Lietuviešu dze-
jas iblase. [Maslinieks G. Elers].
Rīgā, Liesma, 1969. 199 p., 4 leaves of illus. Translations from the
Lithuanian. PG8772.L3V5 DLC;CaAEU.

3724. VIENUOLIS, A., pseud. Taĭ-
na ozera Platialiaĭ; rasskazy i predaniia. Perevod s litovskogo. Vil'-
nius, Vaga, 1972. 282 p.
PG8721.V5T3 PU.

3725. VIRŠULIS, A. Put' geroev.
[Perevod s litovskogo I. Dektoraĭte.
Moskva], Molodaia gvardiia, 1959.
190 p. illus. D802.L5V52 DLC; DS;
CSt-H; IU; MH.

3726. WICHERT, Julia (Kajrukszti-
sowa). Antologia poezji litewskiej
... z przedmową Artura Górskiego.
Warszawa, Instytut popierania nauki,
1939. xxxvi,279 p.
491.922Cw633 PU; NNC.

3727. ŽILINSKAITĖ, Vytautė. An-
gel nad gorodom; iumoristicheskie
rasskazy. Perevod s litovskogo F.Dek-
tora. Moskva, Sovetskiĭ pisatel',
1972. 182 p. illus. At head of title: Vitaute Zhilinskaite.
PG8722.36.I4Z51 PU; CaOTU; CU-S;DLC;
IU; MH; NjP.

3728. --- Der himmelblaue Maikä-
fer; Humoresken und Satiren. [Aus dem

Litauischen von Irene Brewing.
1.Aufl.] Berlin, Eulenspiegel, 1970.
141 p. PG8722.36.I4H5 DLC.

3729. ŽUKAUSKAS, Albinas. Trudna-
ia, radost'; stikhotvoreniia. Avtoriz.
per. s litovskogo. [Leningrad, Sov.
pisatel', Leningradskoe otd-nie,1970]
190 p. ill. At head of title: Al'-
binas Zhukauskas. MH.

3730. ŽYMANTIENĖ, Julija (Beniuše-
viciūtė). Die Schwiegertochter. Petras Kurmelis. Topylis. Aus dem Russischen übers. von Anneliese Globig,
Marlene Milack und Wilhelm Plackmeyer]
Berlin, Aufbau-Verlag, [1973]. 127 p.
PG8721.Z9A6 1973 PU.

XIII.5.c.7. ORIGINAL WORKS IN FOR-
EIGN LANGUAGES ON LI-
THUANIAN THEME

3731. BITĖL', Piatro Ivanovich.
Zamki i liudzi. Gistarichnaia poéma.
[Mastakh A. Kashkurėvich]. Minsk,Be-
larus', 1968. 102 p. illus.
PG2835.2.B5Z2 DLC.

3732. CHODŹKO, Ignacy. Pisma.
Wyd. nowe. Wilno, J. Zawadzki,1880.
Partial contents.--t.1-2. Obrazy li-
tewskie.--t.3. Podania litewskie.
PG7158.C54 1880 InU; CaAEU(1-2);CtY;
MH; MiU; NNC.

3733. JUNGFER, Victor. Irka; Roman. Karlsbad, [1945]. 382 p. "Es
ist ein farbiges Bild des litauisch-
en Volkstums, das hier entworfen
wird". 838J955I PU.

3734. --- Der Weg der Skaringa;
Roman. München, Ger., 1940. 288 p.
At head of title: Victor Georg Jung-
herr, [pseud.].   PT2619.U46W4 PU.

3735. KONDRATOWICZ, Ludwik. Már-
gis (Márgiris). Išvertė ir eiliuotą
įžangą parašė Antanas Valaitis. Įvadą parašė Mykolas Biržiška. [Kaunas],
Sakalas, [1936].[Xerox copy, 1977].
150 p. At head of title: Liudvikas
Kondratavičius (Vladislovas Syrokom-
la). PG7158.K57M319 1936a PU.

3736. KRASZEWSKI, Józef Ignacy.
Witolorauda; giesme isz padawimu Lie-
tuwos. Lietuwiszkay iszgulde su isz-
reiszkimais nepaprastu żodżiu J.A.W.
Lietuwis, [pseud.] Poznaniuje, Kasztu J.I. Kraszewskio, 1881. [Xerox copy, 1975]. viii,320 p.
PG7158.K75W55165 1975a PU.

3737. KWIATKOWSKI, Józef. Lietu-

vaitė; apysaka. Guldė P.G. Chicago,
Ill., Turtu ir spauda "Kataliko",
1906. At head of title: Juozas
Kvietkovskius. L826Kw ICLJF; CtY;
NN; OCl; WaS.

3738. MICKIEWICZ, Adam. Conrad
Wallenrod. An historical poem. Tr.
from the Polish by Michael H. Dzie-
wicki. London, T. Richardson and
Son, 1883. PG7158.M5Z34 DLC(1883,
1841, 1925 ed.); CU(1925 ed.); GU(
1925 ed.); KU(1925 ed.); MH(1841,
1882...); MU(1925 ed.); MiU(1882,
1925 ed.); NIC(1925 ed.); OCl(1925);
ODW(1925 ed.); TxU(1841 ed.).

3739. --- Diedai ir Gražina. Tr.
into Lituanian by Jr. Jonas,[pseud.]
[s.l., s.n.], 1899. 1 v. (Vertimai,
t.1) Translation of Dziady, pt.2
and Grażyna. RP.

3740. --- Dziadów część III w
podobiźnie autografu Adama Mickiewicza. Wydał Józef Kallenbach. W Krakowie, Nakł. Polskiej Akademji Umiejętności; skład główny w Księgarni
Gebethnera i Wolfa, 1925. vii,126
p. facsims. PG7158.M5D72 1925 DLC;
CSt; KU; MH; MiU(1925, 1967 ed.);MU;
NNC(1925, 1967 ed.); NcD(1967 ed.);
NjP(1967 ed.).

3741. --- Dziady; poema. War-
szawa, Bibljoteka Polska,[19-].
257 p. (Wielka bibljoteka, nr.41).
PG7158.M5D72 DLC(19- , 1947 ed.);
CaBVaU(1916, 1944 and 1952 ed.);InU
(1901 ed.); CLU(1970 ed.); CU(1947ed)
CtY(1929 ed.); MB(1885, 1947 ed.);
MH(1916, 1920, 1922, 1929, 1968,1970
ed.); MiU(1929 ed.); MiD(1947 ed.);
NN(1906, 1916 ed.); NNC(1947,1970ed.)
OCl(1907 ed.); WU(1929 ed.); WaU(
1933 ed.).

3742. --- Forefathers. Translated from the Polish by H.M. the King
of Poland. Bookham, Surrey,[1943].
Translation of Dziady.
PG7158.M5Z32 DLC; ,iU; WU.

3743. --- ---; parts one and two
in one volume. Translated from the
Polish by Count Potocki of Montalk.
London, Right Review, 1944. 60 p.
Translation of Dziady, pt.1-2.
Huk55M58gD98 1944 CtY; KU; MH; NNC;
OCl.

3744. --- Forefathers' eve (pro-
logue and scenes 1-5). Translated
from the Polish by Dorothea Prall
Radin. Edited by George Rapall Noyes.
[London, Eng.], School of Slavonic
Studies in the University of London,
King's college,[1925]. vii,45 p.
(Masterpieces of the Slavonic lite-
ratures) PG7158.M5Z33 DLC; CaBVaU;

CU; IU; ICU(1968 ed.); DeU(1968 ed.)
MB; MH(1925,1968 ed.); MiU; MiEM(
1968 ed.); NN; NBuU; NjR(1968 ed.);
OCl; WaS.

3745. --- Gražina. [Vertė Just.
Marcinkevičius]. Konradas Valenrodas. [Vertė V. Mykolaitis-Putinas].
2.leidimas. Kaunas, Šviesa, 1967.
98 p. PG7158.M5G715 1967 PU.

3746. --- Grażyna, powieść litewska. London, Eng., M.I. Kolin
Ltd.,[1941]. 51 p. (Książnica naro-
dowa). PG7158.M5G7 DLC(1941, 1944,
1951, 1956 ed.); CaBVaU(1935, 1953ed)
CoU(1960 ed.); CtY(1947, 1935 ed.);
CU(1922, 1945 ed.); ICU(1928 ed.);
MB(1894 ed.); MH(1925, 1947, 1953,
1956 ed.); MiU(1928, 1952 ed.); NN(
1894 ed.); OU(1925 ed.); PU; PCamA(
1925, 1928, 1929 ed.); WU(1925,1929,
1935 ed.).

3747. --- Grazyna; a tale of Lithuania. Translated from the Polish
by Dorothea Prall Radin. IN Poet
Lore (Boston, Mass.), 1940, v.46, no.
1, p. 3-43. Detached copy.
834M62gEr CU.

3748. --- Herr Thaddäus; oder,
Der letzte Eintritt in Lithauen.
Übersetzt von Siegfried Lipiner.Leip-
zig, Breitkopf und Härtel, 1882.
xvi,313 p. (His Poetische Werke,Bd.1)
PG7158.M5P18G3L76 CaAEU(1882 ed.);
GU(1898 ed.); NN(1936 ed.); RPB(
1882 ed.).

3749. --- Konrad Wallenrod; powieść historyczna z dziejów litewskich i pruskich. Petersburg, Drukiem
K. Kraya, 1828. viii, 88 p. Wydanie nakładem autora. PG7158.M5K6
DLC(1828, 187-, 1878, 1924, 1943,
1964 ed.); CaBVaU(1924 ed.); CLSU(
1924 ed.); CU(1946 ed.); CtY(1922,
1924, 1943 ed.); ICU(1861 ed.); InU(
1890 ed.); MH(1828, 1894, 1897, 1924
ed.); MiU(1924 ed.); NN(1897, 1943ed)
NNC(1828, 1924, 1946 ed.); OU(1924ed)
PCamA(1861, 1924, 1926 ed.); WU(1861,
1924, 1930 ed.).

3750. --- Konradas Valenrodas;
lietuvių ir prusų žygių istorinė apysaka. Vertė V. Mykolaitis-Putinas.
[Iliustracijos iš originalo, 1851 metų Paryžiaus leidinio - dail. J. Ty-
siewicz. Konrad Valenrod a historical story from the campains of Lithuanians and Prussians. Brooklyn, N.Y.
Gabija, [1953]. 96 p. illus.
PG7158.M5K8L7 1953 CaAEU; NN.

3751. --- Pan Tadeusz; czyli, Os-
tatni zajazd na Litwie. Historja
szlachecka z r. 1811 i 1812, we dwu-
nastu księgach, wierszem... Wydanie

Alexandra Jełowieckiego s popiersiem
autora. Paryż, 1934. 2 v.
PG7158.M5P3 1834 DLC(1834, 1921,
1949, 1950, 1954, 1956, 1957 ed.);
CaBVaU(1897, 1921, 1950 ed.); CLSU(
1945 ed.); CLU(1963 ed.); CSt(1949ed)
CSf(1964 ed.); CtY(1928, 1931, 1945,
1949, 1950, 1954 ed.); CoU(1959 ed.)
CU(1882, 1945, 1949, 1950, 1954 ed.)
ICU(1949, 1967 ed.); IEN(1950, 1966
ed.); IEdS(1950 ed.); IU(1882, 1959,
1963 ed.); InU(1898, 1945, 1968 ed.)
KU(1934, 1945 ed.); KyU(1954 ed.);
MB(1883, 1953, 1954 ed.); MH(1923,
1925, 1929, 1945, 1949, 1966,1969ed.)
MiU(1912, 1925, 1934 ed.); MiD(1950
ed.); MiDW(1953); MNF(1966 ed.); NB
(1967 ed.); NN(1834, 1921, 1945,1949,
1950, 1954, 1959 ed.); NNC(1886,1923,
1929, 1934, 1945, 1946, 1948, 1950,
1954 ed.); NIC(1958 ed.); NSyU(1962
ed.); NcD(1958, 1959 ed.); NcU(1964,
1966 ed.); NBuU(1920, 1954 ed.);
NBuC(1929, 1950 ed.); OU(1954 ed.);
OCl(1906, 1928, 1933, 1950, 1956,
1959 ed.); OClW(1967 ed.); OrP(1954
ed.); PP(1916 ed.); PU(1961 ed.);
PSt(1925, 1949, 1950 ed.); PCamA(
1923, 1931, 1945, 1950 ed.); ViU(
1950 ed.); WU(1928, 1934 ed.)

3752. --- ---; or, The last foray
in Lithuania; a story of life among
gentlefolk in the years 1811 & 1812
...tr. from the Polish by George Rapall Noyes. London; Toronto, J.M.
Dent, 1917. PG7158.M5P CSt(1917ed.)
CaBVaU(1930 ed.); CaBVa(1930, 1962
ed.); CLSU(1962 ed.); CtY(1962 ed.);
CU(1917, 1962 ed.); CoU(1917, 1930
ed.); DLC(1930, 1968 ed.); FU(1930
ed.); IEN(1917 ed.); IdU(1917 ed.);
INS(1930 ed.); InE(1930 ed.); InU(
1949, 1962, 1964 ed.); ICU(1964);
MH(1930, 1962, 1964 ed.); MWelC(1949
ed.); MiDW(1962 ed.); MtU(1917 ed.);
MdBJ(1917 ed.); MiU(1917, 1962 ed.);
NN(1962 ed.); NNC(1962, 1964 ed.);
NIC(1917 ed.); NcD(1917 ed.); NCU(
1962 ed.); NjP(1962 ed.); NjN(1962
ed.); OrL(1917 ed.); OrU(1962 ed.);
OrPR(1917 ed.); OU(1917, 1930 ed.);
OOxM(1917 ed.); OrStbM(1930 ed.);PU(
1917 ed.); PBm(1917 ed.); PHC(1930ed)
ViU(1917, 1962 ed.); KMK(1964 ed.).

3753. --- Ponas Tadas; arba, Paskutinis antpuolis Lietuvoje; bajorų
nuotykiai iš 1811 ir 1812 metų. Vertė V. Mykolaitis-Putinas ir Justinas
Marcinkevičius. [Iliustracijos M.E.
Andriolio]. Vilnius, Vaga, 1974.
477 p. At head of title: Adomas Mickevičius. PG7158.M5P31655 PU;DLC.

3754. --- Vėlinės, parašė A. Mickevičius, vertė "Varpas". Pasveiki-
nimai dienos 24 gruodžio 1898 m.
Išleido kuopelė Vinco Kudirkos atmin-
čiai. Tilžėje, Spausdinta pas J.

Schoenkę, 1900. 68 p.
Huk55.M58uW94v CtY.

3755. REUTT, Marya. Z dziejów po-
gańskiej Litwy; opowiadania historyczne dla młodzieży: Wajdiewutis. Min-
dowe. Gedymin. Dwaj bracia(Kiejstut
i Olgierd). Warszawa, [s.d.]. 1 v.
491.922R313 PU.

3756. RODZIEWICZÓWNA, Maria. De-
wajtis; powieść... Wyd. nowe. Lwów,
Nakł. Wydawnictwa polskiego, [s.d.].
353 p. port. 491.922R615.2 PU;ICU.

3757. --- --- Wydanie dziesiąte.
Poznań, Wydawnictwo polskie R. Weg-
nera, [1931]. 328 p. (Her Pisma,
tom 1). NN; BHS; DCU; InU; MH; NNC.

3758. --- --- Rzym, Polska YMCA,
1945. 269 p. PG7158.R69D3 1945
CaAEU.

3759. --- --- Kraków, Wydawn. Literackie, [1957]. 337 p. (Biblioteka Polska). 1 v. DLC-P4;MH;MiU;OU.

3760. --- Dievaitis; šių laikų
apysaka. Autorei maloniai sutikus
lietuvių kalbon išvertė Kazys Puida.
Šiauliuose, I. Brevdos & K. Puidos
lėšomis, 1908. 308 p. MB; OKentU.

3761. SCHONDOCH, 14th cent. Lietuvos karaliaus krikštas; vizijinė
poema iš XIV amžiaus. Vertė A. Tyruolis. Chicago, Ill., M. Morkūnas,
1976. 30 p. illus. Translation of
Der Litauer. English title: Baptism
of the King of Lithuania; a poem from
14th century. PT1651.S35L77L7 1976
CaAEU.

3762. SUCHEWIRT, Peter. Žygis į
Lietuvą; istorinė poema iš 1377 metų.
Vertė A. Tyruolis. [Brooklyn, N.Y.,
Karys], 1977. 36 p. PT1656.S82V619
PU.

3763. WICHERT, Ernst. Gesammelte
Werke. 8.Aufl. Dresden, Ger., C.
Reissner, 1900-1902. 6 v. (v.1-3,
16-18) PT2558.A1 1902 DLC; NcU.

3764. --- Litauische Geschichten.
2.Aufl. Dresden und Leipzig, Ger.,
C. Reissner, 1900-1901. 2 v. (His
Gesammelte Werke, v. 16-17)
PT2558.L6 1900 DLC; NcU.

3765. --- --- 3. und 4.Aufl.
Dresden und Leipzig, C. Reissner,
1914. 2 v. 491.922W633 PU; DLC.

3766. --- --- [Another edition].
Hrsg. von P. Wichert. Berlin-Charlot-
tenburg, Ger., Volksverband der Bü-
cherfreunde Wegweiser-Verlag, [1927].
472 p. ill., ports. PT2558.L6 CU.

3767. --- --- Einmalige Ausg.
Hamburg, Ger., Deutsche Hausbücherei
[1934]. 317 p. illus.
PT2558.L6 1934 DLC.

XIII.5.c.8. LITHUANIAN AUTHORS WRITING IN FOREIGN LANGUAGES

3768. LES AMIS DE MILOSZ. Cahiers. Paris, Éditions André Silvaire, 1969. 1 v. (Cahiers de l'Association, 3). KMK; KU; MeU.

3769. BALTRUŠAITIS, Jurgis. Derevo v ogne. [Stikhi. Sostavil IÙozas Tumiãlis. Vil'nius, Vaga, 1969. 535 p. PG3453B23D4 PU; CaAEU;CaOTU CaBVaU;CSt; CtY; CoU; CU; FMU; IaU; IU; MH; MiU; MnU; MB; NN; NNC; NIC; NjP; NRU; OU; RPB; WU; WaU; DLC; MiEM.

3770. --- Gornaĩa tropa; vtoraĩa kniga stikhov. Moskva, Skorpion,1912. 181 p. At head of title: IÙ. Baltrushaĩtis. Microfilm. Tumba, Sweden, International Documentation Centre [1973]. 4 sheets 9 x 12 cm. WU.

3771. --- --- Moskva, Skorpion, 1912. [Ann Arbor, Mich., Univ. Microfilms, 1972]. 167 p. At head of title: IÙ. Baltrushaĩtis. CaBVaU.

3772. --- Lilĩã i serp. 3.kniga stikhov. Parizh, YMCA-Press, 1948. 225 p. illus.
PG3476.B2868L5 DLC; CaAEU; CSt; PU; PPULC.

3773. --- Žemės laiptai. Kalnų takas. [Eilėraščiai]. Vertė L.Broga. Vilnius, Vaga, 1973. 278 p. port. Translation of Zemnye stupeni and Gornaĩa tropa. PG8721.B3Z416 DLC; OKentU.

3774. --- Žemės pakopos; elegijos, giesmės, poemos. Iš rusų kalbos vertė J. Valaitis. Tübingen,Ger., 1947. 157 p. PG3453.B23Z36 DLC; CaAEU; CtY; PU; PPULC; OCl; WU.

3775. --- Zemnyĩã stupeni; elegiĩ, piesni, poėmy. Moskva, Skorpion, 1911. 212 p. At head of title: IÙ. Baltrushaĩtis. Reproduced by xerography 1970.
PG3453.B23Z4 1970 PU.

3776. --- --- Moskva, Skorpion, 1911. 212 p. Microfiche. Tumba, Sweden, International Documentation Cetre [1973]. 3 sheets 9 x 12 cm. At head of title: IÙ. Baltrushaĩtis.
PG02.9 CaAEU(microfiche); WU.

3777. BELLEMIN-NOËL, Jean. Poèmes d'adolescence de Milosz; le cahier déchiré. Paris, Lettres modernes, 1972. 135 p. facsims (Avant-Siècle, 13). PQ2625.I558C23B44 1972 CaAEU; CaOTP; CaOOU; CaQMM; CLSU; CU; CSt; CtY; CtW; CU; CU-SB; CNoS; CU-S; DLC; FU; IaU; InU; IU; MH; MU; MiDW; MiU; NNC; NIC; NcD; NjP; NRU; OKentU; OU; PU; TxHR; TU; ViU; ViBlbV; WU; WaU.

3778. --- Le texte et l'avant-texte; les brouillons d'un poème de Milosz. Paris; Larousse, [1972]. 143 p. (Collection L) PQ2625.I558C43B44 1972 CaAEU; CaQMM; CLU; CSt; CtY; CtW; CU; CU-SB; CFS; DLC; ICU; MH; MiU; MiEM; MoSW; MU;NN; NIC; NjP; NcD; NcU; OU; PSt; TxHR; ViU; WU.

3779. BUDRYS, Algis. The Amsirs and the Iron thorn. Greewich, Conn., Fawcett, [cl967]. 159 p. (A Fawcett gold medal book). OClU; CNoS.

3780. --- Budrys' inferno. New York, N.Y., Berkley Pub. Corp.,1963. 160 p. (A Berkley medallion book, F 799) CSt; OU.

3781. --- The iron thorn. London, Eng., Gollancz, 1968. 188 p. PR6052.U22I27 1969 CaAEU; CaOTP; CU-S; ViU.

3782. --- The unexpected dimension. New York, N.Y., Ballantine Books,[cl960]. 159 p. (An Originan Ballantine book, 388K). CSt; AzU.

3783. --- Who. New York, N.Y., Pyramid Books, [1958]. 157 p. (Pyramid books). PR6052.U22W6 1958 CaAEU; AzU; CSt; FTaSU.

3784. --- --- New York, N.Y., Lancer Books, [1968,cl958]. 191 p. OU; OClUr; KU.

3785. GODAY, Armand. Milosz, le poète de l'amour. Paris, A. Silvaire, 1960. 282 p. illus. PG2625.I558Z7G5 CaAEU; ICU; InU;MH; NNC; NIC; OrU.

3786. KLEMENTAS, Antanas Jackus. Žemaitiška giesmelė. [Paruošė V. Vanagas]. Vilnius, Vaga, 1972. 192 p. illus. (Versmės) Several poems in Polish with parallel Lithuanian translations. PG8721.K59Z25 1972 DLC; NN; WU.

3787. MILOSZ, Oscar Vladislas. L'amoureuse initiation; extrait des Mémoires du chevalier Waldemar de L... Paris, Grasset, 1910. 290 p. NjP.

3788. --- ---; roman. [Fribourg],

Egloff, [1944]. 266 p. (His Oeuvres complètes, 2). MH; IaU; NcU.

3789. --- --- Préf. de Gilbert Sigaux. Lausanne, Société coopérative éditions rencontre, [1961,c1958] 277 p. (Prix rencontre, 8). IU; WU.

3790. --- --- (Extrait des Mémoires du chevalier Waldemar de L...) Paris, A. Silvaire, [1958]. 248 p. (His Oeuvres complètes, t.5). PQ2625.I558A65 DLC; IU; MH; MnU;MiU NIC; NcD; LNHT; TxHR; TxU.

3791. --- Les arcanes. Paris, Egloff, [1948]. 176 p. (His OEuvres complètes, t.8. Philosophie, 2) IU; CaBVaU; CaOTP; MiU; NIC; NcD; NcGU; TxU.

3792. --- Ars Magna. Paris, A. Sauerwein, 1924. 77 p. CaBVaU;MH.

3793. --- --- Suivi de Les origines ibériques du peuple juif, L'apocalypse de Saint-Jean déchiffrée, La clef de l'apocalypse. Paris, A. Silvaire,[1961]. 202 p. (His OEuvres complètes, 7). MiU; MH; InU; NcD; TxLT.

3794. --- Le Cahier déchiré. Paris, A. Silvaire, 1969. 63 p. At head of title: O.V. de L. Milosz. PQ2625.I558C3 1969 DLC; CaAEU;CaBVaU CU-SC; CU-S; CU-SB; CLU; CSt; CtY; FU; IU; KMK; MoSW; MnU; MiDW; MiU;MU MB; NN; NNC; NBuU; NcU; NbU; OrU;OU; WU.

3795. --- La clef de l'Apocalypse. Paris, [Imp. Firmin-Didot],1938. 7 p. MH.

3796. --- La confession de Lemuel. Paris, Connaissance, 1922. 83 p. PQ2625.I558C6 WU; NN.

3797. --- Connaissez-vous? Milosz; choix de textes, présentés par Jacques Buge. Paris, A. Silvaire, [1965]. 126 p. illus., ports.,facsims. Bibliography: p. [121]-124. IU.

3798. --- Contes et fabliaux de la vieille Lithuanie. Paris, A. Silvaire, 1972. 224 p. PQ2625.I558C6 1972 DLC.

3799. --- Dix-sept lettres de Milosz [à Armand Guibert. Paris],GLM, [1953]. 16, 4 p. IU; KU; NN; NjP; WU.

3800. --- Fourteen poems; translated, and with an introd., by Kenneth Rexroth. Illustrated by Edward Hagedorn. San Francisco, Calif., Peregrine Press, 1952. [61] p. illus. "129 copies... all of which are signed by the traslator, the artist,and the printer." English and French. PQ2625.I558A6 1952 DLC; CLU-C; CoU; IEN; IaU; ICU; NN; NjP.

3801. --- Lettres inédites à Christian Gauss dont une en fac-similé hors texte. Paris, A. Silvaire, c1976. 90 p. PQ2625.I558Z52G27 1976 CaAEU; DLC.

3802. --- Mephiboseth. Paris,Egloff,[1946]. 154,[4] p. (His OEuvres complètes, 4). At head of title: O.V. de L.-Milosz. Imprint on cover Librairie Les Lettres. PQ2625.I558M4 1946 DLC; AU; CU-S(1946 ed.); CU(1914 ed.); DGU(1945ed.) IaU; InU; IU; KyU LU; MH; MiU; NN(1913 ed.); NIC; NbU; NcGU(1945 ed.); NcD; PU(1945 ed.); TxU; TU(1945 ed.); CaBVaU(1914 ed.); MWelC.

3803.--Miguel de Mañara, misterio en seis cuadros. Buenos Aires, Emecé editores, [1947]. 111 p. OU.

3804 --- Miguel Mañara, a mystery in six scenes. Tr. from the French by Edward J.O'Brien. [Boston, Mass., R.G. Badger, 19--]. p. 224-264.(Poet lore plays, new ser.) MnS.

3805. --- --- In Poet lore (Boston, Mass.), 1919, v.30, no.2, p.224-264. PN2P7 vol.30 DLC; CaBVaU;MB; NN; OCl; WaU.

3806. --- Miguel Mañara; mystère en six tableaux. Avant-propos d'Armand Godoy. Paris, Bernard Grasset, [1935]. 137 p. At head of title: O.V. de Milosz. PQ2625.I558M5 DLC; MWelC; NcD; NjP; PSt.

3807. --- --- Paris, Egloff,1945. 115 p. (His OEuvres complètes, 3). MH.

3808. --- --- [and] Faust; traduction fragmentaire. Paris, Librairie Les Lettres, [1957]. 135 p. (His OEuvres complètes, 3) PQ2625.I558M5 1957 DLC; MH; NIC; MiU; TxHR; ViU; VtMiM.

3809. --- Miguel Manara; šešių paveikslų misterija. Vertė Antanas Vaičiulaitis. [Iliustracijos V.O. Vitkaus]. Chicago, Ill., Lietuviškos knygos klubas, 1977. 94 p. PQ2625.I558M519 1977 PU.

3810. --- Milosz; choix de textes présentés par Jacque Buge. Paris, A. Silvaire,[1965]. 126 p. illus., facsims., ports. (Connaissez-vous?) PQ2625.I558A6 1965 DLC.

3811. --- Milosz, 1877-1939. Choix établi par Jean Bellemin-Noël. Paris, A. Silvaire, 1967. 160 p. (Maximes et pensées) PQ2625.I558A6 1967 DLC; CU; MoU; MiU; MU; NNC; NcD; NcU; TxU; WU.

3812. --- Milosz, 1977-1939, Apollinaire, 1880-1918, Toulouse,[30 novembre-29 décembre] 1967, Centre régional de documentation pédagogique. Toulouse, Centre régional de documentation pédagogique, 1967. ii, 13 p. PQ2625.I558Z76 DLC; IU; MiU.

3813. --- O.V. de L. Milosz; une étude par Jean Rousselot, oeuvres choisies. [Paris], P. Seghers,[1949] 219 p. illus., ports., facsims. (Poètes d'aujourd'hui, 17) Bibliography: p. [211]-216. PQ2625.I558A6 1949 DLC; CaBVaU; CU; CLSU; CtY; GEU; GU; IEN; IaU; ICU; LU; MA; MH; NcD; NjP; NcGU; OCl;OU; OrU; PHC; PSt; TxU; ViU; WU(1955 ed.)

3814. --- OEuvres complètes. Paris, Librairie Les Lettres,[19--] 12 v. Some vols. published by Egloff; some by A. Silvaire. Variations in volume numbering; U.C. Library set numbered from list in v.5. Contents.--t.0. La vie et l'oeuvre de O.V. de L. Milosz.--t.1. Poésies I: Le poème des décadences. Les sept solitudes.--t.2. Poésies II: Les éléments. Adramandon. La confession de Lémuel. Demiers poèmes.--t.3. Théatre I: Miguel Mañara. Traduction fragmentaire de Faust.--t.4. Théatre II: Méphiboseth. Scènes de "Don Juan" --t.5. Roman: L'amoureuse initiation.--t.6. Contes et fabliaux de la vieille Lithuanie.--t.7. Philosophie I: Ars Magna. Les origines ibèriques du peuple juif. L'Apocalypse de Saint Jean déchiffré. La clef de l'Apocalypse.--t.8. Philosophie II: Les arcanes.--t.9. Contes lithuaniens de ma mère l'Oye. Dainos. Les origines de la nation lithuanienne. --t.10. Chefs-d'oeuvre lyrique du nord.--t.11. Correspondance. Varia. PQ2625.M155A1 1946 CU; C; IEN; OrU.

3815. --- --- Introduction par Edmond Jaloux. [Fribourg], Egloff, [1944-1963]. 10 v. front. 10 v. Vols. 7-10 have imprint: Paris, A. Silvaire. Contents.--t.1. Poèmes. --t.2. L'amoureuse initiation.--t.3. Miguel Mañara.--t.4. Méphiboseth. --t.5-6. Contes et fabliaux de la vieille Lithuanie.--t.7. Ars Magna, Les origines ibèrique du peuple juif. L'Apocalypse de Saint Jean déchiffrée. La clef de l'Apocalypse.--t.8. Les Arcanes.--t.9. Contes lithuaniens de ma mère l'oye. Dainos. Les

origines de la nation lithuanniene. --t.10. Chef-d'oeuvre lyriques du Nord; Angleterre, Allemagne. NN; NNC; NjP; NcD; CLU; CSt; CtY;ICU; KU; LU; MH; MiDW; MU; OU; WaU.

3816. --- --- Paris, A. Silvaire, [1946- c1945-]. 11 v. Imprint varies: t.4,6 & 8 (1946-1948) are published by Egloff; t.3 (1957) by Les Lettres. t.6 of theis set was t.5 in the Egloff arrangement. PQ2625.I558 1945 CaBVaU; CaAEU; OrU.

3817. --- Los orígines ibéricos del pueblo judie... Versión de Lysandro Z.D. Galtier, con una noticia preliminar del mismo, un autógrafo del autor y un frontispicio de V.K. Jonynas. Buenos Aires, [Estabicimiento gráfico de las Ediciones católicas argentinas, 1935]. 106 p. front, facsim. At head of title: O.W. de Lubicz Milosz. GN547.M5 DLC;CtY;CU.

3818. --- Poemas. Traducción de Augusto D'Halmar,[pseud.]. Santiago, Chile, Nascimiento, 1953. 204 p. NN; CU; DPU; TxU.

3819. --- ---; selección y traducción de Lysandro Z.D. Galtier, con un retrato inédito y un poema autógrafo del autor. Buenos Aires, Ediciones "Huella", [1941]. 77 p. front., facsim. (Colección "Huella". Cuaderno no.2] At head of title: O.W. de Lubicz Milosz. PQ2625.I558A55 DLC.

3820. --- Le poème des dćadences. Paris, Girard et Villerelle, [1899]. 72 p. At head of title: O.W.Milosz. NN; NIC.

3821.--Poèmes, 1895-1927. Paris, J.O. Fourcade, [1929]. 132 p. No. 126 in an edition of 270 copies. Hfp.mi88 CtY.

3822. --- --- Préf. de P.L. Flouquet. Lettre autographe de O.V. de L. Milosz. Paris, A. Magné, [1939]. 94 p. illus. (Cahiers des poetes catholiques). PQ2625.I558A17 1938 WU; MB; OrU.

3823. --- --- Introd. par E. Jaloux. [Fribourg], Egloff, [1944]. 162 p. port. (His OEuvre complètes,1) MH; NcU.

3824. --- --- Avec une préf. de Jean de Boschère. [Marselle], R.Laffont, [1944]. 164 p. (Sous le signe d'Arion, 7). PQ2625.I558A17 1944 DLC; CLSU; CtY; DNW; IEN; ICU; ICRL; NN.

3825. --- --- Paris, Librairie

Les Lettres, [1956]. 140 p. (Collection Origine, 2). IU; CaBVaU; CU; DLC; IaU; InU; KU; LU; MH; MiU;MdBJ; NN; OCl; PPiU; PU; TxU; WU.

3826. --- Poésies. Textes, notes et variantes établis par Jacques Buge. Paris, A. Silvaire, [1960]. 2 v. (His OEuvres complètes, 1-2) Contents.--t.1. Le poème des décadences. Les sept solitudes.--t.2. Les éléments. Autres poèmes. Symphonies. Nihumim. Adramandoni, etc. PQ2625.I558A17 1960 DLC; LNHT; MB; MH; MiU; NIC; NhD; NjP; NjR; RPB; TxLT.

3827. --- Saul de Tarse; mystère en quatre tableaux. Suivi de Daïnos et de diverses traductions. Paris, A. Silvaire, [1970]. 188 p. (His OEuvres complètes, t.11) PQ2625.I558S3 1970 DLC; CaQMM; CU; CU-SB; CU-S; InU; MH; MWelC; NBuU; NN; NcD; NcGU; NbU; OCl; PU; RPB; TxU; ViU; WU; LU.

3828. --- Soixante-quinze lettres inédites et sept documents originaux. Paris, A. Silvaire,[1969]. 164 p. plates. Letters to L. and J. Vogt. PQ2625.I558Z53 DLC;CaAEU; CaBVaU; CLSU; CFS; CSt; CtY; CLU; CNoS; CU; CU-SC; CU-SB; IEN; ICU; IaU; InU; IU; LU; MB; MH; MiU;MiEM; MoSW; MU; NN; NNC; NIC; NBuU; NjP; NcU; RPB; WU; WaU.

3829. --- Textes inédits de O.V. de L. Milisz, suivis de lettres inédites de Paul Valéry, Antoine Bourdelle, André Suarès, Jules Supervielle. Paris, A. Silvaire, [1959]. 107 p. illus. PQ2625.I558T4 DLC; CU; ICU; MH; MiU; NNC; NjP; KU;OrU; WU.

3830. --- Trois symphonies. Drei Symphonien. [Gedichte. Texte original français avec traduction allemande en regard[. Traduit en allemand par Walter Eckstein. Gravures sur bois par Karl Schmid. [Erlenbach; Zürich, Éd. Daphnis, 1966]. [43] p. 4 plates. At head of title: Oscar Vladislas de L. Milosz. 200 copies printed. No. 198. PQ2625.I558T7 1966 DLC; IU; WU.

3831. --- Wybór poezji. Z upoważnieniem autora przeł. Bronisława Ostrowska. [Rys. J.J. Wronieckiego]. Poznań, Ostoja, 1919. 65 p. MH.

3832. MILOSZ. Textes et documents inédits présentés par Armand Guibert. [Villeneuve-lès-Avignon, P. Seghers, 1942]. 103 p. ports., facsims. (Poésie, 42) "Cahier spécial de Poésie 42" PQ2625.I558Z75 DLC;CtY;CU.

3833. ROUSSELOT, Jean. O.V. de L. Milosz; une étude par Jean Rousselot, une bibliographie, une chronologie bio-bibliographique: Milosz et son temps. Paris, Seghers, 1972. 200 p. plates. Bibliography: p. [195-200]. PQ2625.I558Z84 DLC; CaAEU; CLU; CSt; IaU; IU; MiDW; MU; NRU; PSt; TxHR; ViU.

3834. SAULAITIS, Marija. And you. Introd. by Charles Angoff. New York, N.Y., Manyland Books, [1972]. 37 p. PS3569.A788A8 DLC; NN; RPB.

3835. ZOBARSKAS, Stepas. Young love and other infidelities. Introd. by Charles Angoff. New York, N.Y., Manyland Books, [1971]. 115 p. PZ4Z85Yo DLC; FTaSU; GU; ICU; IaU; NN.

XIII.6. THEATRE

3836. AKADEMINIO OPEROS IR BALETO teatro baletas. [Aliodija Ruzgaitė, Henrikas Liandzbergas. Vilnius, Vaga, 1976]. [96] p. (chiefly illus.] [Ballet of the Academic Theatre of opera and ballet]. GV1786.V5A5 PU.

3837. MALCIENĖ, Marijana. Lietuvos kino istorijos apybraiža (1919-1970) [Concise history of cinematography in Lithuania]. Vilnius, Mintis, 1974. 175 p. On t.p.: Lietuvos TSR Mokslų akademijos Istorijos institutas. PN1993.5.L5M3 PU;DLC.

3838. MILLER, Antoni Witold. Teatr polski i muzyka na Litwie jako strażnice kultury zachodu (1745-1865). Studjum z dziejów kultury polskiej. Wilno, Nakł. Wyd. im. Bozchów Łopacińskich, 1936. 245 p. plates., ports. PN2859.L5M5 DLC; NN.

3839. ROSTOVAITĖ, Tatjana. Scenoje, lietuvių dramaturgija; teatro kritikos etiudai. [Lithuanian drama; a critical review]. Vilnius, Mintis, 1977. 133 p. PN2859.L5R6 PU.

3840. SRUOGA, Balys. Mūsų teatro raida. [The development of our theatre]. In Kemežys, V., ed. Lietuva 1918-1938. Kaunas, 1938. 947.52.L625 PU; CtTMF; ICCC; ICLJF.

3841. VAIČIŪNIENĖ, Teofilija. Scena ir gyvenimas. [Stage and life] Vilnius, Vaga, 263 p. PN2728.V28A3 PU.

3842. VILNA. UNIVERSITETAS. Universiteto kiemo teatras. [University theatre]. [Atsak. redaktorius V.

Zabarauskas]. Vilnius, [Vilniaus universiteto Leidybinis skyrius], 1975. 30 p. PN2726.V5U5 PU.

3843. ZABARAUSKAS, Vitalius. Bronius Babkauskas. Vilnius, Lietuvos TSR Teatro draugija, 1973. 87 p., [16] leaves of plates. PN2728.B25Z3 PU.

3844. ŽILEVIČIUS, Juozas. Lietuviškas teatras. [Lithuanian theatre]. In Studentų Žodis (Thompson, Conn.), 1943, no.4, v.11, p.87-91. ICCC; OKentU.

XIII.7. MUSIC

XIII.7.a. GENERAL WORKS

3845. AMBRAZAS, Algirdas. ĪUozas Gruodis; ocherk zhizni i tvorchestva. Leningrad, Muzyka, Leningradskoe otd-nie, 1964. 63 p. ports. MH;WU.

3846. ANTANAS BUDRIŪNAS, straipsniai, amžininkų atsiminimai. [A.Budriūnas, his life and works. Sudarė ir parengė S. Yla]. Vilnius, Vaga, 1974. 271 p., [9] leaves of plates. ML423.B83A8 DLC; PU.

3847. BACEVIČIUS, V[ytautas]. La musique Lithuanienne. In Menestrel (Paris), Année 91, 1929, p.353-354. *MA-Music Division--NN.

3848. BAGDANSKIS, Jonas. The Lithuanian musical scene. [Translated from the Lithuanian by Olimija Armalytė]. Vilnius, Mintis, 1974. 119 p. ML309.L5B3 PU; DLC.

3849. BUDRECKAS, Ladas. Juozo Naujalio muzikinė veikla Lietuvoje. [Juozas Naujalis and his life as a musician in Lithuania]. In Aidai (Brooklyn, N.Y.), 1973, no.8, p.356-365. See serials consulted.

3850. GAUDRIMAS, Juozas. Balys Dvarionas. Moskva, Sovetslǐí kompozitor, 1960. 29 p. ports. ML410.D98G4 DLC; CtY; FMU; IU; NIC.

3851. JUODPUSIS, Vaclovas. Juozas Pakalnis. Vilnius, Vaga, 1972. 75 p. illus., music, 8 leaves of illus. ML410.P143J8 DLC.

3852. KAROSAS, Juozas. Garsų keliais; dainavimo metodikos, muzikos istorijos, muzikos formų ir instrumentų bruožai. [A sketch of singing methods, the history of music, etc.] Kaunas, 1936. 120 p. illus. Li-

thuanian misic on p. 87-92. 780K ICCC.

3853. KAṬKUS, Donatas. Lietuvos kvartetas. [Lithuanian quartet]. Vilnius, Vaga, 1971. 126 p. ML1157.L5K3 PU; DLC; MH.

3854. LANDSBERGIS, Vytautas. Sonata vesny; tvorchestvo M.K. Chǐurlenisa. Leningrad, Muzyka, 1971. 326 p. illus., music, plates(part.col), ports. At head of title: V. Landsbergis. Translation of Pavasario sonata. Bibliography of M.K. Čiurlionis works: p. 292-[313]. ML410.C6L48 DLC; CaOTU; KU.

3855. --- Tvorchestvo Chǐurlenisa; Sonata vesny. Izd. 2-e, dop. Leningrad, Muzyka, Leningr. otd-nie, 1975. 279 p.,[20] leaves of plates. illus. Bibliography of M.K. Čiurlionis works: p. 256-[275]. Discography: p. 276-277. Bibliography: p. 277-279. ML410.C6L48 1975 DLC.

3856. MATULAITYTĖ, Aldona. Konstantinas Galkauskas. Vilnius, Vaga, 1975. 117 p. ML410.G155M3 PU.

3857. NAKAS, Vytautas. Gražina: the first Lithuanian national opera. Some aspects of Jurgis Karnavičius' life and analysis of the libreto by Kazys Inčiūra. At head of title: Vytas Nakas. In Lituanus (Chicago, Ill.), v.21, no.1, 1975, p.45-62. See serials consulted.

3858. --- Muzikinės ir dramatinės eigos vystymasis Jurgio Karnavičiaus "Gražinos" operoje. Musical and dramatic development in Jurgis Karnavičius opera "Gražina". In Institute of Lithuanian Studies. Lituanistikos instituto 1973 metų suvažiavimo darbai. Chicago, Ill., 1975. p.221-225. Summary in English. DK511.L2I63 1975 CaAEU; PU.

3859. NARBUTIENĖ, Ona. Eduardas Bal'sis; ocherk tvorchestva. Leningrad, Muzyka, Leningr. otd-nie,1975. 79 p. illus. ML410.B19N4 DLC.

3860. --- Eduardas Balsys; kūrybos apybraiža. [Creative works of Eduardas Balsys]. Vilnius, Vaga, 1971. 83 p. ML410.B185N3 PU; MH.

3861. --- Juozas Indra. Vilnius, Lietuvos TSR Teatro draugija, 1975. 117 p. ML420.I57N3 PU.

3862.--Juozas Naujalis; straipsniai, laiškai, dokumentai, amžininkų atsiminimai, etc. [Juozas Naujalis...]. Sustatė Ona Narbutienė. Vilnius, Vaga, 1968. 333 p. illus., port.,

music. Bibliography: p. 318-[324].
ML410.N287N4 DLC; CtY; ICLJF;OKentU.

3863. PETRAUSKAS, Mikas. Straipsniai, laiškai, amžininkų atsiminimai.
[Sudarė ir paaiškinimus parašė Jūratė Burokaitė]. Vilnius, Vaga, 1976.
341 p. [Articles, letters and recollections of Mikas Petrauskas contemporaries]. ML410.P45A3 PU.

3864. PRESSE, Arkadius. La musique Lithuanienne. In Courrier musical et théatral (Paris), Année 30,
1928, p. 28, 70 and 102.
*MA--NN(Music Collection); also
ML5.C71 DLC(1-[4], 9-[16], 24-34);
CaQMM(32-36); ICN(7-16, 27-37); MB(
[7]-[9], 12); NN([4,7-16,18-25,27]-
[36]; NRU(23-[26-27]-37).

3865. ŠIMKUS, Stasys. Straipsniai, dokumentai, laiškai. Amžininkų
atsiminimai. [Essays, documents,letters and recollections of S.Šimkus
contemporaries]. [Sudarė ir paaiškinimus parašė D. Palionytė]. Vilnius,
Mintis, 1967. 494 p.
ML410.S58A3 PU.

3866. ŠIMUTIS, Leonardas Juozapas.
Lithuanian music and the characteristics of the Lithuanian folk songs.
Chicago, Ill., 1949. Thesis(M.A.)--
De Paul University, Chicago, Ill.,
1949. ICD.

3867. --- Lietuvių musikologija.
Lithuanian musicology. In Institute of Lithuanian Studies. Lituanistikos instituto 1973 metų suvažiavimo darbai. Chicago, Ill., 1975.
p.227-233. DK511.L2I63 1975
CaAEU; PU.

3868. TAMULYTĖ, Loreta. Vytautas
Klova. Vilnius, Vaga, 1973. 63 p.,
5 leaves of plates. illus.
ML410.K54T3 PU; DLC.

3869. TAURAGIS, Adeodatas. Litauische Musik; Gestern und Heute. [
Deutsche Übersetzung von I. Vladimirovienė]. Vilnius, Gintaras, 1972.
230 p. illus., music, photos. Discography: p. 223-[231]. Bibliography: p. 215-[222]. NcU.

3870. --- Lithuanian music; past
and present. [Translated by M. Ginsburgas and N. Kameneckaitė]. Vilnius,
Gintaras, 1971. 223 p.
ML309.L5T35 PU.

3871. ŽILEVIČIUS, Juozas. The
Juozas Žilevičius Library of Lithuanian musicology. Translated by
Leonardas J. Šimutis. [Chicago, Ill.,
J. Žilevičius Library of Lithuanian
Musicology, 1973. 25 p.

E184.L7Z51 PU; CaAEU.

3872. --- Lietuvis vargonininkas
išeivijoje. Brooklyn, N.Y., Vargonininkų-muzikų sąjunga, 1971. 304
p. illus. Summary in English: The
Lithuanian organist in exile].
ML27.U5A44 DLC.

XIII.7.b. SCORES AND MUSIC

3873. BACEVIČIUS, Vytautas. Dvi
groteskos. Deux grotesques. Zwei
Grotesken. Op.20... Wien, Universal-Edition,[c1938]. 19 p. Publ.
pl. no. 10971. For piano. "Herausgegeben von Litauischen Staatskonservatorium" *MYD--NN(Music Coll.)

3874. --- Pirmas žodis. Premier
mot. Das erste Wort. Op.18... Wien,
Universal-Edition, [c1938]. 18 p.
Publ. pl. no. U.E. 10970. For piano. "Herausgegeben von Litauischen
Staatskonservatorium"
*MYD--NN(Music coll.)

3875. BUDRIŪNAS, Bronius. Sidabrinė diena. Libretto. Lithuanian].
Sidabrinė diena; trijų veiksmų operetė. [Chicago, Ill.], Lietuvių meno ansamblis Dainava, [1972]. 155 p.
At head of title: Anatolijus Kairys.
Music by B. Budriūnas; words by Anatolijus Kairys. ML50.B943S5 1972
DLC; OKentU; PU.

3876. ČIURLIONIS, Mikalojus Konstantinas. Kūriniai fortepijonui.
[Piano works]. Parengė ir redagavo
Jadvyga Čiurlionytė. 2.papildytas
leidimas. Vilnius, Vaga, 1975. 262
p. port. CaOTU.

3877. --- [In the fores. Phonodisc]. Miške; simfoninė poema. Jūra; simfoninė poema, redakcija E.
Balsio. [In the forest. The sea].
Moskva, Melodiîa, [196-?]. Matrix
no. 013977-013978. 2 s. 12 in.
33 1/3 rpm. Maskvos Valst. filharmonijos simfoninis orkestras, B.Dvarionas conductor. M1002 DLC.

3878. --- Poėma "More", dlîa
bol'shogo simfonicheskogo orkestra s
organom. [Red. Ė. Bal'sis]. Leningrad, Muzyka,[Leningradskoe otd-nie],
1965. score (176 p.)
M1002.C533J9 DLC.

3879. --- [PRELIUDAI. Organ]. Preliudai ir fugos. Vilnius, Valstybinė grožinės literatūros leidykla,
1959. 84 p Contains 20 preludes
for organ; 9 canons; 17 fuges, and
4 preludes for piano. M7.C57P7 DLC.

3880. --- [Preludes, piano. Selections. Phonodisc.] Preliudii dlia f-no. Moskva, Melodiia, [196-.]. Matrix no. 012339-012340. 2 s. 12 in. 33 1/3 rpm. microgroove. At head of title: M. Chiurlenis. V.Landsbergis, piano. M1002.C33 DLC.

3881. --- [In the forest] V lesu; simfonicheskaia poėma. Miške. [Red. T. Makachinasa]. Leningrad, Muzyka, Leningradskoe otd-nie, 1975. score (63) p.) M1002.C33I5 DLC; CaOTU. At head of title: M.K. Chiurlenis.

3882. DVARIONAS, Balys. [Pieces, piano]. 12[i.e. Dvylika] pjesių fortepijonui. Vilnius, Vaga, 1971. 34 p. M25.D888P4 CaOTU.

3883. GRUODIS, Juozas. Rytiečių šokis. Danse orientale. Orientalischer Tanz. Wien, Im Kommissionverlag der Universal-Edition, [cl938]. 4 p. Publ. pl. no. 10957. For piano. "Herausgegeben von litauischen Staatskonservatorium" *MYD---NN(Music Coll.).

3884. JAKUBĖNAS, Vl[adas]. [Rhapsody, piano, no.1]. Rapsodija no.1. Kaunas, J. Petronis, cl944. 7 p. M25.J348R4 MB.

3885. JUZELIŪNAS, Julius. Afrikanskie ėskizy, dlia simfonicheskogo orkestra. Leningrad, Sovetskii kompozitor, 1962. score (163 p.). At head of title: IUlius IUzeliunas. For orchestra. M1045.J98A3 DLC.

3886. --- [Concerto, organ solo] Kontsert dlia organa. Koncertas vargonams. Leningrad, Muzyka, Leningr. otd-nie, 1974. 43 p. At head of title: IUlius IUzeliunas. M9.J89K6 DLC; CaOTU.

3887. --- [Quartet, strings, no.3] Styginis kvartetas nr.3. String quartet no.3. Vilnius, Vaga, 1972.[11] p. miniature score (12-46 p.). Pref. by J. Antanavičius in Lithuanian, English and Russian. M452.J985 no.3 DLC.

3888. KAČINSKAS, Jeronimas. Missa in honorem immaculati cordis Beatae Mariae Virginis, occasione 700 anniversarii Baptismi Mindaugi Regis Lituaniae, for mixed choir and soprano, alto, tenor and bass solos with organ acc. and 7 brass instruments (ad libitum). Toledo, Ohio, Gregorian Institute of America,cl952. score (69 p.) Brown Music Collection M2010.K33I5 1952 MB.

3889. KANKLĖS. Mėnesiniai leidiniai. [The Harp. Monthly. no.1-56]

Metai 1-5; 1917-1921. South Boston, Mass., [Lietuvių muzikos konservatorija, 1917-1921. 56 nos. in 1 v. Edited by Mikas Petrauskas, each number consisting of one of his compositions. The first twenty of these are catalogued separately. M2898 MB.

3890. PETRAUSKAS, Mikas. Apvesdinkite ir mane; trijų veiksmų operetė. Pagal A.N. Ostrovskio žodžius sulietuvino ir leiles parašė M. Rastenis. Kaunas, Švytyrys, 1921. Vocal score (79 p.). Comic opera, Lithuanian words. *MS--NN.

3891. --- Eglė, žalčių karalienė. Šešių aktų opera. Žodžius, libretto parašė Mikas Petrauskas, panaudodamas veikalą tuo pat vardu Žalčių karalienė Aleksandro Fromo ir liaudies folkloru. [Vokale partitura]. Išleido Gabijos Fondas. [Eglė, Queen of the Snakes. An opera in six acts. Libretto and music by Mikas Petrauskas... Vocal score. Published by the Lithuanian music and drama society Gabija]. South Boston, Mass., 1924. [5], 240 p. M1503.P496E3 PU; MB.

3892. --- Vieno veiksmo fantastiška opera. A one-act fantastic opera "Girių karalius". The King of the forest. So.Boston, Mass., The Lithuanian Conservatory of Music, 1919. Vocal score (78 p.). L8127 MB.

3893. RAČIŪNAS, Antanas. [Sonata, 2 pianos]. Sonata dlia dvukh fortepiano. Sonata dviem fortepijonams. Leningrad, Sov. kompozitor, 1972. score (39 p.) Kontsertnyi repertuar pianista. At head of title: A. Rachiunas. CaOTU.

3894. --- [Sonatina, violin & piano]. Sonatina dlia skripki i fortepiano. Leningrad, Sovetskii kompozitor, 1963. score (28 p.) and part. At head of title: A. Rachiunas. M219.R123 DLC.

3895. --- [Symphony, no.6. Phonodisc]. Simfoniia no.6. Moskva, Melodiia, [196-.]. Matrix no.020728. 1 s. 12 in. 33 1/3 rpm. With Žigaitis, R.D. Jaunystė; Gobulskis, Benjaminas. Concerto-fantasy. LTSR Valst. filharmonijos simfoninis orkestras: J. Domarkas, conductor. M1004 DLC.

3896. --- Simfoniia no.7. [Symphony, no.7]; dlia simfonicheskogo orkestra. Leningrad, Muzyka, 1975. Miniature score (159 p.). At head of title: A. Rachiunas. M1001.R135 no.7 DLC.

3897. --- [Works, violoncello & piano. Selections. Phonodisc]. Tanets, Kolybel'naia, Utro. Vses. studiia gramzapisi. [196-.]. Matrix no. 010593. 2 s. 12 in. 33 1/3 rpm. microgroove. At head of title: A. Rachiūnas. M. Shederovas, violoncello; R. Shederova, piano. With: Karnavičius, Jurgis. Poėma, violoncello & piano. Gaīzhauskas, IUrgis. Quartet, strings, no.2. DLC.

3898. SCARMOLIN, A. Louis. Lithuanian rhapsody, no.1. Op.197. Cleveland, Ohio, Ludwig music publ., 1945. 10 p. Condensed score, band. *MV--NN(Music Coll.).

3899. SĄSIUVINYS LIETUVIŠKOS DAInos, no.4,5. [Collection of Lithuanian songs]. So.Boston, Mass., Lietuvių muzikos konservatorija, 1918-1919. 2 parts. Edited by Mikas Petrauskas; music by him, words by various writers. Partial contents.--sąs.4. Mišriems balsams (kvartetams arba chorams). [For mixed voices (quartets or choruses)].--sąs.5. Dviem balsam. [For two voices (for schools)]. 4040a.237 MB.

3900. ŠIMKUS, Stasys. Plaukia sau laivelis. [Sudarė K. Kaveckas]. Vilnius, Vaga, [196-.]. score. M1766.L4S5 CaOTU.

XIII.7.c. HARMONIZED FOLKSONGS AND HYMNS

3901. KOVOTOJŲ GIESMĖS. 2.laida. [The songs of warriors...]. Surinktos revoliucijonierių mintis. Philadelphia, Pa., Spauda "Kovos",1914. [Xerox copy, 1975]. 45 p. PG8715.K65 PU.

3902. LITUANICA, Lietuvių skautų tuntas, Chicago. 101 [i.e. Šimtas viena] daina. [One hundred and one songs]. Chicago, Ill., 1955. 122 p. illus. M1766.L4L5 DLC.

3903. REVOLIUCIJOS GIESMĖS; prirengtos vyrų chorams ant dviejų, trijų ir keturių balsų. [Revolutionary songs; for male choirs...]. So. Boston, Mass., Spauda ir laida "Keleivio", 1908. [Xerox copy, 1976] [16] p. PG8715.R43 1908a PU.

3904. SKRISK DAINUŽE; dainynas. [Song book]. Vilnius, Valstybinė grožinės literatūros leidykla, 1958. 128 p. music with text. L784LO ICLJF.

XIII.8. ART

XIII.8.a. GENERAL WORKS

3905. ACCORATO APELLO DEI GIOVANI artisti lituani per la salvaguardia del patrimonio culturale nazionale (M.K. Čiurlionis). In Elta Press(Roma), 1972, no.12, p.8-13. See serials consulted.

3906. CHERVONNAIA, Svetlana Mikhĭlovna. Lietuvių dailės ryšiai. [Connections of Lithuanian art]. Iš rusų kalbos vertė Laima Patiubavičienė. Vilnius, Vaga, 1977. 235 p. At head of title: Svetlana Červonaja. N6995.L5C45 PU.

3907. ESTREICHER, Karol. Grobowiec Władysława Jagiełły. Kraków, 1953. 45 p. NA6178.E73 PU.

3908. JUCEVIČIUS, Feliksas. Menas spalvų ir formų žaisme. [Art of colour and form]. [Putnam, Conn., Immaculata spaustuvė, 1975. 237 p. Bibliography: p. 231-235. N7435.J8 PU; DLC.

3909. KATO, Ichiro. Mikalojus Konstantinas Čiurlionis, the Lithuanian composer and painter, and the correlation between pictorial and musical composition. In Journal of Baltic Studies (Brooklyn, N.Y.), no.1, v.7, 1976, p.40-44. See serials consulted.

3910. LIETUVIS DAILININKAS IŠEIVIjoje. [Lithuanian artist in exile]. Redagavo Algimantas Kezys. Chicago, Ill., Lietuviai Jėzuitai ir Jaunimo Centras, 1974. 176 p. TR680.L54 PU.

3911. LIETUVIŲ DAILĖS DRAUGIJA. 1926 metų Lietuvos dailininkų pavasario paroda. Kovo 27d.-balandžio 12 d., Kaunas. [Spring exhibition of the works of Lithuanian artists,1926] Kaunas, 1926. 947.52L6226 PU.

3912. LIETUVOS TSR DAILĖ. [The art of Soviet Lithuania. Įžanginio straipsnio autoriai ir albumo sudarytojai: J. Umbrasas, L. Jasiulis. Leningradas, Aurora, 1972]. 32,[32] p., 71 leaves of illus. (Piat'desiat let SSSR). Lithuanian, English and Russian. N6995.L5L46 DLC; CaOTP;CaBVaU CLU; CSt; IaAS; IU; MH; NjR; OKentU; OrU; PU; WU.

3913. MIKĖNAITĖ, A. Litovskoe narodnoe iskusstvo. Vil'nĭus, Khudozh. muzeĭ Litovskoĭ SSR, 1968. 13 p. At head of title: A. Mikenaĭtė]. NK976.L5M5 DLC.

3914. NEW YORK. RIVERSIDE MUSEUM. Lithuanian international art exhibition. 1st- 1958- . New York,N.Y. illus. N6995.L5N4 DLC; MH.

3915. OBST, Jan. Sztuka litewska. Wilno, Księgarnia Stowarz. Nauczycielstwa Polskiego, [n.d.]. 11 p. illus. Reprint from "Litwa i Ruś" 750.0 ICBM.

3916. RANNIT, Aleksis. In search of a philosophical background of M. K. Čiurlionis. In Lituanus (Chicago, Ill.), no.2, v.21, 1975, p.5-14. See serials consulted.

3917. --- Time in M.K. Čiurlionis. In Journal of Baltic Studies (Brooklyn, N.Y.), no.1, v.7, 1976, p.31-39. See serials consulted.

3918. REKLAITIS, Povilas Viktoras. Keistenybės Lietuvos ikonografijos senovėje. [Peculiarities in the early Lithuanian iconography]. In Aidai (Brooklyn,N.Y.), no.8, 1973, p.351-355. See serials consulted.

3919. RESPUBLIKINĖ DAILĖS PARODA LIETUVOS TSR 20-mečiui PAMINĖTI,1960. Katalog. [Katalog sostavili P. Gudinas i S. Ÿakshtas. Red. S. Ÿakshtas] Vil'niûs, Vil'niûsskiĭ gos. khudozh. muzeĭ, 1960. 285 p. 74 illus. At head of title: Ministerstvo kul'tury Litovskoĭ SSR, Soĭuz. khudozhnikov Litovskoĭ SSR, Vil'niûsskiĭ gosudarstvennyĭ khudozhestvennyĭ muzeĭ. Includes bio-bibliographical notices of Lithuanian artists. ICIU.

3920. SAVICKAS, Augustinas. Bespokoĭnoe puteshetvie. Avtorizovannyĭ perevod s litovskogo D. Kyĭv. Moskva, Sov. Khudozhnik, 1977. 324 p. illus. ND699.S34A42 DLC.

3921. --- Peisažas lietuvių tapyboje. [Landscape painting in Lithuania]. Vilnius,[s.n.], 1965. 326 p. ND1360.S3 PU; DLC; MH.

3922. VIESULAS, Romas. Lietuvio dailininko problema gyvenant svetur. Ethnic problems of the Lithuanian artist living abroad. In Institute of Lithuanian Studies. Lituanistikos instituto 1973 metų suvažiavimo darbai. Chicago, Ill., 1975. p.213-219. Summary in English. DK511.L2I63 1975 CaAEU; PU.

3923. --- Why the world does not know Čiurlionis. In Lituanus(Chicago, Ill.), no.2, v.21, 1975, p.39-50. See serials consulted.

XIII.8.b. PAINTING

3924. ADOMAS GALDIKAS TAPYBOS PAroda; katalogas. [The catalogue of the exhibition of Adomas Galdikas works]. Kaunas, Valst. M.K.Čiurlionio dailės muziejus, 1969. 1 v. (unpaged). illus. OKentU.

3925. ADOMONIS, Tadas. Vincas Grybas. [V.Grybas his life and works]. [Vilnius], Valstybinė politinės ir mokslinės literatūros leidykla, 1959. 150 p. NB699.G75A5 PU.

3926. BAGDONAS, Juozas. Juozas Bagdonas. [J. Bagdonas his life and works]. [Paruošė ir suredagavo Paulius Jurkus]. New York,N.Y., Lietuvių bendruomenės Vaižganto Kultūros klubas New Yorke, 1972. 80 p. N6999.B33J87 DLC; PU; OKentU.

3927. BAL'CHIÛNENE, Galina Iosifovna. M.K. Chiurlenis; k 100-letiÛu so dnÏa rozhdeniÏa. Moskva, Znanie, 1975. 20 p.,[8] leaves of plates. illus. (Novoe v zhizni, nauke, tekhnike. SeriÏa iskustvo, 5). NX6.N6 1975 no.5 DLC.

3928. BUDRYS, Stasys. PÏatras Rimsha. [P. Rimša his life and works] Moskva, Sovetskiĭ Khudozhnik, 1961. 61 p. port., illus. MH.

3929. CHIÛRLENIS. [Perevod s litovskogo]. Moskva, Iskusstvo, 1971. 111 p. illus. ND699.C6C45 PU; CtY; IaU; MoU; NjP; TxU.

3930. ČIURLIONIS, Mikalojus Konstantinas. M.K. Čiurlionis. M.K.Chiurlenis. 32 reprodukcijos. [4.leidimas. Redakcinė komisija: V. Čiurlionytė-Karužienė et al.]. Vilnius, Vaga, 1970. xxxiii p., 32 leaves of plates. Text by Antanas Venclova. Lithuanian English, French, German and Russian. fND699.C6V4 1970 OKentU.

3931. --- Mikalojus Konstantinas Čiurlionis; reprodukcijos. Reproduktsiĭ. Reproductions. Abbildungen. Vilnius, Vaga, 1976. 31 p., and 35 col. reproductions 40 x 30 cm. In Lithuanian, Russian, English, French, and German. ND1978.C58C58 DLC.

3932. ČIURLIONIS, Mikalojus Konstantinas. Pasaulio sutvėrimas. [Creation of the world]. Text by Vytautas Landsbergis. Vilnius, Vaga,1971. 10 p., 13 col. plates. ND1978.C58A55 DLC; PU.

3933. --- Zodiako ženklai. [M.K. Čiurlionis and his Signs of the Zodiac. Text by V. Landsbergis. Ed. by J. Grigienė]. Vilnius, Vaga, 1967. 19 p., 12 col. plates. In Lithuanian Russian, English, French, and German.

3934. --- --- Dvylika M.K. Čiurlionies paveikslų "Zodiako ženklai". Igno Šlapelio tekstas. [M.K.Čiurlionis and his Signs of Zodiac]. [5] p., 12 mounted plates. port.Kaunas,1927. A759.75C499 PU.

3935. ČIURLIONIUI 100. [Čiurlionis, 100th anniversary of his birth]. Sudarė Jonas Bruveris. Vilnius, Vaga, 1977. 348 p. ND699.C6C49 PU.

3936. GALDIKAS, Adomas. Adomas Galdikas; a color odyssey by Charlotte Willard with an essay by Waldemar George. New York, N.Y., October House, c1973. 171 p. illus. ND699.G32W54 DLC.

3937. --- Adomas Galdikas. Juozas Girnius... [et al.]. So. Boston, Mass., Lietuvių enciklopedijos leidykla, 1975. 191 p. illus. ND699.G32G57 DLC.

3938. GEORGE, Waldemar. Galdikas. Paris, Éditions Arts et Lettres, [1931]. 1 v. (unpaged) mostly illus. (Les paintres contemporains). 947.52G133yG PU; ICLJF.

3939. GUDYNAS, Pranas. Vytautas Mackevičius. Vilnius, Vaga, 1971. 111 p. illus. Summary in Russian, English and German. ND699.M22G78 DLC; MH; NNC.

3940. JANKUS, Jurgis. Alfonso Dargio dailės kūryba. [The creative art of A. Dargis]. In Aidai (Brooklyn, N.Y.), no.6, 1973, p.260-264. See serials consulted.

3941. JAUTOKAITĖ, Saulė. The art of Pranas Gailius. In Lituanus (Chicago, Ill.), no.3, v.20, 1974, p.37-39. See serials consulted.

3942. JOKUBONIS, Gediminas. Gediminas Jokubonis. [Teksto autorius Pranas Gudynas]. Vilnius,Vaga,1976. 8 p.,[16] leaves of plates. NB699.J6G8 PU.

3943. JUKONEN, Hennes. M.K. Čiurlionis, lietualainen taidemaalari. [M.K. Čiurlionis a Lithuanian painter] [Helsinki], 1926. 20 p. Offprint from Eripainos Juosimiehesta. 947.52C497yJ PU.

3944. KAROSAS, Juozas. Nueitas kelias; atsiminimai. [The covered distance; recollections]. Vilnius, Vaga, 302 p. ML410.K27A3 PU.

3945. KORSAKAITĖ, Ingrida. Antanas Gudaitis; piešiniai. [Paintings of A. Gudaitis]. Vilnius, Vaga,1973. 108 p. NC269.G82K67 PU; DLC; InU; IU; MH; OKentU.

3946. LANDSBERGIS, Vytautas. Čiurlionio dailė. [Art of Čiurlionis] Vilnius, Vaga, 1976. 397 p.,[32] leaves of plates. illus. Bibliography of M.K.Čiurlionis works: p. 286-[375]. ML410.C6L36 DLC.

3947. LIETUVOS TAPYBA. [Lithuanian painting. Sudarė Pranas Gudynas] Vilnius, Vaga, 1976. 394 p. (chiefly col. illus.). In Lithuanian, Russian, English, and German.. ND695.L5L52 PU.

3948. ŁUBIEŃSKA, Dolores. Życie i śmierć artysty. Warszawa, Kultura, 1975. 3 leaves. illus. Bound with Chervonnaia, S. Malarskie sonaty. Warszawa, 1975. ND699.C6L92 1975 CaAEU.

3949. NASVYTIS, Mindaugas. Dailininko Viktoro Vizgirdos meninis kelias. [V. Vizgirda and his creative art]. In Aidai(Brooklyn, N.Y.), no. 9, 1972, p.379-383. See serials consulted.

3950. PETRULIS, Algirdas. Algirdas Petrulis; reprodukcijos. [Text by Pranas Gudynas]. Vilnius, Vaga, 1972. 15 p., 16 col.plates. DK699.P45G8 PU.

3951. PUZINAS, Paul. Puzinas. [By Frederic Whitaker, introd. by A. Puzinas] New York, N.Y., Austra Publications, 1975. [72] p. (chiefly col. illus. ND699.P89W45 DLC.

3952. ROZINER, Feliks Iakovlevich. Gimn solntsu [Chiulėnis]; iskusstvodecheskaia povest'. [Moskva, Molodaia gvardiia, 1974]. 188 p. ND699.C5R6 PU.

3953. SAVICKAS, Augustinas. Augustinas Savickas; reprodukcijos. Vilnius, Vaga, 1969. 15 p. plates. In Lithuanian, English, French, German, and Russian. OKentU.

3954. SKOLEVIČIENĖ, Jovita and Jasiulis, Leonas. Napoleonas Petrulis. Vilnius, Vaga, 1975. 103 p. illus. Summary in English and Russian. NB699.P45S5 PU; DLC.

3955. TAPYBA. [Painting]. [Sudarė B. Uogintas] Vilnius, Vaga, 1971. 118 p. (chiefly illus.). In Lithuanian, English, French, German, and Russian. ND695.L5T31 PU; DLC.

3956. TAPYBA. [Painting]. [Leidini parengė A. Stasiulevičius]. Vilnius, Vaga, 1976. 126 p. ND695.L5T33 PU.

3957. VAITKŪNAS, Gytis. Mikalojus Konstantinas Čiurlionis. [Übersetzung aus dem litauischen Manuskript Edmund Danner. Aufnahmen Klaus G. Beyer. Dresden, Verlag de Kunst, [1975]. 278 p. ND699.C6V42 PU; DLC

3958. VAŠTOKAS, Joan M. M.K.Čiurlionis; abstraction and the visionary experience. In Lituanus(Chicago, Ill.), no.2, v.21, 1975, p.15-38. See serials consulted.

3959. WEIDLÉ, Wladimir. Un peintre-musicien, Nicolas Tchourlionis. In Le Mois (Paris), v.9, no.100,1939, p.177-185. AP20.M68 v.9 DLC; see also serials consulted.

XIII.8.c. SCULPTURE, GRAPHIC ART,
WOOD CARVING AND
APPLIED ART

3960. BUDRYS, Stasys. Bronius Vyšniauskas. [Biography of B. Vyšniauskas]. Vilnius, Vaga, 1969. [29] p. illus. (Šiuolaikiniai lietuvių dailininkai) Summary in English and Russian. NB699.V9B8 DLC;PU.

3961. BULIS, Jonas. Karikatūros. [Caricatures]. Vilnius, Valstybinė grožinės literatūros leidykla,1956. 138 p. (chiefly illus.), port. At head of title: Lumbis, [pseud.]. NC1579.B8A5 OKentU.

3962. GALDIKAS, Valerijonas. Valerijono Galdiko linoraižiniai Maironio "Pavasario balsams". [V. Galdikas. Linocuts for the book of poems by Maironis]. Vilnius, Vaga, 1970. [13] p. of illus. CtY.

3963. GEDMINAS, Antanas and Galkus, Juozas. Lietuvos plakatas. [Albumas. Lithuanian posters; album] Vilnius, Mintis, 1971. 176 p. illus. Summaries in English and Russian. NC1807.L5G4 DLC; DSI;MB; MH; NNC; OKentU; PU.

3964. GYVENIMO ŽINGSNIAI; jubiliejinė grafika. [...Jubilee of the graphic art]. Vilnius, Vaga, 1967. [8] p. and 39 plates. NE676.L5G9 PU.

3965. KEZYS, Algimantas. Form and content. Photos by Algimantas Kezys. Chicago, Ill., Morkūnas,1972. xii p., 64 leaves of photographs.

"Simultaneously published in Lithuanian under the title "Foto Kompozicijos" TR650.K43 1972 CaAEU; DLC.

3966. KLOVA, Boleslovas. Lietuvių monumentalioji dekoratyvinė tapyba; freska, grafitas mozaika. [Lithuanian decorative art...]. Vilnius, Vaga, 1975. ND2768.L77K56 PU.

3967. KORSAKAITĖ, Ingrida. Al'bina Makunaite. Moskva, Sov. Khudozhnik, 1972. 119 p. illus. NE1156.5.M34K67 DLC; CU-SB; IU; MB; MU; NjP; WU.

3968. --- Arūnas Tarabilda. Vilnius, Vaga, 1971. 71 p. illus.,port. Summaries in English and Russian. MB; MH; NNC.

3969. KULESHOVA, Vera Nikolaevna. Stasis Ushinskas. Moskva, Sovetskiĭ, khudozhnik, 1973. 158 p. illus. ND699.U75K8 PU; DLC; CU; NjP; PPT.

3970. KUZMINSKIS, Jonas. Ekslibrisai. [Ex Libris. Sudarė ir apipavidalino A. Gediminas]. Vilnius, Vaga, 1976. 63 p. In Lithuanian, English and Russian. NE678.K84G4 PU.

3971. LIETUVIŲ FOTOGRAFŲ IŠEIVIJOje paroda 1972. [Lithuanian photographers' exhibition in exile. Redagavo Algimantas Kezys]. Chicago, Ill., Lietuvių Foto Archyvas, 1972]. 80 p. (chiefly illus.). TR654.L54 PU.

3972. LIETUVIŲ FOTOGRAFŲ IŠEIVIJOje paroda 1973. [Lithuanian photographers' exhibition in exile, 1973. Redagavo Algimantas Kezys]. Chicago, Ill., Lietuvių Foto Archyvas. 1974. 1o3 p. (Chiefly illus.) TR654.L54 1973 PU.

3973. LIETUVIŲ GRAFIKA, 1968,1969, 1970. [Lithuanian graphic art, 1968-1970. Leidinį parengė Rimtautas Gibavičius]. Vilnius, Vaga, 1971. 157 p. (chiefly illus.), port. In Lithuanian, English and Russian. NE676.L5L54 OKentU; CU; DLC; IU;ICIU; MH; MiU; MnU; MdBJ; NIC; PU; WU; WaU.

3974. LIETUVIŲ TARYBINĖ DAILĖ; skulptura. [Soviet Lithuanian art; sculpture. Vilnius], Valstybinė politinės ir mokslinės literatūros leidykla, 1961. xxxii p., 143 plates. In Lithuanian and Russian. MiEM.

3975. LIETUVOS FOTOGRAFIJOS MENO paroda. Katalogas; [Lietuva-69. Photography exhibition in Lithuania,1969; a catalogue. Comp. by S. Krivickas]. Vilnius, Vaga, 1969. 15 p., 144 plates. In Lithuanian, English, German and Russian. At head of title: Lietuvos draugystės ir kultūrinių ryšių su užsienio šalimis draugija. TR6.L5 OKentU.

3976. PAKELIŪNAS, Algirdas. Dailininko Algirdo Pakeliūno grafikos parodos katalogas. [Exhibition catalogue of A. Pakeliūnas graphic works. Paruošė Povilas Valaika; ats. redaktorius Jonas Baltušis] Kaunas LTSR Dailininkų s-gos, Kauno skyrius,1976. [28] p. illus. At head of title: Kauno viešoji biblioteka. NE678.P25V35 DLC.

3977. --- Kauno senamiestis. [The old section of the City of Kaunas. Medžio raižiniai. Teksto autorė Marija Matušakaitė. Vilnius, Vaga, 1973]. [4] p., 12 plates. NE678.P35K3 PU.

3978. PLIKIONYTĖ, Joana. Joanos Plikionytės iliustracijos A. Churgino poezijos rinkiniui "Ir tavo širdy" [Illustrations of J. Plikionytė for a selected poems "In your heart too" by A. Churginas]. Vilnius, Vaga, 1972.]12] p. illus. Added title page: Aleksys Churginas. Ir tavo širdy. CtY.

3979. REKLAITIS, Povilas Viktoras. Die Stadtansichten Alt Litauens in der Graphik des 16 bis 19 Jahrhunderts. Lüneburg, Ger., Nordostdeutsches Kulturwerk, 1972. 60,36 p. illus. DK511.L2R4 DLC; CU-SB; GU; InNd; MiDW; OKentU; ViU; WU.

3980. ROZINAS, S. Vilnius; linoleumo raižiniai. [Vilnius; linoleum cuts]. Moskva, Moskovskoe otd-nie khudozh. fonda SSSR, 1957. 3 p., 10 col.plates (in portfolio). NE678.R6A56 DLC; IU; NN.

3981. SATYRA IR JUMORAS 1961;dailės paroda. [Satire and humor 1961; art exhibition. Spaudai paruošė: P. Gudynas ir S. Jakštas]. Vilnius,Vilniaus valstybinis dailės muziejus, 1961. 45 p. illus., ports. (Juokas --dalykas rimtas). NC1576.S2 DLC.

3982. SKULPTŪRA. [Sculpture. Sudarė Vladas Vildžiūnas. Redakcinė komisija: Alfonsas Ambraziūnas, Antanas Gedminas, Gediminas Jokūbonis]. Vilnius, Vaga, 1974. [11] p.,[64] leaves of plates. NB955.L5S61 PU; MH.

3983. TAIKOMOJI--DEKORATYVINĖ dailė. [Applied and decorative art; album of photographs. Edited by Juozas Adomonis]. Vilnius, Vaga, 1969. vii, 119 p. illus. In Lithuanian, English, German, and Russian.

NK976.L5T12 CaAEU; CU-SB; MB; MH; MiU; MdU; OrU; PU; WaU.

3984. TIKHOMIROVA, Marina Aleksandrovna. Litovskoe zoloto. Vil'nius, Vaga, 1973. 53 p. illus. NK6000.T54 PU; CaOTU; DLC; IU; MH; MU; NNC; NjP; PSt.

3985. THE TWELVE RAVENS; a Lithuanian fairy tale. Text by Paulius Jurkus. Wood-cuts by Vaclovas Ratas. Munich, Ger., T.J. Vizgirda, 1949. 29 p. illus. (Lithuania, country and nation, 27). PZ8T92 DLC; CtY; InU; PU.

3986. VAN DER MARCK, Jan. The modulated monochrome of Kazys Varnelis. In Arts Canada (Ottawa, Ont.), 1971, no.160-161, p.34-36. N1.C21 CaAEU; see also serials consulted under title "Canadian Art".

3987. VILNA. UNIVERSITETAS. BIBLIOTEKA. Ekslibrisai Vilniaus Valstybinio V. Kapsuko universiteto Biblioteka. [Book plates in the Vilnius University library]. Vilnius, Vaga, 1970. 46 p. illus. On verso of title page: A. Augaitis. In Lithuanian, English, and Russian. Z994.L28 V5 DLC; CaAEU; CSt; CU; InU; IU;MiU; NIC; RPB.

3988. THE YOUNGER GENERATION OF graphic artists in Lithuania. In Lituanus (Chicago, Ill.), no.2, v.19, 1973, p. 55-66. See serials consulted.

3989. ŽEMAITYTĖ, Zita. Domicelė Tarabildienė. Vilnius, Vaga, 1973. 143 p. illus. N6999.T37Z45 DLC;MB; MH; NNC; OKentU; PU.

3990. ŽILIUS, Vladas. Vlado Žiliaus raižiniai Petro Vaičiūno poetinėms miniatiūroms "Gyvenimo preliudai" Engravings to the poetical miniatures Prelude of Life by P. Vaičiūnas. Vilnius, Vaga, 1969. 16 p. illus. MH.

3991. ŽMUIDZINAVIČIUS, Antanas. Velniai; dailininko Antano Žmuidzinavičiaus kolekcija. [Wood cuts of the devil's images; a collection]. 3.leidimas. Paruošė P. Porutis. Vilnius, Vaga, 1973. 113 p. ill. In Lithuanian, English, German, and Russian. NK550.Z6P85 1973 CaAEU; DLC.

XIII.9. ARCHITECTURE

XIII.9.a. GENERAL STUDIES

3992. BUDREIKA, Eduardas. Arkhitektura Sovetskoĭ Litvy. Leningrad, Stroĭ-izdat, 1971. 111 p. NA1195.L5B8 PU; CaOTU; CU-SB; DLC; IU; MB; MH; MU; MdU; NIC; NjP; ViU; WU.

3993. LIETUVOS PILYS. [Castles of Lithuania. Ats. redaktorius J. Jurginis. Red. G. Gustaitė. Dailininkas K. Katkus. Spalvotos nuotraukos Z. Kazėno. Vilnius, Mintis, 1971.] 304 p. illus. At head of title: Lietuvos TSR Mokslų akademija, Istorijos institutas. DK511.L2L4219 DLC; CaAEU; CtY; CU; ICU; ICIU; InU; IU; MH; NNC; NjP; PU; PPiU; OKentU; WaU.

3994. MAŽOJI ARCHITEKTŪRA. Arkhitektura malykh form. [Sudarė ir parengė K. Čerbulėnas, F. Bielinskis, K. Šešelgis. kn.1-]. Vilnius, Vaga, 1970- . illus. (Lietuvių liaudies menas, t.9, etc.) NA1195.L5M37 PU; ICBM; ICCC; MH; OKentU.

3995. PAEVSKIĬ, Lev. Dostoprimechatel'nosti vilenskago Sv. Troĭtskago monastyrĭa...(na osnovaniĭ pol'skikh istochnikov). Vil'na, [s.n., s.d.]. 947.52P136 PU.

3996. SCHLICHTING, Richard and OSMANN, L. Schlösser und Herrensitze in Litauen. In His Bilder aus Litauen. Kowno, 1917. p.97-116. DK511.L26S34 CSt-H; CaAEU; CSt; NN; NjP; PU.

3997. SCHMID, Bernhard. Litauische Backsteinbauten: Neu Traken und St. Nikolas zu Wilna, die Kirche in Sapyschkis, Deutsche Steinmetzen in Litauen. In Deutsche Kunst und Denkmalpflege (Berlin; Wien), v.20, 1918. See serials consulted.

XIII.9.b. URBAN ARCHITEKTURE

3998. KAIRIŪKŠTYTĖ-JACINIENĖ, Halina and BARŠAUSKAS, Juozas. Pažaislis. [The church of Pažaislis]. Vilnius, Valstybinė politinės ir mokslinės literatūros leidykla, 1960. 82 p. illus. (Lietuvos TSR architektūros paminklai, 1) NA5695.P3K3 OKentU.

3999. KITKAUSKAS, Napalys. Vilnius Cathedral. [Translated from the Lithuanian by Juozas Butkus]. Vilnius, Mintis, 1977. 77 p. NA5697.V48K5 PU.

4000. --- Vil'nĭusskiĭ kafedral'nyĭ sobor. [Perevod s litovskogo

L. Chernoĭ]. Vil'nĭus, Mintis, 1977. 63 p. NA5697.V48K517 PU.

4001. KULPAVIČIUS, Alfredas. Der Barock in den Sakralbauten Litauens. Darmstadt, 1951. Thesis (PhD)--Technische Hochschule, Darmstadt. Ger.DaTH.

4002. REMEIKIS, Tomas. Preliminary results and prospects of controlled urbanization in Lithuania. In Institute of Lithuanian Studies. Lituanistikos instituto suvažiavimo darbai. Chicago, Ill., 1971. p.191-226. DK511.L2I57 1971 DLC; CaAEU; InNd; MiU; NIC; NRU; PU.

4003. RUSSKAĬA VIL'NA; prilozhenie k puteshevstviĭu po sv. miestam russkim. Vil'na, Tip. A.G. Syrkina, 1865. 62p., 5 plates. fold.plan. At head of title: A.N. Murav'ev. Avery Ak5681R91 NNC.

4004. --- [Another edition].Sanktpeterburg, 1864. [2],43 p. Slav 5301.1. MH.

4005. VILNIAUS ARCHITEKTŪROS VYStymosi bruožai. [An outline of the development of the architecture of Vilnius]. In Vilnius; architektūra iki XX amžiaus pradžios. Kaunas,1958. p.7-[20]. In Lithuanian and Russian. NA1197.V5V52 DLC; InU; ICU; IU; MiD; ICLJF; NN.

4006. ZAHORSKI, Władysław. Kościół św. Michała i klasztory panien Bernardynek w Wilnie. In Kwartalnik litewski. Petersburg, 1910. t.4. 947.52Z13 PU; see also serials consulted.

XIII.9.c. RURAL ARCHITEKTURE

4007. GIMBUTAS, Leonidas. Žemės ūkio statyba. Bendroji dalis: Statybos medžiagos ir trobesių dalys. Kaunas, Aukštesniosios technikos mokyklos leidinys, 1929. 436,[10] p. [Rural architecture; materials and parts of the buildings]. NA8200.G54 PU.

4008. JURGINIS, Juozas. Alytaus ekonomijos dvarų pastatai 1649 metais. [Buildings in the district of Alytus in 1649]. Vilnius, LTSRMAII, 1972. 54 p. (Acta historica Lithuanica, 8) At head of title: Lietuvos TSR Mokslų akademijos, Istorijos institutas. Summary in Russian. NA8206.L5J8 PU; CU; DLC; InU; OKentU.

4009. LIETUVIŲ LIAUDIES ARCHITEK-

tūra. [Lithuanian folk architekture]
Vilnius, Mintis, 1965- . v. ill.
At head of title: Kauno politechnikos
institutas. K. Šešelgis [et al.]
Summaries in German and Russian.
NA4110.L54 CaOTU; CU; DLC; MH; NN.

4010. MIELKE, R. Dorf und Bauern-
haus in Ostpreussen. In Das Land (
Berlin), nr.4, 1915, p. 41-45.
CaOTU; ICJ; see also serials consulted.

4011. OBST, Jan. Nasze dwory
wiejskie.. Wilno, Księgarnia Stow.
naucz. polskiego, [19-]. p. [95]-
124. illus., plates. "Otbitka z
Kwartalnika Litewskiego"
NA7566.P602 DLC; MH.

4012. RÄNK, Gustav. Baltic farm-
house types, their regional distri-
bution and historical stratification.
In Laos. Etudes comparées de folklore ou d'ethnologie regional. Comparative studies of folklore and regional ethnology. (Stockholm), v.1,
1951. GR1.L36 DLC; CaOTU; CaQMM;
ICU; InU; IU; KyU; NN; NIC; NcD; OCl;
OCU; see also serials consulted.

4013. VITAUSKAS, A. Molio statyba Padubysio valsčiuje. [Clay constructions in the municipality of Pa-
dubysis]. In Gimtasai Kraštas (Šiauliai), no.17-18, 1938, p. 194-202.
Mr. B.Kviklys, Chicago, Ill., has it
See also serials consulted.

4014. ŽERVYNŲ KAIMAS. [The village
of Žervynai]. Bendra redakcija Kazio
Šešelgio. Vilnius, Periodika, 1974.
47, 108 p. illus. (Lietuvių liaudies architektūros paminklai, 1) At
head of title: Lietuvos TSR Aukštojo
ir specialiojo vidurinio mokslo ministerija. Vilniaus inžinierinis statybos institutas. Summaries in English, German and Russian.
NA1197.Z47Z47 PU; DLC.

XIII.10. EDUCATION

XIII.10.a. HISTORY OF EDUCATION

XIII.10.a.1. GENERAL STUDIES

4015. HIRSCHBERG, Adolf. Szkolnictwo na ziemiach północnowschodnich. Wilno, 1928. Pszedruck z
Kurjera Wileńskiego. 947.52H518 PU.

4016. RUKŠA, Antanas. Dėstomosios
kalbos ir lietuvių kalbos klausimas
senajame Vilniaus universitete. Languages of instruction and the use of
Lithuanian at the Old University of

Vilnius to 1832. In Lietuvių Tautos
Praeitis (Chicago, Ill.), v.3, kn.2,
1973. p.53-81. Summary in English.
See serials consulted.

4017. STUDENTAI LIETUVIAI UŽSIENIO
universitetuose, Nepriklausomoje Lietuvoje ir jų organizacijos. [Lithua-
nian students abroad, in independent
Lithuania and their organizations.By
R. Krasauskas, J. Girnius and V. Liu-
levičius]. In Lietuvių Enciklopedija, So.Boston, Mass., 1963. v.29, p.
64-71. AE60.L5L5 v.23 DLC; CaAEU;
CaOTP; CaOTU; CLU; CU; CtY; DNLM; IC;
ICCC; ICU; InU; IU; KU; MH; MrIU; NNC;
NN; NcU; NRU; OCl; OU; PSt; PU; WU;
WaU.

XIII.10.a.2. EDUCATION BEFORE 1795

4018. AVIŽONIS, Konstantinas. Švietimas Lietuvoje XVII amžiaus pirmoje
pusėje. [Education in Lithuania in
the first part of the 17th century].
In Lietuvos Praeitis (Kaunas),
v.1, 1940. DK511.L2A233 v.1 DLC;
see also serials consulted.

4019. BARTNICKA, Kalina. Po jubi-
leuszu 200-lecia utworzenia Komisji
Edukacji Narodowej. In Rozprawy z
dziejów oświaty(Wrocław), t.18, 1975,
p.77-101. See serials consulted.

4020. GRABSKI, Władysław. Pierwszy budżet Komisji Edukacji Narodowej
1773-1776. In Rozprawy z dziejów
oświaty (Wrocław), t.18, 1975, p.3-
38. See serials consulted.

4021. KUKULSKI, Zygmunt, ed. Pier-
wiastkowe przepisy pedagogiczne Komisji Edukacji Narodowej z lat 1773-
1776. Lublin, Lubelski komitet...,
1923. 184 p. At head of title: Wydanie jubileuszowe w 150-tą rocznicę
utworzenia Komisji Edukacji Narodowej.
QO--NN.

4022. LEWICKI, Józef. Komisja E-
dukacji Narodowej w świetle ustawo-
dawstwa szkolnego... Warszawa, Książka Polska, 1932. 370.9438L584 PU.

4023. --- Ustawodawstwo szkolne
za czasów Komisji Edukacji Narodowej;
rozporządzenia, ustawy pedagogiczne
i organizacyjne, 1773-1793. Zebrał
i zaopatrzył wstępem krytycznym oraz
przepisami Józefa Lewickiego. Kraków, Nakł. M. Arcta, 1925. lxxvii,
456 p. (Biblioteka polskich pisarzy
pedagogicznych, nr.2) LB2924.P6L4
DLC.

4024. RAČKAUSKAS, Jonas A. Education in Lithuania prior to the dissolution of the Jesuit Order (1773). At head of title: J.A. Rackauskas. In Lituanus (Chicago, Ill.), no.1, v.22, 1976, p.5-41. See serials consulted.

4025. --- The educational commission of Poland and Lithuania, 1773-1794. In Lituanus (Chicago, Ill.), no.4, v.19, 1973, p.63-70. See serials consulted.

4026. --- Edukacinės komisijos nurodymai parapijų mokykloms, 1774. The parish school regulation of 1774 and parish schools in Lithuania under the Educational Commission, 1773-1794. In Institute of Lithuanian Studies. Lituanistikos instituto 1971 metų suvažiavimo darbai. Chicago, Ill., 1971. p.63-84. Summary in English. DK511.L2I57 DLC; CaAEU; InNd; MiU; NIC; NRU; PU.

4027. --- Lietuvos ir Lenkijos Edukacinė Komisija. [The Educational Commission of Poland and Lithuania]. In LKMASD, v.8 p.399-420. See serials consulted.

4028. --- School visitations and inspections under the Commission for National Education of the kingdom of Poland and the Grand Duchy of Lithuania (1773-1794). In Lituanus(Chicago, Ill.), no.4, v.22, 1976, p. 5-44. See serials consulted.

4029. SZYBIAK, Irena. Szkolnictwo Komisji Edukacji Narodowej w Wielkim Księstwie Litewskim. Wrocław, Zakład Narodowy im. Ossolińskich, 1973. 260 p. LA841.S96 PU.

XIII.10.a.3. EDUCATION, 1795-1918

4030. PRO"EKT NOVAGO USTROĬSTVA uchilishch Vilenskago Uchebnogo Okruga. Projekt nowego urządzenia szkół w wydziale naukowym Wileńskim. Vil'na, 1825. D1376 KU

4031. RUSSIA. MINISTERSTVO NARODNAGO PROSVESHCHENIIA. Istoricheskiĭ obzor dei͡atel'nosti Ministersva Narodnago Prosvi͡eshchenii͡a, 1802-1902. Sostavil S.V. Rozhdestvenskiĭ. S.-Peterburg, 1902. 785 p. LA831.7.A55 DLC; CSt; MU; NN; NNC.

4032. UCHEBNYI͡A ZAVEDENII͡A V ZApadnykh guberni͡akh 1802-1804. In Russia. Ministerstvo Narodnago Prosveshchenii͡a. Sbornik materialov... S.-Peterburg, 1893. T.2. LA830.A43 v.2 DLC; NN; see also serials consulted.

XIII.10.a.5. EDUCATION IN SOVIET LITHUANIA

4033. ATAMUKAS, Solomonas. Nauja Lietuva, nauji kadrai. [A new Lithuania and new cadres]. Vilnius, Mintis, 1974. 236 p. JN6745.A98K692 DLC.

4034. BUDGINIENĖ, A. Darbas su atsiliekančiais iš lietuvių kalbos rašybos. [Work with the students who fall behind in written Lithuanian language]. Vilnius, Periodika, 1973. 61 p. At head of title: Lietuvos TSR Ministrų Tarybos Valstybinis profesinio techninio mokymo kabinetas. Respublikinis mokymo metodikos kabinetas. PG8519.B8 DLC.

4035. KUR MOKYTIS 1973 METAIS. Informacija apie tolesnį mokymąsi ir specialybės įgijimą respublikos mokymo ir mokslo įstaigose. [Which learning institutions to attend in 1973; a guide to a continuing learning and acquiring of a professional skil. Sudarytojas A. Šulcas]. Kaunas, Šviesa, 1973. 75 p. T136.L5K85 PU.

4036. LIAUDIES ŠVIETIMAS; vyriausybinių dokumentų rinkinys. [Education in Soviet Lithuania... Sudarė J. Kavaliauskas]. Kaunas, Šviesa, 1973. 302 p. At head of title: Lietuvos TSR Švietimo ministerija. LA853.L48L43 DLC; PU.

4037. LIAUDIES ŠVIETIMO PROBLEMOS ir uždaviniai. [Education of masses, its problems and tasks. Sudarė A. Sniečkus et al.]. Vilnius, Mintis, 1972. 248 p. LA853.L48L45 PU; DLC.

4038. LITHUANIAN SSR. CENTRINĖ STATISTIKOS VALDYBA. Narodnoe obrazovanie, nauka i kul'tura v Litovskoĭ SSR. T͡Sentralnoe statisticheskoe upravlenie pri Sovete Ministreov Litovskoĭ SSR; redaktor V.V. Grigaĭte. Vil'ni͡us,[s.n.], 1972. 317 p. LA853.L48L53 1972 DLC.

4039. PEDAGOGIKOS MOKSLŲ VYSTYMAsis Tarybų Lietuvoje. Respublikinės mokslinės konferencijos medžiaga. [The development of teaching in Soviet Lithuania... Red. kolegija: B.Bitinas (atsak. red.) ir kiti]. Vilnius,1969. 160 p. At head of title: Lietuvos TSR mokslinio tyrimo institutas. LA853.L48P4 DLC; MH.

4040. PROCUTA, Genutis. Pedagoginių ir psichologinių mokslų padėtis Lietuvoje. [The situation of the educational and psychological sciences in Soviet Lithuania]. In Metmenys (Chicago, Ill.), no.23, 1972, p.164-173. See serials consulted.

4041. RUKŠA, Antanas. Kai kurios
šių dienų Lietuvos švietimo problemos.
[Some educational problems in Soviet Lithuania]. London, Nida Press,
]1973]. 75 p. Atspaudas iš "Europos
Lietuvio" 1972 m. nr.40-50 ir 1973 m.
nr.1-6. LA853.L48R8 PU.

4042. ŠIMKUS, Sigizmundas Juozas.
Internacionalinis ir patriotinis auk-
lėjimas. [International and patriotic
education in Lithuania]. Vilnius,
Mintis, 1973. 302 p.,[24] leaves of
plates. illus. Bibliography: p.293-
[302]. MH.

4043. VILNA. MOKYKLŲ MOKSLINIO
TYRIMO INSTITUTAS. Gimtosios kalbos
mokymas pradinėse klasėse; iš trečių-
jų respublikinių "Pedagoginių skaitymų" medžiagos. [The teaching of Lithuanian language in the primary
grades]. Kaunas, Valstybinė pedagoginės literatūros leidykla, 1960.
LB1577.L5V5 DLC; MiEM.

4044. VILNA. MOKYKLŲ MOKSLINIO
TYRIMO INSTITUTAS. Iš lietuvių kal-
bos ir literatūros mokytojų darbo pa-
tirties. [Experiences of teachers in
Lithuanian language and literature.
Sudarė Z. Alaunienė ir E. Savickaitė.
Kaunas, Šviesa, 1964. 95 p. (Mokyto-
jo bibliotekėlė). LB1577.L5V52 DLC.

4045. --- Kai kurie Lietuvos
TSR pedagoginės minties ir švietimo
istorijos klausimai; MMTI mokslinės
konferencijos pranešimų tezės. Vilnius, 1965. 50 p. At head of title:
LTSR Švietimo ministerija. Mokyklų
mokslinio tyrimo institutas. [Some
Soviet Lithuanian educational ideas
and questions of educational history]
LA853.L48V52 DLC.

4046. --- Mokyklų mokslinio tyrimo instituto 1966 m. mokslinės konferencijos pranešimų tezės. [Reports of
the Soviet Lithuanian Research institute on education, 1966]. Vilnius,
1966. 102 p. At head of title: Lietuvos TSR Švietimo ministerija. Mokyklų mokslinio tyrimo institutas.
LA853.L48V53 DLC.

XIII.10.a.6. LITHUANIAN EDUCATION IN
OTHER COUNTRIES

4047. BARYCZ, Henryk. Polacy na
studiach w Rzymie w epoce Odrodzenia
1440-1600. Kraków, Polska Akademia
Umiejętności; skł. gł. w księg. Gebethnera i Wolffa, 1938. iv, 274 p.
(Polska Akademia Umiejętności. Archivum komisji do dziejów oświaty i
szkolnictwa w Polsce, nr.4)

DG814.B29 ICU; DLC.

4048. ČIŽIŪNAS, Vaclovas. Lietuvių švietimas tremtyje; žvilgsnis po-
rai dešimtmečių sukakus. Lithuanian
education in Displaced Persons Camps.
In Lietuvių Tautos Praeitis (Chicago,
Ill.), v.3, kn.1, 1971, p.135-164.
Summary in English. See serials consulted.

4049. LIETUVIŲ ŠVIETIMAS VOKIETI-
joje; vaikų darželių, pradžios mokyklų, progimnazijų, gimnazijų, specia-
lių mokyklų ir kursų, veikusių 1944-
1950 m. apžvalgos su žemėlapiu bei
252 nuotraukomis. Priede lietuvių
švietimas Austrijoje su 10 nuotraukų.
Redagavo Vincentas Liulevičius. [Edu-
cation of Lithuanians in Germany and
Austria...1944-1950]. Chicago, Ill.,
Kultūrai remti draugija, 1969. 639p.
LA721.81.L53 DLC.

4050. MASILIONIS, Juozas. Čikagos
aukštesnioji lituanistikos mokykla,
1950-1975: dvidešimt penkių metų
veiklos apžvalga. [The school of Lithuanian studies in Chicago, Ill.,
1950-1975; 25th anniversary. Chicago, Ill.], Čikagos aukštesniosios lituanistikos mokyklos, Tėvų komiteto
leidinys, 1975. 216 p.
LD7501.C4C76 DLC.

4051. MEDZIUKAS, Ignas. Šv. Kazimiero lituanistinė šeštadieninė mokykla, 1949-1974. [Lithuanian St.Ca-
simir Saturday School in Los Angeles,
Calif., 1949-1974]. Los Angeles,
1975. 64 p. E184.L7M4 PU.

4052. PENKIOLIKMETIS CHICAGOS TOL-
minkiemyje, 1959-1975. Kristijono Donelaičio mokyklų sukaktuvinis leidinys. [The 15th anniversary issue to
commemorate the K.Donelaitis School
in Chicago, Ill. Redakcinis kolektyvas: Danutė Bindokienė, Jonas Bagdonas, Julius Širka]. Chicago, Ill.,
1975. 314 p. E184.L7P39 PU.

4053. PUZINAS, Jonas. Pabaltijo
universiteto 30 metų sukaktį minint.
Žiupsnelis faktinės medžiagos iš ar-
chyvinių dokumentų ir prisiminimų.
The 30th anniversary of the establishment of the Baltic University:
some factual archival material and
memoirs. In Lietuvių Tautos Praeitis
(Chicago, Ill.), v.4, bk.1, 1977, p.
7-52. See serials consulted; also
offprint: LF3194.P54P8 PU.

4054. RUDNYTS'KYĬ, Ĭaroslav B[oh-
dan]. Slavic and Baltic universities in exile. Winnipeg, 1949. 16
p. (Slavistica, 4). PG1.S63 DLC;
CaOTU; CaBVaU; CtY; MH; MiU; NN;NNC.

4055. STARKUS, Jonas. Seinų "Žiburio" gimnazija. I laidos 10 metų sukakties proga. ["Žiburio" High School of Seinai; 10th anniversary of the First graduating class]. [Marijampolė], 1935. [Xerox copy, 1977] 47 p. LF4446.L3S8 1935a PU.

XIII.10.b. EDUCATIONAL INSTITUTIONS

XIII.10.b.1. PRIMARY, SECONDARY, AND SPECIAL SCHOOLS.

4056. LITHUANIA. ŽEMĖS ŪKIO DEPARTAMENTAS. Žemesniosios žemės ūkio mokyklos; taisyklės, programos ir kt. [Agricultural schools; by-laws, programs, et.]. Kaunas, Spindulio b-vė, 1929. 56 p. illus. S535.L5A57 DLC.

4057. LITHUANIAN SSR. ŠVIETIMO MINISTERIJA. Aštuonmečių mokyklų programos. Lietuvių kalba ir literatūra V-VIII klasei. [Eight year sch school programme: Lithuanian language and literature]. Kaunas, Valstybinė pedagoginės literatūros leidykla, 1963. 51 p. 373.475L776 a IEN.

4058. --- Vidurinių mokyklų programos. Literatūra IX-XI klasei. [High School programmes; literature] Kaunas, Valstybinė pedagoginės literatūros leidykla, 1963. 49 p. IEN.

4059. RAČKAUSKAS, Jonas A. Pradinis švietimas Lietuvoje iki trečiojo padalinimo. [Primary education in Lithuania before the third partition of 1795]. In Lietuvių Tautos Praeitis (Chicago, Ill.), v.3, kn.1,1971, p.63-134. Summary in English. See serials consulted.

4060. VIDURINIŲ MOKYKLŲ PROGRAMOS. Oficialus leidinys. [High School programmes; official edition]. Kaunas, Švietimo ministerijos, Knygų leidimo k-jos leidinys, 1939.[Xerox copy, 1977]. 199 p. pages 47-48 wanting. LB1617.L5A4 1939a PU(xerox).

XIII.10.b.2. UNIVERSITIES, ACADEMIES, ETC.

4061. BEDNARSKI, Stanisław. Geneza Akademji wileńskiej. In Vilna. Uniwersytet. Księga pamiątkowa ku uczczeniu CCCL rocznicy założenia i wskrzeszenia Uniwersytetu Wileńskie-go. Wilno, 1931. v.1, p.1-22. LF4425.V56A5 DLC; CaBVaU; MH; NcD; PU.

4062. BIČIŪNAS, Jonas. Pirmosios Jėzuitų kolegijos įsteigimas Lietuvoje-Vilniuje, 1570 m. [The founding of the first college in Lithuania, 1570]. In Tautos Praeitis,(Chicago, Ill.), v.3, kn.3/4, 1967, p.3-93. See serials consulted.

4063. LIELIŃSKI, Józef. Szkoła sztuk pięknych. In His Uniwersytet Wileński. Kraków, 1899-1900. v.2, p.736-765. 947.52.B476 PU; DCU; KU; MH; NN; NNC; PPULC.

4064. BIRŽIŠKA, Mykolas. Vilniaus universitetas vokiečių okupacijos metais. [University of Vilnius during the German occupation, 1941-1944]. Schweinfurt, 1947. [Xerox copy, 1977] 22 p. Iš "Tėviškės Garsas", nr.85-94. LF4425.V5B51 1947a PU.

4065. KAUNAS. UNIVERSITETAS. Vytauto Didžiojo Universiteto 1939 m. rudens semestro kalendorius. [The calendar of the University of Vytautas the Great for 1939]. Kaunas, VDU Kanceliarijos leidinys, 1939. [Xerox copy, 1977]. 111 p. LF4445.A5 1939a PU.

4066. KONČIUS, Ignas. Stepono Batoro universitetas Vilniuje. [The S. Batory university in Vilnius]. In Tautos Praeitis (Chicago, Ill.), v.2, kn.2, 1965, p. 143-160. See serials consulted.

4067. LIETUVOS TSR MOKSLŲ AKADEMIJA, Vilna. LIETUVIŲ KALBOS IR LITERATŪROS INSTITUTAS. Lietuvių kalbos ir literatūros institutas. [Institute of Lithuanian language and literature in Vilnius. Parengė A. Seselskytė]. Vilnius, Mintis, 1973. 77 p. illus. AS262.L49 PU; InU.

4068. LIETUVOS UNIVERSITETAS,1579-1803-1922. [University of Lithuania]. Redagavo Pranas Čepėnas. Chicago, Ill., Lietuvių profesorių draugija Amerikoje, 1972. xvl, 896 p. illus. Added t.p.: The University of Lithuania. Table of contents also in English; summary in English. "Mokslo personalo spausdinių bibliografija, 1922-1944," by Povilas Dilys: p.785-816. LF4445.L53 DLC; CaAEU; InNd; NjP; PU.

4069. LITHUANIAN S.S.R. AUKŠTOJO IR SPECIALIOJO VIDURINIO MOKSLO MINISTERIJA. Stojamųjų egzaminų į aukštasias mokyklas programos. [Entrance examinatio programmes for Colleges and Universities]. Vilnius, 1969.

79 p. At head of title: Lietuvos TSR Aukštojo ir specialiojo vidurinio mokslo ministerija. LA853.L48A429 DLC.

4070. --- --- [Another edition]. Vilnius, 1971. 75,[4] p. At head of title: Lietuvos TSR Aukštojo ir specialiojo vidurinio mokslo ministerija. Mokslinis metodikos kabinetas. LA853.L4A43 DLC.

4071. --- --- [Another edition]. Vilnius, 1975. 83 p. LA853.L48A45 PU.

7072. LITHUANIAN S.S.R. VALSTYBINIS AUKŠTOJO IR SPECIALIOJO VIDURINIO MOKSLO KOMITETAS. [The University of Soviet Lithuania]. Lietuvos TSR aukštosios mokyklos. Kaunas, Šviesa, 1 1964. 129 p. LA853.L48L5 DLC;IEN; MH; MH-Ed.

4073. POLAND. LAWS, STATUTES, ET ETC. Zbiór ustaw i rosporządzeń o studjach uniwersyteckich, oraz innych przepisów ważnych dla studentów uniwersytetu... w Wilnie. Wilno, 1926. 374 p. DLC-L.

4074. POPŁATEK, J[an]. Religiosi ordinis S.Basilii Magni qui in Academia et Universitatae Vilnensi Societate Jesu gradibus academicis ornati sunt. In Analecta Ordinis S.Basilii Magni (Roma), t.4, 1932, p. 211-218. See serials consulted.

4075. PUZINAS, Jonas. Lietuvos universiteto vaidmuo lietuvių tautinei kultūrai. [The importance of the University of Lithuanian to the Lithuanian culture]. In Naujoji Viltis (Chicago, Ill.), no6, 1974, p.4-13. See serials consulted.

4076. RABIKAUSKAS, Paulius. Vilniaus Akademija naujose Lietuvos leidiniuose. [Academy of Vilnius in the new Lithuanian publications]. In Aidai (Brooklyn,N.Y.), no.3, 1972, p. 75-91; no.4, p.147-153. See serials consulted.

4077. RAINYS, Juozas. Vytauto Didžiojo Universitetas ir Žemės Ūkio Akademija. [University of Lithuania and Academy of Agriculture]. In Kemežys, V., ed. Lietuva, 1918-1938. Kaunas, 1938. 947.52.L625 PU; CtTMF; ICLJF; ICCC.

4078. ŠIAULIŲ K.PREIKŠO PEDAGOGInis institutas. [Teachers' college in Šiauliai]. [Redakcinė kolegija: A. Bitinienė, B. Preskienis(ats.red.), K. Župerka. Šiauliai, Šiaulių K.Pr Preikšo Pedagoginis institutas, 1973]. 135 p. LF4446.S5S5 PU.

4079. VALIUS, Mečys and DAGYS, Jonas. Biologijos instituto mokslo tiriamųjų darbų apžvalga 1946-1950 m. laikotarpyje. [The review of scientific research by the Institute of Biology during the years 1946-1950]. In Lietuvos TSR Mokslų akademija,Vilna. Biologijos institutas. Darbai, v.1, 1951, p.13-29. See serials consulted.

4080. VALIUŠKEVIČIŪTĖ, Apolonija. Kauno meno mokykla. [The Academy of Arts in Kaunas]. Vilnius, Vaga,1971. 152 p., 32 leaves of illus. At head of title: Lietuvos TSR Mokslų akademija. Istorijos institutas. N332.L753K38 DLC; CU; InU; IU; MB;MH; NNC; OKentU; PPiU.

4081. VILNA. UNIVERSITETAS. Vilniaus universiteto 1942/43 mokslo metų pavasario semestro paskaitų tvarkaraščiai. [Syllabus of the University of Vilnius for 1942/43]. Vilnius, 1943. [Xerox copy, 1976]. 73 p. LF4425.V5A3 1943a PU.

4082. VILNA. UNIVERSITETAS. HUMANITARINIŲ MOKSLŲ FAKULTETAS. Vilniaus universiteto humanitarinių mokslų fakulteto reguliaminas. Humanitarinių mokslų fakulteto tarybos priimtas 1941.X.31, Universiteto senato patvirtintas 1942.I.12. Vilnius, 1942.[Xerox copy, 1976]. 31 p.[Regulations of the Department of Humanities and Social sciences]. LF4425.V5A4 1942a PU.

4083. VILNIAUS UNIVERSITETAS. [Sudarė L. Tapinas]. Kaunas, Šviesa, 1975. 1 portfolio ([8] p.,[15] leavea of plates. illus. Text in Lithuanian, English, French, and Russian. LF4425.V5V54 PU.

4084. VILNIAUS UNIVERSITETO ISTOrija, 1579-1803. [A history of the University of Vilnius, 1579-1803. Ats. redaktorius V. Merkys]. Vilnius, Mokslas, 1976. 316 p. LF4425.V56 V52 PU.

XIII.10.b.3. LEARNED SOCIETIES

4085. MOKSLO, KULTŪROS IR ŠVIETIMo draugijos. [Lithuanian Learned Institutions and Societies. Ats. redaktorius Vytautas Merkys]. Vilnius, Mokslas, 1975. 250 p. (Iš lietuvių kultūros istorijos, 8). On leaf preceding t.p.: Lietuvos TSR Mokslų akademija. Istorijos institutas. Summaries in Russian. DK511.L212M64 DLC.

4086. TREADGOLD, Donald W. Baltic

studies as viewed by an outsider. In Bulletin of Baltic Studies (Tacoma, Wash.), no.4, 1970, p.14-21. See serials consulted.

4087. VARDYS, Stanley V. Baltijos valstybių studijos vakaruose; padėtis ir perspektyvos. The status and prospects of Baltic Studies in the West. In Institute of Lithuanian Studies. Lituanistikos instituto 1971 metų suvažiavimo darbai. Chicago, Ill., 1971. p.271-280. Summary in English. DK511.L2I57 DLC; CaAEU InNd; MiU; NIC; NRU; PU.

4088. YLA, Stasys. Antrasis LK Mokslininkų ir mokslo megėjų suvažiavimas 1936. [The second conference of Lithuanian Catholic Scientists 1936]. In Lietuvių Katalikų mokslo akademija, Roma. Suvažiavimo darbai, v.2, p.457-471. See serials consulted.

4089. --- Lietuvių katalikų mokslo akademija. [The Lithuanian Catholic Academy of Sciences]. In Aidai (Brooklyn,N.Y.), no.10, 1972, p.409-413). See serials consulted.

XIII.10.b.4. ARCHIVES, GALLERIES, LIBRARIES AND MUSEUMS

4090. KASPERAVIČIUS, Julius. Lietuvos TSR muziejai. [The museums of Soviet Lithuania]. 2., pataisytas ir papildytas leidimas. Vilnius, Mintis, 1977. 127. AM61.L5K3 1977

4091. LIETUVOS TSR BIBLIOTEKŲ DARBUOTOJŲ MOKSLINĖ KONFERENCIJA, 2d, Vilnius, 1965. Medžiagos rinkinys. [Proceedings of the Lithuanian conference of librarians. Sudarytojai: St. Elsbergas, P. Kizis ir Kl. Sinkevičius]. Vilnius, 1967. 349 p. At head of title: Lietuvos TSR Valstybinė Respublikinė Biblioteka. CU; CLSU; MH.

4092. LITHUANIAN AMERICAN ART CLUB, Chicago. Čiurlionio vardo galerija. [Art gallery of Čiurlionis]. [Chicago, Ill., 1957.. 30] p. (chiefly illus., ports) N531.C5L5 DLC.

4093. MAŽIULIS, Antanas. Kraštotyros muziejai Lietuvoje ir svetur. Ethnographic museums in Lithuania and abroad. In Institute of Lithuanian Studies. Lituanistikos instituto 1973 metų suvažiavimo darbai. Chicago, Ill., 1975. p. 235-246. Summary in English. DK511.L2I63 1975 CaAEU; PU.

4094. MISIŪNIENĖ, I. Trakų istorijos muziejus. [History museum of Trakai]. Vilnius, Mintis, 1967. 28 p. illus. GN37.T7M5 DLC; CtY; MH; PU.

4095. MUSEUMS OF VILNIUS. [Teksto autorius J. Kasperavičius. Iš lietuvių kalbos vertė V. Udrienė]. Vilnius, Mintis, 1977. [12] p. AM61.V5M PU.

4096. RAČKAUSKAS, Vladas Karolis. Petro Cvirkos memorialinis muziejus; exponatų katalogas ir ekskursijų vadovas. [The memorial museum of Petras Cvirka; a catalogue and guide]. Vilnius, Valstybinė politinės ir mokslinės literatūros leidykla, 1960. 160 p. illus. Balt.9650.68.810 MH; CLU. At head of t.: K.Vairas-Račkauskas.

4097 RYGIEL, Stefan. W Wileńskiej bibljotece publicznej i uniwersyteckiej. Kraków, 1925. 10 p. "Powiększona odbitka z 4-go zeszytu Silva Rerum" B8828.1. MH.

4098. SKRODENIS, Stasys. Baubliai. Vilnius, Mintis, 1974. [31] p. ill. GN36.L57S55 PU; DLC.

4099. TOMCZAK, Andrzej. Zarys dziejów archiwów Polskich. Część I: do wybuchu I Wojny Światowej. Wyd.2. Toruń, Uniwersytet Mikołaja Kopernika, 1974- . v. (Skrypty i teksty pomocnicze-Uniwersytet Mikolaja Kopernika). CD1741.T65 DLC.

4100. VILNA. LIETUVOS TSR VALSTYBINĖ RESPUBLIKINĖ BIBLIOTEKA. Lietuvos TSR bibliotekos; pagrindinės žinios apie respublikos bibliotekas. [Libraries of Soviet Lithuania... Sudarytojos: E. Košinskienė, G. Tamošiūnaitė]. Vilnius, Mintis, 1977. 231 p. Z821.7.V52 PU.

4101. VILNA. UNIVERSITETAS. BIBLIOTEKA. Vilniaus Valstybinis V.Kapsuko universitetas, Mokslinė biblioteka, 400. [Research library of the V. Kapsukas State University of Vilnius. Parengė Jurgis Tornau. Foto nuotraukos Mečislovo Sakalausko].Vilnius, Vaga, 1970. 108 p. illus. Summary in Russian and English. Z821.7.V543 DLC; CaAEU; CLU; CSt;CU; IU; MiU; NN; OClW; OKentU; PU; ICU.

4102. VILNA. VALSTYBINIS DAILĖS MUZIEJUS. Lietuvos XVIII-XIX a. dailė. Piešiniai. Katalogas. [Lithuanian art of 18th and 19th cent.Paintings; a catalogue. Sudarė P. Svičiulienė. Atsak. redaktorius P. Gudynas]. Vilnius, 1972. 104 p. At head of title: Lietuvos TSR dailės muziejus. NC268.L5V5 PU.

4103. --- Vakarų Europos XV-XIX a. tapyba Vilniaus Paveikslų galerijoje. [West European paintings of 15th-19th centuries in the Art gallery of Vilnius. Paruošė P. Juodelis] Vilnius, 1973. 24 p. At head of title: Lietuvos TSR Dailės muziejus. N3368.A85 PU.

4104. VILNA. VALSTYBINIS DAILĖS MUZIEJUS. PAVEIKSLŲ GALERIJA. Kartinnaia galereia. [Putevoditel']. Perevod s litovs. Pranas Gudynas et al.]. Vil'nius, Mintis, 1969. 94 p. illus. N3368.A85 DLC; MH; MiU.

4105. --- Paveikslų galerija. [The Art gallery in Vilnius]. Vilnius Mintis, 1968. 80 p. illus. At hea head of title: P. Gudynas [et al.] N3368.A87 DLC.

4106. CANCELLED.

4107. ŽILEVIČIUS, Juozas. The Juozas Žilevičius Library of Lithuanian Musicology. Translated by Leonardas J. Šimutis. [Chicago, Ill., J.Žilevičius Library of Lithuanian Musicology, 1973]. 25 p. E184.L7Z51 PU; CaAEU.

XIII.11. HISTORY OF THE BOOK; LITHUANIAN PUBLISHING AND JOURNALISM

4108. BIRŽIŠKA, Vaclovas. The American-Lithuanian publications, 1875 to 1910. [Boulder, Colo.,1959] p. [396]-408. Reproduced by xerography, 1972, from Journal of Central European Affairs, v.18, no.4. PG8740.B5 PU.

4109. BUDRECKIS, Algirdas. Vilniaus "Vairas" ir jo tautiška linkmė. [Journal "Vairas"(Vilnius) and its national character]. In Naujoji Viltis(Chicago, Ill.), no.5, 1973, p.13-29; no.6, p.27-34; no.7, p.15-39. See serials consulted.

4110. CZARNECKI, Jerzy, pseud. Rzut oka na historję książki wileńskiej. Kraków, 1932. 45 p. His real name Tadeusz Turkowski. Otbitka. 491.922C998 PU; NN(Turkowski, T.)

4111. --- Wilno w dziejach książki polskiej. Wilno, J. Zawadzki, 1928. 24 p. His real name Tadeusz Turkowski. Bound with His RZUT oka na historję książki. 491.922C998 PU.

4112. DAMBRAUSKAS, Aleksandras.

Šv. Kazimiero draugija, jos kūrimasis ir pirmųjų 25 metų veikimas, 1906-1931. [Saint Casimir society and its development during 1906-1931. Kaunas, Šv.Kazimiero draugija, 1932. 140 p. illus., ports. (Šv.Kazimiero draugijos jubiliejinis leidinys, nr.533) DK511.L2A27 DLC.

4113. DOKUMENTAS API LITYNIŠKAS litaras lietuviškoje literatūroje. [Document about Latin alphabet in the Lithuanian literature]. Tilsit, O.v. Mauderode, 1899. Perspausdintas iš "Varpo". 891.926D687 PU.

4114. ĒNTUZIASTY RASPROSTRANENIIA pechati; opyt rasprostraniteleĭ pechati Prenaĭskogo raĭona. [Perevod s litovskogo iazyka]. Vil'nius, Gazetno-zhurnal'noe izd-vo, 1964. 42 p. illus., ports. At head of title: Ministerstvo sviazi Litovskoĭ SSR. Respublikanskaia direktsiia Soiuzpechati. CSt-H.

4115. KORSAKAS, Kostas. The first Lithuanian printed book. Moscow, 1948. 6 leaves. At head of title: The U.S.S.R. Society for cultural relations with foreign countries. GAH p.v. 292--NN.

4116. LAUCEVIČIUS, Edmundas. XV-XVIII a. knygų įrišimai Lietuvos bibliotekose. [The book binding of 15th -18th centuries in the libraries of Lithuania] Z270.L5L3 PU.

4117. LOEBER, Dietrich A. Baltic authors under Soviet law; regular publishing and Samizdat. In Conference on Baltic Studies, 3d, University of Toronto, 1972. Problems of mininations. San Jose, Calif., 1973. p. 175-192. HC243.C65 1972 DLC; CaBVaU; CSt; CtY; CU; GAT; ICIU; IU; InU; ICarbS; InNd; MB; MH; MiU; NN; NNC; NjP; NBuU; NBuC; NmU; OkU; RPB; UU; WU; WaU.

4118. PETRAUSKIENĖ, Irena. Vilniaus akademijos spaustuvė, 1575-1773. [Printing services of Vilnius Academy, 1575-1773]. Vilnius, Mokslas, 1976. 243 p. Z166.V5P4 PU.

4119. RAGUOTIENĖ, Genovaitė. Šimtas knygos mįslių. [One hundred riddles of the book]. Vilnius, Vaga, 1974. 439 p. Z4.Z9 PU.

4120. ŠEŠPLAUKIS, Alfonsas. The Martynas Mažvydas Cathechism of 1547. In Lituanus (Chicago, Ill.), v.19, no.3, 1973, p. 3-19. See serials consulted.

4121. SPAUDA IR SPAUSTUVĖS. [Publishing and Printing houses in Lithuania. Redakcinė kolegija: Juozas Jurginis(ats. redaktorius) et al.].Vilnius, Mintis, 1972. 295 p. (Iš lietuvių kultūros istorijos, 7) On page preceding t.p.: Lietuvos TSR Mokslų akademija, Istorijos institutas. CtY; InU.

4122. STOLZMAN, Małgorzata. Czasopisma wileńskie Adama Honorego Kirkora. [Kraków, Państwowe Wydawnictwo Naukowe, Oddział w Krakowie,1973]. 162 p. PG7003.K73 zesz.26 PU.

4123. "TIESOS" KELIAS, 1917-1977; Lietuvos komunistinės spaudos istorijos puslapiai. [A history of the Lithuanian Communist press; "Tiesa", 1917-1977. Redakcinė komisija: R. Šarmaitis (pirmininkas), S. Bistrickas, A. Laurinčiukas, D. Šniukas, A. Viršulis]. Vilnius, Mintis, 1977. 210 p. PN5279.V54T5 PU.

4124. TOPOLSKA, Maria. Książka na Litwie i Białorusi w latach 1553-1660; analyza statystyczna. In Odrodzenie i reformacja w Polsce(Warszawa), t.21, 1976, p.145-164. See serials consulted.

4125. 1934-1964[i.e. Tūkstantis devyni šimtai trisdešimt ketvirti-tūkstantis devyni šimtai šešiadešimt ketvirtų] m. "Šluota"; karikatūros. Litovskiĭ satiricheskiĭ zhurnal "Shluota"(Metla). [Sudarytojas J. Bulota. Vilnius], LKP CK laikraščių ir žurnalų leidykla, [1964]. 7 p.,[56] p. of illus., (part.col.), ports. NC1578.T8 DLC.

4126. VLADIMIROVAS, Levas. Frantsisk Skorina; pervopechatnik Vil'-niŭsskiĭ. Vil'niŭs, Mokslas, 1975. 64 p. Z232S615.V5 PU; DLC.

4127. ŽURNALISTIKA. [Journalism]. Redagavo Juozas Prunskis. Chicago, Ill., Išleido Lietuvių žurnalistų sąjunga, 1974. 291 p. illus. PN4797.Z8 DLC; PU.

AUTHOR INDEX

Abelkis, Povilas see Tulpė, P., pseud.
Abramauskas, Stasys, 1819.
Abramavičius, Girša, 136.
Abramavičius, Vladas, 137-138.
Adamus Bremensis, 11th cent., 1453-1454.
Adlerfelt, Gustaf, 1372-1373.
Adlys, Petras, joint author, 696.
Adomaitis, J., 1192.
Adomas Juodasai, pseud. see Lastas, Adomas.
Adomauskas, Liudas, 1780.
Adomavičiūtė, Stefanija, 1698.
Adomėnas, Vincas, 3166.
Adomonis, Juozas, ed., 3983.
Adomonis, Tadas, 3925.
Aer, Elvi, joint comp., 72.
Afanas'ev, B.L., ed., 581.
Agapov, Sergeĭ Vasil'evich, 99.
Aišbė; Aišbė, A.; Aišbė, B., pseud, see Kriščiukaitis, Antanas.
Aidukaitė-Ragauskienė, R. see Ragauskienė, R. (Aidukaitė)
Aidulis, Juozas, 2574, 2657, 3239-3240.
Akademiĭa Navuk BSSR, Minsk. Instytut historyĭ, 1374-1375.
Aksamitas, Pranas, ed., 1780, 1788, 1791.
Akstinas, Bronius, 303, 309, 310.
Alantas, Vytautas, 1683, 2444, 2575, 2736-2738, 3167.
Alantas, Vytautas, ed., 3502.
Alaunienė, Z., comp., 4044.
Alderfeld, Gustav,
Alekna, Antanas, 139.
Aleknavičius, B., photo, 434.
Aleknavičius, Kajetonas, 2278, 2315, 3241.
Aleksa, Osvaldas, 2739.
Aleksa-Angarietis, Zigmas, 1184, 1718.
Aleksandravičius, Jonas see Aistis, Jonas.
Aleksandravičius, V., ill., 3379.
Aleksandriškis, Jonas see Aistis, Jonas.
Aleksandrov, V.A., ed., 678.
Aleksynas, Kostas, ed., 2115-2116.
Alionis, Algirdas, 3242.
Ališas, Venancijus, pseud., 3243.
Ališauskas, Kazys, 893-894, 1611.
Aliūnas, S., Dr., pseud. see Baronas, Aloyzas.
Almenas, Kazys, 2740-2741.
Amalviškis, Rimas, pseud. see Jūra, Klemensas.

Ambrasas, Arvydas, 3244.
Ambrasas, Kazys Juozas, 2413-2414.
Ambrazas, Algirdas, 140, 3845.
Ambrazas, Vytautas, 2348.
Ambrazas, V., ed., 2247.
Ambrazevičius, Juozas, 877, 2445, 2576-2577.
Ambrazevičius, Juozas, ed., 3305.
Ambrazevičius, V. illus., 436.
Ambraziūnas, Alfonsas, ed., 3982.
Amburger, Erik, comp., 124.
Amerikos lietuvių darbininkų literatūros draugija, 1505.
Amerikos lietuvių ekonominis centras, 719.
Amerikos lietuvių congresas, Detroit (1969), 720.
Amis de Milosz, Les, 3768.
Andersen, Henning, 2177.
Anderson, Edgars, 1308-1310, 1542.
Andersson, Ingvar, 1376-1377.
Andriekus, Leonardas, 3245-3246.
Andriekus, Leonardas, ed., 538.
Andrijauskas, V., joint tr., 109.
Andriulis, V., comp., 40.
Andriušis, Pulgis, 2742-2744.
Androšiūnienė, L., 1270.
Andziulaitis, Juozas, 2659.
Andziulytė-Ruginienė, Marija, 2000.
Angarietis, Zigmas see Aleksa-Angarietis, Zigmas.
Angelus, Oskar, 2178.
Anglickis, Stasys, 3247-3248.
Aničas, Jonas, 1023, 1751, 1781-1782.
Aničas, Jonas, ed., 1283, 2009.
Anichas, I. see Aničas, Jonas.
Antkowski, Ferdynand, 2179.
Antoniewicz, Jerzy, 1298.
Antoniewicz, Karol Bołoz, 2279.
Antoniewicz, Włodzimierz, 2151.
Anysas, Martynas, 1906.
Apalia-Šidlienė, Dz., 615.
Apanavičius, Martynas, 1025.
Apanavičius, Martynas, joint comp., 1043.
Aputis, Juozas, 2745-2748.
Arbusow, Leonid, 2039.
Areška, Vitas, 2446, 2578.
Armalytė, Olimpija, tr., 382, 540, 3848.
Arminas, Aleksandras see Ališas, Venancijus, pseud.
Armentrout, Ruth, tr., 129, 2260.
Armon, Witold, 9.
Arnašius, Stasys, 1058, 1719.
Arnold, Udo, 1879.
Artemov, Vladimir Alekseevich, ed., 2299.

Breichmanas, Gediminas, ed., 764.
Breichmanienė, Genovaitė, 2138.
Breimeris, Feliksas, 3285.
Bretkūnas, Jonas, 2280.
Brewing, Irene, tr., 3615, 3648-
  3651, 3655, 3700, 3728.
Bričkus, Viktoras, illus., 3480.
Briedis, Juozas, 1185.
Brizgys, Vincentas, 2024.
Brodskiĭ, D., tr., 3708.
Broga, L., tr., 3773.
Brown, Zvie A., 1633.
Brundza, Kazys, 616.
Brunner, Otto, joint ed., 939.
Bruožis, Ansas, 1867.
Bruveris, Jonas, comp., 165, 3935.
Byblys, Vladas, 1225.
Bubnis, V. see Bubnys, Vytautas.
Bubnys, Vytautas, 2792-2795, 3600-
  3601.
Bucevičienė, Stasė, 3286.
Buch, Alfred, tr., 2292.
Buch, Tamara, 2292, 2389.
Buchienė (Meiksinaitė), Tamara
  see Buch, Tamara.
Bučys, Algimantas, 2529.
Bučys, Petras, Vysk. see Bučys,
  Pranciškus Petras, Bp.
Bučys, Pranciškus Petras, Bp.,
  2050-2051.
Būdavas, Stasius, 2796-2797.
Buddensieg, Hermann, tr., 3683.
Budginienė, A., 2319, 4034.
Budraitis, Petras, 1837.
Budreckas, Ladas, 158, 3849.
Budreckis, Algirdas, 965, 1546-
  1548, 4109.
Budreckis, Algirdas Martin, joint
  author, 756.
Budreckis, Algirdas Martin, comp.
  & ed., 748.
Budreika, Eduardas, 3992.
Budriūnas, Bronius, 3875.
Budrys, Ajay, 1618.
Budrys, Algirdas Jonas see Budrys,
  Algis.
Budrys, Algis, 3779-3784.
Budrys, Dzidas, 1157.
Budrys, Jonas see Klajūnas,
  Jonas, pseud.
Budrys, Rimantas, 611-612, 2798-
  2800, 3602.
Budrys, Rimantas, comp., 248.
Budrys, Stasys, 159, 1880, 3928,
  3960.
Budrytė, Stasė, comp., 2656.
Būdvytis, Pranas V., 3287.
Būdvytis Svyrūnėlis, Pr. V. see
  Būdvytis, Pranas V.
Bufienė, Teklė, 12, 2433.
Buivydaitė, Bronė, 3288.
Bukelienė, Elena, 2581.
Bukontas, Alfonsas, 3289-3291.
Bulavas, Juozas, ed., 790, 1028.
Bulis, Jonas, 3961.
Bulota, Juozas, 2801.
Bulota, Juozas, comp., 4125.
Bulota, Juozas, ed., 2626.
Buračas, Antanas, 100.

Buračas, Antanas, joint author,
  1157.
Burokaitė, Jūratė, comp., 3863.
Burokevičius, Mykolas, 1660, 1699.
Burokevičius, Mykolas, ed., 1235,
  1712.
Burwell, Michael, 2187.
Bušackis, Brunonas, 160.
Bušmienė, Stasė, 42, 161.
Būtėnas, Julius, 162, 357-358,
  2453-2454, 2530.
Būtėnas, Julius, comp., 2679-3628.
Būtėnas, Petras, 2374.
Būtėnas, Vladas, 723.
Būtėnas, Vladas see also Ramojus,
  Vladas.
Butkevičius, Izidorius, 1204.
Butkų Juzė, pseud. see Butkus,
  Juozas.
Butkus, Juozas (1893-1947), 1911,
  2679, 3173.
Butkus, Juozas, tr., 382, 540, 3999.
Butkus, Juozas, joint tr., 382.
Butkus, V., ed., 622.
Butrimas, Edmundas, 3174.
Byczkowa, Margarita E., 1068, 1379.
Byras, Antanas, 3292.

Cadzow, John F., 54-55, 1594.
Campana, Cristoforo, joint author,
  1776.
Çap, Biruta, 163.
Čapskis, M., joint ed., 1027.
Caro, Jakob, 1470.
Čeginskas, Kajetonas Julius, 338.
Čekienė, Emilija, 724.
Čekuolis, A., 2802.
Čenienė, Jovita, comp., 2321-2324.
Čepaitis, V., tr., 3133, 3575, 3578.
Čepas, R., comp., 2690.
Čepėnas, Pranas, 339, 1426.
Čepėnas, Pranas, ed., 4068.
Čepienė, Irena, 2148.
Čepskis, M., joint ed., 1027.
Čerbulėnas, K., comp. & ed., 3994.
Čerkeliūnas, Kęstutis, ed., 1116
Černeckis, V., joint author, 1819.
Černius, Rimas, 90.
Černius, Rimas, joint author, 2447.
Černius, Vytautas, 725.
Červonaja, Svetlana see Chervon-
  naĭa, Svetlana Mikhaĭlovna
Česnulevičiūtė, Petrė, 2582.
Česnulis, Petras, 761, 988.
Chankowski, Stanisław, 1556.
Characiejus, Alfonsas, 1251.
Chekman, V. K., 2188, 2227.
Chernevskiĭ, Petr Osipovich, 2.
Chernoĭ, L., tr., 4000.
Chervonnaĭa, Svetlana Mikhaĭlovna,
  3906.
Chienas, Menašas, 1793-1795.
Chłopocka, Helena, 1489.
Chodynicki, Henryk, 891.
Chodynicki, Kazimierz, 1509.
Chodźko, Ignacy, 3732.

Garunkštis, A., ed., 606.
Gasiūnas, Jonas, 729.
Gaučys, Povilas, 2629.
Gaudrimas, Juozas, 169, 3850.
Gause, Fritz, 1881.
Gecys, Casimir C. see Gečys, Kazys.
Gečys, Kazys, 1124.
Geda, Sigitas, 3311-3313.
Gedgaudas, Česlovas, 118, 1352.
Gedminas, Antanas, 3963.
Gedminas, Antanas, comp. & ed., 3770.
Gedminas, Antanas, joint ed., 3982.
Gedvilas, Leonas, joint author, 2371.
Gedvilas, Leonas, comp., 2252.
Gedvilas, Leonas, ed., 2371.
Gedvilas, Mečyslovas, 1621.
Gėlė, Zigmas, pseud. see Gaidama-
   vičius, Zigmas.
Gelžinis, Martynas, 634.
Geniušienė, E.Š. see Geniūshene,
   Ė. Sh.
Geniūshene, Ė.Sh. (Geniušienė, E.Š.)
   2236, 2353.
Genytė-Šmaižienė, Viktorija, 3314.
Genzelis, Bronius, 360, 1963.
Genzelis, Bronius, comp., 1963.
Georg, Waldemar, 3936, 3938.
Georg, Waldemar, joint author, 3936.
Geralavičius, Vytautas, 1275.
Gerke, Aleksei Aleksandrovich, ed.,
   599.
Germantas, pseud., 1701, 1702.
Gerulaitis, Karolis, 545.
Gerulis, Petras, 2078.
Gerullis, Georg, 170, 170a, 1433,
   2194-2195.
Gerutis, Albertas, 1383, 1746.
Gerutis, J., pseud. see Balvočius,
   Jonas.
Gibavičius, Rimtautas, comp., 3973.
Gibavičius, Rimtautas, illus.,
   3438, 3553.
Gidžiūnas, Viktoras, 56, 2028-2030.
Gieczys, Kazimierz see Gečys,
   Kazys.
Giedra, Balys, 793.
Giedra, Vincas, 2842-2843, 3315-3316.
Giedraitis, Antanas, 2098-2099,
   2844-2846.
Giedraitis, Romualdas see Spalis,
   Romualdas.
Giedraitis-Giedrius, Antanas see
   Giedraitis, Antanas.
Giedrius, A., pseud. see Giedrai-
   tis, Antanas.
Gieysztor, Aleksander, 1384.
Gil'debrand, German see Hildebrand,
   Hermann.
Gimbutas, Jurgis, 171, 1125, 2166.
Gimbutas, Leonidas, 4007.
Gimbutas, Marija (Alseikaitė), 1300,
   2065-2067, 2079.
Ginaitė, Sara, 1286.
Gineitis, Leonas, 2462.
Gineitis, Leonas, joint ed., 2681.
Ginsburgas, M., tr., 1820, 3870.
Gintautas, J. pseud. see Staugai-
   tis, Justinas.
Gira, Liudas, 172, 2584.

Girčys, Vytautas, joint author, 1729.
Girdenis, Aleksas, ed., 2430.
Girdzijauskas, J., 2383.
Girdzijauskas, J., comp., 2475-2476,
   2662.
Girdzijauskas, Vytautas, 2847-2848.
Girich, G., ed., 440.
Girkontaitė, Ramutė, 3317.
Girnius, Juozas, 173, 1966.
Girnius, Juozas, joint author, 4017.
Girnius, Juozas, ed. 3937.
Girnius, Saulius A., 174.
Gisevius, Eduard Karl Samuel, 668,
   2463.
Glagolevas, V., 1254-1255.
Glemža, Jonas, 1271.
Gliauda, Jurgis, pseud. see Gliau-
   dys, Jurgis.
Gliaudys, Jurgis, 1732-1733, 2464,
   2849-2852.
Glinskii, F.A., 624.
Glinskis, Juozas, 2853, 3178-3179.
Globig, Anneliese, tr., 3730.
Godoy, Armand, 175, 3785.
Goetz, Leopold Karl, 1161-1162.
Golawski, Michał, 1385.
Goldas, M., 3, 63, 1703.
Goldas, M., comp., 1700.
Goldhagen Erich, 1090.
Górski, Ryszard, ed., 2086.
Gorski, Tadeusz, 176, 2002.
Gorskii, Sergei, 1320.
Goštautas, Jonas, 361.
Grabauskaitė, Kristina , joint ed.,
   523.
Grabis, R., IA., ed., 2181.
Grabski, Władysław, 4020.
Grabowsky, Adolf, 342.
Graičiūnas, Jonas, 3318-3320.
Grauslys, Alfonsas, 1967.
Gray, Louis Herbert, ed., 2069.
Gražbylys, Petras, pseud., 2309.
Gražys, Remigijus, 3321.
Gražytė, Ilona see Gražytė-Mazi-
   liauskienė, Ilona.
Gražytė-Maziliauskienė, Ilona, 2465,
   2565, 2585-2586.
Greene, Victor R., 343, 730.
Grekov, Igor' Borisovich, 1353.
Gricius, Alfonsas, 3322-3324.
Gricius, Augustinas, 362, 2532,
   2854-2855, 3180-3181, 3611-3612.
Grickevičius, Valentinas, 125.
Grienberger, Theodor R. von, 2068.
Grigaitė, V. V., ed., 374, 4038.
Grigaitis, Alfonsas, 1014.
Grigaitytė, A., comp., 1940.
Grigalavičienė, Elena, joint author,
   666.
Grigaliūnas, Stanislovas, 820.
Grigas, Kazys, 2100.
Grigas, Kazys, ed., 1792.
Grigas, R., ed., 1246, 1283-1284.
Grigelienė, A., ed., 579-580.
Grigelis, A., ed., 25, 587, 608.
Grigelis, I., ed.,
Grigialene, A. see Grigelienė, A.
Grigialis, A.A. see Grigelis, A.
Grigienė, J., ed., 3934.

Juodpalytė, Genovaitė, joint author, 2435.
Juodpusis, Vaclovas, 187, 3851.
Juodvalkis, Jonas, 1918.
Juozapavičius, Pranas, 188.
Juozėnas, L., 2877.
Jūra, Klemensas, 3350.
Jūragis, Juozas Almis, ed., 2651.
Jurašienė, Aušra Marija, 2533.
Jurėnas, A., ed., 2139.
Jurėnas, Eduardas, illus., 3416,3676.
Jurevičius, A., 102.
Jurevičius, Juozas, 189, 1126.
Jurevičiūtė, E., ed., 1199.
Jurevičiūtė, Irena, 2435.
Jurgaitienė, V., 1723.
Jurgaitis, Algirdas, 584.
Jurgaitis, Algirdas, joint ed., 586.
Jurgela, Constantine Rudyard, 997, 1358.
Jurgela, Petras, 1127.
Jurgelionis, Kleofas, 3351.
Jurgėnas, Ed., ed., 1767.
Jurginis, Juozas, 190, 1574, 1665-1666, 2006-2008, 4008.
Jurginis, Juozas, ed., 1791, 3993, 4121.
Jurkiewicz, J., 344.
Jurkūnas, Ignas, 367.
Jurkūnas, Jonas, joint author, 881.
Jurkūnas, Vytautas (jaunesnysis), illus., 3264.
Jurkūnas-Scheynius, Ignas see Jurkūnas, Ignas.
Jurkus, Paulius, 700, 3352, 3985.
Jurkus, Paulius, ed., 2654, 3926.
Jurkus, Paulius, comp. & ed., 3926.
Juronienė, Genovaitė, 1783.
Juškienė, Elena, comp., 94.
Juzeliūnas, Julius, 3885-3887.

K.A.K., pseud. see Kaupas, Antanas
K, D.S., 2329.
K.P.W., pseud. see Viksva, Pranciškus.
Kabašinskas, P., comp., 1199.
Kabelka, J., joint ed., 2681.
Kacenbergas, J., photo, 442.
Kačinskas, Jeronimas, 3888.
Kačiulis, Justinas, 2588.
Kadžytė, Liuda, 2330.
Kahle, Wilhelm, 2044.
Kairienė, Aldona (Baužinskaitė) see Baužinskaitė-Kairienė, Aldona.
Kairiūkštytė-Jacinienė, Halina,1205, 3998.
Kairys, Anatolijus, 2878, 3188,3353, 3619, 3875.
Kairys, Anatolijus, joint ed., 2654.
Kaleininkas, Dominikas see Laukis, Joseph (Juozas).
Kalinauskas, Bronius, 2372.
Kalinauskas, Vytautas, illus., 2372, 2656, 3032, 3398, 3554.
Kalinka, Waleryan, 803.
Kalinouski, Kastus' see Kalinauskas, Konstantinas.
Kalinovskiǐ, Kastus' see Kalinaus-

kas, Konstantinas.
Kalnėnas, Juozas, pseud. see Andziulaitis, Juozas.
Kalniņš, Bruno, 275.
Kamantauskas, Viktoras, 2331.
Kamenetskaite, N., tr., 3870.
Kamenetsky, Ihor, 1900.
Kamienecki, Witold, 1515.
Kaminauskas, V.J., illus., 3614.
Kamiński, A., 17, 1905.
Kancevičius, Vytautas, 1622.
Kancevičius, Vytautas, comp., 1184.
Kancevičius, Vytautas, ed., 1624.
Kanet, Roger E., 18.
Kaniauskas, M., comp., 231.
Kanovich, Gregoriǐ, tr., 3688.
Kanovichius, G. see Kanovičius, G.
Kanovičius, G., tr., 3604, 3688, 3701.
Kantautas, Adam, 58.
Kantautas, Adam, comp., 4.
Kantautas, Filomena, joint comp., 4.
Kapačinskas, Juozas, 712.
Kaplanas, Isakas, tr., 3622, 3667, 3680-3681, 3702.
Kaplanas, Jokūbas, 2311.
Kapnys, Stasys, 2879.
Kapsukas, Vincas, 368.
Kapsukas-Mickevičius, Vincas see Kapsukas, Vincas.
Karalius, Vytautas, 3354.
Karbach, Oscar, joint author, 1101.
Karčiauskas, Mykolas, 3355-3356.
Kardelis, Jonas, 1919.
Kardelytė, Jadvyga, 2425.
Kareivis, J.D., pseud., 2880.
Kaributas, Juozas, 2691.
Karka, Jonas, joint ed., 774.
Karosas, Juozas, 3852, 3944.
Karosas, Viktoras, 1003.
Karosas, Vytautas, 3357.
Karpavičienė, L., comp., 2338.
Karpavičius, Kazimieras see Karpius, Kazys S.
Karpavičius, P., joint author, 415.
Karpius, Kazys S., 2081, 2881-2882.
Karvelio, J. ir J. Rinkevičiaus knygynas, 59.
Karvelis, Kazys, 1272.
Karvelis, Petras, 276.
Karvelis, Vladas, 1636-1638.
Karvelytė, Ada, 3358.
Karvialis, Vladas see Karvelis, Vladas.
Karvojus, pseud. see Kaupas, Antanas.
Karys, Jonas K., 1220.
Kašauskas, Raimondas, 2883-2884.
Kashkurėvich, A., ed., 3731.
Kashprovski, Yevgeni Ivanovich, 1499.
Kaškelis, Juozas, 569.
Kaslas, Bronius J., 277, 925, 931, 945-946, 998, 1322, 1623.
Kaslas, Bronius J., comp., 999, 1460.
Kaslas-Kazlauskas, Bronius see Kaslas, Bronius, J.
Kasperavičius, Julius, 4090, 4095.
Kasperunas, Georgiǐ Vladimirovich, 2885.

Lituanistikos institutas. Suvažia-
vimo darbai see Institute of
Lithuanian Studies. Lituanistikos
instituto...metų suvažiavimo dar-
bai.
Liudžius, Juozas, 2698.
Liudžiuvienė, Petronelė, 199.
Liulevičienė, Monika see Nendrė,
O., pseud.
Liulevičius, Vincentas, 702, 749.
1363.
Liulevičius, Vincentas, joint
author, 4017.
Liulevičius, Vincentas, ed., 200,
1428, 1810, 4049.
Loeber, Dietrich A., 2481, 4117.
Loewe, Karl von, ed. & tr., 826.
Logminas, B., 626.
Lofewski, Erich von, 2113.
Lopaev, Sofroniĭ Semenovich, 882.
Lossowski, Piotr, 346, 915, 957-958,
1327, 1602.
Lowery, Sidney, 1328-1329.
Łowmiański, Henrik, 692, 828.
Lubenow, Hedwig, 1890.
Lubicz-Milosz, O.W. de see Milosz,
Oscar Vladislas.
Lubieniecki, Stanisław, 2047.
Łubieńska, Dolores, 3948.
Lukaševičius, Henrikas, 1924, 2934.
Lukinskas, Romualdas, 2935-2936.
Lukoševičienė, Irena, 703.
Lukoševičius, Jonas, 704.
Lukoševičius, Mireilee, tr., 3576.
Lukošiūnas, Algimantas, joint
author, 51.
Lukša, Juozas see Daumantas,
Juozas, pseud.
Lukšaitė, Ingė, ed., 1054.
Lumbis, pseud. see Bulis, Jonas.
Lušys, Stasys, 1811.
Luther, Martin, 2285.
Lydinis, pseud., 3200.

MacCulloch, John Arnott, 2069.
Mackienė, S., joint author, 2306.
Maceina, Antanas, 201, 705, 714,
1785, 1812, 1972-1979.
Mačernis, Vytautas, 3379-3380.
Macevičius, Juozas, 2645, 3381-3384,
3626-3627.
Macijauskas, Jonas, 2937, 3628.
Macijauskas, Jonas, comp., 127.
Macijauskienė, Marija, 2547, 2938.
Maciuika, Benedict V. see Mačiui-
ka, Benediktas Vytenis.
Mačiuika, Benediktas Vytenis, 283,
693, 1149-1153, 1277.
Mačiuika, Vytautas, 3385.
Mačiukevičius, Jonas, 2939-2942,
3386, 3629.
Maciulevičius, Jonas see Maironis,
Jonas.
Mačiulis, Jonas, 2943.
Mačiulis, Jonas see Maironis,
Jonas.

Mačiūnas, Vincas, 45, 75, 202, 203,
2482, 2596-2597.
Mackevičius, Bronius, 2699, 3387-
3388, 3630.
Mackevičius, Mečys, 799, 1631.
McKinstry, Betty, joint comp., 72.
Mackus, Algimantas, 3389-3393.
Mačys, Vladas, 874.
Mager, Friedrich, 1200.
Maiminas, Jefremas, 1168.
Maironis, Jonas, 1429, 3394-3395.
Maironis-Mačiulis, Jonas see
Maironis, Jonas.
Maksimaitis, Mindaugas, 796.
Maksimavičius, J., joint author,
1079.
Makūnaitė, Albina, illus., 3132,
3136, 3400, 3451.
Malcas, E., tr., 3612, 3680, 3694.
Malcienė, Marijana, 3837.
Maldeikis, Petras, 204, 883.
Maldonis, Alfonsas, 3396-3398, 3631-
3633.
Maldonis, Alfonsas, comp., 3670.
Maldonis, Alfonsas, joint ed., 132,
2554, 2944, 3393.
Maldutis, Julius, 1196.
Maldžiūnaitė, S., 627.
Maleczyńska, Ewa, 1395.
Mališauskas, Vaclovas, ed., 1183,
1198, 1201, 1233.
Malishauskas, V. see Mališauskas,
Vaclovas.
Maliukevičius, R., ed., 2690.
Mal'tsas, E. see Malcas, E.
Maniušis, Juozas, 323, 1238-1240.
Marcelis, Albertas, 1707.
Marcijonas, A., 1042.
Marcinkevičius, Antanas, 2945.
Marcinkevičius, Jonas, 2946.
Marcinkevičius, Juozas, 3201, 3399.
Marcinkevičius, Justinas, 3202-3203,
3400-3405, 3634-3640.
Marcinkevičius, Justinas, ed., 2641-
2642, 3521, 3697.
Marcinkevičius-Mantautas, Aleksand-
ras, ed., 379, 2712.
Marciński, Maciej Franciszek, 2337.
Mareckaitė, G., comp., 3664.
Margalis, Juozas, pseud. see
Šnapštys, Juozas.
Margeris, Algirdas, 1015, 2947.
Margevičius, K., joint comp. & ed.,
2241.
Margevičius, P., joint author, 3021.
Markevičius, Anelius, 2948-2949,
3641.
Markiavichius, Anelius see Marke-
vičius, Anelius.
Martin, André, 1768, 2011.
Martinaitis, Ignas, illus., 2896,
3539.
Martinaitis, Marcelijus, 2483, 3406-
3410.
Martinaitis, Marcelijus, comp., 3723.
Martinaitis, M., ed., 3244.
Martínez Beretche, José Pedro, 1625.
Martinkus, Vytautas, 2950-2951, 3411.

New York (City). Public Library.
  Slavonic division. The Research
  Libraries, 66.
New York. Riverside Museum, 3914.
Nezabitauskis, Adolfas, 223.
Nezavitauskis, Liudvikas, 1085.
Nežinomas, pseud. see Ralys, Je-
  ronimas.
Niemcewicz, Julian Ursyn, 1550.
Niemojewski, Stanisław, 1930.
Niessel, Henri Albert, 1931.
Nimtz-Wendlandt, Wanda, ed., 1932.
Niunka, Vladas, 1786.
Nol'de, Boris Ėmmanuilovich, Baron,
  1544.
Norbutas, Vytautas, 2983.
Noreika, Zigmuntas, 1021.
Norkevičienė, R., comp., 2387.
Norkevičienė, R., joint ed., 2252.
Norkus, Jonas, 2253.
Norkus, Jonas, ed., 2491.
Norvilas, Algis, 1748.
Novickis, Birutė, ed., 1063.
Nowicki, Edward, joint author, 548.
Nyka-Niliūnas, Alfonsas see Čip-
  kus, Alfonsas.

Obelienius, Juozas, 400.
Obst, Jan, 3515, 4011.
Ochmański, Jerzy, 2037.
Ochmański, Jerzy, ed., 1367.
Öller, Ragnar, tr. & ed., 3672.
Oginski, Michał K., 1527-1528.
Okulicz, Jerzy, 1305.
Olechnowiczius, K. see Aleknavi-
  čius, Kajetonas.
Olekienė, O., 2254.
Onaitis, Vytautas, 3452.
Orda, J., 664.
Orentaitė, Birutė, 436.
Orintaitė, Petronėlė, 2984-2986,3453,
Osmann, L., joint author, 3996.
Osmolskis, P., illus., 2677, 2744,
  3300.
Ost, Horst G., tr., 1893.
Ostrauskas, Kostas, 2567, 3207.
Otrębski, Jan Szczepan, 2426.
Oželienė, Sofija, 1933.
Ozerov, Lev Adol'fovich, 3674.
Ozerov, Lev Adol'fovich, tr., 2547,
  3644, 3665, 3625.
Ozerovas, Levas see Ozerov, Lev
  Adol'fovich.

Pabaltijo tautų susiartinimo kongre-
  sas, 5th, Kaunas, (1939), 934.
Pabijūnas, Algimantas, 3454-3456.
Padaužų dramos skyrius, pseud.: Iš-
  naros see Išnaros.
Paevskiĭ, Lev, 3995.
Pagėgis, Algimantas, pseud. see
  Mackus, Algimantas.
Pagirys, M., comp., 380.
Pakalka, Jonas, 884.
Pakalnis, Antanas, 2705, 2987,3672a.

Pakalniškis, Aleksandras, 684, 1847,
  1934, 2989.
Pakalniškis, Kazimieras, 1188.
Pakalniškytė, Milda, joint ed., 523.
Pakarklis, Povilas, 2014.
Pakeliūnas, Algirdas, 3976-3977.
Pakštas, Kazys, 643.
Pakštienė, Janina, 224-226.
Pakuckas, Česlovas, 590-591.
Palanta, pseud. see Byras, Antanas.
Pal'chinskaĭte, Violetta see Pal-
  činskaitė, Violeta.
Palčiauskas R., illus., 2261, 2626,
  3249, 3472.
Palčinskaitė, Violeta, 3457, 3673.
Paleckis, Justas, 1603, 2706-2707,
  3458-3459, 3674-3675.
Palilionis, Petras, 3460.
Palionis, Jonas, 2255.
Palionytė, D., comp., 3865.
Palmaitis, Lėtas, 2211.
Paltarokas, Kazimieras, 1056.
Panucevič, Vaclaŭ, 2015.
Paparonis, pseud. see Šmulkštys,
  Antanas.
Papečkienė, Sigita, comp., 2694.
Papritz, Johannes, joint ed., 939.
Papšys, Antanas, 418.
Paraščiakas, A., joint comp., 132,
  2554.
Parojus, Juozas, 3461-3462.
Pasaulio Lietuvių Bendruomenė, 377,
  706-707, 1686.
Pasaulio Lietuvių Bendruomenė. Sei-
  mas. 4th, Washington, (1973),708.
Pashuto, Vladimir Torent'evich, 290.
Paškauskaitė, J., illus., 3403-3404.
Paškauskaitė, Lili, illus., 2683,
  3261.
Paškauskas, Jurgis, 2708.
Paškevičius, Juozas, 592-595.
Passarge, Ludwig, 291.
Passendorfer, Edward, 596.
Paszkiewicz, Henryk, 1480a, 1485,
  1502.
Patackas, Gintaras, 3463.
Paterson, Adrian, tr., 2134.
Paukštelis, Juozas, 2709, 2990,2992-
  2993, 3208, 3675a, 3676.
Paulauskienė, Aldona, joint author,
  2354.
Pauliukonis, Pranas, 1197.
Pautieniūtė, Teresė, 3464.
Paužuolis, Juozapas, 1935.
Pavalkis, Victor, 1772.
Pavilionytė, D., joint author, 682.
Paweł Włodkowc z Brudzewa, 326.
Pawiński, Adolf, 1529.
Payne, Pierre Stephen Robert, 1000.
Pažėraitė, Karolė, 2994-2995.
Pažūsis, F., comp., 1679.
Pažusis, Lionginas, 2412.
Peackok, Kenneth, 2135, 2145.
Pečkauskaitė, Marija, 227, 327, 378,
  1064, 2710, 2996-2999, 3677.
Pelėda, Lazdynų, pseud. see Pšibi-
  liauskienė, Sofija (Ivanauskaitė).
Penkauskas, Pranas, 1439, 1493.
Perlbach, Max, 1472.
Perlbach, Max, comp., 1463, 1892.

Pučkoriūtė, L., illus., 3701.
Puida, Kazys, 3023.
Pugevičius, Casimir, ed., 84.
Puikūnas, Jonas Mingirdas, comp. & ed., 2114.
Puišytė, Aldona, 3466.
Pukelevičiūtė, Birutė, 3024.
Pukys, P., 437.
Pulokienė, I., joint author, 107.
Pupkis, Aldonas, comp., 2310.
Puronas, Vytautas, ed., 1147.
Puronas, Vytautas, joint author, 1241.
Pušinis, Bronius, 1940.
Puškoriūtė, L., illus., 2058.
Pusta, Karel Robert, 1049.
Putinas, pseud. see Mykolaitis, Vincas.
Putinas, V. Mykolaitis see Mykolaitis, Vincas.
Putvinskis, Vladas, 379, 2712.
Putvinskis-Pūtvis, Vladas see Putvinskis, Vladas.
Puzinas, A., 3951.
Puzinas, Jonas, 233, 348, 644, 665, 1333, 1440, 1687, 1826, 1851,1861, 4053, 4075.
Puzinas, Paul, 3951.
Puzyna, Józef Edward, 1476.

Quennerstedt, August Wilhelm, ed., 1410.

R., H., 1226.
Rabačiauskaitė, A., comp., 3351.
Rabikauskas, Paulius, 234, 307, 2033, 4076.
Račiūnas, Antanas, 3893-3897.
Račkauskas, Jonas A., 29, 4024-4028, 4059.
Račkauskas, Kazimieras, 1245.
Račkauskas, Konstantinas, 806.
Račkauskas, V.K., comp., 536-537.
Račkauskas, Vladas Karolis, 235, 2713, 4096.
Račkus, Aleksandras M., 1223.
Radloff, W., 1100.
Radzevičius, Bronius, 3467.
Radžius, Aleksandras, 3468-3469.
Radziwiłł, Albrycht Stanisław,1531.
Ränk, Gustav, 4012.
Ragaišienė, Vanda, ed., 1829.
Ragana, Šatrijos, pseud. see Pečkauskaitė, Marija.
Ragauskas, Jonas, 1787.
Ragauskienė, R. (Aidukaitė), 3025.
Ragažinskas, Povilas, 236.
Raguotienė, Genovaitė, 4119.
Raguotis, Bronius, 237.
Raila, Bronys, 752, 1941, 2496.
Rainys, Juozas, 4077.
Raišupis, Matas, 1774.
Railys, Jeronimas, 3026.
Rakūnas, Algirdas, 1057.
Ramanauskaitė-Pažūsienė, T., comp., 2139.

Ramanauskas, Antanas, 3027.
Ramm, Boris IAkovlevich, 1506, 2016-2018.
Ramojus, Vladas, 1614.
Ramojus, Vladas see also Butėnas, Vladas.
Ramonaitė, Valerija, 2386.
Ramonas, K., illus., 2739.
Ramonas, Vincas, 3028-3029.
Ran, Leyzer, comp. & ed., 1107.
Rannit, Aleksis, 3916-3917.
Rasa, Rėnė, pseud., 3030.
Raščius, Pranas, 3470-3472.
Rasikas, R., 574.
Raslavičienė, Regina see Rasa, Rėnė, pseud.
Rastenis, Nadas, tr., 3587.
Rastenis, Vincas, ed., 1606.
Raštikis, Stasys, 901, 1942.
Ratas, Vaclovas, illus., 3985.
Rathfelders, Hermanis, 292.
Ratnikas, Jonas, 3473.
Rauch, Georg von, 1334.
Rauduvė, Petras, illus., 3458, 3505, 3541.
Raulinaitis, Z., 1411.
Raumer, Kurt von, 1585.
Rautinš, Danutė, tr., 2135.
Redaway, W.F., ed., 1381.
Reddaway, P., joint author, 1731.
Regel, Konstantin, 620.
Regratis, Artūras, pseud., 2714-2715.
Reicher, Michał, 685.
Reikalas, Kęstas, 2568-2571.
Reimeris, Vacys, 329, 753, 3474-3475, 3687.
Reimeris, Vacys, ed., 2640, 2702.
Reimeris, Vacys, joint ed., 2715, 3393.
Reinhard, Marcel, 645.
Reĭtern, V.E., ed., 1074.
Rekašius, Zenonas, 694.
Rėklaitienė, Janina see Reklaitis, Janine (Kanauka).
Reklaitis, Janine (Kanauka), 2257-2258.
Reklaitis, Povilas Viktoras, 5, 6, 3979.
Remanė, Lieselotte, tr., 3599,3660.
Remeika, Jonas, 330.
Remeikis, Thomas, 1629, 4002.
Renner, Hans von, 293.
Respublikiniai sanitarinio švietimo namai, 1114.
Reutt, Marya, 3755.
Rhesa, Ludwig Jedimin, tr., 3304.
Riasanovsky, Nicholas V., 1412.
Rieckenberg, H., 1901.
Rimaitis, J., 1775, 2020.
Rimaitis, Juozas, joint author, 1023, 1751.
Rimantienė, Rimutė (Jablonskytė), 600, 666, 1306.
Rimkevičius, Vytautas, 3031-3033, 3210, 3211, 3688.
Rimklavichius, Vitautas see Rimkevičius, Vytautas.
Rimkus, Petras, 384, 3034.
Rimošius, pseud. see Savickis, Jurgis.

Satunovskiĭ, Leon Mikhaĭlovich, ed., 1244.
Saudargienė, Ava see Saudargienė, Vlada R.
Saudargienė, Vlada R., 2717.
Sauka, Leonardas, joint comp., 2656.
Saukaitytė, Dalia, 3488.
Saulaitis, Antanas, 1119.
Saulaitis, Marija, 3489, 3834.
Saulaitytė, Marija Jurgita see Saulaitis, Marija.
Saulius, Vytautas, ed., 3379.
Šavelis, Rimantas, 3045, 3490.
Savickaitė, E., joint comp., 4044.
Savickas, Augustinas, 130, 3920-3921, 3953.
Savickis, Jurgis, 2718, 3046-3047.
Savukynas, Bronys, comp., 2276-2277, 2408.
Scarmolin, A. Louis, 3898.
Schaeder, Hildegard, 948.
Schaper, Edzard Hellmuth, 1336-1337.
Scheynius, pseud. see Jurkūnas, Ignas.
Schiemann, Theodor, 1338.
Schleicher, August, ed. & tr., 2092, 2342.
Schlichting, Richard, 3996.
Schmalstieg, William Riegel, 2213a, 2214-2219, 2265.
Schmalstieg, William Riegel, tr., 129, 2213a, 2260.
Schmid, Bernhard, 3997.
Schmidt, Axel Johan, 1339.
Schnitzer, Marc L., 2303.
Schondoch, 14th cent., 3762.
Schoeps, Hans Joachim, 1895.
Schramm, Gottfried, historian, 1072.
Schröder, Ingeborg, tr., 3635.
Schröder, Otto, 1615.
Sealey, Danguolė, 3491-3493.
Sealey, Danguolė, tr., 3712.
Šeinius, Ignas, pseud. see Jurkūnas, Ignas.
Šeižys, Mykolas, 3494-3495.
Selelionis, Eduardas, 3496.
Selimas, pseud. see Kaupas, Antanas.
Semaška, Algimantas, joint author, 410.
Šemerys, Salys, 3497-3498.
Semkowicz, Aleksander, 1474.
Senas, Vincas, pseud. see Jackson, V.J.
Senkus, Juozas, 2427-2428.
Senn, Alfred, 2060, 2220, 2343, 2406.
Senn, Alfred, tr., 2060.
Senn, Alfred Erich, 69, 239, 771, 886, 917-918, 1597-1599, 1604.
Senn, Alfred Erich, joint author, 1596.
Sepkus, Lionginas, 2499.
Seraphim, August, 875a.
Seraphim, Hans Jürgen, 331.
Seraphim, Peter Heinz, 646.
Serapinas, Rapolas, comp. & tr., 1983.
Sereiskis, Benjaminas, 95.

Sergeenkov, Mikhail Mikhaĭlovich, 383-384.
Šešelgis, Aleksandras, Joint author, 44.
Šešelgis, Kazys, 4009.
Šešelgis, Kazys, ed., 1859, 4014.
Šešelgis, Kazys, joint comp. & ed., 3994.
Seselskytė, Adėlė, comp., 2248, 4067.
Seselskytė, Adėlė (Ada), joint comp., 2116.
Šešplaukis, Alfonsas, 70, 2500-2501, 3499-3500, 4120.
Šešplaukis, Alfonsas, comp., 2502.
Šešplaukis, Alfonsas, tr., 3761-3762.
Šeštokas, Konstantinas, 1789.
Sezemanas, Vosylius, ed., 1983.
Shaforenko, N., tr., 3642, 3678.
Shailitskiĭ, V.I., ed., 1954.
Sharmaitis, R. see Šarmaitis, R.
Shartse, Olga, 3577.
Shatriės Ragana, pseud. see Pečkauskaitė, Marija.
Shaw, Joseph Thomas, ed., 8.
Shein, Pavel Vasil'evich, comp., 2088.
Shelepin, I.V., 1413.
Shlygina, N.V., joint editor, 678.
Shmigel'skis, K. see Šmigelskis, K.
Shub, Anatole, 1740.
Shustikov, Nikolaĭ Ivanovich, 1669.
Sidabraitė, Alė, pseud. see Žalinkevičaitė, Elena.
Sideravičius, Rimantas, 2503-2504.
Šidlauskas, Adomas see Vilainis, A., pseud.
Šidlauskas, Domas, 2053.
Šidlauskas, Kazys, 1817.
Sidzikauskas, Vaclovas, 807.
Siew, Liebermann, 1010.
Šikšnys, Marcelinas, 2719.
Šilbajoris, Rimvydas, 2505, 2549-2550, 2572-2573, 2603-2609.
Šilbajoris, Rimvydas, comp., 525.
Šilbajoris, Rimvydas, ed., 526.
Šileikis, Mikas, illus., 3453.
Šilelis, L., pseud. see Šimutis, Leonardas.
Šimkūnas, Romualdas, 439.
Šimkūnas, V., joint ed., 34.
Šimkus, Alfredas, 3501.
Šimkus, Jonas, 2506-2507, 3048-3049.
Šimkus, Morkus, ed., 920, 1370.
Šimkus, Sigizmundas Juozas, 4042.
Šimkus, Stasys, 3865, 3900.
Šimkus, Vladas, 3690-3691.
Simonaitytė, Ieva, 3050-3055, 3692-3693.
Šimonis, K., illus., 2925.
Sims-Černeckytė, Marija, 3502.
Šimukonienė, Gražina, comp., 2648.
Šimutis, Leonardas, 3220.
Šimutis, Leonardas Juozapas, 3866-3867.
Šimutis, Leonardas Juozapas, tr., 760, 3871, 4107.

TITLE INDEX

LIST OF SERIALS CONSULTED

AND

ANALYZED MONOGRAPHS WITH LOCATIONS AND HOLDINGS

ACTA BALTICA, v.1- ; 1960 61- . Königstein im Taunus, Institutum Balti-
cum. Annual. DK511.B25A5 DLC(1-) AzTeS(1-) CaAEU(1-) CaOTU(1-) CaBVaU;
CLU(1-) CU(3-) CoU(4,6) CU-Riv(5-) CSt-H; CSt(1-) CtY(1-) GU(4,6) ICU(1-)
InU(1-6) KMK(7-) KyU(1-) MH(1-) MnU(1-) MiEM(1-) MB(1-) MoU(1-) MoSW(6-)
NN(1-) NIC(1-) NbU(1-) NcD(4,6) NNC(4-) OClW(7-) OKentU(1960-1972)
OrCS(4-) PU(1-) PPiU; PV(5-) TxHR(1-) WU(1-)

AIDAI; mėnesinis kultūros žurnalas. [Echoes: cultural magazine] München,
Ger.; Kennebunk Port, Me.; Brooklyn, N.Y., 1945- . Monthly. In United
States Published by Franciscan Fathers, Kennebunk Port, Me. since Oct.
1949 and in Brooklyn, N.Y. since Oct. 1952. AP95.L5A4 DLC(1952-) CtTMF(
1946,no.9(21-)-1963) CtY(1957-) ICCC(1945-1946,no.6,7,8; 1947-1949,no.22-
23,25-26; 1950-1956) ICLJF(1945-1946, 1951, 1957-1970-) ICWA; MH(1957-);
NN(1-); PU(1947-) OKentU(Sept.1945-Oct.1946; v.1,no.1-v.3,no.12 on microfilm; 1947-1973 bound-)

AKADEMIE DER WISSENSCHAFTEN, BERLIN. Sitzungsberichte. Bd. 1- ; 1882-1921.
Berlin. Monthly. Supersedes its Monatsberichte and continued in classes.
AS182.B35 DLC(1-) CLU(1-) CSt(1-) CaQMM(1882-96,1915-1921) CaOTU(1-)
CU(1-) CtY(1-) DSG(1-) ICU(1-) MH(1-) MiU(1-) NN(1-) NNC(1-) NbU(1-)
NjP(1-) OCU(1-) PU(1-) WaU(1-)

AKADEMIE DER WISSENSCHAFTEN, Munich. KOMMISSION FÜR ORTSNAMENFORSCHUNG.
Studia onomastica monacensia. 1- ; 1956- . München. CU(1-) DLC;IU(1-)
MdBJ; MH(1-) MiDW(1-) NBuU(Studia onomastica) PU(1-)

AKADEMIIA NAUK S.S.S.R. Bulletin. s3,v1-32,1860-1888; s4,v.1-4,1890-1894;
s5,v.1-25,1894-1906; s6,v.1-21,1907-1927. sl see Bulletin scientifique;
s2 see Classe historico-philologique. Bulletin and Classe physico-mathé-
matique. Bulletin. s4,v.1-4 also as s3,v.33-36. From s5,v.1 second
title in Russian. 1928- in sections which see under its Izvestiīa.
AS262.S34 DLC(1-s4,v.[1-4]-s6,v.[4]-[8]-[10-12]-21) CSfA([5], s5,v.1-6,
[20]-25; s6,v.[1]-21) CSt(s6,v.6,19-20) CU; CaQMM(1-s4,v.[1-4]-s6,v.21)
CaOOG(1-12,[14,24-29],s5,v.1-[16]-s6,v.[1-8]-[19,20]) CaOTR: CaOTU(1,[3-5]-
7,11[12],14,24,s5,v.1-s6,v.21) CoD(s6,v.16-21) CtY; DA(1-32; s5,v.1-s6,
v.21) DGS(s4,v.[1-4]-s6,v.21) DSI-M(s4,v.[4]-s5,v.[9]-s6,v.[4]-[8],10-13,
15-[19-21]) IC(1-s5,v.25) ICF(s5,v.1-s6,v.21) ICJ(1-s4,v.[4]-s6,v.21)
ICN(1-32) ICU(1-32;s5,v.[12]-s6,v.11]19-21) IU; IaAS(1-32; s4,v.2; s5,v.1-
s6,v.21) IaU([1-6],s5,v.14-16,[22-24],s6,v.[1-6],13,15-21) InIA(s5,v.1-25)
MB(1-s6,v[12]) MBA(1-s6,v.[7-8]10-21) MBN(1-s4.[3-4]-s6,v.21) MH; MH-A(1-
s5,v.24; s6,v.1-4) MH-F(1-s5,v.[19]s6,v.[8]-13) MH-G(s6,v.6-21) MH-Z(14-
[18,25],s5,v.2-17,22-24; s6,v.1-21) MSM(s6,v.[6-8]-[11-12]-[20],21) MWhB;
MdBJ; MdBP(s5,v.[13]-[20]; s6,v.5-21) MiU; MnU(1-26; s4,v.[4]-s6,v.[1])
MoSA(1-32; s4,v.36; s5,v.1-s6,v.[9]-16) MoSB; MoU(s5,v.13-s6,v.21)
N([4-s5,v.22]-s6,v.[4]-21) NBB(s5,v[18],21-s6,v.21) NBuB([1-17]-32; s5,
v.1-[17]-s6,v.21) NIC(1-s6,v.[1]-[8]-21) NN(1-s4,v.[4]-s5,v.[5]-s6,v.21)
NNA(1-32; s5,v.1-s6,v.11) NNBG(8,12-17,26; s4,v.3-6; s5,v.1,8-9,12) NNC-M(
1-28) NNC(1-s4,v.3; s5,v.1-s6,v.21) NNCoC(22-[28]-s6,v.3) NNE(s6,v.[1-13])
NNM(1-[14]-32; s5,v.1-s6,v.21) NRU(s4,v.1-s6,v.21) NSU(1-30) NhU(s4,v.4;
s5,v.1,[2-4]-(9]-[13,17]-s6,v.4,6-9,12-13) NcD; NcU(s5,v.3-6,8,10-s6,v.21)
NhD(1-32; s5,v.2-s6,v.7) Nh(s5,v.8-s6,v.13,15-21) NjP(1-32; s5,v.1-s6,v.21)
NjR(1-s5,v.24) OCU(s5,v.16,[17,20]-s6,v.4,15-18,20-21) OCl([1-s6,v.21])
OClW(1-s6,v.[6]-13,15-21) OO([3-32],s5,v.1-18,[20]-s6,v.[5]-13,15-21) OU(1-
s5,v.[19-24]; s6,v.1-[3-10]-21) PBm(1-s5,v.24) PP(s5,v.3-s6,v.21) PPAN;
PPAP; PU(1-31; s4,v.1-3; s5,v.1-[4-5]-s6,v.21) TxU(1-32; s5,v.1-6,v.21)
RPB(s5,v.1-s6,v.21) WU(s4,v.[1-s6,v.21]) WaU(1-s4,v.2; s5,v.1-s6,v.21)

AKADEMIIA NAUK SSSR. Izvestiīa. Seriīa istorii i filosofii. T.1-9, nr.3;
1944-mai iiun' 1952. Moskva. ill. 6 nos. a year. AS262.A6247 DLC(1-)
CaOTU([1]-[3-4]-[6]-) CSt-H([1]-[3]-[5]-) CU(1-[3]-) CtY(1-[3-4]-) DDO(1,
[2-6]) ICU(1,[2],4) IaU(1-) MH -) MiDW(5-) NiC(1-) NN(1,[2]-[4])

NNC(1944-) NSU([1946-1948]-) NcD(4,6-) OU(5) OrU; PPAP(4-) PU(3,[4],6-)
WaU([1-4]-)

AKADEMIĪA NAUK SSSR. INSTITUT ARKHEOLOGII. Kratkie soobshcheniīa o dokladakh i polevykh issledovaniīakh. T.1- ; 1939 . Moskva. DK30.A173
DLC(9-) CaOONM(no.[6-50]-) CaQMAI(66-) DDO(11-30,34-35,37-) ICRL(1-) ICU(
2-3,5-6,10) MH-P(4-) NIC([13-34]-) OU(11-16,48-) PU-Mu([2-27]-)

AKADEMIĪA NAUK SSSR. INSTITUT OKEANOLOGIĪ. Trudy. 1- ; 1948- . Moskva.
GC1.A4 DLC(1-2,5-) CaQMAI(22-); CtY(6,12-13) ICRL(1-) MdBJ(1-4,6-13,15,17-)
NIC(2-13,15,17-) NNC(2-5) NNM(8) KU; CoDGS

ALTERTUM. 1- ; 1955- . Berlin, Akademie der Wissenschaften. Sektion für
Altertumswissenschaft. DE1.A35 DLC(1-) AzU(1-) CaAE(1,12-) CaMWU(1-7)
CaNSHD(14-) CaOOU(1-) CaOTU(1-) CaOWA(1-7,10-) CaQMU(1-7) CLU([1-3]-) CoU(
12-) CSt; CU(1-) CU-SB(1-) DDO(1-) FTaSU(14-) GU(14) IaU(1-) ICMcC(1-3,5-)
ICU(1-) InNd(1-) InU([1]-) IU(1-) KMK(1-) KyU(2-) LNHT(5-) MdBJ(6-) MdU(
1-) MH(1-) MH-AH; MiDW(2-) MiU(1-) MnU([1]-) MoU(8-) MWalB(1-3) N(1-7)
NbU(14-) NcRS(12-) NcU(1-) NIC(1-) NjP(1-) NjR(1-) NBuU; NN(1-) NNC(1-)
OCU(1-) OkS(14-) OrU(1-) PPiPT(14-) PPiU(9-) PSt(1-) PU(1-) RPB([1]-)
UU (1-7,10-) ViU(1-7) VtU(15-) WU(1-) WaU([1]-)

ALTERTUMSGESELLSCHAFT PRUSSIA, KÖNIGSBERG. Sitzungsberichte. Bd.1- ,
Hft.1- ; 1874- . Königsberg i.Pr. 1875- . GN814.P8A3 DLC(1-21,27-28,
31,33) MH(1-22) MH-P(2,5-6,8-) NN(3-6,8,10-18) NNC(1-22) PU-Mu(22-24,
1900-1922)

ALTPREUSSEN; Vierteljahrschrift für Vor- und Frühgeschichte. (Königsberg.
Universität. Seminar für Vor- und Frühgeschichte; Königsberg. Prussia-
Museum) v.1-9, no.1-2, May 1935-44. 9 v. MH(1-)

ALTPREUSSISCHE FORSCHUNGEN. Bd.1-20; 1923 24-1943. Königsberg in Pr.,
Gräfe und Unzer, 1924-43. 20 v. Semiannual. At head of title: Histo-
rische Kommission für ost- und west-preussische Landesforschung. Includes
"Bibliographie der Geschichte von Ost- und Westpreussen". DD491.04A17
DLC(15-) MH([1]-) NN([12]-) NNC(1-) PU(1,7-15,16,no.1,17-20)

ALTPREUSSISCHE GESCHLECHTERKUNDE. Ja. 1- ; 1927- . Königsberg in Pr.
Annual. Vols. 16 and 17 issued together. "Blätter des Vereins für Fa-
milienforschung in Ost- und Westpreussen. CS670.A45 DLC(16-17)

--- N.F. Jahrg. 1- ; Hft. 1- ; April 1953- . NN

ANALECTA ORDINIS S.BASILII MAGNI. Tomus 1-6; 1924-1949. Series 2, t.1- ;
1949- . Roma. ill. Tom 1-6 is published in Zhovkova with added title
page and most of text in Ukrainian. Series 2 also called Analecta OSBM
series 2, sectio 2. Text in Latin or Ukrainian. Mzd900.B3A12 CtY; CoU;
DCU; DDO(1-) NN(1-) NcD; PU

ANTROPOLOGICHESKOE OBSHCHESTVO, LENINGRAD. VOENNO-MEDITSINSKAĪA AKADEMIĪA.
Trudy. 1-5; 1893-1899. GN2.A93 DLC; DSI-E([1]-3) MB(1-3) MH([1],5) MH-P

ARCHIV FÜR SLAVISCHE PHILOLOGIE. v.1-42,no.3-4; 1875-1929. Berlin. Suspended May 1920-Oct. 1922. Index 1-34. PG1.A8 DLC(1-) CaAEU(no.1-482 on
microfiche) CaBVaU; CaOTU; CoU; CtY(1-) CU; DDO;FTaSU; ICN; ICU; MB; MH;
MdBJ(26-42) MiU; MnU; NIC; NN; NNC; NBU(1-31) NjP; OO; OClW(1-2) TNJ(29-34)
TxU(23,37) WU; WaU

ARCHIVUM PHILOLOGICUM. Commentationes ordinis philologorum Universitatis
Vitauti Magni. Kaunas, Humanitariniu Mokslu Fakultetas, 1930-39. 8 v.
illus. Contains articles on Baltic linguistics in Lithuanian, French or
German. P9.A7 DLC(1-) CU(1-) CaAEU(5) ICU(1-5) ICCC(5) MH(2-) MoK(1-)
MoU(1-) NN(1-) PU(1-6,8)

ARKHITEKTURNOE NASLEDSTVO. AKADEMIĪA ARKHITEKTURY SSSR. INSTITUT ISTORII I
TEORII ARKHITEKTURY. no.1- ; 1951- . Moscow. illus., plates, plans.
NA17.A614 DLC(1-2 CtY(1,6) CU(6-) DS(8-) InU(1-) IU(1-) MH(1,4-5,7-)
NcD(7-) NN(1-) NNC(1-) NRU([3-16]-) PSt(3-) WU(6-)

ATEITIS; katalikiškojo jaunimo žurnalas. Nr.1- ; vasaris 1911- . Kaunas;
München, Ger.; Tübingen, Ger.; Schwäbische Gmünde, Ger.; Brooklyn, N.Y.

illus., ports. Monthly except July and August. AP95.L5A8 DLC(1953, 1953-)
CaOONL(1954,no.2-10; 1955-1958; 1960-1963; 1965-1966) CSt-H([2-4]-7; 1914-
1918) CtPAM(1911,no.2,5,11-12; 1912,no.4,6-7,8; 1913,no.1-4,9-12; 1914,no.
2-3,7-12; 1915,1916,no.2,4; 1917-1922,1923,no.1; 1924,no.2-3,5-6; 1925-
1927,1928,no.1,4-10,12; 1929-1930,no.1-7,11-12; 1932,no.6; 1933,no.6-7,
9-10,11-12; 1934,no.3-4,6-8,12; 1935,no.1,2,8-9,11; 1936,no.1-6,10,11;
1937,no.1-2,4,11-12; 1938,no.1(13),2(14),3(15); 1939,no.1-2,5,8; 1940,no.5;
1946-1970-) CtTMF(1911-1914,1919-1940, 1946-1970-) ICCC(1911-1912; 1913,
no.1-7,9; 1914,1916,no.2-6; 1917,no.2-6,8,12; 1918,no.6,9-12; 1919,no.1-2;
1920-1922-1924,[1925],1926-1936; 1938,no.1-6; 1938 39-1939/40; 1946-1956-)
ICLJF(1911; 1937-1939; 1951-1965; 1967-1970-) NN(1914,1950-) PU(1911,no.
1-12) OKentU(1944,no.211,212,237,238,241-250; 1948,no.8; 1949,no.1; 1951,
no.9; 1957,no.2; 1970,no.7,9; 1971,no.2-3; 1953-)

ATENEUM WILEŃSKIE; czasopismo naukowe, poświęcone badaniom przeszłości ziem
Wielkiego Księstwa Litewskiego. Wilno, Towarzystwo Przyjaciół Nauk, 1923-
1939. 14 v. illus., plate, maps, tables. Quarterly. DK511.L2A77 DLC(2-
[6]) CaBVaU; CoU(v.7,no.3-4) CU(1-) CLU(8-) CtY(1-) ICU; ICLJF(v.6,no.1-4)
KU(1-24) MH(1-14) MiU(1-) NN(1-[6-7]-) NNC(7-8) PU(1-13)

ATHENAEUM; kalbos, literaturos, istorijos ir geografijos žurnalas. Kaunas,
Teologijos-filosofijos fakultetas, 1930-1938. 9 v. CU(1-) ICU(1-7)
ICCC(1931,1933-1934) MH(11-) NN(1-5,7-) NNC(1-5,7-[11]-) PU(1-9) WaU(1,4-)

BALTIC AND SCANDINAVIAN COUNTRIES. v.1-5,no.2(no.1-12); Aug.1935-April,1939.
Thorn (Toruń); Leyden; [etc.], Baltic Institute, 1935-39. 5 v. Title
varies: vol.1-2, 1935-Dec.1936 as Baltic Countries. D965.A1B3 DLC(1-)
CLSU(1-) CLU(1-) CU(1-) CaQOG(1,[2],3) CtY([1]-[5]) ICU(1-4) IEN(3-5)
MB(1-) MH(1-) MiU(1-) McM([2-5]) MnHi(1-) MnU(4-5) NN(1-) NNC(1-) NNU(1-2)
NPV(4-5) NR(1-) NcD(1-) NjP(1-) OCU(1-]4],5) OCl(1-) OU(1-) PU([1]-[4])
WU(1-)

BALTIC LINGUISTICS, edited by Thomas F. Magner and William R. Schmalstieg.
University Park, Pa., Pennsylvania State University Press, [1970] 177 p.
Contains chiefly papers presented at a symposium held at Pennsylvania
State University, April 5-6, 1968. PG8002.B3 DLC; AAP; CaAEU; CLSU; CaOTP;
CaBVaU; CLU; CU; CtY; CSt; CoU; FU; FTaSU; GU; IEN; ICU; IaU; InU; KU; KyU;
LU; MiU; MiEM; MoSW; MnU; MB; MoU; MtU; MU; NBuU; NcGU; NjR NSyU; NbU; NRU;
NcD; NjP; NIC; NNR; N; NNC; OU; OrU; OkU; OKentU; PSt; TNJ; TU; TxU; UU;
ViBlbV; ViU; WU; WaU

BALTIC REVIEW. No.1-38; Dec.1953-Aug.1971. New York, N.Y. Committee for a
free Estonia, Latvia and Lithuania. Supersedes The Baltic Review published in Stockholm, 1945-49. Nos.1-10, Dec.1953-March 29,1957, with numbers
6-10 printed. DK511.B25B318 DLC(1-) AMAU(1-) AzTeS(29-) AzU(1-) CaBVaU(
37-) CaAEU(1-3,5,7-8,10,12,15-16,19-31-38) CaOOCC(33-) CaQMM(14-) CaOTU(
1-)CaWA(34-38) CLU(9-) CU(4-) CtY(1-) IEdS([19-36]) IEN(1-) LU MH(1-)
MdBJ(4-) MnU(1,5-) MU(33-) NN(1-) NcU(1-) NjR(19-) NIC(8-) NNC(1-) NjP(1-)
OU(1-) OKentU(1961-1971) PU(1-) PV(37-) TxSaT(37-) TxU(31-) ViU(4-) WU(1-)
WaU(1-3) KU(2-)

BALTIJAS VĒSTURNIEKU KONFERENCE, 1st. RIGA, 1937. Runas un referāti. Riga,
1938. DK511.B25B35 DLC; CSmH; NNC; PPULC; PU.

BALTISCHE HEFTE. Bd.1- ; Oct. 1954- , Grossbiewende, Ger. illus., plates,
ports. Quarterly. Began publication with Oct. 1954 issue. Issued in 1951
as supplement to Baltische Briefe; 1952-53, as supplement to Baltische
Rundschau. Includes section Baltische familiengeschichtliche Nachrichten.
DK511.B25B36 DLC(4-) CLU(5-) CtY(2-) ICU(1-) MH(1-) NN(1-) PU(2-)

BEGEGNUNG. Bd.1- ; Feb. 1946- . Köln, Verlag "Wort und Werk". Monthly.
Began publication with Feb. 1946 issue. AP30.B28 DLC(1-) CLU; CtY(4-)
CU(7-) CSt; IaU MH(1-4) NN(4-7) NIC(2-) NNC(1-) PU(1-2) TxU

BEITRÄGE ZUR MEERESKUNDE. Hft. 1- ; 1961- . Berlin, Akademie-Verlag.
GC1.B35 DLC; CLSU-H(1-) CLU; CoFS(22-) CU-SB(22) FTaSU(1-) IU(1-) KMK(1-)
KU(1-) MdBJ(1-) NN(1-) NhD(1-6,9-) NNC(1-6,10-) TxHR(1-6,9-) WaU(1-)
WU(2 3-)

BERLIN. FREIE UNIVERSITÄT. OSTEUROPA-INSTITUT. Forschungen zur Osteuro-
päischen Geschichte. Bd.1- ; 1954- . Wiesbaden, Ger. DRl.B45 DLC(1-)
CaAEU(1-) CaBVaU(1-) CaNBFU(1-) CaOWA(13-) CaQML(11-) CLU(1,3-) CoU(8-)
CSt(1-3) CtY(1-) CU(4-) DDO(1-) DS(8-) FU; GEU(1-) GU(1-) IaAS(1-) IaU(1-)
ICN(3-4) ICU(1-) IEN(1-) InU(1,2) IU(1-) LU(3,10-11) MB(1-) MdBJ; MH(1-)
MiDW(1-) MiEM(1-) MiU(1-) MnU(1-) MoSW(1-) NbU(1-) NcU(1-6) NIC(1-)
NjP(1-) NjR(1-) NNC(1-) OrU(1-) TxHR(1-) UU(1-) ViU(1-) WaU(1-) WU(1-)

BOOKS ABROAD; an international literary quarterly. v.1- ; Jan. 1927- .
Norman, Okla. illus. Subtitle varies slightly. Issues for 1927-1929
published by the University of Oklahoma; 1960- by the University of Okla-
homa Press. Z1007.B717 DLC; ABS; AzTeS; CaW; CaMW; CU-Riv; CaBVaU; CaBVa;
CSt; CoDI; CoU; CoDU; CoCC; CaAEU; DAU; DNAL; DS; FDS; FM; GDS; IRA; IU;
ICJ; InCW; ICN; KT; KMK; LNL; MtBC; MeP; MtU; MtBC; MBdAF; MiU; MBtS; MB;
NN; NcU; NdU; Nc; NcRS; NIC; NNU; NGrnUN; OO; OCl; OOxM; OrCS; OC; OrU;
Or; OU; OkTU; OAkU; OCU; PPiD; PHC; PBm; PSC; PU; PCarlD; P; PPULC; PPSC;
TU; TxDW; TxLT; ULA; VHS; VtMM; ViU; WaSP; WaS; WyU; WAL

BOTANICHESKII ZHURNAL. (Russkoe botanicheskoe obshchestvo) Leningrad.
T.1- ; 1916- . Leningrad. v. illus., plates, maps. Frequency varies.
Summaries in English, German and French. Vol.1-16,1916-1931 as the soci-
ety's Zhurnal. QK1.V713 DLC(1-) CaOOAg; CaBVaU; CaOON(24-) CaOTU; CU(1-)
CU-I; CSt; DA(1-) GU; ICJ(1-3,9[10]-15) MWhB([14]) MdBJ(1-2) MnU(1-[21]-)
ICF(27,1942-) ICU([8-16]) InIA(1-) MH-A([15]-[17]-[20]-[23-26]-[28])
MoSB(1-) N(1-5) NIC-A(11-) NcD; NYBT(12-) NjP(20) OCL(1-5) OrCS; PPAN(1-)
WvU

BULLETIN OF BALTIC STUDIES. Tacoma, Wash.; Brooklyn, N.Y. Association for
the Advancement of Baltic Studies. Quarterly. DK511.B25B78 DLC; MH;
OKentU

CANADIAN ART. v.1- ; Oct.-Nov.1943- . Ottawa. ill. Bimonthly from Oct.
to June 1943- . 4 no. a year. Frequency varies. Supersedes Maritime
Art. Issues for 1958- called also no.59- Title varies: 1943-66, Canadian Art. Issued 1943-winter 1953 under the direction of a board repre-
senting the National Gallery of Canada and various art associations;
spring 1953- by Society for Art Publications. Part of the illustrative
matter is colored, part mounted. Some no. accompanied by phonodiscs.
Issues for 1967 accompanied by a "tabloid insert" with title Artscan which
is cataloged independently in this library (call no: 705 CANA) N1.C25 DLC
AzTeS; CaAEU; CaBViC; CaMW; CaOONL; CaSRL; CaOTU; CtY; CtNIC; CoD; HU; IC;
IaU; KT; MiU; MdBJ; MB; NN; NdU; NRU; NhD; NcD; NBuG; OC; OU; PPULC; P;
PBm; TxLT.

DEUTSCHE GEOLOGISCHE GESELLSCHAFT, BERLIN. Zeitschrift der deutschen geo-
logischen Gesellschaft. 1- ; 1849- . Berlin, W. Hertz. illus., plates,
maps, tables. Quarterly. Each volume includes "Verhandlungen". QE1.D4
DLC(1-66,69-70,73-78,80-88) CaOTU(1-) CaQMM(1-86) CSt(1-) CtY(1-) DI-GS(1-)
FTaSU; FU; GU; ICU(1-) IU(1-) CLEA; InU(21-48,56-) IaAS; ICJ; KyU; KU; LU;
MH; MH-Z(1-) MdBJ(1-) MiU(1-) MnU(2,4-) MBdAF; NIC(1-) NN(1-) NNC(1-)
NjP(1-) OClW(1-16,24-); OU(1-) OCU; OU; OO; OkU; PU(3-4,11-12,[42])
PPAN(1-) PSt; PBL; PBm; TxU(1-) TxDAM; TxLT; WvU; WaU(1-)

DEUTSCHE KUNST UND DENKMALPFLEGE. 1-35, 1899-1933; ns v.1-15, no.7/8; 1934-
1942/43. Berlin; Wien; München. Vol.1-24, 1899-1922 as Denkmalpflege.
Supersedes an earlier publication with the same title, issued 1899-1943.
Issues for 1952-. IU(1-8) MH(1-[23]-) MiU([22-23]) NNC(3-) NjP(32-) NN([23,
30], 31,33-)

DIRVA [The Field]; tautinės minties svaitraštis. Nr.1- ; rugp. 1916- .
Cleveland, Ohio. Weekly; Twice a week. OKentU(1946, nos. 26-39,41-52;
1952; 1957-1961; 1963-1965)

DOCUMENTS ON INTERNATIONAL AFFAIRS. 1928- ; London, New York, [etc.] Oxford
University Press 1929- . "Prepared...to accompany and supplement the annual Survey of International affairs produced by Professor Arnold J. Toynbee." 1932- issued under the auspices of the Royal Institute of International affairs. "Norway and the war, September 1939-December 1940, edited
by Monica Curtis" was published in the advance of the regular 1940 volume.

D442.S82 DLC(1928-1937) AzTeS; CaAEU(1-) CaBViP; CaOLU(1928-1931) CaQMM(
1934-1937) CaAMS([1928-1932,1934[) CaOTP(1938-) C(1-) CCC(1-) CL(1-) CLU(
1-) CLSU(1-) CU; CoD(1928-) CoDU(1928-1937) CoU; Ct(1930-1933) CtHT(1-)
CtNIC(1931,1934-1937) CtW(1931,1935-1936) CtY(1-) CtY-L(1-) CStbS; CSt-H;
DCE(1-) DN; FU; GEU; GU(1933-) ICN(1-) ICU(1928-1937) IEN(1929-) IEN-L(
1928-1929) IU(1-) IaGG(1928,1931-1936) IaU(1-) IaU-L(1930) In(1-) IdU;
InU(1929-) IdPl; KyU(1930-1932, 1934-) LU(3,5-11,14) MA(1-) MB(1-) MH(1-)
MBAt(1934-1936) MCM(1930-1932) MdBP(1929-1934) MeB MH-L(1-) MNS(1928-1932)
MWC(1-) MWelC(1-) MWiW(1-) MdAN(1-) MdBJ(1-) MiD(1-) MiU(1928-1937) MoU(1-)
MiU-L(1-) MnM(1929,1935) MnSJ(1-) MnU(1-) MnU-L; N(1-) NAW(1-) NB(1928-
1937) NBC(1-) NBu(1-) NBuG([1929-1936]) NCH(1-) NN(1-) NNA(1-) NNB(1-)
NNC(1-) NNC-T(1930-) NNCoC(1-) NNQ(1-) NNU(1-) NNU-C(1930,34-37) NPV(1-)
NR(1929-35 NRU(1-) NSU(1-) NbU(1928,30) NcD(1-) NcU(1-) NjNbN(1-) NjP(1-)
NjR(1930,32-33,35-38) OC(1929-31,34-37) OCU(1-) OCl(1-) OClW(1935-) ODa(
1929-) OO(1928-37) OOxM(1936) OU(1928-33,35-) OkU([1929,31-37]) PBL(1935-
37) PBm(1934,36) PHC(1-) PPAP(1-) PPi(1928-36) PU(1-) RPB(1-) TNJ(1-)
TxU(1-) VLxW(1928-) WAL(1-) WM(1-) WU(1929-) WaS(1-) WaU(1-) WvU(1930,33-
34) WyU(1928-37)

DONUM BALTICUM. To professor Christian S. Stang on the occasion of his
seventieth birthday, 15 March, 1970. Ed. by Velta Rūke-Draviņa. Stock-
holm, Almquist & Wiksell, 1970. xiv, 598 p. ill. In English, French,
German, Latvian, Lithuanian or Russian. PG8002.D6 DLC; CaAEU; CaBVaU;
CaQMM; CtY; CU-SB; CLU; ICU; IU; IaU; InU; ICIU; InNd; LU; MH; MU; MnU;
NN; NNC; NIC; NjP; NbU; NcU; OU; PU; PSt; TxU; ViU; WU; WaU

DRAUGAS; lietuvių katalikų laikraštis. 1- ; liepa 1909- . Wolkes Barre,
Pa.; Chicago, Ill. Weekly; daily since 1916. CtTMF(1,nos.3-8,20-21; 2,
no.5-9,17,22,25,27,32) CtPAM; DLL; ICCC(1909; liepa-gruodis) ICD; IU([1917]-
[1929]) OKentU(nos.152-304,1919; 1920; 1923-1924; 1944; 1972; 1973)

EAST EUROPEAN QUARTERLY. v.1- ; 1967- . Boulder, Colo., University of
Colorado. v. DR1.E33DLC AMAU; AzTeS(3-) AzU(1-) CaAEU(1-) CaBVaS(1-)
CaBVaU(1-) CaNSHD(1-) CaOKQ(2-) CaOLU(1-) MBU(1-) MCM(1-) MdBJ(1-) MdU(1-)
MH(1-) MiEM([2]) MiU(1-) MnSSC(1-) MnU(2-)

ELTA PRESS; Servizio d'informazioni Lituane. 1- ; 1954- . Rome. DLC(
[1]-) CtPAM([1954-1960]-[1967])

ETNOGRAFIA POLSKA. 1- ; 1958- . Wrocław, Zakład Narodowy im. Ossolińskich.
ill., ports., maps. Annual. Issued by Dzial IV. of the Institut Historii
Kultury Materialnej of the Polska Akademia Nauk. GN585.P6E8 DLC(1-) CU(1-)
CSt(3,5) ICU(1-) InU(1-) IU(5-) MB(1-) MH-P(1-) MiU(3-4) NIC(12-) NNC(1-)
NSyU(10-) PU(5-) TxHR(4-) WaU(1-)

EURASIA SEPTENTRIONALIS ANTIGNA; bulletin et mémoires consacrés à l'archéologie et l'ethnographie de l'Europe orientale et de l'Asie du Nord. no.1-12;
1926-1938. Helsingfors. GN700.E8 DLC(1-8) CMC(1-11) CSt(8) CU; CtY(1-9)
DDO(1-10,12) ICU(1-11) ICF; IU(2) NIC; NN; NNC; NNM; NbU; OCU(2) OCl; PU
PBm(9-10)

GEOGRAFICHESKOE OBSHCHESTVO SSSR. Zapiski. Sanktpeterburg, V.Bezobrazov,
1861-1864. 4 v. illus., ports, fold. maps. 4 nos. a year. Supersedes the
society's Viestnik. Issued by the society under its earlier name: Russkoe
Geograficheskoe Obshchestvo. 1865- divided into 3 distinct journals.
Superseded in 1866-1867 by the society's Zapiski po obshchei geografii,
Zapiski po otdieleniiu etnografii, and Zapiski po otdieleniiu statistiki.
Other journals with the same title were issued by the society 1846-1859
and 194- . G23.G229 DLC CU(2-3) NN; NcU; NNA(1,3) NNC([1-2,4])

GEOGRAFICHESKOE OBSHCHESTVO SSSR. Zapiski po otdieleniiu statistiki. T.1-
17; 1866-1915. Petrograd; S.-Peterburg. 29 v. ill., maps. Supercedes in
part the society's Zapiski, published in 1861-64. Issued by the society
under the earlier name Russkoe Geograficheskoe Obshchestvo. Ceased publication 1915. G23.G2293 DLC(1-[11]-13,[16-17]) CSt-H(3-4,[10-11],13-14) CU(1-
[8-13]) FU; MH([1-12]) MH-P([7]) MH-Z([1]) NN(1-[7-8],10-14) NNA(1-4,[7-8,
10-12]-14) NNC([7]) PPAN([4],6) PPAP(1-2)

GEOGRAFINIS METRAŠTIS. v.1- ; 1958- . Vilnius. Issued by Lietuvos TSR
Mokslo akademija, Vilna. Geologijos ir geografijos institutas and Lietuvos

TSR Geografinė draugija. Gl.G3135 DLC(1-) CtPAM(1-) CtY(1-) CU(1-) DI-GS;
ICU(1-) InU(1-) IU(1-) MH(1-) MH-Z(3-) MoKL(1-2,5) MWhB(1-2,5) NN(1-) NNM(
1-) PPAN(1-) PU(1-) WyU(6-) NNC(1-)

GEOLOGISCHE UND PALEONTOLOGISCHE ABHANDLUNGEN. Jena, G. Fischer, 1882-1933.
  23 v. ill., plates, maps, tables, diagr. QE1.G492 DLC([8]-10,12-23) AzU;
  CaBVaU; CaOOG; CoU; CU(1-10,12-23);CU-Riv.; CPT(1-10,12-18) CSfA([2],6,8,
  [10],17) CSt([ns v.2-4,6,8]) CtY(1-18) DI-GS; DGS; FTaSU; GEU; ICJ(1-10,
  12-[23]) ICU([1-14]-23) IU; IaU(1-4) ICarbS; ICRL; ICF; MB; MH-Z(1-10,12-
  23) MdBJ; MdBP(1-6,8-19) MiU MBdAF; NN(1-10;12-23) NNC(1-10,12-23) NNM(1-4;
  ns v.1-6,8-19) NjP; PPAN; PU; RPB(2,no.3) TxU(6-11,13-23) WaU

GESCHICHTE IN WISSENSCHAFT UND UNTERRICHT. Bd.1- ; April 1950- . Stutt-
  gart, Ger. D1.G66 DLC([4]-) ArU(21-) CaBVaU(7-) CaOKQ(17-) CaOLU(18-)
  CaOTU(19-) CaOWA([21]-) CaOWtU(1-7,11,13,15-) CaQML(19-) CLSU(18-) CLU(2-)
  CoFS([16]-) CoU(9-) CSt(15-) CtU([9]-) CtY([1-5]-) CU(12-) CU-Riv.(17-)
  DeU(18) DAU; GEU(9,11,13-) IaU(13-) ICU(9-) InND([18]-) IU(8-) InU; KyU(8-)
  MdBJ(12-) MH([1-5]-) MiDW(2-) MiEM([8-10]-[12-19]-) MiU([16]-) MnU([12]-)
  MoU(15-) MWalB(19-) NIC(1-) NjP(2-3) NjR([2]-) NN(1-) NNC(2-) OO(15-) OU;
  OrU(21-) PPiU(14-) PSC(20-) PU([18]-) TxHR(11-) UPB([21]-) WaU(11-) WU(2-)

GESELLSCHAFT FÜR ERDKUNDE ZU BERLIN. Zeitschrift. 1-6, 1853-1856; ns v.1-
  19, 1856-1865; s3, v.1-36, 1886-1901; 1902-1944. Superseded by Erde.
  1853-1865 as Zeitschrift für allgemeine Erdkunde. Gl3.G5 DLC(1-ns v.18;
  s3 v.1-36; 1902-1914,21-) CaBVaU; CaOLU(ns v.2-6) CaOOG(23-) CaOON(s3, v.
  23-36,1902-1914) CaOTR(1902-[14]) CaOTU(s3,v.20-) CSfA(s3,v.25-36; 1902-
  1916) CSt(1-s3,v.35) CU(1-) CtY(1-) DA(1914-) DGS(s3,v.9,21-) DSI-E(s3,v.
  24-[28-36]; 1902-[16]) DSI-M(s3,v.30-) DWB(s3,v.34-) CLSU; CLU(1-5; ns v.1-
  1921,27-29,33-[36-37]38) I(1-ns v.15) IC(s3,v.1-36; 1902-1910) ICF(s3,v34-)
  IaU(1908-11,13,-15[21-24]-[32]-35) IaAS; ICU(1-) IEN(s3,v.33-36; 1902-1907)
  IU(1-s3,v.36; 1902-1916) IaU([1921-1924]-[32]-35) KU; LU(1-) MA(1-ns v.6)
  MB(1-s3,v.36; 1902-1917[19]-) MBAt(1902-1915) MCM(6-ns v.3) MH(s3,
  v.[19-28]-36; 1902-1916 21-22) MH-P(1902-[16]) MH-Z(s3,v.1-36[1921]-)
  MSM(1928-) MWC(1-) MWhB(s3,v.8-14,18-36) MdBJ(3-ns v.1,4-8,12-[18]-s3,v.16,
  18-19,34-36) MdBP(s3,v.3-36; 1902-[16]19-21) MiU(1-) MnU(1-ns v.[1-19]-s3,
  v.36[1902-1931]-) MoU(s3,v.1-) N(1-s3,v.36; 1902-1921,23-) NCH(1-ns v.13)
  NIC(1-) NN(1-) NNA(1-) NNC(1-) NNCoo(s3,v.8,10,13,15,20-31) NNM(s3,v.5-)
  NNU(1928-[30]-32) NSU(1-s3,v.20) NjP(1-) NjR([9]13) OC(1-ns v.1) OCU(1922-)
  OCl(1-s3,v.36; 1902-1914) OkU; OU(1-) PPAN(s3,v.23-) PPAP(1-) PPGeo; PPAmP;
  PBL; PPL; PPF(s3,v.12-17) PPi(s3,v.1-36; 1902-1910,13) PU(s3,v.24-27) TxU;
  WU(1-ns v.18; s3,v.1-[36]; 1902-)

GESELLSCHAFT FÜR GESCHICHTE UND ALTERTUMSKUNDE, RIGA. Mitteilungen aus der
  livländischen Geschichte. v.1-25, no.4, 1836-1937. Riga. 25v. Name of
  the association varies. Superseded by its Mitteilungen aus der baltischen
  Geschichte. DK511.B25M63 DLC(1-[20-21]-25) CLU([9]17-23) CSt(24) CSt-H(21)
  CU(1-) DSI-E([13]-[18-25]) ICU(1-23) MH(1-25) MnU(1-2,4-25) NN(1-[21-24]25)
  PU(17-20) PU-Mu(17-20)

DASGRÖSSERE DEUTSCHLAND; Wochenschrift für deutsche Welt- und Kolonialpolitik. Bd.1-5; 1914-Nov.1918. Weimar, Ger.; Dresden, Ger. JN3934.A3 DLC(
  [1]-5) CSt-H(1-[5]) CtY([1-2,4]) ICN([1]-5) ICU([1-2]) IEN([1-2]) MB(1,no.
  24,26,28,35) MH(1-[4]) MWelC([1-4]) MiU; NN(1,[2-4]) NIC([5]) NjP(1-3)
  OU; TxU(4) WE

HAGUE, ACADEMY OF INTERNATIONAL LAW. Recueil des cours. T.1- ; 1923- .
  Paris, Recueil sirey, etc. ports. Not to be confused with its Cours et
  conférences. JX74.H3 DLC(1-) CaBVaU; CaOOSC; CaQMM(1-) CaOTU(1-) CL(1-)
  CLU(1-) CSt(1-) CU(1-) CStlS; CoU(1-) Ct(1-) CtY-L(1-) DCE(1-)
  DPU; FTaSU; FU; GU-L; GEU; ICU(1-) IEN(1-) IEN-L(1-) IU(1-) IaU-L(1-) IaAS;
  InU(1-25,31-) KyU(1-) LU-L; LNHT(1-66) MA(11-) MBAt(1-2) MCM(1-) MH(1-)
  MH-L(1-) MWiW(1-) MdAN(1-) MdBJ(1-) MiU(1-) MiU-L(1-) MnU(1-) MnU-L; MoU(-)
  NCH(11-15,47-50) NN(1-) NNB(1-) NNC(1-) NBuU; NBuU-L; NNU(1-42,47-) NSU(1-)
  NbU(1-) NcD(1-) NcD-L(1-28,44) NjP(1-) NmU(1-30) OCU(1-) OO(1-66) OU(1-)
  PPiU(1-) PPB; PSC(1-) PU(1-) PBm; PU-L(1-) RPB(1-) ScU; TxDaM(1-56) TU;
  TxU(1-) VU(1-) ViU; WU(1-) WaU(1-) WvU(1-)

HANSISCHE GESCHITSBLÄTTER. Jg.1- , 1871- . Leipzig, Ger., Verein für han-
  sische Geschichte. DD801.H17H3 DLC(1-) CLU(1-) CU(1-) CaOTU(1-3) CtY(1-)
  ICU(1-) IU(1-26) IaU(1-23) MB(1-) MH(1-) MnU(1-23) NN(1-) NNC(1-) NjP(1-)
  NNU-H(1-43,46-56) OCl(1-) PU(1-) WU(1-) WaU(1-47,59)

HISTORISCHE ZEITSCHRIFT. v.1- , 1859- . München, J. G. Gotta, 1859-19- .
Quarterly. D.1H6 DLC(1-) CaCEU(1-180 on microfilm, 179-189,205) CaQMM(1-)
CLU(1-14,17-164-) CU(1-) CtY(1-165-) IEN(1-) KU(1-) LU(1-) MiU(1-) NIC(1-
167-) NN(1-167-) NNC(1-163-) NNF(1-) NRU(1-) NjP(1-) NjR(1-) OU(1-) PU(1-)
TxU(1-165-) VU(1-) WaU(1-)

Į LAISVĘ. [To freedom: a journal of Friends of the Lithuanian Front]
1- ; 1941- . Kaunas; Los Angeles, Calif.; Rolling Hills Estates, Calif.,
Lietuvių Fronto Bičiuliai. ill. June 25, 1941- December 31, 1942, daily
newspaper in Kaunas. 1943-1944 suspended by German occupational authori-
ties and published in Marijampole, Utena, Telšiai, etc. as irregular underground newspaper, total 34 nos.; 1948 published only 3 nos. in Germany.
Since December 1953 published in United States. DK511.L2A2325 DLC(20-)
CaOONL; ICJLF(6-33; 1955-1963) ICWA(47-48,[84-85]; 1969-1970) OKentU(nos.
1-2,1948; 1953-1957, 1964-1972 bound. nos. 15-23, 1958-1960) nos.28-29,
1961; no.30, 1962) PU(nos.1-56, 1953-1972-)

Imperatorskoe russkoe geograficheskoe obshchestvo see Geograficheskoe obshchestvo SSSR.

INDOGERMANISCHE FORSCHUNGEN; Zeitschrift für indogermanische Sprach- und
Altertumskunde. Bd.1- ; 1891 . Strassbourg; Berlin, K. J. Trübner;
[etc.] illus., plates. Suspended between June 1944 and May 1948.
P501.I4 DLC(1-) CaOOG(1-) CaOTU(1-) CLU(1-37) CSt(1-) CU(1-) CtY(1-)
DCU(1-) ICN(1-) IEN(1-) IU(1-) IaU(1-) InU(1-) KU(1-) MB(1-) MH(1-) MiU(1-)
MdBJ(1-) MnU(1-) NIC(1-) NN(1-) NNC(1-) NbU(1-) NcD(1-) NcU(1-) NhD(1-)
NjP(1-) OCU(1-36,44-45) OClW(1-10,33-37,40-) OU(1-) PBM(1-) PU(1-)
TNJ(1-) TxU(1-) WaU(1-)

INDOGERMANISCHES JAHRBUCH. Bd.1- ; 1913- . Strassburg, K. J. Trübner,
[etc.] 1914- . Z7049.A7I8 DLC(1-) CaQMM(1-) CLU(1-) CSt(1-) CU(1-) CtY;
CoDU(11) CtW(1-7) DCU(1) ICU(1-) IEN(1-) IU(1-) InU(1-) MH(1-) MdBJ(1-20)
MiU(1-) MnU(1-) MoSW(1-) MoU(1-) CLSU(1-28) KyU(1-12,14-) LU(24-26,29)
MiDW(1-21) NIC(1) NN(1-) NNC(1-) NNCoC(1-) NNU(1-17) NNU-H(1-) NRU(1)
NbU(1-) NcU(1-) NjP(1-) OCU(1-) OClW(14-) OO(13-23) OU(1-) PBM(1-) PU(1-)
PPT(15-29) RPB(1-) TxU(1-) VU(1-20,29)

INSTITUTE OF LITHUANIAN STUDIES. Lituanistikos instituto 1971 metų suva-
žiavimo darbai. Proceedings of the Institute of Lithuanian Studies, 1971.
Spaudai paruošė, Thomas Remeikis. Chicago, Ill., Lietuanistikos institu-
tas, 1971. 280 p. illus. Lithuanian or English. Summaries in English.
Includes bibliographies. DK511L2I57 1971 DLC; Ca_AEU; InNd; MiU; NIC; NRU;
PU.

INTERNATIONAL CONGRESS OF LINGUISTS. Proceedings. 1st- , 1928- .
P21.I58 DLC AAP; CaBVaU; CtY; CLU; CU; CSt; DCaE; DGW-C; DSI; FTaSU; FU;
KyU; KU; ICU; ICN; IEN; MH; MtU: MB; MeB; MiU; NBuU; NjP; NN; NNC; OU; OCU;
OClW; OrU; PPAmP; PU; RPB; ScU; TxU; WU

JAHRBUCH DER ALBERTUS-UNIVERSITÄT ZU KÖNIGSBERG in Pr. Freiburg in Br.,
1951- . v.(Der Göttinger Arbeitskreis. Veröffentlichung) LF2901.C53
DLC(1952-) CaAEU(2-10) CaBVaU; CSt-H; CLU(1-) CU(1-) CtY(1954-1955) DS;
ICU(2-) IU(1-) MoU(1-) MH; NIC(2-) NNC(1-) NCU(1-) NBuU; NjP; OrU; WaU

JAHRBUCH DES DALTISCHEN DEUTSCHTUMS. 1955- . Lüneburg, Ger. v. ill.
In Auftrag der deutsch-baltischen Landsmannschaft i. Br. herausgegeben von
der Carl-Schirrer Gesellschaft. DK511.B25J3 DLC(1915-) CaBVaU(1969-) CtY(
1955-) CU(1966-) ICU; MH(1955-) MnU(1966-) NcD(1963-) NIC(1955-) NN(1955-)

JAHRBÜCHER FÜR GESCHICHTE OSTEUROPAS. Bd. 1-6,no.2-4; 1936-1941. Breslau,
Ger. ns v.1- ; 1953- . Supersedes Jahrbücher für Kultur und Geschichte
der Slaven. D1.J3 DLC(1-) CSt(1-) CU(1-) CtY(1-) MH(1-) MiU(1-) NN(1-)
NNC(1-) NIC(nsv.1-) CaAEU(ns v.14-) CaBVaU; CaOTY; CaBVaS; CaQML

JĘZYK POLSKI. 1- ; 1916- . Kraków, Towarzystwo miloṡników języka polskiego. PG6001.J48 DLC; CaBVaU; CaQTU; CSt-B; CU(6-) CtY([26,32]-) ICU(38-)
KyU; NIC(36-) NNC(11,13-15) NN([1-3]-) NjP; OU; MH; MiU; PU; PPiU; WU(3,9-
13, 15-16, 18-23)

JOURNAL OF BALTIC STUDIES. 1- ; 1972- . Brooklyn, N.Y., Allentown, Pa.,
Association for the Advancement of Baltic Studies. Quarterly. Continues

Bulletin of Baltic Studies by v.3, Spring 1972. DK511.B25B78 DLC([3]-)
AzTeS(3-) CaOOCC(3-) CaQTY(4-) CaOLU(3-) CLU(3-) CSt-H(3-) CLobS(5-)
CtY(3-) CU-S(3-) FTaSU([5]-) InU(3-) ICU(3-) ICarbS([4]-) InNd(4-) MH(1-)
MiMtpT([3]-) NCH(3-) NN(3-) NjP(3-) NNC(3-) NhD(3-) OrU(3-) PV(3-) PBL(3-)
PSt(3-) PU(3-) RPB(5-) TNJ(3-) TxHR([5]-) VtU(3-) WU(3-)

JOURNAL OF INDO-EUROPEAN STUDIES. v.1-   ; January 1973- . Hattiesburg,
Miss. University of Southern Mississippi.   v. illus. CB201.J68
DLC(1-) AzU(1-) AzTeS(2-) AU(2-) CaBVaU(1-) CaOTU(1-) CaAEU(2-) CaBVaS(2-)
CaOONL(1-) CaQMG([1]-) CaQMU(1-) CaMWU(1-) CaNBFU(1-) CaOLU(1-) CaOONM(1-)
CaOTY(1-) CaOWA(1-) CaOWtU(1-) CaQML(1-) CLSU(1-) CLU(1-) CLobS(1-) CSt(1-)
CU(1-) CU-Riv(1-) CoU(1-) CtW(1-) CtY(1-) CU-SB(1-) DGW(1-) DeU(2-) FU(1-)
GASU(1-) GU(1-) GEU(1-) GDS(1-) ICarbS(1-) ICU(1-) IU(1-) IaAS(1-) IaU(1-)
InNd(1-) InU(1-) ICIU(3-) INS(1-) KU(1-) LNHT(1-) MH(1-) MiDW(1-) MU(1-)
MiEM(1-) MiU(1-) MnU(1-) MoU(1-) MBMU(1-) MWelC(1-) MdBJ(1-) NIC(1-) NNC(
1-) NNStJ(1-) NmU(1-) NRU(2-) NbU(1-) NcD(1-) NcGU(1-) NcU(1-) NCWsW(1-)
NhD(1-) NjP(1-) NSyU(1-) OU(1-) OkU(1-) OrU(1-) OCU)1-) OkS(1-) PPiD(1-)
PPiU(1-) PU(1-) PPD(1-) PSt(1-) PV(2-) RPB(3-) ScU(1-) TxCM(2-) TxHR(1-)
TxU(1-) UU(1-) ViU(1-) VtU(1-) WaU(1-) WyU(1-) WU(1-)

KARYS; pasaulio lietuvių karių-veteranų mėnesinis žurnalas. [The Warrior]
Metai 1- ; 1950- . Brooklyn, N.Y. 10 nos. a year. CtPAM(1952, 1954,
1956-1961, 1963-1964) DLC(1951-1953) ICWA; NN(1950-) OKentU(1950-1952;
1953, nos. 1-5,7-8,12; 1957, nos.5,10;[1958], nos.2,4,9,10; 1960, no.2;
1961, no.10; 1963, nos.4,8-10; 1967; 1969, nos.2-5; 1970, nos.4,8; 1971,
nos.5,6; 1972, nos.3-5; 1973, nos.1-3,5).

KAUNAS. ANTANO SMETONOS LITUANISTIKOS INSTITUTAS. LIETUVOS ISTORIJOS
SKYRIUS. Lietuvos praeitis. t.1-2; 1940-1941. DK511.L2A233 DLC; NN

KAUNAS. UNIVERSITETAS. MATEMATIKOS-GAMTOS FAKULTETAS. Darbai... Mémoires
de la Faculté des sciences de l'Université de Vytautas le Grand. Kaunas,
1923-39. 13 v. illus., plates, maps, facsims, tables, diagrams. Text in
Lithuanian, German, or English. Summaries in German for Lithuanian articles. Q60.K14 DLC(1-) CU(1-6) DNAL(1-) DGS(5-7,9,13) DSI(6,no.2-3; 7-9; 10,
no.2; 11; 12,no.1) ICU(3-11) MH-G(5,7,9) NIC-A(1-) NN(1-) NbU(2-) NNC(1-3)
NBG(1,3-) NNM(3,5-) NjP(1923,1929) RPB(2; 6,no.2-3; 7-9; 10,no.1; 11; 13)
CtY(3-)

KOSMOS; gamtos ir šalinių mokslų illiustruotas žurnalas. Kaunas, 1920-40.
Monthly. ICBM(1,no.2-3,1920-1921; 3-4,no.2,1922-1923) ICCC(1920-1925,no.
1-2,4-6; 1926-1927,no.1-3,6-12; 1928,no.1; 1929-1931; 1938,no.1-3)

KWARTALNIK HISTORYCZNY. T.1-   ; 1887-   . Lemberg, Polskie Towarzystwo
Historyczne. Quarterly. Dl.K85 DLC(10-12,16-32,34-) CaAEU(66-) CU(1-41)
CtY(1-) IUC(65-) KU(66-) MH(1-) MdBJ([8-12,19-26]-33,46-52) MnU(1-) NN(1-)
NIC(62-) OCl(51-) PU(65-)

KWARTALNIK LITEWSKI. Tom 1-5; 1910-1911(Rok 1, Tom 1-4, 1910; Rok 2, Tom 5,
1911). Edited by Jan Obst. Sanktpeterburg. Quarterly. Rok 2 begins with
Tom 5. 947.PK979 PU(1-4) ICLJF(1-2) MH(1,5)

DAS LAND; Zeitschrift für die sozialen und Volkstümlichen Angelegenheiten der
Landbevölkerung. Berlin, 1895-[1932] illus. Oct.1894-Sept.1922, semimonthly; Oct.1922-1932, monthly. CaOTU; ICJ

LAOS. Etudes compareés de folklore ou d'ethnologie regionale. Comparative
studies of folklore and regional ethnology. t.1-3; 1951-1955. Stockholm,
Almquist & Wiksell. 3 v. illus., maps. GR1.L36 DLC(1-) CaOTU(1-) CU(1-)
CaQMM(1-) ICU(1-) InU(1-) IU(1-) KyU(1-) MH(1-) MiU(1-) MiDW(1-) MiEM(1-)
NN(1-) NIC(1-) NcD(1-3) NcU(2-3) OCl(1-) OCU(1-)

LATVIJAS VĒSTURES INSTITUTA ŽURNĀLS. 1- gads; 1937-   . Riga, Latvijas vēstures institūta izdevums, 1937-   . illus., plates, ports. Quarterly.
DK511.L15L35 DLC; NN

LIETUVIŲ KATALIKŲ MOKSLO AKADEMIJA, ROME. Metraštis. 1-   ; 1965-   . Roma.
v. (Its leidinys) Some articles have summaries in English or French.
AS222.L5A2 DLC(1-) CaAEU(1-) CtPAM(1-) CtY(1-) ICU(1-) MB(2-) NN(1-) PU(1-)
OKentU(1965,1967) WU(1-5)

LIETUVIŲ KATALIKŲ MOKSLO AKADEMIJA, ROME. Suvašiavimo darbai. 1- ; 1957-
Roma. (Its leidinys) Summaries in English, French, or German. Each vol.
has also a distinctive title. BX839.R6L49 DLC(4-5-) CaAEU(4-) ICU(4-)
MB; PU; PPULC

LIETUVIŲ TAUTOS PRAEITIS. Lithuanian historical review. Tomas 3- ; kn.9-
; 1971- . Chicago, Ill., Lietuvių istorijos draugija. v. illus.
Lithuanian with summaries in English. Continues Tautos Praeitis.
DK511.L2A276 DLC; CaAEU

Lietuvos praeitis see Kaunas. Antano Smetonos lituanistikos institutas.
Lietuvos istorijos skyrius. Lietuvos Praeitis.

LIETUVOS TSR MOKSLO AKADEMIJA, VILNA. Darbai. Serija A. T.1- ; 1955- .
Vilnius, Valstybinė politinės ir mokslinės literatūros leidykla. illus.,
maps. Semiannual. Supersedes in part the Academy's "Žinynas" (1947-1953).
Text in Lithuanian and Russian with summaries in the other language.
AS262.V422 DLC(1955-) CaOTU(1968-) CL(1955-) CLU(1962-) CU(1955-) CtY(1955-
ICU(1960-) KyU(1955-) MCM(1955) MH(1-) NN(1955-) NIC(1964-) NcU; NcD; NNC(
1966-) OKentU(1972) OU; PPiU(1966-) PU(1-) PSt(1967-) RPB(1966-) ViU;
WU(1966-) WaU(1957-)

LIETUVOS TSR MOKSLŲ AKADEMIJA, VILNA. Darbai. Serija B. T.1- ; 1955 .
Vilnius, Valstybinė politinės ir mokslinės literatūros leidykla. illus.,
maps. 3 nos. a year. Supersedes in part the Academy's "Žinynas" (1947-
1953) Text in Lithuanian or Russian with summaries in the other language.
Q4.L52 DLC(1955-) CLU(1962-) CU(1955-) CU-A(1962-) CU-Riv(1963-) CtY(1955-
DNAL(1955-) GAT(1955-) ICRL(1955-) IU(1962-) ICU(1965-) IaAS(1966-) LNHT(
1962-) MH(1955-) MoKL(1964-) MWhB(1957-) NN(1955-) NNC(1962-) NcU(1962-)
NcD; OKentU(1972) OrU(1955-) PU(1955-) PPF(1967) ScU(1956-) TOU(1960)

LIETUVOS TSR MOKSLŲ AKADEMIJA, VILNA. Darbai. Serija C. T.1- ; 1960- .
Vilnius, Valstybinė politinės ir mokslinės literatūros leidykla. 3 nos. a
year. Text in Lithuanian or Russian with summaries in the other language.
QH301.L52 DLC; CU(1960-) CtY1961-) CLSU-H(1960-) DNAL(1960-) DNLM(1960-)
IaAS(1966-) IU(1966-) LU; MoKL(1967-) MH(1960-) NN(1960-) NIC(1960-)
OKentU(1972)

LIETUVOS TSR MOKSLŲ AKADEMIJA, VILNA. BIOLOGIJOS INSTITUTAS. Darbai. Trudy.
Vilnius, 1951-59. 4 v. No more published. QH301.L53 DLC(1-) CU; DNAL(
1-) MH(1-) NN(1-) PPAN(1-) PU

LIETUVOS TSR MOKSLŲ AKADEMIJA, VILNA. EKONOMIKOS INSTITUTAS. Darbai. 1- ;
19   . Vilnius. HC337.L5L45 DLC(3-) CU(2-) MH(2-) NN(8-)

LIETUVOS TSR MOKSLŲ AKADEMIJA, VILNA. GEOLOGIJOS IR GEOGRAFIJOS INSTITUTAS.
Collected papers for the XIX International Geographic Congress. Edited by
V. Gudelis. Vilnius, 1960. 482 p. illus., maps. Text in English or
Russian with summaries in Lithuanian. GB3.I45 1960 ac DLC; CaAEU; CaMWU;
CU; CFS; ICU; NNC; PPULC; TxU; WU

LIETUVOS TSR MOKSLŲ AKADEMIJA, VILNA. GEOLOGIJOS IR GEOGRAFIJOS INSTITUTAS.
Collected papers for the XXI session of the International Geological Con-
gress. Edited by V. Gudelis. Vilnius, 1960. 445 p. illus., ports, maps.
English and Russian. QE1.L4483 DLC; CU; DI-GS; ICU; MH-Z; NNC; PPULC

LIETUVOS TSR MOKSLŲ AKADEMIJA, VILNA. GEOLOGIJOS IR GEOGRAFIJOS INSTITUTAS.
Moksliniai Pranešimai. 1, 1955- . Added T. P. and summaries in Russian.
QE1.L448 DLC(1-) CaOOGB(1-) CtY; CU(1-) FTaSU; ICU(1-) InU(5-8) MWhB(1-)
NN(1-) PPAN(1-) WyU(4,12-)

LIETUVOS ŪKIS; mėnesinis visuomenės ūkio ir finansų laikraštis. Finansų
ministerijos leidinys. T.[1]-6,(Metai[1]-7; gruodis 1921-gruodis 1928.
Kaunas, Valstybės spaustuvė [etc.], 1921-28. 6 v. in 2. Monthly.
HC337.L5A16 DLC; CtPAM(no.1-75) NN(no.1-67,69-75)

LITAUISCHE LITERARISCHE GESELLSCHAFT, TILSIT. Mitteilungen. Bd. 1-6 (Heft
1-31) 1880-1912. Heidelberg, C. Winter, 1883-1912. 6 v. illus., plates,
maps, plans. Irregular. PG8503.L7 DLC([1]-6) BM(1-6) CtY(v.2,no.10) IU;

ICU; MH; MiU(1-6) NN(1-6) NNU-H(4-6) NjP(1-[5],6) NBuC; OClW(1-6) OCCU; OU;
PU(no.2-11,13-14,17,23-24-30)

LITHUANIA. FINANSŲ DEPARTAMENTAS. Wietschaftliche Informationen des Finanzdepartements der Republik Litauen. no.1-63; 1930-1933. Kaunas. Monthly.
HC337.L5A33 DLC; NN(1-4)

LITHUANIAN SSR. VALSTYBINĖ ARCHITEKTŪROS PAMINKLŲ APSAUGOS INSPEKCIJA. T.1-
1958- . Vilnius. illus., facsims., plans. Annual. Summaries in Russian. NA9.L5 DLC(1-) MH

LITUANISTIKOS DARBAI. LITHUANIAN STUDIES. 1- . Čikaga, Lituanistikos in-
stitutas, 1966- . v. illus. Yearbook of the Institute of Lithuanian
Studies. Includes English summaries. DK511.L2A264 DLC(1-) CaOTU(1-)
CaQML(1-) CU(1-) ICU(1-) MH(1-) NIC(1-) NN(1-) PSt(1-) PU(1-) WU(1-)

LITUANUS. V.1- ; 1954 . Brooklyn, N.Y., Lithuanian Student Association.
Quarterly. Issues for Nov., 1954-Dec., 1957 lack volume numbering but con-
stitute volumes 1-3. DK511.L2L78 CaAeu(7-) CaOWA(4-) CaBVaU(3-) CaSSU;
CaMWU(10-) CaNSHD(12-) CaNBFU([5]-) CaOKQ(v.5-) CaOLU([13]-) CaOOCC([10]
[12]-) CaOOU(]3]-[5]-) CaOPAL(v.11-12,14-) CaOTU(11-) CaOTP; CaOWA(5-)
CaQML(v.13-) ArU([1]-) CL([1]-) CLI(3-) CLSU(1-) CLU(1-) CoD(3-) CoFS(8-)
CStcIU(7-) CtY([1-2]-[6]-) CU(3-) CU-SB([13]-) DGW([9]-) DLC(1-) DS(6-)
FTaSU(1-) FU([2]-) IaAS(14-) IaU(1-) ICU(16-) IEdS(7-12,14-) IEN(12-) IU;
InNd(4-) INS(v.12-) InU(8-) KAS([6]-10,12-) KU(1-) KyU(1-) LU([4-5]11-)
MB([3]-) MdBJ(1-) MdBP; MdU(10-) MH(1-) MiDM(1-) MiEM(12-) MiMtpT(6-)
MnCS; MoSU(4-) MoSW([15]-) MShM(1-) MsU([1]-) MtBC(2-) MWelC(6-) NB(6-)
NcD(10-) NcU(4-) NhD(5-) NIC(2-4[5]-) NN(1-) NNC(8-) NNU(11-) NRRI; NRU(4-)
OrCS([1]-) OrPU(12-) OU; OKentU(1954-) PPiU([14]-) PSt(8-) PU(1-) PV(12-)
ThJ(3-) TxDaM(1-) ULA(5-) UU([1]-) ViU(5-7) WaU([10]-) WU(10-)

LUND. UNIVERSITET. SLAVISKA INSTITUTET. SPRÅKLIGA BIDRAG. Meddelanden
från seminarierna för slaviska språk... no.1, 1951. Title varies.
AzU(8-14) CLSU(1-) CLU(10-) CoU(1-) CtY; CU(7-) DLC(2-) FU(9-) ICU(8-)
InU(1-) IU(3-) KU([5]-) MH(3-) MnU([2]-) NbC(8-) NNC(1-) OCl(6-) OU; NN;
PU(8,16-) ViU(12-) WaU([2]) WU

LUND. UNIVERSITET. SLAVISKA INSTITUTET. Årsbok. PG1.L8 DLC; CLU(1-)
CLSU(1-) CSt; CoU(1-) CtY(1-) FTS(1-) IEN(1-) IU(1-) IaU(1-) MH(1-) NN(1-)
MnU(1-) MdBJ(1-) MiU(1-) N91-) NNC(1-) NjP(1-) OCl(1-) NNU-W; PU(1-) TxU;
VU(1-) WU(1-) WaU(1-)

MATERIALY I ISSLEDOVANIĪA PO ARKHEOLOGII SSSR. Materiau et recherches
d'archéologie de l'URSS. no.1- ; 1940- . Moskva; Leningrad, Izdatelstvo
Akademii nauk SSSR. v. illus., plates, diagrs. DK30.M3 DLC(1-) CaBVaU;
CaAEU(11-13,15-28,30,33-41,43-44,46-53,56-55,58-77,79-95,97-100,102-128,
131,136,139-142,144-146,148,150-158,160-161,163-169,172-174,176-180,182,185)
CLSU([7-55]58-) CLU([1-85]-) CU(1-5,7-52) CaOONM(15,18-20,24-52,54-77,85)
CtY(1-40,42-52,54-75,77-81,85-86,91) DDO(3,7,9-) DSI(7-8,12,14-) FMU(45)
FU(38,43-44) InU([2-91]) KMK([7-77]) MoU(7,9-43[47-91]-) NIC([1-54]-)
NNC([1-77]) NNM([7,9-13,15-52[55-71]) NNU([1-57]) NcD(63) OCl(19,33,35,38)
OU(34-35,37,43) OrU([3-85]) PU-MU(2-3,7-) RPB([14-77]) TxU(18,26,38,58,60,
63,72) WU(7,9-)

MATERIALY K POZNANIĪU GEOLOGICHESKOGO STROENIĪA SSSR. Novaīa seriīa. Vyp.
1- ; 1941- . Moskva. illus., maps. QE276.M28 DLC; InU; NN

MATERIALY STAROŻYTNE. Warszawa, Państwowe Wydawnictwo Naukowe, 1956- .
illus., maps, annual. DK409.M3 DLC; CaOTRM(2-8) CaOTU(1-) CoU(2-) CSt(4-5)
CtY(1-) CU(1-) ICF(1-) ICU(1-) IU(1-) MB(10-) MH-P(1-) MiU; MoU(1-) NIC(10-)
NN(1-) NNM(1-) PU-MU(1-) WU(1-)

METMENYS; jaunosios kartos kultūros žurnalas. 1- ; 1959- . [Chicago],
Ill. Irregular. AP95.L5M4 DLC(1-) CLU(7-) CtY(1-) ICWA; MH(1-) NN(1-)
PU(1-) OU(1-2,6-7,9,12,14,16-) OKentU(1959-1972-)

METRAŠTIS, 1950. [Yearbook, 1950 with collection of essays] Redagavo L. Andriekus. Kennebunk Port, Me., Tėvai Pranciškonai, 1949. 221 p. ill.,
ports. DK511.L223M59 1949 CaAEU; MH

LE MOIS; synthèse de l'activité mondiale. 1- ; Jan. 1931- . Paris, Maulde et Renou [1931-].   v. illus(maps), plates, ports., diagr. AP20.M67
DLC(1-96,98-112) CaOLU(25-36,40-96) CaQMM(23,25-28) CaOOP(1-) CSt-H(24-34,
42-83) IaU(97-) MH(1-) MWelC(8-) MNS(8-) NN(1-) NNU(8-) NPV(61-) NcD(1-)
NcU(17-18,41-42,41,44,46-51) ICU; MB

MOSCOW. UNIVERSITET. Izvestiia. 1- ; 1865-1872. CLU[1871] CU[1871] KU;
NNC(1870) ViU

MŪSŲ SPARNAI. 1- ; 1950- . Chicago, Ill., Lietuvių evangelikų reformatų
leidinys. DLC(1952) ICC(1953,nos. 3-4; 1954,no.5; 1955, nos.8-9. OKentU(
1953,no.3; 1961,nos.11-12; 1963,nos.13,14; 1964,no.16; 1965,nos.18-19;
1967,no.22; 1971,no.30)

MŪSŲ ŽINYNAS; karo mokslo ir istorijos žurnalas. Kaunas, Krašto apsaugos
ministerija, Karo mokslo skyrius, 1921-40. 38 v. Quarterly, 1921-1928;
monthly, 1929-1940. U4.M8 DLC(v.5,no.24; 10-13; 16-23) CtTMF(1921-1925)
NN(28-32)

NASH KRAĬ. v.1-6, no.9-10; Oct.1925-Sept.-Oct. 1930. Minsk. DK511.N5A17
DLC MH(no.6-7 to 8-9, 1926) NN([1-5],6)

NAUJOJI VILTIS; politikos ir kultūros žurnalas. no.1- ; 1970- . Chicago,
Ill.; Cleveland, Ohio, Lietuvių studentų tautininkų korporacija Neo-Lithuania. DLC(1-) OKentU(1970-1974,nos.1-6)

NAUKA I SZTUKA. Rok 1,nr.1- ; 1945- . Warszawa. Volume and number desig-
nation irregular. DLC[1946,50-51];MH; NN([2-4]) CoU([1-]])

DAS NEUE DEUTSCHLAND. Jg.1-11; Oct.1912-Oct.1923. Berlin; Gotha, Ger.
DLC(3-10) CU; CSt-H([2]-[7-11]) ICU(9) MnU(1-10) NN([3],10-11) NjP

NEUE PREUSSISCHE PROVINZIAL-BLÄTTER. Bd.1-12, 1846-1851; Folge 3, Bd.1-12,
1852-1857; Folge 3, Bd.1-11, 1858-1866. Königsberg in Pr., In Commission
bei Tag & Koch[etc.], 1846-66. 35 v. in 18. plates, maps, tables. Monthly, 1846-1861; quarterly, 1864-1866. Supersedes Preussische Provinzial-
Blätter. Suspended 1862-1863. Series 2 has added title page: Preussische
Provinzial-Blätter. Merged into Altpreussische Monatsschrift. DD491-04A2
DLC(1-) ICU(1-15,17-18,[20-21]-[27]) ICN(s2,v.[12],s3,v.[1]-4) IEN(s1-s3,
v.2) IU(1-) MH(1-) MH-Z(1-s3,v.[11]) MnU(1-) NNC(1-) NNUT(1-) NjP(1-)

NORDISK KULTUR. no.1- ; 1936- . Stockholm, A. Bonnier. Not issued in
chronological order: no.1 & 30 publ. in 1936; no.2, 1938; no.5, 1939.
913.48.N751b KU; CLU(6,9,24-25) CU(1-30) CtY(1-) DLC(1-) ICN(1-) IRA(1-)
LU; MH(1-30) MdBJ(1-) MnU(1-27) NN(1-30) NNC(1-) NIC(1-) NBuG(1-30) NcD;
NcU; TU; WU(1-)

NUMISMATIST. Baltimore, Md., American numismatic society, Philadelphia,
1888- . CJ1.N8 DLC(4-10[13,15-16]-) AzU(1-) CaBVaU; CaOOP(4-) C([41]-)
CL(50-) CSf(37-) CU([53]-) CoD(30,36-37,42-44,49-51) Ct(4-) AzTeS(40-[45]-)
CtHT([26-27],29,[30]) CtHW(1-45) CtHi(1-) CtY([15]-20,[23-39]) DSI-M(20-21,
[25]-) MdBJ(33,35-[37]-[43]-46) FU([30,43-44]) H(25-) ICN(34-) ICR(1-)
IEN([36,40-41]) LNHT(1-) MB(18-20,25-) MH(1,[2]-) MHi([9],12-[52]) MSM([31-
46]) MWA(13-14,[21,24-25],30-43) MdBE(31-) MdBP([29-30]-[34]-) MeBa(30-)
Mi([25],38-) MiD(3-) MiD-B([7-8]) MiU(7-15,17-21) MnHi([22,28-32]-) MnNC(
36-[42]) MoS([42]-) MdBJ(33,35-[37]-[43]-46,56-) N(21⁸2,25],28,[29]-[33],
1912-20) NN(7-) NNAN(20-65,68,76-) NNC(26-[30,37-38,40,43,45]) NNHi(26-)
NIC([13,15]-[21-41]) NBB(22-33) NBuG([3]-[6],8-9,46-) NR(30-35,38-40,42-
46,49-) NbHi([37]) NbO(21-26,39-) NjR([22-24,26]-[29],32,[37-38,40-48]-55)
NjP; NvU([36-39]) OC([25],50-) OCl(33-) OClMA(33-) OClWHi([1-17]) OHi([1],
11,[12],14-[23]-43,45-[47]-) OO([17,22,30]) PEr(44-) PP(23-24,41-) PPi(1-)
PPHi([24-53]) RP(50-) RPB[34-35]-37,39-[43]-47,49-51,53-) TMG([50]-) TN(
30-31) TxU(4-) VR(1-) WMM(42-) WaS(7-[12-14]-[20]-[22]-24,26-) WaSp(27-)

OCHERKI PO ISTORII GEOLOGICHESKIKH ZNANII. Vyp.1- ; 1953- . Moskva, Izd-
vo Akademii nauk SSSR. illus., ports. Issued by Institut geologicheskikh
of Akademiia nauk SSSR. QE13.R9A562 DLC(1-) CaOOG(9-) CaOTU; CLU(11-) CU(
1-) CSt(3-) DSI(1-) ICJ(1-) ICRL(1-) IU(1-) MH(5-) MnU(1-) NIC(8-) NN(3-4)
NNC; NNM(1-2,4) OkU(4-) OU; ViU(1-3)

ODAL; Monatschrift für Blut und Boden. Jg.1- ; July 1932- . Berlin.
Title varies: Deutsche Agrarpolitik. S7.015 DLC; CtY(7-) DNAL([2-3]- ·
[6]-) IEN(1-) IU; MiU; N; NN(1-4),[7-9],10-) NNC; ViBlbV

ODRODZENIE I REFORMACJA W POLSCE. (Polska akademia nauk. Instytut histo-
rii) Warsaw. T.1- ; 1956- . DK425.03 DLC(1-) CaOTU(1-) CSt(1-) CU(1-)
ICU(1-) IU(1-) MB(1-) MH(1-) MiDW(1-) NIC(1,14-) NjP(8-) NN(1-) NNC(1-5)
PU(1-) WaU(4-) WU(1-)

OSTDEUTSCHE WISSENSCHAFT. Bd.1- ; 1954- . Munich, (Ostdeutscher Kultur-
rat); R. Oldenbourg. "Jahrbuch der Ostdeutschen Kulturrates," 1954- .
AS181.08 DLC(1-) CaBVaU(1-) ICU(6-) InU; KU(1-) MH(1-) MiDW(1-) MiU(6-)
MnU(10-) NcD(1-) NIC(1-) NN(1-) NNC(1-) OCl(1-) TxHR(6-) WaU(1-)

OSTRECHT; Monatsschrift für das Recht der osteuropäischen Staaten. Jg.1-3,
September 1925-März 1927. Berlin. C. Heynemann. 3 v. United with
Zeitschrift für Ostrecht to form N.S. of Zeitschrift für osteuropäisches
Recht. DLC-L; CtY-L; IEN-L(1-3) MH-L; NN

PAMIĘTNIK FIZYJOGRAFICZNY. Warszawa. v.1-27, 1881-1922. Continued
Warszawa, Wydawn. Geologiczne, 1955- . QE276.5.P3 DLC DNAL(27) DAS;
DI-GS; ICJ; MH-P(1-3,9,12-16,18-20,23,25-27) MH; MBdAF(1-2,23-25) NN(12-
15,18-19,26-27) NNM(2-3,9,12-16,18-20,22-27)

PAMIĘTNIK LITERACKI. 1- ; 1902- . Warszawa,[etc.], Polska akademia nauk.
Instytut badań literackich. Suspended 1940-1945. PG7001.P3 DLC(33-38,
41-45) CaBVaU; CaOTU([1-49],50-) CtY(46-) CU; CSt; CLU; ICU(47-) MB; NIC;
NcD(1-) NN(1-27) NNC; NBuU; NjP; NcU; PU(44-) PPiU; TxU; ViU; WU(1-6,8-11,
13-15,17-18,31-32,34-35)

PĖDSAKAI; kultūros ir visuomenės žurnalas. nr.1-3 to 4; liepos mėn. 1946-
kovas 1947. Fulda, Ger., Mūsų Viltis. PG8501.P42 PU; OKent(1946-1947)

POLAND. ARMIA. WOJSKOWE BIURO HISTORICZNE. Przegląd historycznowojskowy,
wydawany przez Wojskowe biuro historyczne... Rocznik 1- ; 1929- .
Warszawa. illus., maps. D25.P6 DLC; NN; PU

POLSKA AKADEMIA UMIEJĘTNOŚCI, KRAKÓW. Bulletin international de l'Academie
des sciences de Cracovie. Comptes rendus des seances... Cracovie, Impr.
de l'Université, 1889-1900. v. illus., plates(part col.), diagrs.
Monthly except Aug. and Sept. In the volume for 1889 the numbers are
separately paged. French and German text. Continued after 1900 in two
series: "Bulletin International de l'Academie... Classe de philologie.
Classe d'histoire et de philosophie," and "Bulletin international de l'Academie... Classe des sciences mathematiques et naturelles." AS142.K83 DLC;
CaQMM(1890-1900) CaOON(1890-1900) CaOTR; CU; CtY; DGS; DNLM; ICJ([1897-
1898]-1900) ICU(1898-1900) IaAS(1890-1900) MH-Z; MdBJ(1891-1900) MiU; MnU(
1890-1900) MoSB(1892-1900) NIC(1896-1900) NN(1890-92,1894,1897-1900) NNC(
[1889]-1900) NjP([1889-1898]-1900) OU(1890-1900) PPAN; PPAP(1889-[1893-
1894]-1900) RPB([1899-1900) WaU

POLSKA AKADEMIA UMIEJĘTNOŚCI, KRAKÓW. Sprawozdania z czynności i posiedzeń.
T.1- ; 1896- . Kraków. 10 nos. a year. Vols.1-24,1896-1919, issued
under the Society's earlier name: Akademia Umiejętności. AS142.K82 DLC(
3-5,7,15,16) CaBVaU; IaAS(1-[4-5]-[10]-[15]-[25]-48,50-52) ICJ(19-[29-30]-
[42]-[44]) InU; KU; MnU; MH([3],26-30) NN(10-15) NNC; OCl(43-) PU

POLSKA AKADEMIA UMIEJĘTNOŚCI, KRAKÓW. KOMISJA DO BADANIA HISTORII, FILOSOFII
W POLSCE. Archivum. T.1-6. Kraków, Nakład. Akademii Umiejętności; Skł.
Gł. w Księg. Gebethnera i Wolffa, 1917-37. 6 v. in 3. B99.P62P6 DLC(6)
CtY; MB(1-6) NCJ(1-5) NN(1-2) NNC(1-2,4-6) WaU

POLSKA AKADEMIA UMIEJĘTNOŚCI, KRAKÓW. KOMISJA ANTROPOLOGICZNA. Zbiór wiadomości do antropologii krajowej. T.1-18; 1875-1895. Kraków, Nakł. Akademii Umiejętności, 1875-1895. GN2.P5822 DLC(1-10,12-18) CtY; DNLM(1-13)
MH; NN(2,4-18) NNM; NNC; OCl

POLSKA AKADEMIA UMIEJĘTNOŚCI, KRAKÓW. WYDZIAŁ HISTORYCZNO-FILOZOFICZNY.
Rozprawy. T.1- ; 1874- . Kraków, Nakład Akademii Umiejętności; Skład
Głowny w Księgarni G. Gebethnera. Vol. 1-25, 1874-1891 include the Soci-

ety's reports of its meetings: Sprawozdania z posiedzeń. AS142.K85 DLC(
1-s2,v.44,46-) CaBVaU; CaOTR(22-s2,v.30,32-41) CtY; CSt; CU(s2,v.6,8,11-
12,14-21,24-42) DGS(1-) ICU(16) MH(1-) MiU; NN(s2,v.8,11,38) NNC(s2,v.38,
41) OU; PPAP(21-24;s2,v.3-5,7-[31-33]-) WaU

POLSKIE TOWARZYSTWO GEOLOGICZNE. Roeznik. T.1- ; 1921-1922- . Kraków.
illus. Began publication with 1921-22. "Wydano z zasiłku Wydziału nauki
Ministerstva oświaty". Title also in French: Annales de la Société géo-
logigne de Pologne. *QPA--NN; CaOTU; CaOOG(1-) CtY; CU; DLC(1-14) DSI;
DI-GS; IU(1-11) ICRL; ICU; LU; MBdAF; MCM; MiU(2) MB; MdBJ(3) NcD; NNC;
NNM(1-) NjP(1-) OClW(1-14) OCU; PPAN(1-14) WU(3-[8-9])

POWSZECHNY ZJAZD HISTORYKÓW POLSKICH. Referaty. 1- ; Warszawa, Polskie
Towarzystwo Historyczne. Irregular. Title varies: Pamiętnik Zjazdu
Historyków Polskich. DK401.P8943 DLC(4-5) CSt-H(9) ICU(9) MH(9) MiU(9)
NN(2,4-5,9) NNC(9) OU(9) PU(5-6) RPB(9) WU

PRAEITIS. Kaunas, Lietuvos istorijos draugija, 1930-33. 2 v. illus., maps.
DK511.L2P75 DLC(1-2) CaAEU(1-2) ICU(1-2; microfilm) KU(1-2) PU(1-2)

PRZEGLĄD ARCHEOLOGICZNY; czasopismo poświęcona archeologii. Poznań, Zaklad
Narodowy im. Ossolinskich. v.   ; illus., ports, maps. Began publica-
tion in 1919. Publication suspended 1940-1945. DK409.P7 DLC(7-19,26-)
CtY; CoU; CSt; CU; InU; ICU; MB; IEN(5-) IU([5]) NIC; NN(2-) NNC; NNM([1])
OU; PU; ViU

PRZEGLĄD HISTORYCZNO-WOJSKOWY see Poland. Armia. Wojskowe biuro history
czne. Przegląd historyczno-wojskowy.

PRZEGLĄD HISTORYCZNY. T.1- ; 1905- . Warszawa, Państwowe Wydawn. Naukowe
[etc.]. Suspended 1940-1945. Vol. 21-35 also called Series 2, v. 1-15.
DK401.P915 DLC(1-) AAP; CaBVaU; CLU; CtY(45-) CaAEU(58-) ICU(47,49-) IU;
ICRL; KU; MiU(46) NIC(45-) NBuU; NN(1,[2]-) NNC; NcD; NjP; NSyU; OU; PU;
PSt; TxU; WaU

PRZEGLĄD POWSZECHNY; miesięcznik poświęcony sprawom religijnym, kulturalnym
i społecznym. Rok 1- ; 1898- . Warszawa, Wydawn. Księży Jezuitów.
Monthly. Publication suspended 1940-1946. AP54.P78 DLC; BM(59,no.175,177;
60, no.178,179; 230,no.10(703), etc.) CaOTU(209) CtY; IU; InU; NN; NNC

REFORMACJA W POLSCE. Warszawa, Skład Główny w Księgarni Trzaska, Evert
Michalski, 1921-1938. 18 v. Summaries in French. BR420.P7R4 DLC(1-8)
CtY(7-8) MiU(4, no.13-16) NN(1-8)

RICERCHE SLAVISTICHE. V.1- ; 1952- . Roma, G. Casini. DR25.R5 DLC(1)
CaBVaU; CU(1-) CLU(6-) CtY(1-) ICU(1-) MH(1-3) NN(1-) NjP(1-) NcD(1-2)
OrU; OU; OrPS; PU(1-) RPB(1-) TxU; TU; UU

ROCZNIK SŁAWISTYCZNY. Revue slavistique. 1- ; 1908- . Kraków. Nakl.
Studium Slowiańskiego Uniw. Jagiellońskiego. PG1.R6 DLC; CaOTU; CaBVaU;
CU(1-13) CtY(1-2,7,9-[16]) CSt; CLU; ICU(1-14) KU; LU; MH(1-14) MiU NIC;
NNC(1-13) NcU(18-) NBuU; NcD(10-) NjP; NN; OClW; OU; PU(1,3-5,7-14) TU;
UU; ViU; WaU; WU

ROCZNIKI BIBLIOTECZNE. Organ naukowy bibliotek szkół wyzszych. 1- ;
1957- . Wrocław, Państwowe Wydawn. Naukowe. illus., ports., quarterly.
Summaries in French and German. Z671.R66 DLC(1-) CLU(4-)

Royal Institute of International Affairs. Documents on international
affairs see Documents on international affairs.

Royal Institute of International Affairs. Survey of international affairs
see Survey of international affairs.

ROZPRAWY Z DZIEJÓW OŚWIATY. T.1- ; 1958- . Wrocław, Zakład Narodowy im.
Ossolińskich. Issued by Pracownia Dziejów Oświaty of the Polish Akademia
nauk. L51.R68 DLC(1-) CaBVaU(8-) IU(1-) CLU; MB(1-) MH(1-) MiDW; MiEM(1-)
NjP(12-) WaU(5-)

RUSSIA. MINISTERSTVO PROSVESHCHENIĬA. Arkhiv; sbornik materialow dlīa istorii prosveshcheniīa v Rossii, izvlechennykh iz Arkhiva Ministerstva narodnago prosvīeshcheniīa. S.-Peterburg, Izd. Ministerstva nar. prosvīeshcheniīa, 1893-1898. 3 v. tables. LA830.A43 DLC: NN

RUSSKAIĀ STARINA. 1-176; 1870-1918. Petrograd: Sanktpeterburg. illus.,
plates, ports., maps. Monthly, 1870-1917; bimonthly, 1918. Ceased publication 1918. AK1.R863 DLC(1-172) CaBVaU; CSt(1-4) CSt-H(1-173) CU(1-
172) CtY(1-[161]-[164]-[168]-171) MH(1-152,157,[158]-[160]-172) NN(1-[15]-
[169]-170,[173],175) NNC(1-168,173) OrU; PPT

--- New York, N.Y., Readex Microprint, 1961. 7 boxes. (Russian Historical
sources) MICP.S.75-1 KyU; CaAEU; PPT

RUSSKIĬ ARKHIV; istoriko-literaturnyĭ sbornik. 1-55; 1863-1917. Moskva.
illus., plates, ports. Twelve nos. a year, 1863-1880 and 1885- ; six
nos. a year, 1881-1884. Ceased publication 1917. DK1.R865 DLC(1-[43]-
[51]-53) CLU([1-19]) CSt-H(1-53) CU([1-23]-54) CtY(1-49,52) MB(1-32) KMK;
MH(1-53) ICU(1-13,15-20,22-29,31-33,35-36,38-42-55) NN(1-20,22-28,31-[34]-
[53]-55) NNC(1-[18]-[23]-[27]-31,33-[42]-55) NjP([9-10,20,22]) OrU

ŠALTINIS. Metai 1-15; kovas 1926- birželis 1940. Marijampolė, Tėvai Ma-
rijonai, 1926-1940. Weekly. CtTMF(1926-1927, 1932-1940) ICCC([1926-1940,
no.1-25]) NN(1926; 1933-[1935])

SANTARVĖ; rezistencinis visuomeninių ir kultūros reikalų žurnalas. London.
Lietuvių Rezistencinė Santarvė, 1953-1958. 42 nos. Irregular.
AP95.L5Š26 PU(6-42) DLC(1953) OKentU(1953,no.3; 1954, no.3,6,10; 1955,
no.4-5; 1957,no.2; 1958,no.1)

SAVIVALDYBĖ; mėnesinis Lietuvos savivaldybių laikraštis. Metai 1-18; birž.
1923-liepa 1940. [Kaunas], Savivaldybių departamentas [etc.], 1923-40.
illus., ports., diagrs. Monthly. Subtitle varies. JS6130.5.AlS3 DLC(
1923-1937) CtPAM(1931-1938)

SĖJA; tautinės demokratinės minties laikraštis. [The Sowing] Metai 1- ;
1953- . Melrose Park, Ill., Varpininkų leidinių fondas. DLC(1956-)
OKentU(no.2,1954; nos.1,8,1957; nos.1-2,5-7,1958; nos.1-5,1959; nos.2-3,
5-6,1960; nos.1-5,1961; nos.1-4,1962; nos.1-6,1963; nos.2-6,1964; nos.1-
3,1965;nos.1-3,1966; nos.1-4,1967; nos.1-3(1968); nos.1,4,1969; nos.1-2,
1970)

THE SLAVONIC AND EAST EUROPEAN REVIEW; a survey of the peoples of Eastern
Europe, their history, economics, philosophy and literature. V.1- ;
June 1922- . London [etc.], Eyre & Spottiswoode; [etc.]. 3 nos. a
year, 1922-Jul.1939; annual. 1939/1940-1941; Semiannual, Mar.1943- .
Title varies: June 1922-Dec.1927, The Slavonic Review; Mar.1928-Dec.1930,
The Slavonic (and East European) Review; Mar.1931- The Slavonic and East
European Review. Imprint varies. D377.AlS65 DLC(1-) CaOTP(1-) CaAEU(4,
6-7,20,22,25-31,33-38,40-41,44) CaOTU(1-) CLU(1-) CU(1-) CtY(1-) ICU(1-)
MH(1-) MdBJ(1-) MnU(1-) MoU(1-) NN(1-) NNC(1-) NjP(4-) OCl(1-) PP(1-)
TxU(1-) WaS(1-)

SOVETSKIE ARKHIVY. 1- ; 1966- . Moskva. illus., ports., bimonthly.
Supersedes Voprosy arkhivovedeniīa. Organ of Slavnoe arkhivnoe upravl-
lenie. CD1710.S6 DLC(no.2,1966-) AAP([1970]-) CaNBFU(1967-) CLU(1966-)
CSt-H(1966-) CtY(1969-) CU(1966-) FU(1968-) ICU(1966-) InLP(1970-) InU(
1966-1967) MdBJ(1966-) MH(1966-) MiU(1966-) NIC([1969]-) NjP(1966-)
TNJ(1966-) ViU; WU([1966]-) WaU(1966-)

DIE SPRACHE; Zeitschrift für sprachwissenschaft. V.1- ; 1949- . Wien,
A. Sexl. [Im Auftrage der Wiener Sprachgesellschaft." P3.S6 DLC(1-2)
CLU(1-) CU(2) CoU(1-) CtY(1-) DCU(1-) ICU(1,[2]) IEN(1-) IU(1-) IaU(1-)
KU(1-) KyU(1-) MH(1-) MdBJ(1-) MdU(1-) MiDW(1-) MiU(1-) MnU(1-) NIC(1-)
NN(1-) NNC(1-) NNM(1-) NcD(1-) NcU(1-) OU(1-) OkU(1-) PSt(1-) PU(1-)
RPB(1-) TxDAM(1-) TxHR(1-) TxU(1-) VU(1-) WU(1-) WvU([1]-)

STUDI BALTICI. 1-8, 1931-1940; [New series] 1(9)- , 1952- . [Roma] L.
S. Olschki. (Academia toscana di scienze e lettere "La Colombia". Studi,

2) PG8001.S8 DLC CaOTU; CtY(1-) CtPAM(1-4,6,9-10) NN(1-) NNC(1-)
NjCa(1-) OU(1,9) PU(1-) WU(1-)

STUDIA ONOMASTICA MONACENSIA; hrsg. von der Kommission für Ortsnamenforschung, Bayerische Akademie der Wissenschaft. München, Verlag der Bayer-
ischen Akademie der Wissenschaften, in Kommission bei Beck, 1956- .
CU(1-) DLC; IU(1-) MH(1-) MdBJ; MiDW(1-) NBuU; PU(1-)

STUDIA Z DZIEJÓW ZSRR I EUROPY ŚRODKOWEJ. T.1- ; 1965- . Wrocław, Zak-
ład Narodowy im. Ossolińskich. Summaries in Russian and English.
D410.S85 DLC; CaBVaU; CtY; CU; CSt-H; ICU; MiU; NIC; NjP; NNC; NSyU;
OU; UU

STUDIA ŹRÓDLOZNAWCZE. Commentationes. v.1- ; 1957- . Warszawa [etc.]
Państwowe Wydawn. Naukowe. v. illus., facsims. Irregular. Issued by
Instytut Historii of the Polska Akademia Nauk. Summaries in French,
English, or other languages. D13.S853 DLC(2-) CaBVaU CaOTU CSt IU; ICU;
INU(2) MB; MH(1-) NN(1-) PU; WaU(1-) WU(1-)

SUOMALAINEN TIEDEAKATEMIA, HELSINGFORS. SUOMALAISEN TIEDEAKATEMIAN TOIMI-
TUKSIA. Annales Academiae scientiarum fennicae. Ser. B. T.1-60; 1909-
1946. Helsinki, Suomalaisen tiedeakatemian kustantama, 1909-1946. 60 v.
Q60.H53 DLC(1-34,36-49,51-) CaOON(1-) CaQMM(1-) CaOG(6,8-9[14-34],36-49,
51-) CaOTU(17,42-) CSt(1-) CLU(38-49,51-) CU([8,21,28]) CtY(1-) IU([29],
34-49,51-) KU(34-) MH(1-) MdBJ(1-41,43-49,51-) MiU(19,21,23-) MnU(1-[38],
42,[45]) NIC(34-49,51-) NN(17,19-49,51-) NNC(1-) NcD(33-) NhD(1-) NjP(1-)
OU(1-) RPB(1-) PPAN(1-) WU(1-)

SURVEY OF INTERNATIONAL AFFAIRS. V.1- ; 1920/1923- . London, Eng.;
New York, N.Y., Oxford University Press [etc.]. Irregular. D442.S8 DLC;
CaAEU(1920/1923-1963) AU(1920-1938) CL(1924-) CaOTP(1-) CtY-L(1-) FTS(1-)
DA(1929,36-) IaAS(1924,33-) IEN(1-) MSM(1-4) MiU-L(1-) MdBP(1920/1923-33)
MdU(1924,32-38) MiU(1-) N(1-15) NBG(1930-) NNC(1-) NcU(1-) ODa(1920-37)
OOxM(1920-24,26-38) PU(1930-) PEI(1920/1923-) PU-L(1926-) RPB(1920-37)
TNG(1925) TNJ(1925-) WM(1920-38) WyU(1920-25,27-33)

TAUTA IR ŽODIS. Epe lituana; sumptibus Ordinis philologorum Universitatis
lituaniensis edita. Kn.1-7; 1923-1931. Kaunas, Humanitarinių mokslų
fakulteto leidinys, 1923-1931. 7 v. illus., ports. Irregular.
PG8501.T3 DLC; CU; ICU(1-5,7) ICCC(1-7) MH(1-7) MoU(6) NIC(6) NN(1-7)
NNC(1-5) PU(1-6) WU(1-7) CaAEU(1,6)

TAUTOS PRAEITIS; isotorijos ir gretimųjų sričių neperiodinis žurnalas.
T.1-2; book 1-8; 1959-1970. Chicago, Lietuvių istorijos draugija. illus.
facsims. Irregular. In Lithuanian with summaries in English. Each book
has 4 nos. DK511.L2A276 DLC(1-) CaOONL(no.1-8) CaOTU(1-) ICCC(v.1,kn.1-
2) ICBM(v.2,kn.1-2,5-6) ICLJF(kn.1-4; 1959-1962) InU([2]) KU(v.1,kn.1)
MH(1-) NN(1-) PU(1-) OKentU(1-3)

TECHNIKOS ŽODIS. 1- ; balandis 1951- . Chicago, American Lithuanian
Engineers and Architects. Monthly; bimonthly. DLC([3]) ICCC(1952,no.1-
4,6-8,10; 1953,no.1-4,6,7) OKentU(1953,no.3; 1957,no.3; 1960,no.5-6; 1961,
no.1-5; 1962,no.1,2; 1964,no.2,5; 1965,no.1-2,5-6; 1966,no.2-4; 1967,no.
3-4; 1968,no.2; 1969,no.1).

TEISĖ; teisės mokslų ir praktikos žurnalas. Nr.1-52. Kaunas, Lietuvos
teisininkų draugija, 1922-1940. 52 nos. Quarterly. ICBM(1-35).

TEISININKŲ ŽINIOS. Nr.1-26; lapkr.1952-gruod.1958. Chicago, Lietuvių
teisininkų draugija, 1952-1958. 26 nos. Irregular. DLC-L(1-) MH-L(1-)
ICCC(1953,no.2) OKentU(1953,no.3)

TĖVYNĖS SARGAS; politikos ir socialinių mokslų žurnalas. Nr.1- ; 1947- .
Reutlingen, Ger.; Chicago, Ill., Lietuvių krikščionių demokratų partija.
Irregular. DK511.L2A57 DLC CtPAM(1947-1965) ICCC(1947-1948, 1951-1954)
ICLJF(1947-1949, 1951-1955) MH(2,no.1-2 3,5-6/7) OKentU(1947-1972) PU(1-)

TOWARZYSTWO NAUKOWE WARSZAWSKIE. Sprawozdania z posiedzeń Wydziału I-IV.
Rok 1- 1-36,no.6; 1908-1938. Warszawa, Monthly. Vol.1,no.9 never

published. Suspended 1918-1925. AS262.W323 DLC(1-31) CaOTR(29-30)
CaOOAg(1929-1938) CPT(28-30) CU(6,19-31) CtY(1-24,26-31) ICJ(11/18-3)
IU(26-31) MBA(1-6) MH(1-31) MH-P(22-31) MWhB(1-6) NIC-A(22-31) NN(1-31)
NNC(24-29) NNM(1-[10]-31) NcD(19-31) NjP(29-30) PPAN(1-31) PU(1-[11],19-
27,29) RPB(1-[30],31) WaU(6-31)

VARPAS; neperiodinis žurnalas. Nr.1- ; 1953- . Brooklyn, N.Y., Varpininkų leidinių fondas. Irregular. 57.92V438 PU(1-5-) DLC(1-) ICLJF(6)
NN(1-) OKentU(1953-1972,nos.1-2,5-9,11; 1965,no.6)

WARSAW. INSTYTUT GEOLOGICZNY. Biuletyn. No.1 ; 1938- . Warszawa.
Formed by the union of its Sprawozdania and Posiedzenia... QE276.5.W362
DLC(no.[1-161]-) CLU(no.[1-142]-) CU([1-136]-) CtY([1-44]) IaU([24-60]-)
IU([1-79]-) KU([1-24]-) KyU(97-) MdBJ([1-90]-) MiD([13-32]-) NIC([71-107]-
NbU([8-132])

WIĘŻ 1958- . Warszawa, [RSW "Prasa"] illus., ports. Monthly. AP54.W57
DLC(1-) CaBVaU(6-) CaOTU(1-) MH(3-) NcD([10]-)

Z DZIEJÓW STOSUNKÓW POLSKO-RADZIECKICH; studia i materiały. 1- ; 1965- .
Warszawa, Polska akademia nauk. Zakład historii stosunków Polsko-Radziec-
kich. DK418.5R9Z2 DLC(1-) ICU(1-) CaBVaU; CLU; MH(1-) MiU(1-) NIC(2-)
NjP(1-) NN(1-) NNC(1-) WU(1-)

ZEITSCHRIFT FÜR GEOPOLITIK IN GEMEINSCHAFT UND POLITIK. Bad Godesberg; etc.
1- Jahrg.; Jan.1924- . Suspended 1945-50. 1924-55 as Zeitschrift für
geopolitik. 1956- by the Institut für geosoziologie und politik. Ab-
sorbed Weltpolitik und weltwirtschaft in Ja. 1927; Gemeinschaft und politik in Ja. 1956. D410.Z4 DLC(1-) CLU([1]10-) CSt-H(1-6,12-) CU(1-) CoG(3-
CoU(1-) CtY(1-) DCU(15-) DI-GS(1-[11]) ICJ(1-[11]) ICU(1-) IEN(6-) IU(1-)
IaU(1-[11]) MB(1-[11]) MH(1-) MH-L(1-) MWC(5-) MdBJ(1-) MiU(1-) MnU(1-)
NBuG(11-[13]) NN(1-) NNA(1-) NNC([8]-) NR([11]-) NcD(15-) NcU(7-[9],11-
[15]) NhD(1-) NjP(1-) OAU(12-) OCl(11-) OU(1-[3]-) TxU([1],8-[16-17]-)
WU(1-) WaU(1-)

ZEITSCHRIFT FÜR OSTFORSCHUNG; Länder und Völker im östlichen Mitteleuropa.
Jahrg. 1- ; 1952- . Marburg/Lahn, Johann Gottfried Herder-Forschungs-
rat; N. G. Elwert. illus., maps. 4 nos. a year. DR1.Z4 DLC(1-) AMAU(2-)
CaAEU(1-) CaQMM(1-) CLU(8-) CU([104],5-) CtY([1]-) FU(9-) IU(1-) InU(1-)
KyU(6-) MH(1-) MiDW(1-) MdBJ(1-) MnU(1-) NIC(1-) NnCl(1-) NN(1-) NjP(1-)
OCU(10-) PSt(1-) PU(1-) TxHR(9-)

ZEITSCHRIFT FÜR OSTRECHT. Berlin, C. Heynemann, 1927-34. 8 v. Monthly.
Formed by merging of Ostrecht and Zeitschrift für osteuropäisches Recht.
CtY-L;DLC-L; ICU; MH-L; MdBJ; MiU-L; NN(1-[7]-8) NNB; NNC; OrU;

ZEITSCHRIFT FÜR POLITIK. Bd.1-35, 1907-1945; Neue Folge. Bd.1- ; 1954- .
Berlin, C. Heymann. JA14.Z67 CaAEU(ns 1-3,5-13,15-17-) CU(12-) CtY(1-)
DLC(1-) MH(1-) NiU(1-) MdBJ(1-) MnU(1-) MoU(1-) NN(1-) NNC(1-) NjP(1-)
OClW(1-) WU(1-)

ZEITSCHRIFT FÜR VERGLEICHENDE SPRACHFORSCHUNG AUF DEM GEBIETE DER INDOGER-
MANISCHEN SPRACHEN. Bd.1- ; 1852- . Berlin [etc.]. F. Dümmler; [etc.]
Bimonthly. 1-22, 1852-1874 as Zeitschrift für vergleichende Sprachfor-
schung auf dem Gebiete des deutschen, griechischen und lateinischen. 21-40
also as ns v.1-20. Suspended 1945-1947. P501.Z5 DLC(Fragments) CSt(1-)
CU(1-) CaQMM(1-37) CoDU(58-59) CtY(1-) ICU(1-20,23,25-28,30-[68]-) IU(1-)
IEN(1-) InU(2) KU(1-66,69-) KyU(1-) OCU(1-) OClW(1-66,68-) OU(1-46,48,50-)
OC(5-10,24-25) ODW(1-30) OO(28-29[45],48) CaAEU(1-58; 1852-1931) CaOTU(
1-) CLU(1-53,55-) CtW(1-) DGW([10-16,18-30]) DSI([29,34-35]-) [39]-[43])
ICN(1-) IaU(1-60) LNHT([23],47-[58]) LU(1-50) MB(1-) MH(1-) MNF(11[12]-
[17]-[23]) MWelC(23-27) MWiW(1-) MdBJ(1-) MiU(1-) MnU(1-) MoSU(60-)
MoSW(1-) NCH(1-) NIC(1-) NN(1-) NNC(1-) NNCoC(1-48) NNU(1-50,56-60) NcU(1-
NNU-H(1-53) NNUT(1-13) NRU(1-62) NbU(1-) NdC(63-) NhD(1-) NjP(1-) PSC(1-20
PEL(25-38,41-46) PPiU(25-46) PU(1-67,69-) PBL(1-49,51-) TxU(1-[66]
TNJ(8-10,12,15,41-43,50-52) VU(1-[66]) WU(1-)

ŽEMĖTVARKA IR MELIORACIJA. Kaunas, Lietuvos matininkų ir kultūrtechnikų sąjunga. 1926-40. Quarterly.; bimonthly. TC801.Z4 DLC(1930-1940) DNAL

ŽIDINYS; literatūros, mokslo, visuomenės ir akademinio gyvenimo mėnesinis
žurnalas. Metai 1-17, no.1-6; gruodis 1924-birž.1940. Kaunas, Studentų
ateitininkų sąjunga,1924-40. Monthly. 57.92.Z67 PU(t.5-6,1927,lacks nr.
10; 1928-1933, lacks nr.4; 1934, lacks nr.1,4-6; 1935-1936, lacks nr.1,7,
12; 1937-1940) CtPAM(1924-1940) CtTMF(1925-1940) ICCC(1924-1940,nr.1-4)
ICWA; OKentU(1928,nos.5-6; 1929,nos.1-7,10,11; 1930-1931,nos.1-2,4,7-9,
12; 1932,nos.1,5-6; 1933,nos.2,7; 1934,nos.1-10,12; 1935; 1936,no.10;
1937,nos.7,10-11; 1938,nos.1-3,11-12; 1939,nos.1-4,7-11; 1940,nos.1-4)